BIBLICAL STUDIES ALTERNATIVELY

An Introductory Reader

BIBLICAL STUDIES
ALTERNATIVELY
An Introductory Reader

SUSANNE SCHOLZ
Merrimack College

Prentice
Hall

Upper Saddle River, New Jersey 07458

Library of Congress Cataloging-in-Publication Data

Biblical studies alternatively: an introductory reader / [compiled by] Susanne Scholz.
    p. cm.
  Includes bibliographical references and indexes.
  ISBN 0-13-045429-X
  1. Bible-Social scientific criticism. 2. Sociology, Biblical. I. Scholz, Susanne

BS521.88.B53 2003
220'.07'2—dc21

2002042534

VP, Editorial Director: Charlyce Jones-Owen
Senior Acquisitions Editor: Ross Miller
Assistant Editor: Wendy Yurash
Editorial Assistant: Carla Worner
Senior Managing Editor: Jan Stephan
Production Liaison: Fran Russello
Project Manager: Marty Sopher/Lithokraft II
Prepress and Manufacturing Buyer: Brian Mackey
Cover Art Director: Jayne Conte
Cover Designer: Bruce Kenselaar
Cover Art: Holly Cannell, "Fluid Transition"
Marketing Manager: Chris Ruel
Marketing Assistant: Kimberly Daum

This book was set in 10/12 Palatino by Lithokraft II
and was printed and bound by R. R. Donnelley & Sons Company.
The cover was printed by Coral Graphics.

© 2003 by Pearson Education, Inc.
Upper Saddle River, New Jersey 07458

Printed in the United States of America

10 9 8 7 6 5 4 3 2 1

ISBN: 0-13-045429-X

Pearson Education Ltd., *London*
Pearson Education Australia PTY. Limited, *Sydney*
Pearson Education Singapore, Pte. Ltd
Pearson Education North Asia Ltd, *Hong Kong*
Pearson Education Canada, Ltd., *Toronto*
Pearson Educación de Mexico, S.A. de C.V.
Pearson Education—Japan, *Tokyo*
Pearson Education Malaysia, Pte. Ltd
Pearson Education, *Upper Saddle River, New Jersey*

Rabbi Tarfon and the elders were reclining
in the upper story of Nithza's house in Lod.

The question was asked before them.
"Which is greater, study or action?"
Rabbi Tarfon responded, "Action is greater."
Rabbi Akiva responded, "Study is greater."
Then everyone said:
"Study is greater, because study brings forth action."

Babylonian Talmud, Tractate Kiddushin 40b.

In Loving Memory

To My Grandmother,
An Avid and Committed Reader of the Bible,
Anni Knobloch, geb. Püschel
(1913–1999)

Contents

PART I. INTRODUCTORY MATTERS

PART II. THE RHETORIC OF GENDER

Chapter 3. Ethnic Perspectives on the Bible

Chapter 4. Christian Anti-Judaism and Biblical Interpretation

PART IV. THE RHETORIC OF CLASS

Chapter 1. God and the Option for the Poor

Chapter 2. Economic Justice as a Biblical Concern

Chapter 3. Liberation and Oppression in the Book of Exodus

Preface

The Bible is an international bestseller, sustaining the religious life of many people around the globe. Yet many academic courses in the West explore only the historical meaning of this text, sacred to Christianity and Judaism, and so they cut off the study of the Bible from questions of contemporary meaning. *Biblical Studies Alternatively* is an anthology that brings both together: scholarly research as well as discussions on the meaning of the Bible in our world.

The anthology shows that the Bible can be reduced to neither a pietistic appreciation nor its historical origins. Both approaches are important in their respective contexts: among Christian and Jewish readers on the one hand and biblical scholars on the other hand. Yet, both approaches also lack each other's insight. The pietistic stance ignores the wealth of scholarly work; the historical analysis neglects the strong desire for meaning. Integrating both insights, *Biblical Studies Alternatively* invites readers to appreciate the continuing cultural, political, and religious relevance of the Bible as suggested by biblical scholars. The four sections of the anthology—*Introductory Matters, The Rhetoric of Gender, The Rhetoric of Race/Ethnicity,* and *The Rhetoric of Class*—present a wide range of scholarly articles that introduce the Bible as an influential document of past and present culture, politics, and religion.

During the last decades, many researchers have become quite interested in reading the Bible as a cultural artifact. Their interpretations left the traditional confinements of a field that examined biblical texts primarily with historical and archaeological questions in mind. Once, there were good reasons for interpreting the Bible in the historical setting of the ancient Near East and early Christianity. When Christian institutions held great authority over biblical meaning, the historical approach was a bold challenge to religious and political power. Many Pentecostal and fundamentalist Christians continue to reject this challenge and still consider historical readings of the Bible as unacceptable. Yet, in our time, Christian institutions do no longer hold unquestioned religious authority or political power. Especially in comparison to their past status in Western societies, many of today's Christian institutions are relatively marginalized—politically, culturally, and economically. Whose interpretation of the Bible is still regarded as a challenge to Christian institutions, which have become as diverse as contemporary Western society? For the last two hundred years, scholars have worked hard and successfully to establish the right of interpreting the Bible with scientific methodologies, and so anybody may now publish her or his views on the Bible.

Consequently, historical criticism is no longer most challenging for the students in our classrooms. Whether they are secular or Christian evangelical, students in the West wonder why they should study the Bible in an academic environment in the first place. What do they gain from the exercise? Why should they spend a whole semester on a single book that has at best a perfunctory place in the public realm of today's Western society? This anthology recognizes the changed status of biblical scholarship as well as the changed purpose of an introductory course on the Bible. It is no longer enough to present biblical texts as historical relics, as many introductory textbooks advise. No longer do students perceive the church as a publicly powerful institution. Religion is a private matter and so, to students, it is an obvious fact that the Bible belongs to the past that is read as a religiously inspirational text. In such an environment scholars have to demonstrate that the Bible offers more than individual piety or historical data. If they want to ensure the intellectual and cultural significance of the Bible for the twenty-first century, biblical studies courses have to provide an alternative. They have to demonstrate the cultural impact and the intellectual contributions of the Bible for our understanding of the world in which we live.

Biblical Studies Alternatively provides the scholarly resources for this task. Discussing biblical stories and poems in the context of gender, race/ethnicity, and class—analytical categories that are standard for contemporary intellectual discourse, the anthology introduces the Bible as a culturally, politically, and religiously indispensable resource of our time.

ACKNOWLEDGMENTS

This anthology has developed over time and with the support of many. Let me begin by thanking the acquisition editor of Prentice Hall, Ross Miller, who found merit in the idea of introducing the Bible alternatively. Thanks also to the Prentice Hall reviewers, Beth LaRocca-Pitts, Duke Divinity School, Pamela J. Milne, University of Windso, and William Gregory Carey, Lancaster Theological Seminary, who offered valuable advice and suggestions for the final version of the manuscript. I am grateful to the staff members of the Burke Library at Union Theological Seminary, NY, where I was able to finalize this anthology in Spring 2002. It is always with great pleasure to work at the Burke Library and to take advantage of its outstanding resources. I also want to thank my students of the course "Introduction to Biblical Studies: Interpretation and Culture" who gave me valuable feedback on materials for this anthology during the years 1998 to 2001. I thank Peter Havholm, professor of English, Richard H. Bell, professor of Philosophy, and Josephine Wright, professor of Music and Black Studies, for their professional support and advice. I thank my sophomore research assistant Teodora I. Zheleva for her diligent and reliable help in Fall 2001. Many thanks to Chris Herlinger, journalist and my proofreader, who made sure to catch any potential or real Germanism in my writing. Last but not least, special thanks to Lorraine Keating, entrepreneur and always first reader of my many drafts, for her honest and encouraging criticism from beginning to end.

Grateful acknowledgment is made to the various publishers and authors who generously granted permission to reprint their articles in this volume.

Introduction

1. WHY STUDY THE BIBLE ACADEMICALLY? AN OPENING COMMENT

Most people in western societies know something about the Bible, but they know almost nothing about its academic study. They learn about the Bible in church, synagogue, or from television, movies, and the Internet, and have perhaps read parts of the Bible in their childhood or adolescence. They know that people debate the biblical creation story in the context of teaching evolution in high schools, but they might not know where to find this narrative in the Bible. Of course, they have heard of Jesus—although they probably do not know much about scholarly discussions on Jesus as a historical figure. In fact, many would not even consider the academic study of the Bible a necessity because, to them, the Bible has religious, rather than scholarly, value.

The view that the Bible serves religious purposes is widespread among many people. In a telephone poll by the Princeton Religion Research Center, 81 percent of the 1,005 interviewed Americans regarded the Bible as the actual or inspired word of God.[1] Polls in other countries yield other results. In Britain, for instance, only 44 percent of the interviewees regarded the Bible as the word of God. Still, even this much lower number is impressive. It suggests that the Bible enjoys substantial prestige in people's hearts, and so people rarely respond unemotionally to biblical talk. Some carry deep wounds from childhood exposure to biblical teachings. Others get annoyed and angry when they read biblical stories that they find hard to understand and to believe. Still others find life, trust, and faith in biblical words.

The emotional responsiveness to biblical matters and the relative inexperience in approaching the Bible with an intellectually open, nuanced, and reasoned attitude make it often difficult to introduce the Bible academically. Sometimes, people have very definite ideas how the Bible should be studied and what the scholarly issues ought to be. When they realize that their expectations differ from the actual work done, some begin to feel disappointed. Others find the whole notion of studying the Bible academically misguided. They demand that the Bible be treated as the word of God, and resist scholarly investigations. Still others refuse to engage in such study because they are irritated by fundamentalist references to the Bible and distrust any biblical discourse, scholarly or not. There are, of course, always those who bring or, in due time, develop an interest in academic research. Yet, in general, the religious and cultural image of the Bible makes the academic teaching a precarious, though very necessary endeavor.

---

[1]Robert Bezilla (ed.), *Religion in America 1992–1993* (Princeton, NJ: The Princeton Religion Research Center, 1993), p. 22. The poll on "Beliefs about the Bible" showed that 32 percent consider the Bible as "the actual Word of God . . . to be taken literally, word for word;" 49 percent consider it as "the inspired Word of God but not everything in it should be taken literally word for word." Only 16 percent consider the Bible as a "Book of fables" and 3 percent are not sure.

This book aims to foster such effort by bringing the fruits of biblical research to students at colleges, universities, or seminaries, and to those interested in academic explorations of biblical meanings. Providing resources about contemporary theory and practice of academic Bible readings, *Biblical Studies Alternatively* demonstrates that the inquiry into biblical text and interpretation enhances our understanding not only about the Bible, but also about the Bible's place in society and society's role in the meanings of the Bible.

2. MODERNITY AND THE STUDY OF THE BIBLE AS HISTORICAL LITERATURE

For the last several centuries, people of the West have come to take their modern worldview for granted. Beginning in the fifteenth century, new developments in science and the colonial expansion of European nations such as Spain, Portugal, or Britain initiated the movements that eventually led to what we call modernity. These events and a renewed focus on the Bible, fostered by the Protestant Reformation that coined the phrase *sola scriptura* (only Scripture), motivated many scientists and philosophers to question the historical events depicted in biblical texts. The historicity of the Bible became a problem in a time when the observation of nature promised near-total understanding of the world and humanity's place in it. Over the course of several centuries, the historical investigation of the Bible developed into the field that we call "biblical studies." The first section of this volume, "Introductory Matters," elaborates further on these developments and their ramifications for the academic study of the Bible. Suffice it to say, the modern mindset has fundamentally changed how people relate to the Bible. They want to know whether or not the mentioned events of the Bible actually happened. They want to know if the Bible is, in a sense, "true." With the emergence of modernity the historicity of biblical texts, events, or characters has been under great scrutiny, defining the academic study of the Bible largely as a historical field.

The historical analysis of the Bible has led to the development of different methods that are commonly classified under the rubric "historical criticism." Numerous hypotheses have addressed the historical origins of the Bible. Research about the historical circumstances of biblical texts has provided a wealth of scholarly speculation, historical reconstruction, and intense debate. These procedures assured that biblical researchers gained respect within academia, particularly since the nineteenth century. Their intellectual insistence that the Bible is not the word of God, but a historical document, weakened the religious appropriation of biblical literature. Among biblical researchers were radical and daring thinkers. For instance, in the 1870s, Bruno Bauer maintained that the historicity of Jesus or Paul cannot be ascertained by scholarly methods.[2]

Religious organizations often responded to such claims by attempting to dismiss scholars from their academic positions. In 1892, the Presbyterian Church subjected biblical scholar Charles A. Briggs to a presbytery trial for heresy. Briggs

---

[2]See Raymond E. Brown, *Introduction to the New Testament* (New York: Doubleday, 1997), p. 816; Albert Schweitzer, *The Quest of the Historical Jesus: A Critical Study of Its Progress from Reimarus to Wrede* (Baltimore: John Hopkins University Press, 1998), p. 137–160.

taught Hebrew and cognate languages at Union Theological Seminary in New York City, at the time a Presbyterian institution. The denomination demanded that Briggs either not apply scientific methodology to the Hebrew Bible or leave his professorial position. Supported by Union's faculty, Briggs did not waiver; he continued his work and kept his job. Yet, the Presbyterian denomination did not accept this situation and cut its ties with the seminary, which has been non-denominational ever since.[3] Many other such stories exist. Most of them demonstrate that scientific conviction persevered over religious authority. Scholars risked, and sometimes lost, their careers when they maintained that the Bible is historical literature like any other document of the past and has to be studied as such.

It is crucial to realize that historical criticism developed within the modern worldview. Scientifically approved methodologies established the meaning of the Bible, limiting it to the original author's intention and setting. The historical meaning counted as objectively "true" and as established independently of interpretive biases. The assumption was the other interpreters, applying the same methods, would get similar results.

Academic teachers published many books that introduce students to the results of such research. Usually, these books are written by scholars in the field, either specializing in Hebrew Bible or New Testament, who provide surveys on the historical developments of biblical texts and events. Assuming the interpretive principles of the modern worldview, the books explore the history of ancient Israel in the context of the ancient Near East, or the history of the early Christian movement in the context of the Hellenistic era. Even today, this modern, or "positivist," approach continues to govern much academic research for it promises unbiased, objective, and scientifically approved results.

Certainly, the development of historical criticism is more complex than this brief description indicates. Many historical critics would readily admit that their historical reconstructions only tentatively outline biblical events. They might also make use of other methods, among them literary and cultural approaches, because a plurality of methods has become a "fact of life" for most biblical scholars. Still, many introductory textbooks reduce the discussion to a historical portrayal of the Bible, whether focused on the Hebrew Bible or the New Testament, and are silent about the specific social locations and hermeneutical interests of their work.

3. WHAT IS "ALTERNATIVE" ABOUT THIS INTRODUCTORY READER?

This volume presents an alternative approach to the modern-historical introduction of the Bible. Covering the Christian canon of the Bible, *Biblical Studies Alternatively* is rooted in the intellectual and philosophical developments of recent decades what is commonly called "postmodernity," an intellectual-cultural discourse that has grown out of modernity and is indebted to modern thought. According to postmodern

---

[3]Robert T. Handy, "The Trials of Charles Briggs (1881–1893)," chap. in *A History of Union Theological Seminary in New York* (New York: Columbia University Press, 1987). See, e.g., also Charles A. Briggs, *The Case Against Professor Briggs* (New York: Scribner, 1892–1893); Charles A. Briggs, *Authority of Holy Scripture: Inaugural Address and Defense, 1891/1893* (New York: Arno Press, 1972).

epistemology—or the theory of knowledge, meaning is not an objective reality, independent from interpreters, but created by readers. Accordingly, this volume invites students to recognize that the Bible has multiple, indeterminate, and infinite meanings, emerging in relation to the Bible's diverse readers and the world.

Since the 1970s, scientists and philosophers have begun to question the notion of objectivity, one of the prime ideas of modernity. Developments in twentieth-century physics replaced the Newtonian view of the world. With or without a constant of the universe, many theorists have come to recognize the multiplicity, indeterminacy, and infinity of interpretive meaning. Quantum physics, in particular, has changed the understanding of the relationship of the observer, the observed, and the observation process. A sentence, such as, "We *select* an experience for recollection, after *evolving* its importance to us," can be stated only *after* scientists recognized that the position of an observer determines whether a neutron is seen as a neutron or a proton.[4] Philosophers speak of the linguistic turn that acknowledges truth as a social construct. As a result, meaning in our postmodern time is no longer regarded as an objective reality, independent from the interpreter. Rather, meaning "arises from the subjective, or ideological, juxtaposing of text with text *on behalf of* specific readers in specific historical/material situations."[5]

These intellectual developments have also affected biblical scholarship. Not long ago modern concerns dominated the field; now many scholars consider the Bible as a "polysemous" book, i.e. a book of multiple meanings, and reject the possibility of extracting objective and single truth from it. They challenge traditional approaches to the Bible that claim objectivity, scientific value-neutrality, and universality of meaning. As postmodern interpreters, they recognize the limitations and locatedness of all knowledge.[6] To them, biblical texts contain many interpretive possibilities; some realized, others still to come. Readers do not simply describe the content of a text or reconstruct its historical meaning. They never define the Bible conclusively. Instead, every interpretive attempt is situated, located, and particular. Different readers create different meanings.

The focus on the readers has profoundly changed the direction of biblical studies. No longer exclusively concerned with the historical origins or the literary forms of the text itself, scholars explore the connections between the Bible, its readers, and the world. Thus understood, biblical studies illuminate societal dynamics which make a number of questions important: Who are the readers? Why do they read the Bible the way they do? What biblical passages do they use and how? What social, political, economic, or religious views do their interpretations promote? How do the interpretations relate to the social, political, economic, or religious status quo?

Postmodern studies of biblical text and interpretation emphasize that, as an inherently ambiguous text, the Bible escapes ultimate definition. This characteristic has perhaps contributed to the Bible's enduring meaning among a wide range of people. Readers come to believe that theirs is the only possible and

---

[4]Gary Taylor, *Cultural Selection* (New York: Basic Books, 1996), p. 18.
[5]G. Aichele and G. Phillips, "Introduction: Exegesis, Eisegesis, Intergesis," *Semeia* 69/70 (1995): 15.
[6]See, e.g., A. K. M. Adams, *What is Postmodern Biblical Criticism?* (Minneapolis: Fortress, 1995); Edgar V. McKnight, *Postmodern Use of the Bible: The Emergence of Reader-Oriented Criticism* (Nashville: Abingdon, 1988).

sensible reading. Yet, once it is understood that different interpreters read the Bible with many different and often contradicting meanings, this claim becomes untenable. Then, the academic study of the Bible is appreciated as an opportunity for viewing biblical meanings as reflections of political, cultural, and religious theories and practices. It is a way of learning to connect the reading of the Bible with the past and the present and, perhaps most importantly, to consider society's involvement in the process of meaning. This anthology aims to nurture such a learning process, and represents an alternative to modern-historical introductions to the Bible.

4. WHY RELATE THE CATEGORIES OF GENDER, RACE/ETHNICITY, AND CLASS TO THE STUDY OF THE BIBLE?

When American scholars began to study these and other categories, their work emerged within the political and social movements of the 1960s. Earlier generations had sometimes explored the history and development of societies viewed through these categories. Yet, their work had been marginalized or was largely unknown until the 1960s. In the case of gender, for instance, feminist historians recovered the memory of the first women's movement of the West, which had been effectively silenced from mainstream historiography, in some textbooks even today.[7] In the case of race/ethnicity, African American thinkers had done significant research on the impact of race on American society during the late nineteenth and early twentieth centuries. Yet their work, too, was relatively unknown and had to be made available to the public again.[8] A concerted effort to comprehend the theoretical implications of ethnicity is only emerging now.[9] In the case of class, Karl Marx and others began to articulate the dynamics of class in the nineteenth century. The confrontation between capitalism and socialism, however, made such work difficult to accomplish within Western academic institutions. Especially in the United States, the study of class has been marginalized, and sometimes even stigmatized, most prominent during the McCarthy era of the 1950s.[10] With the 1960s, however, intellectuals have come to reclaim such work as the basis for understanding the dynamics of society.[11]

---

[7]For examples of such studies see, e.g., Gerda Lerner, *The Majority Finds Its Past: Placing Women in History* (New York: Oxford University Press, 1979); Mary S. Hartman and Louis Banner (eds.), *Clio's Consciousness Raised: New Perspectives on the History of Women* (New York: Octagon, 1976).

[8]For one of the most prominent thinkers, see, e.g., W.E.B. DuBois, *W.E.B. DuBois: A Reader*, ed. Meyer Weinberg (New York: Harper & Row, 1970); Herbert Aptheker, *Annotated Bibliography of the Published Writings of W.E.B. DuBois* (Millwood, NY: Kraus-Thomson Organization, 1973).

[9]For such work within the field of biblical studies, see, e.g., Meir Sternberg, *Hebrews Between Cultures: Group Portraits and National Literature* (Bloomington: Indiana University Press, 1998); Mark G. Brett, *Ethnicity and the Bible* (New York: Brill, 1996); David M. Rhoads, *The Challenge of Diversity: The Witness of Paul and the Gospels* (Minneapolis: Fortress, 1996).

[10]For a critical analysis of this era, see, e.g., Richard Gid Powers, *Not Without Honor: The History of American Anticommunism* (New York: Free Press, 1995); Ellen Schrecker, *No Ivory Towers: McCarthyism and the Universities* (New York: Oxford University Press, 1986).

[11]See, for example, Paula S. Rothenberg, *Race, Class, and Gender in the United States: An Integrated Study* (5th edition; New York: W. H. Freeman, 2000).

Biblical scholars, too, began to apply social categories to their research.[12] They were committed to relating the Bible to contemporary society, politics, and religion, and their work has demonstrated that they have much to contribute to understanding the world in which we live. In the last decades these categories have inspired many studies on the Bible's relationship to social, political, and religious discourse and life. This volume collects such studies documenting the close link between biblical research and the effort to analyze society according to these categories; a link greatly affecting the direction of the academic study of the Bible.

The correlation of the social categories to the Bible illuminates another important dimension of biblical interpretation. It shows that the reading of biblical texts is always a political activity. Examining the Bible from different interpretive positions, it is possible to recognize that interpreters referred to the Bible both in support of and in opposition to political systems of oppression and injustice. As a result, students recognize that biblical meaning depends on interpretive interests. Biblical meaning does not simply wait to be uncovered but is created by readers. This realization makes students question positivist and literalist approaches which claim objectivity, universality, and disinterestedness. Reading the Bible in the context of gender, race/ethnicity, and class, they realize that interpreters from different social locations create different meanings that relate differently to the status quo. They learn to relate the study of the Bible to interpreters and their contexts. Eventually, then, the correlation of the social categories to the Bible demonstrates that the reading of biblical texts, and for that matter the reading of any texts, is a political act.

Relating social categories to the study of the Bible is beneficial for yet another reason. Often, many of today's students have only the vaguest idea about the Bible, but countless experiences related to gender, race/ethnicity, and class. They can speak from the context of their lives how these categories affect society. Put a different way, this anthology helps students to relate from the familiar (i.e. gender etc.) to the unfamiliar (i.e. the Bible). They are encouraged to wonder why they themselves have not made the connection between the Bible and the world. For example, why do they take androcentric interpretations for granted, but not the feminist ones? They learn to appreciate how, to give another example, practices of slavery or discrimination against women were justified with the Bible. They become curious about a particular culture and society after reading biblical interpretations—for instance, from Asia. As a result, the organization of this anthology encourages the development of a critical stance toward one's view on the Bible. In a time when many people in the West know little about the sacred text of Judaism and Christianity, the organization of this book emphasizes familiar categories to increase curiosity about the unfamiliar, namely biblical text and interpretation.

The connection between the social categories and the study of the Bible addresses another tactical problem. Traditionally, textbooks deal with either the Hebrew Bible or the New Testament, while this volume responds to the growing need for textbooks on the Christian canon of the Bible. The problem is, of course, how to cover the enormous quantity of materials. This anthology solves the problem by focusing on the social categories. They provide the structural coherence to

---

[12]See, e.g., Fernando F. Segovia and Mary Ann Tolbert (eds.), *Reading From This Place*, vol. 1 & 2 (Minneapolis: Fortress, 1995).

cover a wide range of biblical texts and scholarly research that might otherwise seem disconnected or arbitrary. For instance, the section "The Rhetoric of Gender" includes discussions about the characteristics of feminist biblical interpretation in general, articles on a particular narrative from the Hebrew Bible (Gen. 2–3), articles about female characters from the Greek Bible (Mary Magdalene and women in the gospels), and research on a biblical topic related to texts from both the Hebrew and the Greek Bible (heterosexism). In other words, the category of gender makes it structurally logical, almost necessary, to cover both the Hebrew and the Greek Bible. Admittedly, the various sections include relatively few biblical texts and scholarly articles, especially in light of the vast amounts of materials available, and thus many difficult choices had to be made. Still, this volume includes a considerable amount of biblical texts and scholarship, and so guarantees an acceptable survey on the Christian canon of the Bible.

Perhaps most importantly, the organization of this anthology demonstrates that the understanding of the Bible as a polysemous text relates closely to the development of biblical research on gender, race/ethnicity, and class. Scholars have become aware of their interpretive biases and acknowledged openly their political, social, and religious interests, once they began to examine the Bible according to these social categories. Often they themselves have come from communities that endured social and political discrimination and injustice. In fact, such practices frequently motivated their academic work that targets such societal conditions. It has to be emphasized that some of the research included in this anthology uses traditional methodologies, such as historical criticism, and does not necessarily rely on "postmodern" premises. Nevertheless, the articles illustrate the postmodern concept when examined as illustrations for the postmodern notion of the polysemous Bible. Focused on the social categories, they exemplify—sometimes overtly, sometimes covertly—the notion of multiple meanings. In sum, the structure of *Biblical Studies Alternatively* integrates seamlessly with the overarching premise of postmodern biblical studies.

5. WHAT ARE THE CRITERIA FOR SELECTING THE ARTICLES OF THIS ANTHOLOGY?

A four-fold organization engages biblical texts, topics, and debates on the Christian canon of the Bible. The first section, "Introductory Matters," begins with articles on the historical development of biblical studies as an academic discipline; hermeneutical issues involved in reading the Bible; and the epistemological rationale for the concept of the polysemous Bible. The second section, "The Rhetoric of Gender," presents scholarly work on feminist biblical studies. The third section, "The Rhetoric of Race/Ethnicity," includes research about the Bible in relation to the categories of race and ethnicity. The fourth section, "The Rhetoric of Class," offers research on the Bible in light of class analysis. Introductory comments begin each section, providing brief explanations about the context and content of the articles included.

Several criteria determined which articles to include in the anthology. A first criterion established that the articles cover equally the Hebrew and the Greek Bible, and so several articles deal with the Hebrew Bible, others with the Greek

Bible, and still others include references to both. This relative equilibrium ensures that the collection as a whole does not privilege the Greek Bible over the Hebrew Bible, or vice versa. Although the volume introduces texts and scholarship on the Christian canon, it does not refer to every biblical book or familiar biblical passage. Significant materials had to be excluded. Despite the enormous and, perhaps, impossible task to be comprehensive, some people might be disappointed about the decisions made. Still, the key requirement is fulfilled, namely to introduce texts and scholarship on the Hebrew and the Greek Bible. Yet while the anthology covers evenly the Christian canon of the Bible, the selection favors U.S.-American and Christian-Protestant research for the following reasons. Most innovative work is currently done in the United States and Christian-Protestant scholars currently dominate the field of biblical studies. Although this situation is changing, it still prevails. In addition, the majority of students, registering for an introductory course on the Christian canon of the Bible, come from a Christian background, and thus the Christian bias gives them the tools to understand their own religious heritage. Despite this focus on U.S.-American and Christian-Protestant research, other perspectives are included, such as Jewish, Christian-Catholic and international ones.

Another criterion stipulated that the various segments introduce students to biblical texts, issues, and scholarship related to gender, race/ethnicity, and class. Sometimes it was difficult to decide which topic to include. For instance, interpretations on Gen. 2–3 belong unquestionably into an introductory volume such as this, although the quantity of available research made choices hard. Perhaps more debatable is the inclusion of research on Mary Magdalene, a relatively marginalized figure in the canonical gospel literature. Yet popular interest in this biblical woman and the opportunity to illustrate the history of Christian androcentrism justified the inclusion. Disputable is also the quantity of articles chosen for several topics. For instance, important articles on the book of Exodus were excluded although they have much to contribute for appreciating the Bible as a polysemous text and a reader's role in the meaning-making process. But again, a one-volume survey certainly cannot include every suitable interpretation. As such, the collection should be valued for what it is: an introductory reader. Other more specialized publications have to be consulted for deepening the analysis on the interpretive import of the Bible. This anthology offers only the groundwork for such advanced work.

Another criterion ascertained that the anthology expose students to a variety of scholarly writings existing in the discipline of biblical studies. As a result, some articles come from journals that address a general audience. Others are taken from scholarly journals that target a scholarly audience, and require careful reading from students and generous clarification from instructors. Several essays constituted chapters in monographs. Some were published many years ago, others more recently. Several authors are well-respected scholars in the field; others are more unknown. The range of sources introduces the scope of research available in the field and makes for a diverse reading experience. The volume should therefore not be read unassisted like a continuous narrative. Instead, the variety of articles invites students to pause and consider the spectrum of perspectives and methods applied when dealing with biblical text and interpretation. Not designed as a linear reading experience, the content of this anthology awaits discussion and reflection based on a circular and reflective mode of learning.

6. WHAT CAN YOU EXPECT TO LEARN FROM THIS ANTHOLOGY?

Biblical Studies Alternatively introduces some of the basics about the Bible and biblical scholarship as well as some of the more advanced and theoretical issues related to the study of the Bible in today's world. Concerning the basics, the volume provides a better understanding about prominent biblical passages and questions raised by biblical scholars. Students acquire a basic knowledge about terminology, vocabulary, and scholarly tools characteristic of the academic study of the Bible. They learn to relate the interpretation of the Bible to larger religious debates within Christianity and Judaism, the major faith communities associated with the Hebrew and the Greek Bible. They become able to critically reflect on major biblical texts, characters, and themes in the context of biblical scholarship, and become skilled at distinguishing various hermeneutical approaches. They learn to view the Bible as a complex literary document that requires careful and substantial reflection in order to understand the wide range of meanings given to the Bible by people of the past and the present. In short, students become aware of the enormity of dealing with biblical literature, and learn to respect the reasons why statements, such as "But the Bible says . . . ," are problematic and hermeneutically short-sighted.

In addition to these basic points about the Bible and biblical studies, the anthology provides an understanding about several more advanced issues involved when the Bible is examined as a book of many meanings. Among them are the following: (1) the problems of evaluating different interpretations; (2) the recognition that biblical interpretations emerge from particular cultural, political, and religious contexts; and (3) an appreciation for the intellectual benefits of studying the Bible in the academy. These are certainly the three most central issues for the following discussion although others might come up in the process of reading the Bible as polysemous literature.

A first issue, namely the evaluation of different interpretations, usually emerges in discussions on the plurality of biblical meanings. The question is then raised whether all interpretations are equally valid, a problem disturbing to many. They fear the loss of standards and authoritative norms which establish the validity of one interpretation over another. The worry is based on the accurate observation that there are, in fact, countless interpretations for most biblical passages. Who decides whether or not an interpretation is more valid or "true," to use a highly ambiguous but popular adjective, than another?

The concern about ending up in the morass of "anything goes" should not be taken lightly considering that most people, biblical scholars included, want to hold on to some sort-of truth or evaluative standard. Indeed, the plurality of interpretation is a real problem, but it cannot simply be solved by dismissing the very idea of a polysemous Bible. Rather, the plurality of biblical meanings prompts one of the most important issues related to biblical interpretation and that is the question of ethics—asking who benefits from an interpretation, and who is disempowered by it. The development of evaluative standards presupposes awareness about individual interpretive interests and affiliation to the status quo.

Different solutions to this question of deciding the ethics of biblical interpretations have been exercised in the past. Sometimes people refer to religious-institutional authority to determine the validity of an interpretation. Yet in an academic context it is certainly not enough to refer to such authority. The deference to institutional authority relinquishes the question of standard and ethics to institutional power and avoids serious reflection. Sometimes people suggest taking a vote for or against an interpretation in the effort to solve multiplicity of meaning. This position assumes that an interpretation is to be neglected if it does not gain support from a majority of people. Yet this idea is highly problematic because of its potential to discriminate against marginalized voices. The history of interpretation illustrates abundantly the oppressive nature of this idea. Sometimes people want to simply accept all interpretations, refusing any evaluative process. This position, too, is unsatisfactory on several accounts. Most importantly, the lack of judgment posits a distance to interpretive meaning that ultimately supports the political, social, or religious status quo. It also advances a pretended stance of neutrality, as if biblical meanings do not matter to intellectual understanding. Evaluative indecision or neutrality are therefore most dangerous positions because they always support the powerful and the status quo.

In view of this complex situation, biblical scholars have proposed to focus on the political consequences of biblical interpretations.[13] They look for discussions on the ethics of the various interpretations with questions like: How does an interpretation relate to the political, social, economic, or religious status quo? Does it foster suspicion toward the hierarchical structures of society or does it strengthen them? How does an interpretation relate to the larger social context from which it emerges? Why does an interpretation emphasize only a certain aspect of a biblical text? What does this emphasis disclose about the interpreter's relationship to the status quo of society? How do we as evaluators relate to the interpreter's views on society, politics, or religion? These and related questions take seriously the need to evaluate the merit of different biblical interpretations; this anthology provides resources to become trained for this crucial task.

The anthology brings awareness about another issue: the recognition that biblical meanings emerge within particular cultural, political, and religious contexts. When the Bible is studied as a product of the history of interpretation, one cannot help but see the multifaceted connections among the Bible, its readers, and the world. Such study shows that biblical meanings emerge from the particularities of the social locations of readers. In other words, the Bible does not "say" anything, but its readers articulate biblical meaning, as they see fit. This insight is central for contemporary biblical studies, though it is mostly avoided, ignored, or denied by literalist-modern Bible readers who claim to simply repeat biblical content or to reconstruct historical times. Yet students of *Biblical Studies Alternatively* learn to understand the significance of the locatedness of biblical meaning.

A third issues emerging from the study of this anthology relates to the intellectual benefits of the academic study of the Bible. Often, people—scholars included—maintain that the Bible has little to contribute to academic inquiries about society. To them, the Bible is a religious document of Judaism and Christianity, deservedly limited to the privatized and individualized realm of faith. In secular and multi-religious societies like the United States, they find the teaching of the Bible

---

[13]See, e.g., Daniel Patte, *Ethics of Biblical Interpretation: A Reevaluation* (Louisville, KY: Westminster John Knox Press, 1995); Elisabeth Schüssler Fiorenza, *Rhetoric and Ethic: The Politics of Biblical Studies* (Minneapolis: Fortress Press, 1999).

suspect and out-of-place. Often, discussions on this issue are emotionally loaded and sometimes even hostile. The visibility of Christian fundamentalist claims on biblical meaning has clearly contributed to the almost allergic reactions among many people when they hear suggestions to study the Bible in an academic context. Admittedly, much pedagogical abuse has been committed even in academia. Yet the scholarship presented in this anthology demonstrates that the analysis of biblical meanings in a world defined by plurality enriches intellectual discourse.

Unfortunately, such scholarship, as offered here, is often unknown to the public, although the anthology exemplifies the invaluable benefit of this work. Biblical research, when examined in light of postmodern assumptions, widens the cultural, political, and religious horizon, brings religion out of the privatized realm of Western imagination, connects biblical meanings to the larger realm of human interaction, and deepens intellectual appreciation for the religious, and even non-religious, dimensions of society. Ultimately, the Bible, understood as literature of many meanings, teaches the value of ambiguity. Challenging fundamentalist dualism and literalist certainty, the concept of the polysemous Bible demands flexibility and mobility. Its readers have to acknowledge the locatedness of their views and, at the same time, deal with the many other approaches to the Bible. Confronted with the long history and impressive presence of biblical meanings, readers of the Bible learn to tolerate, accept, and cherish differences as well as to hold on to their own view.

This balancing act in which right or wrong, friend or enemy, truth and relativity are simultaneously held together demands great intellectual maturity and awareness. The academic study of the Bible, if treated as a book of multiple and located meanings, nurtures growth into this direction. It also makes the Bible inherently interesting because this process never ends. Generation after generation is invited to articulate the meanings of the Bible for themselves.

7. POSTSCRIPT: A FUTURE FOR BIBLICAL STUDIES

In 1936, the Council of Church Boards of Education set out to survey courses on the Bible and religion in American universities and colleges. The survey of 828 institutions of higher education demonstrated that Bible courses constituted 29 percent of all religion courses offered. The report mentioned that, according to a 1931–32 study of 100 denominational institutions by Yale University, 30 percent of all religion courses were Bible centered. Even among non-denominational and state schools, Bible courses were more frequently taught than most other subjects in religion. The report concluded optimistically, "The Bible remains the one supreme subject of study in the field of religion in American colleges and universities."[14]

This situation has surely changed at the beginning of the twenty-first century. Despite the lack of a similar survey for more recent years, it is safe to say that the number of Bible courses is declining at American colleges and universities. Demands for a multi-religious and multi-cultural curriculum as well as limited support for the academic study of religions have reduced the number. In addition,

---

[14]Gould Wickey and Ruth A. Eckhart, "A National Survey of Courses in Bible and Religion in American Universities and Colleges: Under the Auspices of the Council of Church Boards of Education," *Christian Education* (October 1936): 22.

student interest in Bible courses is probably declining. Knowing little of the Bible, students are interested in the "big" religious questions. Yet traditional courses in biblical studies rarely engage such questions since academic Bible courses are usually limited to the historical origins of the Bible. As a result, introductory Bible courses rarely communicate the intellectual and socio-political value of the Bible.

Conceptually, *Biblical Studies Alternatively* tries to remedy this situation. Organized by social categories, the volume illustrates the unique contributions of biblical studies to a political, societal, economic, and religious understanding of society, and the interrelationship between the Bible and the world. The future of academic research on the Bible depends on the effort to affirm these connections.

BIBLICAL STUDIES ALTERNATIVELY

An Introductory Reader

PART I

INTRODUCTORY MATTERS

Introductory Comment

The academic study of the Bible is closely linked to the emergence of western modernity in the sixteenth and seventeenth centuries C.E. During this time, scientific and geographic discoveries increasingly challenged the medieval worldview, which was based on the biblical understanding of the world and humanity's place in it. Ultimately, the period of the so-called "enlightenment" displaced the God-centered with a human-centered worldview. Observation and experience substituted the traditional means of knowledge, namely faith in the authority of the Church and the Bible. Many cultural, religious, and scientific developments contributed to this shift. Among them were the colonialist explorations since the end of the fifteenth century, the Protestant reformation, and the invention of the printing press in the early sixteenth century, as well as the increasing intellectual prominence of scientific discoveries that began with Nicolaus Copernicus (1473–1543), continued with Galileo Galilei (1564–1642), and culminated in Isaac Newton's (1643–1727) formulation of the laws of physics in 1687.

These developments prompted scholars to realize that the Bible was no longer a conclusive authority for understanding the world and was actually at odds with the emerging modern worldview. For instance, the geographical discoveries of other continents confronted Europeans with the fact that peoples on these continents had never heard of the biblical God or Jesus. Their religious traditions appeared sometimes to be even older than the biblical one. As a result, European researchers began to focus their attention on the creation stories in the book of Genesis, as these narratives related to the origins of the universe and humanity. Scholars often wanted to reconcile the discrepancies between the Bible's account and the existence of humans unaware of the biblical faith. One of those scholars was Isaac de la Peyreri, whose treatise "The Pre-Adamites," first published in 1655, held that only Jews descended from the first human, Adam, as described in the Bible; other peoples originated from humans living before Adam. Ultimately, Peyreri's influential account did not prevail although some fundamentalist Christians continue to refer to it even today.

Yet the effort of examining the Bible from a modern perspective eventually led to the formation of the academic field called "biblical studies." Gradually, scholars abandoned their apologetic stance towards the Bible and, especially since the nineteenth century, formulated scholarly hypotheses about the historical and literary origins of the Bible, based on scientifically recognized methodologies, later called "historical criticism." The historical focus continues to be of major interest to many people in the West who want to know whether the stories of the Bible "really" happened or how to "believe" in the historicity of Jesus' miracles contradicting scientific explanations. Growing up with a modern mindset, Western people find it thus difficult to appreciate biblical texts in any other way but the historical one. Like many researchers during the early phases of modernity, they intuit the contrast between the biblical and the scientific-modern approach to the world. As a result, they, too, are troubled about the "truth" of the Bible, i.e. the historicity of biblical events. For several centuries, therefore, biblical scholars investigated with great rigor and forcefulness the historical validity of events reported in the Bible.

At the end of the twentieth century, the academic study of the Bible has, however, begun moving away from an exclusively historical approach. The "postmodern" turn that has swept through academia during the last decades has also affected biblical research. With the emergence of postmodern notions that recognize the multiplicity of meaning and the importance of readers in the interpretive process, more and more biblical scholars have begun to abandon objectivist, positivist, and universal convictions characteristic of modernity. Recognizing the prominence of readers and their contexts, many interpreters question that biblical texts have a single, universally valid, and historically determined meaning, once created by a long-deceased author and established independently of an interpreter's interests. Especially scholars from groups previously marginalized in western male academia argue that biblical meanings emerge from the particularities of time and space, and have to be appreciated and examined as such.

The shift from a modern to a postmodern understanding of the interpretive task challenges many commonly accepted notions about the modern ways of knowing. Still relatively new to most people, postmodern views are often resisted and even ridiculed as theories with which "everything goes" or that are "wishy-washy." Such responses are an expression of the threat that many people feel when they begin to acknowledge their experiences of living in a time of great plurality of views, religions, customs, or ideas. Many people prefer to cling to the known in an attempt to avoid an intellectual engagement with the changed conditions in western societies. In contrast, postmodern ideas acknowledge that no philosophy, ideology, or thought offers a single, universally, and objectively "true" meaning. Instead, any text has many different meanings depending on the readers and their social locations. It is time to appreciate this hermeneutical insight and to critically engage the plurality of views on the Bible, whether one applies historical, literary, or cultural methodologies. The articles of this section, "Introductory Matters," introduce the rationale and methodological issues of these developments for biblical studies as they have been emerging since the 1970s.

Four articles illuminate the scholarly direction that acknowledges the multiplicity of biblical meaning and the reader's significance in the interpretive process. Michael D. Coogan examines the reasons for the discrepancy between scholarly, particularly modern-historical, and lay approaches to the Bible. Coogan discusses the importance of biblical authority, the idea of a canon within the canon, and the impact of various exegetical methodologies for scholarly and lay readings. He documents the developments of biblical studies as an academic discipline and contrasts that to lay interest in the Bible as a document of faith. He argues for the need to make biblical scholarship more accessible to lay audiences than done in the past.

Mark Coleridge moves beyond this modern-historical view regarding the development of biblical studies. Examining the relevance of the Bible in his native country, Australia, at the end of the twentieth century, Coleridge wants biblical scholars to reflect more critically on the social impact of their work than they currently do. The article thus raises important questions about the theoretical and cultural significance of the Bible and highlights the political function of the Bible and biblical scholarship in secular countries such as Australia.

Gale A. Yee describes the methodological history of the academic study of the Bible. Outlining the most important interpretive approaches to the Bible, Yee urges readers to consciously identify their ethical responsibilities while they read biblical texts. They have to recognize that their interpretations are always connected to the political, economic, societal, or religious status quo of their respective societies. They thus have to ask themselves how their interpretations serve or critique the powers in place, and relate the quest for biblical meaning to a critical analysis of power.

The last article of this section, written by Mercy Amba Oduyoye, examines the implications of the theoretical insight that focuses on readers and their social locations. Describing the contextual and historical forces in which African Christian women read the Bible, Oduyoye illustrates her argument with interpretations of the infancy narratives of the Gospel of Matthew (Matt. 1–2). The article investigates further the significance of understanding the interrelationship among reader, social location, and the multiplicity of biblical meaning. In sum, this section provides scholarly resources for reflecting on the historical, methodological, and political implications of the postmodern notion that every biblical reading is located, situated, and particular.

The Great Gulf Between Scholars and the Pew

Michael D. Coogan

Three great intellectual revolutions of the 19th and early 20th centuries have profoundly shaped and transformed the way we think of ourselves and our world. The first is Marxism and its derivative, socialism. The dissolution of the Soviet Union and the changes in Eastern Europe may appear to have thoroughly discredited Marxism; such is the message of a letter I recently received from the Campus Crusade for Christ, which headlined its plea for funds with the message "Marx is out, Jesus is in." But many Marxist principles, such as "from each according to his abilities, to each according to his needs," have unalterably changed the social systems of the world, including our own. The particular Marxist system known as Communism has failed, but Marxism in its most basic sense has not.

The second revolution was launched by Charles Darwin's synthesis of evolutionary theory, *The Origin of Species* (1859). Despite occasional and even sustained attacks on the book and its ideas from fringe groups, it is recognized as a turning point, a classic formulation not just of where we came from but who we are. Darwin was right: The fact that monkeys have hands should give us pause.

The third intellectual revolution is that of Sigmund Freud, in some respects the most original. His explanations of the workings of the human psyche have become part of our vocabulary. Terms like ego and id regularly appear in crossword puzzles; Freudian jargon such as inferiority complex, passive-aggressive, and anal-compulsive is commonplace. Though Freud's psychological theories have been considerably modified by subsequent researchers and practitioners, their essential insight holds: As Freud himself is reported to have said of his opponents, they may disagree with us in their writings and lectures, but in their dreams they prove us right.

A fourth major intellectual revolution of the last century and a half has had surprisingly far less impact; it has to do with the Bible.

For almost 2,000 years, the Bible was widely regarded as a unified text, unequivocally the word of God and thus by definition consistent and free from error. The Bible was viewed as an absolute authority, and later, for Protestants, as the sole authority for belief and practice. Biblical views on everything from God to money were accepted without question; in Christian tradition the church in the broadest sense was the indispensable and authenticating interpreter of the Bible, but the Bible was its necessary foundation.

The first challenges to this traditional understanding of the Bible came in the 17th century, from philosophers like Thomas Hobbes[1] and Benedict Spinoza[2] and clerics like Richard Simon,[3] who began the modern study of the Bible in a critical way. (By critical I do not mean negative, but rather free of presuppositions—or at least self-conscious about one's presuppositions.) These pioneers challenged traditional views about the Bible's authority and authorship by appealing to common sense, logic and historical method. By the 19th century their approach had gained considerable momentum. One of the most significant books relating to the New Testament was *The Life of Jesus* (1839) by the German scholar David Strauss, who, for the first time, provided a clear statement of the relationships among the Synoptic Gospels: Matthew, Mark and Luke. For the Hebrew Bible or Christian Old Testament, the most influential work by far was the *Prolegomena to The History of Israel* (1878) by another German, Julius Wellhausen. During the same period thousands of ancient texts—in languages such as Assyrian, Babylonian, Aramaic and later Sumerian and Ugaritic—were excavated, deciphered and translated. Many of these texts had close or even verbatim correspondences with biblical passages, so that the view of the Bible as a unique document without parallel came under irrevocable challenge. Finally, there was an exponential growth of scientific knowledge: The Bible was simply not true, or not simply true, in the sense in which it had for so long been considered. Its cosmology, anthropology and chronology were often just wrong.

For the most part, scholars engaged in this new criticism were not only believers but ordained clergy, generally teachers in seminaries. The results of their work may be summarized as follows: The Bible is not one book by a single author, but, as the Bible itself clearly indicates, it is many books, by many authors who wrote over the course of more than a thousand years. Moreover, the Bible contains different points of view and often contradictory understandings and formulations of the nature of God and of our relationship with him and with other human beings. The Bible is not in any simple sense the word of God, but rather the words of Amos and Isaiah, of Luke and Paul.

Nor is the authorship that the Bible credits to various ancient figures historically accurate. Moses did not write the Torah (the Pentateuch, that is, the first five books of the Bible); David did not write most of the Psalms; Solomon did not write the Song of Solomon or Ecclesiastes; Isaiah did not write the entire book attributed to him; Paul did not write the letters to Timothy or Titus or several others published under his name; and it is unlikely that the apostles Matthew, James, Jude, Peter and John had anything to do with the canonical books ascribed to them.

Closely related to issues of authorship and even more significant is the question of consistency. It became clear, for example, that there was no way to

---

[1] See Thomas Hobbes, *Leviathan* (1651).
[2] See Benedict Spinoza, *Tractatus Thrologico-Politicus* (1670).
[3] See Richard Simon, *A Critical History of the Old Testament* (1678).

harmonize certain conflicting biblical details. For example, was the conquest of the land of Canaan by the Israelites a rapid series of military victories or a slow process of assimilation? Was Jesus born in a stable or in a house? In Bethlehem or Nazareth? Did his active career last several years or only a few months? Was he absolutely or only theoretically opposed to divorce? Freed from dogmatic constraints, some scholars also pointed out that the Bible did not speak with one voice on more profound theological issues as well. There were different views about the paternity of Jesus, different interpretations of the confessional statement "Jesus is the son of God."

The result, then, of what is now called the historical-critical method was an understanding of the Bible as a collection of historically conditioned documents, reflecting the biases, backgrounds and idiosyncrasies of its authors. But this understanding has had remarkably little effect on the way most people in our culture, whether religious or not, think of the Bible. This is evident in the way it is quoted by politicians, popes and pundits, and is most evident to me in the students I have taught for the last 20 years. The intellectual revolution that can be summed up in the phrase "the historical-critical method" has had virtually no impact; most people today view the Bible not very differently from the way scholars and laity alike viewed it before the Enlightenment—naively and precritically.

Why have the results of the historical-critical method, though broadly accepted by biblical scholars, had so little influence? Partly because the churches correctly perceived the results of biblical scholarship as an implicit and even explicit challenge to their authority. If the Bible is not true in any simple sense of that term, not free from error and not consistent, then so too must be subsequent formulations, whether conciliar, pontifical or episcopal. Christian leaders especially have therefore restricted the exposure of most people to the Bible. Although the Bible is acknowledged in theory as an authority, much of it has simply been ignored. For centuries there has been a kind of canon within the canon, a selection of biblical texts read in liturgical contexts that are therefore the principal contact most believers have with the Bible. Conspicuously absent from lectionaries are most or all of such books as Joshua, with its violent extermination of the inhabitants of the land of Canaan at divine command, or Judges, with its horrifying narratives of patriarchy and sexual assault in chapters 11 and 19—to say nothing of the Song of Solomon, with its charged eroticism, or of Job, with its radical challenge to the dominant biblical view of a just and caring God. Imagine if one Sunday these words were read from a pulpit as the day's lesson:

> "So I commend enjoyment, for there is nothing better for people under the sun than to eat, and drink, and be merry, for this will go with them in their toil through the few days of life that God gives them under the sun. . . . Everything that confronts them is vanity, since the same fate comes to all, to the righteous and the wicked, to the good and the evil, to the clean and the unclean, to those who sacrifice and those who do not sacrifice. As are the good, so are the sinners; those who swear are like those who shun an oath. This is an evil in all that happens under the sun, that the same fate comes to everyone. Moreover, the hearts of all are full of evil; madness is in their hearts while they live, and after that they go to the dead. But whoever is joined with all the living has hope, for

a living dog is better than a dead lion. The living know that they will die, but the dead know nothing; they have no more reward, and even the memory of them is lost. Their love and their hate and their envy have already perished; never again will they have any share in all that happens under the sun" (Ecclesiastes 8:15; 9:2–6 [NRSV]).

The skeptical theism of Ecclesiastes (Qoheleth) with its apparent hedonism has been a scandal almost since the book was written, as the scribal note at its end attests;* it is no wonder that Ecclesiastes has, practically speaking, been dropped from the Bible used by the churches.

Nor do wedding ceremonies any longer feature one of the typical, and relatively few, extended biblical texts about marriage:

"Wives, be subject to your husbands as you are to the Lord. For the husband is the head of the wife just as Christ is the head of the church, the body of which he is the Savior. Just as the church is subject to Christ, so also wives ought to be, in everything, to their husbands" (Ephesians 5:22–24 [NRSV]; compare 1 Corinthians 11:3; Colossians 3:18).

How can this be reconciled with Galatians 3:28: "There is no longer Jew or Greek, there is no longer slave or free, there is no longer male and female; for all of you are one in Christ Jesus"?

Similarly, can the sadistic torture at divine initiative of "all who do not have the seal of God on their foreheads" (Revelations 9:3–5), or any number of other passages from that book of fantasy, be reconciled with the command to be merciful even as the Father is merciful (Luke 6:36; compare Matthew 5:43–45)?

Biblical passages like those just quoted are not the words of the Lord, at least not in the sense that Christians hear them as such. But they are in the Bible, and by what criterion are they less significant or less authoritative than others? There is a contradiction in the attitude of Christians toward the Bible. On the one hand it is an icon, to be venerated—according to a recent survey more than 90 percent of households in the United States own a Bible; on the other hand, it is ignored, or at best sanitized and bowdlerized, reduced essentially to what people want it to say or think it should say.

Students regularly ask me, "Why weren't we ever told this is in the Bible?" In part, the answer is that they could not be trusted to read the Bible: It is a dangerous, even subversive collection. Exposure to such texts would require considerable explanation of the Bible as an inconsistent text with various, and in some ways incomplete, views on such topics as divine justice and mercy, the afterlife, and the status of women.

The idea of a canon within the canon is an ancient one, first formulated by Marcion in the second century. Based on his reading of Paul, Marcion cavalierly

---

*Apparently, this was thought necessary to bring the book into an acceptably orthodox mode: "The end of the matter; all has been heard. Fear God, and keep all his commandments; for that is the whole duty of everyone. For God will bring every deed into judgment, including every secret thing, whether good or evil" (Ecclesiastes 12:13–14).

rejected the Old Testament as heretical. Although Marcion's view itself was rejected, it nevertheless had considerable influence. If "the righteousness of God has been disclosed apart from the Law" (Romans 3:21) so that "now we are discharged from the Law" (Romans 7:6; compare Galatians 2:21), then what significance could the Law—the Torah—have for Christians? No matter that Paul's view is debated within the pages of the New Testament, in the letter of James and especially in the Gospel of Matthew (5:17–19), where we find what can best be understood as a direct attack on Paul's teaching by a Jewish Christian writer.

Thus, most Christian thinkers, following Paul rather than Matthew or James, have rejected the binding force of hundreds of biblical laws. Their only enduring significance is predictive or typological: They point somehow to Jesus. Still, most Christians have accepted, more or less, the enduring authority of such laws as the Ten Commandments. I say more or less, because although if asked, most Christians would claim to observe them, they have not read them; one commandment, at least, is consistently and institutionally violated, that prohibiting the making of images (Exodus 20:4–6). The long tradition of religious art depicting biblical heroes and even God clearly violates the second commandment, as the ancient iconoclasts and the more recent Puritans recognized.

Thus, within institutional Christianity, we can discern a selective approach toward biblical texts, as well as a resistance to the texts motivated by an at least unconscious fear of the implications of the historical-critical method. That method is correctly perceived as calling into question not just the authority of the Bible, but also the authority derived from the Bible.

But institutional Christianity is not the only party responsible for this situation. That widely accepted scholarly ideas have not penetrated the thinking of the laity is partly the fault of biblical scholars themselves. One area especially lacking in courage is Bible translation. Many translations do not convey exactly what the original biblical languages—Hebrew, Aramaic and Greek—say. In this way translators avoid shocking people by making the Bible seem like one book with internal consistency, rather than an anthology exhibiting development of doctrines and a concomitant inconsistency.

For example, the high mythology of some biblical traditions is often softened by a backreading of monotheism, a principle that developed only relatively late in the biblical period. Thus biblical texts repeatedly refer to a group of divinities called "the sons of God" (see, for example, Job 1:6, in Hebrew), associated with Yahweh, the personal name of the God of Israel. Most translations render the phrase with something vague like "heavenly beings" (NRSV, Job 1:6) or "members of the court of heaven" (REB, Job 1:6), obscuring the idea of a high god presiding over an assembly of other deities, a concept the Israelites shared with their ancient Near Eastern neighbors.

Another example is the repeated references to angels. The development of an elaborate angelology is, like monotheism, a late phenomenon that should not be retrojected anachronistically. The angels who appear in biblical texts dated prior to the fifth century B.C.E. are simply minor deities, messengers of the assembly of the gods, much like Iris, Hermes (Mercury) and other gods of classical mythology.

Similarly anachronistic is reading every reference to the "spirit" of God as though it referred to what later came to represent the third person of the Trinity. As in Genesis 1:1, the translation "spirit" is often just wrong. It is not "the spirit of God" that swept over the waters (see, for example, the REB translation), but simply "a wind from God" (see also Genesis 8:1). In many translations we find a tendentious capitalization of the word "spirit," as in Matthew 12:28 (casting out demons by the "Spirit of God").

To preserve the uniqueness of Israel, translators draw overly sharp contrasts between Israel's practices and those of its neighbors. Various forms of a Hebrew root meaning "to prophesy" are used in the Bible for both prophets of Yahweh and prophets of Baal, the Canaanite storm-god. Both Elijah and his adversaries on Mount Carmel are prophets, yet in most translations of 1 Kings 18:29 the latter "rave" rather than prophesy, though the Hebrew word is the same.

For the author of the Gospel of Matthew, as for most of his Christian contemporaries and their successors, the Hebrew Bible was essentially a set of codes decipherable only with the key of Christian belief. Matthew applies this principle with a wooden literalism that can have comic effects: According to Matthew 21:7. Jesus sat on two donkeys at the same time when he entered Jerusalem. This is in fulfillment, as the text tells us, of Zechariah 9:9, which contains a prophecy that the author of Matthew misread.* Only the most recent translations of Matthew 21:7 honestly, render "he sat on them," traditionally softened to "he sat thereon."

This tendency to bowdlerize the Bible also appears in the inclusive language of newer translations. The Bible is overwhelmingly patriarchal. But how different it sounds when the psalmist's or Paul's exclusively male language is broadened to include women. "Happy the man who . . . delights in the Law . . ." at the beginning of Psalm 1 becomes "Happy are those who . . . ," as if women could study the Law; and Paul now routinely addresses his "brothers and sisters" rather than just his brothers, as in the original (Romans 1:13; 1 Corinthians 1:10; Galatians 1:11; 1 Thessalonians 2:1, etc.). Such changes may be defensible for a Bible used in a liturgical context, when the words are understood to address a modern audience, but surely some Bible translation should accurately render the imperfect, gender-specific language of the original books.

Biblical studies have also been both sidelined and trivialized. Most biblical scholars, like me, became interested in the Bible for what may be characterized as essentially pious reasons. But a modern, critical study of the Bible can be discomforting. Because study may lead to disbelief, it is easier to focus on the constant new discoveries instead of the Bible itself. (Those discoveries should of course be interpreted not just for their relevance to the Bible, but in their own right.)

The Bible is probably civilization's most overstudied book. Since academics have to publish to get jobs and keep them, and since there are fewer and fewer

---

*Zechariah foretells that a king will arise for Jerusalem triumphant "riding on a donkey, on a colt, the foal of a donkey." This is an example of parallelism, in which the repetition of an idea in different words is analogous to a musical variation on a theme. There is only one animal, however. The author of Matthew misread this, so he has Jesus entering Jerusalem riding on two animals.

original things to say about the primary texts, biblical studies have often moved, understandably, to the fringes. Enormous amounts of time and energy are spent performing minute analyses of texts, themes and artifacts that more sensible historians regard as insignificant, or on studying studies of the Bible.

The timidity and centrifugal force of such studies have also resulted in a lack of popularization, perhaps better termed "accessible scholarship" by Richard Friedman. Biblical scholars often feel that expressing their methods and results in nontechnical language is beneath them. To some extent this is a product of the American academic system, which values the esoteric over the elegant. Thus biblical scholars often leave the field to the pious and ignorant.

For the latter the Bible is too often little more than an anthology of quotations to be sampled and drawn on as argument or emotion requires. The result is that in religious education, as in political and often even theological discourse, as well as in hierarchical pronouncements, the role of the Bible is to provide support from presumably unquestioned authority; it is essentially a series of proof texts.

But absolutizing part of the Bible, quoting it out of context, is risky and misguided. If the Bible is accepted as an unquestioned authority, appealed to in support of a position against, say, abortion or capital punishment—these activities are wrong, it is asserted, because the Bible says: "Thou shalt not kill"—then on what basis is the Bible not followed in its support of slavery or the subordination of women? But if we recognize that at least some of the Bible's beliefs and practices are a product of their times and hence irrelevant for a contemporary audience, then the process of biblical criticism has begun, and its consequences are far-reaching.

The impact of biblical criticism is not solely negative, however. To study the Bible critically, not as the word of God in a simple sense but as the words of human beings, is to recognize the essential task of historians and believers as well—seeking meaning in experience or, in the classic formulation, faith seeking understanding. The Bible is a record of such quests, by men and women who are our forebears as well as our predecessors: We belong to their community.

To put it somewhat differently: Whether viewed positivistically or seen as an inspired text, the Bible is the beginning of a trajectory leading toward full freedom and equality for all persons. This movement has its initial historical stimulus, perhaps, in the Exodus, the liberation of Hebrew slaves from Egyptian bondage. This event, which they saw as divinely caused, has served as a model for ancient Israel and its heirs, Judaism, Christianity and Islam—a model for interpreting subsequent events such as the repeated deliverances of Israel and of the Jewish people, the "exodus" of Jesus (for that is what Luke 9:31 calls his death) and the *hegira* of Muhammed. It has also served as a model of conduct: "You shall not oppress a resident alien: you know the heart of an alien, for you were aliens in the land of Egypt" (Exodus 23:9); that is, you should treat others as God treated you. Or, as Jesus is reported to have said, "Be merciful, just as your Father is merciful" (Luke 6:36). Or, as another prophet was told: "Did he not find you an orphan and shelter you? Did he not find you wandering and guide you? Did he not find you needy, and give you abundance? So as for the orphan, do not oppress him, and as for the beggar, do not scold him; and as for your Lord's blessing, declare it" (The Qur'an, Sura 93).

Viewed as a historically conditioned anthology, then, the Bible can be understood not as a complete and infallible guide to the details of human conduct, but as a series of signposts pointing the way to a goal that its authors, like us, had not yet reached but were moving toward. There is, in other words, a continuity between our times and those of Moses and Amos and Jesus. Their formulations, like ours and all those in-between, are imperfect, but that too is reason for optimism: They were not specially privileged, their experience of the divine was not qualitatively different from our own.

Life in the Crypt or Why Bother with Biblical Studies?[1]

Mark Coleridge

The question, Why bother with biblical studies?, is one which came to haunt me as I hacked through doctoral work in early middle age; and it nags at me now as I bid farewell to student days and settle to life as a biblical scholar of sorts. Having spent the best part of three years doing the most intense and detailed work on two chapters of Luke,[2] I am now of a mood and mind to address some of the larger questions which floated through my mind in that time—questions which I was quite unable to tackle in the thesis, but which I have the freedom to tackle now. I trust these questions are not wildly idiosyncratic.

By and large, we tend to *assume* the importance of what we do; the question of why never seems to enter our head. You need not be Maurice Blanchot to note, as he does, that "one can certainly write without asking why one writes."[3] Of

---

[1]This essay began as a paper prepared for and presented to the Fellowship for Biblical Studies in Melbourne, Australia. I have removed some of the more arcane local references, but have preferred to leave intact those which the non-Australian reader might find something less than completely bewildering.

[2]Mark Coleridge, *The Birth of the Lukan Narrative: Narrative as Christology in Luke 1–2* (JSNTS 88; Sheffield: JSOT Press, 1993).

[3]M. Blanchot, "Literature and the Right to Death," in *The Gaze of Orpheus and Other Literary Essays* (trans. L. Davis; Barrytown NY: Station Hill Press, 1981), p. 21.

course, the relentless routine of teaching and writing (and whatever else life brings) leaves little time for the luxury of distance which such questions demand. But there may be a moment to stand apart from the routine and to ponder such questions—a moment of contemplative ease such as this essay affords.

THE SCOPE OF THE QUESTION

The answer you give to the question, Why bother? will depend upon how broadly you set the context of biblical study. Are we talking about biblical study within the religious group—synagogue or church? Or is it more a matter of biblical study within the academy? Or even within the society writ large? Such questions arise only in situations like ours in Australia where religious group and academy have for the most part gone their different ways, and where society as a whole follows a different path again, listening occasionally to the voice of the academy when it suits and almost never to the voice of religion.[4]

At the *personal* level, some very obvious answers to the question, Why bother?, suggest themselves. For example: I believe the Bible to be the word of God; I am in need of the job and salary; it is the only thing I am really qualified to do.

If we take *the synagogue or church* as the context of our question, then answers are again not far to seek. The task of the biblical scholar is to teach in theological colleges and faculties; to provide an enrichment or renewal of faith for members of the religious group; to bolster ideological or doctrinal positions; to safeguard the tradition and resist fragmentation; to overcome past misreadings of Scripture, to rid the Bible of false usage and so provide either legitimation or delegitimation; to blow the whistle on dogmatism; to provide the prophetic edge in areas such as peace, justice and the environment. The list could of course continue.

If we take the *academy* as the context of our question, then answers are a little more elusive but still close enough to hand. The task of the biblical scholar is to trace the formation of the biblical texts; to explore the history of their reading; to identify the way in which the Bible functions *qua* text; to describe the work and perhaps the intention of the biblical authors; to locate the biblical texts within the context of the history of religions—and so on.

But if we take *society writ large* as the context—as I do in this essay—then the question becomes very perplexing indeed. The task of the biblical scholar is . . . what? Perhaps to provide, from the margin, social or cultural criticism of a kind? To show how the Bible is "the great code" not just of Western art as Blake claimed, but perhaps even of Western culture.[5] Perhaps to offer a critique of ideology, especially of the totalitarian variety? Or . . . what? The question was less perplexing

---

[4]It is sobering to think that when the Australian Government recently summoned a National Ideas Summit to ponder and imagine the nation's future, not a single religious figure was invited—not even, I fear to report, a biblical scholar.

[5]Blake claimed that the Bible was the great code of art, but it was Northrop Frye who in his book, *The Great Code: The Bible and Literature* (New York & London: Harcourt Brace Jovanovich, 1982), extended Blake's sense of the Bible to see it as the great code not just of Western art but of Western culture.

once upon a time when the biblical scholar functioned as the guardian of the common myth, the grand legitimating and unifying narrative of Western culture. But that is far from being the case now, though it is always possible, I suppose, to bury the head in the sand and carry on as if it *were* still so. But assuming this is not so, the question becomes: What might be the social function(s) of biblical criticism or the biblical critic *now?*

THE CONTEXT OF THE QUESTION

So much for the scope of the question: now for its context. To establish that, I turn first to the figure of Jean-François Lyotard. Lyotard, Professor of Philosophy at the University of Paris at Vincennes, hit the headlines in 1979 with his essay, *The Postmodern Condition: A Report on Knowledge.*[6] Since then he has come to be one of the more interesting and influential voices in the Gallic chorus of deconstruction: with Derrida, Lacan, Bataille and all the rest. In *The Postmodern Condition*, Lyotard claims that we live in a moment where the meta-narratives of yore no longer apply. He identifies two great myths or narrative archetypes used to legitimize science, or more precisely institutional scientific research.[7] These he calls "the dialectic of the Spirit" (the more contemplative, Germanic, Hegelian of the two) and "the emancipation of humanity" (more activist and Gallic, looking as it does to the Enlightenment and the French Revolution). With the collapse of these legitimizing meta-narratives, as Lyotard sees it, a performativity criterion takes their place. Performance—understood as that which helps the social system to function better—is what now legitimates. Instead of legitimation by means of master-narrative, we have (and need)—claims Lyotard—legitimation by performativity.[8]

The biblical critic is not exempt from such questions of legitimation. What legitimizes our work as a contribution to society? The question has very practical ramifications, one of which might be phrased as a question: Why should an avowedly secular government fund biblical study in a university? Do we still look to the myths of "the dialectic of the Spirit" or "the emancipation of humanity" to legitimize our work? Or are we prepared to accept Lyotard's performativity criterion? If so, how does biblical criticism help the social system perform or function better?

Lyotard claims that it is not merely the legitimizing meta-narratives of science or knowledge which have ceased to function. Master-narratives in general have suffered the same fate. We struggle to believe in political or historical teleologies, or in the great "actors" or "subjects" of history—the nation-state, the proletariat, the party, the West, even the New World Order, so recently touted as new myth and so quickly discredited. According to Lyotard, this does not lead to the dissolution of the social bond, or to "the disintegration of social aggregates into a

[6]J.-F. Lyotard, *The Postmodern Condition: A Report on Knowledge* (trans. G. Bennington and B. Massumi; Manchester: University of Manchester Press, 1984).
[7]See especially pp. 31–37.
[8]See pp. 41–53.

mass of individual atoms."[9] Such claims, he writes, are "haunted by the paradisaic representation of a lost 'organic' society."[10] Perhaps; but if the process Lyotard describes does not lead to the complete dissolution of the social bond, it does, I think, lead to a privatisation of discourse, a situation in which each of Habermas' "communities of discourse" engages in vigorous internal conversation, sparing hardly a glance for other communities of discourse. The Fellowship for Biblical Studies may meet here and chat away biblically; but what of, say, the Fellowship for Psychoanalytic Research just down the corridor? Have we anything to hear from or say to each other?

The same question might be put to biblical study itself as specialisation grows more intense, and as various fields of research develop their own horizons, questions and vocabulary. Take the example of two fields of NT study which happen to interest me—narrative criticism and social science criticism. Somewhere down the track they may converge; but for the moment they seem to be hurtling in different directions, developing a set of theoretical assumptions and a vocabulary which, if not wholly private, are arcane enough.

Is it possible now, with the disappearance of an overarching mythic discourse, to create any community of discourse—both within the disciplines and among them? May we speak of a grand project which we share—or may we speak only of personal projects? Has the possibility of the grand project gone with the master-narrative?

Such questions are posed at a moment when not only the meta-narratives have fled, but when some question the entire narrative impulse and enterprise. Painters for example, even some novelists, have rejected narrative as bourgeois and escapist in the light of the appalling dislocations of this century.[11] In the light of such dislocations, how can we responsibly resort to the more or less smooth continuities and connectedness of narrative? For the Bible, the impulse and enterprise of which is so profoundly narrative, this can seem to make life very awkward; it can seem to make Scripture the opium of the people, with very little indeed to offer society as a whole.

The question becomes more acute in a situation like ours in *Australia* where it is difficult for the Bible to claim any greater authority than the Koran or the newspaper, and where religion has always been marginal, at least to public life in a way not true of a country like the USA. Werner Kelber may be right that interpretation is "our essential mode of survival;"[12] but what might this now mean of the Bible in Australia now? George Steiner may claim that "the lamps of explication must burn unquenched before the tabernacle . . . ;"[13] but again what might

---

[9]Lyotard, *Postmodern Condition*, p. 15.

[10]Lyotard, *Postmodern Condition*, p. 15.

[11]On which see the remarks of J. Tambling, *Narrative and Ideology* (Philadelphia: Open University Press, 1991), pp. 95–96, where he focuses particularly on the critique of narrative (especially nineteenth century narrative) made by the Marxist literary critic George Lukács.

[12]W. Kelber, "Narrative as Interpretation and Interpretation of Narrative: Hermeneutical Reflections on the Gospels," *Semeia* 39 (1987), p. 127.

[13]G. Steiner, *Real Presences: Is There Anything in What We Say?* (London & Boston: Faber & Faber, 1989), p. 40.

this mean now in Australia where there seems to be either no temple or so many temples that it's difficult to know in which the tabernacle might be found, to know where we might burn our lamps . . . and perhaps even why we should waste our oil?

At this point, let me introduce the figure of San Keen, about whom I know less than I do about Lyotard. I gather he is American and that he has written a lot of very popular books.[14] But it was not his books which caught my eye; it was a TV commercial advertising sessions which Keen was to conduct in Melbourne. It was the title of the sessions which struck me most: "Creating Your Own Mythic Journeys." Helping people do that seems to be Sam's specialty; and if what Lyotard says is right, then it is no wonder Sam is doing a roaring trade. As far as I know, Keen is not normally associated with the New Age movement; but his title suggests that he is in tune with its deeper impulses, which tend to be radically individualistic. According to Keen, not only do you create your *own* mythic journeys, but, given the plural "journeys," you may create as many as you like. Solipsism such as this, it seems, is fertile.

Somehow we need to find a way between the contrived fertility of Keen and the equally contrived sterility of Lyotard. Is solipsism the only way beyond the kind of desolation Lyotard describes? I refuse to accept that it is; and I suspect that Scripture might open for us a different way. In search of that way, I turn to consider exegesis under the aspect of mourning.

EXEGESIS IN THE CRYPT[15]

It was Freud who first explored the deeper recesses of the experience of mourning; and his work has been developed further by analysts such as Nicholas Abraham and Maria Torok.[16] Following Freud, they speak of successful and unsuccessful mourning. In the case of successful mourning, the beloved (the lost "who" or "what") is introjected; the dead one is, as it were, wholly digested and becomes part of the mourner. In the case of unsuccessful mourning, however, the process of introjection works only to a point. The beloved is not wholly introjected; the mourner is unable to give the beloved wholly up to the annihilation of death. At this point, there is born a fantasy which may turn morbid but need not. The part of the beloved which cannot be absorbed is kept, as the analysts say, in the wall of the ego, where there forms a niche or, more properly, a *crypt*.

It is possible to understand the whole of Scripture as testimony to a people's persistently unsuccessful mourning of the *mirabilia Dei*, and therefore as an

---

[14]Among the books which made Keen's reputation are titles such as *Apology for Wonder* (New York: Harper & Row, 1969) and *To A Dancing God* (New York: Harper & Row, 1970). He has produced a stream of works since then.

[15]In what follows I draw upon two papers of the Australian poet and critical theorist, Kevin Hart—"Crypt as Gift," given in Melbourne to a conference on liturgical language, and "Reading Scrypture," given at the International Conference of the American Academy of Religion held in Melbourne in July, 1992. As far as I know, neither paper has as yet been published.

[16]See N. Abraham and M. Torok, *The Wolf Man's Magic Word: A Cryptonomy* (trans. N. Rand; Minneapolis: University of Minnesota Press, 1987).

elaborate and by no means morbid fantasy. We cannot forget, cannot wholly introject the *mirabilia Dei*. Nor would we want to; and therefore our Scripture becomes Scryp*t*ure—spelt with a "y," a crypt at its heart. It is possible to understand biblical criticism also as a fantasy born of unsuccessful mourning. The critic laments the lost narrative, the authoritative master-narrative which made things whole and so gave meaning. In this sense, exegesis may be understood as a perhaps perverse refusal to let go completely of Lyotard's "paradisaic representation of a lost 'organic' society," though it is possible and probably necessary for exegesis to imagine paradise and an "organic" society differently than does Lyotard.

Exegesis as fantasy may turn morbid, and it will if we live and work in an anachronistic world where things are presumed to be as they once were, as if the Bible still functioned in our society as the kind of master-narrative it once was. The morbid fantasy in this case would show itself as radically privatised discourse, with biblical criticism listening and speaking only to itself. Were that so, the crypt would become a tomb. The fantasy may also prove creative, but only if the moment of mourning is allowed to become a moment of discovery, if the crypt is allowed to become a womb.

In his analysis of the melancholy of mourning, Freud notes evocatively that "[t]he shadow of the object falls across the ego."[17] This may be where we are in biblical studies, at least in this country: we stand in the shadow. The object that we mourn is the Bible as master-narrative of the culture, as overarching myth for society writ large; and it is the shadow of this which falls across our corporate ego. Biblical studies in Australia and elsewhere might in this sense be judged depressed.

One symptom of the shadow here and elsewhere is the chronic weariness of the historical critical method, which has come under fire from various quarters in more or less recent times. What we have seen in the wake of this weariness is a scatter of methods, with all manner of new approaches seeking or claiming to provide biblical studies with a new kind of energy. The scatter of methods suggests that many are trying to flee the shadow, though there is widespread disagreement as to which path we should take. Stephen Moore, for instance, urges the path of iconoclasm. This means for him that we read the Bible through the lens of deconstruction—and he is not alone in taking this path, though the challenges come furiously from certain quarters. Moore's first book, *Literary Criticism and the Gospels: The Theoretical Challenge* argued for the necessity of an iconoclastic moment in biblical studies;[18] and his more recent and more wickedly titled book, *Mark and Luke in Poststructuralist Perspectives: Jesus Begins to Write*,[19] demonstrates in quite spectacular style what he means by that, with wild dionysian voices

---

[17]The phrase is drawn from Freud's essay "Mourning and Melancholia" (1917), and is cited in C. Gilligan, "Mapping the Moral Domain: New Images of Self in Relationship," *Cross Currents* 39/1 (1989), p. 57.

[18]S.D. Moore, *Literary Criticism and the Gospels: The Theoretical Challenge* (New Haven & London: Yale University Press, 1989). See especially his last chapter, "Conclusion: New Testament Criticism and Mythology," where he posits "the necessity of an iconoclastic moment in biblical studies" (p. 176).

[19]S.D. Moore, *Mark and Luke in Poststructuralist Perspectives: Jesus Begins to Write* (New Haven & London: Yale University Press, 1992).

echoing down the corridors of his text and on every page riotous mimicry of the linguistic play of Jacques Derrida and James Joyce, an explosive combination if ever there was one. Moore seems to revel in the kind of break-up Lyotard describes, and to agree with Lyotard that our task now is not to put the bits together again, to remake the master-narrative, but to make ourselves comfortable in the ruins (or the void) in which we find ourselves now. I do not necessarily agree with Moore, and I certainly think there are other ways forward for biblical studies than the path of deconstruction. But Moore remains a very telling symptom of something afoot in the biblical field. The little foxes are in the vineyard.

Part of the scatter of method in biblical studies is the turn to a bewildering array of other disciplines, as Moore's new book testifies—literary criticism, psychoanalysis, philosophy, literature, linguistics, semiotics, narratology, feminist studies, social history, sociology, as well the disciplines which have more conventionally fed biblical studies. At the same time other disciplines—literary criticism, for example—are turning to the Bible in the attempt to move beyond what many judge to be a methodological impasse.

Stephen Prickett is a case in point. Prickett was until recently Professor of English at the Australian National University in Canberra, and while there produced his book, *Words and the Word: Language, Poetics and Biblical Interpretation*,[20] in which he first signalled his lively interest in the Bible and biblical criticism, expressing regret at the cleavage between literary and biblical criticism which he judges to have been to the impoverishment of both.[21] Since his move to Glasgow, Prickett has pursued his interest, and recently published an article[22] in which he claims that the Bible has in quite precise and complex ways conditioned our sense of "the book," and that we cannot understand what we mean by "book" unless we know something of the Bible—in particular of the way it plays with unity and diversity as "the Book of books." Such interest in the Bible and biblical criticism from "outside," from another community of discourse, may stir surprise in us; we might even feel a little flattered, given how quaint and marginal we have been made to seem, at least in Australia.

Willy nilly, we are being called into a larger cultural conversation. We can of course ignore it, but that would be a pity and in the end, I think, irresponsible. When literary critics openly solicit the collaboration of biblical scholars; when postmodernism proclaims the death of all master-narratives and perhaps even of narrative itself; when the New Age urges us to "Do It Yourself"—then we hear the voice of a cultural conversation which extends far beyond the bounds of the religious group or the biblical guild. To hear that voice and answer its call may be what it takes to move beyond Freud's shadow of melancholy. It may enable us to experience mourning as a moment of discovery, to experience mourning as morning.

---

[20]S.D. Prickett, *Words and the Word: Language, Poetics and Biblical Interpretation* (Cambridge: Cambridge University Press, 1986).

[21]See especially his introductory comments on p. 2.

[22]S.D. Prickett, "Inheriting Paper: Words and William Golding," *Literature and Theology* 6/2 (1992), pp. 146–152.

I mean by this a new discovery of the Bible as polyphony, a new discovery of *both* its diversity and unity. It is true that one *kind* of meta-narrative (and with it the Bible understood as one *kind* of meta-narrative) has gone. Any totalising meta-narrative, any master-narrative which seeks or claims to be univocal, has had its day; and this is true of the Bible insofar as it seeks or claims to be a totalising or univocal master-narrative. But this allows, perhaps demands, the discovery of the Bible as *a new kind of meta-narrative*—a meta-narrative not univocal but polyphonic in Mikhail Bakhtin's sense, not monologic but dialogic.[23] Scripture may be the word of God, but the biblical God has many voices and they all speak at once: God speaks polyphonically. To attune ourselves more deeply to the Bible's polyphonic voice, we may need to read more novels, remembering that the peculiarly polyphonic form of the novel (described so tellingly by Bakhtin) takes its cue from the Bible, distantly and indirectly perhaps, but unmistakeably nonetheless. We may be at a point where it is truer than ever that to read the Bible we cannot only read the Bible.

In its refusal to give mastery to any single voice, the Bible is an unusual master-narrative. It is also unusual in the way its narrative unfolds by way of huge dislocations, refusing any sense of the smooth connectedness that some find objectionable in certain kinds of narrative. In that sense, the Bible agrees with the twentieth century painters, writers and whoever else find narrative a problem. Yet it stands irreducibly as a defence of the necessity of narrative in human life and society—and this because it agrees with Isak Dinesen that "[a]ll sorrows can be borne if you put them into a story or tell a story about them."[24] Perhaps narrative is the only way of dealing with the dislocations which make narrative itself so problematical at this time. The Bible insists upon a common narrative, but one which includes a diversity of voices; many stories comprise *the* story. God's story is both single and several. It also insists upon a narrative which at times is most disjointed and the connectedness of which is perceived only by way of struggle. The Bible is no easy read.

To be critics or servants of such a meta-narrative, as we claim to be, means a number of things. First, it means that we reject Lyotard's claim that all meta-narrative has vanished. Frederick Jameson may be closer to the mark in his Foreword to Lyotard's *Postmodern Condition,* where he makes the counter-claim that the meta-narratives have gone underground to become what he calls "the political unconscious."[25] One *kind* of meta-narrative—the univocal or totalising kind'—has gone underground, down into the crypt—and, with it, the Bible understood in those terms. But it is in the crypt that Scripture may be transfigured and emerge again into the light as a new kind of meta-narrative. If the crypt can give birth to

---

[23]See especially his work (available to me only in French translation), *La poétique de Dosto[imacron]evski* (trans. I. Kolitcheff; Paris: Seuil, 1970), especially chap. 1, "Le roman polyphonique de Dosto[imacron]evski et son analyse dans la critique littéraire" (pp. 31–81).

[24]The remark of Isak Dinesen (Karen Blixen) is cited by Hannah Arendt, *The Human Condition* (Garden City NY: Doubleday, 1958), p. 175.

[25]F. Jameson, "Foreword," p. xii.

the Bible as a new kind of meta-narrative, then Jameson's "political unconscious" may give birth to a political conscious in the biblical guild. With the mention of the *polis,* we touch the question of the social, even political function of the biblical critic implied by the sense of the Bible as a new kind of meta-narrative.

Attentive to the Bible's polyphony, the biblical critic is more aware than most that the alternative to univocal or totalising meta-narrative is not the solipsism which would have everyone create their own mythic journeys, with the radical privatisation of discourse which that implies. To discover the Bible as polyphonic master-narrative is to discover a way between Lyotard's "no(meta-) narrative" and Keen's "any narrative." It implies a refusal to yield to the anachronistic demand for a totalising master-narrative, which would have us all once again on a shared mythic journey, and the unrealistic and finally hellish demand that we each create our own master-narrative, that we go alone on a mythic journey of our own making. It is to accept and even struggle for a healthy pluralism which resists both totalisation and privatisation.

We are committed, I presume, to the belief that the Bible has an authority not just for the individual or the religious group, but also for society writ large—though it is plain to most that we need to think and speak of biblical authority in new ways. The discovery of the Bible as polyphonic master-narrative has implications on each of these levels.

a. At the personal level, it may mean a recognition that I am several: a French satirist once remarked that each of us spends so much time and energy wondering "who I am," only to wake one morning to the realisation that "I am several" ("Je suis pluriel"). I am several, but my different voices may sing together to create a single, coherent identity.

b. Within the religious group, the Bible understood in these terms authorises and insists upon a pluralism, a play of diversity and unity, which does not always sit well with religious groups which might prefer to choose between either diversity or unity, privatisation or totalisation.

c. In the academy, it will mean—within biblical criticism itself—a resistance to all totalising interpretations (like fundamentalism) and totalising claims for method (like fundamentalism). It will mean as firm a resistance to all solipsistic interpretations and claims for method. It may mean as well that we resist an excessive specialisation which allows us to hear only one voice in the Bible. Among the disciplines, it will mean that the Bible take its place in the process of converging discourses now in full swing.[26] It will mean a preparedness to collaborate with others—like the literary critics or the critical theorists—who turn to the Bible and biblical criticism in the search for new ways forward. This in turn will mean a preparedness to listen to other

---

[26]As a recent symposium of the Australian Academy of the Humanities made clear. The symposium bore the title, "Beyond the Disciplines: The New Humanities," and the publicity brochure read as follows: "During the last two decades the Humanities have engaged in radical critiques of their own political and epistemological assumptions. Positive outcomes of this self-scrutiny include a redrawing of the boundaries between traditional disciplines, and the establishment of new disciplines—the new Humanities . . . "

discourses, even to learn other languages. We have always held extravagant linguistic competence to be necessary for serious biblical study: now we may be hoisted on our own petard. I find the task very daunting indeed, but I doubt that we have a choice. It will mean finally a sturdy resistance to all weary old dichotomies like science and the Bible: to enter into conversation with, say, quantum physics or astrophysics—themselves mythic discourses—may be part of our task.

d. In society writ large, it will mean, in general terms, that we become purveyors of a vision of the possibility and necessity of conversation between communities of discourse. It will also mean that we know how to speak accessibly about the *model* of conversation which the Bible provides. It will mean that we function as a voice of (let us call it) *hope*—hope that there is an alternative to Lyotard's desolation (one form of which is the economic rationalism now rampant here), that there is an alternative to totalisation and privatisation. This sounds all very bland and inconclusive perhaps, but its social and indeed specifically political implications are real enough.

Pope Paul VI was never a man given to overstatement. Yet it was he who claimed that one of the great tragedies of our time is the cleavage between faith and culture; and the claim has always exercised my mind. I doubt that His Holiness had Australia specifically in mind, but his comment applies to this country in a special way, I think. In this essay I have considered one manifestation of the cleavage between faith and culture in Australia—the cleavage between biblical criticism and society writ large. If there is such a cleavage—and not all would agree with my claim—then we face a choice. We can ignore it and go our merry way; or we can lament it and wanly wish things were different; or we can—as I think we should—seek to understand the cleavage and do something about it, though exactly what is harder to say.

In our place and in our discipline, we stand at a moment which is both threat and promise. The fantasy may destroy or create; the crypt become tomb or womb; the shadow turn to utter darkness or to light. Death of a kind lies the way of either totalisation or privatisation: what we search for, as we grub through the jots and tittles of the text, is life of a kind. We need another way—and by "we" I mean not just the biblical guild nor the synagogue or church, but society writ as large as only we perhaps can write it, society writ large by Holy Writ.

The Author/Text/Reader and Power: Suggestions for a Critical Framework for Biblical Studies

Gale A. Yee

In his introduction to literary theory, Terry Eagleton states that

> one might very roughly periodize the history of modern literary theory into three stages: a preoccupation with the *author* (Romanticism and the nineteenth century); an exclusive concern with the *text* (New Criticism): and a marked shift of attention to the *reader* over recent years.[1]

One may also observe similar periods with special emphases either on the author, the text, or the reader in the study of the Bible.[2] Historical, form, source, tradition, and redaction criticism all focus on the author, more broadly defined to include not only the composer himself[3] but everything involved in the *production* of his text, for example, the preliterary history of the oral traditions that he takes over, the historical world in which he lived and to which he responded, and so on. The main focus of these methods, comprehensively assumed under the "historical-critical" designation, is the reconstruction of history and religion in the biblical world.

Dissatisfaction with the limitations of the historical-critical method has expressed itself within the past fifteen years in different ways. First, the field has seen a shift from author-centered *historical*-critical methods to text-centered *literary*-critical methods. A move has taken place from inquiries into the preliterary stages seeking the historical setting, the more original saying, the various *Sitze-im-Leben,* the circles of tradents, and so on, to the literary texts themselves. The turn to the text foregrounds the aesthetic beauty of the literature and the religious power of its rhetoric. One encounters firsthand the text and not simply the

---

[1]T. Eagleton, *Literary Theory: An Introduction* (Minneapolis: Univ. of Minnesota Press, 1983) 74; emphasis added.

[2]J. Barton, *Reading the Old Testament: Method in Biblical Study* (Philadelphia: Westminster, 1984) 198–207.

[3]I am assuming that the Bible on the whole is a product of male authorship, particularly in his symbolization of woman as evil.

formative historical situations behind the text. This shift from author to text, from production to product, from history to literature, has taken a number of forms, corresponding to the plurality that already exists in contemporary literary theory.[4]

Second, another trajectory in biblical interpretation remains author-centered in approach but moves beyond history to the social world of the biblical text. Scholars here employ the methods and models of cultural anthropology and sociology to shed light on the ancient society and culture of the biblical world. Focus is put on the interrelationships of groups organized in social structures, functioning in harmony or in conflict.[5] The topics of interest from a social-scientific perspective are many and varied. One may investigate the social structure of ancient Israel as a confederation of tribes, as a nation under a monarchy, or as a people under a colonial power. Others can examine kinship, marriage, and inheritance customs; class structures; values systems (for example, honor/shame, purity/impurity); or the social roles of priesthood, ritual, and symbol—all in order to illumine the biblical world of both the Hebrew Bible and New Testament.

Third, along with the move toward text-centered methods, biblical criticism has witnessed the emergence of reader-centered criticism.[6] As the name implies, reader-response or reception theories locate meaning in the experience of the reader and his or her *consumption* of the text:

> The reader makes implicit connections, fills in gaps, draws inferences and tests out hunches; and to do this means drawing on a tacit knowledge of the world in general and of literary conventions in particular. *The text itself is really no more than a series of "cues" to the reader, invitations to construct a piece of language into meaning.* In the terminology of reception theory, the reader "concretizes" the literary work, which is in itself no more than a chain of organized black marks on a page.[7]

Biblical criticism is still undergoing shifts in paradigm from author, to text, to reader, which parallel similar movements emphasizing literary production, written product, or reader consumption in contemporary literary theory. It is possible and quite legitimate to keep the three elements, author, text, and reader, analytically distinct in biblical criticism. The discipline of biblical studies already manifests this heuristic separation in the different emphases placed on each of these three elements during the course of its history of interpretation.

---

[4]See, for example, R. M. Schwartz, ed., *The Book and the Text: The Bible and Literary Theory* (Cambridge, Mass.: Basil Blackwell, 1990). In the turn to the text, one also observes the rhetorical criticism of J. Muilenburg; the focus on narrative poetics in M. Sternberg, R. Alter, A. Berlin, and S. Bar-Efrat; on narratology in M. Bal; on structuralism in D. Jobling; and on deconstruction in P. Miscall.

[5]B. J. Malina, "The Social Sciences and Biblical Interpretation," *The Bible and Liberation: Political and Social Hermeneutics* (ed. N. K. Gottwald; Maryknoll, N.Y.: Orbis Books, 1983) 11–25. N. K. Gottwald, "Sociological Method in the Study of Ancient Israel," in *The Bible and Liberation*, 26–37.

[6]E. V. McKnight, *Post-Modern Use of the Bible: The Emergence of Reader-Oriented Criticism* (Nashville: Abingdon, 1988); idem, *The Bible and the Reader: An Introduction to Literary Criticism* (Philadelphia: Fortress Press, 1985). See *Semeia* 31 (1985) and 48 (1989) for special issues on reader-oriented approaches to biblical texts.

[7]Eagleton, *Literary Theory*, 76; emphasis added. See also the annotated bibliography in J. P. Tompkins, ed., *Reader-Response Criticism: From Formalism to Post-Structuralism* (Baltimore: Johns Hopkins University Press, 1980) 233–72.

Problems arise, however, when one views the essential critical act in studying the Bible solely as the determination of its "meaning," whether this meaning is located in the author, the text, or the reader. Critical analysis then becomes primarily *interpretation* of this foundational text, whose ultimate goal is "meaning" (either the author's, the text's, or the reader's meaning). I will first address the problems in privileging one of these three areas where "meaning" is thought to occur. I will then argue for a shift of focus in biblical study that takes seriously the question of power that influences author, text, and reader in the production, product, and consumption of "meaning."

PRIVILEGING THE AUTHOR

One problem in the exclusive focus on the author in traditional historical criticism is the neglect of the text itself. Obvious reaction to this restriction of meaning to the author is seen in the shift away from historical criticism to more literary-critical investigations of the biblical text in recent years.

The modification of author-centered approaches in the present rise of social-scientific criticism is also not immune to the neglect of the text.[8] In a review several years ago, I criticized a social-scientific study on the ancient Israelite woman by Carol Meyers precisely in this regard.[9] Although Meyers's interdisciplinary approach is informed by the social-scientific and archaeological theories that illuminate the social world of ancient Israel, she has no literary theory to reckon with the biblical text itself. This lack of literary theory accounts for her dismissal of the biblical text in her reconstruction of the ancient Israelite woman. In her endeavor to show that the position of women in ancient Israel was higher than has been appreciated, she overlooks passages in the text itself that would reveal otherwise.

PRIVILEGING THE TEXT

The text-centered literary-critical approaches to the Bible are susceptible to the same criticisms lodged against their literary counterparts, New Criticism, formalism, and structuralism. Severing the text from the author and the reader results in an ahistorical analysis that regards literature primarily as an aesthetic object unto itself rather than a social practice intimately connected to a particular history.[10] The valorization of the text, what Mikhail Bakhtin describes as *"the fetishization of the artistic work artifact,"*[11] ignores the workings of ideology in the text. It disregards

---

[8]D. Jobling ("Sociological and Literary Approaches to the Bible: How Shall the Twain Meet?" *Journal for the Study of the Old Testament* 38 [1987] 85–93) has already discussed this problem in his review of N. K. Gottwald's *The Hebrew Bible: A Socio-Literary Introduction* (Philadelphia: Fortress Press, 1985).

[9]G. A. Yee, review of *Discovering Eve: Ancient Israelite Women in Context*, by C. Meyers, *Catholic Biblical Quarterly* 52 (1990) 530–32.

[10]Eagleton, *Literary Theory*, 91.

[11]M. Bakhtin, "Discourse in Life and Discourse in Art (Concerning Sociological Poetics)," *Contemporary Literary Criticism: Literary and Cultural Studies* (ed. R. C. Davis and R. Schleifer; 2nd ed.; New York: Longman, 1989) 394. See also, Eagleton, *Literary Theory*, 49

the fact that ideology is *produced* by a particular author, culturally constrained by historical time, place, gender, class, and bias, among other things.

Besides ignoring its *production*, the valorization of the text, or the *product*, creates problems in the *consumption* of the text by the reader. These problems become particularly acute when reading the Bible, which has a different normative value in different religious communities. Difficulties lie in the location of meaning primarily in "the text" as *the* inspired word of God. The biblical text is vested with an authority that is literally sacrosanct. The major dilemma is that competing claims to truth become very problematic. The same text can be used for diametrically opposed contexts and theological positions. A work like the book of Exodus can be appropriated by both a right-wing fundamentalist and a Marxist liberation theologian. Genesis 1–3 has been taken up by misogynists and feminists alike to diminish or exalt the status of women. Those who locate meaning exclusively in "the text" must reckon with the issue of competing claims to truth, rather than simply dismissing the opposing view as heretical or bourgeois, male-bashing or sexist. One of the insights of modern literary theory is the recognition of the polyvalent character of the text.[12] In different ways this insight is being taken over by scholars of the Bible.[13] However, religious and denominational constraints often still hinder or preclude the development of a more reader-sensitive doctrine of biblical inspiration.

PRIVILEGING THE READER

The term *eisegesis* is one often employed by biblical scholars to refer to what should *not* be done with regard to the Bible, that is, "reading into" the biblical text what one wants it to mean. It is opposed to *exegesis,* ostensibly the correct way of studying the Bible, where, through historical-critical and some varieties of literary-critical exegesis, one is able to draw "out" of the text its meaning.[14] The negative evaluation of eisegesis is related to two assumptions about the nature of "correct" exegesis: first, that an objective, value-neutral inquiry into the text is possible in a proper exegesis of the text, and, second, that there is *one meaning*, primarily the author's own, that exegesis wants to discern. The suspicion of the reader of the biblical text is closely allied to the determination of both religious and academic communities to control the interpretation of such a founding text. Interpretation is put into the hands of elites and specialists who are equipped (either by the laying on of hands or with academic degrees) to grasp *the meaning* of the text.

---

[12]This is particularly evident in poststructuralism. See Eagleton, *Literary Theory,* 127–50.

[13]See S. Lasine, "Indeterminacy and the Bible: A Review of Literary and Anthropological Theories and Their Application to Biblical Texts," *Hebrew Studies* 27 (1986) 48–80.

[14]See J. H. Hayes and C. R. Holladay, *Biblical Exegesis: A Beginners Handbook* (Atlanta: John Knox, 1982) 5.

Although a plurality of reader-centered literary theorists exists, each having different perspectives on the role of the reader,[15] all of them seem to concur in opposing the conviction of New Criticism that meaning is intrinsic to the literary text totally and exclusively. Taking their cues from their literary colleagues, reader-centered biblical scholars challenge historical-critical methods with their so-called objective, value-neutral search for *the* definitive and universal meaning in the biblical text, thought to be located either in the author's intention or in the world represented by the text. The shift of paradigm to the reader underscores the importance of context and a reader's specific social location or place of interpretation. The positionality of the reader with respect to factors such as gender, race, class, ethnicity, and religion becomes determinative in answering the question, What does the text mean?[16]

Nevertheless, in an engaging article Jane Tompkins maintains that despite their apparently radical divergence from New Criticism, reader-oriented critics are akin to their New Critical associates in presuming that determining "meaning" is the goal of the critical enterprise:

> The essential similarity between New Criticism and reader-response criticism is obscured by the great issue that seems to divide them: whether meaning is to be located in the text or in the reader. The location of meaning, however, is only an issue when one assumes that the specification of meaning is the aim of the critical act. Thus, although New Critics and reader-oriented critics do not locate meaning in the same place, both schools assume that to specify meaning is criticism's ultimate goal.[17]

Tompkins goes on to show that in the classical period, in the Renaissance, and during the Augustan Age, audience response rather than the determination of meaning was the primary critical concern. In classical antiquity, language was considered a form of power that is exerted upon the world. Hence, literary criticism was absorbed in mastering the rhetorical skills that enabled one to wield that power and in exercising ethical control over literary production. In the Renaissance, when poets became dependent upon an aristocratic class for patronage, poems were regarded as a public form of influence, a means of accomplishing

---

[15]S. R. Suleiman, "Introduction: Varieties of Audience-Oriented Criticism," *The Reader in the Text: Essays on Audience and Interpretation* (ed. S. R. Suleiman and I. Crosman; Princeton, N.J.: Princeton Univ. Press, 1980) 3–45. The first two chapters of S. Mailloux, *Interpretive Conventions: The Reader in the Study of American Fiction* (Ithaca, N.Y.: Cornell Univ. Press, 1982) 19–65, provide a helpful critique of psychological and social models of reading.

[16]According to McKnight, *Post-Modern Use of the Bible*, 150: "A reader-oriented approach acknowledges that the contemporary reader's 'intending' of the text is not the same as that of the ancient author and/or the ancient readers. . . . But is there not continuity between the past and the present? Is it not possible that the reader's 'intention' is of a piece with the author's intention and with the meaning and significance found by earlier readers with different views? This will mean not that there is no meaning, but that meanings discovered in different epochs are authentic—that meanings discovered with approaches that are informed by discourse and hermeneutic oriented insights are authentic in the same fashion—not final, but satisfying and authentic."

[17]J. P. Tompkins, "The Reader in History: The Changing Shape of Literary Response," *Reader-Response Criticism*, 201.

specific class-related social transactions. During the Augustan Age, satire commanded the literary scene, and the literary act was regarded as a weapon to be hurled against an adversary, as a partisan activity whose purpose was to advance individual and factional interest. Thus the social functions of literature and the motives of its users were particularly foregrounded in criticism during this time.

Nevertheless, from the late eighteenth century onward, culminating in New Criticism, literature was gradually severed from its social roles and designated as an aesthetic object of contemplation and study. "Once the literary work has been defined as an object of knowledge, as meaning not doing, interpretation becomes the supreme critical act."[18] According to Tompkins, reader-response critics have failed to break out of the New Critical mold that equated criticism with the quest for meaning and explication. She argues for a shift of emphasis "away from the analysis of individual texts toward an investigation of what it is that makes texts visible in the first place." Taking on a political nature in this endeavor, criticism will share a commonality with a long history of criticism prior to formalism in viewing language as a form of power exerted in the world. Questions regarding meaning will be framed more broadly in the complex relationship between discourse and power: "What makes one set of perceptual strategies or literary conventions win out over another? If the world is the product of interpretation, then who or what determines which interpretive system will prevail?"[19]

DISCOURSE AND POWER

Whatever dangers the term *eisegesis* signal for interpreters should not blind them to the fact that all scholarship on the Bible begins with the *act of reading:*

> Be it from the point of view of philology, historical criticism, textual criticism, or on the literary side, close reading, structuralism, or deconstruction, each and every approach to the Bible starts with readings. Readings always in the plural.[20]

Biblical scholars should therefore repudiate the positivist notion of a value-free investigation. Any investigation into the biblical text through whatever method is a reading by a particular reader.

According to Mieke Bal, the exegetical methods themselves are institutionalized sets of codes, or modes of discourse, structured by readers and imposed upon the text by readers.[21] A particular exegetical method functions like a template to

---

[18]Ibid., 222.

[19]Ibid., 225–27.

[20]M. Bal, "Introduction," *Anti-Covenant: Counter-Reading Women's Lives in the Hebrew Bible* (ed. M. Bal; Bible and Literature Series 22; Sheffield, England: Almond, 1989) 11–12.

[21]M. Bal, *Murder and Difference: Gender, Genre, and Scholarship on Sisera's Death* (Bloomington: Indiana Univ. Press, 1988) 2–11. The disciplinary codes, or modes of discourse, that Bal examines are the historical code, the theological code, the anthropological code, and the literary code. The thematic code and the neglected gender code constitute the two transdisciplinary codes.

make some sense of the text or give it some coherence. It gathers the codes in the text and correlates them with its own mode of discourse or code. The synthetic ability of interpretive codes to integrate seemingly diverse and disparate data into a coherent whole accounts for the power of codes as critical instruments. Nevertheless, while acknowledging that codes lead us far into the understanding of the text and its cultural background, Bal argues that *"at the same time* they reveal to what degree their bias imposes, stimulates, or permits a practice of censorship that stems from the restriction and the institutionalization of codes."[22]

The characteristic feature of this censorship in all the exegetical methods paradoxically discloses by way of exclusion the interests, biases, and ideologies of those who utilize them. What is deemed important to study in a particular investigation automatically reveals what is not important to look at. We have already seen how author-centered inquiries invariably neglect the text and reader and how text-centered methods often overlook the author and underestimate the reader. We can expand the author- and text-centered (or production-, product-centered) categories further: examining only powerful men in the biblical world excludes all women and ordinary men. Looking only at elite groups in that world overlooks the common folk, poor people, slaves, and other marginalized populations. A text that recounts only the exploits of great men makes it seem as if these were the only individuals important in the society that produced it. A text told from the perspective of the conquerors will not usually reveal the interests or the pain of the conquered.

By choosing a particular method with which to study a biblical text, a reader automatically sets limits on the kinds of questions that can be asked and on the results of her or his investigation. It therefore behooves a reader to be conscious of what these methodological limitations actually are. Lack of regard to the censorship feature in any exegetical method lulls a reader into a false security that allows "the implicit codes—moral, religious, and aesthetic—to go unnoticed, smuggled in like contraband."[23] It is precisely these implicit codes affecting the conclusions of one's study that divulge one's concerns, prejudices, and ideologies. The real danger in espousing a "value-neutral" perspective in reading is having an ideological agenda without acknowledging it.

At stake in foregrounding the reader is one's ethical responsibility in reading and its concomitant political repercussions. This is especially the case in reading such a foundational work as the Bible, a book that continues to be a powerful standard for people's present-day social, as well as religious, attitudes and behavior. The Bible was not written to be an object of aesthetic beauty or contemplation, but as a persuasive force forming opinion, making judgments, and exerting change. It was a form of power acting upon the world. Hence, Tompkins's suggestion that a shift of critical emphasis focusing on what makes the Bible visible in the first place is particularly relevant. Critical study of the Bible would then be in keeping with the more pragmatic notion of criticism in antiquity that sought to appropriate a

---

[22]Ibid., 9.
[23]Ibid., 136.

text's rhetorical power and to exercise ethical supervision over its uses. Such a criticism poses different questions: How does my reading of the Bible affect my relationships with my spouse, my children, with others in my religious community, my social community, my national community, my global community? Does my reading help in transforming society or does it (sub)consciously affirm the status quo and collude with its sexism, racism, anti-Semitism, classism, and imperialism? Which power groups and interests does my reading serve or not serve? What power groups have a say in determining the "veracity" of my reading?

> However eagerly one attempts to overcome the limitations of reading, every scholar of texts is a reader in the first place. Acknowledging that status, and accounting for the underlying guiding conventions, is a primary ethical responsibility of all scholars. Not only must we acknowledge the relative status of our readings, we also need to analyze the positions of power which underlie the social circulation of readings.[24]

In giving this attention to the reader, I am not advocating a completely reader-centered investigation. In fact, my argument is that one should not privilege any of the three areas author/text/reader as the sole locus of meaning. This includes the reader. Nor am I championing eisegesis, reading into the text what you want it to say. Both the author and the text constrain the reader in some way, just as the reader constrains in some way both the author and the text. Nor am I rejecting meaning as a legitimate pursuit in critical inquiry. Rather, my concern is that the question of meaning be more broadly framed within the relations of discourse and power. What are the social locations of power that make meaning possible in the *production of meaning* in the text and in the *consumption of meaning* by the reader?

In emphasizing the reader, I wish to show three things: first, how all exegetical approaches are a matter of reading; second, how the rejection of the reader, in the mistaken interests of an objective, value-neutral study, makes the reader/investigator unknowingly (or perhaps even knowingly!) complicit in the institutionalized ideologies of the methods, which have for the most part excluded gender, race, and class as specific categories of analysis; and, third, that all readings involve ethical responsibility, particularly in the case of a religiously and socially influential work like the Bible.

I have kept the discussions of author, text, and reader (production, product, consumption) analytically distinct for heuristic reasons. They are, however, very much interconnected, interrelating through the course of history very much like a spiral that is both circular and linear. The ancient biblical writer affects and is affected by the social world in which he lives. In a very real way, he is a product of that world. Nevertheless, he is involved in the production of that world in the production of the literary text. The text that he proffers is his "reading" of the social world he inhabits, a "reading" that describes, legitimates, denounces, satirizes, entertains, and exhorts that social world. In short, through his "reading" of his social world he attempts to create or produce that world. His "reading" becomes a

---

[24]Bal, "Introduction," 15.

product for consumption by other readers, who themselves are products of their own social world. These later readers utilize the ancient text/reading in the production of their own "readings" of their particular world in order to legitimate, satirize, entertain, exhort, and so on, that world.

In order to get beyond the problems of author-centered, text-centered, or reader-centered methods, one should not privilege any of these areas. A critical task in biblical exegesis is developing a theoretical framework that encompasses all three components, author, text, and reader, as they interface with power. This theoretical framework must be able to bridge the fissures among the author (broadly defined to include everyone and everything involved in the production of the text), the autonomous text, and the specific reader, all three in their historical specificities of gender, race, class, and religion. "Meaning" and "truth" in the biblical text involve a dynamic interplay among these three, with power as the pivotal variable. "Meaning" and "truth" must be critically analyzed to determine the answer to the question: Whose meaning and whose truth?

Biblical Interpretation and the Social Location of the Interpreter: African Women's Reading of the Bible

Mercy Amba Oduyoye

THE BIBLE

The most precious common heritage of Christians all over the world and in all ages is the Bible. This rather trite truism may seem simple enough, but it is loaded with pitfalls. One could ask, for example: Which Bible? Whose interpretation? Does one have to have the whole of the Bible? At another level, although reading the Bible as individuals and in groups has been the tradition of some Christian communions, for others this "open Bible" represents a recent experience. A further set of questions could be raised around the fact that the Bible is a *book* to be read. Of what use is it if one cannot read at all or cannot read the language in which the

Bible is presented? Such questions are very real in Africa, given its high level of illiteracy, which defeats even the heroic efforts at translation of the Bible Society.
This essay on the use of the Bible in Africa has such questions as a backdrop.[1]

Muhammad described Jews, Christians, and Muslims as people of the Book.
In fact, the Bible and reading became the distinguishing mark of Christians in
West Africa in the early days of the nineteenth-century missionary enterprise.
Later, when people began to distinguish between Protestantism and Roman
Catholicism, they associated going to Bible class with the former and attending
catechism with the latter. The "open Bible" of the Protestant is exemplified by
the practice of the Harris Movement, which swept West Africa from Liberia to the
Ivory Coast and was taken over by Wesleyan missionaries operating out of the
Gold Coast (Ghana) at the time.

Churches that are part of this movement leave a Bible open and in a conspicuous place in order to symbolize its availability to all. It is said that by reading directly from the Bible and retelling the story of the salvation of humanity by God in
Christ from the principalities and powers, the prophet Harris moved tens of thousands to forsake "their fetishes and to seek a higher religion," one that has *a book*.
The book became the new idol, a carrier of the divine presence. This was the effect
of the Bible as taught from the social location of Western missionaries evangeliz-
ing Africa, without regard for the sociocultural background of the audience.

The open Bible—together with prayers, dreams, and visions—continues to
bring many to God-in-Christ through the African-instituted churches. This phenomenon is greeted with mixed feelings. For Roman Catholics in eastern Africa,
for example, it has resulted in the church's keen interest in "small Christian communities" that attempt to appropriate the biblical message for themselves. This
has led to attempts at co-opting and institutionalizing them. The spontaneous attraction to the Bible is also recognized as an opportunity for teaching. All Christian communions in Africa now recognize this need for "the church" to guide
believers through the Bible.

With that as background, I should like to focus on the following five topics:
(1) the Bible as a symbol of God's presence and protection; (2) the Bible and
African religiocultural contexts; (3) the Bible as the main source of Christian theology in Africa; (4) reading the Bible from the context of African Christian women;
and (5) an example of a Bible reading from an African cultural location.

THE BIBLE AS SYMBOL OF GOD'S PRESENCE AND PROTECTION

The Bible has a special place in the hearts and homes of African Christians. The
question is, How is it appropriated? A couple of stories will suffice to illustrate
this. Living a rover's life, I am often behind in my assessment of how life in Ghana
is changing. I was, thus, completely puzzled when I arrived at a sister's house and
saw an open Bible in the cot of her newborn babe. "You have left your Bible here,"

---

[1]The Africa referred to in this essay excludes Mediterranean as well as Nilotic Africa, the location of
the Christianity of the first millennium.

I called. "No, it is deliberate; it will keep away evil influences." I was dumb-founded: the daughter of a Methodist pastor, with a doctorate in a discipline of the natural sciences, earned in a reputable U.S. university, using the Bible as a talisman! When I told this story in the course of a social occasion in Nigeria, a discussion ensued that revealed many more such uses of the Bible: Christian lawyers who keep a Bible on every shelf of their library; houses built with Bibles buried in their foundations and individuals buried with Bibles in their coffins; Bibles in cars that may never be read but whose presence proves comforting, a sort of Immanuel, or God-with-us.

The Psalms, although well known and well loved, also have a mystique all their own. Specific psalms are prescribed for specific circumstances. Some are to be said with a lit candle and a bowl of water for greater effectiveness as vehicles of petitions. Others, like Psalms 21 and 23, are to be memorized and repeated when danger lurks in one's path. Firm is the belief that the Bible speaks the truth and protects the innocent, so young people have recourse to the Bible as a key system for "divining" whenever a dispute arises, especially concerning petty pilfering and gossip. And of course in most of the English-speaking world of Africa, persons swear on the Bible to tell the truth in the courts of law.

There is also a use of the Bible as guide that involves reading. This we find among those who believe in using a verse a day to guide them. They open the Bible and take as the message from God whatever meets their eyes, often acting that day as much as possible in accordance with the message in question. More systematic individual and family readers make use of daily guides, which add comments, prayers, and hymns to Bible passages to facilitate daily devotions. Bible study groups usually focus on specific books and use a variety of forms, although most churches follow a lexicon developed by themselves, issued by their communion, or borrowed from other communions. Somehow or other, much of the Bible gets read in church.

The Bible is a popular book in Africa, peddled by colporteurs and sold in markets alongside other wares, sometimes even by Muslims. Its price fluctuates according to supply and demand. In many countries it is a best-seller, and in some it is the only book in the mother tongue. Passages, verses, and stories are alluded to in conversations, even by persons who have never stepped into a church. Creative literature written by Africans often quotes or alludes to the Bible.

Bible passages employed in these ways are, like any biblical text, to be studied with the social location of the authors in mind. Many Africans find that the Bible has a ring of truth about it, that its language, proverbs, and ideals of morality and justice are very close to the world they know and understand. It is one of the few books they own or have heard about, and many read it if they can. It may be the only religious book in which God speaks their language, since African-language Korans are few.

The stories I noted above about uses of the Bible in Africa could be compounded endlessly. These stories are not just anecdotes but realities that biblical scholars in Africa have to bear in mind when attempting to communicate their scholarly readings of the Bible.

THE BIBLE AND THE AFRICAN RELIGIOCULTURAL CONTEXT

Why do Africans find the Bible attractive? What's in it for them? In effect, Africans who study the Bible locate themselves within its history, its culture, its social structures, and its obvious assumption that the divine is a reality and is involved in the created order.

J. S. Mbiti provides an overview of this inadequately analyzed aspect of Christianity in Africa.[2] He points out that when black Africans are in direct conversation with the Bible, they experience an affinity with the culture of the Bible— what is "history" in the Bible corresponds to life as they live it. The Bible mirrors life, affirming and confirming African cultural, social, and religious life. For example, the Bible presents events and concepts that are echoed in the African colonial and neocolonial experience: in the takeover of land in Africa by immigrants from Europe; in Africa's economic life at a very basic stage; in migrations, settlements, and the struggle between the urban and the rural, the pastoral and agricultural; and in African ethnic strife and "tribalness." Similarly, the Bible's depiction of social arrangements of families and lineages; of royalty and birthright; of rules governing community interaction; and of caring for the stranger—all these are familiar to Africans as well, as are rules governing what one eats. A dramatic parallel in this regard involves the creation of nations out of ethnic communities and the tensions and challenges of that effort. The primal world of the Bible is thus alive in Africa today, as is exploitation by the global economic order.

In Africa people do not quibble about what they should learn from the Bible: the simple rules of life, ethical and moral, are life-enhancing. Where there is a conflict in the Bible, it is often a case of an old law versus a new law. Such dilemmas are not unknown in the corpus of African wisdom. When all else fails, we create new myths to replace oppressive African myths. In fact, at some points, where the Bible text is clearly a "text of terror" from the standpoint of what we understand to be the project of the living God, we may even need other texts. The Bible has become part of the received wisdom. For the African Christian as for the early white missionary, the Bible has become a standard for evaluating African religion, culture, and society. Since the Bible does not divorce religion from other aspects of life, Africans have felt at home with it. All of life is seen as a whole. Unfortunately, much of this acceptance follows the legalism of the missionary approach, which is still rampant even though the Western churches are under African leadership.

The universal history of Genesis 1-11 confirms several African myths of beginnings, which also seek to explain fundamental puzzles such as the unity and diversity of humanity, the immanence and transcendence of God, the human capacity for good and evil, and God's continued care in spite of human unworthiness. The Bible speaks of God and God's dealings with the world and involvement in human realities. It is the written source of theology, and it challenges, confirms, corrects, modifies, and reshapes the belief in God that informs

---

[2]J. S. Mbiti, *Bible and Theology in African Christianity* (Nairobi: OUP, 1989).

Africa's own religion and causes those who read it to try a fresh approach to God, Christianity, and life. The Bible is the word of life.

At a consultation of Jewish scholars and African Christian theologians (Nairobi, November 1986), a statement was made that proved significant for me: "Scripture is not a European creation." Such a realization frees African Christianity from the insistence that it justify itself before the court of European and American judges. Both the attempts by Mbiti and others to show that Africans use the whole of the Bible and the view of Kwesi Dickson and others who point to the African predilection for the Old Testament are relevant here. We are accountable in our theology to God and to the people to whom we tell it.

If we are selective in Africa, we are not alone in this "sin." When one is being denied justice, the God of justice speaks with exceptional clarity from the pages of the Bible. Yet, as is true elsewhere, not all in Africa go to the Bible with ears and eyes keen to hear and see this God. So then in Africa too one finds a variety of theological emphases coming from the one Bible. African Christians are not alone in being Christocentric: Jesus Christ is our teacher and the example we follow for a life acceptable to God. We are also, to be sure, trinitarian monotheists, but what is unique about our religion is Jesus Christ. So we do need the New Testament and the Hebrew Bible. We need the whole Bible, including what is called the Apocrypha.

THE BIBLE AS MAIN SOURCE OF CHRISTIAN THEOLOGY IN AFRICA

African Christian theologians take the traditional Reformation view that the central source for theology is the Bible. Only when we have had the chance to read for ourselves can we begin the steps toward our own theologizing. For the churches instituted and led by black Africans, the Bible was the only written source for Christian theology, liturgy, and practice. They found in the Bible how God had spoken directly to Adam and Hagar, to Pharaoh through a prophet, and to Joseph through dreams and their interpretation; they found there the use of symbolism, the taking off of shoes, the blessing of water, and many other ritual approaches to religion. They also found sacrifices, healings, and appearances of spirit beings. They understood theology in the Bible as people talking about their encounters with God. Praying is a real and dynamic encounter with God that has power to bring about what is desired. The Bible is used to construct types of ministries and to validate the roles of persons in the congregations.

Preachers and theologians who have a background in formal biblical studies do their theology from the open books of the life around them, the Bible, and other written sources. Theologies worth that name in Africa speak of a salvation that reconciles humanity to God and with creation and that brings a reign of justice, peace, and compassion on earth among human beings. The Kairos Document, which came out of South Africa, has been an open challenge to the historical theology that lies at the foundation of Western Christianity in Africa. It has recalled the story of Jacob and Esau: there is no reconciliation without repentance and restitution. The insistence on working for transformation as the required end of theologizing and as a further source of theology is a word for all Christians everywhere. African biblical scholars are conscious of being part of a faith community to which they are accountable for exposing the truth as they see it.

The narrative theologies exemplified by the sermons of Desmond Tutu and Allan Boesak, the speeches and healing sessions of Emmanuel Milingo together with the written theology of Jean-Marc Elá—these and all the other forms that see the God of the exodus and the gospel at work in Africa demonstrate the liberative use of the Bible in Africa. They have witnessed in the Bible the God who comes to rescue and who promises a future of righteousness and peace. It is this God of the Bible that African theology seeks to present, so that the people may praise and adore God and become partners in the struggles for God's future. Women sing of the exodus in Fanti lyrics, and the God of Moses who caused thousands to cross the river is praised as the God of compassion. Shoes are taken off to remind us of God's holiness and the sacredness of each place that God has given us. Reading the Bible, we are assured that God has not moved away from earth and has not withdrawn from human history, leaving us to our own clever devices. God's story has not been sold to humanity as the Akan folktale alleges; rather, the human situation is seen as infused with the story of God.

In the Bible we have found samples of the revelation of God through human history, reality, and experience. The Bible empowers us to proclaim God's will in the name of Jesus and through the power of the Holy Spirit. The Spirit that came mightily at Pentecost is alive and well and powerful in African Christianity—the Bible affirms this belief as the gifts of the Spirit are experienced in both dramatic and pragmatic modes. The Bible has brought a message of hope to Africa and African Christians; therefore, we hail and love the Bible. If one finds a Bible in a cot in Africa, one should know that it is a symbolic expression of God's continued presence in and care of the whole of creation, especially of those too weak to fend for themselves. In such a cot, then, lie the two loves of African sisters—God and humanity.

READING THE BIBLE FROM THE CONTEXT OF AFRICAN CHRISTIAN WOMEN

WOMEN'S BIBLE STUDY GROUPS

The story of "the Bible in the cot" should be taken together with the story of the Bible that is sung. The first women to appropriate the Bible in Africa heard it read and its stories retold. They met God in the narrative and transmitted their testimonies in "poetic theology," singing, praying, and commenting on the biblical events. These women—mostly farmers, traders, often marketing their own produce and products—also had crucial responsibilities in their families and the larger community. These were women with not a minute to spare, but they still found time for church and churchwomen's groups, where praying, reading, and sharing insights from the Bible were central.

They appropriated the Christian faith not only from sermons but also from listening to the Bible read by the few women who at that time could read. In Bible class there was opportunity to talk about what they had heard, something that they could not do when the Bible was preached as doctrine. In Bible class they had their faith strengthened and were blessed with courage for the journey. Such groups continue not only in rural Africa where the illiteracy rate is high but also in urban communities where people read the Bible for themselves. Reading the Bible as a community of believers has become a practice for empowering women.

It is not often that these groups move on to public issues, but there have been instances when the women have observed that their experience of particular aspects of church and/or society could not be the will of God. When they have judged certain situations to be unjust, these women have usually gone ahead to seek amelioration without politicizing the issue or seeking to enter a protest in the appropriate quarters. Women have taught other women, especially girls, to read. They have passed on survival skills, both economic and societal. Only on very rare occasions have African church-women challenged African culture, even when they have judged its practices to be inhuman and unjust. It is therefore important to call attention to the Presbyterian women of Kenya who, as far back as 1922, formed the Council of the Shield in order to resist female circumcision. This initiative later became the Presbyterian Women's Guild, a group offering courageous resistance to a practice woven into the very fabric of their community life. To sustain their resolve, they needed to stay close to the Bible. Through Bible study meetings and prayers, they learned to live as Christians in the wider community. Bible study groups in girls' boarding schools remain a valuable part of Christian women's culture in most parts of Africa. Nyambura Njoroge's research, although focusing on ethics, deals extensively with the biblical concept that promotes women's dignity and humanity.[3]

WOMEN THEOLOGIANS

Although several of the African women with tertiary education in theology are in fields other than biblical studies, they all resort to the Bible in theologizing and in the construction of Christian ethics in the African context. The particular contexts of these women result in a reading of the Bible that varies as much from the perspectives of African male theologians as from those of the churchwomen discussed above. The churchwomen who are ordained and/or work directly in the institutions of their churches, especially in pastoral roles, also tend to approach the Bible somewhat differently than the women theologians working in academic situations. The critical approach to the Bible possible in a university context is deemed unsuitable in Bible study groups, especially in cases where there is no opportunity for continued contact. The context determines whether the Bible is to be read as shared sustenance, for meditation, as an aid to prayer, or as a source of solace. We concentrate here on Bible study as a written contribution from women seeking to understand or discover God's will for their particular circumstances.

---

[3]N. Njoroge, "The Woman's Child: The Institutional Locus for an African Women's Christian Social Ethic," Ph.D. diss., Princeton Theological Seminary, 1992.

This rereading is empowered by the fact that within the Bible itself there is reinterpretation.

Certain aspects of life in Africa send women theologians to reread their Bibles. Everyone knows from the mass media that life in Africa can be ugly. In spite of this reality, we have evidence of how African women continue to say, "We dare to believe." Women theologians living in Africa, where the daily news sounds like Hebrew Bible narratives without the miraculous deliverances, still dare to believe in a God of love who delivers from adversity. As churchwomen memorized biblical events of deliverance, composed lyrics, and sang them in the midst of adversity, so women theologians write down their cries, confident that God hears and comes to deliver them. In the midst of internecine wars, the Bible is read for the affirmation of family and community as well as for a proper interpretation of hospitality in the African context. The experiences of shifting populations, famine, flood, and other disasters send women to the Bible in search of the God of love, the gracious one who blesses and nourishes the whole of creation. Women see affluence and poverty, misuse of political and economic power, the battle of religions in Africa, and they go to the Bible in search of a word from the God of justice.

In the midst of such conditions, the Bible has been a pivotal tool in the search for meaning. Women have brought their experience into Bible translation seeking accuracy and inclusiveness. Finding dynamic equivalents in African languages to describe women and women's experience has been a challenge to Musimbi Kanyoro of Kenya, who picks up translations of concepts like "help," "wife," and "concubine" that tend to put a negative label on women and that are deduced even when they are not explicit in the text. In addition to the words used of women are the stories told about women in the Bible. Sarah, Tamara, Hannah, Ruth, and Elizabeth are used to validate the unrelenting search of African women for fertility: the message is that God will open the womb, so one must keep on trying and hoping and believing. The struggle between Rachel and Leah to bear sons and the fact that all "special" babies of the Bible are boys come in for a great deal of attention. Women thus seek for a word from God that validates them apart from their child bearing. They look for strong women of the Bible.

The lives of biblical women are reviewed from the perspective of their tenacity arising out of their faith in a God whose purpose for human beings is fullness of life. African women can thus center their thoughts on the salvation, love, and grace of God. Women who read the Bible for themselves or with other women are able to enrich and critique the selective repertoire chosen by men for women, a repertoire that focuses on the alleged inferiority of women and their alleged culpability as the source of sin and evil in the world. They begin to critique both culture and faith as taught and transmitted by men. Teresa Okure's scientific study of the Johannine corpus uncovers a profound meaning of mission and reinterprets the woman at the well in a way that will cause traditional missiologists to sit up and take notice.[4] Those who love to focus on the "embarrassing sex life" of the woman will need to take up their Bibles and read a little more carefully.

---

[4]T. Okure, *The Johannine Approach to Mission* (Tübingen: Mohr, 1988).

When African women who live under active and blatant patriarchy read the Bible, it touches their situation actively and directly. They see the horrors around them and gather courage to expose such horrors and to struggle against them. The affirmation of the dignity and humanity of women drawn from the Bible makes African women audacious. They no longer join in teaching girls to accept and defend their alleged inferiority. Women feel a strong and double affinity with those Gentiles whose admission into the household of God features prominently in the New Testament. In the midst of patriarchy African women seek to live beyond it because they can point to women in the Bible who lived beyond the patriarchy that surrounded them.

Okure points out the need to recognize human sinfulness as "cultural conditioning" and not "the dictate of God." This means that instead of the self-righteous dismissal of those different from us, what women learn from the Bible is that "what is not liberative cannot be of God." She validates these women's readings from their experience by means of a comparison with the response of the crowds to the teaching of Jesus. The crowds, argues Okure, recognized authority in the teaching of Jesus, not in that of the scribes. It is, therefore, quite in order for women to decide which scripture is authoritative. They can detect "what makes sense, what claims their lives and allegiance." When women read the Bible, they hear God affirming their search for community; they see God working through the disadvantaged; and they expect God to act to liberate African women, members of the disadvantaged of humanity. African women theologians like Okure, who have learned not to see biblical texts as normative, are learning to deal wisely with the book, for even with texts about the life and words of Jesus not all can be said to be culturally liberative.

Women theologians in Africa are open to the liberating and empowering themes of the Bible. The Bible has good news for women. The Bible studies of five women published as *Talitha, qumi!* all bring out the empowering elements in the chosen passages.[5] Freedom in Christ summarizes what they live even as they move in a largely oppressive cultural context. They are in tune with the method suggested and practiced by Okure when they reread Scripture, particularly those texts said to embody the eternal and divine will for women in creation, while recognizing that the Bible has both oppressive and liberative elements. While appropriating the liberative strand, the women theologians consistently struggle against the use of its elements for the victimization and marginalization of women. It is in so doing that they draw heavily on the interaction between Jesus and other characters of the New Testament, especially the women. Employing the contextual approach, women reread the stories and from them draw new and empowering meaning.

Musimbi Kanyoro, who coordinated the Bible study sessions at the September 1989 convocation that resulted in the book *Talitha, qumi!* observes: "During the Bible study sessions, it became clear to us that for women to find justice and peace

---

[5]M. A. Oduyoye and M. Kanyoro, eds., *Talitha, qumi! Proceedings of the Convocation of African Women Theologians* (Ibadan: Daystar, 1990).

through the texts of the Bible, they have to try and recover the women participants as well as their possible participation in the life of the text." She also proposes that women read the Scripture side by side with the study of cultures and learn to recognize the boundaries between the two. Her own study of Luke 8:40–46 includes role play, personal reflections, group reflections, and retelling the event from the perspective of the various actors, including that of the mother of the girl Jesus raised, a person who does not say a word during the entire proceedings.[6]

Justine Kahungu Mbwiti, studying John 4:1–42, begins by saying: "We have come into contact with this text of John, which is an interpretation of the life of Jesus. Our reading in faith is therefore an 'interpretation.' What meaning do we make for this day? What questions do we have to put to John?" Here too the response is one of faith seeking meaning and relevance from the biblical narrative.[7] For Okure, one meaning drawn from this biblical event is that if the woman at the well can be redeemed, so can all other sinners who encounter the Christ and engage in dialogue with Jesus through the Gospels. Both Kahungu and Okure underline the testimony of the woman to her own people, the whole village, not just the women and children.

The context of marginalization in the church, the demonization of women's sexuality in both church and society, and the crossroads of the gospel and African culture have all generated intensive Bible studies. Women's actual experiences are discussed in the context of the biblical text. Reflections on slavery, poverty, and lack of recognition have led to studies on how the Bible has been used to support injustices such as apartheid and the lack of adequate compensation for and recognition of women's economic participation. The underlying patriarchal ideology has been traced to African usages, biblical patriarchy, and the Westernization of African society. The Bible is seen by African women as a two-edged sword. On the one hand, it is used to support women's alleged inferiority, polygamy, levirate marriage, the focus on sons, the silence of women, and so on. On the other hand, the same book is seen as a source for resistance of sexual violence and the promotion of the dignity of the women. So like biblical women, African women sing God's victory; they demand justice in the name of God. Some create sisterhood to deal with women's disabilities, such as widowhood and single parenting, and confront structures of injustice with resistance and transforming actions.

The Bible is read by economically poor women and in the context of a poverty that is shared across the "classes"—a conclusion that African family traditions demand. The God of justice and power is seen in the Bible as the God of new life and transformation, and women challenge the church to be in mission to poor women. When women observe and describe the injustice perpetrated in church and society, they pronounce God's judgment and demand that the breaches in community be mended. The Bible is read from current history with little influence of traditional, historical, and doctrinal theology. The tools for biblical exegesis are used but not followed as unbending, once-for-all rules. Jesus is announcing a new

---

[6] M. Kanyoro, "Daughter, Arise (Luke 8:40–46)," *Talitha, qumi!* 54–62.

[7] J. Kahungu Mbwiti, "Jesus and the Samaritan Woman (John 4:1–42)," *Talitha, qumi!* 63–75.

way of living, and each generation has to listen to this message in its own context. One may learn from history, but African women claim the freedom not to see the received interpretation as a static deposit of faith. We read the Bible knowing that no one has the last word on the word of God.

We could characterize this appropriation of the Bible via one's own context as a liberation method. Women are committed to fullness of life in Christ; therefore, they are involved in life-enhancing activities and courses. Reading the Bible, they bring all this experience with them and reflect on the word from God as it comes to them through the Bible. Women's contextual approach to the Bible is anchored in faith in the God who acts continuously in the affairs of creation. Hence, Judith Bahemuka writes: "Revelation is not only a process which began at the time of our ancestors and achieved its fullness in apostolic times, it extends to all history and will never cease."[8] From the Bible, generations have protested many forms of injustice. Today, when African women enumerate the "texts of terror" both in the Bible and in real life, they include cultural texts, racist texts, imperialistic texts, colonial texts, and neocolonial texts, but they continue to hold on to the Bible because in it, also, lie embedded the texts of divine love that empowers.

The primary social determinants of the majority of African women are that they are women and black. Gender discrimination knows no class boundaries. The women writers of Bible studies referred to here cannot be comfortably located in any affluent class. When they talk about poverty, they are not talking of poor cousins, for in Africa you are only as "rich" as family responsibility will allow you to be—and I mean the extended family.

In the very strong conservative and literalist African milieu in which we read the Bible, this liberation method is suspected as subversive, if not altogether unacceptable. We have chosen workshops and other community efforts to give support to one another and provide a forum for self-critique. We can never forget that we live in a religiously pluralistic continent and that our concerned critique of the church and rereading of the Bible may be construed as disloyalty to Christianity in its struggle to show itself as truly African. We also read the Bible as individuals looking for consolation and guidance and sometimes simply to enjoy the sheer beauty of its language and the vividness of its imagery and symbolism. Above all, as women in a continent where the majority of women do not read, we have a context of advocacy. The Bible is a source for the right to fullness of life for all who give and nurture life, and it is as such that women theologians read the Bible.

A survey of the small Christian communities who study the Bible in Kenya reported that most of the participants in these groups were women and children. In one of Nairobi's parishes, 76 percent of the membership of these communities were women.[9] Women's experience in both church and society makes them run to the Bible for consolation and affirmation.

---

[8]J. Bahemuka, "The Hidden Christ in African Traditional Religion," *Jesus in African Christianity. Experimentation and Diversity in African Christology* (ed. J. N. K. Mugambi and L. Magesu; Nairobi: Initiatives, 1989) 1–16.

[9]"Report on Consultation on Methods of Research to Find Out How the Bible Is Being Used in Small Christian Communities in Africa" (Karen-Nairobi, 1989). Sponsored and organized by the Catholic Biblical Centre for Africa and Madagascar (BICAM).

In 1987 women from Umtata in the Transkei of South Africa, of all ages, of different races and marital status, and having a wide variety of interests, commitments, and careers, constituted themselves into a women's theology group. They read the Bible together, discussed "matters of mutual concern," and committed to writing the studies they carried out in order to share them with other women and make them available to men as well.[10] The love of African women for the Bible has moved into a phase in which they consciously seek to share its message as they see it with others. Being South Africans, the Umtata women recognize that they are torn by race, class, culture, and gender, but also that they are united by many things. Indeed, women's common fears unite them: husbands who drink; husbands who are violent; children struggling with growing up; unemployed men around them; rape. One gets much the same list in Kenya and in Algeria. Women are joined together in the struggle to make life a bit more comfortable for those around them—they work eighteen hours a day and always do more than two jobs. They study the Bible together in the context of hope.

Women who read the Bible from the context of relative privilege, such as the professional women who met at the University of Calabar, Nigeria, in 1990, often pick up on the struggles of biblical women on behalf of others.[11] They want the heroines of the Bible to become models for their own struggle to be a liberative force in their communities. It is interesting to note that the Calabar conference was organized by women theologians in the context of the sociopolitical program called "Better Life for Rural Women," which was the brainchild of Mariama Babangida, the wife of the Nigerian head of state. To illustrate this reading of the Bible by African women, I turn now to the infancy narratives of Matthew's Gospel.

AN EXAMPLE OF READING FROM AN AFRICAN CULTURAL LOCATION: THE ANNUNCIATION TO JOSEPH

The following is a reading of the Matthean infancy stories (Matthew 1–2) in the context of the challenge to the churches to stand in solidarity with women. The phrase "Ecumenical Decade: Churches in Solidarity with Women" has revealed a number of assumptions and ambiguities about what the church is understood to be. The most critical of these is the question: Are women not an integral part of the church? While in Africa some women have been baptized into the church, the vast majority have not. They do not belong to an institution called church nor even to the organized religion called Christianity; they have their own faith traditions. The "Ecumenical Decade" is asking for the church's solidarity with all women. A second question has to do with the traditional naming of the church in feminine terms, while the vast majority of the visible leadership (clergy) is made up of men

---

[10]*Umtata Women's Theology Bible Study Series* (Pretoria: C. P. Powell Bible Centre, 1987).

[11]R. Edet and M. Umeagudoso, eds., *Life, Women and Culture: Theological Reflections* (Lagos: African Heritage Research and Publications, 1990).

who are themselves members of this female body. This state of affairs is much in focus because of the parallels it evokes with male-female relations in the human community in general and with certain images in Scripture.

In the Hebrew Scriptures the kinship of Israel and Yahweh is described in terms of marriage. Israel (a man's name) becomes the spouse of Yahweh. This relationship recalls the Canaanite religions in whose context Yahwism grew. Both the congregation of Israel (*qahal*) and the covenant assembly (*'edah*) are feminine in gender, thus reinforcing the femaleness of Israel in relation to Yahweh. This imagery is reproduced in the New Testament, where the kinship of Jesus the Messiah and the church is described by Paul in marital terms (Eph 5:21–33). Here again the gender of both *ekklesia* and *kuriak[emacron]* (kirk, church) is feminine. In the English language one also finds the custom of making the church female. So the church is female, while its rulers, the priests, are male. As Jesus the Messiah husbands the church and is its head, so we have been socialized to believe that it is an anomaly to have a woman as head of a church.

Further, Mary, the mother of Jesus, is sometimes called the prototype of the church, the first to believe that the kingdom of God was about to become a reality. She believed that God could dwell with people. She believed that the chains of the oppressive aspects of traditional community and human relations were about to be broken, that hierarchies would be no more, that the church, the gathering of God's people, would become truly human, and that the presence of God in this new human community would become truly palpable. Indeed, a bleeding woman would touch the garments of Immanuel and be healed. Mary believed that God would come among us and that the human community would be transformed into the fully gathered family of God. This faith of Mary makes her a symbol of the church; thereby another female image is painted.

This female image of the church has encouraged the leadership of the church (mainly male) to appropriate for themselves the headship. Sadly, then, the church of human experience is a male organization (of clergy and prominent laymen) that has to be called into solidarity with women. The church of experience cannot be described as com-passionate nor as being among the people of the world "as one who serves"—nor even as a father living and nurturing both daughters and sons as God does. Women's solidarity with the church is not reciprocated by the church. In the church as in the family, women's services are taken for granted and received without recognition. Why is this?

Reflecting upon the tardiness of some sectors of the church over the issues of the churches' "Ecumenical Decade," it has dawned on me that perhaps it has something to do with this marital image and the way marriage functions in many societies. I am suggesting that the dominant image of the church as a female ruled by the ordained (men) has affected even how we remember our gospel narratives. The "annunciation" in Luke has overshadowed that in Matthew. So I propose to take the events of the coming of Immanuel/God-with-us from the perspective of Joseph, the first man to accept that God would be with us in human form and the man who stood by the woman who was filled with the vision of what that world would look like.

JOSEPH'S DREAMS (MATT 1:18–25; 2:13–15; 2:19–21; 2:22–23)

In Matthew's narrative of the events surrounding the birth of Jesus the Messiah, the role of Joseph is highlighted, thus offering us an opportunity to see God's project with humanity in a holistic manner. The *annunciation* in Matthew is to *Joseph*, a man guided by dreams and visitations from God's angels. When we first meet Joseph, he is described as a son of David in a genealogy geared toward telling us why Jesus of Nazareth was called Son of David later in the narrative (1:1–17). Then follows the saga of the marriage that could not be consummated (1:18–25).

Mary and Joseph were planning to follow the traditional expectations of their culture and community to the effect that young people of marriageable age would get married and start a family. The reverse was an abomination. The story says that Mary was "found to be with child from the Holy Spirit" (v. 18). This explanation of the origin of the pregnancy could only have come from Mary herself. We know of only one other person who shared the secret, her cousin Elizabeth (Luke 1:39–45). Mary and Joseph were living in Galilee in a town called Nazareth. But when Mary accepted this marvel, she left to go to Judaea in the hills to see Elizabeth, for the angel had disclosed that she too was about to deliver a miracle-child. This type of solidarity of women has held the churches' "Ecumenical Decade" together until now. So now we turn to what the solidarity of the churches with women could look like, for, like Mary, many women are pregnant with a new vision of how to live as God's family and in God's world with God among us.

First Dream (Matt 1:18–25).

The gossip about Mary's pregnancy got to Joseph. How, we are not told. But I prefer to imagine Joseph beaming at the sight of Mary, his would-be bride. The whole town is filled with the excitement of the anticipated wedding feast. They hope the wine will last the stipulated number of days. Joseph and Mary and their two families owe it to the town to provide the usual festivity. Joseph begins to rehearse the coming public declaration of approval of their marriage and the blessing that Mary will be like a fruitful vine. "Wait a minute," says Mary, "I have something to tell you." Imagine the painful story Mary had to tell, the shock and disbelief on Joseph's face—the emotions, from anger to despair and disappointment.

Joseph's world begins to crumble around him. Mary has deviated from traditional expectations. As if that were not enough, she is making this outrageous claim—a child of the Holy Spirit indeed! Filled with their different thoughts, they go their separate ways. For Joseph this is a nightmare. Tradition requires that all plans for the union be called off. Tradition demands that he make a public example of this girl who has gone against the norms of society. That night he tosses and turns. Joseph the righteous (Matthew's description of him) agonizes. He suffers with Mary. She is just as distraught and disappointed at the turn of events, if not worse.

The first question: How do I give up a person I love to be disgraced before the whole community, maybe stoned to death (Nazareth was known for that) or burned alive (as happens elsewhere)? Genesis 38:11–26 tells of the response of Judah, Tamar's father-in-law, to the news that Tamar had played the whore and was pregnant: "Bring her out, and let her be burned" (v. 24). These drastic measures were necessary to ensure the purity of the patriarchal line. Joseph's ancestry by the father's line included Abraham, Zadok, David, Mattan, and his own father, Jacob. Mary is telling him the name of the child she is carrying. He does not participate in the choice.

The second question: Can I call this "Immanuel" son of Joseph, when he is in fact "son of the Most High"? Can I hand on my patriarchal line to this Immanuel conceived of the Holy Spirit? Is the line begun by Abraham to end with me? How do I face the family of Jacob? How do I explain the link between Joseph son of Jacob and Jesus son of the Holy Spirit? The discontinuity was too dramatic to pass over lightly. He turns over, wide-eyed; that night was not going to be for resting.

Third question: How do I face my friends, the peer group, the whole clan, and the whole of Nazareth? Am I now the laughingstock of the town? (Joseph twists and turns.) I cannot stand being disgraced, and I cannot bear having Mary disgraced. The way out?

Joseph the righteous responds differently from Judah, Tamar's father-in-law. He will not bring her out. Better call off the marriage quietly. (Having made this painful decision, Joseph falls into an uneasy sleep.) Joseph is then visited by the divine solution to this human dilemma. How is tradition transformed to respond to the will of God, the plan of God to live among God's people? Joseph wants a middle way to conform to tradition only to the extent that the new would not be hurt. God proposes radical solidarity.

The angel of God appears to him and says: "Joseph, son of David, do not be afraid to take Mary as your wife, for the child conceived in her is from the Holy Spirit" (v. 20). Joseph keeps these words in his heart and resolves to act on them. I would like all men to put themselves in Joseph's place, walking around Nazareth facing insults and insinuations. Joseph stands by Mary; Joseph shares Mary's burden. Joseph enables Mary to carry through God's project. Joseph believes Mary's encounter with the Holy Spirit. He stands by her while the whole community wonders, What next? A major tradition is being undermined, and Joseph, son of David, is part of the new move. Imagine the tough journey to Bethlehem. From hotel to hostel to homes they search for accommodation. Joseph is sharing God's project. He is participating with Mary to facilitate God's project. Joseph is helping to look for a place where room could be made. The rest of creation too had been waiting, the stars and the animals are all awaiting the coming of God among creation. Joseph has to be midwife to Mary. Joseph has to provide the encouragement and comfort and security needed to bring "the new" out safely. Mary says, as in the Christmas carol:

> Joseph dearest, Joseph mine,
> help me cradle this child divine.

Joseph sits contemplating this vision of new life at his bosom, while Mary tries to rest from the task, excitement, and wonder of the birth of Immanuel, grateful for the silent and not-so-silent witnesses at the birth of the child of the Most High. Mary blesses God for giving her Joseph, the com-passionate.

Second Dream (Matt 2:13–15).

As if this were not enough, this new life is the cause of a national crisis. This "new" brought in by a woman with the solidarity of a man must not be allowed to live. The event is a threat not only to religious and cultural traditions of the Jews but also to the political situation. So the angel of dreams visits Joseph again: "Get up, take the child and his mother, and flee to Egypt, and remain there." For the sake of this "son" of the Holy Spirit, Joseph is to become a refugee. He will have Mary and the baby to keep him company, but what happens to his carpentry shop? His contribution to Nazareth as a skilled person for the building of projects will be missed, and he will lose income. He will lose contact with friends, colleagues, and family. All for the sake of the "son" of the Holy Spirit and his (Joseph's) decision to stand in solidarity with Mary and her burden from God. So to Egypt the family goes—Jesus, Joseph, Mary—refugees in Egypt living out the meaning of solidarity.

Third Dream (Matt 2:19–21).

Finally, the time comes to move back. The dream comes again: "Get up, take the child and his mother, and go to the land of Israel" (v. 20). But the family cannot stay in Israel for fear of Archelaus (v. 21), now reigning in Judaea.

Fourth Dream (Matt 2:22–23).

As a result of another dream, the family sets off for Nazareth in Galilee. Here Joseph keeps all these things in his heart, and together with Mary they nurture the "son" of the Holy Spirit.

We began with marriage; here we see marriage as partnership. Here there is no master-servant relation that objectifies women. Here is love in action. Such total solidarity, empathy, co-laboring, companionship, and faith in the vision of a woman are what the "Ecumenical Decade" calls the churches to embark upon. First, the "Ecumenical Decade" calls upon the churches to learn to believe women have a new vision of what church and society could look like. Second; the churches are also called upon to reexamine their own and society's traditions and make room for the new to be born.

THE CHURCHES IN SOLIDARITY

There are churches that, like Joseph, have enough faith to stand by women against unbending traditions. These churches, like Joseph, are cradling the visions of the "Ecumenical Decade" and "making room" for their realization. In the first four years of the decade we have found men who, like Judah, the father-in-law of Tamar, are able to say: "The woman is right; I was wrong." Let us look for men who, like Joseph, love and respect the humanity of women and are therefore ready to grant that God works through women. The churches shall be in solidarity with women when, like Joseph, the angel of dreams visits them with the annunciation of the birth of the new life in God's kingdom. This I believe.

We have had happy experiences of churches in solidarity. We have also been faced with painful experiences of churches and persons who seem unable to relate to women, except in hurtful, patronizing, or demeaning ways. Thus, there are churches that do not feel able to leave the past and go to Egypt, that are unable to break with the old structures, that fear the new relationship of women and men that the "Ecumenical Decade" calls for, that are refusing to open themselves to dreams of the new, that are refusing to listen to God's messengers, that cannot even believe that women can be pregnant with the Holy Spirit and bring into being new visions and new perspectives, that have no room for women pregnant with new visions of a community of women and men.

CONCLUSION

Women reading the Bible in Africa are doing so in a context permeated by death and death-dealing forces. These women are not insulated from this context and therefore belong to the social and civic forces seeking to protect and nurture life, to guard and promote the dignity of the human person, and to ensure that neither human life nor the rest of creation is abused. As Christian theologians they bring a spirituality of struggle fueled by hope into this effort of African women. They hope the church will believe and act out the message of salvation. They hope the Spirit of God will move governments and traditional leaders to be just, compassionate, and respectful of human life and women's lives. They hope that in good time the fullness of God's presence will be realized in Africa.

PART II

THE RHETORIC OF GENDER

Introductory Comment

When the Second Women's Movement emerged in Western societies in the 1970s, feminist scholars began to examine the history and politics of gender in biblical research. This section selectively explores some of the issues involved when identifying the Bible as a gendered text with a gendered history of interpretation. Two contrasting factions have developed among Western feminists who considered the value of the Bible for the feminist movement. One group has suggested that the Bible is utterly androcentric, i.e. male-centered, literature. To feminists of this persuasion, the Bible is a detriment to women's rights and has little to contribute to the liberation of women from patriarchal oppression. The other group finds this position too simplistic. Often religiously committed to Christianity or Judaism, these feminists assert that the careful examination of the Bible leads to a more complex and nuanced appreciation of its value than conceded by the first group. Investigating the Bible with scholarly methods and tools, these feminists thus appreciate biblical texts in light of feminist concerns.

Several decades of such work have produced an enormous amount of scholarship, which makes any kind of categorization very difficult. Still, it is possible to distinguish no less than three approaches advanced by feminist biblical scholars. First, they have *re-interpreted* biblical texts to counter patriarchal readings, which have typically discriminated against women. Second, feminist scholars have *recovered* biblical texts and characters that were marginalized or mostly ignored in the patriarchal traditions. Third, they have *identified* androcentric tendencies in biblical text and commentary, and so their interpretations have offered guidance in resisting androcentric imagination and politics. In addition to these three strategies, feminist - interpreters have also begun to relate gender questions to other forms of oppression, as several articles in the sections on race/ethnicity and class illustrate. Sometimes, feminist scholars combine one or the other approach, which makes a clear differentiation not always possible. At other times, they favor one approach over another, as if other feminist strategies do not exist. Yet all of these scholars concur that the Bible is gendered literature with a gendered history of interpretation. Hence, a focus on "The Rhetoric of Gender" characterizes all of their work despite diversity of views and methodologies.

Four sets of articles illustrate concerns and accomplishments of this vibrant area in biblical research. The first set, entitled "The Bible and Feminism," addresses the history of women reading the Bible and the socio-political questions involved in defining biblical interpretations as specifically feminist. Although feminist scholars, trained in the field of biblical studies, have begun to transform the academic study of the Bible only since the 1970s, women have counteracted gender discriminatory readings of the Bible for centuries. Carolyn De Swarte Gifford provides a glimpse at this history. Her article focuses on white American and Protestant women of the nineteenth century and describes how women like Judith Sargent Murray or the Grimké sisters used the Bible to challenge the religious and political gender prejudices of their time. Phyllis A. Bird and Pamela Thimmes move to the current era and address the problem of characterizing interpretations as "feminist." Bird and Thimmes offer different, if not contrasting views, and so demonstrate the plurality of feminist positions in biblical scholarship.

The second set of articles, entitled "The First Woman and Man as a Gender Issue," moves the discussion to a prominent narrative in the Hebrew Bible. The creation stories in Genesis 1–3, highly influential in the Western articulation of gender, are familiar even to the most secular people. Not surprisingly, feminist investigations of these biblical chapters critically examine patriarchal readings and dismantle their pervasiveness even up until today. Helen Schüngel-Straumann surveys the Christian interpretive history of Genesis 1:28, and illustrates the connection between patriarchal practice and biblical interpretation. Phyllis Trible reinterprets a feminist Christian interpretation of the Eve and Adam story in Genesis 2:4–3:24. Characterizing Eve as the pinnacle of divine creation, this interpretation hypothesizes the first woman as the first feminist; the Eve and Adam story becomes a feminist tale in the Bible. Judith Plaskow offers a feminist Jewish *midrash* on Lilith, the first wife of Adam. The *midrash* on Lilith has influenced the Jewish tradition for centuries, and Plaskow's imaginative retelling has significantly contributed to Jewish feminism and re-readings of the Torah. All three essays invite a number of questions: What makes these interpretations feminist? How do they shed light on the biblical discourse on gender? Why do we know androcentric interpretations better than feminist ones? What do we thus learn about contemporary society, culture, and religion?

The third set of essays, entitled "Mary Magdalene and Other Women Disciples," examines representations of women in the New Testament and raises questions about androcentric marginalization and distortion of early Christian women as leaders and influential figures. Jane Schaberg inspects Christian history that characterized Mary Magdalene as a prostitute, and then demonstrates that, instead, Mary Magdalene was a disciple of Jesus. Dorothy A. Lee surveys women in the Gospel narratives, and so provides important insights about women in the early Christian movement and in early Christian texts. Both essays solicit many questions: Why is an early Christian woman like Mary Magdalene remembered as a prostitute when she, more likely, was a disciple of Jesus? What historical, cultural, and political assumptions have reduced her to, at best, a secondary status? Why do movies, such as "Jesus Christ Superstar," continue to present her as a sexual object despite the feminist research of the last decades? Why do we know so little about other important women of early Christianity? What can be done about this androcentric bias in past and present Christianity and Western culture?

The fourth set of articles, entitled "The Issue of Heterosexism," explores the historio-cultural discourse on the Bible and homosexuality as well as questions about the Bible's authority in the context of sexual identity and morality. Susanne Scholz examines selected Internet websites that relate the story of Sodom and Gomorrah in Genesis 19:1–29 to contemporary debates on homosexuality. Martin S. Cohen investigates often-quoted passages in the book of Leviticus that seem to prohibit male homosexuality. Bernadette J. Brooten analyzes interpretations of early Christian theologians regarding Romans 1:26, a passage often mentioned in discussions about biblical views on homosexual behavior. The three articles raise the following questions: Who decides the validity of one interpretation over against another, and why? What do we gain from this or that interpretation in the context of a heterosexist society? What are the problems involved in "proofreading" the Bible? How do we read biblical texts ethically and responsibly in current debates on homosexuality? Why is it still important to refer to the Bible in such debates?

In conclusion, this section on "The Rhetoric of Gender" offers historical, cultural, political, and religious insight into the problems involved when feminists read the Bible. It shows that biblical texts, characters, and issues, formerly ignored or used in support of gender inequality, now become prominent. Eve turns into a premier theologian, and Mary Magdalene is recognized as a disciple of Jesus. The relationship between the Bible and sexual identities is studied, and so feminist scholarship demonstrates that the Bible and the discourse on gender interrelate in manifold ways. Providing a beginning set of resources for appreciating the Bible from gendered perspectives, the section illustrates that the reading of the Bible is never value neutral, objective, or unbiased. Readers from particular social locations with particular political, cultural, and religious agendas create the meaning of a biblical passage, which, in turn, reflects on society and religion. Not containing a single, literal, or monolithic meaning, the Bible is like a prism through which multiple meanings shine, presented by different readers and different interpretive interests. If the interpreters bring feminist perspectives to the Bible, the biblical stories and poems become relevant for theories and practices of gender in culture, politics, and religion. When understood this way, the Bible is clearly a decisive, even mandatory, resource for understanding the rhetoric of gender in the past and in the present.

Chapter 1

The Bible and Feminism

American Women and the Bible:
The Nature of Woman
as a Hermeneutical Issue

Carolyn De Swarte Gifford

For over three and one-half centuries the Christian faith and its sacred book, the Bible, have been a shaping influence in the lives of American women. Americans have turned to the scriptures for insight into the nature of womanhood, certain that they would find in biblical passages God's revelation concerning women, their duties, and their proper sphere. Countless sermons prescribing womanly behavior have been preached from biblical texts. Numerous books and articles of advice for young ladies employed biblical examples of the good woman and her evil opposite. Common speech borrowed biblical phrases to describe womanly attributes. It was both appropriate and inevitable for Americans, a Bible-reading people, to refer to the scriptures for definitions of female and male, ideals of woman- and manhood, and models of activity befitting Christian women and men.

By the late eighteenth and the early nineteenth century a small but growing number of women and men began to reflect on the biblical notion of womanhood, questioning whether traditional scriptural interpretations of the nature of woman did justice to God or to God's creation—woman. Throughout the nineteenth and twentieth centuries the debate over the biblical understanding of womanhood continued, affecting not only religion but all other institutions of American life. Wherever that debate has been carried on—whether politely through articles in denominational magazines on women's right to be delegates to church bodies or in the much more highly charged setting of women's suffrage conventions—the argument has been essentially over the same basic issue: hermeneutics. How shall the scriptures be interpreted and who shall interpret them? These same questions have been raised over and over again in relation to "the woman question," and they have been answered in different ways by various segments of American society. The issue remains unresolved to the present day, as conflicting notions of womanhood and woman's sphere prevail in different religious communities and are reflected in their members' attitudes toward legislative issues, court decisions, business practices, etc. which affect women.

At the close of the eighteenth century a Massachusetts woman, Judith Sargent Murray, wrote an essay entitled "On the Equality of the Sexes" (1790). In it she sought to build a case for opening up more educational opportunities to women since, in her opinion, they were endowed by their creator with minds as sharp as men's. She appended to the body of her essay a letter she had written a decade earlier to a male friend who had attacked her egalitarian stance. He claimed male superiority in intelligence, as in all things, basing his claim on scriptural evidence. Murray replied:

> Not long since, weak and presuming as I was, I amused myself with selecting some arguments from nature, reason and experience, against this so generally received idea [of male superiority]. I confess that to the sacred testimonies I had not recourse. I held them to be merely metaphorical, and thus regarding them, I could not persuade myself that there was any propriety in bringing them to decide in this *very important debate.* However, as you, sir, confine yourself entirely to the sacred oracles, I mean to bend the whole of my artillery against those supposed proofs, which you have thence provided, and from which you have formed an intrenchment *apparently* so invulnerable.[1]

Murray never actually developed an extended counterargument in her letter to meet her friend's scriptural proofs of male superiority. Yet their exchange anticipated issues that would become significant in the following two centuries of discussion on the rights of women.

Murray recognized that it would be necessary for supporters of women's equality to give scriptural justifications for their position since debates were likely to be couched in these terms. She had believed that "arguments from nature,

---

[1] Judith Sargent Murray, "On the Equality of the Sexes," as quoted in *The Feminist Papers* (ed. Alice S. Rossi; New York: Bantam, 1974) 22–23; emphasis in original.

reason and experience" were sufficient to make her point. Her friend's appeals to "sacred oracles," however, alerted her to the fact that biblical proofs were often adduced in debate. While arguments such as Murray's might lend additional strength to a particular position, proofs from scripture held an unassailable authority for many.

Her somewhat facetious remarks indicate that Murray failed to realize precisely how seriously "sacred testimonies" were taken by Americans. She treated them lightly, dismissing them as "merely metaphorical" and not really worthy of being marshaled in support of the weighty matter of equal education for women. When her opponent invoked a traditional argument claiming that Eve's disobedience in the Garden of Eden had caused the Fall and provoked God to decree women's subordination to man in punishment for her sin, Murray responded with her own interpretation of the Adam and Eve story. She suggested that Adam as well as Eve had defied God by eating the fruit from the tree of the knowledge of good and evil. But whereas Eve was motivated by a laudable desire to gain more knowledge, Adam, in accepting Eve's invitation to eat the apple, acted only out of "bare pusillanimous attachment to a woman!"[2] Murray regarded this motive as far less praiseworthy than Eve's hunger to know more.

As the nineteenth century began, women continued the demand for equal schooling for girls begun by Judith Sargent Murray as part of a broader push to educate all children of the young republic. Democratic ideals required that all citizens be intellectually equipped to participate in government. Women, no less than men, needed education in order to train their sons for responsible citizenship. Although it was understood that women would not themselves provide leadership in America's political and economic life—since they must, of course, remain subordinate to men in such matters—they could teach future leaders, not only as mothers but also as school mistresses, a profession opening up for women by the early nineteenth century.

With the wave of reform activity sweeping the country in the second quarter of the century a few brave women began to extend their role as moral arbiters beyond their prescribed sphere. In the 1830s female abolitionists like Angelina Grimké and Abby Kelley Foster began to speak before "promiscuous assemblies"—public gatherings of both males and females—pleading the cause of the slave. In 1840 Lucretia Mott and other women antislavery leaders expected to be seated with the American delegations at the World's Anti-Slavery Convention in London. By the 1850s reformers in favor of temperance, like Susan B. Anthony, rose to voice their opinions in rallies and conferences. Communities of reformers were forced to examine the notion of woman's proper sphere and the biblical undergirding for it.

An early example of the tension between the ideal of woman's domestic sphere and her role as moral arbiter can be seen in the clash between the Grimké sisters, Angelina and Sarah, and the Massachusetts clergy. These southern Quaker women had been speaking against slavery throughout the Northeast, sponsored by abolition societies. Their public role prompted a strongly worded "Pastoral

---

[2]Ibid., 24.

Letter (from) the General Association of Massachusetts to the Churches Under Their Care" (1837), condemning such activities. It is worth quoting at length because it so clearly sets forth opinion current in New England "Orthodoxy" (Congregationalism) about woman's proper sphere and duties, an opinion grounded in a widely held interpretation of scripture, one still voiced today in some segments of American society:

> The appropriate duties and influence of woman are clearly stated in the New Testament. Those duties and that influence are unobtrusive and private, but the source of mighty power.... The power of woman is her dependence, flowing from the consciousness of that weakness which God has given her for her protection, and which keeps her in those departments of life that form the character of individuals, and of the nation. There are social influences which females can use in promoting piety and the great objects of Christian benevolence which we can not too highly recommend.[3]

For the Massachusetts Orthodox (Congregational) clergy the crucial issue was the male/public realm versus the female/private realm. In their opinion female abolitionists (and, later, female temperance reformers and women's rights advocates) overstepped the boundary of the private realm to which God had confined woman. Thus the debate in this instance was not over abolitionism, since some of the Massachusetts clergy supported the antislavery cause. But the spectacle of women defying both God and Saint Paul by their public appearances on behalf of abolition was a horrible one for these clergymen to contemplate. Indeed such women were "unnatural," unwomanly, even monstrous. Throughout the nineteenth and twentieth centuries, those opposing a public role for women used the threat of unnaturalness to frighten women who dared to cross the border from private to public. Scripturally derived epithets such as "disobedient Eve" and "Jezebel woman" were hurled at women and often such name-calling was enough to discourage the more timid from venturing beyond the private realm. Biblical images carried within them enormous capacity to inhibit, as those who employed them knew well. Disobedient Eves challenged not only men but also God; they were not merely stubborn and headstrong but sinful as well. Women's rights reformers would have to develop alternative female biblical images that would empower women, rather than repress them.[4] The task of re-visioning images begun in the nineteenth century still continues today.

In the meantime each small step over the boundary, however hesitant, brought into question the whole concept of separate spheres.[5] Although Angelina

---

[3]"Pastoral Letter (from) the General Association of Massachusetts to the Churches Under Their Care," quoted in *The Feminist Papers*, 305–6. See also Alice S. Rossi's introductory section on women and reform in the nineteenth century (pp. 241–81).

[4]See Carolyn De Swarte Gifford ("Home Protection: The WCTU's Conversion to Woman Suffrage" [unpublished manuscript, 1980]) for a discussion of revisioning images and symbols and the power of symbols to repress.

[5]See Dorothy C. Bass, "'Their Prodigious Influence': Women, Religion and Reform in Ante-Bellum America," *Women of Spirit: Female Leadership in the Jewish and Christian Traditions* (ed. Rosemary Ruether and Eleanor McLaughlin; New York: Simon & Schuster, 1979); and Carolyn De Swarte Gifford, "Women and Social Reform," *Women and Religion in America: The Nineteenth Century* (ed. Rosemary Radford Ruether and Rosemary Skinner Keller; New York: Harper & Row, 1981).

Grimké and Abby Kelley Foster were often shouted down in antislavery meetings, many heard them and were persuaded to the cause of abolition. Although Lucretia Mott and other women delegates from the United States to the World's Anti-Slavery Convention were not allowed to sit with their delegations, the incident provoked a young recruit to the cause, Elizabeth Cady Stanton, to plan a women's rights convention with her new friend Mrs. Mott. They issued a call for the first such meeting eight years later at Seneca Falls, New York. And although Susan B. Anthony was refused permission to speak to rallies of temperance supporters, such a refusal merely served as what twentieth-century feminists would term consciousness-raising events, making them more firmly committed to the struggle for women's rights than they had been previously. The leadership of the nineteenth-century women's rights movement sharpened its reasoning and rhetorical skills through combatting traditional scriptural views of woman's place. In the process they began to formulate new interpretations of scripture.

The New Testament texts to which the Pastoral Letter referred included such passages as 1 Cor 11:3–12 and 14:34–35, Eph 5:22–24, 1 Tim 2:9–15, and 1 Pet 3:1–7, which were continually cited as proof texts for the subordination of women and the circumscribing of their proper sphere. The Grimkés countered with proof texts of their own, passages such as Gal 3:28, which they used to support their view of women as responsible moral beings created equal by God and endowed with consciences capable of being roused against injustice and oppression. When confronted with such clear examples of injustice as slavery in the South and racism in the North, women as well as men must use any means consonant with their consciences to fight these evils.[6]

In Angelina Grimké's *Appeal to the Christian Women of the South* (1836), she suggested that southern women could do four things to overthrow slavery: read, pray, speak out, and act. Their reading material should be the scriptures, which they ought to approach "in the spirit of inquiry and the spirit of prayer. . . . Read the *Bible* then, it contains the words of Jesus, and they are spirit and life. Judge for yourselves whether *he sanctioned* such a system of oppression and crime."[7] The freeing message and acts of Jesus were, for Grimké and others, the criterion by which to interpret the rest of the Bible and to judge one's own ethical choices. The theme of freedom from oppression, which antislavery reformers believed so strongly dominated both the Old and the New Testament, was accompanied by an equally strong subtheme: speaking the truth in defiance of public opinion, the religious hierarchy, and the laws of one's country. Grimké saw the Bible from beginning to end peopled with prophets, apostles, and martyrs willing to suffer for the sake of truth. Abolitionists were the latest in a long line of such persons who could be traced from biblical times to the present, and among those courageous souls were women.

Grimké listed the valiant women of the Bible: Miriam, Deborah, Jael, Huldah, Esther, Elizabeth, Anna, the Samaritan woman, the company of women who

---

[6]Angelina Emily Grimké, *Letters to Catharine Beecher* (Boston: Isaac Knapp, 1836) 118. See also Letter XI.

[7]Angelina Emily Grimké, *Appeal to the Christian Women of the South* (New York: Arno and New York Times, 1969; original 1836) 17; emphasis in original.

followed Jesus to the Cross, Mary the Mother of Jesus, Mary Magdalene, the women on whom the Holy Spirit descended at Pentecost, and the women mentioned by Paul who taught and ministered to the earliest Christian communities. All sorts of women's rights reformers throughout the nineteenth and twentieth centuries—those who worked for equality for women in the churches as well as in the larger society—would lift up these biblical women as models for their own public activity and gain inspiration from their courageous example to persist with reform in the face of ridicule and persecution. For women reformers the Bible evidenced no such differentiated spheres and gender roles in the task of reforming the world as the Massachusetts clergy defended in their Pastoral Letter.

As people chose opposing sides in the controversy over woman's proper sphere, they began to develop alternative interpretations of scripture stemming from different interpretive criteria and appealing to different sets of biblical passages. Those who believed in separate spheres and complementary but unequal roles for male and female articulated what has come to be known as a "subordinationist" or hierarchical interpretation of male-female relationships as found in scripture. They appealed to the second account of creation (Genesis 2 and 3, particularly 2:22); portraits in the Old Testament of good (obedient) wives and bad (disobedient) women; and to the passages in the New Testament epistles cited above, all of which seemed to them to teach the subordination of women. Those who found in the Bible the central theme of freedom from oppression and a more egalitarian view of male-female relationships cited the first account of creation (Genesis 1, particularly 1:26–27); tales of heroic women of scripture; passages indicating that the Holy Spirit empowered both women and men (especially Acts 2:17–18); and Gal 3:28, perhaps the most popular text of women's rights reformers.

The debate over women's proper activities in movements of reform led immediately to an examination of woman's subordinate status in American society generally. Angelina Grimké's sister Sarah replied directly to the Massachusetts clergy's Pastoral Letter in a series of letters of her own, printed together in a widely read collection, "Letters on the Equality of the Sexes and the Condition of Women" (1837). She insisted that Americans face the serious contradiction between the notion of female subordination and the biblical principles of freedom and equality. Like many Americans, Sarah Grimké believed that the nation had been founded on these principles. Struggles for abolition and other reform activities were carried out in order to enable America to embody its ideals. Slaves must be freed if her country was to live up to its high calling, she reasoned, and if slaves, so also women must be freed.

Like her sister Angelina and many other Quakers, Sarah Grimké believed that in Jesus' teachings one could best grasp the egalitarian, liberating theme of the Bible. But whereas Angelina Grimké had, at first, judged only the institution of slavery by the criterion of Jesus' teachings, Sarah Grimké extended that judgment to the institutionalized relationships between men and women. She wrote:

> The Lord Jesus defines the duties of his followers in his Sermon on the Mount. He lays down grand principles by which they should be governed, without any reference to sex or condition. . . . I follow him through all his precepts, and

find him giving the same directions to women as to men, never even referring to the distinction now so strenuously insisted upon between masculine and feminine virtues: this is one of the anti-christian "traditions of men" which are taught instead of the "commandments of God." Men and women are CREATED EQUAL: they are both moral and accountable beings, and whatever is *right* for man to do, is *right* for woman.[8]

Thus for Grimké, the Pastoral Letter of the Massachusetts clergy in its insistence on different spheres and duties for men and women supported "anti-Christian 'traditions of men'" and not the "commandments of God."

If false teachings about women had been disseminated through incorrect translations and biased interpretations of scripture, then different translations and interpretations must be produced which would remain true to the original inspiration of the Bible. Since Grimké had serious doubts about men's ability to carry on such activity without bias, she called for women to do the work. However, she recognized that in order to prepare themselves they must learn Hebrew and Greek, and she did not imagine that women would be admitted either quickly or easily to the study of biblical languages.

Yet a few women were already planning such study, among them Lucy Stone, who was a nineteen-year-old Massachusetts school teacher in 1837 when Grimké wrote her *Letters on the Equality of the Sexes*. As a child, Stone had been horrified by biblical injunctions against women and decided to discover for herself what the Bible really taught in regard to women. She found particularly troubling the segment of Gen 3:16—"Thy desire shall be to thy husband, and he shall rule over thee" (KJV)—popularly known as "the curse of Eve." Stone's mother had explained to her daughter that it was woman's duty to submit to this curse since all women shared in Eve's disobedience and her consequent fallenness. Women's subordinate status was not only part of the order of creation but was also deserved punishment for original sin. Like Lucy Stone's mother, most women humbly accepted what they believed to be God's commandment of submissiveness, but Stone would not do so. She determined to read the Bible in the original languages and entered Oberlin College in 1843 to study Hebrew and Greek. Although Stone did not continue her language work beyond college, she did become a leading women's rights reformer in the nineteenth century, being convinced that there was absolutely no biblical basis for women's subordination.

The traditional translation and interpretation of Gen 3:16 had already been disputed before Stone began her language studies. Sarah Grimké and others even earlier had pointed out that with an alternative translation of verb forms—from "shall" to "will"—the passage could be read as God's prediction of women's lot in a fallen creation rather than God's timeless commandment for women. If the meaning of a text so crucial to a subordinationist view of women could be radically altered by changing one word, it might be possible to reinterpret other passages used to restrict women, thus bringing the whole scriptural underpinning for

---

[8]Sarah M. Grimké, *Letters on the Equality of the Sexes and the Condition of Woman* (New York: Burt Franklin, 1970; original 1838) 16; emphasis in original.

the position into question. Grimké proceeded to do this: she cited further alternative translations and interpretations of other favorite proof texts for women's subordination, drawing upon the work of earlier Quaker scholars who had provided the biblical foundation for their denomination's unprecedented egalitarian treatment of women.[9]

Throughout the next several decades, women continued to call for what might now be termed a feminist exegesis of the Bible. Beginning with the Seneca Falls Convention of 1848, a series of women's rights meetings provided a dramatic and well-publicized forum for discussion of the role that the Bible and religious institutions played in the oppression of women. The call to the first convention clearly stated that inquiry into "the religious condition and rights of woman" as well as their social and civil status would be central on the agenda. A "Declaration of Sentiments," produced by the convention organizers and enthusiastically adopted by those attending, listed among the wrongs committed against women their exclusion from the ministry, from the teaching of theology, and from virtually all public participation in church governance. A resolution unanimously passed by the body succinctly captured the stance toward the Bible and its relation to women taken by the leadership of the women's rights movement almost to the end of the century: "*Resolved,* That woman has too long rested satisfied in the circumscribed limits which corrupt customs and a perverted application of the Scriptures have marked out for her, and that it is time she should move in the enlarged sphere which her great Creator has assigned her."[10] Almost without exception women's rights leaders in the nineteenth century firmly believed that the Bible, correctly interpreted, would disclose God's intention that women be equal to men. Although generations of men might be sexist, God was not. They rather naively assumed that it was simply a matter of encouraging unbiased investigation of the Bible by scholars and nonscholars alike, in order to change American society's definition of womanhood and woman's sphere.

More important for nineteenth-century feminists than the specific details of biblical scholarship were the presuppositions on which the discipline was based. The notion that the Bible was not supernaturally inspired but had evolved naturally over the course of centuries, that it was the historical record of peoples and not the "voice of God," that it could be studied like any other literary work in terms of various genres and its contents located in various historical contexts—all of these presuppositions brought into question the plenary inspiration of scripture. The view of many women's rights leaders was echoed by Heber Newton, Episcopalian popularizer of higher criticism, when he contended that the Bible, while it surely contained God's word, was not, in its entirety, God's word:[11] If these presuppositions were indeed so, there were ramifications extending far beyond the discipline of biblical criticism. Not only could biblical scholars freely pursue their task, but feminists working from those same presuppositions could seriously question biblical

---

[9]Ibid., Letters I–IV, XI, XIV.

[10]Mari Jo and Paul Buhle, *The Concise History of Woman Suffrage: Selections from the Classic Work of Stanton, Anthony, Gage and Harper* (Urbana, IL: University of Illinois Press, 1978) 91.

[11]Brown, "Higher Criticism Comes to America," 206.

authority in the matter of woman's nature and sphere. Although nineteenth-century feminists were not professional biblical scholars, some of them were well aware of the presuppositions, methods, and findings of critical biblical research and on occasion referred to them to support and undergird their attack on traditional views of the authority of scripture and the subordinate position of women.

There was almost certainly no conscious alliance of feminists and biblical scholars during the period. Yet the very existence of a group of serious researchers at work on higher biblical criticism, a growing collection of popular works on the subject, and an increasing number of clergy preaching who were trained in higher critical methods and findings served to provide an intellectual climate somewhat more receptive to a view of the Bible which was at first profoundly disturbing to Americans. That it was disturbing is evidenced by several sensational heresy trials in the 1890s involving biblical scholars. Yet even the trials provided a forum for new views on the Bible. As Henry Preserved Smith of Lane Seminary, one of those tried, observed: "I can truly say that litigation was not to my taste, but I thought it was my duty to carry the case through for its educational value. The wide attention given to my case . . . would help some minds to a better, that is, a more historical, view of the Bible.[12] In much the same way, people who might be "helped to a better view" of the Bible might also be prompted to reexamine some of the traditional attitudes toward women grounded in a correspondingly traditional attitude toward the authority of scripture. Like others before them, women's rights leaders called for such a reexamination in the closing decades of the nineteenth century. But unlike the earlier generation, feminists at the end of the century could point to a growing body of biblical criticism which made possible new approaches to the Bible.

One of those calling for reinterpretation of the scriptural teaching on women in light of the new scholarship was Frances Willard (1839–1898), long-time president of the Women's Christian Temperance Union (WCTU), who sought biblical sanction for an enlarged sphere for women, including equal rights for women within the church. Willard came out of an evangelical Protestant background as did the majority of the powerful organization she led. Many of these temperance women had participated in the mass revival meetings led by Dwight L. Moody during the 1870s, and earlier in the prayer groups and camp meetings of the Holiness movement. Willard herself had been converted at a Holiness revival by Phoebe Palmer (1807–1874), a leader of the movement. In a remarkable book, *The Promise of the Father* (1859), Palmer defended women's call to preach.[13] Although Palmer subscribed to a thoroughly traditional and conservative view of woman's nature and sphere, she cited three biblical passages—Joel 2:28, John 1:4, and Acts 2:17–18—which promised that in "the latter days" God's Holy Spirit would be poured out on women as well as men, enabling those extraordinary persons inspired by the Spirit to preach and prophesy. Unlike the Grimké's and others, she did not claim women's right to preach based on the idea

---

[12]Henry P(reserved) Smith, *The Heretic's Defense: A Footnote to History*, p. 48 (as quoted in Brown, "Higher Criticism Comes to America," 205).

[13]Phoebe Palmer, *The Promise of the Father, or A Neglected Speciality of the Last Days* (Boston: Henry V. Degen, 1859).

that women were equal to men in the sight of God and should not inhabit a separate sphere from men. She insisted, rather, that under inspiration of the Holy Spirit some women might be called to step beyond their proper sphere temporarily and witness to God, returning to that sphere when the moment of inspiration passed.

Grounding the possibility of women's preaching on scriptural texts predicting and describing the inspiration of the Holy Spirit might not seem a particularly fruitful avenue of approach for those defending women's equal rights within the church. Angelina Grimké had pointed this out over two decades earlier in 1837, as she criticized her own sect, the Quakers, for using an argument similar to Phoebe Palmer's in their justification of women's preaching: "Women are regarded [among the Quakers] as equal to men on the ground of *spiritual gifts, not* on the broad ground of *humanity.* Woman may *preach;* this is a *gift;* but woman must *not* make the discipline by which *she herself* is governed.[14] And Phoebe Palmer did not seek for women's rights within the church, asking instead only that women who were truly inspired by the Spirit be allowed to preach and prophesy as did inspired men. Yet during the second half of the nineteenth century, offshoots of the Holiness movement sought to enlarge woman's sphere and provide for women's rights within the church and often called for them within the larger society as well.[15] In the same manner, many WCTU orators and other women involved in the newly created women's missionary societies justified their moves beyond prescribed roles and activities by understanding themselves as participating in a "second Pentecost" in which God demanded new things from women. They saw the end of the nineteenth century as a time of a fresh outpouring of the power of the Holy Spirit—the "latter days" in which women would be empowered by God, in fulfillment of Joel's prophecy, as Palmer had suggested in her book.

Although Palmer and other conservative evangelical women did not believe that women should seek ordination and full lay rights within the church and certainly should not step beyond their proper sphere by demanding suffrage and other rights in the larger society, only one generation later Frances Willard did. She insisted that in "this new day for woman" she should seek a larger sphere, including suffrage and other political and civil rights, full laity rights within the churches, and the right to preach and be fully ordained.[16] Willard had personal experience of the limited sphere which the churches assigned to women. In the 1880 the General Conference of the Methodist Episcopal Church (North) refused to allow her to speak, although she attended as a "fraternal delegate" from the

---

[14]Letter from Angelina Grimké to Theodore Weld and John Greenleaf Whittier, 30 March 1837, *Letters of Theodore Dwight Weld, Angelina Grimké Weld and Sarah Grimké* (ed. Edith H. Barnes and Dwight L. Dumond; Gloucester, MA: Peter Smith, 1965) 431; emphasis in original.

[15]For discussions of the biblical bases of evangelical feminism, see Donald W. Dayton, *Discovering an Evangelical Heritage* (New York: Harper & Row, 1976) chap. 8, "The Evangelical Roots of Feminism," and Nancy Hardesty, Lucille Sider Dayton, and Donald W. Dayton, "Women in the Holiness Movement: Feminism in the Evangelical Tradition," in *Women of Spirit,* ed. R. Ruether and E. McLaughlin.

[16]For discussions of biblical arguments for and against women's rights within the church, see Barbara Brown Zikmund, "The Feminist Thrust of Sectarian Christianity," in *Women of Spirit,* ed. R. Ruether and E. McLaughlin; idem, "The Struggle for the Right to Preach," in *Women and Religion in America,* ed. R. Ruether and R. S. Keller; and idem, "Biblical Arguments and Women's Place in the Church," in *The Bible and Social Reform* (ed. Ernest R. Sandeen; Chico, CA: Scholars Press, 1982).

rapidly growing and powerful WCTU. In 1888 the General Conference voted not to allow the seating of Willard and four other duly elected women delegates. In the midst of Willard's struggles for women's rights within the churches, she wrote *Woman in the Pulpit*, which called once again for women's exegesis:

> We need women commentators to bring out the women's side of the book; we need the stereoscopic view of truth in general, which can only be had when woman's eye and man's together shall discern the perspective of the Bible's full-orbed revelation. I do not at all impugn the good intention of the good men who have been our exegetes, and I bow humbly in presence of their scholarship; but, while they turn their linguistic telescopes on truth, I may be allowed to make a correction for the "personal equation" in the results which they espy.[17]

Willard meant that male interpreters of scripture held a traditional view of woman's nature and sphere which did not allow them to tale a fresh, unbiased look at the material in the texts, although they might sincerely believe that they were doing so. On the other hand, women exegetes, presumably those in particular who were interested in a less restricted position for women, could provide such an unbiased look. For example, Willard found in 1 Corinthians evidence that women did speak and prophesy in the early church, but she warned that such evidence will "hardly be emphasized as we could wish until women share equally in translating the sacred text." Echoing Sarah Grimké nearly a half century earlier, she urged "young women of linguistic talent . . . to make a specialty of Hebrew and New Testament Greek in the interest of their sex."[18]

She further accused men of exegeting scripture in such a way that Christianity "today imposes the heaviest yoke now worn by women upon that most faithful follower of Him who is her emancipator no less that humanity's Saviour."[19] In other words, Christianity had become the instrument of women's subordination contrary to the message and work of the savior it proclaimed. Willard stated explicitly what others before her had only implied, that "universal liberty of person and opinion are now conceded to be Bible-precept principles," and that if one came to the text with those principles in mind one would find instead of a restrictive view of woman's sphere, a liberating word for women which could help to bring them into full equality with men. Willard located this "Bible-precept of universal liberty of person and opinion" in the person of Jesus—his teaching and his action—as indicated in the above quotation which describes Jesus as "woman's emancipator."

When Willard called for young women to learn biblical languages and to acquire theological educations to apply the critical norm she saw in Jesus, she was

---

[17]Frances E. Willard, *Woman in the Pulpit* (Chicago: Woman's Temperance Publication Association, 1889) 21.

[18]Ibid., 31.

[19]Ibid., 23.

demanding what some have termed "interested scholarship," research with a re-
formist purpose and point of view shaping it—in this instance a feminist stance
which would seek through scholarship to make a contribution to the women's
rights movement. In this she would be unlike higher biblical critics of her day who
typically saw themselves doing "pure research," using scientific principles and
methodologies, with no interest in the outcome of the research other than that of
"serving the truth." Willard pointed out in a quotation cited above that men did
indeed come to the texts with biases, and, thus, she implicitly questioned one of
the presuppositions of higher biblical criticism—scientific objectivity—although
she did not elaborate on this in her writings. In raising the issue of the unac-
knowledged patriarchal stance of male translators and interpreters, Willard, in a
far less theologically sophisticated way, anticipated the challenge made by contemporary feminist biblical scholars such as Elisabeth Schüssler Fiorenza against
the claim made by many of their colleagues in the field that their work is value-
neutral and objective.[20]

A few women's rights leaders, among them Elizabeth Cady Stanton, editor
of *The Woman's Bible,* and Matilda Joslyn Gage, author of *Woman, Church and State,*
were definitely not sanguine about the possibility that the biblical record contained any such nonpatriarchal faith. In the appendix to Part II of *The Woman's
Bible,* Stanton wrote:

> In plain English the Bible evidences a degrading teaching in regard to woman.
> Women try to shelter themselves under false translations, interpretations and
> symbolic meanings. It does not occur to them that men learned in the lan-
> guages have revised the book many times, but make no changes in woman's
> position. . . . Though familiar with "the designs of God," trained in Biblical re-
> search and higher criticism . . . yet they cannot twist out of the Old Testament
> or the New Testament a message of justice, liberty, or equality from God to the
> women of the nineteenth century.[21]

Agreeing with Stanton, Gage pointed to research by nineteenth-century archaeologists and explorers who brought to light traces of matriarchal civilizations
ruthlessly supplanted by later patriarchal societies. Gage called for a rebellion by
women against their repression under both church and state.[22]

In compiling *The Woman's Bible,* the method followed by Stanton and her Revising Committee, composed of women who were authors, editors, and ordained
ministers, was to comment on all passages in both Testaments dealing with
women. As this work progressed during the 1890s, Stanton came to the conclusion

---

[20]Elisabeth Schüssler Fiorenza, "Feminist Theology and New Testament Interpretation," *Journal for
the Study of the Old Testament* 22 (1982) 33–35.
[21]Elizabeth Cady Stanton et al., The Revising Committee, *The Woman's Bible,* Part II (New York: European, 1898) 214.
[22]Matilda Joslyn Gage, *Woman, Church and State: The Original Expose of Male Collaboration Against the
Female Sex* (Watertown, MA: Persephone Press, 1980; original 1893) 7–23, 246.

that patriarchy was the very foundation of the Judeo-Christian religion as it had evolved over time. Men in control of institutional religion, be they biblical scholars or ministers, would not make any changes in woman's position because if they should do so, "the bottom falls out of the whole Christian theology." They would not dare to apply the presuppositions, methodology, and findings of over a century of biblical criticism to the position of women as presented in the Bible because this would shake the theological bases of what Stanton might more accurately have termed orthodox or Calvinist theology. Although biblical scholars were beginning to identify and separate out different literary genres in the Bible, identifying some parts as mythological in character, Stanton felt that ordinary worshippers in the pews would never be introduced to the conclusions of such scholarship (although in fact they were in some liberal congregations).

Stanton was a thoroughgoing daughter of Enlightenment liberalism, who tended to judge the Bible not through its own critical norms as Willard would have women do but by the external norm of nineteenth-century liberal thought. At the close of the nineteenth century, she believed, Western civilization had progressed far beyond those earlier civilizations which produced the biblical record in terms of the understanding of the ideals of liberty, justice, and equality. Thus biblical notions should be measured against nineteenth-century liberalism, and when so measured, she implied over and over again in her own commentaries in *The Woman's Bible*, scripture would be found wanting in its teachings. Although it might contain ideas that represented a clear advancement over much of the conventional wisdom of the times in which it was written, it might itself be supplanted by ideas of later centuries.[23] Stanton's thinking here probably represented one of the most radical results of treating the Bible like any other book, one of the presuppositions of many proponents of higher biblical criticism. If the Judeo-Christian belief system was based fundamentally on the oppression of women, as Stanton insisted it was, then in the late nineteenth century it was an inadequate expression of the ideals of liberty, justice, and equality developed by that time. What women needed, she implied, was a different belief system, "a new 'rational religion' deliberately designed 'in harmony with science, common sense and the experience of mankind in natural laws,'" one which would embody the highest ideals of nineteenth-century culture, including as a principal tenet the equality of women in all areas of life.[24] In advocating such a system, Stanton differed fundamentally from Frances Willard, who was still confident that the Bible—and thus Christianity—correctly understood by using the tools of higher criticism for the purpose might be shown to reveal the highest norms of liberty and equality.

---

[23]For examples of Stanton's contention that the ideals expressed in the Bible did not measure up to those of the nineteenth century, see *The Woman's Bible*, Part I, Stanton's commentary on Genesis, pp. 46, 60, 67; on Exodus, pp. 72–73; Part II, Preface, p. 8; Gospel of Mark, p. 131; 1 Corinthians, p. 158. Also see Elizabeth Cady Stanton, letter to the editor in *The Index*, 9 September 1876.

[24]Elizabeth Cady Stanton as quoted in Ellen Carol DuBois's critical commentary on excerpts from *The Woman's Bible* in *Elizabeth Cady Stanton and Susan B. Anthony: Correspondence, Writings, Speeches* (New York: Schocken Books, 1981) 228–29.

If one were to have asked Elizabeth Cady Stanton if it was possible to be both a traditional Christian and a feminist, the answer would probably have been No. As she insisted, "[one] cannot twist out of the Old Testament or the New Testament [in plain English] a message of justice, liberty, or equality from God to the women of the nineteenth century." Apparently she had little hope that the biblical scholars and theologians of her time would undertake the revolutionary hermeneutical task involved in a thorough critique of theological concepts such as creation, sinfulness, and salvation as they had been interpreted for almost two millennia by male theologians.[25] The women's movement as well as professional biblical scholars and theologians failed to grapple with the implications of Stanton's claim that the Judeo-Christian tradition was sexist at its very core. Many women's rights leaders publicly repudiated *The Woman's Bible* and increasingly stepped back from a radical feminist critique of the interlocking institutional structures of religion, economics, and government which restricted women, to concentrate on more narrowly specific goals such as suffrage.

If Stanton was disappointed by the women's movement in her hope for a thorough examination of religion's role in institutionalized sexism, how much more disillusioned might Sarah Grimké and Frances Willard have been had they realized that the entry of trained women into the field of biblical scholarship would not result for nearly a century in the feminist hermeneutics they had demanded. Women began to join the ranks of professional biblical scholars shortly after the organization of the Society of Biblical Literature (SBL), the first woman's name appearing on the membership lists in 1894. However, their numbers were always small, never rising above 10 percent of the total membership and in most years considerably lower than that, and the results of their scholarship published in the journal of their professional association does not indicate that they were concerned with a feminist interpretation of scripture.[26] They do not seem to have made a "specialty of Hebrew and Greek in the interest of their sex," as Frances Willard would have wished.

Such activity continued to come from outside the profession in the work of such isolated scholars as the Reverend Lee Anna Starr, Methodist Protestant minister in Adrian, Michigan, in the early twentieth century, and Dr. Katherine Bushnell, former medical missionary to China and Women's Christian Temperance Union leader during the late nineteenth century. In the 1920s both women produced extended analyses of the treatment of women as recorded in the Bible and interpretations of the theological bases for woman's nature and sphere in the

---

[25]See Beverly Wildung Harrison ("The Early Feminists and the Clergy: A Case Study in the Dynamics of Secularization," *The Review and Expositor* 73 [1975] 41–52) for a discussion of the tensions between evangelical clergy and women's rights leaders, among them Elizabeth Cady Stanton, which resulted in early feminists' disenchantment with their evangelical faith.

[26]For discussions of women's participation in the SBL and for a review of women's struggles during the nineteenth and twentieth centuries to obtain a theological education both outside of and within the seminaries, see Dorothy C. Bass, "Women's Studies and Biblical Studies: An Historical Perspective," *Journal for the Study of the Old Testament* 22 (1982) 6–12; and idem, "Women with a Past: A New Look at the History of Theological Education," *Theological Education* 8 (1972) 213–24.

biblical texts, using their knowledge of biblical languages and scholarship.[27] Both concluded that the Bible correctly translated and interpreted presented a vision of the equality of women and men.

It was not until 1964 that a female professional biblical scholar raised the issue of male domination in the shaping of the Judeo-Christian tradition and urged women to assume an active role in the reshaping of the faith. In that year Margaret Brackenbury Crook, Professor of Religion and Biblical Literature at Smith College and thirty-nine-year member of the SBL, published *Women and Religion.* She proposed to carry out what she termed a "reconnaissance," a survey of women's position in Judaism and Christianity as reflected primarily in the biblical account, drawing on the results of the latest scholarship in her field as well as the disciplines of church history, theology, worship studies, and comparative religion. In her introduction, Crook made clear what she believed such a survey would reveal:

> A masculine monopoly in religion begins when Miriam raises her indignant question: "Does the Lord speak only through Moses?" Since then, in all three of the great religious groups stemming from the land and books of Israel—Judaism, Christianity, and Islam—men have formulated doctrine and established systems of worship offering only meager opportunity for expression of the religious genius of womankind. . . . If a woman born and bred in any of these faiths takes a comprehensive look at the form of theology best known to her, she discovers that it is masculine in administration, in the phrasing of its doctrines, liturgies, and hymns. It is man-formulated, man-argued, man-directed.[28]

Crook repeatedly claimed that her intent was not "feminist" and she meant to display no animosity toward men. She was simply stating the facts of the case on the basis of overwhelming evidence, and those facts clearly showed that women living within the influence of the three religious groups she named were still caught in a man's world. She felt that although women in the United States had made rapid advances in many fields during the twentieth century they had not made an impact on religion. They must now move to the forefront in all areas of religious life, particularly as theologians developing an adequate expression of the "balanced partnership" of women and men which she envisioned for the near future. She boldly asserted that the revolutionary scientific discoveries of the space age ought to stimulate equally new insights about the nature of God and

---

[27]Lee Anna Starr, *The Bible Status of Women* (New York: Fleming Revell, 1926); and Katherine C. Bushnell, *God's Word to Women* (no publishing information, but probably published privately by the author in Oakland, CA, 1923; reissued by Ray B. Munson, Box 52, North Collins, NY 14111); and idem, *The Reverend Doctor and his Doctor Daughter* (Oakland, CA: Katherine C. Bushnell, 1927). This last is a little known and often hilarious account of a dialogue between a rather stuffy clergyman and his physician daughter on the daughter's intention to follow in her father's footsteps by becoming ordained. His "conversion" to the daughter's point of view on the propriety of women being ordained follows rather swiftly after his daughter, using her medical skills, saves her father's life as he chokes on his false tooth which he has swallowed at the height of one of his impassioned arguments against women ministers.

[28]Margaret Brackenbury Crook, *Women and Religion* (Boston: Beacon, 1964) 1, 5.

God's relationship to humankind, retaining fidelity to the profound imagery within the biblical texts, yet phrased in a fresh language produced through a dialogue of women and men. Crook imagined new movements springing up within the Christian traditions in response to challenges arising in the world, a time of turmoil, perhaps even of crisis, yet offering opportunities for constructive change. And women, she insisted, must participate in defining a changing Christian tradition: "The time has come for women to share fully in creating the basic structure of the thought that is to animate these movements, in the forms of devotion, the art and symbolism that must be created to give the new inspiration durability.[29] Crook understood well the necessity that fundamental changes in a religious tradition must be reflected through all aspects of that tradition, so she called for more than just a new translation and interpretation of scripture.

The decade of the sixties saw other women questioning the adequacy of "man-formulated" theology. Even earlier than Crook, theologian and philosopher Valerie Saiving suggested in "The Human Situation: A Feminine View" (1960) that male theologians' definitions of key Judeo-Christian concepts such as sin did not reflect or interpret women's experience and thus needed to be rethought and reformulated in order to get at the depths of meaning behind such concepts.[30] From outside the ranks of academia, Elsie Culver, a professional lay church worker, pointed to the absence of a significant body of research by modern biblical scholars on woman's status and role in the cultures that produced the biblical texts and a discussion of what relevance findings from such research would have for contemporary women. She, like Crook and Saiving, felt that women had been excluded from the realm of theological discourse where the definition and interpretation of reality takes place.[31] If women did not share fully in such definition and interpretation they were relegated to second-class status. All three women were saying in the sixties what Mary Daly would articulate with such powerful imagery and sense of urgency in *Beyond God the Father* (1973): "We have not been free to use our own power to name ourselves, the world, or God. The old naming was not the product of dialogue. . . . Women are now realizing that the universal imposing of names by men has been false because partial.[32]

It was this power of naming, of sharing in the definition and interpretation of reality, for which Sarah and Angelina Grimké, Frances Willard, Elizabeth Cady Stanton, Matilda Joslyn Gage, and other nineteenth-century women longed. Although perhaps only Stanton and Gage would have been prepared to step with Daly beyond Christianity in search of self-definition, they all wished to be in dialogue with men, with the biblical texts, and with God about what it meant to be a woman. They were not content to submit in silence while men "named" them. The decades of the seventies and eighties have seen what might

[29]Ibid., 247–48.
[30]Valerie Saiving (Goldstein), "The Human Situation: A Feminine View," in *Woman-spirit Rising: A Feminist Reader in Religion* (ed. Carol P. Christ and Judith Plaskow; New York: Harper & Row, 1979) 27, 36–41.
[31]Elsie Thomas Culver, *Women in the World of Religion* (Garden City, NY: Doubleday, 1967) 13, 202.
[32]Mary Daly, *Beyond God the Father* (Boston: Beacon, 1973) 8.

be called the beginning of the dialogue about the meaning of being female and male. And it is only a beginning. There is still much more difficult work to be done before women and men together can define and live out the fullest possible meaning of "humanity."

What Makes a Feminist Reading Feminist? A Qualified Answer

Phyllis A. Bird

Neither my published work, nor the other forms of biblical interpretation in which I engage readily fit the description 'feminist reading(s)'. I therefore feel obliged to question the constraints imposed by defining the subject of discussion as 'a reading'. I could formulate my opinion differently by employing a broader understanding of 'reading', but I would still want to make the same points.

My answer to the question addressed to this panel requires definition of the terms 'feminist' and 'reading'. I understand feminism as a critical and constructive stance that claims for woman the full humanity accorded to men, insisting that women be represented equally in all attempts to describe and comprehend human nature and that they be full participants in the assignment and regulation of social roles, rights and responsibilities.[1] Feminism articulates its gender-inclusive view of human nature and responsibility over against historical and contemporary systems of thought and social organization that make males the norm and give men, as a class, power and priority over women. It does this by focusing on women, moving women from the margins to the center of inquiry

[1] Formulated negatively, feminism may be described as a commitment to assert the full humanity of women wherever that is denied, diminished or subordinated to male models.

[2] For me, feminism is also theologically grounded and is central to my theological understanding. To insist that the movement is fundamentally political does not entail denial or qualification of its theological meaning. Nor does its theological grounding exclude common analysis and action with feminists of other or no religious persuasion. My theological understanding does affect my hermeneutics, however, especially when I interpret biblical texts within and for the community of Christian believers. As I shall argue below, the context of interpretation is decisive for hermeneutics.

and action. Feminism begins with critique of existing patriarchal and androcentric forms of thought and organization, and commitment to the realization of alternative forms. It is thus a political movement for change,[2] grounded in social analysis and drawing on women's experience as the primary source for its critical and constructive work.[3]

There is no single feminist program or analysis. Feminist analysis and aims differ in relation to individual and class experience, intersecting loyalties and identities (such as ethnic, national and religious identities), understanding of the root problem, and view of scriptural authority or normativity. As a consequence, specific goals and strategies of feminist action will differ. There is also an essential openness and tentativeness in feminist constructions. When feminism moves from critique of oppressive systems and practices to vision and construction of new alternatives, it moves into the realm of the unknown, and its formulations must be constantly reassessed in the light of new experience.

How does such a movement find expression in biblical interpretation? I am dubious about the possibility or usefulness of identifying a feminist perspective or commitment with any readily discernible feature(s) of the content of a reading viewed in isolation from the circumstances of its production and reception. My initial response to the question addressed to this panel was to say that what makes a feminist reading feminist is a feminist reader—implying first the producer of the reading and secondly, the recipient. I recognize that this is not wholly satisfactory; I can enumerate some signs that fit my own feminist understanding. But I want first to register my discomfort, as a feminist biblical interpreter, with the focus of the question on 'a reading'.

I assume that a 'reading' describes some form of literary (or possibly oral?) production in which a biblical text is interpreted for some audience—that is, it is not simply an immediate and private response to a text, but a communicative act that means to influence a wider audience. For me, the anticipated audience is critical to the production of the reading. A focus on the reading alone narrows attention to a single moment or element in a complex process of communication and does not take account of the occasion, purpose or audience of the work. It makes a discrete literary product carry the full weight of the feminist interpretative agenda in dealing with the Bible or biblical texts.[4]

---

[3]It is also a modern phenomenon of the last two centuries, dependent on economic and technological advances in the West and a natural-rights philosophy grounded in biblical tradition, but not transformed into a global movement drawing upon a variety of cultural and philosophical traditions. The fact that the philosophical roots of the movement may be traced to biblical origins does not, in my view, justify retrojecting feminist perspectives into biblical texts.

[4]This narrower understanding of 'reading' identifies it with literary approaches to interpretation and observes a close identification of 'feminist' interpretation with such approaches, as exemplified in the text-immanent 'readings' of Phyllis Trible, Cheryl Exum, Danna Fewell and Mieke Bal. I am inclined now to extent my definition of 'reading' to encompass all forms of interpretation, following John Barton, *Reading the Old Testament: Method in Biblical Study* (Louisville, KY: Westminster/John Knox Press, rev. edn, 1996). Cf. also Anthony C. Thiselton, *New Horizons in Hermeneutics: The Theory and Practice of Transforming Biblical Reading* (Grand Rapids: Zondervan, 1992). My concern remains nevertheless with those forms of interpretation that do not fit the narrower class of literary approaches.

My complaint arises from the fact that my own approach to the Bible, as a feminist and as a Christian believer, is fundamentally dialogical, requiring as its first step an attempt to formulate the sense of the text in its ancient social and literary context—viewing the text as itself a response to a conversation in the author's own time, an effort to persuade an ancient audience of a new or alternative view. My response to the text comes only after I have clarified its terms—just as my response to a modern dialogue partner demands that I first attempt with all the means at my disposal to hear as accurately and as sympathetically as possible what he or she means to say. I do not imagine that I escape the hermeneutical circle by this sequencing or that my hearing is devoid of bias or interest; I only insist that my first obligation is to the text as a distinct voice, an other whose integrity must be respected in the same manner as a face-to-face conversation partner or a contemporary composition.[5] Thus I want to separate analytically and operationally the horizons of production and reception, even as I acknowledge their inevitable interpenetration. The model of dialogue better suits this aim than the model of 'reading' that collapses the two moments of interpretation.

A reading that attempts only the first descriptive and analytical task may not contain any clearly recognizable feminist message—although I do think that signs of feminist analysis may be observable in the categories and concerns of reconstructing the 'original' message. It may nevertheless play an essential role in feminist response to the text in preaching, Bible study, classroom discussion, and scholarly debate. Feminist aims may be served by readings that do not inscribe feminist messages or values in the text. A reading that contains no explicit feminist critique may serve feminist interests either by providing a springboard for feminist reflection or a fresh interpretation of a text aimed at eliciting broad discussion in which feminist voices may play a role. I see advantages in construing the arena of discussion as broadly as possible and the terms of debate as openly as possible, so as to move feminist interpretation out of the ghetto of exclusive feminist rhetoric. Feminist hermeneutics pertains to the whole work of biblical interpretation and not simply to productions that are recognizible as 'feminist reading'.

This is obviously not the place for a defense of historical-critical method, but in light of the widely accepted view that historical criticism is fundamentally

---

[5]I do not insist that this is the only way, or even *the* 'right' way, to approach the text. I do believe, however, that I have an ethical obligation to the ancient authors to try to hear them as they wished to be heard—despite a history of interpretation that has erased the author or constructed the author in its own image (the concept of canon does not, in my view, cancel the notion of individual authors, whose imprint is indelibly inscribed in the text). As a modern, historically conscious reader, with means of reconstructing the past (however limited), I believe I have an obligation to undertake such reconstruction as these means allow, even when the resulting message is at odds with the church's interpretation and/or my own sensibilities. That obligation is not substantially qualified by the fact that I can never know whether my reconstruction is 'correct' or even close to the 'original' intention (which can only be tested by alternative reconstructions). Nor is it diminished by recognition of multiple authors in the production of the present text (which makes the analysis of speaker and context more complex, but does not invalidate the model). See further below.

antithetical to feminist epistemology and hermeneutics,[6] I must at least insist that it is indispensable to my own feminist understanding of Scripture. I find no tension between historical criticism and feminist commitment, between an attempts to view the past on its own terms and a commitment to change the terms of participation and discourse generated by that past. I see no reason why an attempt to enter sympathetically into the minds or consciousnesses of historical persons and empathize with their feelings, motives and actions should exclude critique and ultimate rejection of those views. Why should an ancient author be denied the critically sensitive hearing demanded by a modern speaker just because he or she cannot speak back? The fact that all historical interpretation, as all cross-cultural interpretation, will fail to represent the other fully or adequately is no reason to abandon the attempt. Dismissal of historical criticism simply means that unexamined assumptions are read into the text. Historical criticism makes no claims concerning the normativity, or representativeness, of the ancient texts; in fact, it alerts readers to the dangers of such assumptions by considering the perspective, location and interests of the ancient author (including class, gender, religious party, etc.).[7]

An underlying problem in much of the debate concerning methods of interpreting biblical texts is differing, and often unstated, assumptions about the normativity of the text, more particularly assumptions about the *way* in which Scripture exercises authority for contemporary belief and practice. Strategies of interpretation are related to notions of the nature and consequences of biblical authority. Without attention to this question discussions of hermeneutical options, feminist or other, remain relatively meaningless, in my view, and fraught with misunderstandings.

With this too-brief excursion into method let me now attempt to identify some signs of feminist orientation in readings of biblical texts, confining my attention to the Old Testament, or Hebrew Bible.[8] For me, the essential signs or ingredients of

---

[6]The notion of a tension between historical-critical scholarship and feminist biblical interpretation in the service of a movement toward social reform is the underlying theme of the volume of essays edited by Adela Yarbro Collins, entitled *Feminist Perspectives on Biblical Scholarship* (SBL Biblical Scholarship in North America, 10; Chico, CA: Scholars Press, 1985). See esp. Collins, 'Introduction' pp. 3–4. The discussion in this volume is dominated by Rankean notions of 'scientific objectivity' that do not seem to me to be essential to distinguishing past and present meanings or to efforts to identify and control reader bias. I find Gordon Leff's views of historical 'objectivity' congenial, as cited from *History and Social Theory* (Garden City, NY: Doubleday, 1971) by Elisabeth Schüssler Fiorenza in 'Remembering the Past in Creating the Future: Historical-Critical Scholarship and Feminist Biblical Interpretation' (in Collins, *Feminist Perspectives,* pp. 43–63, p. 49), and I generally concur with Schüssler Fiorenza's reformulation of the criterion of objectivity when she describes historical judgments as 'intersubjectively understandable and intersubjectively verifiable' ('Remembering the Past', p. 53). I also agree with her in regarding the Bible as a thoroughly androcentric document, but I do not find this sufficient reason to deny it authority as a source for Christian faith—or feminist theology. No historical writing, or experience, has escaped this cultural conditioning. See Bird, 'The Authority of the Bible', in *The New Interpreter's Bible,* I (Nashville: Abingdon Press, 1994), I, pp. 33–64.

[7]Feminist critique joins historical-critical analysis in insisting that the texts that carry the sacred message are human, historically and culturally conditioned vehicles. Feminist analysis of patriarchy is essentially a historical-critical understanding. It needs to be sharpened as a hermeneutical tool, nor blunted or discarded.

[8]I must note briefly that where readings of biblical texts are carried out within or for religious communities, there is no common or neutral language to describe the earliest canon of Scriptures (again the issue of audience is critical to interpretation).

feminist interpretation are *systemic analysis* of gender relations and a *critique* of relationships, norms and expectations that *limit* or subordinate women's thought, action and expression. Highlighting of women alone, either as heroines or victims, does not constitute feminist interpretation, in my view, if it lacks systemic analysis. On the other hand, gender analysis alone, without critique of the asymmetrical distribution of power and prestige within the society is not feminist interpretation, although it may be essential to a feminist reading.

If the combined criteria of systemic gender analysis and critique of androcentric and patriarchal privilege establish a reading as feminist, or at least as indispensable to such an identification, the adequacy of the reading must still be tested. Feminist readings can *distort* ancient meanings to suit modern sensibilities and needs. Are such readings acceptable if they serve feminist goals? What standards of judgment are to be used in assessing readings? Must all readings be accorded equal value? Whom does the reading serve? Who is a competent judge of a reading? Who is a competent reader? For me, these are the critical questions. I have not tried to answer them, because they lie outside the bounds of this assignment.[9] I venture, however, to suggest two further criteria for judging a feminist reading:

(1) It must make sense of women's experience, or 'ring true' for women readers. Here one must immediately ask, Which women?, and recognize the danger of simply conforming to the perceptions of contemporary Western women, European-American women, or other interested parties. Since this danger exists in all readings, however, it can only be controlled by engaging the broadest audience possible and by encouraging dialogue between women of different class and cultural experiences. In the final analysis the rule holds: women have preferred place as judges of a feminist reading.

(2) Ultimately it should make sense to *men* as well. Feminism, and feminist interpretation, is not idiosyncratic, concerned only with female history and female nature, but aims to provide a more adequate account of our gendered human nature and history. Feminist reading should strive, I believe, for universal acceptance (recognizing that no interpretation gains such assent)—even if it seeks only the emancipation and empowerment of women. Its power lies in exposing the limits and distortions of past and prevailing readings and conceptions. I do not underestimate the difficulty of creating a shared world-view—especially where biological and socio-cultural factors are so inextricably intertwined—but feminist goals cannot be achieved by women alone. Feminism is concerned with wholeness, which can only be achieved through dialogue/interchange in which women have positions of power. Feminism seeks to enable that dialogue by empowering women.[10]

---

[9]I recognize as feminist, readings and analyses with which I disagree, as, e.g., treatments of women in patriarchal societies that view them as powerless victims, failing to see how they profit from the system and exercise power within it (cf. Schüssler Fiorenza, 'Remembering the Past', pp. 58–59), or treatments of women's status that equate economic contribution with social recognition and power.

[10]One of the consequences of the patriarchal monopoly of power for social planning is that women are often unable to envision larger goals and may be trapped by a 'victim' mentality or an encapsulated sense of self and world. But they may also be freer to dream the 'impossible.'

A final note on tactics and content of feminist reading. Feminist aims in biblical interpretation may find expression in a wide variety of ways depending on the audience, occasion and desired effect of the reading. Shocking exaggeration or assuming a view opposite to that expressed in the text may achieve recognition of previously unseen or misinterpreted gender perspectives in the text. Lifting up women alone to create a history of biblical women may serve to provide an essential sense of a female past for women (and men) accustomed to viewing the Bible as essentially male history.[11] Feminist midrash can provide a bridge from patriarchal past to feminist future by recasting biblical accounts. Imaginative reconstruction to fill the silences of the text with unseen or unheard women can bring recognition of the limits and biases of the sources so they are not read unconsciously as inclusive. And inclusive readings can claim the whole history and literature for women whether that was the original intention or not. This is hardly an exhaustive catalogue of approaches, but it brings me back to my original point that feminist reading is determined by criteria that lie *outside* the reading itself. These various ways of reading in the service of feminist aims represent different ways of understanding the role of the Bible for the reader. That remains a critical question for determining the adequacy, usefulness or credibility of a reading.

What Makes a Feminist Reading Feminist? Another Perspective

Pamela Thimmes

For several months I asked colleagues, friends and students the question this topic asks me, 'What makes a feminist reading feminist?' Apart from a few serious attempts at fumbled articulation, modest lectures about asking questions that require neat generalizations and playing to type, and even a few silent stares, my hopes for probing questions and ideas and/or musings that might spark the

---

[11]While I rejected such constructions above, I recognize the usefulness of partial and counter treatments in contexts where full analysis is impossible. For laywomen deprived of biblical images of women by a canon and lectionary that contain few images of women, such selective readings may convey an essential feminist message of identification and empowerment.

imagination remained unfulfilled. Perhaps this is a customary response to questions of methodology. Why is this question so difficult to answer? Why do attempts to answer it raise many more difficult questions?

Since this is a question about interpretation, my responses come from a particular socio-political framework: first, my own response recognizes *difference* (there is no such thing as one feminism or a single voice for women); secondly, it comes from a particular social location. The adage 'What you see depends on where you stand', can refer to questions of methodology as much as to the act of writing, or to reading strategies and interpretation. So my own reading and interpretation comes from a particular social location—some of my personal locators mirror majority positions in the academy and society, and some locators clearly position me as a minority in both the academy and society. These locators serve as the lenses through which reading and interpretation proceed.

The question at hand, 'What makes a feminist reading feminist,' is a methodological question. In a search for a starting point I moved beyond the friends/colleagues interview mode to a review of the literature in both biblical studies and literature. It became evident that, while methodological questions marked the early years of feminist literary theory and feminist biblical hermeneutics, until recently there was less attention given to describing and clarifying method, and more emphasis on praxis, literally *doing* feminist hermeneutics.[1] In retrospect, both the diversity of approaches and the continual movement from theory to praxis exemplifies the nature of the discipline. In important ways the development of literary feminism is similar to the development of feminist biblical hermeneutics, and as a practitioner who has had a foot in both disciplines I find myself moving easily back and forth between literary theories and biblical methods in my own reading and interpretation. As a result, I see that similar questions are of concern in both areas. For example, Nina Bayim notes, 'Perhaps the central issue in academic literary feminism right now is theory itself.[2] Similar sentiments are voiced in feminist biblical hermeneutics, but they are framed in terms of cautions. Alice Bach warns, 'Feminist criticism must remain fluid, not fixed, so that each of us can contend with the

---

[1]For example, in literary theory, see Diana Fuss, 'Reading like a Feminist', *differences* 1 (1989), pp. 77–92; Joyce Quiring Erickson, 'What Difference? The Theory and Practice of Feminist Criticism', *Christianity and Literature* 33.1 (1983), pp. 65–74; Elizabeth Gross, 'What is Feminist Theory?', in her *Feminist Challenges: Social and Political Theory* (Boston: Northeastern University Press, 1986); Nina Bayim, 'The Madwoman and her Languages: Why I Don't Do Feminist Literary Theory', in her *Feminist and American Literary History* (New Brunswick, NJ: Rutgers University Press, 1992), pp. 199–213; Josephine Donovan (ed.), *Feminist Literary Criticism: Explorations in Theory* (Lexington: University of Kentucky Press, 1975); Mary Eagleton (ed.), *Feminist Literary Theory: A Reader* (New York: Blackwell, 1986); Elaine Showalter (ed.), *Feminist Criticism: Essays on Women, Literature and Theory* (New York: Pantheon Books, 1985); Gayle Greene and Coppelia Kahn (eds.), *Making a Difference: Feminist Literary Criticism* (New York: Routledge, 1986).
In biblical studies see Elisabeth Schüssler Fiorenza, *But She Said: Feminist Practices of Biblical Interpretation* (Boston: Beacon Press, 1992); as well as *Bread Not Stone* (Boston: Beacon Press, 1984); Janice Capel Anderson, 'Mapping Feminist Biblical Criticism: The American Scene, 1983–1990', *CR* (1991), pp. 21–44; Mary Ann Tolbert, 'Defining the Problem: The Bible and Feminist Hermeneutics', *Semeia* 28 (1983), pp. 113–26; and 'Protestant Feminists and the Bible: On the Horns of a Dilemma', in Alice Bach (ed.), *The Pleasure of her Text: Feminist Readings of Biblical and Historical Texts* (Philadelphia: Trinity Press, 1990), pp. 5–23.
[2]Bayim, 'The Madwoman and her Languages', p. 199.

ripples and waves of the dominant culture, diving into language to recover everything that is duplicitous and resistant and confounding.'[3]

In response to the question 'What makes a feminist reading feminist?' my own thinking moves in a circular pattern, encompassing a number of ideas and presuppositions that find clarity only in partnership with the other elements contained in the circle. This paradigm is marked by particular elements that serve as arcs constituting various portions of the circle and is, at root, an ecological paradigm. That is, no element in the circle works independent of the other elements; rather, this interdependent relationship is what constitutes the circle, and the circle is the methodological enterprise. I see four elements necessary in feminist hermeneutics:

> (1) *Feminism*—is a political category understood and practiced as a liberation movement, critiquing the oppressive structures of society;[4] (2) *Experience*—is not simply a *construct*, it also *constructs*;[5] (3) *Culture* (social location)—mediates our experience, and thus our worldviews or paradigms; (4) *Reading/Interpretation (Language)*—language is more than simply a non-material tool, it is an expression of a particular understanding of reality.[6] It is in language that social locators (gender, race, class, etc.) are first noticed and first submerged.[7]

These elements function together seamlessly in the methodological enterprise, as I understand it. However, I will try to make some specific comments that will clarify the question at hand and the interrelationship of the elements.

I understand *feminism* as both a political term and as a political category because it is, essentially, a liberation movement that not only critiques the oppressive structures of society but, by its various voices and approaches, works for transformation.[8] As a political category feminism grew and grows out of *women's* experience and makes explicit the interconnections among all systems of oppression. Liberation movements work for justice, and ultimately for transformation. So, just

---

[3] Bach (ed.), *The Pleasure of her Text*, pp. ix–x.

[4] Tolbert, 'Defining the Problem', p. 115.

[5] Robert Scholes, 'Reading Like a Man', in Alice Jardine and Pául Smith (eds.), *Men in Feminism* (New York: Methuen, 1987), p. 215.

[6] Roland Barthes, *The Pleasure of the Text* (trans. R. Howard; New York: Hill & Wang, 1975); Basil Bernstein, *Class, Codes, and Control. I. Theoretical Studies towards a Sociology of Language* (4 vols.; London: Routledge & Kegan Paul, 2nd rev. edn, 1974); Roland Champagne, 'A Grammar of the Languages of Culture: Literary Theory and Yury M. Lotman's Semiotics', *Literary History* 9 (1977–78), pp. 205–10; Jonathan Culler, *Structuralist Poetics: Structuralism, Linguistics and the Study of Literature* (Ithaca, NY: Cornell University Press, 1975); Jacques Derrida, *Of Grammatology* (trans. G.C. Spivak; Baltimore: The Johns Hopkins University Press, 1976); *idem*, 'Structure, Sign and Play in the Discourse of the Human Sciences', in R. Macksey and E. Donato (eds.), *The Structuralist Controversy* (Baltimore: The Johns Hopkins University Press, 1970); Joshua A. Fishman, *Readings in the Sociology of Language* (The Hague: Mouton, 1970).

[7] Bach (ed.), *The Pleasure of her Text*, p. xii.

[8] Schweickart reminds us, 'Feminist criticism . . . is a mode of *praxis*. The point is not merely to interpret literature in various ways; the point is to *change the world*. We cannot afford to ignore the activity of reading, for it is here that literature is realized as *praxis*. Literature acts on the world by acting on its readers'. See Patrocino P. Schweickart, 'Toward a Feminist Theory of Reading', in Elizabeth A. Flynn and Patrocinio P. Schweickart (eds.), *Gender and Reading: Essays on Readers, Texts and Contexts* (Baltimore: The Johns Hopkins University Press, 1986), p. 39.

as feminism affirms and promotes the full humanity of women it rejects and denies anything that diminishes the full humanity and equality of women,[9] as well as sexism, racism, classism, ageism, or any other dominance pattern that seeks to separate, alienate and oppress. From the beginning feminism has offered a broad-based critique built from the experience of women, but not exclusive to women. Elisabeth Schüssler Fiorenza suggests,

> A 'feminist' reading . . . must time and again rearticulate the categories and focus its lenses of interpretation in particular historical situations and social contexts. It may not subscribe to a single method of analysis nor adopt a single hermeneutical perspective or mode of approach. It also may not restrict itself to one single reading community or audience . . . At stake here is a theoretical shift from the paradigm of domination to one of radical equality. Emancipatory movements have to create discursive communities based on shared assumptions and values that define boundaries and validate claims to authority.[10]

The ideology that motivates critique (against paradigms of domination) and advocacy (toward a paradigm of radical equality) is an ideology that deconstructs *and* constructs. It is this ideology that is foundational to feminist hermeneutics. However, feminism as both critique and ideology raises a number of questions for feminist interpretation: Because a scholar is a *self-defined feminist*, does that mean any interpretation offered by that scholar is *feminist?* Does the gender of the interpreter automatically presume a feminist or non-feminist reading? Is a particular reading strategy or interpretation feminist because feminists agree that it is? Does placing women's experience, ideas, values, visions at the center of an interpretation make that interpretation feminist?[11] These, and other questions seem to be part of the methodological minefield, part of the contested territory that the academies continue to crawl through in defining, appropriating and utilizing feminist hermeneutical perspectives.

Within the last decade there has been an ongoing conversation about the centrality and importance of *gendered* reading in feminist hermeneutics, bringing this question to the fore. Privileging women's experiences, voices, values, concerns, differences and critiques is the heart of feminist hermeneutics, and will remain so. Gender is a fundamental organizing category of experience and reading is a social activity that involves a complex interweaving of 'structures of power, gender and identity'.[12] We now know that gender is central to any reading experience, and

---

[9]Letty Russell (ed.), *Feminist Interpretation of the Bible* (Philadelphia: Westminster Press, 1985), p. 16.

[10]Elisabeth Schüssler Fiorenza, 'Transforming the Legacy of *The Women's Bible*', in *Searching the Scriptures: A Feminist Introduction*, I, p. 18.

[11]For a discussion that asks many of these questions and provides various views on each question, see Eagleton, *Feminist Literary Theory*, pp. 149–54.

[12]Nancy K. Miller, 'Arachnologies: The Woman, the Text and the Critic', in Nancy K. Miller (ed.), *The Poetics of Gender* (New York: Columbia University Press, 1986), p. 272. Also see Bonnie Zimmerman, 'What Has Never Been: An Overview of Lesbian Feminist Literary Criticism', in Greene and Kahn (eds.), *Making a Difference: Feminist Literary Criticism*, pp. 177–210. Reading, says Annette Kolodny, is a 'learned activity . . . inevitably sex-coded and gender-inflected', quoted in Elaine Showalter, 'Critical Cross-Dressing: Male Feminists and the Woman of the Year', in Jardine and Smith (eds.), *Men in Feminism*, p. 119.

there is provocative research that argues that because the framework of literature (in terms of what is considered classic, good or canonical literature) has been driven by male paradigms, that is, a patriarchal conceptual framework (a situation analogous to the biblical 'canon'), women have been *immasculated* by the very reading process in which they participate.[13] There are also indications that men, reading literature written by women and expressive of women's experience, have a difficult time engaging in and appropriating the framework necessary to the reading and interpretation of those texts.[14]

On the one hand, some would argue that revisionist reading or reading *against* patriarchal texts offers little protection.[15] But what happens to the reader in the reading experience? Harold Bloom cautions, 'You *are* or *become* what you read [my emphases]'.[16] In many cases, the female reader must construct herself as *Other*, when she is required to identify with the male as universal and dominant in a text.[17] In reading, 'what we engage are not texts but paradigms'.[18] Thus the feminist reader, reading biblical texts, is required to be a resisting reader. Kolodny explains, 'we read well, and with pleasure, what we already know how to read; and what we know how to read is to a large extent dependent upon what we have already read (works from which we developed our expectations and learned our interpretative strategies)'.[19]

On the other hand, revisionist readings, reading against the text 'can remind us of the powerful effects readers have on texts, and conversely of the powerful effect texts have on readers . . .'[20] Schweickart notes, 'Feminist criticism . . . is a mode of *praxis*. The point is not merely to interpret literature in various ways; the point is to *change the world*. We cannot afford to ignore the activity of reading, for it is here that literature is realized as *praxis*. Literature acts on the world by acting on its readers.'[21] Joyce Erickson agrees and adds, 'for both feminist and Christian

---

[13]The term was originally coined by Judith Fetterley in *The Resisting Reader: A Feminist Approach to American Fiction* (Bloomington: Indiana University Press, 1987). See Schweickart, 'Toward a Feminist Theory of Reading', pp. 49–50: 'a crucial feature of the process of immasculation is the woman reader's bifurcated response. She reads the text both as a man and as a woman. But in either case, the result is the same; she confirms her position as other'.

[14]See the section Annette Kolodny devotes to structures of signification and reading in 'Dancing through the Minefield: Some Observations on the Theory, Practice and Politics of Feminist Literary Criticism', in *The New Feminist Criticism: Essays on Women, Literature and Theory*, pp. 148–219. Elaine Showalter joins the conversation herself when she reports, 'Heath concludes that a man reading as a feminist always involves a strategy of female impersonation. But is there not also a mode of impersonation involved when a woman reads as a feminist, or indeed, when a woman reads as a woman?', 'Critical Cross-Dressing', pp. 128–29.

[15]See Hélène Cixous, 'Language conceals an invisible adversary because it's the language of men and their grammar', in 'The Laugh of the Medusa', *Signs* 1 (trans. Keith Cohen and Paula Cohen; Summer 1976), pp. 875–93.

[16]Harold Bloom, *Kabbalah and Criticism* (New York: Seabury Press, 1975), p. 96.

[17]Elizabeth Struthers Malbon and Janice Capel Anderson, 'Literary-Critical Methods', in *Searching the Scriptures*, p. 251.

[18]Kolodny, 'Dancing through the Minefield', p. 153.

[19]Kolodny, 'Dancing through the Minefield', p. 154.

[20]Erickson, 'What Difference?', p. 71.

[21]Schweikert, 'Toward a Feminist Theory of Reading', p. 39.

[biblical] critics the high value accorded literature and art is linked to the conviction that they have the power to affect human life, a power that extends into the future'.[22]

These two positions offer plausible arguments. Reading is not done in a vacuum and the activity of reading imperils the status quo. For me the question of what 'reading' we do as biblical critics concerns, not only what reading *is*, but what it *does* to the reader and to the community in which it is read. The old, often asked question, 'does the text construct the reading subject or does the reading subject construct the text?[23] has a place in a discussion about gender and reading. Diana Fuss suggests,

> In reading . . . we bring (old) subject-positions to the text at the same time the actual process of reading constructs (new) subject-positions for us. Consequently, we are always engaged in a 'double reading' . . . in the sense that we are continually caught within and between *at least two* constantly shifting subject-positions (old and new, constructed and constructing) and these positions may often stand in complete contradiction to each other.[24]

Is feminist hermeneutics, then, a reading strategegy, a methodology, that because of its origins, history, and context, can only be done by women? Is gender the only determiner of feminist reading? Fuss notes that 'feminism seems to take for granted among its members a shared identity'.[25] If feminism is understood as a political construct, then fidelity to the ideology must be borne out in the praxis, that is, in the methodologies utilized. For me, then, what makes a feminist reading feminist has less to do *today* with the gender of the person offering the reading and more to do with the coherence the reading has with a feminist ideology. However, I make this statement well aware that there are serious problems inherent in both the appropriation of feminism by men, and with the assumption that men can read like women. Showalter notes that this functional view of reading might be both superficial and politically suspect—can feminist reading be reduced 'to a cognitive skill easily transferable to male texts or critical theories?'[26]

Experience, culture and *reading/interpretation* are difficult to separate in the feminist methodological circle because all are mediated through *social location*. For me, *social location* means that the paradigms or world-views we hold are a result of complex patterns including a number of factors that provide a lens focusing and shaping experience, from which is abstracted a particular view of reality. These factors include gender, age, race, religion, education, class, sexual orientation, physical abilities, geography, environment, politics, culture and family. The

---

[22]Erickson, 'What Difference?', p. 71.
[23]Fuss, 'Reading Like a Feminist', p. 86.
[24]Fuss, 'Reading Like a Feminist', pp. 86–87.
[25]Fuss, 'Reading Like a Feminist', p. 77.
[26]Showalter, 'Critical Cross-Dressing', p. 119.

result is a socially constructed world-view that indicates *place*, or *where I stand*. Mary Ann Tolbert reminds us, 'most of us (though not all) have multiple *perspectives* from which we may interpret texts . . . We do not exist in one social context but many'.[27]

If the four arcs I propose are facets of a feminist reading, the relational nature of these elements serves as a model for the process of reading/interpretation that characterizes a feminist reading. As feminists we bring a shared ideology to the discussion, as well as a variety of interpretative strategies for reading. We need to be reminded that we never *just* read, that we always read *from somewhere*,[28] and that 'reading is, after all, a learned skill, taught according to conventional rules devised by the cultural elite of any literate society. It is thus a kind of socialization into the values and stereotypical roles expected by that society'.[29] There are among us many voices and many *somewheres*, a diversity of experiences, a diversity of readings, and in an ecological framework, diversity is the life-force of the system. We might better ask the methodological question in light of this diversity. 'What makes *feminists' readings* feminist?'[30]

Earlier I noted that feminist hermeneutics has been primarily concerned with the practice of reading. Is there a difference between the theory and practice of feminist hermeneutics? I think not. If we argue there is a difference, we concede that theory is an esoteric luxury and an elitist pastime that has alienated itself from its roots.[31] As a liberation movement founded out of the oppression of women, feminist hermeneutics, in practice and theory, and in partnership with other feminist perspectives,[32] not only works for justice but is actively engaged in transformation—it not only *deconstructs*, it *reconstructs*, and it *constructs*.

At the beginning of this essay I spoke about the parallel routes traveled by literary feminism and feminist biblical hermeneutics. Literary feminists frequently speak about 'second-wave' feminism as the 'discovery that women writers had a literature of their own . . . [33] and now feminists speak about the 'third wave'. If we, as biblical scholars, can talk about a 'second wave' in feminist hermeneutics, it is

---

[27]Mary Ann Tolbert, 'Reading for Liberation', in Fernando F. Segovia and Mary Ann Tolbert (eds.), *Reading from this Place: Social Location and Biblical Interpretation in the United States* (Minneapolis: Fortress Press, 1995), I, p. 274.

[28]Fuss, 'Reading Like a Feminist', p. 89.

[29]Tolbert, 'Reading for Liberation', p. 274.

[30]'Only by emphasizing the differences and multiplicities of knowers and known can hierarchy and dominance be overcome', Anderson, 'Mapping Feminist Biblical Criticism', p. 26.

[31]See Bayim, 'The Madwoman and her Languages', p. 199: 'Feminist hermeneutics oscillates between two perspectives: pluralism and legalism. The pluralist perspective recognizes that the very act of reading implies interpretation, and with any number of readings and individuals engaged in readings, there will be a variety of interpretations—one expects the unexpected and diversity is encouraged. The legalist perspective attempts to "locate the correct positions and marshal women within the ranks".' Of the two perspectives, the pluralist position has dominated biblical studies. Bayim continues, 'As for recent literary theory, it is deeply legalistic and judgmental. Infractions—the wrong theory, theoretical errors, or insouciant disregard for theoretical implications—are crimes. Pluralists "dance"; theorists "storm" or "march"', pp. 199.

[32]Bayim, 'The Madwoman and her Languages', p. 204.

[33]Elaine Showalter, 'Introduction: The Feminist Critical Revolution', in *The New Feminist Criticism*, p. 6. Also see Nina Bayim's assessment of the 'second wave': 'Matters for Interpretation: Feminism and the Teaching of Literature', in *Feminism and Literary History*, pp. 214–15.

very different from that of literary feminists. We cannot claim a 'literature' (in the canonical sense) of our own. Increasingly, though, and particularly with the publication of expressly feminist commentaries and introductions, feminist biblical hermeneutics has moved into a new arena. I would suggest that 'third-wave' feminist hermeneutics is at hand, if not here, the time when feminist monographs, commentaries, dictionaries, etc. that deal with the entire canon (and non-canonical literature) will sit side-by-side on library shelves with the androcentric voices that have dominated the cultural landscape. However, I suspect (and hope) that by the time that horizon is realized we will see that biblical studies has been revolutionized by a multiculturalism that exemplifies both the value of diversity and the importance of social location in any hermeneutic, the foundation of which was laid by feminist hermeneutics.

Chapter 2

The First Woman and Man as a Gender Issue

On the Creation of Man and Woman in Genesis 1–3: The History and Reception of the Texts Reconsidered*

Helen Schüngel-Straumann

1. INTRODUCTION

The texts of Genesis 1–3 are not a unified whole. Genesis 1 was written by a different author, belongs to another period, and shows an appreciation of theological problems that is newer than that of the older reports of Genesis 2–3. This is well known and widely acknowledged. One should, however, always keep in

*Reprinted from T. Schneider (ed.), *Mann und Frau: Grundproblem theologischer Anthropologie* (Freiburg: Herder, 1989): 142–66.

mind that a naive interpretation of the Bible, one that takes the texts literally and mistakes the chronological order of reported events for a historical one, has its (however hidden) effect up to this very day. Similarly, there is a tradition of more than 2000 years and a history of the text's reception which foster anti-woman arguments from which we are still suffering today. These arguments were seldom inherent in the texts themselves; rather, and for various reasons, they were propagated through a long and complicated history of interpretation. That is why everybody reading or listening to these old texts, even a theologian, is, to some extent, biased, as evidenced everywhere in handbooks, dictionaries, essays, and so on.[1]

This historical placing of the origin of both sources means that all traditional arguments which are based on a chronological sequence of Genesis 1 and 2–3 are rendered worthless. Nobody can possibly regard the so-called story of the Fall or the Garden as a further explanation of Genesis 1, as has been the case in the past. We must face up to the fact that even a chain of interpretation of 2000 years' standing may be, quite simply, false.

2. ON THE HISTORY OF THE MAN-WOMAN THEME AND ITS RECEPTION

A. GENESIS 2 AND 3

Beginning with the older texts of Genesis 2 and 3, I should like to answer the question: why could these narratives be used to make women responsible for humankind's sin and evil? There were two major stages leading to this. The first was the interpreting of the Fall in such a way, that the woman's role in it was seen to be greater than the man's. The second was the generalization, *one* woman equals *all* women. In the (Christian) Old Testament there is an indication of a negative interpretation of Genesis in regard to 'The Woman' in the book of Sirach, but this remains the only instance. This late book (from the early second century BCE) contains a sentence which is almost inevitably quoted in all anti-female traditions: 'Of the woman came the beginning of sin, and through her we all die' (Sir. 25.24, AV). Sirach is not included in the canonical books of the churches of the Reformation. It is part of the Septuagint but not of the Hebrew canon. In the so-called Wisdom Literature the woman problem plays an important role. Most of these later texts and writings, which offer advice and help for definite times and situations, are full of anti-woman sentiments. Warnings against the scarlet woman, against adultery, and so forth are very common topoi in this sort of literature, just as in other ancient oriental testaments. This genre is common to all oriental cultures and was carried much beyond the imagination of earlier centuries. To a large extent, the genre stems from old oriental sources, mainly Egyptian. One must not forget the part such didactic literature played in life, especially for the practical

---

[1] Cf. the article on 'Adam', in *TRE*, I, 414–37. There is no article on 'Eve'. All statements concerning women are included in the Adam article, and in another article called 'Woman' (*TRE*, XI, 417–69).

education of male adolescents. To understand such statements as universally valid dogmas about 'The Woman' is to miss the point completely.

The above-quoted verse from Sirach is, however, only the tip of the pre-Christian, literary iceberg. There exists a great number of apocryphal stories, with words of wisdom or apocalyptical content, many of which are preserved in Greek. None of these writings delivers anything new, but they tend to interpret things old and traditional by giving them a new dimension. The whole literate world spoke Greek by then: the traditional Hebrew texts were only understood by a minority, and a real need for new interpretations arose. Due to the changing *Zeitgeist*, everything had to be open-minded and up-to-date. Any trends that might be in the air were taken up and viewed through the eyes of the old traditions. Not long afterwards the writers of the New Testament, especially the letter writers of the second and third generations, explained our Genesis texts with the help of those ancient patterns they already knew. All authors of this period merrily try their hands at this sort of thing, with no fixed canon binding them as yet! Thus, the writers of the New Testament took up the original Hebrew texts, but fell back upon early Jewish-Hellenistic interpretations.

Of the numerous apocryphal stories circulating at that time a few should be mentioned here, as they offer examples of extremely negative interpretations of Old Testament textual traditions: the book of *Jubilees* with its conspicuously tendentious exegesis of the Adam and Eve story (Hebrew copies of *Jubilees* were found in Qumran, proving how widely the book circulated in certain ascetic circles and confirming its pre-Christian origin). Furthermore, *1 Enoch*, especially its Ethiopic version, and the *Testament of the Twelve Patriarchs*, parts of which are dated as late as the beginning of the Common Era, were used and supplemented by Christians.[2]

In addition, there existed a series of stories entitled the *Life of Adam and Eve*, which in the Latin version tended to idealize Adam and place the sole cause of evil upon Eve. Eve goes so far as to ask Adam to kill her, for the loss of Paradise is her fault. Thus, male self-justification is put in the mouth of a woman! Concerning the names Adam and Eve, it remains to be said that they are a product of this late misinterpretation, resulting from the translation into Greek and Latin, whereas the original sources speak of 'man' and 'woman' without using proper names.

Let me give one more example where this tendency to eroticize and demonize becomes evident, with all its devastating consequences for all women. In ch. 5 of the *Testament of the Twelve Patriarchs* Reuben, the eldest of Jacob's sons, gives the following last instruction:

> 1 Women are evil, my children, as they have no power over men, they lure them with their beauty. 2 And if they cannot bewitch them with their beauty, they outdo them with their scheming. 3 For God's Angel spoke unto me thus:

---

[2]For these Apocrypha, including the so-called deuterocanonical books like Ecclesiasticus or the 'Wisdom of Jesus son of Sirach', there is now a new academic German edition (Kümmel 1973–). Some of the volumes relevant for this topic have not been published yet. Thus we have to go back to the older collection of texts by Riessler (1928) and Kautzsch (1900).

women succumb to the spirit of whoring more willingly than men. They contrive in their hearts to scheme against men. They confuse their minds with jewellery. They poison them with their eyes, then capture them with their deeds. 4 For a woman cannot overcome a man openly, she beguiles him with her harlotry . . . ³ (Also cf. *Jubilees* 33).

Here we find an accumulation of the then popular combination of jewellery, beauty and seduction, as well as the affinity of 'Woman' and sexuality. This quotation is typical, since in the original text, referred to by Reuben here, the woman plays no active part in the disgraceful deed—Reuben had taken possession of his father's concubine while she was asleep(!) and while Jacob was away. Nonetheless, the Hellenistic erotic interpretation of this later period blames the woman and her erotic aura for the crime. The same pattern can be shown in countless reinterpretations from those early centuries.

The actual theological problem in the epistles of the New Testament, which derive from this milieu, does not stem from the original text taken from the Old Testament. It is the choice of texts (the Bible has always been read selectively) together with their interpretation against the background of the above-mentioned understanding, which often contradicts the original text. Let me quote another of the epistles, 1 Tim. 2.8–15, which also underlines such tendencies.⁴ Here the woman is introduced as a second-rate creation; she is the only one seduced (cf. Küchler 1986: 9ff.), thus ranking first in the order of sin while second in the order of creation. The literary sequence is changed to a chronological one, which is part of the classical interpretation of the text. The next step, however, is an evaluation of the chronological order, as is also the case with the old tradition. This is against the kerygma of the J source (cf. Küchler 1986: 19). For the statement of seduction a selection is made from Genesis 3, which not only does not accord with the Old Testament text but even contradicts it. The term 'seduction' is used in Genesis 3 only by the serpent, not by the woman. That only the woman committed the sin, as stated in 1 Tim. 2.14, is quite clearly a misrepresentation of the Yahwistic text. Moreover, the sequence in v. 15, 'She shall be saved in childbearing', implies an erotic kind of sin. According to the *talion* principle, the punishment must be in kind, a 'measure for measure' for the sin committed. The meticulous structure of the Timothy pericope suggests a sexual transgression of Eve with the serpent. Quite a number of apocryphal texts are solely concerned with the explicit description of Eve's sin as sexual intercourse with the serpent (*nāhāš* is masculine in Hebrew). Some apocryphal writings even mention the birth of Cain as the 'fruit' of this intercourse (e.g. Küchler 1986: 19, 48).

In 1 Cor. 14.33b–36 there is a late insertion which demands the subordination of the woman in quite an extreme fashion. It refers to a sentence from Gen. 3.16, one of the so-called 'curses'. Here the original early Jewish interpretation of aetiological penal laws is suddenly changed into a command, which is a complete

---

³According to the translation of Becker (1970: 37); cf. Küchler 1986: 442–43, 171–72.

⁴M. Küchler's translation of this text shows the meticulous structure of the epistle and the importance of the argumentation for the letter writer.

reversal of the original statement. Although all recent commentaries deal quite explicitly with the problem of this quotation—it is almost universally accepted that Paul did not write this himself—it is still used against women today (especially in the liturgy)![5]

B. GENESIS 1

In Genesis 1 there is only one passage which involves a woman, that is, the statement on the creation of man and woman in the image of God (1.27). Nevertheless, in the Hellenistic traditions we are not confronted only with the text itself, but also with a whole host of developments and interpretations. The first important obstacle to a proper understanding of this passage is the fact that the term *'ādām* was used by P in the collective sense of 'man'[6] or 'humankind'. In the Hebrew text P never refers to *'ādām* as an individual: this is not questioned by exegetes. Still, early Jewish interpretation read *'ādām* in Genesis 1 as a proper name, due to a misinterpretation of the J texts in Genesis 2 and the following chapter. There Adam and Eve are seen as individuals, and that is why *'ādām* becomes an individual in Genesis 1 also through interpretation, and, consequently, becomes *a man*. Besides, the Greek translation renders *'ādām* as ἄνθρωπος wherever it is not used as a proper name. Although this means 'human being' and includes women, in popular Hellenistic philosophy only the male is regarded as an ἄνθρωπος in the full sense of the word. So, quite frequently the statement on the creation of man and woman in Genesis 1 is perceived as referring to the man only, however subtle the exegesis may be. The word 'image' (εἰκών) is applied solely to the male; God's εἰκών is apparently only a human being in a full sense, namely the man.

There are also rabbinic interpretations denying the god-likeness of the woman; others grant it in a lesser form. Some of those are indeed free-wheeling and even fanciful. Such interpretations often fasten on to the (grammatical) difference between singular and plural in the original text of Gen. 1.27:

> And Elohim created man (*'ādām*) in his own image, in the image of Elohim he created *him;* male and female he created *them.*

The change of object in the last sentence, which, in Hebrew, may be logically derived from a collective meaning of the grammatically singular term *'ādām* and its development into 'male and female', led to a negative interpretation for the woman. There is also another tradition in early Jewish exegesis which regards the first human beings as *androgynous* creatures, with the male characteristics always playing the dominant part (i.e. the man always has the frontal face; the woman displays god-likeness only when together with the man in these interpretations, while the man possesses it also on his own and outside this tradition!) I shall ignore here these interpretative trends as well as the Gnostic concepts and the Nag

---

[5]Cf., e.g., Klauck 1984: 104–106, and the literature cited Küchler 1986: 54ff.

[6]The terms 'man' or 'mankind' which I sometimes use here, especially in the translation of specific passages, are inclusive. Their usage should not conceal the fact that both genders are referred to by these terms.

Hammadi texts (some of which also have a positive Adam tradition that is, however, strongly dualistic). Here I shall confine myself to those interpretations which continue to have an effect in the New Testament and transmit a tradition which is negative towards women.[7]

The Jewish philosopher Philo undoubtedly played a crucial role in the philosophical architecture and further development of such thoughts. He combined the statements of Gen. 1.26 and the following verses with the Logos: the ensuing construct had grave consequences, especially for the further mingling of philosophical ideas with New Testament ones. Whether or not this constituted a direct influence on the New Testament is of little importance; what counts is the summary of the traditional body of thought which was then worked into a philosophical system incorporating Greek concepts.

I shall deal here with some examples from the New Testament in which these early Jewish interpretations are taken up. The exegesis of the New Testament is yet again selective in confusing the traditional interpretation of Genesis 2–3 with that of Gen. 1.26 and the following verses. This process of mingling interpretations, telescoping them into one another, leads to discrimination against women. Thus, the anti-woman features of the ancient tradition have a snowball effect.

The moving force behind the Christian tradition was Paul, insofar that he combined ancient interpretations of Genesis with his Christology. Paul introduced the typological pair of opposites: Adam-Christ (Rom. 5), first human and perfect human, the first bringing sin into this world, the latter salvation. This typological concept must see Adam as an individual, as it also sees Christ as a person, a human being. Since Christ is male, Adam is, accordingly, male too. 'The woman' does not even enter this comparison, although this does not become immediately apparent.

Paul adopts Jewish tradition in several places, particularly in 1 Corinthians 11, where he constructs a hierarchy which quite distinctly diminishes the godlikeness of 'the woman'.[8] In his hierarchy of descent only the member at the top, the male, is God's image in the full sense. God is the original, Christ his actual image. Christ is the head of the man, who is the head of the woman'. Thus, a line of descent ensues from it: God, Christ, man, woman. Against the backdrop of the antifemale interpretation of Genesis 2–3, which Paul combines here with the abovementioned early Jewish interpretation of Gen. 1.27, he jumps to a conclusion which is not in accordance with the original text of Genesis 1: Paul says something different from the P source.

The meticulous construction of 1 Corinthians 11 shows that Paul is not concerned with a mere question of decorum only. Very few other New Testament passages contain so many chains of argument. Looking more closely, it seems obvious that Paul does not use the original (Hebrew) passages from Genesis but the Greek translation, the Septuagint; and he uses those traditions which misinterpret the change from singular to plural in the Hebrew of 1.27, arguing that

---

[7]More on this problem area in Jervell 1960 and Schaller 1961; on pp. 187–90 Schaller lists all instances from the New Testament with allusions to, or interpretations of, Genesis 1 and 2.

[8]Cf. the text in Küchler 1986: n. 5 and its exegesis, pp. 73ff.

women are godlike to a limited extent only. Paul made use of this interpretation, which is derogatory towards women, since it fitted his Adam-Christ typology nicely. The devastating theological consequences for the Christian image of women are widely known.[9] Of all the Pauline statements (and there are others I do not wish to discuss here), this one was destined to become so momentous! Max Küchler examined these and some other passages in the letters of the New Testament and asked why the anti-woman arguments were so powerful. He concluded that it was

> because of an exegesis created by men for men, which interpreted and retold the Bible to women's disadvantage. These exegetes seized every chance to interpret any peculiarities in form or content in such a way that women were kept in their place regarding their conduct and position, but also their confidence and their rights, thus presenting the Biblical-Jewish ethics as God's plan of creation (Küchler 1986: 114).

3. TEXTS

A. GENESIS 2–3

Once again I shall start with Genesis 2 and 3 for practical and historical reasons, since the more recent text of Genesis 1 is meant as a theological correction of the J narratives. These tales must by no means be regarded as isolated texts. They are part of the more comprehensive complex of the original story, in which the author unfolds humankind's addiction to sin in its various guises. One story alone is not enough to describe this addiction to its full extent, hence the use of several approaches. Men and their acts of violence play an important part in all these tales of sin: Cain, Lamech, the sons of the gods and, finally, the men who build a tower 'with its top in the heavens' (NEB), making a name for themselves. Tradition's choice fell on the first story for reasons already mentioned: because a woman plays an active part in it.

Notably, the original story is told aetiologically for the most part, differing greatly from historiography in its genre and intention. The framework of creation right up to the Flood was prescribed for both biblical authors by old oriental sources. What counts is what is being made here of the old traditional texts, that is, how the given material is being re-interpreted and transformed. (This is the case not only in regard to J, but also to P.)

Fortunately, we find a similar myth concerning the beginning of history in Ezekiel 28, a myth which deals with *'ādām. 'ādām* lives blamelessly on a mountain of God and is put in a garden. *'ādām* sins (out of arrogance), *'ādām* is banished by a

---

[9]Cf. the numerous, unfortunately very scattered, papers by E. Gossmann on anthropology in the Middle Ages, especially the 10 volumes in progress in the series *Archiv für philosophie- and theologiegeschichtliche Frauenforschung* (vols. 1–4 have been published so far). They comprise evidence, documentation, and female counter-traditions.

guardian cherub. The text of Genesis 2–3 is also based on this older pattern as far as the traditional history is concerned. However, J transforms this myth. The core of the J narrative contains the term *'ādām* ('man', 'mankind'), created from the *'ᵃdāmâ. 'ādām* is given a command, disobeys it, and is driven from the garden. Anything else is added by J, which means that what he is really interested in is the woman! The verses on the creation of the woman, the dialogue between the woman and the serpent, and the so-called curses do not fit into this context. What is new in the J text?

1. The Creation of 'The Woman' (Gen. 2.18–24).

Genesis 2 is told aetiologically. The whole scene is orientated towards v. 23, the so-called formula of relationship:

> Now this, at last—
> bone from my bones,
> flesh from my flesh! (NEB)

At last the man has found a more suitable companion than the animals. Yahweh's act of creation is described in detail. He takes a rib and 'builds it up into a woman' (for the creation of the man the verb 'to form' was used). The word for 'rib' (*ṣēla'*) is perhaps derived from a Sumerian play on words, in which the corresponding term means 'life' as well as 'woman'. The aetiological aim of the text accounts for God's using a material other than the one used for the creation of *'ādām:* thus the relations between the sexes are explained descriptively. The question, 'Which material is more precious—the *'ᵃdāmâ* or the rib?'—is futile. In both cases, in the creation of *'ādām* and of the woman, Yahweh is the sole creator. The scene does not depict a birth, as is written in many popular feminist interpretations, as if the man pretends to produce the woman. Indeed, mediaeval artists often depicted the scene in this manner, but J does not. *'ādām* plays absolutely no part in the act of creation as he is fast asleep.

Another misunderstanding of this text concerns the term *'ēzer,* 'help'. A closer look at the word reveals that it does not imply anything subordinate, like the help of a maidservant. The masculine word *'ēzer* is used here in lieu of the more common feminine form *'ezrâ. 'ēzer* is applied to God in half of the references dealing with the kind of help that man cannot give, as Trible has pointed out (1973). And that help is not limited to an assistance in producing children, something the text does not even mention.

The J narrative must not be seen against the background of our modern way of asking questions, but against its contemporary environment (cf. the materials in Lieberman 1975). Its statements diverge considerably from the ancient oriental myths. For one thing, no tale from Mesopotamian literature has ever been discovered dealing solely with the creation of women. In the Gilgamesh epic a woman (a prostitute) is 'used' only for a short time to make a human being of the hero. Afterwards he teams up with men again. The woman has only to serve a single purpose there, whereas J regards her as a permanent, equal partner, corresponding to the man as a genuine counterpart.[10]

Both man and woman are created by God and gifted for a joyous, permanent living together. One interpretation of the Song of Solomon tries to read this as an explanation or illustration of this God-given togetherness (cf. Trible 1973). The text of Genesis 3 tells us that things are not like that *de facto*.

2. The So-Called 'Fall'.

Genesis 3 tries to state reasons why the life of humankind is determined by suffering and limitations. This text is particularly concerned with the original relationship between man and woman, whereas Genesis 4 demonstrates the relations between brothers. Sin or its origin is not explained. It is a description without the naming of a guilty party.[11] Thus, to ask whether the woman is to be blamed for the origin of sin is to miss the point completely. The dialogue between the woman and the serpent is added by J. The complete texts of Genesis 2 and 3 talk of Yahweh-Elohim, whereas the term Elohim is always used on its own within the dialogue. It is not known whether J discovered this masterpiece of a well-turned phrase, or whether he invented it himself. And besides, the main character is in fact the serpent, not the woman.

Traditionally there is a great variety of different interpretations of the complex Serpent-Tree-Seduction, since the serpent is a heavily symbolic animal in the positive as well as in the negative sense. In the Gilgamesh epic there was already a serpent furtively eating the hero's herb of life from the rim of the well.

As an animal that sheds its skin, the serpent becomes a symbol of life as well as death. The interpretation of the later tradition, which views the serpent as the devil or Satan, is explicitly excluded by the first sentence of Genesis 3. There it is described as an animal created by Yahweh-Elohim, a creature, not a divine hostile power. The latest interpretation of the serpent as a symbol of the Canaanite fertility cult, which also symbolizes the Canaanite Baal and his sexual potency, seems the most convincing. Moreover, the Hebrew for serpent is masculine (*nāḥāš*). During the times of the kings the dispute with the Canaanite cults became extraordinarily vehement. The male Baal was the great counterpart to Yahweh, Israel's God. That is why J relegates the serpent to a subordinate place.[12]

---

[10]If J really dates back to the period of Solomon, it is extraordinary for that period in its emphasis on a one-to-one personal relationship. Polygamy was the rule then, after all. This could be an argument against dating this text back to such an early period.

[11]Thus also the general phrasing of the command not to eat the fruit of a certain tree: there is no emphasis on anything moral or ritual.

[12]This further supports a later dating, since during the period of Solomon this dispute is hardly perceptible. It increases about the time of Hosea. What is extremely difficult to understand is the damnation of the serpent at the end of Genesis 3, considering that the bronze serpent was worshipped in the temple of Jerusalem until the reign of Hezekiah towards the end of the eighth century BCE; cf. 2 Kgs 18.4.

It is certainly of importance for the exegete to determine at what time J was written. The material and its embedding in a certain period is made valid by the way the author chooses and arranges it according to his own situation. This does not imply that statements only hold true for particular historical situations. I would assume that the author wants to describe something basically valid for humankind, not something restricted to Israel. All interpretations that try to put the statements concerning the serpent or the woman in certain historical or ritual contexts therefore raise problems.

Two notions remain to be explicitly refuted: first, the transgression mentioned here is not of a sexual nature. Secondly, the woman cannot be called 'seductress'. Only of the serpent is it said in definite terms that it 'tricks' (= 'deceives').[13] Woman and man eat *together* from the forbidden tree, although, it must be admitted, the woman eats first and then the man follows her example.

But why does J allow only the woman to deal with the serpent? Where is the man? This is anchored in given patterns of old oriental iconography. Urs Winter and Silvia Schroer have illustrated, with a vast amount of pictorial material, that the tree is always combined with a woman, originally with a goddess. Tree-Serpent-Goddess belonged together as a fixed motif. Hence, J could not but link the woman with the tree when making use of the motif of the tree and the serpent. Everybody is influenced by their own time and its imagination. Furthermore, an attachment to certain conventional forms was much more necessary in the old orient than today. J was probably bound by given pictures, which he could not change at will. The motif of Woman-Tree-Serpent is one single complex and therefore, from the outset, devoid of any value judgment.

I have already explained briefly what the actual sin of the first human beings consists of. The lack of specific terminology shows that it cannot be just one single sinful act. Not before Genesis 4 do we find a term for 'sin'. J seems to be concerned with a statement about sin as a basic occurrence which took place before all individual transgressions. He lives at a time when it is essential for the believing Israelite to obey God's commands.

Obedience means life, transgression means death. The sum of all wisdom is the fear of God, which the author exemplifies with the 'tree of knowing good and evil'. This is a special matter of concern for J (because the given tale in the history of tradition calls it the 'tree of life' in the middle of the garden). This statement about 'good and evil' in its totality is not just a moral issue. It has been interpreted as 'learning about life', 'losing naivety', 'entering history', 'understanding contexts', 'rising to a higher level of civilization', and so on. The term *yāda'*, which is used here, has a wide range of meanings. *yāda'* can mean 'to make oneself acquainted with something', 'get intimate', 'become experienced'—without fear. *yāda'* can be used for the deepest knowledge of God as well as the carnal knowledge of man and wife. J uses it in this sense in Gen. 4.1: 'Now Adam knew Eve his wife, and she conceived and bore Cain'. 'Knowing good and evil' thus comprises the sexual component but extends this meaning further. The complex occurrences of Genesis 3 must by no means be limited to a sexual interpretation.

What is the author's intention in Genesis 3? Are human beings supposed to remain ignorant and naive? Or is this a disapproval of wisdom, which could also be symbolized by the serpent (as is frequently written)? Or is this a condemnation of progress?

It seems to me that, *contra* such interpretations, J is concerned with another matter. According to him man receives from God all he needs, but there are limits. These limits are clearly defined by the words of the serpent: 'You will be like God'.

---

[13] The Hebrew term used here has no erotic meaning. Such interpretations must therefore be dismissed.

It does not say, 'You will be like Yahweh'. This is something an Israelite theologian could never be brought to say. Instead he says, 'You will be like Elohim'! To become divine or like Elohim, not to stay human, is the temptation. Elohim are the Canaanite gods, and the remark is dropped by the serpent which, among other things, is almost certainly a Canaanite symbol (see above). Elohim is a term for those gods which were known not only in Israel but also among its neighbouring peoples. The transgression in Genesis 3, therefore, means ignoring set limits and wishing to become like Elohim, instead of staying human. The author comes back to the same theme in the last narrative of Genesis 1–11, the narrative about the building of the tower. It is not a decline of knowledge or real wisdom which must be coupled with the fear of God. Nevertheless, J rejects certain kinds of arrogant knowledge, which attempt to challenge God.

By breaking the command (specific, single commands do not exist as yet: because the author refers to all humankind, he refers to a general willingness to obey God) man destroys the trust between himself and Yahweh. (In Genesis 2 Yahweh takes a walk in the garden, in Genesis 3 the appearance of God becomes danger.) Moreover, unity among humans is at stake, man's existence becomes disharmony and strife through his own fault.

This is how the biblical author deals with the difficult problem of evil: God created a good 'garden', but other factors intervene. He offers no explanation for evil; neither does the Bible as a whole. Evil exists on earth, but no scapegoat is made to be responsible. Neither the woman nor an extraterrestial power is held responsible for it in the J tales.

Finally, a word on the so-called curses. As mentioned in the remarks on the history of tradition, the curses are not included in the old source. *'ādām* is put in the garden; *'ādām* sins; *'ādām* is driven out of the garden. The loss of the garden is the actual punishment. J describes with these poetical verses the situation of his contemporaries. It is not as if it were God's intention. This holds true with respect to the relationship between God and man, the relationship between the sexes, the hard work in the field for the man, and the pain of childbirth for the woman. Genesis 2 explains how it was intended according to God's plan of creation. The aetiological verses also demonstrate the perversion of the original plan, the situation that should not have been. If this holds true, every attempt at changing this misery must be a step in the right direction. Yet, unfortunately, once again a double standard is in operation. If we were concerned here with God-given punishments which must not be changed, these verses would forbid any relief for the man's work, for example the introduction of tractors or such like. However, these verses were only called upon when it was attempted to improve woman's lot, for example by a birth with reduced pain (cf. Keel 1975; 74–76). The exegesis of the sentence and he shall rule over you' was fateful. The phrasing 'he shall be your master' verbally paved the way for the impression that it is an unconditional, all-embracing command. It is, however, the description of a given miserable situation which J related in the past tense. Just as with the other descriptions of given conditions, this sentence explains what happened against God's will at the time when J lives. In other words, a woman steps in the direction intended by God, whenever and wherever she tries to shake off the unjust, oppressive rule of the man. Thus, the feminist movement could be interpreted as a movement towards the original plan of creation which J did not find in his own lifetime.[14]

The question arises: who can and will use this text as legitimation? Wherever male-dominated theology and ideology want to oppress 'the woman', they still fall back on such passages as suitable starting points. Such an interest in legitimation existed in the era of the Israelite and Judahite kings. Since the rule of Solomon, at the latest, a legitimation of the monarchy served the interest of wide sections of the population. The story of Joseph probably centres upon the question: may a brother rule over a brother? This is answered in the affirmative in certain circles and under certain conditions: if the brother acts like a real brother and not like a despot. A similar question, may the man rule over the woman?, is answered by the author of Genesis 2–3 with a definite 'no!'. Such a rule results from sin, from transgression, and is an expression which signifies breaking away from God, and a perversion of the order that God wanted.

Much remains to be said, for example, concerning the names given to 'the woman' in Genesis 2 and 3. And what remains of the many negative arguments used by tradition? Much of it is still common currency. The J narratives do not deny their origin in a patriarchal society. J is necessarily a man of his time too. But whereas nobody dares to reintroduce slavery today by reference to isolated biblical verses, the contrary holds in regard to the question of man and woman. Isolated sentences from Genesis are still referred to as arguments for the subordination of women. And yet, J was concerned with the woman as a full human being, wherever he might have gathered his material. Contrary to later attempts to demonize 'the woman', and contrary to the most recent ones to make an original goddess of her, this has to be stressed. The woman is no goddess and the man is no little Lord God. In opposition to the popular belief of his time and all later disparagements, this biblical theologian depicts 'the woman' as an equal and equally human partner of 'the man'. Both woman and man are created directly by God; both man and woman are fallible. J wanted to show their *togetherness;* he does not look at what they are in her or his own right.

B. GENESIS 1

The later text of the P source suggests some new trends. In the interest of clarity, the interpretative procedure will be inverted: evaluation of the source will precede an exegesis of the details.[15]

Genesis 1 certainly commands a high degree of authority because of its position in the Bible, its succinctness, and the content of its statement regarding the theological core. Man's place in creation, the relationship between God and man,

---

[14]Genesis 2 and the love songs of the Song of Songs describe such an original relationship.

[15]At first each single text has to be interpreted individually, and as precisely as possible at that. Then it has to be evaluated critically. Although this is common procedure, preconceptions sometimes remain unnoticed (a sentence taken from the Decalogue is of more importance than a dated purity law in a cultic, ritual context of the Old Testament). When assessing values, it may happen that a text from the Old Testament can claim more importance than an exegesis of that text in the New Testament, all the more so if the exegesis is distorted. Cf. Haag 1980: 2–16. Regarding these problems and the dialogue between biblical and systematic theology cf. also Oeming 1987.

between human beings themselves and with the whole of creation, is given a theological explanation.

In the following I shall confine myself to the statements concerning humankind. Genesis 1 relates the creation of humankind after all other acts of creation, namely by rendering a decision made by God in v. 26.

> [26a]Then Elohim said,
>   [b]Let us make man in our image and likeness
>   [c]to rule the fish in the sea, the birds of heaven, the cattle, all
>   wild animals on earth, and all reptiles that crawl
>   upon the earth (NEB).

In v. 26b the choice of words introduces two different expressions for 'image': firstly, *ṣelem*, meaning something like a picture, figure, statue of a king; and secondly *d*[e]*mût*, 'something similar to'. This careful phrasing—Hebrew tends to paraphrase complicated matters with different terms—may indicate that the author cannot finds the words for expressing what he means to say. The term *d*[e]*mût* is also used by Ezekiel, a contemporary who operates within the priestly tradition when he describes his visions: 'There was a semblance . . . I saw something looking like . . . ' (Ezek. 1, 5, 16, 22, 26). Likewise, the P author wants to express that he lacks the suitable words. The statement is further delimited by the use of the plural: God joins up with his heavenly hosts in a manner of speaking ('Let us. . . '). The divine (Elohim) corresponds to humankind (*'ādām*) as a whole.

These three lines, the poetically phrased middle section of this account, embody the essence of the whole. The text quoted contains a controversial switch from the singular to the plural; twice the term *ṣelem* occurs, and there is a new differentiation between male and female, which is placed exactly in the middle of this succinct text. Thus it is part of the good creation executed by God himself, as is expressed three times(!) in this verse with the verb *bārā'*, 'create'. What is rendered vividly in Genesis 2—God himself says it is not good for the man to be alone—is summed up here in a single sentence on the image and likeness of God. Humankind as a whole, in female and male manifestation, is God's image. The author of Genesis 1 would have probably failed to understand the division of human body and mind, or a statement limited to the soul only.

The third part of this complex, v. 28, renders God's blessing for man and woman, which is always phrased in the plural. The statements of this text, which is extraordinarily charged with theological significance, have to be regarded, first and foremost, against their own background. P gives an account of humankind's station and task against the background of ancient oriental concepts of the world and humankind. (There, humanity is created as a mass to make work easier for the gods. In Genesis, however, humanity possesses an intrinsic value.) The text itself explains what is meant by the image of God: the final clause of v. 26 mentions ruling, and this is repeated at the end of v. 28. P relies on the ancient oriental ideology of the monarchy found quite frequently in Egypt where the king or queen represented the deity. Recent research confirms this.[16] In Israel's environment only single

---

[16]Cf. Ockinga 1984; Zenger 1983; Gross 1981: 244–64.

outstanding persons qualify for that, whereas P regards all human beings as God's representatives. Humankind's rule over creation—like a good shepherd who leads and protects his people—means acceptance of *responsibility*. As God's representative, humankind is responsible for the creatures, just as God is for the whole of creation. The democratization of an ancient oriental concept is particularly impressive in this case. Just as in Genesis 2, where man is to till and keep the garden, he is given a task here. Thus, work and task are based on God's good creation for both, man and woman. God is present in that which is made in his image, so he is present in humankind's acceptance of responsibility for the created world. It is important that humans are only allowed to rule over the rest of creation. Accordingly, animals may not be killed and humans are not to rule over other humans: it is God's privilege to rule over humanity. The author of Genesis 1 thus shifted the concepts of his environment on purpose. First, human rule over other humans is excluded; secondly, humans are qualified clearly as male and female. So this statement *explicitly* excludes men's rule over women! Oddly enough, this has not been noticed before. An analysis of the wording in Gen. 1.26–28 results in precisely this, however: man and woman rule over the rest of creation, and this implies only too clearly that one gender may not claim power over the other. Thus P says the same as the vivid narrative tale of Genesis 2–3, albeit in quite a rational and theologically differentiated language. Genesis 2–3 must have been known to the writer of P, and his response may be interpreted as follows. Whenever the man rules over the woman and she suffers from such rule, this is against the aim of creation, a perversion of the original plan. If there was any room for doubt regarding this plan in Genesis 2–3, P purposefully corrected it, made it more precise. Thus this source confirms my exegesis of Genesis 2–3, which is shared by most exegetes today. J regards the man's rule over the woman as a consequence of sin, whereas the Priestly source mentions no explicit sin-tale. Instead he presents, in poetical/rhythmic form, a Creation/Image-of-God statement.

P does not reappear until Genesis 5, where a statement about human God-likeness and its continuation is repeated. This is mentioned for the third time after the Flood. Now humanity is allowed to kill animals, but not to shed the blood of another person. 'He that sheds the blood of a man, for that man his blood shall be shed; for in the image (*ṣelem*) of Elohim has God made man (*'ādām*)!' (Gen. 9.6, NEB). Whoever attacks the image (three times *'ādām*) also attacks the prototype, God. Undoubtedly *'ādām* once again refers to both man and woman, or else the killing of women would be permitted. This underlines the interpretation of Gen. 1.26–28, which forbids human beings to rule over other human beings or to exploit them. Violence in its worst form is explicitly forbidden with reference to humankind, created as *ṣelem*. There are no further references to the image of God in P apart from these three.

Genesis 1 installs both man and woman as rulers. The last line of the middle section ('Male and female he created them') is significant, and not only because of the subsequent blessing of fertility. Naturally the woman is indispensible here, but the order to rule is repeated in v. 28, actually in the plural form. So man and woman share the task of responsibility for ruling the world, and of filling the yet empty earth. Viewed from yet another perspective, this also implies that man and woman function as God's representatives of his image only when they share this responsibility. This is the governing principle. Still, this does not imply that humans are to fulfil their task as couples only. Whenever one gender rules the world *alone*, the originally intended order is perverted. The order to rule, to *master* the world, has in fact mainly been effective for males. It is about time that the female share is reclaimed! Since the statement on the God-likeness of the woman excludes the notion that the man may assume power over her—and vice versa, but that is not the problem in this day and age—the anthropological and theological consequences of such a succinct statement on the very first page of the Bible must be reconsidered.[17]

Eve and Adam: Genesis 2–3 Reread

Phyllis Trible

On the whole, the Women's Liberation Movement is hostile to the Bible, even as it claims that the Bible is hostile to women. The Yahwist account of creation and fall in Genesis 2–3 provides a strong proof text for that claim. Accepting centuries of (male) exegesis, many feminists interpret this story as legitimating male supremacy and female subordination.[1] They read to reject. My suggestion is that we reread to understand and to appropriate. Ambiguity characterizes the meaning of 'adham

---

[17]This is exactly where the anthropological and theological statements intertwine. In addition to the anthropological consequences, the theological ones could only be hinted at: if humankind is godlike in its male and female manifestation only, this anthropological statement must have an influence on the image of God. Woman and man reflect something divine; so their prototype must be divine. If man and woman represent something divine and fulfil their cultural task together, we have to seek for the female part in the image of God today. On the basis of Gen. 1.26–28 the God of the Old Testament cannot be regarded as purely male. As all God talk is subject to the second commandment, inasmuch as verbal images could be created, a 'purely male' concept of God would be like a 'carved image' or a 'likeness', an idol, just like a 'goddess' would be an idol. From the theological point of view it is clear that all images are only temporary: all God talk is analogous, that is, the unlikeness of the applied term is always greater than its likeness. And yet the imbalance in favour of a male manner of speaking in referring to God is quite remarkable. At this very moment it is a matter of great concern to create an awareness of this and correct it from the feminist point of view.

Cf. the following with respect to this problem: Laut 1983; Raurell 1989; Ruether 1983; Schüngel-Straumann 1987; Schüssler Fiorenza 1984; Straham 1987; Wacker 1987.

in Genesis 2–3. On the one hand, man is the first creature formed (2:7). The Lord God puts him in the garden "to till it and keep it," a job identified with the male (cf. 3:17–19). On the other hand, *'adham* is a generic term for humankind. In commanding *'adham* not to eat of the tree of the knowledge of good and evil, the Deity is speaking to both the man and the woman (2:16–17). Until the differentiation of female and male (2:21–23), *'adham* is basically androgynous: one creature incorporating two sexes.

Concern for sexuality, specifically for the creation of woman, comes last in the story, after the making of the garden, the trees, and the animals. Some commentators allege female subordination based on this order of events.[2] They contrast it with Genesis 1:27 where God creates *'adham* as male and female in one act.[3] Thereby they infer that whereas the Priests recognized the equality of the sexes, the Yahwist made woman a second, subordinate, inferior sex.[4] But the last may be first, as both the biblical theologian and the literary critic know. Thus the Yahwist account moves to its climax, not its decline, in the creation of woman.[5] She is not an afterthought; she is the culmination. Genesis 1 itself supports this interpretation, for there male and female are indeed the last and truly the crown of all creatures. The last is also first where beginnings and endings are parallel. In Hebrew literature, the central concerns of a unit often appear at the beginning and the end as an *inclusio* device.[6] Genesis 2 evinces this structure. The creation of man first and of woman last constitutes a ring composition whereby the two creatures are parallel. In no way does the order disparage woman. Content and context augment this reading.

The context for the advent of woman is a divine judgment: "It is not good that *'adham* should be alone; I will make him a helper fit for him" (2:18). The phrase needing explication is "helper fit for him." In the Old Testament the word *helper* (*'ezer*) has many usages. It can be a proper name for a male.[7] In our story, it describes the animals and the woman. In some passages, it characterizes Deity. God is the helper of Israel. As helper Yahweh creates and saves.[8] Thus *'ezer* is a relational term; it designates a beneficial relationship; and it pertains to God, people, and animals. By itself, the word does not specify positions within relationships; more particularly, it does not imply inferiority. Position results from additional content or from context. Accordingly, what kind of relationship does *'ezer* entail in Genesis 2:18, 20? Our answer comes in two ways: (1) The word *neged*, which joins *'ezer*, connotes equality: a helper who is a counterpart.[9] (2) The animals are helpers, but they fail to fit *'adham*. There is physical, perhaps psychic, rapport between *'adham* and the animals, for Yahweh forms (*yasar*) them both out of the ground (*'adhamah*). Yet their similarity is not equality. *'Adham* names them and thereby exercises power over them. No fit helper is among them. And thus the narrative moves to woman. . . . God is the helper superior to man; the animals are helpers inferior to man; woman is the helper equal to man.

Let us pursue the issue by examining the account of the creation of woman ([verses] 21–22). This episode concludes the story even as the creation of man commences it. . . . The ring composition suggests an interpretation of woman and man as equals. To establish this meaning, structure and content must mesh. They do. In both episodes, Yahweh alone creates. For the last creation the Lord God "caused a deep sleep (*tardemah*) to fall upon the man." Man has no part in making woman; he is out of it. He exercises no control over her existence. He is neither participant nor spectator nor consultant at her birth. Like man, woman owes her life solely to God. For both of them, the origin of life is a divine mystery. Another parallel of equality is creation out of raw materials: dust for man and a rib for woman. Yahweh chooses these fragile materials and in both cases processes them before human beings happen. As Yahweh shapes dust and then breathes into it to form man, so Yahweh takes out the rib and then builds it into woman.[10] To call woman "Adam's rib" is to misread the text, which states carefully and clearly that the extracted bone required divine labor to become female, a datum scarcely designed to bolster the male ego. Moreover, to claim that the rib means inferiority or subordination is to assign the man qualities over the woman which are not in the narrative itself. Superiority, strength, aggressiveness, dominance, and power do not characterize man in Genesis 2. By contrast, he is formed from dirt; his life hangs by a breath which he does not control; and he himself remains silent and passive while the Deity plans and interprets his existence.

The rib means solidarity and equality. *'Adham* recognizes this meaning in a poem:[11]

> This at last is bone of bones
>   and flesh of my flesh.
> She shall be called *'ishshah* [woman]
>   because she was taken out of *'ish* [man]. (2:23)

The pun proclaims both the similarity and the differentiation of female and male. Before this episode the Yahwist has used only the generic term *'adham*. No exclusively male reference has appeared. Only with the specific creation of woman (*'ishshah*) occurs the first specific terms for man as male (*'ish*). In other words, sexuality is simultaneous for woman and man. The sexes are interrelated and interdependent. Man as male does not precede woman as female but happens concurrently with her. Hence, the first act in Genesis 2 is the creation of androgyny (2:7), and the last is the creation of sexuality (2:23).[12] Male embodies female, and female embodies male. The two are neither dichotomies nor duplicates. The birth of woman corresponds to the birth of man but does not copy it. Only in responding to the female does the man discover himself as male. No longer a passive creature, *'ish* comes alive in meeting *'ishshah*.

Some read into the poem a naming motif. The man names the woman and thereby has power and authority over her.[13] But again . . . reread. Neither the verb nor the noun *name* is in the poem. We find instead the verb *gara'*, to call: "She shall be called woman." Now, in the Yahwist primeval history this verb does not function as a synonym or parallel or substitute for *name*. The typical formula for naming is the verb *to call* plus the explicit object *name*. This formula applies to Deity, people, places, and animals. For example, in Genesis 4 we read:

> Cain built a city Fand *called* the *name* of the city after the
>   *name* of his son Enoch. (v. 17)

> And Adam knew his wife again, and she bore a son and
>   *called* his *name* Seth. (v. 25)
> To Seth also a son was born and he *called* his *name*
>   Enoch. (v. 26a)
> At that time men began to *call* upon the *name* of the Lord.
>   (v. 26b)

Genesis 2:23 has the verb *call* but does not have the object *name*. Its absence signifies the absence of a naming motif in the poem. The presence of both the verb *call* and the noun *name* in the episode of the animals strengthens the point:

> So out of the ground the Lord God formed every beast of the field and every bird of the air, and brought them to the man to see what he would *call* them; and whatever the man *called* every living creature, that was its *name*. The man gave *names* to all cattle, and to the birds of the air, and to every beast of the field. (2:19–20)

In calling the animals by name, *'adham* establishes supremacy over them and fails to find a fit helper. In calling woman, *'adham* does not name her and does find in her a counterpart. Female and male are equal sexes. Neither has authority over the other.[14]

A further observation secures the argument: *Woman* itself is not a name. It is a common noun; it is not a proper noun. It designates gender; it does not specify person. *'Adham* recognizes sexuality by the words *'ishshah* and *'ish*. This recognition is not an act of naming to assert the power of male over female. Quite the contrary. But the true skeptic is already asking: What about Genesis 3:20, where "the man called his wife's name Eve"? We must wait to consider that question. Meanwhile, the words of the ancient poem as well as their context proclaim sexuality originating in the unity of *'adham*. From this one (androgynous) creature come two (female and male). The two return to their original unity as *'ish* and *'ishshah* become one flesh (2:24):[15] another instance of the ring composition.

Next the differences which spell harmony and equality yield to the differences of disobedience and disaster. The serpent speaks to the woman. Why to the woman and not to the man? The simplest answer is that we do not know. The Yahwist does not tell us anymore than he explains why the tree of the knowledge of good and evil was in the garden. But the silence of the text stimulates speculations, many of which only confirm the patriarchal mentality which conceived them. Cassuto identifies serpent and woman, maintaining that the cunning of the serpent is "in reality" the cunning of the woman.[16] He impugns her further by declaring that "for the very reason that a woman's imagination surpasses a man's, it was the woman who was enticed first." Though more gentle in his assessment, von Rad avers that "in the history of Yahweh religion, it has always been the women who have shown an inclination for obscure astrological cults" (a claim which he does not document).[17] Consequently, he holds that the woman "confronts the obscure allurements and mysteries that beset our limited life more directly than the man does," and then he calls her a "temptress." Paul Ricoeur says that woman "represents the point of weakness," as the entire story "gives evidence of a very masculine resentment."[18] McKenzie links the "moral weakness" of the woman with her "sexual attraction" and holds that the latter ruined both the woman and the man.[19]

But the narrative does not say any of these things. It does not sustain the judgment that woman is weaker or more cunning or more sexual than man. Both have the same Creator, who explicitly uses the word *good* to introduce the creation of woman (2:18). Both are equal in birth. There is complete rapport, physical, psychological, sociological, and theological, between them: bone of bone and flesh of flesh. If there be moral frailty in one, it is moral frailty in two. Further, they are equal in responsibility and in judgment, in shame and in guilt, in redemption and in grace. What the narrative says about the nature of woman it also says about the nature of man.

Why does the serpent speak to the woman and not to the man? Let a female speculate. If the serpent is "more subtle" than its fellow creatures, the woman is more appealing than her husband. Throughout the myth, she is the more intelligent one, the more aggressive one, and the one with greater sensibilities.[20] Perhaps the woman elevates the animal world by conversing theologically with the serpent. At any rate, she understands the hermeneutical task. In quoting God, she interprets the prohibition ("neither shall you touch it"). The woman is both theologian and translator. She contemplates the tree, taking into account all the possibilities. The tree is good for food; it satisfies the physical drives. It pleases the eyes; it is esthetically and emotionally desirable. Above all, it is coveted as the source of wisdom *(haskîl).* Thus the woman is fully aware when she acts, her vision encompassing the gamut of life. She takes the fruit, and she eats. The initiative and the decision are hers alone. There is no consultation with her husband. She seeks neither his advice nor his permission. She acts independently.

By contrast, the man is a silent, passive, and bland recipient: "She also gave some to her husband, and he ate." The narrator makes no attempt to depict the husband as reluctant or hesitating. The man does not theologize; he does not contemplate; he does not envision the full possibilities of the occasion. His one act is belly oriented, and it is an act of quiescence, not of initiative. The man is not dominant; he is not aggressive; he is not a decision maker. Even though the prohibition not to eat of the tree appears before the female was specifically created, she knows that it applies to her. She has interpreted it, and now she struggles with the temptation to disobey. But not the man, to whom the prohibition came directly (2:16). He follows his wife without question or comment, thereby denying his own individuality. If the woman be intelligent, sensitive, and ingenious, the man is passive, brutish, and inept. These character portrayals are truly extraordinary in a culture dominated by men. I stress their contrast not to promote female chauvinism but to undercut patriarchal interpretations alien to the text.

The contrast between woman and man fades after their acts of disobedience. They are one in the new knowledge of their nakedness (3:7). They are one in hearing and in hiding. They flee from the sound of the Lord God in the Garden (3:8). First to the man come questions of responsibility (3:9, 11), but the man fails to be responsible: "The woman whom Thou gavest to be with me, she gave me fruit of the tree, and I ate" (3:12). Here the man does not blame the woman; he does not say that the woman seduced him;[21] he blames the Deity. The verb which he uses for both the Deity and the woman is *ntn* (cf. 3:6). . . . This verb neither means nor implies seduction in this context or in the lexicon. Again, if the Yahwist intended to make woman the temptress, he missed a choice opportunity. The woman's response supports the point. "The serpent beguiled me, and I ate" (3:13). Only here occurs the strong verb *nsh'*, meaning to deceive, to seduce. God accepts this subject-verb combination when, immediately following the woman's accusation, Yahweh says to the serpent, "Because you have done this, cursed are you above all animals" (3:14).

Though the tempter (the serpent) is cursed,[22] the woman and the man are not. But they are judged, and the judgments are commentaries on the disastrous effects of their shared disobedience. They show how terrible human life has become as it stands between creation and grace. We misread if we assume that these judgments are mandates. They describe; they do not prescribe. They protest; they do not condone. Of special concern are the words telling the woman that her husband shall rule over her (3:16). This statement is not license for male supremacy, but rather it is condemnation of that very pattern.[23] Subjugation and supremacy are perversions of creation. Through disobedience, the woman has become slave. Her initiative and her freedom vanish. The man is corrupted also, for he has become master, ruling over the one who is his God-given equal. The subordination of female to male signifies their shared sin.[24] This sin vitiates all relationships: between animals and human beings (3:15); mothers and children (3:16); husbands and wives (3:16); people and the soil (3:17–18); humanity and its work (3:19). Whereas in creation man and woman know harmony and equality, in sin they know alienation and discord. Grace makes possible a new beginning.

A further observation about these judgments: they are culturally conditioned. Husband and work (childbearing) define the woman; wife and work (farming) define the man. A literal reading of the story limits both creatures and limits the story. To be faithful translators, we must recognize that women as well as men move beyond these culturally defined roles, even as the intentionality and function of the myth move beyond its original setting. Whatever forms stereotyping takes in our own culture, they are judgments upon our common sin and disobedience. The suffering and oppression we women and men know now are marks of our fall, not of our creation.

At this place of sin and judgment, "the man calls his wife's name Eve" (3:20), thereby asserting his rule over her. The naming itself faults the man for corrupting a relationship of mutuality and equality. And so Yahweh evicts the primeval couple from the Garden, yet with signals of grace.[25] Interestingly, the conclusion of the story does not specify the sexes in flight. Instead the narrator resumes use of the generic and androgynous term *'adham* with which the story began and thereby completes an overall ring composition (3:22–24).

Visiting the Garden of Eden in the days of the Women's Movement, we need no longer accept the traditional exegesis of Genesis 2–3. Rather than legitimating the patriarchal culture from which it comes, the myth places that culture under judgment. And thus it functions to liberate, not to enslave. This function we can recover and appropriate. The Yahwist narrative tells us who we are (creatures of equality and mutuality); it tells us who we have become (creatures of oppression); and so it opens possibilities for change, for a return to our true liberation under God. In other words, the story calls female and male to repent.

Notes

1. *See inter alia,* Kate Millett, *Sexual Politics* (New York: Doubleday, 1970), pp. 51–54; Eva Figes, *Patriarchal Attitudes* (Greenwich, Conn.: Fawcett, 1970), pp. 38f; Mary Daly, "The Courage to See," *The Christian Century,* September 22, 1971, p. 1110; Sheila D. Collins, "Toward a Feminist Theology," *The Christian Century,* August 2, 1972, p. 798; Lilly Rivlin, "Lilith: The First Woman," *Ms.,* December 1972, pp. 93, 114.

2. Cf. E. Jacob, *Theology of the Old Testament* (New York: Harper & Bros., 1958), pp. 172f; S. H. Hooke, "Genesis," *Peake's Commentary on the Bible* (London: Thomas Nelson, 1962), p. 179.

3. E.g., Elizabeth Cady Stanton observed that Genesis 1:26–28 "dignifies woman as an important factor in the creation, equal in power and glory with man," while Genesis 2 "makes her a mere afterthought" (*The Woman's Bible,* Part I [New York: European Publishing Company, 1895], p. 20). See also Elsie Adams and Mary Louise Briscoe, *Up Against the Wall, Mother . . .* (Beverly Hills: Glencoe Press, 1971), p. 4.

4. Cf. Eugene H. Maly, "Genesis," *The Jerome Biblical Commentary* (Englewood Cliffs, N.J.: Prentice-Hall, 1968), p. 12: "But woman's existence, psychologically and in the social order, is dependent on man."

5. See John L. McKenzie, "The Literary Characteristics of Gen. 2–3," *Theological Studies,* Vol. 15 (1954), p. 559; John A. Bailey, "Initiation and the Primal Woman in Gilgamesh and Genesis 2–3," *Journal of Biblical Literature,* June 1970, p. 143. Bailey writes emphatically of the remarkable importance and position of the woman in Genesis 2–3, "all the more extraordinary when one realizes that this is the only account of the creation of woman as such in ancient Near Eastern literature." He hedges, however, in seeing the themes of helper and naming (Genesis 2:18–23) as indicative of a "certain subordination" of woman to man. These reservations are unnecessary; see below. Cf. also Claus Westermann, *Genesis, Biblischer Kommentar* G (Neukerchener-Vluyn: Newkirchener Verlag, 1970), p. 312.

6. James Muilenburg, "Form Criticism and Beyond," *Journal of Biblical Literature,* March 1969, pp. 9f; Mitchell Dahood, "Psalm I," *The Anchor Bible* (New York: Doubleday, 1966), *passim* and esp. p. 5.

7. See 1 Chronicles 4:4; 12:9; Nehemiah 3:19.

8. See Psalm 121:2, 124:8; 146:5; 33:20; 115:9–11; Exodus 18:4; Deuteronomy 33:7, 26, 29.

9. L. Koehler and W. Baumgartner, *Lexicon in Veteris Testamenti Libros* (Leiden: E. J. Brill, 1958), pp. 591f.

10. The verb *bnh* (to build) suggests considerable labor. It is used of towns, towers, altars, and fortifications, as well as of the primeval woman (Koehler-Baumgartner, op. cit., p. 134). In Genesis 2:22, it may mean the fashioning of clay around the rib (Ruth Amiran, "Myths of the Creation of Man and the Jericho Statues," *BASOR,* No. 167 [October 1962], p. 24).

11. See Walter Brueggemann, "Of the Same Flesh and Bone (Gen. 2:23a)," *Catholic Biblical Quarterly,* October 1970, pp. 532–42.

12. In proposing as primary an androgynous interpretation of *'adham,* I find virtually no support from (male) biblical scholars. But my view stands as documented from the text, and I take refuge among a remnant of ancient (male) rabbis (see George Foot Moore, *Judaism* [Cambridge, Mass.: Harvard University Press, 1927]), I, 453; also Joseph Campbell, *The Hero with a Thousand Faces* (Meridian Books, The World Publishing Company, 1970), pp. 152ff., 279f.

13. See e.g., G. von Rad, *Genesis* (Philadelphia: Westminster Press, 1961), pp. 80–82; John H. Marks, "Genesis," *The Interpreter's One-Volume Commentary on the Bible* (Nashville: Abingdon Press, 1971), p. 5; Bailey, op. cit., p. 143.

14. Cf. Westermann, op. cit., pp. 316ff.

15. Verse 24 probably mirrors a matriarchal society (so Von Rad, op. cit., p. 83). If the myth were designed to support patriarchy, it is difficult to explain how this verse survived without proper alteration. Westermann contends, however, that an emphasis on matriarchy misunderstands the point of the verse, which is the total communion of woman and man (ibid., p. 317).

16. U. Cassuto, *A Commentary on the Book of Genesis,* Part I (Jerusalem: Magnes Press, n.d.), pp. 142f.

17. Von Rad, op. cit., pp. 87f.

18. Ricoeur departs from the traditional interpretation of the woman when he writes: *"Eve n'est donc pas la femme en tant que 'deuxieme sexe'; toute femme et tout homme sont Adam; tout homme et toute*

femme sont Eve." But the fourth clause of his sentence obscures this complete identity of Adam and Eve: *"toute femme peche 'en Adam, tout homme est seduit 'en Eve."* By switching from an active to a passive verb, Ricoeur makes only the woman directly responsible for both sinning and seducing. (Paul Ricoeur, *Finitude et Culpabilite*, II. *La Symbolique du Mal*, Aubier, Editions Montaigne [Paris: 1960]. Cf. Paul Ricoeur, *The Symbolism of Evil* [Boston: Beacon Press, 1969], p. 255).

19. McKenzie, op. cit., p. 570.
20. See Bailey, op. cit., p. 148.
21. See Westermann, op. cit., p. 340.
22. For a discussion of the serpent, see Ricoeur, *The Symbolism of Evil*, op. cit., pp. 255–60.
23. Cf. Edwin M. Good, *Irony in the Old Testament* (Philadelphia: Westminster Press, 1965), p. 84, note 4: "Is it not surprising that, in a culture where the subordination of woman to man was a virtually unquestioned social principle, the etiology of the subordination should be in the context of man's primal sin? Perhaps woman's subordination was not unquestioned in Israel." Cf. also Henricus Renckens, *Israel's Concept of the Beginning* (New York: Herder & Herder, 1964), pp. 127f.
24. *Contra* Westermann, op. cit., p. 357.
25. Von Rad, op. cit., pp. 94, 148.

"Not a Jot, Not a Tittle: Genesis 2–3 after Twenty Years"

(1995 CE)

Phyllis Trible

In the early 1970s, feminist interpretation of the Bible was a cloud no bigger than a woman's hand. Knowing that such clouds can become mighty storms, I began to grapple with two certainties in my life: a love for the Bible and a commitment to feminism. Some friends told me that the twain shall never meet, but I sensed that they had already met within me. The challenge was to articulate the encounter.

I began with a favorite text, the story of the Garden in Genesis 2–3. Throughout the ages people have used this text to legitimate patriarchy as the will of God. They maintained that it subordinates woman to man in creation, depicts her as his seducer, curses her, and authorizes man to rule over her. Well acquainted with the traditional reading, I asked myself a question: If, as it certainly appears, this story is so terribly patriarchal, how come I like it? How come I feel no anger in reading it and no embarrassment in claiming it? How come it gives me a sense of well being despite its tragic ending? Feminist (not feminine) intuition told me that the story invites another interpretation. My job was to find it.

Three clues prepared the way. The first was a childhood memory. A missionary on furlough, whose name I do not know, taught Bible stories to a group of little girls of whom I was one. She said, "Everything that God created got better and better. What was the last thing God created?" Thoroughly indoctrinated, we replied in unison and with vigor, "Man!" She countered. "No, woman." Hers is not the exegesis I now espouse, but nonetheless to this day I am grateful for her insight.

The second clue came in a lecture delivered at Union Theological Seminary in the 1950s by Professor Samuel Terrien. Checking my notes years later, I found this statement: "The portrayal of the man in the garden is not the portrayal of a patriarch. Whereas the woman is depicted as alert, intelligent, and sensitive, the man comes off as passive, bland, and belly-oriented." Whether or not these are Professor Terrien's exact words, they confirm my intuition of a nonpatriarchal perspective at work in the story.

The third clue was a footnote in a study of biblical irony by Professor Edwin M. Good. Writing about Genesis 3:16, he asked, "Is it not surprising that, in a culture where the subordination of woman to man was a virtually unquestioned social principle, the etiology of the subordination should be in the context of man's primal sin? Perhaps woman's subordination was not unquestioned in Israel."[1] For me this blessed footnote removed centuries of misguided interpretation.

Fortified by these clues, I sought an alternative to the patriarchal understanding of Genesis 2–3. An invitation in 1972 to read a paper to the faculty of Andover Newton Theological School provided the first forum for testing my ideas.[2] A section of that paper became a short article, published the next year in the *Andover Newton Quarterly*.[3] Other publications reprinted the article,[4] and it appears again in this volume. Meanwhile, in 1978 a lengthy study expanded the short article and changed some of the interpretation.[5]

The most significant change concerned the use and meaning in Genesis 2:7–22a of the word *ha-a'dam* (or *'adam*, without the definite article *ha*). In the second paragraph of the short article I tried to hold together three meanings: the male creature (the traditional reading), the generic term for humankind, and the androgynous creature. This effort showed my early struggles with an ambiguous text. By the time I developed the lengthy study, these struggles had led to a fourth meaning that superseded the others. Though later in the story *ha-'adam* specifies the male and still later acquires a generic usage, in Genesis 2:7–22a, the word does not carry a male, generic, or androgynous meaning.[6] Instead, it signifies a sexually undifferentiated creature: neither male (nor female) nor a combination of the two.

To talk about this sexually undifferentiated creature, I offered the translation of *ha-'adam* as "the earth creature." That translation served two purposes: to move away from gender-specific language and to suggest the pun present in the sentence, "Yhwh God formed *ha-'adam* (the earth creature) from the dust of *ha-'adama* (the earth)" (2:7). Another translation has since come along: "Yhwh God formed the human from the dust of the humus." How I arrived at this reading I do not remember, but it captures well in English the Hebrew pun. And it also eschews gender identification.

The idea that *ha-'adam* in Genesis 2:7 connotes a sexually undifferentiated creature has stirred various responses—grammatical, conceptual, and literary. Grammatically the noun *'adam* is masculine gender as are all the pronouns that refer to it. (Hebrew offers only two genders, masculine and feminine: the neuter is unavailable.) Grammarians know well that no exact equation obtains between gender and sexual identity.[7] For example, that the noun *sùs* in Hebrew is masculine does not mean that every Hebrew horse is male; that the noun *alopeks* in Greek is feminine does not mean that every Greek fox is female; that the noun *khatifa* in Arabic is feminine does not mean that there was ever a female caliph; that the noun *nauta* in Latin is feminine does not mean that the Roman sailor was female. Similarly, the masculine gender of *'adam* does not itself specify a male creature.

If one insists, however, upon an equation of gender and sex for the word *'adam* in Genesis 2:7, then one must recognize the comparable significance of the feminine grammatical gender of the word *'adama* (earth or humus). Not only does the feminine *'adama* exist in the story prior to the masculine *'adam*, but also the latter comes out of the former. From this perspective the "female" both precedes the "male" and provides the material from which he is formed. The "male," then, is subordinate to the "female." By such reasoning, the argument for the primacy of the male, based on the gender of the word *'adam*, turns unwittingly against itself. But grammar is not the issue.

To the conceptual observation that a sexually undifferentiated earth creature would not be "a human being,"[8] the proper rejoinder is "most surely." In the story humanity unfolds gradually. The first creature lacks not just sexual identity but also direct speech and social identity. These features appear only when the earth creature becomes two creatures, female and male (2:22b–23). And the two emerge simultaneously, not sequentially. The reality can be no other way; male requires female and female requires male. Each sex depends upon the other for its separate identity. The forming of the "human from the humus" only begins the process that eventuates in full humanity.

Literary objections to an understanding of the first creature as sexually undifferentiated have focused on two observations: the absence of parallels in other biblical texts and the absence of a linguistic marker to designate a shift in the use and meaning of the word *'adam* from sexually undifferentiated to male (cf. 2:22b–3:21).[9] The first observation confirms the point it seeks to counter. Genesis 2:7–22a reports on a unique creature for whom, by definition and narrative sequence, there can be no parallels. With the advent of female and male (2:22b–23), the earth creature is no more. The rest of the Bible then assumes the existence of the two sexes.

The second observation, regarding the absence of a linguistic marker to differentiate between the use of *'adam* for the sexually undifferentiated creature and for the male, evokes two different responses, one identifying a linguistic marker and the other relativizing the need for such a marker. On the one hand, a marker is present in 2:22 where the word *ha-'adam*, occurring twice, bears different meanings. In the first part of the verse the word signifies the earth creature: "And the side that Yhwh God took from the earth creature (*ha-'adam*) he made into woman (*'issa*). . . ." The appearance of the noun *'issa*, indeed the appearance of woman, radically alters the situation. New to the story, *'issa* designates the first sexually identified creature and thereby changes the meaning of *ha-'adam*. Accordingly, in the latter part of the verse *ha-'adam* acquires the second meaning, man the male: ". . . he made into woman (*'issa*) and brought her to the man (*ha-'adam*)." Coming between two occurrences of *ha-adam*, the advent of woman changes the meaning of that word. She makes the difference structurally and narratively. Over against the emphases of a patriarchal culture, the story highlights her creation. By contrast, the man's creation emerges from the leftovers. The word *'issa* is the linguistic marker that shifts the meaning of *ha-'adam*.

On the other hand, the demand for a linguistic marker may hoist one on one's own petard. An examination of the use of *ha-'adam* at the ending of the story exposes the flaw. In 3:21 the term specifies the man as he appears in parallel to the woman: "Yhwh God made for the man (*ha-'adam*) and for his woman (*'issa*) garments of skin. . . ." Given this indisputable meaning of *ha-'adam* as male, what is one to make of the meaning of this same word in the very next verse where the parallel word *'issa* does not appear: "Behold, *ha-'adam* has become like one of us . . . " (3:22)? Does the noun refer only to the man, by analogy with its use in 3:21? If so, then the woman has not "become like one of us" and thus is not subject to punishment by God. Furthermore, what is one to make of the grammatical masculine singular pronouns identifying the one expelled from the garden? "Therefore Yhwh God sent *him* forth from the garden of Eden to till the ground from which *he* was taken" (3:23). Do these pronouns refer exclusively to the man? Again, what is one to make of the second appearance in this section of the noun *ha-'adam* without the accompanying phrase "and his woman"? Yhwh God "drove out *ha-'adam*" (3:24). If *ha-'adam* has (or must have) the single meaning of man the male throughout the story, then at the end only the man, not the woman, is driven out of the garden.[10]

No exegete accepts such a conclusion. To the contrary, commentator after commentator assigns a generic meaning to the masculine singular noun *ha-'adam* at the end of the story (3:22–24) and so declares that the woman is expelled from the garden along with the man.[11] I agree with this interpretation and want to underscore its meaning for the relationship of female and male. One sign of their shared disobedience in eating the forbidden fruit is patriarchy, the rule of the man over the woman (3:16). One component of patriarchy is so-called generic language. In vocabulary and effect it subsumes the woman to the man. It renders him visible (hence, *ha-'adam*) and her invisible (hence, the absence of the phrase "and his *'issa*" in 3:22–24 in contrast to its presence in 3:21).

What evidence is available for the generic interpretation of *ha-'adam* in the ending of the story? Is there a linguistic marker to signal a shift from the exclusively male use of the word in 3:21 and the generic use in 3:22?[12] That is difficult to find. The clauses "Yahweh God made" (3:21) and "Yhwh God said" (3:22) are parallel, indicating continuity between the two verses. Yet differences in discourse follow. In 3:21 narrated discourse uses the phrase "for *'adam* and his woman"; in 3:22 direct discourse has the deity say, "Behold, *ha-'adam* has become. . . ." If the difference in discourse be used to argue for a shift in the meaning of *ha-'adam* from male to generic, that argument gets undercut in 3:24 where narrated discourse picks up on the deity's use of the single term *ha-'adam*: "He drove out *ha-'adam*." In other words, no linguistic marker signals the shift in meaning between these two uses of the noun *ha-'adam*. And yet no scholar (of whom I am aware) disputes the shift.[13]

By analogy, then, the presumed lack of a linguistic marker to indicate a shift in the meaning of *ha-'adam* near the beginning of the story is of no consequence. To require a marker there would expose the flaw in the unquestioned acceptance of two meanings for *ha-'adam* near the end. In neither place, the beginning or the end of the story, does the lack of a literary marker invalidate the proposed interpretations of *ha-'adam*.

If exegetes throughout the ages have discerned two uses of the word *'adam* in the story, male and generic, then why not three? They work structurally and narratively. At the start, before the creation of woman and man, *ha-'adam* designates a single sexually undifferentiated creature (2:7–22a). In the middle, beginning with the creation of woman and man, *'adam* designates only the male creature (2:22b–3:21). At the close, after the shared disobedience of the woman and the man, *'adam* designates the couple (3:22–24). It becomes generic language that highlights the male and hides the female.

These three uses of *'adam* illustrate well the many ambiguities that permeate Genesis 2–3. The more I live with the story the more I appreciate such ambiguities and their power to evoke diverse responses. Though traditional readings tend to neglect ambiguity, it nevertheless endures to challenge those very readings. Patriarchy, then, has no lasting claim on this story. Indeed, in the years since I began to articulate a nonpatriarchal interpretation, the text has never failed me.[14] Despite voices to the contrary, it remains a foundational document for developing a feminist biblical theology.[15]

In inviting me to contribute to this volume, the editors asked whether, after more than twenty years, I had changed my mind in any significant way about my understanding of Genesis 2–3. If they mean my views as set forth in the short article reprinted here, then the answer is yes. The discussion of the word *'adam* explicates an important change. If they mean, however, the lengthy study that followed the short article, the answer is no. Not a jot, not a title.

Notes

1. Edwin M. Good, *Irony in the Old Testament* (Philadelphia: Westminster Press, 1965), p. 84. Cf. the second edition published in 1981 in Sheffield by the University of Sheffield Press.

2. This paper became Phyllis Trible, "Depatriarchalizing in Biblical Interpretation," *Journal of the American Academy of Religion* 41 (1973): 30–48.

3. Phyllis Trible, "Eve and Adam: Genesis 2–3 Reread," *Andover Newton Quarterly* (March 1973): 251–58.

4. E.g., Phyllis Tribe, "Eve and Adam: Genesis 2–3 Reread," in Carol P. Christ and Judith Plaskow, editors, *Womanspirit Rising: A Feminist Reader in Religion* (New York: Harper & Row, 1979), pp. 74–83; cf. the 1992 edition. See also Trible, "Eve and Adam: Genesis 2–3 Reread," in Marcia Stubbs and Sylvan Barnet, editors, *The Little, Brown Reader* (Boston: Scott, Foresman and Company, 1989), pp. 1015–24.

5. Phyllis Trible, *God and the Rhetoric of Sexuality* (Philadelphia: Fortress Press, 1978), pp. 72–143.

6. Cf. note 17 in Trible, *God and the Rhetoric of Sexuality*, p. 141.

7. See Bruce K. Waltke and M. O'Connor, *An Introduction to Biblical Hebrew Syntax* (Winona Lake, Ind.: Eisenbrauns, 1990), pp. 99–101.

8. See Elizabeth Achtemeier, "The Impossible Possibility: Evaluating the Feminist Approach to Bible and Theology," *Interpretation* 42 (1988): 51.

9. See most recently Terence E. Fretheim, "The Book of Genesis," *The New Interpreter's Bible* (Nashville: Abingdon Press, 1994), p. 353.

10. Cf. Jean M. Higgins, "The Myth of Eve: The Temptress," *Journal of the American Academy of Religion* 44 (1976): 645.

11. E.g., Fretheim, "The Book of Genesis," p. 353; Claus Westermann, *Genesis I–II: A Commentary*, translated by John J. Scullion (Minneapolis: Augsburg Publishing House, 1974), pp. 271–75.

12. To be sure, the very first line of the next story shows that the woman did leave the garden with the man. Adam and Eve mate to produce Cain (4:1). But a resort to extrinsic evidence changes the rules of the literary game. The point is to find intrinsic evidence for the shift in the meaning and use of *ha-'adam*.

13. Cf. the contradictory stance of Fretheim who first declares that the word *'adam* "should be read with the same [male] meaning throughout" and later declares that "we should note that *'adam* functions generically" in 3:22–24. (Fretheim, "The Book of Genesis," pp. 353, 364.)

14. *Contra*, e.g., Pamela J. Milne, "Eve and Adam: A Feminist Reading," in Harvey Minkoff, editor, *Approaches to the Bible* (Washington, D.C.: Biblical Archaeology Society, 1995), vol. 2, pp. 259–69. Feminists who support the patriarchal reading ironically capitulate to the view they assail.

15. Cf. Phyllis Trible, "Treasures Old and New: Biblical Theology and the Challenge of Feminism," in Francis Watson, editor, *The Open Text* (London: SCM Press Ltd., 1993), pp. 32–56.

Epilogue: The Coming of Lilith

*Judith Plaskow**

In the beginning the Lord God formed Adam and Lilith from the dust of the ground and breathed into their nostrils the breath of life. Created from the same source, both having been formed from the ground, they were equal in all ways. Adam, man that he was, didn't like this situation, and he looked for ways to change it. He said, "I'll have my figs now, Lilith," ordering her to wait on him, and he tried to leave to her the daily tasks of life in the garden. But Lilith wasn't one to take any nonsense; she picked herself up, uttered God's holy name, and flew away. "Well, now, Lord," complained Adam, "that uppity woman you sent me has gone and deserted me." The Lord, inclined to be sympathetic, sent his messengers after Lilith, telling her to shape up and return to Adam or face dire punishment. She, however, preferring anything to living with Adam, decided to stay right where she was. And so God, after more careful consideration this time, caused a deep sleep to fall upon Adam, and out of one of his ribs created for him a second companion, Eve.

---

*With Karen Bloomquist, Margaret Early, and Elizabeth Farians.

From Simon and Schuster "Epilogue: The Coming of Lilith", in *Religion and Sexism: Images of Women in Jewish and Christian Traditions* (1974). 341–343. Copyright by Indiana University Press. Reprinted by permission.

For a time Eve and Adam had quite a good thing going. Adam was happy now, and Eve, though she occasionally sensed capacities within herself that remained undeveloped, was basically satisfied with the role of Adam's wife and helper. The only thing that really disturbed her was the excluding closeness of the relationship between Adam and God. Adam and God just seemed to have more in common, being both men, and Adam came to identify with God more and more. After a while that made God a bit uncomfortable too, and he started going over in his mind whether he might not have made a mistake in letting Adam talk him into banishing Lilith and creating Eve, in light of the power that had given Adam.

Meanwhile Lilith, all alone, attempted from time to time to rejoin the human community in the garden. After her first fruitless attempt to breach its walls, Adam worked hard to build them stronger, even getting Eve to help him. He told her fearsome stories of the demon Lilith who threatens women in childbirth and steals children from their cradles in the middle of the night. The second time Lilith came she stormed the garden's main gate, and a great battle between her and Adam ensued, in which she was finally defeated. This time, however, before Lilith got away, Eve got a glimpse of her and saw she was a woman like herself.

After this encounter, seeds of curiosity and doubt began to grow in Eve's mind. Was Lilith indeed just another woman? Adam had said she was a demon. Another woman! The very idea attracted Eve. She had never seen another creature like herself before. And how beautiful and strong Lilith had looked! How bravely she had fought! Slowly, slowly, Eve began to think about the limits of her own life within the garden.

One day, after many months of strange and disturbing thoughts, Eve, wandering around the edge of the garden, noticed a young apple tree she and Adam had planted, and saw that one of its branches stretched over the garden wall. Spontaneously she tried to climb it, and struggling to the top, swung herself over the wall.

She had not wandered long on the other side before she met the one she had come to find, for Lilith was waiting. At first sight of her, Eve remembered the tales of Adam and was frightened, but Lilith understood and greeted her kindly. "Who are you?" they asked each other, "What is your story?" And they sat and spoke together, of the past and then of the future. They talked not once, but many times, and for many hours. They taught each other many things, and told each other stories, and laughed together, and cried, over and over, till the bond of sisterhood grew between them.

Meanwhile, back in the garden, Adam was puzzled by Eve's comings and goings, and disturbed by what he sensed to be her new attitude toward him. He talked to God about it, and God, having his own problems with Adam and a somewhat broader perspective, was able to help him out a little—but he, too, was confused. Something had failed to go according to plan. As in the days of Abraham, he needed counsel from his children. "I am who I am," thought God, "but I must become who I will become."

And God and Adam were expectant and afraid the day Eve and Lilith returned to the garden, bursting with possibilities, ready to rebuild it together.

"Lilith Revisited" (1995 CE)

Judith Plaskow

Writing "The Coming of Lilith" was one of the few experiences I have ever had of serving as a medium for words and images beyond my own conscious powers. I wrote the Lilith story in 1972 at the Grailville conference on Women Exploring Theology. I had spent the week in a morning group with Karen Bloomquist, Margaret Early, and Elizabeth Farians, exploring and analyzing the early feminist consciousness-raising process as a religious experience. As we repeatedly returned to and shared our own most powerful moments of feminist transformation, we struggled to find a theological vocabulary for expressing those experiences. At the end of our time together, we realized that, although we could not formulate a "feminist theology" apart from particular religious frameworks, we did have a tale we wanted to tell. While the rest of the group was happy to discuss the elements of our journey and leave it at that, I sat down after our last session to see whether I could actually write a story. Rather to my surprise, the words came pouring out of me, and "The Coming of Lilith" was born.

As I read the tale at the final large group gathering at Grailville that night, and as I have reheard or reread it many times since, I repeatedly have been struck by two things: the power of the story to capture a very particular moment in the history of feminism, and the complexity of the issues and feelings it raises and evokes. The spontaneous applause at the first reading, the immediate decision of Rosemary Ruether to publish "The Coming of Lilith" as the epilogue to *Religion and Sexism*, the feelings of delighted recognition numerous women have expressed to me over the years testify to the extent to which the story has touched a chord in many readers. It is clear to me that my ability to write a story that has evoked such a response was rooted in my having spent a week in the Grailville group, immersing myself in the process and content of feminist consciousness-raising. "The Coming of Lilith" works because its method and message are the same: it is a tale of sisterhood that came out of a powerful experience of sisterhood.

While the success of the piece was not accidental, then, in the sense that I and the group at Grailville were trying to articulate experiences that we knew were shared by a much larger community of women, many of the issues the story raises,

From "Lilith Revisited." In *Eve and Adam: Jewish, Christian, and Muslim Readings on Genesis and Gender*, ed. Kristen E. Kvam, Linda S. Schearing, and Valarie H. Ziegler. Copyright by Indiana University Press. Reprinted by permission.

I was not aware of at the time of writing. Thus Rosemary Ruether's discussion of "The Coming of Lilith" in the preface to *Religion and Sexism* quite amazed me when I first read it. She wrote that the "parable turns male misogynist theology upside down, revealing it for what it is, a projection of male insecurity and demand for dominance." She also commented that "the fearsomeness of Lilith in the male imagination preserves a recognition of suppressed power and creativity in women."[1] While I agreed that these things were there in the story, I certainly had not had such profundities in mind when I wrote it! It was only afterward that I came to see Lilith as a classic example of male projection. Lilith is not a demon; rather she is a woman named a demon by a tradition that does not know what to do with strong women. In a somewhat different vein, it was only when I came out as a lesbian more than a decade after writing the story that I first was struck by the potentially sexual nature of the energy between Eve and Lilith. The erotic possibilities in the intensity of their encounter and their care for each other seem so clear to me now that I am astonished I didn't see them earlier.

One of the elements of "The Coming of Lilith" that I often have been challenged on over the years is the maleness of God in the story. Some women have argued that, in making God male, I adopted and reinforced the patriarchal perspective that I was simultaneously criticizing. This was a deliberate decision on my part, and I still completely stand by it. The story is not saying that God in God's reality is actually male. It is playing with our perceptions of God at a particular point in history. The God of the original medieval Lilith midrash is certainly male. He sides with Adam in the struggle with Lilith for reasons that are utterly mysterious. In 1972 also, God was male.[2] Feminists were beginning to raise questions about male images of God but were moving only in the most tentative ways toward alternative concepts and metaphors. It was the process of consciousness-raising and the long, slow experimentation with new images and liturgies that were gradually to make possible a new understanding of the sacred. In this sense, the coming together of Eve and Lilith precipitates a change in (our perceptions of) God. In depicting God Godself as reflecting on that change I was drawing on what has always been one of my favorite aspects of the Jewish tradition: the fact that God is understood as growing through interaction with and challenge from human beings. In alluding to Abraham's argument with God over Sodom and Gomorrah, I was trying to place the feminist challenge in the larger context of fateful divine/human dialogues within Judaism.

I continue to be proud of "The Coming of Lilith." then, and even were I to want to change it, I do not feel it is quite fully mine to do so. I think it still stands as an expression of the original, heady round of consciousness-raising, an expression that perhaps provides a taste of the moment to those who were not part of it. But if the story as story seems to have had a life of its own apart from me, such is not the case with the theoretical and theological context in which it was originally embedded.[3] My understanding of Lilith as a Jewish story is entirely different from what it was twenty-four years ago, and I would write about its theological meaning and import from a completely different perspective.

Today, when I look at the larger framework in which "The Coming of Lilith" was initially presented, I am shocked by the Christianness of the religious language that we/I chose to impose on our feminist experiences, describing them in terms of "conversion," "grace," and "mission." I do not think that my willingness to use this language stemmed simply from the fact that I was working with three Christian women. Especially since the language is heavily Protestant and two of the women were Catholics, I assume these terms were as much a product of my own immersion in Protestant theology in graduate school as of the influence of the group. I was certainly aware at the time of the tension between this vocabulary and my own Jewish identity, but there was as yet no Jewish feminist discussion of theological issues offering an alternative language and conceptual framework.

Were I reflecting today on the religious dimension of feminism, I would try to remain close to the experiences being described rather than impose on them the foreign vocabulary of any particular tradition. When I think back to the larger conference at Grailville, for example, and especially the contributions of a group that was working on images of God. I see that in coming to a new sense of ourselves as agents in the world with power to shape our destinies, many feminists also experienced a sense of connection to larger currents of power and energy in the universe.[4] One can talk about the relationship of such experiences to specific theological concepts, but one does not *need* the concepts to authorize the experiences, and using traditional language may serve to mask the freshness and iconoclasm of the consciousness-raising process.

Were I interested in using traditional language to interpret feminist experience, however, I now see a much closer fit between the shared communal self-understanding of feminism and Judaism than I do between feminism and an individualistic Protestantism. Central both to our group reflections and the Lilith story is the notion that insight and empowerment emerge from the experience of community. Eve and Lilith by themselves are each isolated and powerless. Their ability to transform the garden and God results from their coming together; it is sisterhood that grows them into consciousness and action. This notion that human personhood is fundamentally social, that one stands in relation to God always as a member of a people, is also central to Judaism.[5] Moreover, rather than using the term "mission" to describe the expansive dimension of feminism, I would now talk about Eve and Lilith's transformation of the garden in terms of *tikkun olam* (repair of the world). While mission to me implies a somewhat condescending "I know better than you what is good for you," *tikkun olam* refers to the obligation and project of healing the world from the ontological and social brokenness that has marked it from creation. In contemporary usage, the concept of *tikkun olam* brings together mystical and social understandings of repair within Judaism in a way that fuses spirituality with a commitment to social justice.[6] By creating a more just social order, either through the liberation of women or commitment to other issues, one is also healing the alienation and separation within God. This, of course, is precisely what Eve and Lilith are doing at the end of the story.

What is most striking to me in revisiting Lilith, however, and most glaringly absent in terms of Jewish categories and analysis, is any understanding of the story as midrash. In referring to "The Coming of Lilith" in the framing material, I consistently label it a myth.[7] This points to a rather interesting paradox. On the one hand, for all that I was willing to adopt a Protestant vocabulary, when our group's convoluted theological discussion was over and done, I/we returned to the old Jewish mode of storytelling to capture the truths we had arrived at. On the other hand, in doing so, I had no conscious awareness of standing in a long Jewish tradition of using midrash as a way of expressing religious insight and grappling with religious questions.

Judaism, unlike Christianity, has no continuous history of systematic theological discourse. A tradition in which deed is more central than creed, it deals with theological issues not through the elaboration of doctrine but through engagement with biblical narratives. Midrash is a form of biblical interpretation that often begins from a question, silence, gap, or contradiction in a biblical story and writes the story forward in response to the interpreter's questions. Thus the original Lilith midrash (see p. 204 of this volume) emerged from the contradiction between the creation narratives in Genesis 1 and Genesis 2. Because in Genesis 1, the man and woman are created simultaneously and apparently equally, while in Genesis 2 Eve is created from Adam's rib, the rabbis wondered whether the stories might not describe two different events in the history of creation. Their response was that, indeed, Adam did have a first wife named Lilith, who fled the garden when Adam tried to subordinate her. God sent three angels after her to bring her back, at which point in the midrash Lilith turns into a demon, killing new babies in retaliation for the deaths of her own children.8 Midrash as a major technique of interpretation is not limited to this particular narrative, of course. Rabbinic midrash on countless biblical characters and texts functions as a vehicle for exploring religious questions in a way that makes room for disagreement, ambiguity, and complexity.

In the last decade or so, Jewish feminists have begun to use midrash as an important way of both reconnecting with and transforming tradition. Just as rabbinic midrash often begins from some gap or silence in the biblical text, Jewish feminists are using midrash to explore and fill in the great silence that surrounds women's history and experience. Just as the rabbis brought their own questions to the Bible and found there answers that supported their religious world view, so Jewish women are asking new questions of biblical narratives and, in the process of responding, recreating tradition. The flexibility and creativity of midrash, its power to reinvent, easily lends itself to feminist use. What was Sarah thinking and feeling when Abraham took the son she had born at the age of ninety and brought him to the top of Mount Moriah as a sacrifice? How did she feel when God told Abraham to get up and journey to a new land, leaving the home that they had made together? What was the reaction of Miriam when God struck her with leprosy for challenging the authority of Moses, but left Aaron unblemished? Lacking responses to these and many other questions, feminists are creating them through midrash, and, in doing so, engaging with Jewish tradition in a vital and open-ended way.

My story, "The Coming of Lilith," both does and does not fit into this recent explosion of feminist midrash. First of all, unlike most examples of the genre, it is a midrash on a midrash, and not on a biblical text. In beginning from the Lilith story in the *Alphabet of Ben Sira* rather than from Genesis, I comment on the biblical creation narrative only indirectly. Second, and more significantly, I did not intend to write an interpretation of the traditional midrash but to capture the experience of consciousness-raising within a religious framework. I cannot remember now how I had even heard of Lilith, but I borrowed her tale because it fit my contemporary need. I did not realize that in retelling her story, I was doing for the traditional midrash what it had already done for the biblical text. And yet, once the story was completed, it *read* as a midrash on a midrash of creation, and to that extent stands in the stream of Jewish feminist midrash that was to follow.

Revisiting Lilith twenty-four years later, then, it feels very apt to me that, in the context of this book, the midrash appears as a selection on Jewish egalitarian interpretation. I find it interesting that, in beginning from consciousness-raising as a religious experience and moving from there into Protestant theological categories, I nonetheless ended up with a story that, in content and form, reflects important aspects of Jewish tradition. Insofar as "The Coming of Lilith" has spoken to a generation of readers about the transformative implications of feminism, it testifies to the power of story and the power of midrash to create and communicate religious meaning.

Notes

1. Rosemary Radford Ruether, *Religion and Sexism: Images of Women in the Jewish and Christian Traditions* (New York: Simon & Schuster, 1974), p. 12.

2. See my "The Coming of Lilith: Toward a Feminist Theology," in Carol P. Christ and Judith Plaskow, editors, *Womanspirit Rising: A Feminist Reader in Religion,* (New York: Harper & Row, 1979), pp. 198–209.

3. "Singleness/Community Group," *Women Exploring Theology at Graüville,* packet from Church Women United, 1972. See also my discussion in Judith Plaskow, *Standing Again at Sinai: Judaism from a Feminist Perspective* (San Francisco: Harper & Row, 1990), pp. 86, 143f.

4. Plaskow, *Standing Again at Sinai,* pp. 79–81.

5. Plaskow, *Standing Again at Sinai,* pp. 217–20.

6. See "The Coming of Lilith," in *Womanspirit Rising,* p. 205, and the selection in this volume.

7. The version of the story in Louis Ginzberg's *Legends of the Jews* (rpt., Philadelphia: Jewish Publication Society of America, 1968), vol. 1, p. 65, is somewhat different from the one that appears here.

Chapter 3

Mary Magdalene and Other Women Disciples

How Mary Magdalene Became a Whore

Jane Schaberg

Mention the name Mary Magdalene and most people will free-associate the word "whore," albeit the repentant whore whose love for Jesus led him to forgive her. In *Jesus Christ-Superstar,* Andrew Lloyd Webber and Timothy Rice's 1970s musical, she is depicted as a prostitute platonically in love with Jesus, not having a sexual affair with him but obsessed and baffled by him, not knowing how to love him. At about the same time as *Jesus Christ-Superstar,* in Franco Zeffirelli's TV movie *Jesus of Nazareth,* Anne Bancroft plays the Magdalene as a prostitute of angry intelligence, in contrast to Jesus' disbelieving male disciples. More recently, in Martin Scorsese's controversial film *The Last Temptation of Christ* (based on the 1955 novel by Nikos Kazantzakis), the Magdalene is a tattooed prostitute to whom Jesus was attracted physically—his last temptation.

In the popular mind Mary Magdalene represents the repentant sinner, lifted from the depths of whoredom by her romantic love for Jesus—proof that even the lowliest can be saved through repentance and devotion.

Yet this is a very different picture from the one the Gospels give us. How did this happen? And when? And why?

In all four Gospels the Magdalene participates in Jesus' Galilean ministry, she follows him to Jerusalem, she mourns at his crucifixion and, on the first Easter, she goes to his tomb and finds it empty. Except in the Gospel of Luke, she is said to have been sent with a commission to proclaim to the disciples that Jesus had been raised from the dead. According to the three accounts in Matthew 28:1–10, John 20:14–18, and Mark 16:9 (the Marcan addition*), she is the first to whom the risen Jesus appears. In short, Mary Magdalene is the primary witness to the fundamental data of early Christian faith.

The earliest reference to the Magdalene in Jesus' life comes during his Galilean ministry. In Luke, in a passage without parallels in the other Gospels, we learn that while traveling with his disciples, Jesus healed some women of evil spirits and infirmities. One of them—the first named—is the Magdalene, from whom Jesus exorcised seven demons:

> "[H]e went on through cities and villages, proclaiming and bringing the good news of the kingdom of God. The twelve were with him, as well as some women who had been cured of evil spirits and infirmities: Mary, called Magdalene, from whom seven demons had gone out, Joanna, the wife of Herod's steward Chuza, and Susanna, and many others, who provided for them out of their resources" (Luke 8:1–3).

Mary is called Magdalene because she is from the town of Magdala, generally identified with the site of Migdal on the western shore of the Sea of Galilee. She, along with other women, travels with Jesus and the 12 disciples.

But, as we shall see, as early as the period when the Gospels were written (late first to second centuries C.E.*), the Magdalene's role is gradually diminished and distorted. In the Pauline corpus, she is not mentioned at all, not even in the passage in 1 Corinthians 15:3–8 that lists those to whom Jesus made post-resurrection appearances.

In the passage from Luke we just looked at, she and the other women are cast in a subordinate role of service and support to the males in the movement. In Luke (and in Acts, which was probably written by the same author) the 12 disciples—all men—are the major witnesses and leaders.

But does this reflect the actual experience of Jesus' original followers? In the passage from Luke, the women "provided for them out of their resources." The

---

*The Marcan addition is the longer ending of Mark (16:9–20) found in many manuscripts. It is accepted as canonical, although printed in smaller type in many translations. According to most scholars, it was not written by Mark but added later. Some scholars think 16:9–20 is dependent on the other Gospels and summarizes their narratives of resurrection appearances; other scholars regard it as independent tradition.

*C.E. (Common Era), used by this author, is the alternate designation corresponding to A.D. often used in scholarly literature.

Greek verb translated here as "provided for" is *diakonein,* which means to serve, wait on, minister to as a deacon. Although some ancient manuscript authorities have the women ministering to "him" (that is, to Jesus alone), instead of "them," the canonical text of Luke 8:3 has "them." In Mark 15:41 and Matthew 27:55, however, the women, including the Magdalene, who watched Jesus' crucifixion from afar, are identified as women who had followed Jesus from Galilee, ministering to *him.* That Luke has the women ministering to the disciples is consistent with his general tendency to subordinate the role of women.

Although these women travel with Jesus, none of them is ever given the title of "disciple" by the Gospel writers.

One scholar, Ben Witherington, has said that for a woman "to leave home and travel with a rabbi was not only unheard of, it was scandalous. Even more scandalous was the fact that women, both respectable and not, were among Jesus' traveling companions."[1] But do we really know this? If it was so scandalous, why did the scandal leave no mark on the traditions?[2] Why was the fact that women traveled with Jesus never explicitly defended in the Gospels? And on what basis does Witherington conclude that some of the women who traveled with Jesus were not "respectable"? Perhaps he is thinking of Mary Magdalene as a whore, a subject to which we will return.

What kind of service did the women traveling with Jesus provide? Some see it as domestic—shopping, cooking, sewing, serving meals, the work of a traditional wife. On the other hand, behind this passage in Luke 8:1–3 may be a tradition that women were significant figures in the table fellowship and intellectual leadership of the Jesus movement. In the early Christian community, the Greek noun *diakonia* (which is related to the verb *diakonian* used in Luke 8:3) referred to eucharistic table service and to proclamation of God's word.

Others have suggested that these women were wealthy philanthropists or benefactors. Yet it is widely agreed that most members of the earliest Jesus movement were poor. Writing in the 80s or 90s, Luke often places wealthy women in support roles (see Acts 13:50, 17:4,12,34), but this cannot be accepted as accurate historical memory. This passage from Luke, therefore, cannot give us reliable information about Mary Magdalene's social status or life's work.

At a meeting of scholars where I recently gave a paper on this subject, a professor of New Testament suggested that this passage proved that the Magdalene was a whore: "How else could a woman be wealthy?" he said. That women should be regarded as prostitutes simply because they had resources reflects the same kind of mindset we find in those who somehow conclude from Jesus' exorcism of seven demons from the Magdalene that she had been a whore. There is simply no reason to connect this healing with previous prostitution—or immorality, for that matter.

The next time we meet the Magdalene is at the crucifixion in Jerusalem. Matthew, Mark, Luke and John all name her as a witness to the crucifixion. In Mark and Matthew we learn that among the "women looking on from afar" was Mary Magdalene (Mark 15:40; Matthew 27:55–56). Mark also identifies the women present as those "who when he was in Galilee followed him and ministered to him" (Mark 15:41; compare Matthew 27:55–56). Although Luke does not mention any of the women by name at the crucifixion scene, he does state that "the women who had followed him from Galilee" were there (Luke 23:49), and when he names them later in the scene at the tomb (Luke 24:10), Mary Magdalene is among them. In John, she is standing at the cross with Jesus' mother, among others (John 19:25).

The Magdalene watches as Jesus is laid in the tomb (Mark 15:46–47; Matthew 27:59–61; Luke 23:55). She returns to the tomb on Sunday. The accounts of what happens at the tomb vary. In Mark, the women bring spices to anoint Jesus. They see that the stone has been rolled away from the door of the tomb. Entering the tomb, they are amazed to see a young man in a white robe. He tells them that Jesus of Nazareth has been raised and is not there. He instructs the women to tell the disciples and Peter that Jesus is going before them to Galilee, where "you will see him." The women, however, flee from the tomb, "for trembling and astonishment had come upon them; and they said nothing to any one, for they were afraid" (Mark 16:1–8). Most scholars think that the Gospel of Mark, our earliest Gospel, ended here at verse 8, with the women's silence. Most scholars think also that Matthew and Luke then used and edited Mark's Gospel as they wrote their own.*

In Matthew, Mary Magdalene goes toward dawn with "the other Mary" to see the sepulcher. There is an earthquake at the tomb, "for an angel of the Lord descended from heaven and came and rolled back the stone." The angel tells the women to "go quickly and tell his disciples that he has risen from the dead, and behold, he is going before you to Galilee; there you will see him." The women are full of great joy as well as fear, and they run to tell the disciples. As they run, Jesus meets them and tells them again to tell his brothers to go to Galilee where they will see him (Matthew 28:1–10).

In Luke the women find the stone already rolled away; they go into the tomb and are perplexed not to find the body of Jesus. Two men "in dazzling apparel" ask them why they seek the living among the dead. They remind the women that Jesus told them while he was still in Galilee "that the Son of man must be delivered into the hands of sinful men, and be crucified, and on the third day rise." The women remember the words. On their own, they decide to tell the 11 and others. But the apostles consider their words "an idle tale" and they do not believe them (Luke 24:1–11).

In John, the Magdalene comes alone to the tomb early Easter morning. She finds the stone has been taken away. She runs and tells Simon Peter and "the other disciple, the one whom Jesus loved" that "They have taken the Lord out of the tomb and we do not know where they have laid him." Peter and the other disciple run to the tomb, find it empty and see Jesus' burial linens. They leave, and Mary Magdalene is alone, weeping outside the tomb. She stoops and looks inside the tomb, and sees two angels sitting there. They ask her why she is weeping. She replies, "Because they have taken away my Lord, and I do not know where they have laid

---

*The two-source theory of the literary relationship among the Synoptic Gospels holds that Mark has been used by Matthew and Luke. They also use a second, hypothetical source, simply called Q for the German word *quelle* (source). (See Helmut Koester and Stephen J. Patterson, "The Gospel of Thomas—Does It Contain Authentic Sayings of Jesus?" BR, April 1990.) Further, Matthew and Luke each have access to special sources of written or oral information (M and L). The Gospel of John is viewed as having no direct literary relationship with the synoptics.

him." She turns around and sees Jesus standing there, but she does not recognize him. He too asks her why she weeps, and, thinking he is the gardener, she says, "Sir, if you have carried him away, tell me where you have laid him, and I will take him away." Jesus speaks her name, "Mary," and she recognizes him. He tells her to tell his brothers, "I am ascending to my Father and your Father, to my God and your God." She goes and tells the disciples, "I have seen the Lord" (John 20:1–18).

In John, then, the Magdalene is the first to see the risen Lord. The Marcan addition shares this view: "Now when he arose on the first day, he appeared first to Mary Magdalene" (Mark 16:9). In Matthew, she and the other Mary are first to see him.

So how did this woman who traveled with Jesus in Galilee and was a witness to these epochal events become known as a whore? Nothing in the texts that name her indicates that she had such a past. The most that can be said is that she traveled with Jesus in Galilee where he exorcised demons from her, and she had resources of her own with which to serve.

It is clear that the text itself does not stigmatize the Magdalene as a whore. The first step in giving her this sullied past lies in interpretation. In early Christian interpretation, women mentioned in several passages became identified with the Magdalene, even though these texts do not explicitly name her as the woman involved.

The most important motif that links some of these stories to the Magdalene—and on which much interpretation is hung—is the motif of anointing. The Magdalene, it will be recalled, came to Jesus' tomb on the first Easter with spices to anoint him (Mark 16:1; see also Luke 24:1). Jesus was, of course, called the Anointed One (*Christos*, in Greek). So it is perhaps natural that the unnamed woman who anoints Jesus' head in Mark 14:3–9 and Matthew 26:6–13 is identified in early tradition as the Magdalene, especially because in these precrucifixion passages this anointing is explicitly said to be for Jesus' burial. Adapting this motif of anointing, in Luke 7:36–50 a woman "who was a sinner" anoints Jesus' feet. Jesus tells Simon, "Her sins, which are many, are forgiven, for she loved much; but he who is forgiven little, loves little." Here too later tradition identifies the woman as the Magdalene. The identification is made easier because in John 12:1–3 a woman named Mary at Lazarus' home in Bethany anoints Jesus' feet (see also John 11:2).

Thus, in one of the passages that became associated with Mary Magdalene, there is a woman named Mary; she is therefore assumed (although this Mary is from Bethany) to be the Magdalene. In other passages, no name is given to the woman, but she is nevertheless identified in later tradition as Mary Magdalene. In one episode the unnamed woman is a public sinner, "a woman of the city" (Luke 7:36–50); her sin, it is clearly implied, is sexual. Sexual sin is the link between this passage and others in later tradition sometimes considered to be about Mary Magdalene: the story of an unnamed woman caught in the act of committing adultery (John 7:53–8:11) and the story of the Samaritan woman said to have had five husbands and to be living with a man not her husband (John 4:8–29).

These identifications—"conflation" is the technical term by which scholars tell us these stories were all combined—produced the beginnings of a "biography" of this remarkable woman who clearly was more important to the story of

Jesus than the Gospel writers explicitly indicated. The initial motives behind this conflation may have been benign, even creative, but the conflation ended up as a basis for degrading the Magdalene.

The identification of her sin in later legend as prostitution has its source in the story of the "sinner" in Luke 7:36–50. This identification fulfills the desire—or the need—to downgrade the Magdalene, as well as the desire to attach to female sexuality the notions of evil, repentance and mercy. One scholar believes the later legend of the Magdalene as prostitute was "brought into existence by the powerful undertow of misogyny in Christianity, which associates women with the dangers and degradation of the flesh."[3] The need for a penitent whore-heroine in Christian mythology shaped the understanding of passages like this that did or might (in the Christian imagination) concern her. In the words of this same scholar, Marina Warner, the development of the prostitution legend represents "Christianity's fear of women, its identification of physical beauty with temptation, and its practice of bodily mortification."[4]

I would add that the legend-making process also reflects a Christian reaction against female power and the authority of this major witness to the crucial data of Christianity, especially the resurrection.

Precisely how early this conflation produced the legend of Mary Magdalene's whoredom, we do not know. Origen (c 185-c. 254) and John Chrysostom (c 347–407) comment that Mary Magdalene was a wholly unsuitable first witness to Jesus' resurrection. So the legend, or basic aspects of it, may already have been in place at this time. In the sixth century, Pope Gregory the Great gave prestige and authoritative sanction to this conflation in his homilies.[5] The earliest extant text that harmonizes the episodes into a single, concise, coherent narrative of the Magdalene's "life" appears to be a tenth-century sermon attributed to Odo of Cluny.[6]

Especially influential was a legend about her last 30 years, supposedly spent in Provence, France. Its fully developed and relatively stable form is that told by Jacobus de Voragine in his immensely popular *Legenda Aurea* (*Golden Legend*) in the mid-13th century.[7] In this telling, very little attention is paid to the Magdalene's presence in the passion and resurrection scenes; the emphasis, instead, is on her sin and repentance, and on love. Her story as told here shows that anyone, even the most sinful, can be forgiven. In her life after the ascension of Jesus, the Magdalene is said to have traveled widely, to have undergone many trials and to have spent her last 30 years in isolation. Actually, the ultimate source of this life of solitude is a legend about the prostitute Mary of Egypt, who did penance naked and wrapped in her hair in a desert retreat. By the ninth century this story was blended into that of the Magdalene. In this telling the prostitute has become a recluse; the Magdalene of the Gospels has all but disappeared.

Beginning in the 16th century, modern scholarship began to deharmonize the Gospels—instead of trying to make them consistent, scholars began to appreciate their differences and what lay behind those differences. In 1517 a scholar named Jacques Lefèvre d'Etaples published a critique of the traditional view of Mary Magdalene as repentant whore.[8] Within the next three years, 15 major treatises were written on the controversy. Lefèvre d'Etaples was censured by the theological faculty of the Sorbonne. His works were placed on the Vatican's *Index Lil rorum Prohibitorum* (*List of Prohibited Books*). The controversy over the Magdalene, however, continued to rage for the next 350 years.

Today it's official. Roman Catholic and Protestant doctrines agree with that of Eastern Orthodoxy in distinguishing among three separate female Gospel characters: Mary Magdalene, Mary of Bethany and the unnamed "sinner" in Luke 7. Thus, the Magdalene can no longer be identified as a sinner. And of course the links between the Magdalene and the Samaritan woman caught in the act of adultery (John 7:53–8:11) and between the Magdalene and the Samaritan woman who had five husbands and was living with a man not her husband (John 4:8–29) were always so weak as to require little modern scholarship to break them.

But unofficially—in popular piety and among those adhering to unexamined assumptions—the Magdalene is still the ex-whore. For example, tales of Mary Magdalene's lustful early life and repentance take up half of Marlee Alex's 1987 book for children entitled *Mary Magdalene: A Woman Who Showed Her Gratitude*.[9] According to this account, the Magdalene "was not famous for the great things she did or said, but she goes down in history as a woman who truly loved Jesus with all her heart and was not embarrassed to show it despite criticism from others." This description is of course still based on the conflated passages, especially Luke 7 in which an unnamed sinner anoints Jesus. Relegated to a relatively minor position are those New Testament passages that actually mention the Magdalene. In those texts, she is remembered for the great things she did (she followed Jesus and was present at the cross and at the tomb) and for what she said (that the tomb was empty and that he was raised from the dead).

Another tradition about the Magdalene is preserved in several Gnostic works of the second to fourth centuries, including the Gospel of Thomas, the Gospel of Philip, the *Sophia of Jesus Christ, Dialogue of the Savior, Pistis Sophia* and the Gospel of Mary (Magdalene). These Gnostic works preserve a tradition about a rivalry, or conflict, between the Magdalene and Peter or other male disciples. When she is challenged by Peter, Jesus (or, in one instance, Levi) defends her. Neither silenced nor excluded, the Magdalene speaks boldly and powerfully, entering into dialogue with the risen Jesus and comforting, correcting and encouraging the male disciples. She is a visionary, praised for her superior spiritual understanding and often identified as the intimate "companion" of the Savior. In the Gospel of Philip (63:34–64:10), Jesus is said to have kissed her often. An erotic element is also present in the Gospel of Mary: "The Savior loved [her] more than the rest of woman" and "He loved her more than us [the male disciples]."

But unlike the Magdalene of later Western art and legend, the Gnostic Magdalene had not been a prostitute or sinner.[10] She does not represent repentance nor forgiveness nor regenerate sexuality.

If the erotic element in the Gnostic works does not reflect the tradition of an earlier sinful life, what does it signify? According to Elaine Pagels, "The hint of an erotic relationship between [Jesus] and Mary Magdalene may indicate claims to mystical communion; throughout history, mystics of many traditions have chosen sexual metaphors to describe their experiences."[11]

It is likely that Mary Magdalene functioned in Gnostic circles not only as the representative of the female followers of Jesus, but also as a symbol of the importance and leadership of women among the Gnostics.[12] She may have been a role model on which some women based their claim to power. Women may have played important roles in these communities, both as leaders and as sources of revelation and authority.

This probably reflects the egalitarianism within the Jesus movement, itself rooted in the egalitarian form(s) of Judaism. As one scholar, Rosemary Ruether, has argued, "The tradition of Mary Magdalene as a sinner was developed in orthodox Christianity primarily to displace the apostolic authority claimed for women through her name."[13] From the Gnostic materials, we can glimpse what was displaced, distorted, lost and overlaid by the legend of Mary Magdalene as the whore.

Now we can begin to restore the Magdalene to her rightful place, as we look more deeply into the Gospel episodes in which she appears—and those in which she does not appear. Despite her importance, the Gospels themselves have neglected to tell us much about her. We are not told of her call by Jesus (nor of any other woman's call, only of the call of males). No discussion or teaching during his ministry involves her. Only the figure(s) at the empty tomb and the risen Jesus speak to her. Dialogue with her as an individual occurs only in John 20:1–18. Outside of the Gospels, she is mentioned nowhere else in the New Testament.

Yet the trace of her great significance remains. She travels with Jesus in Galilee and goes up with him to Jerusalem. She is there at the crucifixion and at the empty tomb. The risen Jesus appears first to her,[14] and it is she who carries the word of his resurrection to the male disciples. In this loyalty, courage and religious insight is the foundation of her lasting memory.

Notes

1. Ben Witherington III. "On the Road with Mary Magdalene. Joanna, Susanna and Other Disciples—Luke 8:1–2", *Zeitschrift für die Neutestamentliche Wissenschaft* 70 (1979), pp. 244–245.

2. John 4:27 is the only exception, though it has nothing to do with travel. Jesus' disciples find him with the Samaritan woman: "They were astonished that it was speaking with a woman, but no one said, 'What do you want?' or 'Why are you speaking with her?'"

3. Marna Warner, *Alone of All Her Sex* (New York: Knopf. 1976), pp. 225–232. Elisabeth Schussler Fiorenza has rightly remarked that the post-New Testament distortion of the image of Mary Magdalene signals a deep distortion in the attitudes toward, and in the self-understanding and identity of the Christian woman and man ("Mary Magdalene: Apostle to the Apostles." *Union Theological Seminary Journal* [April, 1975], p. 5; *Der Vergessener Partner* [Düsseldorf. Ger.: Patmos Verlag, 1964], pp. 57–59). That distortion calls for precise documentation and correction by historians. See also Pheme Perkins. "'I Have Seen the Lord' (John 20:18): Women Witnesses to the Resurrection," *Interpretation* 46 (1992), pp. 31–41.

4. Warner, *Alone of All*, p. 232.

5. Pope Gregory, *XL Homiliarum Evangelia* 2.25. 76:1188–1196 in *Patrologiae Latina*, ed. Jacques Migne (Paris, 1844 *et seq.*).

6. Odo of Cluny, *De Maria Magdalene & triduo Christi Disceptatio.*

7. Jacobus de Voragine, *Legenda aurea*, ed. T. Graesse (Dresden, 1846); English transl.: Granger Ryan and Helmut Rippergar, *The Golden Legend of Jacobus de Voragine* (New York: Longmans. 1941: reprint: New York: Arno, 1969), pp. 355–364.

8. Jacques Lefevre d'Etaples, *De Maria Magdalene & triduo Christi Disceptatio* (Paris. 1517).

9. Marlee Alex, *Mary Magdalene: A Woman Who Showed Her Gratitude* (Grand Rapids, MI: Eerdmans, 1987).

10. Rather, another gnostic figure. Sophia (Wisdom), is associated with a fall through love and an agony of remorse.

11. Elaine Pagels, *The Gnostic Gospels* (New York: Random House, 1979), p. 18.

12. See D.M. Parrot, "Gnostic and Orthodox Disciples in the Second and Third Centuries." *Nag Hammadi, Gnosticism, and Early Christianity,* ed. CW. Hedrick and R. Hodgson, Jr. (Peabody, MA: Hendrickson, 1986), pp. 218–219.

13. Rosemary Ruether, Women-Church (San Francisco: Harper & Row, 1985), n. 1. p. 286. Contrast Pheme Perkins (*The Gnostic Dialogue* [New York: Paulist, 1980], n. 10, p. 136), who thinks that the role of Mary Magdalene in Gnostic texts is not evidence that the Gnostics upheld community leadership by women. Her role, however, is not the only evidence for this.

14. This tradition is probably historical, despite the fact that in Luke 24:34, as in 1 Corinthians 15:5, the first appearance is said to be to Peter (Cephas). John 20:8 presents the unnamed Beloved Disciple as the first to believe. Already in the New Testament period, the Magdalene's role was in the process of being diminished and distorted. In the memories, traditions and rethinking of the Pauline and Lucan communities, her prominence was challenged by that of Peter: in Johannine circles, by that of the Beloved Disciple.

Presence or Absence? The Question of Women Disciples at the Last Supper

Dorothy A. Lee

In theology and spirituality, the dynamic between presence and absence is a paradoxical way of speaking of the elusive mystery of God. For women the same motif, translated into their experience of church and theology, takes on a new connotation which feels more like contradiction than paradox. Nowhere is the tension more obvious than in the passion narratives of the Gospels, where women as disciples are conspicuous both for their presence and their absence. The purpose of this article is to discuss the dynamic of presence/absence at the Last Supper within the broader context of women in the passion and resurrection narratives.

WOMEN AND THE GOSPEL OF LUKE

Quentin Quesnell has has put forward a significant argument that women are present at the Last Supper in Luke's narrative.[1] This makes Luke, although not the earliest Gospel to be written, an appropriate place to begin the discussion. Quesnell

---

[1]Q. Quesnell, "The Women at Luke's Supper" in R. J. Cassidy and P. J. Scharper (eds.), *Political Issues in Luke-Acts* (Maryknoll, NY: Orbis Books, 1983) 59–79. See also Rosalie Ryan, "The Women from Galilee and Discipleship in Luke", *Biblical Theology Bulletin* 15 (1985) 58.

believes that the disciples who have followed Jesus from Galilee remain with him through the events that take place in Jerusalem, including the Last Supper. Given Luke's explicit mention of women disciples on the journey to Jerusalem, Quesnell argues, there is no reason to suppose their absence from the Last Supper.[2] Certainly it is the case that, unlike Mark, Luke mentions these women early in the course of the Galilœan ministry (especially Mary Magdalene, Joanna, Susanna; Luke 8:2b–3a) and groups them with the twelve (v. 1). The women have been recipients of Jesus' healing and/or exorcising power (v. 2a) and have given up their wealth (v. 3b; see Luke 18:28/pars.) to follow Jesus and exercise ministry (διακονέω, v. 3b).[3] Moreover it is clear from this that, for Luke, the group of disciples which follows Jesus to Jerusalem is a large one and by no means restricted to the twelve (see 6:17, 8:3, 10:1–20, 19:37).[4]

The positive role of women as disciples carries through into the passion narrative where women are present at the cross,[5] the twelve, on the other hand, are apparently absent. The women are present along with a group of "those known to him" (πάντες οἱ γνωστοὶ αὐτοῦ, 23:49), which probably refers to an unstructured group of Jesus' relatives and family friends (see 2:44).[6] Luke's narrative implies, therefore, that the twelve share Peter's cowardice and shame (22:61–62; see vv. 31–34).[7] The women, in contrast, are witnesses to the resurrection and empty tomb (24:4–7) and the first to be initiated into the dynamic "remembering" of the community (vv. 6–8).[8] When they proclaim faithfully the message of the resurrection to "the eleven and all the others" they are not believed (vv. 9–11). Just as, in a positive way, the twelve and the women are grouped together at 8:1–3 as faithful followers

---

[2]Quesnell, "Luke's Supper", 59–61, 67–69.

[3]See Ben Witherington, "On the Road with Mary Magdalene, Joanna, Susanna, and Other Disciples—Luke 8:1–3", *Zeitschrift für die neutestamentliche Wissenschaft* 70 (1979) 243–248, and *Women and the Genesis of Christianity* (Cambridge: Cambridge University Press, 1990) 110–112. Witherington argues that the women's contribution consists of traditional female roles of "hospitality and service" (*Genesis of Christianity*, 112). For a helpful critique of this view, see David C. Sim, "The Women Followers of Jesus: The Implications of Luke 8:1–3", *Heythrop Journal* 30 (1989) 51–62. Sim sees the contribution of the women as the pooling of resources; there is no implication that the function of the women was to perform traditional menial tasks; like the men, "they were expected to be faithful and attentive students" (p. 60).

[4]Although Luke uses the term "disciple" less frequently than the other gospels, he uses it in a broader sense (see, for example, the mission of the seventy-two at 10:1–20). In Acts "disciples" refer to christians in general (for example, Acts 6:1). The feminine form μαθήτρια is used of Tabitha (Dorcas) at Acts 9:36, the only occasion it is used in the singular of a woman. One of the inexplicable features of Lukan usage is that the term ceases at Luke 2:45 and does not recur until Acts 6:1. See K. H. Rengstorf, "μαθητής", *Theological Dictionary of the New Testament* 4, 415–461.

[5]A separate group from the Gailiaean women are the mourning women of Jerusalem, part of a larger crowd which follows Jesus to the cross (23:23–31). According to J. Massyngbaerde Ford, *My Enemy is My Guest: Jesus and Violence in Luke* (Maryknoll, NY: Orbis, 1984) 128–30, these mourners are disciples of Jesus "prepared to share the same fate as he" (p. 130).

[6]See R. Bultmann, "γνωστός", *Theological Dictionary of the New Testament* 1, 718–9, and E. Schweizer, *The Good News According to Luke* (London: SPCK, 1984) 362; against this, see Joseph A. Fitzmyer, *The Gospel According to Luke X–XXIV* (New York: Doubleday, 1985) 1520.

[7]Jesus' words at Luke 22:32b—" and you, when once you have turned back, strengthen your brothers"—imply loss of faith by Peter's fellow-disciples; see I. Howard Marshall, *The Gospel of Luke: A Commentary on the Greek Text* (Exeter: Paternoster, 1978) 822.

[8]According to J. D. Kingsbury, *Conflict in Luke: Jesus, Authorities, Disciples* (Minneapolis: Fortress, 1991) 132–3, the women disciples at the tomb are the first to make the transition to spiritual enlightenment.

of Jesus, so now the eleven and the women are juxtaposed in a negative way, in the crucifixion and empty tomb stories. The harmony of their earlier relationship is disturbed by the events of the passion.

This harmony is not restored until the beginning of Acts, where the christian community—consisting of women and men—comes to birth in the gift of the Spirit (Acts 2:1–13). The twelve have first to re-group themselves after the treachery and loss of Judas Iscariot (Acts 1:16–19); the women and relatives of Jesus need no such re-grouping (1:12–26). Both groups play a symbolic role for Luke, just as they have on the journey to Jerusalem, and at the cross and empty tomb.[9] Together they stand for the new community, the new Israel, and it is no accident that we first meet them in Acts in the context of prayer (1:14a). Moreover the gift of the Holy Spirit is bestowed on all present ("all flesh"),[10] so that the daughters prophesy with the sons (2:17) and each hears the "mighty acts of God" in her or his own tongue (2:11)—a prophecy which is prefigured in the infancy narratives where women prophesy as well as men (Elisabeth, Mary, Anna; Luke 1:39–55, 2:36–38). The new community embraces the giftedness of women, acknowledging the divine Spirit dwelling in them and clothing them with "power from on high" (Luke 24:4; see Acts 1:8).[11]

In the light of this, Quesnell would seem to have a strong case in arguing for the probability of women's presence at Luke's Last Supper. The term "disciples" occurs four times throughout the narrative of Luke 22. Given its association with the larger group of Jesus' disciples, it is hard to see why it should not be read in its customary sense here too. This means that in the scene immediately preceding the Last Supper (22:7–13), the reader assumes that the term "disciples" refers to a large group: "'Where is the guest room, where I may eat the Passover *with my disciples?*'" (22:11). Nevertheless the narrative of the Last Supper moves unexpectedly in a different direction: "And when the hour came, he reclined *and the apostles with him*" (Luke 22:14).[12] On the few occasions in Luke's Gospel where the term "apostle" is used, it refers to the twelve (see 6:13; 9:1, 10; 24:10). The text, therefore, cannot be read to imply the presence of others beside the twelve; Luke words the introduction carefully to make it clear that this is a special occasion for the twelve alone. Whether this narrowing of the term extends to the following episode on the Mount of Olives (23:39–46) is not made clear by the narrative.

That only the twelve are present at the Lukan Last Supper is supported also by the short discourse following the Meal which refers to those present "judging the twelve tribes of Israel" (Luke 22:30). Quesnell tries to argue that this need not exclude the presence of others.[13] However, it does draw out the numerical symbolism

---

[9]Against this view, see Gerd Lüdemann, *Early Christianity According to the Traditions in Acts: A Commentary* (London: SCM, 1987) 27, who, influenced by the Western reading of Acts 1:14, suggests that the women are wives of the apostles.

[10]See Joseph A. Grassi, *God Makes Me Laugh: A New Approach to Luke* (Wilmington, DE: Glazier, 1986) 66–8, 72.

[11]See Charles H. Talbert, *Reading Luke: A Literary and Theological Commentary on the Third Gospel* (New York: Crossroad, 1982) 90–93.

[12]In other banquet stories, Luke begins with a description of those present: for example, 5:29, 7:36–37, 10:38; in the case of the latter two there is no implication that the disciples are present.

[13]Quesnell, "Luke's Supper," 64–5.

which is so important in Luke's understanding of the twelve. Indeed it is an argument in favour of the presence only of the twelve because precisely here Luke's symbolics are operative. Just as the Passover is the meal of the old Israel, so the Lord's Supper is the meal of the new community.[14] The presence of the twelve represents for Luke the point of transition from the old community to the new. That the twelve are both male and Jewish is implicit in Luke's narrative and contributes (presumably) to the authenticity of the symbolism. The "apostles", as Luke understands them, bridge the gap between the old and the new.

At the same time, it is important to note that Luke underscores the presence of the twelve at the Last Supper because they, more than others, need to hear Jesus' message of servant leadership (22:24–30). This is made clear by their quarrel about greatness (22:24).[15] Their ministry is to be of a different order from that of the world. It is to be centered in hospitality and service; its authority is to be grounded in self-giving love for the other rather than hierarchical structures of domination. In many respects, the women in Luke's Gospel already exemplify this model of ministry. Indeed the Gospel begins in the perceptive insight and self-giving of Mary of Nazareth who, as the first christian in Luke's Gospel, courageously places herself at the service of God (1:38).[16] She understands the overturning of power which the good news implies (1:47–55). In this sense, it is not the women but the inner group of the twelve which needs the lesson of the Last Supper.[17]

What can we conclude from this in regard to Luke's account of the Last Supper? However attractive Quesnell's argument, we cannot impose consistency on Luke's narrative. Despite the enthusiasm of some scholars for Luke's positive portrayal of women, his presentation is in fact more ambiguous.[18] In the resurrection narrative, for example, the women receive no appearance of the risen Lord, despite their fidelity; Peter appears to be the primary witness to the resurrection (24:34). Moreover in Acts, the focus on women's discipleship and ministry is lost sight of as the narrative proceeds. Luke's focus becomes so intensely directed on

---

[14]Luke emphasises the Passover link more than the other Synoptics; see Fitzmyer, *Luke,* 2, 1378, 1390–92.

[15]For Kingsbury, *Conflict in Luke,* 127–31, Luke presents the disciples, particularly in the passion narrative, as examples of spiritual immaturity and incomprehension.

[16]So Fitzmyer, *The Gospel According to Luke I-X* (New York: Doubleday, 1981) 341, 725, and Francis J. Moloney, *Woman, First among the Faithful: A New Testament Study* (Melbourne: Dove, 1984) 47–8.

[17]For other examples of exemplary behaviour by women in Luke, see 1:39–45, 2:36–38, 7:36–49, 8:2, 8:42b–48, 10:38–42, 13:20–21, 15:8–10, 18:1–8, 12:1–4. See Jane Kopas, "Jesus and Women: Luke's Gospel", *Theology Today* 43 (1986) 192–202.

[18]On the androcentrism of Luke in more recent feminist writings, see Elisabeth Schüssler Fiorenza, *In Memory of Her: A Feminist Theological Reconstruction of Christian Origins* (London: SCM, 1983) 50–53, and "Theological Criteria and Historical Reconstruction: Martha and Mary: Luke 10:38–42", *Colloquy* 53 (Berkeley, CA: Center for Hermeneutical Studies, 1986) 1–12; also Elisabeth Moltmann-Wendel, *The Women Around Jesus: Reflections on Authentic Personhood* (London: SCM, 1982) 142–4; Jane Schaberg, "Luke", in Carol A. Newsom and Sharon H. Ringe (eds.), *The Women's Bible Commentary* (London: SPCK, 1992) 275–92; and especially Mary Rose D'Angelo, "Women in Luke-Acts: A Redactional View", *Journal of Biblical Literature* 109 (1990) 441–61. According to D'Angelo (pp. 448–60), Luke is concerned to educate women but also to present them as docile and controllable, in order to avoid misunderstanding in the public sphere; as a result, women are prominent yet also distanced from ministry.

the inclusion of the Gentiles that the inclusion of women, which is a strong characteristic of the Gospel, is hardly a theme of Acts beyond Pentecost. The same contradiction is apparent in the story of the Last Supper. It is true that it would make more sense of Luke's narrative that all the disciples, including women, are present at the Supper. Nonetheless, in Luke's anxiety to stress the symbolic function of the twelve, the role of the women is relativised. In the key events surrounding Jesus' passion and resurrection in Jerusalem, the discipleship of women is strongly visible at some points and strangely invisible at others. There seems no consistent rationale in Luke's theology for this motif of presence/absence.

WOMEN AND THE GOSPEL OF MARK

Assuming Mark to be one of the major sources on which Luke depends, we may well expect to find a similar dynamic in Mark as in Luke. Winsome Munro takes a negative view of Mark's presentation of women, arguing that the evangelist leaves women invisible until the last moment (15:40–41), where he has no choice but to disclose their (rather shocking) presence on the journey from Galilee to Jerusalem.[19] It is certainly true that Mark makes no explicit mention of women disciples on the journey to Jerusalem as Luke does. Munro's point, however, is a debatable one.[20] There is no reason to assume in the early parts of Mark's Gospel that "disciple" is a term reserved only for males.[21] In fact, Mark does not explicitly mention women earlier in the Gospel as disciples because only in the passion and empty tomb narratives is the response of male and female disciples differentiated.

Mark's story of the Easter events is bounded on either side by the fidelity of women disciples: the unnamed woman of the anointing (14:3–9) and the women disciples at the cross and empty tomb (15:40–41, 16:1–8). Whether the empty tomb story signifies fidelity or infidelity is, however, a moot point. Do the women disciples flee from the tomb in silence as a sign of disobedience to the angelic command (16:7)? Or is their response an indication of a deeper fear, a sense of awe accompanied by holy silence? An impressive case has been put forward by a number of scholars who have seen in the women's reaction to the resurrection a parallel to that of the men in regard to the cross. According to this

---

[19]W. Munro, "Women Disciples in Mark?", *Catholic Biblical Quarterly* 44 (1982) 225–41.

[20]See Ched Myers, *Binding the Strong Man: A Political Reading of Mark's Story of Jesus* (New York: Orbis, 1988) 407: "Far from being 'invisible' in Mark . . . women emerge as the true disciples."

[21]A number of scholars have argued that after Mark 3:13 the term 'disciples' is identified with the twelve; for example, R. Bultmann, *The History of the Synoptic Tradition* (Oxford: Blackwell, 1963) 67; and Leonhard Goppelt, *Theology of the New Testament* (Grand Rapids: Eerdmans, 1983) I.210–11. Against this, see Martin Hengel, *The Charismatic Leader and His Followers* (Edinburgh: Clark, 1981) 81–82; Ernest Best, *Disciples and Discipleship: The Gospel According to Mark* (Edinburgh: Clark, 1986), 131–61; and Vincent Taylor, *The Gospel According to St. Mark* (London: Macmillan, 1952) 230. See Michael J. Wilkins, *The Concept of Disciple in Matthew's Gospel as Reflected in the Use of the Term Μαθητής* (Leiden: Brill, 1988) 166–7.

theory, all disciples, whether male or female, prove themselves inadequate and in need of the miracle of faith.[22]

There is an equally strong, and in my view stronger, case for the other view: that the fear and silence of the women is a response (albeit temporary) to the awesome and ineffable power of God witnessed in the empty tomb.[23] In this interpretation, the women's reaction is not only not disobedient, it is entirely appropriate in response to an epiphany. This interpretation is supported by Mark's previous allusions to the discipleship of women in the context of the passion narrative. First there is the anointing at Bethany (14:3–9), which intrudes into the story of Judas' betrayal (14:1–2, 10–11) and prefigures what the evangelist will later reveal about the women. Secondly, the revelation of women's presence (15:40–41) happens at perhaps the most dramatic point in the Gospel: immediately following the death of Jesus and the centurion's confession (15:37, 39). Mark now reveals to the reader that women have been among Jesus' companions and disciples from the first because, in contrast to the men who have betrayed, fled or denied their Lord, they have remained faithful. The language of these verses is the technical terminology of discipleship and ministry (ἀκολονθέω διακονέω).[24]

Mark's account of the women's presence at cross and empty tomb is deeply ironical. For the evangelist, the twelve fail in the dual role which Jesus has assigned to them. In the first place, they are to "be with him" in his ministry as companions (ἵνα ωσιν μετ᾿ αὐτοῦ, Mark 3:14), supporting as well as learning from him. Where the twelve fail in this role, the women's faithful presence carries it through;[25] they succeed in "being with him" in a situation where to be with Jesus is a frightening option.[26] Their faithful presence extends also, as we have seen, to the empty tomb. The three women who are at the three key narrative points of cross, burial and empty tomb[27]—Mary Magdalene, Mary the mother of James and Joses, and Salome—correspond to the three privileged males, Peter, James and

---

[22]See, for example, John D. Crossan, "Empty Tomb and Absent Lord (Mark 16:1–8)" in W. H. Kelber (ed.), *The Passion in Mark: Studies on Mark 14–16* (Philadelphia: Fortress, 1976) 149; Thomas E. Boomershine, "Mark 16:8 and the Apostolic Commission" *Journal of Biblical Literature* 100 (1981) 225–39; T. E. Boomershine and G. L. Bartholomew, "The Narrative Technique of Mark 16:8", *Journal of Biblical Literature* (1981) 213–23; Norman Perrin, *The Resurrection Narratives. A New Approach* (London: SCM, 1977) 30–35; and Mary Ann Tolbert, "Mark", in Newson and Ringe, *Women's Bible Commentary*, 273–4.

[23]For this view, see R. H. Lightfoot, *The Gospel Message of Saint Mark* (Oxford: Clarendon, 1950) 80–97; David Catchpole, "The Fearful Silence of the Women at the Tomb: A Study in Markan Theology" *Journal of Theology for Southern Africa* 18 (1977) 3–10; also Donald Senior, *The Passion of Jesus in the Gospel of Mark* (Wilmington, DE: Glazier, 1984) 137; and Athol Gill, "Women Ministers in the Gospel of Mark" *Australian Biblical Review* 35 (1987) 18–19. Elizabeth Struthers Malbon, "Fallible Followers: Women and Men in the Gospel of Mark", *Semeia* 28 (1983) 44–6, believes the silence and fear "are as much signs of the limits of humanity in the presence of divinity as signs of fallibility as followers . . . " (p. 44).

[24]See W. D. Davies, *The Setting of the Sermon on the Mount* (Cambridge: Cambridge University Press, 1964) 422–3. Against this, see the discussion on "following" by Jack D. Kingsbury, "The Verb *Akolouthein* ('To Follow') as an Index of Matthew's View of His Community", *Journal of Biblical Literature* 97 (1978) 57–62.

[25]According to Moltmann-Wendel, *Women Around Jesus*, 110–111, the women fulfil Jesus' teaching at 9:35 on serving as the true mode of discipleship and leadership.

[26]The same irony is also present in the burial of Jesus by Joseph of Arimathaea (15:42–46): it is not one of the twelve who lovingly buries Jesus but a wealthy outsider—probably even a member of the Sanhedrin (Luke 23:51); see Senior, *Passion of Jesus in Mark*, 132–134.

[27]See Perrin, *Resurrection Narratives*, 19–20.

John. In contrast to the three men who are unable to stay awake and share Jesus' suffering at Gethsemane, the three women steadfastly share the intimacy of Jesus' death and burial.[28] Similarly, the second part of the apostolic commission is fulfilled by the women. According to 3:14, the twelve are appointed "in order that he might send them out (ἀποστέλλω) to proclaim"[29] At the empty tomb, it is not the twelve who are given the message and sent out to proclaim, but the women (16:7). Here again the apostolic role of the twelve is forfeited to the women.[30]

When we turn from this to Mark's narrative of the Last Supper, we find a situation which is at first glance similar to Luke's presentation. In the preparation for Passover, Mark refers to οἱ μαθηταί (14:12, 13, 14, 16; see also 14:32) and at v. 17 suddenly narrows the focus: "when evening fell he came *with the twelve.*" Moreover the scenes following the Last Supper are unclear. Some features of the narrative imply only the presence of the twelve. Jesus' prophecy, for example, that all πάντες will desert him (14:27), is fulfilled at the arrest: "and leaving they all πάντες fled" (14:50).[31] On the other hand, there are features that suggest a wider group. At the Last Supper, Jesus refers to the betrayer as "one of the twelve, who dips with me into the bowl" (14:19) which makes sense only if others are present beside the twelve. The young man who flees naked (14:51–52) does not seem to be one of the twelve, since the narrator goes to the trouble of explaining that he is a disciple who has followed Jesus συνηκολούθει αὐτῷ, 14:51).[32] Since none of the twelve would be described in this way so late into the narrative, we can only conclude that Mark, or the tradition behind him, presupposes the presence of a wider group at Jesus' arrest. As in the case of Luke's account, it is difficult to know who is actually present.

In other respects, however, Mark is very different from Luke, particularly in the theology which emerges in the final chapters of Mark's Gospel. At the heart of the Markan passion narrative is the anomalous contrast between the failure of the twelve in their apostolic role and the fidelity of the women.[33] The motif of

---

[28]The fact that Mark describes these women as watching the crucifixion "from afar" does not invalidate the point. As Susanne Heine rightly comments (*Women and Early Christianity: Are the Feminist Scholars Right?* [London: SCM, 1987], 77–8), the presence of the women at the cross and the tomb is politically dangerous, given that Jesus is crucified as an enemy of the (Roman) state; see also Frank J. Matera, *Passion Narratives and Gospel Theologies. Interpreting the Synoptics Through their Passion Stories* (New York: Paulist, 1986) 48, and Moltmann-Wendel, *Women Around Jesus,* 111. Against this, see Struthers Malbon, "Fallible Followers", 43.

[29]According to Elisabeth Schüssler Fiorenza, "The Twelve", in L. Swidler and A. Swidler (eds.), *Women Priests: A Catholic Commentary on the Vatican Declaration* (New York: Paulist, 1977) 114, the twelve have no symbolic significance in Mark vis-à-vis the new Israel. See also Best, *Disciples and Discipleship,* 158–61, who argues that Mark is uninterested in the twelve and sees them as having no post-Easter role.

[30]See Elisabeth Schüssler Fiorenza, "The Twelve and the Discipleship of Equals" in M. L. Uhr (ed.), *Changing Church and Changing World* (Australia: Millenium Books, 1992) 117: "Far from being the exemplars of apostolic discipleship, the Twelve are the negative blueprint of right discipleship."

[31]Senior, *The Passion in Mark,* 84. For the link with Mark 13:14–20, see Matera, *Passion Narratives,* 27

[32]On the meaning of this episode as symbolic of the "nakedness" of the disciples at this point in the narrative, see H. Fleddermann, "The Flight of a Naked Young Man (Mark 14:51–52)", *Catholic Biblical Quarterly* 41 (1979) 412–18.

[33]As Schüssler Fiorenza rightly points out (*In Memory of Her,* 319), this polemic against the twelve primarily revolves around the issue of "right leadership".

presence/absence functions ironically, as we have seen: narrative expectations are overturned in the unexpected presence of the women and absence of the men. The same dynamic undergirds the narrative of Mark 14 with its contrast between the two "Supper" stories. In the first, the nameless woman (herself a symbol of presence/absence) recognises Jesus' death and responds in faith and love.[34] So important is this moment of insight that the woman's symbolic action is placed at the heart of the proclamation of the gospel (14:9). In the second, the Lord's Supper is bounded on one side by the betrayal (14:18–21), and on the other by the denial and flight (14:27–31) of the twelve. Supper is contrasted with Supper, as assumptions of female invisibility and male visibility are overturned.

Thus in spite of its awkwardness at certain points, Mark's narrative through passion and resurrection is concerned with a reversal of human values in which insiders become outsiders and outsiders become insiders (see 10:31). In this presentation, women as disciples take on (almost by default) a major narrative and theological role. They represent the outsiders—the poor and marginalised—who are open and receptive to the kingdom, in contrast to the powerful who resist or oppose it. Above all, by their presence/absence, the women reveal the way in which God is present: not in power and self-assertion, but rather at those points of vulnerability and powerlessness where, in human terms, God is presumed to be absent.[35] The presence/absence of the women in Mark becomes symbolic, in other words, of the way the kingdom operates in the world.

WOMEN AND THE GOSPEL OF MATTHEW

Matthew's account of the passion is close to Mark's and therefore displays many of the characteristics we have already noted. Matthew follows the overall Markan structure so that women once again bound the passion narrative with their faithful and insightful presence (26:6–13, 27:55–56, 61).[36] The major point of difference is the account of the resurrection where the women at the empty tomb (this time only Magdalene and "the other Mary", 28:1) encounter in person the risen Christ; he is present to them in a way which goes beyond the terse Markan narrative. Nevertheless Matthew's narrative has its own dynamic in regard to the discipleship of women, which is not easy to understand. While in Mark the relationship between presence and absence is both ironical and paradoxical, in Matthew the dynamic is much less ironical and strains the narrative to the point of contradiction. Presence and absence exist in uneasy relationship within Matthew's narrative.

---

[34]According to Tolbert, "Mark", the portrayal of the woman coheres with the way women have been presented earlier in the Gospel: "Most women . . . are anonymous, act boldly without letting traditional customs or conventions prevent their faithful service, seek no fame or status for themselves, and show the fruitfulness of faith in the kingdom." (p. 272; see also pp. 270–71).

[35]See Dorothy A. Lee-Pollard, "Powerlessness as Power: A Key Emphasis in the Gospel of Mark", *Scottish Journal of Theology* 40 (1987) 1–16.

[36]See the chiastic structuring suggested by Elaine M. Wainwright, *Towards a Feminist Critical Reading of the Gospel According to Matthew* (Berlin: Walter de Gruyter, 1991) 122–3.

In Matthew's Gospel the tension between presence and absence is clearest in the narrative of the resurrection. Matthew has two appearances of the risen Lord: the first to the two women near the empty tomb and the second to the eleven on the mountain in Galilee. The guards, on the other hand, witness both the earthquake and the appearance of the angelic messenger at the tomb (vv.2–3), but later are bribed to deny it (vv. 11–15).[37]

This "hierarchy" of responses is in some tension with the order of appearances and commissionings. The main appearance of the risen Christ is to the eleven on the mountain in Galilee (28:16–20) because it is there that the church receives its commission for mission: the eleven, not the women, are given authority to baptise and teach. Except for the guards, whose status is unchanged, the position of the men and women is here inverted. Whereas in terms of *response* the order was:

> women (positive response)
> men (qualified response)
> guards/religious leaders (negative response),[38]

now in terms of *appearance and commission* it has shifted to:

> men (commission for mission)
> women (commission for meeting between eleven and Jesus)
> guards ("commission" to deny resurrection)

There are also other difficulties with the narrative, particularly in the opening episode. The angelic message (vv. 5, 7) is reiterated by Jesus in almost identical wording (v. 10), making the appearance of the Lord to the women seem redundant.[39] Moreover the angel—unlike Jesus—speaks of the encounter in Galilee in the second person plural ("there *you* will see him", v. 7), implying that the women are to be present at the meeting, which of course they are not. At the same time, the narrator is careful not to dismiss the women's role; they still retain their importance as witnesses to the resurrection.[40] These narrative inconsistencies suggest an uneven editing of earlier traditions in which the women originally played a more prominent role.[41] Here in Matthew's redaction we find a contradictory dynamic between presence and absence.

---

[37]On the contrast between the women and the guards, see Daniel Patte, *The Gospel According to Matthew: A Structural Commentary on Matthew's Faith* (Philadelphia: Fortress, 1987) 394–7.

[38]The women approach Jesus ($\pi\rho\sigma\epsilon\lambda\theta o\acute{u}\sigma\alpha\iota$), clasp his feet ($\dot{\epsilon}\kappa\rho\acute{\alpha}\tau\eta\sigma\alpha\nu$) and worship him ($\pi\rho\sigma\epsilon\kappa\acute{u}\nu\eta\sigma\alpha\nu$, v. 9). The response of the eleven on the other hand is more cautious and less wholehearted: they see ($\dot{\iota}\delta o\nu\tau\epsilon$s), worship ($\pi\rho\sigma\epsilon\kappa\acute{u}\nu\eta\sigma\alpha\nu$) and some of them doubt ($o\acute{\iota}$ $\delta\grave{\epsilon}$ $\dot{\epsilon}\delta\acute{\iota}o'''\tau\alpha\sigma\alpha\nu$, v. 17). See Wainwright, *Gospel According to Matthew*, 145–6.

[39]F. W. Beare, *The Gospel According to Matthew* (Oxford: Blackwell, 1981) 542.

[40]As is pointed out by E. Schweizer, *The Good News According to Matthew* (London: SPCK, 1975) 523–4, the women in Matthew do not come to the tomb to anoint the body; instead they are "turned into witnesses" (p. 524).

[41]Wainwright, *Gospel According to Matthew*, 353, sees "tension, ambiguity and anomaly" as characteristic of Matthew's presentation of women as a whole; she demonstrates the way in which male, patriarchal tradition and female counter-tradition stand in considerable tension within the Gospel (pp. 316–52).

How does this relate to Matthew's presentation of the Last Supper? Matthew contains the same ambiguity that we have found in the other Synoptics. The term οἱ μαθηταί is used in an unspecified way until the actual Passover (οι μαθηταί, 26:8, 17, 19, 26, 35, 36, 40, 45, 56; οἱ δώδεκα, 26:14, 20, 47) where it is suddenly narrowed to the twelve: "When it was evening, he took his place *with the twelve*" (26:20).[42] The confusion is not so obvious in Matthew as in Mark, however, since Matthew makes no reference to the flight of the naked disciple. This could be a way of tidying Mark's narrative and making it clear that only the twelve (or, more strictly, the eleven) are present in the events following the Last Supper. On the other hand, it could be part of Matthew's tendency to tone down Mark's disapproval of the disciples.[43] Even though Matthew refers to οἱ μαθηται in Gethsemane at two points where Mark speaks more vaguely of "them" (Matt 26:40, 45/ Mark 14:37, 41), it is still unclear whether all the disciples are asleep or just the inner circle (Peter and the two "sons of Zebedee", 26:37). The same problem is present at 26:45–46 (see Mark 14:41–42): does Jesus address these remarks to all the assembled group or only the three? Are all the disciples present at the arrest or again only the three?

In spite of the confusion, Matthew is clear about the exclusive presence of the twelve at the Last Supper. Nevertheless, this certainty creates a sharp tension within the narrative. As in Mark, the women in Matthew are absent at the Last Supper but present at the cross (Matt 27:55–56); they do not fail their Lord as do the twelve (see Matt 26:31–35, 56b, 69–75).[44] They are present at the tomb but inexplicably absent for the Great Commission. These tensions are already evident at the beginning of Matthew's Gospel, where four Old Testament women are anomalously present in a patrilineal genealogy (1:3, 5, 6; also v. 16).[45] However, unlike Mark, Matthew never manages to deal theologically with the tension between women's presence and absence; in his hands, it becomes a contradiction. The twelve, for all their failing at the cross and empty tomb, are given authority at the resurrection; whereas the women, who are faithful in their presence at the cross

---

[42]For a discussion of the term μαθητής in Matthew, see Wilkins, *Disciple in Matthew's Gospel*, 126–172, and Ulrich Luz, "The Disciples in the Gospel according to Matthew", in G. Stanton (ed.), *The Interpretation of Matthew* (Philadelphia: Fortress, 1983) 98–128. On the relation between μαθητής and gender, see Janice Capel Anderson, "Matthew: Gender and Reading", *Semeia* 28 (1983) 20, who argues that their gender prevents the women being classified as disciples; see also Kingsbury, "The Verb *Akolouthein*", 61, and Wainwright, *Gospel According to Matthew*, 330–39.

[43]On this see G. Barth, "Matthew's Understanding of the Law" in G. Bornkamm, G. Barth, and H. J. Held, *Tradition and Interpretation in Matthew* (2nd ed.; London: SCM, 1982) 105–112.

[44]See, for example, the "mother of the sons of Zebedee" whose two brief appearances in Matthew—with her sons on the journey to Galilee and at the foot of the cross—represent a small parable of discipleship: "She has exchanged the places of spiritual honour, which seemed to her so desirable, for the places of execution. She has acted differently from her sons and exposed herself to the danger of arrest" (Moltmann-Wendel, *The Women Around Jesus*, 126–127). On the fidelity of women throughout Matthew's passion narrative, see Amy-Jill Levine, "Matthew", in Newson and Ringe, *Women's Bible Commentary*, 261–2.

[45]See Raymond E. Brown, *The Birth of the Messiah: A Commentary on the Infancy Narratives in Matthew and Luke* (New York: Doubleday, 1977), 71–4; Capel Anderson, "Matthew", 7–10; Donald Senior, "Gospel Portrait: Images and Symbols from the Synoptic Tradition", in D. Donnelly (ed.) *Mary, Woman of Nazareth. Biblical and Theological Perspectives* (New York: Paulist, 1989) 97–103; Wainwright, *Gospel According to Matthew*, 155–76, and Edwin D. Freed, "The Women in Matthew's Genealogy", *Journal for the Study of the New Testament* 29 (1987) 3–19.

and empty tomb, are excluded from the Last Supper and Great Commission and the authority with which both are invested. Matthew's Gospel leaves us in the final analysis with a disturbing and irresolvable tension between male and female, presence and absence, authority and disempowerment.

WOMEN AND THE GOSPEL OF JOHN

Although John's account of the Last Supper has no direct parallel with the institution of the eucharist (see John 6:51–58), only in this Gospel is there a real possibility for women's presence at the Last Supper.[46] At the beginning of the Last Supper narrative, the fourth evangelist speaks of Jesus loving "his own" (ἀγαπήσας τοὺς ἰδίους τοὺς ἐν τῷκόσμῳ) and loving them "to the end" (εἰς τέλος ἠγάπησεν αὐτούς, 13:1b). Later in the footwashing, "his own" are identified as "disciples" (τοὺς πόδας τῶν μαθητῶν, 13:5). Unlike the Synoptics, John does not list the twelve, although he is familiar with the tradition and names several of them. The twelve are mentioned four times, though appearing in only one episode, and play a minor role in the Gospel (6:67, 70, 71; 20:24). There is no reason to assume therefore that "his own"—the disciples gathered at the footwashing—are limited to the twelve. The presence of a wider group coheres with John's overall tendency to minimise the role of the twelve and focus on the more inclusive category of discipleship.[47]

There are a number of disciples in John's Gospel outside the twelve who belong among "his own", most of whom are women.[48] In the story of the raising of Lazarus we are told of Jesus' love for Martha, Mary and Lazarus (ἠγάπα, 11:5). This is a particularly significant allusion, since Mary of Bethany prefigures the footwashing by anointing Jesus and drying his feet with her hair (11:2, 12:3).[49] The mother of Jesus is also among those loved by Jesus. His love for her is handed over to the beloved disciple at the foot of the cross at the founding moment of the christian community (19:27).[50] As a result, the beloved disciple takes the mother of Jesus "into his own" (εἰς τὰ ἴδια; see also 1:11). Mary Magdalene hears and recognises the voice of the Good Shepherd at the empty tomb, revealing herself to be among "his own" (20:16; see 10:3–5, 14–16, 20). Finally, the beloved disciple is one whose very name places him pre-eminently among "his own" and who is named among those present at the Last Supper. Nowhere in John's Gospel is there any

---

[46]See Schüssler Fiorenza, *In Memory of Her*, 325.

[47]See Raymond E. Brown, *The Community of the Beloved Disciple: The Life, Loves, and Hates of an Individual Church in New Testament Times* (New York: Paulist, 1979) 81–88, 186, 191.

[48]See Brown, *Community*, 191–2.

[49]So Sandra M. Schneiders, "Women in the Fourth Gospel and the Role of Women in the Contemporary Church" *Biblical Theology Bulletin* 12 (1982) 42; see also J. R. Michaels, "John 12:1–22", *Interpretation* 43 (1989) 287–91, and John C. Thomas, *Footwashing in John 13 and the Johannine Community* (Sheffield: Sheffield Academic Press, 1991) 57–60, 82.

[50]See Raymond E. Brown, *The Gospel According to John XIII-XXI* (New York: Doubleday, 1966) 922–927; C. K. Barrett, *The Gospel According to St. John* (2nd ed.; London: SPCK, 1978) 552; and R. Alan Culpepper, *Anatomy of the Fourth Gospel, A Study in Literary Design* (Philadelphia: Fortress, 1983) 133–4.

[51]See, for example, Brown, *Community*, 31–34; Rudolf Schnackenburg, *The Gospel According to St. John* (London: Burns & Oates, 1982) 3,375–388, especially pp. 383–7.

indication that he belongs among the twelve. If he is indeed outside the twelve, as is likely, it is significant that he has so prominent a role at the Supper (13:23–26).[51]

It is a characteristic of John's Gospel, moreover, that women disciples (and also the beloved disciple) are included in places where we might expect the activity and testimony of Peter and the twelve.[52] The mother of Jesus initiates the ministry of Jesus by her faith (2:5), even though the disciples who first come to Jesus or are called by him are all males, traditionally associated with the twelve (1:35–51). The Samaritan woman is the first to act in an apostolic role in the Gospel and is contrasted both with Nicodemus and with Jesus' disciples (an unspecified group) who lack understanding (4:27–38).[53] Martha of Bethany makes the key messianic confession of the Gospel (11:27), a confession reserved for Peter in the Synoptics (Mark 8:29 / pars.).[54] Mary Magdalene is the first to receive an appearance of the risen Christ; her search for him continues where Peter and the beloved disciple have returned home (20:10).[55] Her faith is prior to that of Peter and the twelve (see 20:9) and she is the first to receive an appearance of the Lord (20:14),[56] she is the first to be named by him, to acclaim him and to receive the apostolic commission (20:16–18).[57]

On this basis, there is no reason to assume the absence of women at any of the major narrative points of the Gospel. The group which John designates as "disciples" is wider than the twelve and includes women as well as men. Both at the foot of the cross and in the resurrection narratives, women and men are co-equally present as models of faith, discipleship and apostolicity. The mother of Jesus and the beloved disciple present at the foot of the cross symbolise the founding of the believing community out of the death of Jesus (19:26–27); Mary Magdalene and Thomas receive personal appearances of the risen Lord and act as a bridge between the resurrection of Jesus and the Easter faith of the new community (20:1–2, 11–18, 24–29). Similarly, at the Last Supper there is no reason to deny women's presence alongside the men. Not only the passion and resurrection narratives, but indeed the tenor of the whole Gospel warrants such a conclusion. Women's presence is more securely located in this Gospel than in any of the others.

WOMEN AND THE HISTORICAL JESUS

From the discussion so far, we can see how vague and even contradictory the relationship is between disciples and the twelve in the Gospel narratives, particularly in relation to women. There is a strong implication, coming especially from the

---

[52]Brown, *Community*, 189–92.

[53]See Mary M. Pazdan, "Nicodemus and the Samaritan Woman: Contrasting Models of Discipleship", *Biblical Theology Bulletin* 17 (1987) 145–8; Culpepper, *Anatomy*, 137; Ben Witherington, *Women in the Earliest Churches* (Cambridge University Press, 1988) 175, and Schneiders, "Women", 40.

[54]Schneiders, "Women", 41.

[55]On the problem of the status of the beloved disciple's faith at 20:8–9, see Brown, *John* 2.987.

[56]See Schüssler Fiorenza, *In Memory of Her*, 332–3.

[57]See Gail R. O'Day, "John", in newson and Ringe, *Women's Bible Commentary*, 300–302. Schüssler Fiorenza sums up the role of women in the Fourth Gospel (*In Memory of Her*, 326): "at crucial points of the narrative women emerge as exemplary disciples and apostolic witnesses".

Synoptics and Acts, that originally women played a greater role in early traditions and the twelve a lesser role. The position of the twelve in the Gospel narratives is certainly an ambiguous one and points to a complex pre-history.[58] On the one hand, multiple attestation points to the twelve as an integral element of early traditions: the Synoptics, Q, Acts, John and Paul. On the other hand, it is clear that the notion of the twelve grew in importance in the latter decades of the first century C.E., in some places more than others. In the Johannine tradition, as we have seen, and also the Pauline tradition, the concept of the twelve does not have much significance. Moreover Paul's notion of what constitutes an apostle is broad enough to include an unspecified number outside the twelve, including himself, James, the Lord's brother, and Junia (a woman)—almost certainly reflecting early tradition (see especially 1 Cor 5:5–10; also Gal 1:19, Rom 16:7).[59] Even Luke, who makes most of the twelve and is far more restrictive than Paul in his understanding of "apostle",[60] does not have a major role for the twelve after Pentecost; their function seems more representative than actual. After the martyrdom of the apostle James (Acts 12:1–2), the twelve are not re-constituted.[61]

There are also historical problems with the status of the twelve within the ministry of Jesus. Given the undeniable Jewishness of Jesus, it is not easy to explain the appointment of the twelve or the nature of the role given them.[62] One possibility is that their appointment has more to do with Jesus' eschatological sense of the kingdom of God than the forming of a new community in opposition to Judaism (see Rev 21:14).[63] It is also unlikely that the twelve were equivalent to, or even identified with, the "apostles" in Jesus' ministry.[64] Thus while the tradition of the twelve is an early one, it is almost impossible to guess its original status. There is even the possibility that it is an early post-Easter construct.[65] If the latter, it

---

[58]See R. H. Rengstorf; "$\delta\omega\delta\epsilon\kappa\alpha$", *Theological Dictionary of the New Testament* 2, 325–328 and Taylor, *St. Mark*, 619–27.

[59]On the feminine name "Junia", see Bernadette Brooten, "'Junia . . . Outstanding among the Apostles' (Romans 16:7)", in *Women Priests*, 141–4; also Brendan Byrne, *Paul and the Christian Woman* (Homebush: St. Paul Publications, 1988) 69–74

[60]On this, see Quesnell, "Women at Luke's Supper", 65–6, and Elisabeth Schüssler Fiorenza, "The Apostleship of Women in Early Christianity" in *Women Priests,* 135–40.

[61]See Lüdemann, *Early Christianity,* 33, and Schüssler Fiorenza, "The Twelve and the Discipleship of Equals", 118–119.

[62]Witherington, *Genesis of Christianity,* 111, finds nothing problematic in the view that "[Jesus] affirmed the headship and authority of the man when He chose Twelve men from among His disciples to be leaders of the community". For Madeleine I. Boucher, "Women and the Apostolic Community," in Swidler and Swidler, *Women Priests,* 153, Jesus is simply acting "according to the social norm he knew".

[63]Schüssler Fiorenza, "The Twelve", 119–120, argues that the role of the twelve in Luke is essentially an eschatological one. See the statement of the Executive Board of the Catholic Biblical Association of America, "Women and Priestly Ministry: The New Testament Evidence", *Catholic Biblical Quarterly* 41 (1979) 610–611.

[64]See Schüssler Fiorenza, "The Twelve and the Discipleship of Equals", 111–14, and Rengstorf, "$\mu\alpha\theta\eta\tau\acute{\eta}$s", 450–52.

[65]Schüssler Fiorenza, "The Twelve," 116; the suggestion goes back to Wellhausen, *Einleitung in die Drei Ersten Evangelien* (2nd ed.; Berlin: Georg Reimer, 1911) 138–47. Against this, see Joachim Jeremias, *New Testament Theology* (London: SCM, 1971) 233–4; also E. P. Sanders, *Jesus and Judaism* (London: SCM, 1985) 98–106, who argues, however, that nothing can be known of the significance Jesus gave to the twelve.

may have arisen out of the earliest community's experience of rejection in its mission to Israel. Whatever conclusion we draw on this issue, one point remains. Whether embedded in the ministry of the historical Jesus or not, the notion of the twelve owes much of its significance to later redaction. Such redactional activity explains why the larger group of disciples who shared Jesus' final Meal were written out of later traditions of the Last Supper. The traces of their presence, however, can still be seen in the uneven editing of those traditions, particularly within the Synoptic framework.[66]

There are more obvious indications from the practice of the historical Jesus that women disciples were among those present at the Last Supper. At the very least, the Last Supper was a "fellowship" meal, reflecting Jesus' practice of table-fellowship and symbolising the hospitality, bonding in friendship and spirituality shared by Jesus' disciples (see Mark 3:31–35/pars.).[67] It is indisputable that women, along with other marginalised and alienated groups, were present on such occasions. The Gospels record a number of stories which include women in Jesus' table sharing (e.g. Mark 14:3–9/Matt 26:6–13; Luke 7:36–50, 11:38–42; John 12:1–8). On these occasions women play a significant role, acting as ideal disciples or models of christian ministry. Behind these stories lie historical traditions of Jesus' radical inclusion of women in his table-sharing and ministry generally.[68]

This of course has implications for other groups among Jesus' disciples, quite apart from women: the poor, tax-collectors, children. It is hard to conclude from this that, on the critical occasion of his final meal, Jesus excluded disciples such as these. It is hard to believe that Jesus departed from the radical inclusiveness which so characterised his ministry,[69] and caused such offence to members of the religious establishment. Elsewhere in the Gospels Jesus condemns this kind of exclusiveness, and calls for hospitality and openness of heart (for example, Mark 9:38–40/Luke 9:49–50). The point is more forceful if the Last Supper was in fact a Passover meal (as the Synoptics present it).[70] It is even less probable that Jesus would have celebrated Passover apart from the band of disciples who had accompanied his pilgrimage from Galilee. Why would the women disciples and other male disciples have been excluded? Why, for that matter, would children have been excluded? Passover was a time of family celebration which included men, women and children, each of whom had a vital role to play in the ritual.[71] It is highly improbable that Jesus would have departed from Jewish practice to celebrate the feast only with a select few of his disciples. Where would the rest of his disciples have celebrated Passover? That Jesus excluded most of his

---

[66]See Schnackenburg, *St. John*, 3.385–6.

[67]See Jeremias, *Theology*, 114–21, 169.

[68]Jeremias, *Theology*, 223–7.

[69]On Jesus' praxis of "inclusive wholeness", see Schüssler Fiorenza, *In Memory of Her*, 118–30.

[70]As is argued by Jeremias, *The Eucharistic Words of Jesus* (Oxford: Blackwell, 1955) 1–60; see also Fitzmyer, *Luke*, 2.1378–9. Against this, see D. E. Nineham, *Saint Mark* (Harmondsworth: Penguin, 1963) 455–8 and E. Schweizer, *The Good News According to Mark* (London: SPCK, 1970) 294–7; Taylor, *St. Mark*, 535–539, leaves the question open.

[71]See Quesnell, "Women at Luke's Supper", 70–71.

disciples, including women, from his last meal, whether or not this was a Passover meal, contradicts both the Judaism which nurtured him and also the table-praxis of his ministry.

CONCLUSION

The question of women's presence or absence at the Last Supper is a complex one, taking us into the intricate dynamics of history, tradition and redaction within the Gospels. The confusion of the Synoptic accounts and the evidence of the Fourth Gospel suggest an early tradition—going back to the historical Jesus—of a wide group of disciples at the Last Supper. This group would undoubtedly include the presence of women whom Jesus included in his "discipleship of equals" and table community.[72] This means that between the historical events of Jesus' last days and the writing of the Synoptic Gospels, the tradition of the twelve has intervened in such a way as to displace other groups of disciples. Nevertheless the displacement is by no means complete and the footprints of women can still be traced. We are left with the uneasy testimony of texts which both conceal and reveal; in which women are both present and absent.

It would be an easy thing, on this basis, to dismiss the Synoptic accounts of the Last Supper as the result of androcentric redaction. Androcentrism is undeniable even within the most sacred traditions of the New Testament; nevertheless it is not the whole story. In the painful struggle of the early christian communities in relation to Judaism—first as insiders and later as outsiders—the notion of the twelve became important for a number of them in justifying their identity. By the time we reach the Synoptic Gospels, the tradition of the twelve is so entrenched that it can be used in a variety of ways, both positive and negative. To varying degrees, the Synoptic Gospels expose the faithlessness of the twelve and contrast it with the fidelity of the women. However, whereas Luke and Matthew have a positive focus on the role of the twelve for its symbolic import, Mark uses the same tradition in a way which seems to undermine it.

The hermeneutical implications of these reflections are two-sided. In the first place, as interpreters of Scripture we need to acknowledge the androcentrism of our interpretation of these texts. Leonardo da Vinci's painting of the Last Supper, which presents only the twelve with Jesus, arises out of a long tradition of reading the text in this way—though it is not the only way the tradition has presented the Last Supper.[73] At the same time, the Gospels themselves need to be read with an awareness of the androcentric bias which is embedded in their narrative and

---

[72]Schüssler Fiorenza, *In Memory of Her*, 140–51.

[73]See Dorothy Irvin, "The Ministry of Women in the Early Church: The Archaeological Evidence", *Duke Divinity Review* 45 (1980) 76–86, quoted in Inger Marie Lindboe, "Recent Literature: Development and Perspectives in New Testament Research on Women" *Studia theologica* 43 (1989) 157, who argues from second century catacombs that one of the main figures at the Last Supper is identifiably female. See T. F. Torrance, *The Ministry of Women* (Edinburgh: Handsel, 1992) 1–4, who points to an early catacomb in which Priscilla is depicted as one of seven presbyters concelebrating the eucharist.

theological framework. Just as we develop awareness of other aspects of the biblical worldview which are alien to our own, so we need to develop a similar awareness in relation to issues of gender. Feminist readings of biblical narrative have endeavoured to stress this point in a number of ways.[74]

Secondly, however, a "hermeneutics of suspicion" can only ever be the first step to an authentic reading of the text. We need to recognise also the ways in which the New Testament has transcended the limitations of its environment. As Susanne Heine points out, we need to distinguish between the claim or promise of the gospel and its translation into practice, if only to realise that the latter is always partial.[75] The absence of women at the Last Supper along with their paradoxical/contradictory presence at other critical points in the story of Jesus' passion and resurrection, testify to both dimensions: "the claim and its betrayal." The liberating gospel of Jesus stands in some tension with the androcentrism which reflects the compromise of later generations. The two are not easily separable: presence and absence coalesce in these stories in a complex way. However, at a deeper level of interpretation—sometimes reading "against the grain",[76] sometimes reading in harmony with the narrative as a whole—a different picture emerges. It is women's graced presence at the Supper, just as it is at cross and empty tomb, which is finally where the gospel is to be found for us today.

---

[74]See especially Schüssler Fiorenza, *In Memory of Her*, 3–40, and *Bread Not Stone: The Challenge of Feminist Biblical Interpretation* (Edinburgh: Clark, 1984) 1–22. See also Sandra M. Schneiders, *The Revelatory Text: Interpreting the New Testament as Sacred Scripture* (San Francisco: Harper, 1991) 181–6; Mary Ann Tolbert, "Defining the Problem: The Bible and Feminist Hermeneutics", *Semeia* 28 (1983) 113–126; and Pheme Perkins, "Women in the Bible and Its World", *Interpretation* 42 (1988) 33–44. See also the four Old Testament narrative studies in Phyllis Trible, *Texts of Terror: Literary-Feminist Readings of Biblical Narratives* (Philadelphia: Fortress, 1984). For a different approach to the same issue, see Heine, *Women and Early Christianity*, 1–13.

[75]*Women and Early Christianity*, 147–54.

[76]See Wainwright, *Gospel According to Matthew*, 39–42.

Chapter 4

The Issue of Heterosexism

Sodom and Gomorrah
(Genesis 19:1–29) on the Internet:

The Implications of the Internet
for the Study of the Bible

Susanne Scholz

Disclaimer: Unless otherwise noted, the websites discussed in this article were active on the day of publication. Due to the transitory nature of some websites, some of these links may no longer be active. The opinions expressed in these websites are not necessarily those of the author or the Journal.

INTRODUCTION

When the Internet became accessible to the wider American public during the 1990s, people reacted in several ways. One group worried about the societal consequences of this technology. They imagined that in the near future people would become incapable to communicate directly with one another and instead prefer to share their most intimate experiences via email and in the chat rooms of the Internet. This group feared that people would turn into emotionally alienated, digitally dependent creatures.

In contrast to this rather pessimistic assessment, another group greeted the Internet enthusiastically. This reaction swept over the United States. The Internet appeared to be a new god, providing ultimate freedom from time and space. Connected to a computer with a modem, one could be anywhere. The Internet promised access to the vast treasures of human civilizations from the past and present. People anticipated eagerly that computers would soon provide access to huge amounts of information and knowledge with a simple key stroke. Everything outside the realm of the Internet appeared to be extremely limited and removed from society's bright future. Reaching the remotest corners of the planet, the World Wide Web (WWW) shrunk any distance to a digital moment of transmission. For many people, the Internet seemed the perfect technological tool that might save them from human finitude. No religion, no theological concept, and no biblical story has provided this collective sense of salvation in recent decades.

A mediating position has certainly been another reaction to the Internet. By now many people have accepted the presence of the Internet in their daily lives. Even though they do not believe that the digital world will change the world as we know it, they use the Web to see what people in Cyberspace do and say. This response to the Internet is more cautious compared to the other two reactions. However, over time it might become the general attitude toward the WWW.

Initially, the enthusiastic response dominated the assessment of the digital world. The worriers were barely audible. Who wanted to be on their side when the Internet would allow us to overcome all human limitations? However, only a few years after the American public has accepted the presence of *.com* in radio, television, and address books, the situation seems to have changed. The Internet is losing its mystery. Even those speculating in the stock market have become hesitant to invest into emerging Internet companies. Research has also shown that factors, such as class, race, and gender, limit people's access to computers and thus the Internet. Digital practices reflect existing social structures (see Ebo). The technology-eager United States has sobered up from the initial euphoric response to the Web.[1]

The Internet has still grown enormously. Personal, organizational, and commercial Web pages abound. Selling and buying have become regular online procedures. Most searches lead to thousands of Web pages, which require days of reading or a systematic elimination process to refine one's search. Some scholars compare the relative anarchy of the Web with the early stages of printing when

---

[1]Describing this process, Calcutt maintained that the initial enthusiasm of online users is "an expression of the desire in each and every one of us to escape our mutual alienation and reconnect with each other." Calcutt called this experience "the 'one world' feeling." It wanes the more we go online and become used to the Internet as a part of the society in which we live: "So it is that the more being online becomes everyday experience as lived in our anti-social society, the more its universalizing potential tends to be obscured, and even forgotten entirely" (126).

publishers had not yet invented books but faced only unnumbered and loose sheets. It was then that printers invented a method to organize the stacks of individual papers. They enclosed them in covers, included tables of content, chapters, and indexes, and learned to advertise their products. Similarly, the Web is still in its early stages, consisting of "an undifferentiated mass of information in cyberspace." It is not yet "categorized, organised, packaged and presented in a way that makes it a pleasurable and satisfying prospect for today's information buyers" (Spender: 60). At the same time the Internet is an uncensored medium. If one has the money and the skill to create a Web page, one can do so. In that sense the Internet is a "great equalizer" (for a critical assessment, see Wolf). Opinions and issues become visible that often remained more hidden in the pre-Internet culture. Thus, the digital world represents an exquisite environment to examine contemporary perceptions and views on almost any subject.

The Bible has also been a subject on the Internet. Biblical topics, names, and even particular texts appear in thousands of Web pages. Organizations and individuals create Web pages to inform the Internet public about their biblical interpretations, religious views and convictions. In other words, the Internet is also a rich storage house for understanding the role of the Bible in contemporary culture.

THE STORY OF SODOM AND GOMORRAH ON THE INTERNET

Many people, even those with limited biblical knowledge, know of Sodom and Gomorrah. Although those people may not remember that the story is told in the book of Genesis, they probably know that the cities were destroyed for some sort of evil doing, often associated with sexual depravity. It is, therefore, not surprising that a search on the Internet for "Sodom and Gomorrah" yields thousands of hits. To be precise, on July 18, 1999 the search engine *Excite* offered 7,219 and *Yahoo* 4,594 hits. This number is huge, particularly if compared to the scholarly work on Genesis 19. For example, *Old Testament Abstracts*, the thrice-yearly bibliography of literature relating to the Old Testament, lists twenty-six entries related to Genesis 19:1–29 for the ten-year period from 1989 to 1998. Less than thirty scholarly articles discuss the story in contrast to thousands of Web pages. The comparison indicates that Sodom and Gomorrah play a significant role in the imagination of Internet users.

Many Web pages on Sodom and Gomorrah fall into three categories. The first category contains Web pages that offer literal readings of Genesis 19 to argue for or against homosexuality. Characterized as "prooftexting," this approach is a common interpretive method for typically non-academic sites. The second category are those Web sites that use archaeology to prove the historicity of Sodom and Gomorrah. The third category are Web sites that have commercial interests related to Genesis 19. The following analysis explores sample Web pages of these categories towards a threefold purpose. The examination demonstrates how Sodom and Gomorrah have infiltrated popular digital culture. It assesses the importance of the digital appropriations for biblical studies. And it helps to understand the role of the Bible in contemporary society.

It was not always easy to decide which Web page deserved detailed scrutiny. Over time, however, four criteria emerged that determined the value of a Web page. The first criterion related to the digital life span of a Web page. All Web pages examined in this article have been available since January 1998. Some authors changed the look of their site but they usually did not change the content. The second criterion concerned the depth of the argumentation. The selected Web pages offer better discussions than others. The third criterion established whether a Web site contained an unexpected or unusual appropriation of Sodom and Gomorrah. The fourth criterion related to the aesthetic quality of a Web page. Most Web pages examined in this article have a particularly intriguing look. All criteria helped to select representative Web pages for the analysis about Sodom and Gomorrah on the Internet.

PROOFTEXTING FOR AND AGAINST HOMOSEXUALITY

Numerous Web pages appropriate the story of Sodom and Gomorrah in their discussions on homosexuality. Created by religious organizations and individuals, some Web pages argue for the rejection of homosexuality, whereas others plead for acceptance. All of them illustrate the religious and cultural function of Genesis 19 inside and outside the digital world (for examples from the printed world, see Goldberg, Hallam). The Web pages also exemplify that regardless of their view on homosexuality many Web sites share a similar interpretive premise. Reading Genesis 19, authors of Web pages assume that they simply repeat what "the Bible says." They construct their "message" under the banner of a literal reading. They fail to understand that as readers they are involved in the interpretive process before they even open the Bible. They are the ones who choose and arrange the various biblical passages to support their particular views.[2]

Three Web pages illustrate the anti-gay stance. The home page of "Christian Friends" (http://www.lovejesus.org/), a group of born-again Christians, provides a link to a section called "Devotional Reading." An article on "Sodomy" appears in the collection. Ben Drake is the credited author. The characterization of "Sodomy" as "devotional reading" has an ironic twist which is probably not intended (http://www.lovejesus.org/sodomy.htm). The essay explains that the word "sodomy" has its etymological origin in Genesis 19. Based on this explanation, the page describes the content of the biblical tale. Drake stresses that no other sin but sodomy "warrants this kind of treatment," namely the destruction of the two cities. The article concludes: "Here we see there was one righteous in Sodom (apparently none in Gomorrah) and as soon as he was removed, all the rest were destroyed. THAT is what God thinks of this awful sin."

---

[2]See the brief and good summary on this epistemological issue in Walter Truett Anderson, (ed.), "Introduction: What's Going on Here?" chap. in *The Truth About The Truth: De-Confusing and Re-constructing the Postmodern Word* (New York: Putnam Book, 1995).

The "Christian Friends" and the author of this particular article, Drake, maintain that Sodom was destroyed because the inhabitants committed what the contemporary word "sodomy" signifies. Drake's preconceived notion about the meaning of "sodomy" informs the interpretation. Accordingly, homosexuality was already rejected during biblical times. The argumentation, however, indicates that Drake is not aware of his hermeneutical reading process. He believes to present what the Bible says about "sodomy." He does not realize that he projects the contemporary meaning of "sodomy" back into the biblical story to get the interpretation that supports his view on homosexuality. In other words, Drake fails to understand that his preconceived view about homosexuality determines the outcome of his interpretation.

Another Web page argues similarly. It is more informative than the previous one because of its detailed argumentation. Thus, it exposes its hermeneutical assumptions more clearly than Drake's essay. The author, Mark A. Copeland, calls himself "simply a Christian," who is a preacher of a congregation in Florida. He offers what he calls a "non-sectarian approach to the Scriptures" (http://www.christianlibrary.org/authors/Mark_A_Copeland/back.htm). Copeland believes that his interpretations "are simply the result of my own personal studies of God's Word" and thus unhindered by denominational or creedal doctrine. He believes that "God has spoken fully and completely through His Son Jesus Christ and His apostle and prophets whose words are contained in the Bible." From the beginning then, his interpretive approach is evident. Copeland considers the Bible as divinely inspired as the Word of God.

This naïve hermeneutical stance is carried out in an essay entitled "Homosexuality—A Christian Perspective" (http://www.christianlibrary.org/authors/Mark_A_Copeland/hom.htm), one of Copeland's numerous "Executable Outlines" (http://www.christianlibrary.org/authors/Mark_A_Copeland/home.htm). The page acknowledges that his discussion of homosexuality is "an effort to speak the truth in love on a volatile subject." The essay contains seven sections. One addresses specifically "What the Bible Teaches About Homosexuality"(http://www.christianlibrary.org/authors/Mark_A_Copeland/hom/hom_03.htm).

The discussion begins with a question: "Assuming that one accepts the Bible to be the Word of God, and as such the final authority on issues it discusses, what then does it have to say about the subject of homosexuality?" Posed as a question, the statement maintains not only that the Bible is the final authority, but also that the Bible addresses the issue of homosexuality. Copeland sees himself as the neutral deliverer of the biblical message on homosexuality because he accepts the Bible as the word of God. The Bible "tells" him what to believe, a major interpretive premise of the fundamentalist approach (see Boone, Wilcox).

This conviction shapes the argumentation of the whole essay. Quoting from the New Testament (2 Pet 2:6), Copeland asks why the two cities Sodom and Gomorrah suffered such "unique judgment." He answers his question by emphasizing the importance of Genesis 19:5. This verse proves that "homosexual conduct was 'a grievous sin' in the days of the patriarchs." The Sodomites sinned because they wanted to know the visitors "carnally." Copeland rejects the notion of "homosexual theologians" that the "sin" of the Sodomites was their inhospitable behavior towards the visitors.

Three basic ideas characterize Copeland's interpretation. First, he suggests that only homosexual theologians consider inhospitality the sin of the Sodomites. Disliking those who present the argument, Copeland simply rejects the interpretive possibility. However, several commentators consider inhospitality as the "sin" of the Sodomites without disclosing their sexual orientation (Parker: 6–8; Wenham: 54–55; Visotzky: 77–78). Second, Copeland underlines the importance of the verb "to know." He refers to Genesis 4:1, 17, Lot's response in Genesis 19:6–7, and other texts from the Hebrew Bible and the Greek Testament (e.g. Lev 18:22; 20:13; 1 Cor 6:9–10; Rom 1:18–23) to ascertain that the verb means "to have sexual intercourse." The biblical connections allow him to regard Genesis 19 as a story against homosexuality. Third, Copeland stresses that the Bible is the Word of God. Consequently, one either accepts the Bible as the Word of God and its "simple" message or one rejects both.

> I can understand that those who do not believe in God or who do not accept the Bible as the Word of God would strongly disagree with such an evaluation of homosexuality. . . . May those who profess to accept the Bible as the last word never hesitate to accept what it says, no matter, how "politically incorrect" our society might say it is.

Caught in this dualism of either accepting or rejecting the Bible as the word of God, Copeland understands those who do not consider the Bible as the word of God. He appreciates their decision to reject the biblical message. However, Copeland accepts the message since he believes that the Bible is the Word of God.

A third Web page further illustrates how Web sites mention Genesis 19 to argue against homosexuality. The page belongs to a radio program called "Cutting Edge," which is "dedicated to warning and informing God's people" (http://cuttingedge.org/radio.html). Belonging to a "fundamental independent Baptist Church," the site maintains that the Bible is "the only revelation of God and His Son, Jesus Christ." Different from the previously described Web page, this page does not simply cite biblical texts to dismiss homosexuality. The page also claims to present "spiritual insights into 'The New World Order' so startling you'll never look at the news the same way again." Thus, Genesis 19 is only a part of a much larger argument. Since the end of the world and the second arrival of the Messiah are near, the program has a threefold goal. It "explain(s) the goals and aspirations of the New World Order," shows "how its implementation will affect the average American citizen and family," and explains "how families are being influenced now, before we actually move into this system." In other words, the page belongs to a group of fundamentalist Christians who present a political analysis from their particular Christian perspective.

One section relates directly to the story of Sodom and Gomorrah and is entitled "America: Guilty of Sin of Sodom" (http://cuttingedge.org/ce1063.htm). The section is the transcript of a show once aired by radio host David Bay. He parallels the situation of the biblical towns Sodom and Gomorrah to contemporary America:

> The sin of Sodom . . . [was] taking control of that society. Everyone was taught in every state institution, from schools to churches, that homosexuality was just as valid and desirable as heterosexuality. . . . This same situation is now developing in America, as we move to teach our children the same lie straight out of the pit of hell. If the Lord Jesus Christ tarries, America will produce the same type of society as did Sodom and Gomorrah. America is the new Sodom.

The radio host obviously criticizes the growing acceptance of homosexuality, which in his view was the sin of Sodom and Gomorrah. It once led to the destruction of the two cities. Now it threatens the United States of America, the new Sodom. Like the previous two examples, this Web page advances an anti-gay stance with an interpretation of Genesis 19. Claiming to repeat only the biblical message, the author does not acknowledge that his opposition to homosexuality shapes his reading of the Bible.

The anti-gay stance is not the only one found on the Internet. Genesis 19 is a popular text also for those who counter this view. They, too, post their Web pages. Three Web sites shall illustrate their argumentation. The Web page of the "Universal Fellowship of Metropolitan Community Churches," "a worldwide fellowship of Christian congregations serving all people, with a special outreach to the world's g/l/b/t communities" (http://www.ufmcchq.com/menu.htm) provides a link to a paper entitled, "Homosexuality and the Bible . . . Bad News? Or Good News?" (http://www.ufmcchq.com/handb.htm) by Nathan L. Meckley. He explains that "sadly, the Bible is often used as a weapon to 'bash' gays and lesbians. "In a reconciliatory tone he emphasizes that "such hurtful things are not a reflection of Christ, or the way God wants the church to be, or even what the Bible really says." In fact, Meckley maintains that the Bible supports gays and lesbians: "The Bible does have Good News for gays and lesbians, and it does not say what you may have thought it did about homosexuals." He explicates this position in a paper entitled, "Sodom, Creation, and the Law" (http://www.ufmcchq.com/sodom/htm). There he states that the sin of Sodom was not homosexuality. According to Meckley, this view is a "misinterpretation of Scripture." It ignores biblical references which describe the reasons for the destruction of the two cities. For instance, Ezekiel 16:49–50, "an equally inspired book of the Bible," maintains that the sin of Sodom and Gomorrah was pride and inhospitality.

As a member of The Universal Fellowship of Metropolitan Community Churches (UFMCC), "a worldwide fellowship of Christian congregations serving all people and especially gay/lesbian/bisexual/transgender communities," Meckley obviously supports a pro-gay position. However, his interpretation relies on a reading strategy similar to his opponents. He simply quotes selected biblical passages, mentioning one verse to explain another. Like the anti-gay Web authors, Meckley bases his argument on a literal reading of the Bible.

This common interpretive method, which is so typical for popular discourse on the Bible, appears also in many other pro-gay Web sites. An example is the Web site of "Whosoever: An Online Magazine For Gay, Lesbian, Bisexual and Trans-gendered Christians" (http://www.whosoever.org/). Inspired by John 3:16, the home page describes the overall purpose of this magazine: "*Whosoever* strives to assure gays, lesbians, bisexuals and transgendered persons that they are in-cluded when the Bible says 'whosoever believeth in him should not perish but have everlasting life.'" A quote from the Bible justifies the stance of the pro-gay online magazine.

The page provides a link to biblical passages "used to condemn homo-sexuality" (http://www.whosoever.org/bible/index.html). The editor, Candace Chellew, explains the reason for this section:

> Of the negative or critical e-mails I receive from critics of this magazine and its mission, I'd estimate 90% of them advise me to read my Bible. Specifically, I am urged to read at least one or all of the six passages we as GLBT Christians know as the "clobber passages." These are the verses, we're told, where God con-demns homosexuality in no uncertain terms. . . . In this section of *Whosoever* we explore the six "clobber" passages and several other verses used as "proof-texts" of homosexuality's condemnation.

Genesis 18–19 is one of those passages (http://www.whosoever.org/bible/genesis.htm). Summarizing the content of the story, Chellew states that "it is unclear from these few verses whether God demolished the city because the citi-zens: 1. were uncharitable and abusive to strangers, 2. wanted to rape people, 3. engaged in homosexual acts." The interpreter then maintains that "the Church has traditionally accepted the third explanation" whereas "the first explanation is *clearly* the correct one" (emphasis added). To prove that the sin of Sodom and Gomorrah did not consist in the inhabitants' sexual preference but in their inhos-pitality, Chellew lists other biblical texts mentioning Sodom and Gomorrah. She concludes: "We are faced with the inescapable and rather amusing conclusion that the condemned activities in Sodom had nothing to do with sodomy."

By referring to biblical texts, Chellew maintains that the story condemns the inhospitality and idolatry of the inhabitants, not their homosexuality. Although the position defended is the opposite from the anti-gay Web pages, the methodol-ogy is similar. Chellew's final argument is a good example:

> NOWHERE in the Scriptures does it say that the sin of Sodom and Gomorrah was homosexual sex. Even if the specific point of the story was concerning a sexual matter, rather than hospitality, the issue is rape not homosexuality. Jesus claimed the issue was simply one of showing hospitality to strangers (Luke 10:12). How ironic that those who discriminate against homosexuals seem to be true practitioners of the sin of Sodom.

Like many Web pages, this one also claims to reiterate the biblical text. Only this time Genesis 19 is not used as "a clobber passage." Joined with other biblical pas-sages, Genesis 19 criticizes inhospitality. However, neither Chellew nor her oppo-nents realize that they prooftext their position.

A third example is a Web page that lists several Jewish sources to support a pro-gay stance. The site is particularly interesting because it includes extrabiblical texts. Published by the "Interfaith Working Group," the page is entitled "What was the sin of Sodom?" It offers a collection of classical Jewish texts related to Genesis 19 (http://www.iwgonline.org/docs/sodom.html). Robert Kaiser, the compiler and commentator of the site, explains that "classical Jewish texts concur that God did *not* destroy Sodom and Gomorrah because their inhabitants were homosexual. Not at all. Rather, the cities were destroyed because the inhabitants were nasty, depraved, and uncompromisingly greedy" (emphasis in the original). Kaiser then presents seven texts, adds a bibliography of more sources, and concludes: "So the next time someone tries to use Genesis 19 as an excuse to justify homophobia, we can educate them by giving them these sources to read and consider." The compiler is hopeful. He believes that more and more sources will convince his opponents to view Genesis 19 in a different way. Kaiser seems unaware that the participants in this debate share a similar methodological premise despite their opposing views. They quote biblical texts to support their preconceived views. Both sides, however, fail to address their common hermeneutical assumptions. They agree on two accounts. To them, the Bible is authoritative, and readers do not construct their interpretations.

The examples illustrate that, in the digital world, Genesis 19 plays a central role for discussions on homosexuality. The Web pages also show the methodological similarity between opponents and proponents of homosexuality. The Internet is for them another communication avenue to air their positions and to gain power in the contemporary discussion on homosexuality. The Web pages also demonstrate that the digital debate is relatively polarized. Web pages are either for or against homosexuality. To prove one or the other view, interpreters rely on the same methodological approach to the Bible—they proftext.

PROVING SODOM AND GOMORRAH WITH ARCHAEOLOGY

A significant number of Web pages presents archaeological findings to prove that the cities of Sodom and Gomorrah existed and were destroyed as described in the biblical account. A home page, entitled "Welcome to the Mysteries of the Bible," is a good example of this recurrent interest (http://www.biblemysteries.com/). The author of the page, Michael S. Sanders, welcomes Web surfers with this invitation: "Every week participate in an exploration of another Bible Mystery." The site supposedly advances "scholarly rather than religious" views. The link "Previous Lectures" opens a long list of articles. Two are entitled "Sodom & Gomorrah" and "Sodom & Gomorrah—Part II."

In the first lecture Sanders states that Bible scholars and archaeologists are uncertain about the precise location of Sodom and Gomorrah and three other cities mentioned in Genesis 14:3 (http://www.biblemysteries.com/library/deadsea/). However, he claims to settle the uncertainties with his lecture. Referring to scholarly research, Sanders identifies the location of the two cities. The work of two American archaeologists, Arabic names of five archaeological sites, and the archaeological site of *Bab edh-Dhra* prove that the discovered sites are not the original locations of the towns. Archaeologists found only the secondary towns that people built after Sodom and Gomorrah were destroyed. The ruins of the original Sodom and Gomorrah are now flooded by the Dead Sea. This hypothesis enables Sanders to suggest an early date for Genesis 19. Openly dismissing scholarly hypotheses on the historical literary development of the biblical narrative, he regards the story as an eye-witness report.

> The Biblical account could NOT have been made up by scribes after the Babylonian Exile. We will prove categorically that the work of Rast and Schaub absolutely confirms the Biblical account and that account must at least have been contemporary. How else could the "writer" know that an area which is the most barren surface of the earth could in ancient times have supported an enormous population when today nobody lives anywhere near there. . . .

Sanders refers to Walter E. Rast and R. Thomas Schaub's work to argue for a literal reading of the biblical tale, although neither scholar supports this position. In other words, Sanders skews archaeological discoveries and biblical scholarship to prove that the biblical events happened as described in Genesis 19.

His second lecture continues this effort (http://www.biblemysteries.com/lectures/sodom2/). Again, Sanders uses archaeological findings to justify the historical correctness of the biblical account. He rejects the dates of biblical scholarship and describes his view about the events, among "the major Mysteries of the Bible."

> My revised chronology dates the Exodus to the end of the early Bronze Age and the final destruction of these sites coincides with the area-wide catastrophe which occurred at that time with the mass migrations and disruptions that followed. The vast cemeteries were therefore begun some 1,800 years earlier using conventional dating figures (much less using the conventional chronology) and were created as a result of the mass slaughter that took place at the time of the destruction of Sodom and Gomorrah as recounted in the Bible.

In his effort to validate the biblical account. Sanders subordinates the archaeological data to the biblical text like many early "biblical archaeologists." However, he argues for a biblical chronology that has little support from the scholarly community. In his view Sodom and Gomorrah were destroyed in 1882 B.C.E. To give his argumentation scholarly weight, he includes satellite images from the area. In his opinion, they show that the excavated sites represent only the relocated cities further away from the Dead Sea (http://www.biblemysteries.com/library/deadsea).

As the description indicates, Sanders' presentation is problematic for several reasons. His work is driven primarily by religious conviction. With the help of archaeology, he hopes to demonstrate the reliability and the validity of a literal reading of Genesis 19. He calls himself a "biblical scholar," although he does not disclose his credentials. Despite his intention to present scholarly views, he is only superficially interested in scholarly work. He quotes his own words from one lecture to another, but he does not engage scholarship. The origins of his sources are unclear, and some bibliographical references are outdated.[3]

Another archaeological site openly admits its religious interests (http://www.netlink.co.uk/users/cmc96/sodom.html).[4] The title, "Sodom & Gomorrah: Read how these lost cities, now found, were revealed and why they were destroyed; Was Sodom and Gomorrah a preview of what is to come again soon?!" reflects a theme common to many fundamentalist Web pages. The page aims to prove that the two cities once existed and were later destroyed. The author uses references to Genesis 19 and archaeological findings, a quote from an assyriologist, and objections from "skeptics" to support this position. Moreover, he argues that "aerial or satellite pictures" and "balls of burnt sulphur" are "scientific proof that actual fire and brimstone rained down upon this area" (i.e. Sodom and Gomorrah).

The author of the page also suggests that the story is a prediction of the near future. He states first that the archaeological findings provide the "physical evidence in these last days of man's rule . . . so that all mankind will have undeniable proof that what the Bible says is TRUE." Then he continues: "These discoveries indicate that the Second Coming of Christ could well be very soon." Archaeological findings enhance the fundamentalist Christian message of doom. The page concludes:

> Exhaustive research has ascertained the following: These 5 [cities]—specified in the Bible—are the only known sites in the world covered by pellets of burnt sulphur. For pictures of Sodom and Gomorrah send for the video below!! It's on film.

Lacking a bibliography for the "exhaustive research," the Web page insists that archaeology proves the historical reliability of Sodom and Gomorrah. The page ends with an invitation to order a video entitled "Surprising Discoveries: Lost Cities by the Dead Sea; Exciting Discoveries Beneath the Dead Sea (Over 2 Hours of Compulsive Viewing)" as if the video offered visual evidence for the existence of Sodom and Gomorrah.

Claiming the historical reliability of the biblical narrative, both sample Web pages use archaeology to give their interpretation scientific weight. However, their references to archaeological data are incomplete, outdated, and a mélange of scattered quotes and photos. Sometimes commercial interests take over. In one case the selling of a video ends the discussion about the historicity of Sodom and Gomorrah. This tendency towards commercialism becomes the openly acknowledged purpose of Web pages in the third category.

---

[3]For example, he mentions the journal, *Biblical Archaeology Review,* which published several more recent articles on Sodom and Gomorrah (21, 4 [1995]: 9–10; 22, 4 [1996]: 10; 23, 1 [1997]: 70). Sanders includes only an article from 1980. He claims that the article was published in 1978 but the correct bibliographical reference is: "Have Sodom and Gomorrah Been Found?" *Biblical Archaeology Review* 6, 5 (1980): 27–36.

[4]This site was no longer available on July 18, 1999. For a similar Web page visit http://www.biblerevelations.org/ronwyatt.htm.

COMMERCIAL, CULTURAL, AND FANTASTIC REFERENCES

Numerous Web pages try to catch the attention of Web surfers to buy an item on Sodom and Gomorrah. For instance, *filmnoir.com* sells a colorful poster of the movie "Sodom and Gomorrah" (1963) for $65.00 (www.filmnoir.com/sodom.htm) The top line of the poster reads: "Inside their hearts no good existed . . . inside their cities no God!" Connotations about the immorality, societal chaos, and sexual corruption inspired the colors. They are all kept in somber tones of red, brown, and yellow.

Also for sale are religious videos that want to prove the historicity of the biblical story. The Web page of "The Wellspring Collection" is an example of a conservative Christian company that uses the Internet for such commercial outreach. Entitled "Acts of Faith" (http://www.wellmedia.com/collection/spirit/itb.html),one of their videos features Genesis 19. The advertisement states that the film "introduces us to some of the Bible's first great heroes." The four heroes and their stories are "Noah and The Flood, Abraham and Sarah, Sodom and Gomorrah—Lot and His Wife, [and] Abraham and Isaac." The list indicates the special attention given to Sodom and Gomorrah. The names of the towns precede the hero, i.e. Lot. The 56-minute video costs $14.95.

Entitled "Sodom & Gomorrah: A Tail [*sic*] of Two Cities," another video exploits the sexual connotations of Genesis 19. The video sells for $28.95 from a company that specializes in pornographic videos, books, and photos. The Web page explains that "not too often do we get Biblical stories adapted to porno scripts, and it's not hard to guess why. But here, it works, and again, it's not hard to guess why—the story of Sodom and Gomorrah is tailor-made for the blue screen" (http://search.excaliburfilms.com/moviepgs/sodom.htm). Videos like this one perpetuate the idea that God destroyed Sodom and Gomorrah because of the inhabitants' sexual corruption. The strategy is simple. The video makers rely on connotations of evilness and sexual depravity to seduce their audience to buy the film.[5]

Songs and paintings also feature the biblical story. The Web page by "Scarlett Rose," a Montana-based religious music group, contains a song entitled "Sodom & Gomorrah" (http://www.scarletrose.com/songs.html#s&g):

you think you know me	remember Lot!
you don't have a clue	they were at his door
well I've been listening	he tried to leave but they wanted some more
listening to you	filled with lust
you put me down	and evil desire
any way you can	but what they got
I think you know just who I am	was a pillar of fire
	CHORUS

---

[5]For the same business strategy from the fashion industry, see "Clothing from Gomorrah's Closet" http://www.gomorrah.com.

CHORUS

Sodom & gomorrah

look what's coming for ya'!

Sodom & gomorrah

don't say I didn't warn ya'!

you think you know it

you know the times

you look around

you don't see signs

I know you know it

you know it's true

but you don't know

what might happen to you

CHORUS

Only the chorus and the second strophe refer explictly to Genesis 19. The chorus identifies the pronoun "you" with Sodom and Gomorrah and the pronoun "I" as the warning voice of God. The song appropriates the story as if it will happen again in the very near future. Scarlet Rose, the "I" voice of God, sings the song to warm "you," the listeners identified with Sodom and Gomorrah. "You" should remember what happened to Lot. Similarly, the group's homepage mentions that "Scarlet Rose is striving to be a one stop center for Christian sound recording . . . from concept [*sic*] to completion!" (http://www.scarletrose.com.faq.html.).

Another Web page illustrates the cultural and educational potential of the Internet. It presents the painting "The Destruction of Sodom" (http://sunsite. unc.edu/cgfa/dore/p-dore11.htm) by the book illustrator Gustave Dore who lived in France from 1833 to 1883. The author of the Web page, Carol L. Gerten, started the site "so that I could make fine art easily available over the Web, in hopes that others would enjoy it as much as I do." The site exemplifies that the Internet has indeed enormous potential to store cultural resources, including art on Genesis 19, and to make them accessible beyond museums.

Trivial references to Genesis 19 appear in many Web pages. One page, no longer on-line, belonging to "Jon" featured photos of cats and dogs, one of which showed two cats named "Sodom and Gomorrah," while two other photos depicted each cat individually. Who would have thought to name a cat this way! Another page (http://www.chank.com/fonts/sodom.html) sells a font called "Sodom and Gomorrah." Yet another outlet for trivial references about Sodom and Gomorrah are jokes. The home page of "Reverend Fun" (http://www.gospelcom.net/rev-fun/ 02-96/rf-02-96art.shtml) provides a link to a cartoon in which one thin white male throws another thin white bespectacled male into the air. The text underneath the image reads: "Of all the sins that the people of Sodom and Gomorrah committed casting lots was the worst" (see similar sites at http://www.ladyhawk.com/ jam27.html and http://www.jokepost.com/one.html). Flattening the narrative to a simple and shallow joke, the story of Sodom and Gomorrah seems to lack any profound and serious meaning. It is as if the religious fervor that inspires so many other Web pages is completely absent here. Sodom and Gomorrah are no longer synonyms for evil. They have become harmless, vapid placeholders in silly jokes.

Perhaps the most unexpected reference to Sodom and Gomorrah centers on UFOs. This page, entitled "UFOlogy: Is Disclosure on the Horizon" (http://www/geocities.com/Areas51/Shadowlands/6583/ufology.html), discusses every conceivable topic related to contacts with aliens. The link "Extraterrestrials" (http://www.geocities.com/Areas51/Shadowlands/6583/et.html) opens a site called "Extraterrestrials: Ancient Cultures/ET Timeline" (http://www. geocities.com/Areas51/Shadowlands/6583/et03.html). Beginning with the year "310,000,000 B.C., the first evidence of man . . . in 'Ethiopia, Africa' and 'Tanzania'," the timeline mentions Sodom and Gomorrah at the year "1900 B.C." A description states: "There is strong evidence that the Bible's ancient cities of 'Sodom and Gomorrah' next to the Dead Sea, were destroyed by a nuclear explosion. Sand vitrications found in Iraq next to the Dead Sea [*sic!*] resemble those produced by an atomic bomb. Notice it's called the Dead Sea! High salt content." The site sparkles with depictions of aliens, stars, and UFOs. Imaginatively incorporating names, themes, and events that include Genesis 19, the page does, however, not disclose the sources of information.

Commercial, cultural, and fantastic references to Sodom and Gomorrah pull the biblical story into the trivia of contemporary life. At the same time the references show that digital culture is steeped in allusions to Genesis 19. Whenever the names of Sodom and Gomorrah are mentioned, people respond. Their minds do not run blank, even if they do not know the Bible and they think of themselves as secular. The range of meanings for Sodom and Gomorrah is impressive. Evilness, sexual depravity, and even pet names are among the connotations. Sodom and Gomorrah continue to inspire the imagination of people.

ACCOUNTING FOR THE NEXUS OF BIBLE AND CULTURE

The Internet is like a new "gold rush" or "Wild West" where fortunes are made and new stakes are claimed. People make lots of money by inventing new digital services and offering their goods online. Web pages on Sodom and Gomorrah are bountiful, fanciful, and imaginative; they all have an agenda. Some refer to the story to reject homosexuality, others to defend it. Several pages want to prove the historicity of the biblical account and use every old and new discovery to promulgate their convictions. Numerous Web sites mention Sodom and Gomorrah to enlarge their sales of pornographic items, to come up with a joke, or to present their account of the universe. In their eagerness to communicate and to make money, individuals and groups rush to let the world know how they approach Sodom and Gomorrah. The Internet gives them the opportunity to create and post Web pages on any subject of their whimsy. What can biblical scholars learn from this anarchic situation of the new "Wild West"?

First, the Internet demonstrates that "culture" cannot and should not be ignored in biblical studies. Scholars have begun to study the Bible in culture as a formal topic only since the 1980s.[6] Reading *in front of* the biblical text, researchers

---

[6]For an overview of this historical development in the discipline of biblical studies see West. For an introduction about the development of biblical cultural studies, see Exum and Moore. The growing interest in the Bible and culture found an early expression in the six-volume series edited by Gaustad and Harrelson. The volumes were the result of the centennial celebration of the Society of Biblical Studies in 1980.

have become interested to focus on readers and their contexts. The examination of references to Sodom and Gomorrah shares this growing interest to understand the connections between Bible and (digital) culture. The analysis guarantees that the many different approaches to the Bible are not lost, left unexamined, or unnoticed. The task becomes to trace biblical interpretations of past and present societies and to examine the values of these interpretations for reading the Bible today. This work has to include the Internet, one of the newest technological developments in which culture finds expression.[7]

Second, the Web pages exemplify that biblical interpretations reflect societal conflicts. When biblical scholars examine cultural areas such as the Internet, the field has the opportunity to get involved in understanding society. The research then contributes to "unravel the network of social, political, and economic factors which regulate both the production and the reception of literature"—i.e. the Bible (Lefevere: 189). The Web pages on Sodom and Gomorrah illustrate this point. The growing gap between literal Bible readers and secular forces in Western societies finds digital expression in the two basic approaches to Genesis 19. On the one hand, Genesis 19 constitutes "authoritative evidence" for views for or against homosexuality and for the historical accuracy of the Bible. On the other hand, many trivial references to Sodom and Gomorrah indicate that the largely secular society does not take seriously the content or meaning of the Bible. Sodom and Gomorrah receive attention in shallow jokes or catchy titles. Although mediating positions exist in this polarized discussion, they appear rarely in the digital world and thus remain in the background. The Web pages demonstrate that the Bible represents both a contested and a marginalized area of discourse in contemporary society.

If Web pages on Sodom and Gomorrah reflect social, political, and economic factors of society, how do professional readers of the Bible take them into account? Some might think that it is possible to interpret Genesis 19 regardless of such factors. Instead they might want to focus on the text itself or the history behind the biblical narrative. But much is to be gained from the integration of the digital world into biblical studies. As an expression of the world, the Internet provides a window to see how contemporary society treats the Bible and what the treatment discloses about society. In the case of Genesis 19 the digital world contributes to understanding the role and function of Sodom and Gomorrah in the context of contemporary struggles over sexuality, biblical authority, and secular indifference towards the Bible. These struggles are not new for scholars of the Bible but new for the analysis of the digital world. By taking this world into account, biblical scholars provide new evidence for the seriousness of these matters in contemporary Western culture.

Third, the situation on the Internet concerning Genesis 19 demonstrates that biblical studies have to reach out to the wider academic and non-academic world. The analysis documents that scholarly discourse is strangely absent on the Web. This situation is certainly not limited to biblical studies. Many academics lament

---

[7]See also Paula M. Cooey who urged to study the significance of new technologies like the Internet for the humanities (4).

the dearth of academic sites. Others debate about the merits of posting lecture notes on the Web. In the meantime literal and trivial assessments flood the Internet where they remain unchallenged. Search engines do not list scholarly discussions on Genesis 19.[8] Are they not yet available, or do search engines not find them because they are deeply buried in the computer networks of universities? Several issues might be involved. The resistance of posting scholarly work on the Web could be related to copyright protection. Once scholarly ideas, lectures, or papers are available to the world at large, they can be accessed for free. Professors might resist to give away their intellectual work. They might also be concerned that free access to scholarly work could reduce the number of students who have to pay for the privilege of attending colleges and universities. It could also be that researchers in biblical studies do not yet know enough about computer technology to make full use of the Web. Whatever the reasons, the lack of scholarly information on Genesis 19 constitutes a problem for the representation of Sodom and Gomorrah in the digital world.

The absence of biblical studies is also a problem for the reputation of the field. If biblical studies do not become visible and accessible to the general public, institutions of higher education might question the rationale for spending money on the field. Those in power at such institutions might come to believe that literal or trivial Bible readings are all there is to reading the Bible. The academic study of the Bible is often not known to them. Scholars from other disciplines might also start to think that biblical studies are disconnected from contemporary intellectual explorations. Therefore, the critical examination of the nexus of Bible and (digital) culture enhances the understanding of society and the appreciation for biblical studies. Sodom and Gomorrah are a case in point.

Bibliography

Anderson, Walter Truett (ed.) 1995 *The Truth About The Truth: De-Confusing and Re-constructing the Postmodern Word*. New York: Putnam.

Boone, Kathleen C. 1989 *The Bible Tells Them So: The Discourse of Protestant Fundamentalism*. Albany: State University of New York Press.

Calcutt, Andrew 1999 *White Noise: An A-Z of the Contradictions in Cyberspace*. New York: St. Martin.

Paula M. Cooey 1998 "Transformations of Humanistic Studies in the 21st Century: Opportunities and Perils." *Religious Studies News* February: 4.

Exum, J. Cheryl and Stephen D. Moore 1997 "Biblical Studies/Cultural Studies." Pp. 19–45 in *Biblical Studies/Cultural Studies*. Edited by J. C. Exum. Sheffield: Sheffield Academic Press.

Gaustad, Edwin S. and Walter Harrelson (eds.) 1982–85 *The Bible in American Culture*. 6 Volumes. Philadelphia and Chico: Fortress and Scholars.

Goldberg, Jonathan (ed.) 1994 *Reclaiming Sodom*. New York: Routledge.

Gunkel, Hermann 1997 *Genesis*. Translated by Mark E. Biddle. Macon, GA: Mercer.

Hallam, Paul 1993 *The Book of Sodom*. London: Verso.

Hamilton, Victor P. 1995 *The Book of Genesis: Chapters 18–50*. Grand Rapids: Eerdmans.

Lefevere, Andre. 1987 "'Beyond Interpretation' on the Business of (Re)Writing." *Comparative Literature Studies* 24, 1: 17–39.

Ebo, Bosah (ed.) 1998 *Cyberghetto or Cybertopia? Race, Class, and Gender on the Internet*. Westport: Praeger.

---

[8]An exception is the site by Michael Carden, a doctoral student from Australia: http://student.uq.edu.au/~101014/1SODOM.html.

Parker, Simon B. 1991 "The Hebrew Bible and Homosexuality." *Quarterly Review* 11, 3: 4–19.

Rast, Walter E. and R. Thomas Schaub (eds.) 1981 *The Southeastern Dead Sea Plain Expedition: An Interim Report of the 1977 Season* Ann Arbor, MI: American Schools of Oriental Research.

Spender, Dale 1995 *Nattering on the Net: Women, Power and Cyberspace*. North Melbourne: Spinifex.

Storey, John (ed.) 1996 *What is Cultural Studies? A Reader*. New York: Arnold.

Wenham, Gordon J. 1994 *Genesis 16–50*. World Biblical Commentary 2. Waco: Word.

West, Gerald O. 1995 *A Biblical Hermeneutics of Liberation: Reading the Bible in the South African Context.* Maryknoll: Orbis.

Visotzky, Burton L. 1996 *The Genesis of Ethics*. New York: Crown.

Wilcox, Clyde. 1992 *God's Warriors: The Christian Right in Twentieth-Century America*. Baltimore: Johns Hopkins University Press.

Wolf, Alexia 1998 "Exposing the Great Equalizer: Demythologizing Internet Equity." Pp. 15–32 in *Cyberghetto or Cybertopia? Race, Class, and Gender on the Internet*. Edited by B. Ebo. Westport: Praeger.

The Biblical Prohibition of Homosexual Intercourse

Martin Samuel Cohen

The decision by the United Church of Canada last summer to ordain homosexual candidates for the ministry has caused a great deal of furor across the country. Under normal circumstances, I would not feel obliged to comment on a debate which has no bearing on the Jewish community, but since a great deal of fuel is almost daily being thrown on the fire in the form of references, learned and less so, to the alleged Biblical prohibition of homosexuality, and since almost all of those references are based on what seems to me to be a flawed understanding of the context in which the Biblical verses in question appear, I would like to suggest what seems to me to be the correct interpretation of the prohibition that stands at the centre of the controversy.

Twice in the Torah, we find prohibitions of homosexual behaviour.[1] At Leviticus 18:22, we read, "You shall not have sexual intercourse with another man, for such is abominable behaviour." Again, at Leviticus 20:13, we read a similar remark:

Copyright 1990, The Haworth Press, Binghamton, NY. *Journal of Homosexuality*, "The Biblical Prohibition of Homosexual Intercourse (Lev. 18:22; 20:13)," vol. 19, no. 4 (1990): 3–20. Reprinted by permission.

"Two men who have sexual intercourse with each other have committed an abomination; they shall be put to death and the fault is theirs alone."[2] The Torah is silent as regards the reasons for this prohibition, beyond stating that such activity is abominable, just as it is silent regarding the motivation behind all the other sexual prohibitions.[3] Before beginning to explain what seems to me to be the meaning of these verses, however, there are several givens that I think it necessary to state. First of all, abominable does not mean unnatural. On the contrary, if a need is felt to derive some sort of Scriptural opinion on the "naturalness" of homosexuality, it would seem reasonable to suppose that the Torah is tacitly admitting that homosexual intercourse is something which some people would, under normal circumstances, find attractive; the Torah elsewhere seems only to prohibit types of sexual activity in which people would otherwise engage.[4] It can be, therefore, assumed that the point of these prohibitions is not to outlaw something contrary to nature, human or otherwise. It isn't unnatural to eat pork, only forbidden, and the same thing can be said of homosexual intercourse. Furthermore, the assumption on the part of many that this prohibition reflects some sort of primitive understanding of human sexuality developed in hoary antiquity when mankind lived under the fantasy that sexual orientation was a matter of choice (and hence something that could be dictated to any individual by a higher authority) must, in the absence of proof to the contrary, be considered itself a fantasy. In other words, since no modern I know perceives him or herself consciously to have chosen his or her sexual orientation, the burden of proof must lie on anyone who would claim that the ancients *did* perceive sexual orientation to be a matter of free choice. It can be presumed, therefore, that the point of the prohibition is not to convince homosexuals to turn to heterosexuality. Finally, it must be stated that there is no justification at all for assuming that the prohibitions of homosexual intercourse is to be read in light of the story of the destruction of Sodom. Although it is true that the mob of male hooligans who surround Lot's home after he has taken the angelic visitors in as his guests do scream that they wish to abuse his guests sexually, there is nothing at all in the text of Genesis 19 to suggest that this story is meant to be taken as an etiological explanation of the (later) prohibition of homosexual intercourse. Although the Sodomite hordes are condemned as miscreants who must suffer a ghastly fate for their sins, the Bible does not suggest, even tacitly, that it is because of their misdeeds that homosexual intercourse must forever more be forbidden, any more than it suggests that the rape of Dinah would be a good reason to prohibit heterosexual intercourse. On the contrary, there is nothing in the context of Leviticus 19 or 20 to suggest that it is violent homosexual rape that is being prohibited, as opposed to mature, tender homosexual love. To assume that the text of Leviticus means to prohibit homosexual rape only is to ignore completely the context in which the verses appear.

Having said all that, the task at hand is to determine what the context is in which the Torah prohibits male homosexual intercourse. Our first observation, and this is most relevant to many of the speakers in the United Church debate, is that there is no cogent reason to separate the Biblical prohibitions regarding homosexual behaviour from their contexts. Neither the Massoretes nor any later Biblical commentators find any justification for removing the verses in question from their larger frameworks and it is, therefore, the first job of the exegete to identify those larger frames and to understand first and foremost how these verses fit into the larger picture. A careful analysis of context yields other conclusions vital for a proper appreciation of the text. For example, the assumption which one hears stated over and over that it is the impossibility of procreative result that renders homosexual intercourse abominable is firmly belied by the context in which the prohibition is stated. Almost all of the other prohibitions of Leviticus 18 and 20 could easily lead to offspring, yet they are firmly forbidden. On the other hand, Scripture nowhere suggests that intercourse with post-menopausal or infertile women is to be discouraged.[5] The only conclusion justified by context is that procreative potential is no factor in the decision regarding the abominability of homosexual intercourse. Another relevant observation based on the context in which the verses in question appear is that the Torah shows no apparent interest in the question of sexual orientation. Nowhere does the Torah suggest that one ought not have homosexual inclinations or desires, only that one may not engage in homosexual intercourse. On other occasions, the Torah does deal with the question of the desire that motivates sin. Not only, for example, is theft prohibited, but the coveting of one's neighbour's possessions, which presumably is the prelude to theft, is also formally prohibited by the tenth of the Ten Commandments. Not only is adultery formally forbidden, but lusting after one's neighbour's wife is specifically mentioned as a passion forbidden the pious Israelite.[6] Here, there is no suggestion of the sort that might suggest that one must not conceive homosexual desires. That the Biblical text supposes that people have homosexual desires is obvious from the very fact that the fulfillment of such desires is prohibited. But that same Biblical text that tacitly owns up to the existence of those desires does not suggest one should somehow try not to have them in the same way that one is supposed to try to avoid the kind of desire that might lead to theft or adultery. The logical conclusion is that desire for homosexual intercourse is largely irrelevant, I suppose, in the same way that the law is unconcerned whether a given Israelite does or does not find a particular forbidden food to be something under other circumstances he might have desired. A further observation based on the language of the passages themselves is that it is specifically the homosexual equivalent of *mishkeve 'ishah*, presumably meaning homosexual anal intercourse, that is prohibited. Other forms of sexual activity between men are not discussed and it seems wrong to conclude from the silence of the text that other types of sexual activity are obviously forbidden as well. On the contrary, the text seems quite concerned that the reader understand exactly what kind of sexual activity is under discussion and I do not see any reason to assume that the text does not mean what it says. Finally, it seems to me highly relevant that the text can only be understood to be discussing male homosexuality. The context in which the verses appear, as I have already pointed out, requires that the verses be taken as referring to men, and this is hardly only because the language is couched in words of masculine gender.[7] Grammar aside, the fact that the Hebrew literally reads "You shall not have intercourse with a man of the type one generally has with women . . . " guarantees that the prohibition is being directed towards men. To assume that the Biblical author was sufficiently naive so as to have been unaware of the phenomenon of female homosexuality seems too facile a solution to a thorny problem.

It seems to me that to understand the significance of the prohibition, we must first devote some time discussing what semen meant to the ancients, as it seems clear to me that it is the special quality of semen itself that generates the reason for the prohibition. First of all, that would explain the lack of interest in lesbianism. Secondly, it would explain the absence of procreative angle in the discussion: semen has many appropriate uses, only one of which is directly procreative, but apparently anal intercourse between men is not one of them. Thirdly, it would explain why the Torah does not prohibit the desire, but only the act: it is not homosexuality itself that is of interest here in the first place, only the fact that certain types of homosexual activity yield a misuse of semen which must, therefore, be curbed. Finally, it would explain why the Torah is only interested in intercourse itself: because there is something about homosexual intercourse between men that is itself objectionable. The prohibition is therefore precisely as stated and the act forbidden was not meant in the first place to serve as a mask or a catch-all phrase for all other types of sexual activity between members of the same sex.

One of the most complicated, yet most potentially rewarding tasks that the Torah sets for mankind is the division of the world into its sacred and profane components, presumably as an exercise in coming closer to the Creator by recognizing the sacred in the creation. This idea is expressed in a wide range of metaphoric, symbolic, and mythological contexts, yet all have in common the simple idea that the world is made up of God-like and un-God-like elements and that the ultimate act of piety is the drawing of a clear distinction between the two domains. Sometimes this is expressed in terms of holy and profane, sometimes in terms of pure and impure. It is expressed in terms of good and bad, of light and dark, of bloody and bloodless, of clean and dirty, of leavened and unleavened, of Sabbath and weekday, and in terms of sacerdotal and lay. All of these are variations on a common theme, but whether the Israelite is being careful to defecate only outside the boundaries of the camp, whether he is bidden to bury the blood before he may eat the slaughter, or whether he is bidden to keep separate milk, the physical embodiment of motherhood, from meat, the raw flesh that suggests war and slaughter, he is still being told simply to divide the world down into two realms, one like God (i.e., the clean, the pure, the unleavened, the sabbatical) and one antithetical to God.[8] Sometimes, the exercise is even simpler, for example when the Israelite is bidden simply to divide things which do not belong together, even though neither of the two is obviously more godlike than the other. Thus, we may posit that when the Israelite is bidden to avoid mixing diverse grains in a common field or to avoid yoking diverse species under a common yoke, or to avoid tampering with a neighbor's landmark so as to obfuscate the correct boundary between neighboring pieces of property, he is merely being commanded to practice this type of universal separation in instances where the consequences of failure might not be so dire.[9] This notion of separation pervades almost all aspects of Pentateuchal legislation and can certainly be considered a cornerstone of ancient Israelite piety. To paraphrase the Saturday evening liturgy, just as God Himself set the standard by separating light from darkness, Israel from the nations and the Sabbath from the rest of the week, so must Israel learn to emulate God even in this and to spend its pious efforts analyzing all corners of existence and erecting metaphysical barriers between the sacred and profane realms.

Perhaps the most obvious of all these metaphoric realms of distinction is the division that all cultures and religions know between life and death. God is called the source of all life, the fountain of life, He Who liveth forever, the author of life, the life of the universe, and the living God at countless places in Scripture and liturgy. The connection between God and the idea of life is so deeply ingrained in the Jewish consciousness, that the Hebrew word for "alive," *chai,* has become an unwitting circumlocution for the name of God among countless Jews who have chosen, especially in our day, to express their Jewish identity by wearing necklaces bearing this otherwise inexplicable legend.[10] The opposite of life, of course, is death, and it is in this context we must understand the horror of corpse and carrion that pervades Biblical law. The corpse is the most potent source of impurity; the corpse alone can render people impure who are merely to be found under the same roof.[11] The laws connected with the disposal of the dead are matters of grave import as well, and it is no doubt significant that the Bible chooses to conclude its selection of stories about Abraham with the elaborate retelling of the special care with which he went about purchasing precisely the correct sepulchre for Sarah. Finally, the extraordinary purification ritual for one who had come into contact with a corpse set forth in such great detail in the nineteenth chapter of the Book of Numbers points with undeniable force towards the gravity with which Scripture views the status of any individual contaminated through contact with a corpse. Given the force of these Scriptural phenomena, then, it is no wonder that one of the primary metaphoric ranges in which these dividing the world rituals are developed has to do with the division of the physical universe into the realm of life and the realm of death.

The world divides down rather easily, then, into three great spheres: the living, the dead and the inanimate. Most things in the world fall easily into one or the other category, although rabbinic exegesis of the relevant Scriptural passages provided endless gradations and refinements of the basic law. But, nonetheless, there are still certain existents that seem to rest precariously on the cusp between life and death, and to these items the Law must turn special attention. Of these, the twin fluids of life deserve special mention. The ancients seem to have believed that human reproduction was somehow effected by the intermingling of semen and menstrual blood, a conclusion obviously reached through observation rather than through exegesis and one not all that incorrect in a pre-microscopic sort of way. This theory is supported by the use of the Hebrew *zera'* in various passages. Literally, the word means "seed," but it is used of women as well as of men, which suggests that the ancients imagined the respective seeds of men and women to be suspended in their respective vital fluids.[12] It was only to be expected, therefore, that these two fluids, neither exactly alive, yet both somehow the stuff of life, would be accorded special attention in the Israelite drive to effect consequential ritual separation of life from death. I have already mentioned the special Israelite interest in blood. Not only must the blood be poured out on the ground "like water" before the meat may be eaten, but later rabbinic law developed an entire procedure for soaking and salting meat in order to draw out any excess blood, a ritual which goes beyond the letter of Pentateuchal law but which stays quite close to its spirit. Furthermore, the blood was closely connected with the spirit of life.[13] In fact, the explanatory phrase *ki haddam hu' hannefesh* "for the blood is the soul" became the standard Biblical aside.[14] Given this overweening interest in blood of all kinds, it stands to reason that menstrual blood would be given even more careful scrutiny and, in fact, its special qualities are clearly noted in Scripture. Best known, probably, is the fact that it contaminates the woman in her menses and renders her unclean for a week.[15] After nine months of gestation, the uterine bleeding that accompanies childbirth is deemed especially potent: it renders the new mother impure for months.[16] In later rabbinic literature, a wide variety of superstitious beliefs grew up around the menstruant, not the least strongly stated of which suggests that if a menstruating woman even passes between two men towards the beginning of her monthly period, one of them must die.[17]

It would follow from this type of thinking that semen too ought to occupy a special place in the ritual nexus that separates the pure from the impure and the living from the dead, and this is, in fact, the case. According to Biblical law, seminal ejaculation in and of itself is enough to render a man impure.[18] Furthermore, the ejaculate itself is a source of impurity and can render a garment of cloth or leather impure.[19] Even more to the point, the ejaculate even renders the woman who receives it impure; both partners require subsequent ritual purification.[20] Semen is not a living substance, yet as the stuff of life, it must be treated with the greatest care. It has enormous procreative power, yet most of the time it does not function procreatively at all. Yet, presumably, this is in accordance with the will of God, who created the human reproductive system in such a way that requires that vast quantities of semen be spent in vain. It comes as no surprise, therefore, that the establishment of the precise contexts in which semen may be ejaculated is a matter of prime concern to the Biblical legislator. This, I believe, is the context of the Levitical lists of forbidden and illicit sexual liaisons, set as they are in two chapters following the longest Biblical exposition of the various laws relating to ritual purity and impurity.

The books of the Torah all follow a certain rhythm, beginning with introductory material, reaching an apogee of interest in their central chapters and finishing with closing material meant to tie up loose ends and introduce the following book. Thus perceived, for example, it is no less clear that it is the narrative detailing the birth of Jacob and his wresting of the birthrite from Esau that constitutes the central point of the Book of Genesis than it is that it is the story of the theophany at Sinai that is the obvious high point of the Book of Exodus.

The Book of Leviticus, which contains almost no narrative at all, maintains nonetheless this rhythm in the way it presents its material. Clearly, it is the section of laws relating to purity and impurity that are the "point" of the book. The section begins in chapter 11 with the dietary laws, here cast almost exclusively in terms of purity, impurity and abomination. The text goes on, in chapter 12, to discuss the purity laws relating to childbirth and, in chapters 13 and 14, the elaborate text relating to the leper and his purification. Chapter 15 begins to turn to sexual matters, touching upon the case of a man who suffers from an ongoing discharge, then continuing on with the case (which we have discussed just above) of a man who has a normal (i.e., voluntary) seminal emission and with the cases of women who have normal and abnormal menstrual discharges. Chapters 16 and 17 discuss the ritual for the Day of Atonement, describing the day as a day of purification and expiation and making special, unexpected reference to the special care that the Israelite must take in handling blood. In chapter 18, the text turns back to sexual matters, offering a long list of prohibited sexual relationships, including, in verse 22, the prohibition of male homosexual intercourse. Once the text turns to the purity situation surrounding the twin stuffs of life, the progression of ideas seems clear and cogent: the text moves from abnormal seminal discharge to normal ejaculation, then turns to abnormal and normal menstrual flow. Having dealt with semen and blood in normal and abnormal but naturally occurring contexts, the text now turns to voluntary activity.[21] In chapter 17, we have a series of unexpected, and to a certain extent, unique passages. The Israelite is warned against the slaughter of animals in any but the correct sacrificial context. "Bloodguilt shall be imputed to that man, for he has shed (illicit) blood and that man shall be cut off from his people so that the Children of Israel (may be encouraged thereby) to bring any sacrifices which they might make in the open to God, that is, to the door of the Tent of Meeting, to the priest . . . " Later, the Deuteronomist specifically has to allow the slaughter of meat in a non-sacrificial context, but this was apparently not the view of the priestly legislator whose opinions are codified in this section of Leviticus—our passage considers all slaughter to have ritual implications.[22] The point, then, of this passage is to specify that sacrifice offered outside the Temple is acceptable as long as the carcass is brought to the priest so that he might sprinkle the blood against the altar of the Lord.[23] Then, beginning with verse 10, the text turns its attention to blood eaters of all types, declaring that "the life of the flesh is in the blood" and ordaining that one who does "partake of the blood of any flesh shall be cut off."[24] The text might logically be expected, at this point, to turn to questions of voluntary (i.e., non-conjugal, waking) acts of seminal ejaculation, and that is exactly what we do find.

The eighteenth chapter of Leviticus presents a long list of sexual prohibitions. I think that the context in which they appear precludes our conclusion that the various varieties of sexual deviancy are included (or that other varieties are excluded) because they are the practice of relatively small groups within larger society, because they do not or ought not lead to pregnancy or because they are morally wrong.[25] The list of sexual prohibitions presented includes those forms of sexual behaviour which require unacceptable uses of semen and which are, therefore, the counterpart of the list of the various illicit uses to which blood may be put that appears in the previous chapter. As a substance that is clearly the essence of life, yet which is equally clearly not alive, semen (like blood) falls into an odd category in the ritual division of the world and its existents into God-like and un-God-like domains. To put it another way, all substances that are neither alive nor inanimate confuse the basic premise of the system of purity that underlies Biblical law and require special treatment, and semen is *so* potent a substance so as to require an actual delineation of licit and illicit uses. There are three categories to consider: licit situations which do not render impure, licit situations which do render the parties who come into contact with the semen impure, and illicit situations which, since they are forbidden, transcend the laws of purity. Having dealt with the first two in the preceding chapters, the Biblical text now turns to the final category. It is in this category that the Bible forbids homosexual intercourse between men.

The eighteenth chapter of Leviticus begins with an introductory passage pointing out that the prohibitions about to be introduced are, in fact, the regular practices both of the Egyptians, whose land Israel has left, and the Canaanites, to whose land Israel has yet to come. The Israelites, on the other hand, are bidden to follow the law of God, to walk in His ways and "to keep (God's) statutes and ordinances that a man might do and thereby live."[26] The statement has the ring of Biblical cliche, but the meaning is actually rather subtle—the Israelite who would live must cling to the ways of the Life of the Universe. The stage is therefore set for the introduction of a long list of separation rituals (or anti-rituals, as the list contains solely prohibitions) which present the regular Israelite effort to divide the world down into the domains of life and death. It is instructive to consider not only what is listed, but also what forms of sexual activity are not mentioned. The list begins with various types of forbidden incest, mostly with female family members of various types (mother, step-mother, sister, half-sister, granddaughter and so forth) but also with one's father.[27]

When the text concludes that line of thought, it continues with other, more special cases, forbidding first of all intercourse with a menstruant woman and with another's wife. The text then presents a verse which, according to the traditional interpretation is completely out of place, but which, I think may hold the key to understanding the entire passage. This verse forbids men from offering their *zera'* to Molech, a pagan deity of some sort.[28] Traditionally, this is presumed to refer to some sort of child sacrifice, the word *zera'* here having the secondary meaning of "offspring."[29] The problem in interpreting the verse in the traditional way is that it has no connection with its context and can only be presumed to have been included in this passage by virtue of the use of the word *zera'*, which the text uses in the preceding verse as well, albeit in a different sense. The only way to make this particular prohibition germane to its context would be to assume that *zera'* here does not refer to offspring at all and that the prohibition here has nothing to do with child sacrifice at all, despite the universal assumption in rabbinic sources that it does.[30] If we take *zera'* literally to mean "semen," just as it did in the preceding verse, then perhaps we have reference here to some obscure pagan ritual in which semen itself was offered to the god. This would fit the context and have the added advantage of no longer requiring us to imagine that the word *zera'* has two different meanings in two adjacent verses.[31] The passage then concludes by forbidding homosexual intercourse between men, intercourse between men and animals and, finally, between women and animals, which is in fact the first and only sexual prohibition directed towards women on this list. Finally, the text offers a stern warning to anyone who would violate any of the prohibitions.

The passage, then, prohibits three kinds of sexual act: incest of various varieties, male homosexual intercourse and male and female bestiality. All have in common the single factor that they result in an improper use of semen and this can be demonstrated in several ways. First of all, it explains why the only prohibition directed towards women has to do with dumb animals. Generally speaking, men are in control of their seminal flow. They are therefore the ones being addressed, even when the prohibited kind of intercourse is heterosexual in nature. If men are considered the perpetrators if semen is improperly spilt during sexual contact with women, then how much the more so are they responsible for impropriety when committed with animals. The only time a woman can be held responsible, in fact, is when her partner is itself an animal; in this unique case, a woman must bear the responsibility for the improperly spilt semen of her animal partner. Second of all, it explains why the prohibition of bringing one's seed to Molech is included: even though it does not involve intercourse, it still involves an abuse of seminal emission of some sort. Thirdly, it explains why, instead of being taken as an anomalous insertion into an otherwise well-organized pericope and therefore omitted when the various sexual prohibitions are rehearsed two chapters later, the Molech prohibition was actually brought to the fore in the repetition of these commandments in chapter 20, where it not only introduces all the rest, but actually sets the tone by declaring that God Himself will deal with any man (and his family as well) who commits this particular offense.[32] Fourthly, it explains why other forms of sexual abuse are absent from this passage. The text, for example, ignores instances of sexual crime where no improper use of semen is made, as in the case of rape or seduction, both of which are treated in some detail elsewhere in the Pentateuchal text.[33] Also absent are illicit relations between priests and divorcees or converts, and the prohibition of sacral (or lay) prostitutes, which for all their illegality, presumably do not result in semen being used improperly.[34] It therefore follows that the misuse of semen is a category of offense unto itself, sometimes matching other areas of sexual misconduct, sometimes not. Finally, it explains the use of the term *to'evah* to characterize the nature of these sins. The term *to'evah*, derived from a verbal root meaning "to abhor," is used at Leviticus 18:22 and 20:13 to qualify the sin of homosexuality and again in Leviticus 18:27 as a more general qualifier for all the sexual prohibitions listed in the pericope. The term is widely used in Scripture, often metaphorically, to denote wickedness and unchastity, but when divested of its larger connotations, it seems to refer specifically to sins against the kind of pious dividing up of the world into pure and impure realms. Thus the term is used of forbidden foods at Deuteronomy 14:3 ("Eat no *to'evah!*") because the forbidden foods have the special ability to introduce impure stuff into the human body and it is used of witchcraft and sorcery at Deuteronomy 18:9, which introduce impurity into the midst of the people. When the prophet Malachi used the term to refer to intermarriage with the daughters (not the sons!) of idolatrous nations (if such be the proper interpretation of Malachi 2:11), he probably meant that intermarriage is forbidden first and foremost because it blurs the division between the holy people and the heathen nations.[35]

It follows from all of this that the prohibition of homosexual intercourse between men appears in Scripture as an example of an act that treats the stuff of life carelessly and in a way that, for whatever reason, Scripture considers inimical to the careful delineation of the boundary between the sacred and the profane. Any attempt to describe the Scriptural prohibition of male homosexual intercourse as an instance of Biblical outrage against men of homosexual orientation or as a

divine condemnation of love between men is based, I think, on a faulty understanding of the nature of Biblical context, nuance and style. By extrapolation, one
would have to assume the Bible meant to forbid men to love their pets as well.

Notes and References

1. Regarding the specific prohibition of homosexual intercourse with one's father, see below, note
27. In this essay, the abbreviation BT stands for Babylonian Talmud and M stands for Mishnah. Both
sigla are followed directly by the name of the tractate to which reference is being made. Torah is the
Hebrew name for the first five books of the Bible, considered by the synagogue as the oldest and most
authoritative section of Scripture.

2. This is more of an accurate paraphrase than a direct translation. The Hebrew for sexual intercourse is *mishkeve 'ishah*, literally, "the laying-down of a woman." Since the verb is a masculine form
and since the entire context suggests that these prohibitions are being directed towards men rather
than towards women, it seems correct to translate *mishkeve 'ishah* simply as sexual intercourse and to
use the phrase "another man" to suggest that the Torah is speaking of two men who are engaging in
the type of sexual activity in which generally men and women engage. Presumably, the Torah is referring to anal intercourse between men.

3. The statements at Leviticus 18:2 and 18:24 (repeated at 20:22–23) to the effect that these various
sexual acts are prohibited because they were the impure acts both of the Egyptians and of the Canaanite
nations whom God proposes to drive out from before the conquering Israelites is hardly the reason the
acts are impure and abominable in the first place. Those nations also engaged in many other rituals, sacrifice and prayer among them, which Torah does not find abominable at all once they are divested of
their pagan overtones and recast as acts of Jewish worship. The text goes on in both chapters to adjure
the people to obey these laws lest the land spew them forth just as it is about to spew forth the indigenous nations. The point can hardly be that Israel is prohibited these various forms of sexual activity
because they were the habits of the nations God is about to clear out of the land. If it was because of their
sexual misconduct that those nations are being evicted from their native soil, there must be something
inherently wrong with them. The question we are going to address is just what that wrong thing is.

4. The obvious parallel is to the dietary prohibitions. Only edible foods that, were they not to have
been forbidden, would be eaten freely are prohibited. The assumption is that normal, natural people
would eat all the forbidden foods had the Torah not come forward to forbid them.

5. In fact, the rabbinic interpretation of Exodus 21:10, in which the Torah sets down that sexual sat-
isfaction is one of the three obligations husbands bear towards their wives, makes special point of emphasizing that this duty devolves upon husbands even when their wives cannot possibly become
pregnant, for instance when they are already pregnant or beyond their childbearing years. The major
rabbinic sources are discussed in detail in David Feldman's book *Marital Relations, Birth Control and
Abortion in Jewish Law* (New York, 1968), pp. 60–80.

6. Exodus 20:17.

7. The Torah almost always speaks in the masculine singular, but that is usually considered a convention of Biblical speech rather than a sign that only men are included in a given prohibition or commandment. "Thou shalt not kill" is stated with a masculine singular imperative, but no commentator
has ever concluded that women *are* permitted to murder other people.

8. Defecation outside the camp: Deuteronomy 23:13–14; burying the blood before eating the
slaughter: Leviticus 17:13–16; eating milk with meat: Exodus 23:19 and 34:26 and Deuteronomy 14:21
according to the universal rabbinic interpretation.

9. Mixing diverse grains: Deuteronomy 22:9; yoking diverse species under the same yoke:
Deuteronomy 22:10; tampering with a landmark: Deuteronomy 19:14.

10. The *chai* (as it is called) has almost overtaken the so-called Star of David as the Jewish symbol
par excellence. The marker set up by the municipality of Rohrbach, a small village near Heidelberg
where I lived for two years, to memorialize the site of the synagogue burnt down on Krystallnacht has
cut into it at its centre an enormous Hebrew *chai*. When I asked a member of the town council what
those two Hebrew letters signified, he told me it was the name of God. His utter ignorance of Hebrew
notwithstanding, I think he had somehow hit upon a truth. When set into the context of the study of
so-called practical Kabbalah, I cannot think of any other way to explain the use of *chai* as an amulet except to suppose it is a version of God's name.

11. Numbers 19:14. Other sources of impurity require physical contact to transfer their impurity
further.

12. As, for example, at Leviticus 12:1, where the text posits that a given woman might "cast forth
her seed and give birth to a male." The rabbis took it for granted that the text meant to suggest that the

sex of the offspring was determined by the order in which the parents cast forth their seed during intercourse, as set forth in BT Niddah 31a, a source widely quoted in relevant literature. This also explains, of course, why women no longer menstruate after they conceive.

13. Cf., for example, Genesis 9:5: "But you may not eat of the flesh with its life-blood (literally, with its blood-soul) in it."

14. This remark appears, for example, at Deuteronomy 12:23.

15. Leviticus 15:19–24, 18:19 and 20:18. It is not without interest (as we shall see presently) that these last two passages occur in the same contexts in which homosexual intercourse is forbidden. The verse in Leviticus 20 is especially revealing in this context: "A man who has intercourse with a menstruating woman (Hebrew: *'ishah davah*) and who uncovers her nakedness has disturbed her source (i.e., the uterine source of her blood) and (as a result) she has exposed the source of her blood. The two of them are to be cut off from the bosom of the people."

16. For thirty-three days for a boy and for sixty-six days for a girl; see Leviticus 12:1–8.

17. BT Pesachim 111a. If she passes between them towards the end of her menses, she only induces strife between them. The text says, more literally, that she kills one of them, not merely that he will die.

18. Leviticus 15:16–18. Ibn Ezra's assumption that this refers to involuntary ejaculation seems unwarranted by the language of the passage. The evolution of rabbinic efforts to depart from the obvious legal implications of this passage is quite interesting. In a passage in BT Bava Qamma 82b, for example, it is stated that one of the ten *taqqanot* (enactments) of Ezra was the requirement that men bathe in the ritual bath after any seminal ejaculation. The Talmud observes that this is, in fact, a Scriptural requirement, as clearly stated in our passage. To this, the text explains that the passage in Leviticus only requires immersion in a ritual bath for men who have experienced seminal ejaculation if they wish to partake of *terumah* (the produce tax reserved for priestly consumption which had to be eaten in a state of purity) or *qodashim* (the portions of sacrificial meat which were permitted for consumption). Ezra's enactment specifically extended this requirement to any who would study Torah as well. Thus, even with the added provision, the rabbinic interpretation of the passage still ends up far less stringent than the simple meaning of the Pentateuchal text would seem to suggest. The reality of the situation is that the rabbis did not require ritual immersion after seminal ejaculation. Limiting the meaning of the Biblical text to two extinct categories merely allowed them formally to abrogate any further application of the law, now perceived as rabbinic (even Ezra counts as a rabbi) extrapolation, rather than Scriptural edict. In a long discussion at BT Berakhot 22a-b, the Talmud takes another approach to the tradition regarding Ezra's enactment, declaring that, in fact, he only meant to require washing in nine *kabin* of water, rather than total immersion in a ritual bath. Even that requirement is scaled down, at least according to certain theories presented in the text, to apply only to involuntary seminal ejaculation and then only when the man in question is in good health.

19. Ibid.

20. Leviticus 15:18. Rashi's remark that this is a "royal decree" (i.e., a divine law that could not otherwise have been derived from Scriptural law) and that her impurity is specifically *not* occasioned by her contact with the semen seems forced.

21. It is not without interest that, since the Torah itself orders husbands to engage their wives sexually, conjugal sexual intercourse is discussed here in the context of natural, involuntary seminal emission. Conjugal intercourse is involuntary in the sense that it is divinely legislated.

22. See Deuteronomy 12:20–28.

23. Cf. Deuteronomy 12:13–16. Leviticus 17:7 suggests that this legislation was enacted to stem sacrifices to goat-gods, a remark Rashi and Ibn Ezra take at face value despite its great obscurity.

24. It is interesting that the legislation at verses 11–14 seems to suppose that eating the meat of hunted animals is licit as long as the blood is poured out on the ground and covered up with earth. This is apparently meant to be understood in distinction to the laws in verses 2–10, which suppose that all slaughter must be taken to the priest so that he may pour the blood out on the altar. There is no contradiction if we presume that verses 11–14 are discussing animals killed on the hunt, while verses 2–10 are discussing slaughtered domesticated animals, or if we imagine that verses 2–10 only apply to oxen, sheep and goats, while verses 11–14 lay down the general rule for (other) animals and birds.

25. In any event, the Scriptural point of view is that things are morally wrong because they are forbidden by God, not the other way around.

26. Leviticus 18:5.

27. The Talmud (BT Sanhedrin 54a) presumes that homosexual intercourse with one's father is what is being forbidden and that the text mentions this, even though it would be forbidden anyway (because of the prohibition of homosexual intercourse between any two men), to make the sinner guilty of two separate violations. Rabbi Judah's opinion, also cited in the Talmud, that when the text here refers to one's father it means to be making reference to one's father's wife, is cited approvingly by

Rashi, who relies on the parallel passage in Leviticus 20. The text is rather moot and could be read reasonably both ways.

28. Molech is identified in 1 Kings 11:7 as a god of the Ammonites, but the name there should probably be read as Milkom, as in verses 5 and 33 of that chapter, a fact already reflected in the Septuagint. The often repeated suggestion that the name Molech is merely the Hebrew word for king (correctly vocalized *melech*) with the vowel pointing for the Hebrew term of opprobrium *boshet* ("shame") seems cogent, especially given the propensity of the Biblical text to give the name with a definite article (a detail we have omitted from our translation) and, especially, the evidence of Isaiah 30:33, where the same deity is apparently referred to as Melech (or rather, using the definite article, as The Melech, i.e., The King.) The final word on Molech worship, at least for the time being, is George C. Heider's *The Cult of Molek: A Reassessment*, published in 1985 as the forty-third supplement to the *Journal for the Study of the Old Testament*.

29. Cf. Rashi, ad loc. In some Biblical passages, for example 2 Kings 23:10 or Jeremiah 32:35, it cannot be disputed that Molech worship is described as child sacrifice, yet in those very passages where the meaning is clear the word *zera'* is *not* used and the text refers specifically to "sons and daughters." Possibly the presence of the passage in Leviticus 18 and 20 reflects a later misunderstanding of the meaning of *zera'* in an earlier source, a misunderstanding which supposes it to be taken literally and which may well reflect a different sort of abominable practice with which the priestly legislator was aware. Be all that as it may, the fact remains that the passage in Leviticus is really rather unambiguous if context is taken into account and the need for contemporary historical substantiation of such a practice is set aside.

30. See the sources collected at BT Sanhedrin 62b.

31. Ritual offerings of semen were not unknown in antiquity. Epiphanius, for example, cites the example of the Alexandrian Phibionites as follows: "After they have intercourse in the passion of fornication, they raise their own blasphemy toward heaven. The woman and the man take the fluid of the emission of the man into their hands. They stand, turn towards heaven, their hands besmeared with the uncleanness and pray . . . bringing to the Father of the Nature of All that which they have on their hands and they say, 'We offer to thee this gift, the body of Christ.' And then they eat it, their own ignominy and say. 'This is the body of Christ and this is the Passover for the sake of which our bodies suffer and are forced to confess the suffering of Christ.' Similarly also with the woman: when she happens to be in the flowing of the blood, they gather the blood of menstruation of her uncleanness and eat it together and say, 'This is the blood of Christ.'" This is Mircea Eliade's modification of Stephan Benko's translation of Epiphanius' *Panarion* 26.27.1ff. Benko's original translation appeared in the *Vigilae Christianae* 2(1967), pp. 109–110 and Eliade's modification, in his article, "Spirit, Light and Seed," first published in *History of Religions 11:1* (August 1971), pp. 1–30 and subsequently reprinted in *Occultism, Witchcraft and Cultural Fashions: Essays in Comparative Religions* (Chicago and London, 1976), pp. 93–119.

32. The order in chapter 20, except for the Molech passage, is not that different from chapter 18. First, we have the Molech law, which is expanded from one to eight verses. Then we have the prohibition (absent from chapter 18) of cursing one's parents, of adultery, of incest with step-mother and daughter-in-law, of homosexual intercourse between men, of marriage of mother and daughter as co-wives, of sexual relations between a man and an animal and of relations between a woman and an animal. The text continues then with various incestuous possibilities, outlawing them all.

33. Seduction is forbidden (or rather, its consequences are made explicit) at Exodus 22:15–17 and rape at Deuteronomy 22:23–29. Neither is mentioned in our passage, because for all their nefariousness, neither crime involves the misuse of semen *per se*.

34. The marriage of priest and divorcee is forbidden at Leviticus 21:7. The union of a priest and a convert, although not explicitly mentioned in the passage, was inferred by the rabbis. Prostitution, at least in its sacral variety, it outlawed at Deuteronomy 23:18. Again here, the point is that these types of sexual activity are forbidden, but if they do occur, no misuse of semen is considered to have taken place.

35. Cf. the explanation Bar Kappara offered to Judah the Patriach (as recorded at BT Nedarim 51a) of the word *to'evah*. He explained that it was a sort of acronym which stood for the words *to'eh 'atah bah*, which I would translate "you err in this." I think he means to say that Scripture uses the term specifically with reference to homosexuality because it is often misperceived by men, who cannot fathom why anal intercourse with a woman should not be considered a misuse of semen, but similar relations with another man should. Because the two seem so similar, it is likely that one might err, hence the special effort of Scripture to avert such an error by specifically labelling homosexual intercourse a *to'evah*.

Patristic Interpretations
of Romans 1:26*

Bernadette J. Brooten

Rom 1:26 occurs in the context of Paul's discussion of idolatry (Rom 1:18–32). According to Paul, idol worship had serious consequences. Rom 1:24–27 reads (RSV):

> Therefore God gave them up in the lusts of their hearts to impurity, to the dishonoring of their bodies among themselves, because they exchanged the truth about God for a lie and worshipped and served the creature rather than the Creator who is blessed for ever! Amen.
>
> For this reason God gave them up to dishonorable passions. Their women exchanged natural relations for unnatural (αἵ τε γὰρ θήλειαι αὐτῶν μετήλλαξαν τὴν φυσικὴν χρῆσιν εἰς τὴν παρὰ φύσιν), and the men likewise gave up natural relations with women and were consumed with passion for one another, men committing shameless acts with men and receiving in their own persons the due penalty for their error.

This is the only passage in the entire Bible referring explicitly to lesbians. Ancient Israelite law forbade male homosexual relations, but did not make reference to women (Lev 18:22, 20:13).

Interpretations of Rom 1:26 occur only rarely in the patristic sources. When the verse is quoted at all, it is usually the first half, 'God gave them up to dishonorable passions,' which is quoted without comment (e.g., Origen often does this).[1] The interpretations which do occur fall into two categories. According to the one, Paul is referring here, not to lesbians, but rather to unnatural heterosexual intercourse. According to the other lesbians are indeed meant. Anastasius and Augustine are examples of the unnatural heterosexual intercourse interpretation, while John Chrysostom and Clement of Alexandria would be examples of the second category.

According to scholia found in two manuscripts of the *Paedagogus* of Clement of Alexandria, Anastasius interpreted the verse as follows: 'Clearly they do not go into one another (ἀλλήλαις), but rather offer themselves to the men.'[2] He thus

*This paper was written as part of the 'Frau und Christentum' project of the Institute for Ecumenical Studies, University of Tübingen, under the sponsorship of the Stiftung Volkswagenwerk.

From "Patristic Interpretations of Romans 1:26." In *Studia Patristica xviii*, vol. 1, ed. Elizabeth A. Livingstone, 287–290. Kalamazoo: Cistercian Publications, 1985.

seems to dispute the possibility of sexual relations between women at all. Augustine also took the verse as referring to unnatural heterosexual intercourse. For him unnatural means that which does not allow for procreation, such as anal intercourse: 'But as regards any part of the body which is not meant for generative purposes, should a man use even his own wife in it, it is against nature and flagitious.'[3] Augustine sees sexual intercourse with a prostitute as less evil than nonprocreative forms of marital intercourse, because the former is at least not contrary to nature.

How is it possible to interpret the verse as not referring to sexual relations between women? It is the case that, with respect to the women, Paul speaks only of their having 'exchanged natural relations for unnatural.' Thus, one inclined to overlook the existence of lesbians could take vss. 26 and 27 as not parallel to each other, in spite of the ὁμοίως, 'similarly,' of v. 27.

One should note, however, that Augustine does not totally dispute the possibility of love relations between women. In fact, he specifically warns nuns about lesbian existence: 'The love which you bear to each other must be not carnal, but spiritual.'[4]

According to the second category of interpretation, Rom 1:26 does refer to lesbians. John Chrysostom, in his commentary on Romans, writes that the women in question were without excuse, because they did have access to lawful intercourse, making unnecessary this 'monstrous depravity.' Chrysostom further notes that it is 'more disgraceful that the women should seek this type of intercourse, since they ought to have a greater sense of shame than men.'[5] Thus, for Chrysostom, lesbian existence and male homosexuality are not parallel to each other, for women and men are not meant to be alike. The man was designed to be the teacher of the woman, the woman the helpmate of the man. Gender roles and a polarization of the sexes are essential to his interpretation of Rom 1:26–27. Homosexual men become, in essence, women and cease to be men or rather blur the differences between women and men.[6] A similar concern with the blurring of gender role distinctions occurs in Chrysostom's tractates on spiritual marriage.[7]

Moving behind Chrysostom to an earlier historical stage, we find that Clement of Alexandria similarly devotes much greater attention to male homosexuality than to lesbian existence. Like Chrysostom, he is concerned that through homosexuality men become like women. Clement emphasizes that men's hair and clothing should not resemble women's hair and clothing. Men should wear a beard as a sign of their stronger nature and their right to rule. Women should be veiled and with covered faces. It is in the context of the necessity of gender differentiation with respect to clothing and hair that Clement discusses homosexuality: 'men passively play the role of women, and women behave like men (ἀνδρίζονται) in that women, contrary to nature, are given in marriage and marry'.[8]

Augustine is likewise concerned about gender distinction with respect to hair, writing that monks should not believe that celibacy means they are no longer men. Monks should avoid long hair, which could create the impression that they are available to be bought. Women should veil themselves, for woman, unlike man, does not through her body show that she is made in the image of God. Man is meant to rule and woman to be subordinate (*illa regit, haec regitur; illa dominatur, haec subditur*).[9]

To sum up thus far, neither those commentators who interpret Rom 1:26 as referring to heterosexual intercourse, nor those who take it as referring to lesbians interpret v. 26 (on women) as parallel to v. 27 (on men). This is in keeping with these authors' view that the very deep differences between women and men which they posit must be preserved.

Patristic references to lesbians must be viewed in their Graeco-Roman context. References to lesbians in the Graeco-Roman world are relatively more numerous than in earlier periods, which could indicate that lesbians were living more openly than previously. For example, while the Hebrew Bible does not forbid lesbian existence, post-biblical Jewish writings do discuss whether it is forbidden: Pseudo-Phocylides[10] (1st C.?), the Tannaitic midrash Sifra and other rabbinic writings,[11] Asclepiades,[12] the writer of epigrams (3rd C. BC), Seneca the Elder[13] (1st C. BC), Martial[14] (1st C.), possibly Juvenal[15] (1st/2nd C.), Phaedrus[16] (1st C.), Plutarch[17] (1st C.), Lucian[18] (2nd C.), Pseudo-Lucian[19] (?), the mathematician Ptolemy[20] (2nd C.), the astrologer Vettius Valens[21] (2nd C.), the astrologer Manetho[22] (4th C.), the medical writer Caelius Aurelianus[23] (5th C.) and others also mention lesbians, usually in a derogatory fashion. This is different from discussions of male homosexuality in ancient sources, some of which are accepting and others of which are negative. It is this nearly thorough rejection of love between women in both ancient and non-Christian and Christian sources which causes me to question the thesis posed by John Boswell in *Christianity, Social Tolerance and Homosexuality* (Chicago, 1980) that a broad strand of tolerance of homosexuality existed in the early church. Boswell pays little attention to the sources on women, although he does quote a number of those which I have quoted to you and I have learned much from him.[24] Nevertheless, I believe that his thesis does not apply to women and is therefore inaccurate.

The pre-Christian and Christian Sappho interpretation of the Hellenistic and Roman periods further confirms the general rejection of lesbian existence. The earliest Sappho biography, P. Oxy. 1800, fr. 1 (2nd/3rd C.), notes that, 'She has been accused by some of immorality (ἄτακτος [οὐ]σα τὸν τρόπον) and of being a lover of women (γυναικε[ρασ]τρία).' According to Horace she was *mascula Sappho*.[25] Both Plutarch[26] and Maximus of Tyre[27] compared her with Socrates, who was known for his preference for men. Ovid says that she loved girls and cast into poetic form the legend that she fell in love with a man, Phaon, who did not love her in return.[28] According to the Suda,[29] Sappho was accused by some of 'shameful love' (αἰσχρὰ φιλία) for women. Thus, beginning in the Roman period we find an increasing preoccupation with Sappho's love for women, usually combined with disapproval of that love. Tatian describes Sappho as a ἑταίρα and as a 'love-crazy harlot of a woman, who sang her own licentiousness' (γύναιον πορνικὸν ἐρωτομανές, καὶ τὴν ἑαυτῆς ἀσέλγειαν ᾄδει).[30] The context is a list of disparaging remarks concerning fourteen Greek women writers, the works of nearly all of whom are lost to us. Tatian must have been familiar with the negative Sappho interpretation before him, which, in turn, may have arisen in reaction to women's, possibly women poets', appealing to Sappho. The Christian father's rejection of lesbian existence may have contributed to Sappho's poetry not being handed down, so that before the discovery of the Oxyrhynchus papyri, nearly all of it was lost to us.

Other scattered references to lesbians include two derogatory mentions by Terullian of *frictrices*,[31] from *frico*, 'to rub,' probably parallel to the most common Greek word for lesbian, τρίβας, from τρίβω, 'to rub.'

In sum, Christianity entered a world in which male writers were commenting more frequently on lesbian existence than previously, nearly always negatively, which is different from ancient discussions of male homosexuality. Similarly, patristic interpretations of Rom 1:26 indicate that the authors in question did not view lesbian existence as parallel to male homosexuality. Either they interpreted Rom 1:26 as not referring to lesbians at all—denying that love relations between women are possible to a strong motif in the history of writing about women's sexuality and women—or they took it as referring to lesbians, but focused much greater attention on male homosexuality. Male homosexuality has always received greater attention in the literature, probably because men and men's sexuality are simply seen as more important. Clement, Chrysostom and Augustine are especially concerned about sharp gender differentiation, of which clothing and hairstyle form important components. They view a blurring of gender distinctions through clothing, hairstyle and same-sex love as dangerous because it contradicts the natural, God-ordained hierarchy of man over women. I would like to add that I find this connection between Rom 1:26–27 and 1 Cor 11:2–16 (on hairstyle, the hierarchical relationship between the sexes and possibly veiling) to be helpful in understanding Paul, i.e., exegetically convincing.

Notes

1. E.g., Origen, *Comm. Lam.* 45 (*GCS* 6: 255, 20-textual variant); *Comm. Matt.* 123 (*GCS* 41: 64): 12 (*GCS* 41: 102). It is not possible to discuss in this paper all of the patristic references to Rom 1:26. Among the more interesting of those not discussed are: Tertullian, *De cor.* 6, 1(*CC*2: 1046–47); Hippolytus, *Refutatio* v. 7. 16–19 (*GCS* 26: 82.11–83.8), which deals with the Naasenes; *Acta Thomae* § 55, ed. R.A. Lipsius, M. Bonnet (Leipzig, 1903; repr.: Hildesheim, 1959), vol. 2/2, p. 172; Ambrosiaster, *Ad Hom*, i. 26 (*CSEL* 81, 1: 51, 1–15); Pseudo-Julian of Toledo, *Ars grammatica, poetica et rhetorica* 6, 49, ed. W.M. Lindsay (Oxford, 1922), pp. 31–32. I would like to express special appreciation to Prof. Dr. Walter Thiele and the Vetus Latina Institut of Beuron in the Federal Republic of Germany for making available to me the catalogue of the Latin references to Rom 1:26 in early Christian literature. Also very helpful was the *Biblia Patristica* produced by the Centre d'Analyse et de Documentation Patristiques (Paris, 1975–), *ad loc.*

2. *PG* 8: 501–2, n. 9; *GCS* 12: 331, 6–8.

3. *De nupt. et concup.* xx. 35 (*CSEL* 42: 289); cf. *De bono coni.* 11 (*CSEL* 41: 202–3).

4. *Epist.* 211. 14 (*PL* 33: 964).

5. *In epist. ad Rom., Hom.* 4 (*PG* 60: 417).

6. *In epist. ad Rom., Hom.* 4 (*PG* 60: 415–22).

7. Ed. and tr. J. Dumortier (Paris, 1955). For a translation with introduction and notes, see Elizabeth Clark, *Jerome, Chrysostom, and Friends. Essays and Translations*. Studies in Women and Religion 2 (New York, 1979) pp. 158–248.

8. *Paed.* 3.3.21 (*GCS* 12: 249). See the whole of 3.3.15.1–25.3 (*GCS* 12: 244–51); see also *Paed.* 2.10.83.1–115.5 (*GCS* 12: 208–26).

9. *De op. monach.* 31.39–32.40 (*CSEL* 41:590–94; *PL* 40: 578–80). esp. 32.40 (*CSEL* 41:594; *PL* 40:580). For an extensive analysis of Augustine's theological anthropology of woman, see Kari E. Borresen, *Subordination and Equivalence. The Nature and Role of Woman in Augustine and Thomas Aquinas* (Washington, D.C., 1981) pp. 1–140.

10. *The Sentences of Pseudo-Phocylides* 192, ed. and tr. P.W. van der Horst (Leiden, 1978) pp. 239–40.

11. *Sifra Leviticus* 18. 3 (337a); *y.* Gi[tldot][tldot]in 49c. 60–61; *b. Shabbath* 65a (see Rashi); *b. Yebamoth* 76a (see Rashi).

12. *Anth. Pal.* v. 206, ed. H. Stadtmueller (Leipzig, 1894), vol. 1: pp. 168–69; see schol. B:ὡς τριβάδας διάβαλλει).

13. *Contrav.* 1.2.23, ed. and tr. M. Winterbottom (Cambridge, MA, 1974) vol. 1: pp. 86–87 (LCL); see also Seneca the Younger, *Epist.* 95.21, ed. L.D. Reynolds (Oxford, 1966), vol. 2: p. 387.

14. *Epigr.* 1.90; 7.67, 70, ed. W.M. Lindsay (Oxford, 1959).

15. *Sat.* 6. 306–13, ed. W.V. Clausen (Oxford, 1959) p. 82.

16. *Lib. fab.* 16, ed. A. Guaglianone (Turin, 1969) pp. 66–67.

17. *Vit., Lyc.* 18.9, ed. K. Ziegler (Leipzig, 1973) vol. 3, 2: pp. 29–30.

18. *Dial. meretr.* 3, ed. C. Mras (Berlin, 1930) pp. 19–22.

19. *Amor.* 19–28, ed. and tr. M.D. MacLeod (Cambridge, MA, 1967) vol. 8 (Lucian): pp. 178–95 (LCL).

20. *Tetrabiblos* 3.14; 4.5, ed. and tr. F.E. Robbins (Cambridge, MA, 1956) pp. 368–71; 402–5 (LCL).

21. *Anthol. lib.* 2.36, ed. W. Kroll (Berlin, 1908) p. 111.

22. *Apotelesmat.* 4.24, ed. A. Koechly (Leipzig, 1858) p. 75.

23. *Tard. pass.* 4.9.132–33, ed. and tr. I. E. Drabkin (Chicago, 1950) pp. 900–3.

24. See, e.g., Boswell's translation of Clement of Alexandria, *Paed.* 2.10 (pp. 355–59) and of John Chrysostom, *In epist. ad Rom., Hom.* 4 (pp. 359–62). His discussion of the patristic sources is to be found primarily in chap. 6, 'Theological Traditions' (pp. 137–66). It includes a treatment of Clement, Chrysostom and Augustine, as well as of the marginal gloss by Anastasius (p. 158). On pp. 82–84, he discusses some of the Roman-period sources.

25. *Epist.* 1.19.28, ed. A. Kiessling, rev. R. Heinze (Berlin, 1961) pt. 3, p. 184. See also Horace's reference to Folia of Arminum, to whom he attributes *mascula libido, Epod.* 5.41–46, ed. E.C. Wickham, rev. H.W. Garrod (Oxford, 1952).

26. Mor. 406a, ed. M. Pohlenz, W. Sieveking (Leipzig, 1929) vol. 3: p. 51.

27. *Philos.* 18.7, ed. H. Hobein (Leipzig, 1910) p. 227.

28. *Tristia* 2.365–66, ed. S.G. Owen (Oxford, 1915); *Heroides* [XV], ed. R. Ehwald (Leipzig, 1907; 1916 ed. unavailable to me), pp. 173–79 (authorship disputed); cf. also Ovid, *Metamorph* 9 666–797, ed. O. Korn, rev. R. Ehwald, M.v. Albrecht (Zürich, 1966) vol. 2:115–25.

29. Ed. A. Adler (Leipzig, 1928–38; repr.: Stuttgart, 1967–71) vol. 1, 4: p. 323.

30. *Oratio ad Graecos* 33, ed. and tr. M. Whittaker (Oxford, 1982) pp. 60, 62 (translation my own).

31. *De res.* 16.6 (CC 2:939); *De pallio* 4.9 (CC 2:745).

PART III

THE RHETORIC OF RACE/ETHNICITY

Introductory Comment

The end of Western colonialism in the Third World and the success of the Civil Rights movement in the United States have put the issue of race and ethnicity on the progressive political agenda for decades. As a result, scholars have begun to investigate the history and politics of race and ethnicity in biblical studies. The sometimes reticent, but nonetheless occurring discourse on these issues in Western society and academia, as well as the growing number of biblical scholars who themselves come from racial and ethnic groups have increased the demand for such work. After all, for most of its history, the academic discipline of biblical studies, similar to other academic fields, was created and defined by white male scholars of Europe or European descent. Under such conditions, "The Rhetoric of Race/Ethnicity" played, at best, a marginal role—although issues of race and ethnicity permeated the field, albeit subconsciously, but with overt political, economic, and religious consequences for people of color. To uncover such practice and theory, the relationship between the Bible and race/ethnicity has to be understood. This section includes a limited, yet representative number of articles that characterize this burgeoning research area in biblical studies.

Much has been written on the concepts of race and ethnicity because neither term has a self-evident or fixed meaning. Despite the claim of nineteenth-century scientists and their heirs, race or ethnicity are not based in nature or genetics. Instead, both terms are social constructs which are historically and culturally defined. Sometimes the terms are used interchangeably, as in the phrase "ethnic minorities,"[1] which suggests similar characteristics for both terms. The following definition refers to the commonalities of both terms:

> Ethnic and racial groups [are] social groups, singled out as such for social interest, whether good or bad, either from inside or outside the differentiated groups, on the basis of certain cultural [i.e. ethnic] or physical [i.e. racial] characteristics.[2]

Both terms (ethnicity, race) refer to human groups, one focuses on the cultural and the other on the physical aspects of the group members. The precise usage of the terms, however, depends on the particular historical and socio-political

---

[1]Kenneth Leech, "Ethnicity," in *Dictionary of Ethics, Theology and Society*, ed. Paul Barry Clarke and Andrew Linzey (London/New York: Routledge, 1996), p.321.

[2]Fernando F. Segovia, "Racial and Ethnic Minorities in Biblical Studies," in *Ethnicity and the Bible*, ed. Mark G. Brett. (Leiden: E.J. Brill, 1996), p. 470n.

circumstances. Sometimes, instead of the similarities, the differences of both terms are stressed, as in this definition:

> Race is a pseudo-biological concept, closely related to colour, and racism is a structural and cultural reality which results in discrimination and disadvantage. Ethnicity, on the other hand, defines the characteristics of a group which sees itself as distinct. Ethnicity is not necessarily related to race, colour or religion though these will often affect it.[3]

Race and ethnicity, then, describe ideas and practices in Western history and culture that sometimes overlap and at other times differ. Biblical scholars have used both concepts to examine biblical texts and their interpretations.

Four sets of articles illustrate the discussions on race and ethnicity in biblical studies. The first set, entitled "A Baptismal Formula For Racial and Ethnic Justice," presents two essays focused on a highly influential text of the New Testament, namely Galatians 3:28. The three articles look at the possibilities for creating just and egalitarian societies and invite discussions on the interconnectedness of racial and ethnic inequality to gender and class. Christopher D. Stanley elaborates on the significance of this biblical passage for the socio-ethnic dynamics during the Hellenistic era in which early Christians lived. Elisabeth Schüssler Fiorenza articulates the difficulties of early Christians who tried to live according to the egalitarian ethos of Gal. 3:28 in a society that was hierarchically structured by gender, ethnicity, and class. Both essays invite reflections on developing egalitarian models of society in a world filled with aggressive actions of racial oppression and ethnic cleansing.

The second set of articles, entitled "The Dispute about Slavery in America," describes the various usages of the Bible in nineteenth-century America. The articles describe how interpreters of that time referred to the Bible in support of or in opposition to the practice of slavery. Surveying old and discredited argumentations, the essays provide the opportunity to question standards for reading the Bible and to examine critically the issue of biblical authority. Caroline L. Shanks surveys the theological debate raging in nineteenth-century America, particularly during the 1830–1840s. Gene Rice describes the interpretive history of another influential passage that was used to justify racial discrimination. Focused on Genesis 9:18–27, the so-called "curse of Ham," the article shows how this biblical passage was read to discriminate against Black people in Africa and the United States. Jennifer A. Glancy investigates the cultural authority of the Bible in past and present discussions on slavery, particularly in regard to the so-called household codes of the New Testament, and so exemplifies the Bible's continuing role in American society, politics, and religion.

The third set of essays, entitled "Ethnic Perspectives on the Bible," exemplifies the great variety of concerns and directions of current developments in

---

[3]Ibid.

biblical research. The articles are internationally and culturally diverse, and discuss biblical matters from African American, indigenous Latin American and African perspectives. These articles, of course, introduce only selectively the debates about the Bible from various racial and ethnic perspectives, and yet they provide a solid introduction to such research. Vincent L. Wimbush reflects on the theoretical implications of reading the Bible within the African American experience. His analysis elaborates on the notion that a reader's "world" shapes a reader's understanding of the Bible. He shows why this insight is particularly apparent from an African American perspective. Justin S. Ukpong surveys the history of the Bible in Africa since the 1930s, emphasizing the increasing significance of "ordinary readers" and their African contexts for biblical interpretation in Africa, particularly since the 1990s. After two theoretical articles, the work of Dalila Nayap-Pot interprets a particular biblical book from a particular ethnic context. Reading the book of Ruth from the perspective of Latin American indigenous women, Nayap-Pot illustrates the validity of the notion that a reader's social location shapes the interpretation.

All three articles, then, invite reflections on the multiple meanings of the Bible in the context of diverse ethnic and racial locations. They raise several questions: Is the textual meaning of a biblical passage ultimately infinite because a biblical meaning is intricately linked with a reader's social location? If so, what are the criteria for determining the validity of one interpretation over against another? Furthermore, how do we explain that the idea about the interrelatedness of biblical meaning and social location emerges only when ethnically and racially marginalized groups enter the field of biblical studies? What do we learn about the benefits of diversity and plurality for the understanding of the Bible in particular and of the world in general?

The fourth set of articles, entitled "Christian Anti-Judaism in Biblical Interpretations," provides resources for another significant area related to the rethoric of race and ethnicity, namely the issue of anti-Judaism in Christian interpretations of the Bible. Until today, many Christians learn theologically prejudiced and discriminatory ideas about Jews. These notions have historically led to the devaluation of the Hebrew Bible as part of the Christian canon and created a negative image for Jewish groups such as the pharisees, contemporaries of Jesus. The selected articles examine various aspects of Christian anti-Judaism to create awareness about anti-Judaism in Christian history and interpretation of the Bible. Arthur E. Zannoni examines the Christian negligence to value the Hebrew Bible as much as the Greek Bible, and so provides guidance for Christians to remedy the situation. Michael Cook investigates the significance of anti-Jewish passages in the New Testament, such as Matthew 23, and surveys Christian attempts to reconcile the anti-Judaism that they find in their sacred literature.

Both essays encourage discussions on Christian-Jewish relations in light of the Christian difficulties to respect and value the religion from which Christianity emerged. How can Christians read biblical passages that have been used to ridicule Jewish customs and even led to the murder of Jews in past centuries? Should Jews be concerned with this Christian problem, and if so, how? How can Christians learn to welcome people from other religious traditions, including Jews, so that they will feel welcomed and respected for their different religious convictions and as human beings?

This section provides a potpourri of biblical scholarship, as it illuminates issues of race and ethnicity. The articles demonstrate that biblical texts, characters, and topics, formerly marginalized and ignored by white and male scholars, appear in a very different light. Contexts and "worlds" of readers become as important as biblical texts. In fact, scholars of ethnically and racially marginalized groups emphasize the significance of reading texts as part of context. They posit that the meaning of a text emerges only through readers' eyes and relates to their social locations. Texts do not stand by themselves as if their meaning were waiting to be uncovered. Readers create meaning, and thus the reading of the Bible is a practice shaped by social, cultural, and religious location. Interpreters have the task of illuminating this connection, to make apparent the confluence of reader, social location, and the interpretation of the text. Like feminist scholars, scholars of racial and ethnic perspectives reject the notion of an unbiased, objective, and distanced Bible. To them, the Bible is a valued text because it enables them to shed light on racism and ethnocentrism and to imagine alternative worlds and relationships among humans from different races and ethnicities.

Chapter 1

A Baptismal Formula for Racial and Ethnic Justice

'Neither Jew nor Greek': Ethnic Conflict in Graeco-Roman Society

Christopher D. Stanley

From the middle of the first century BCE, we have sporadic reports of social unrest involving Jewish communities in the cities of Asia Minor, Syria, Palestine, Egypt, and Parthian-controlled Mesopotamia. Our primary sources for these conflicts are the writings of Josephus (notably the *Jewish Antiquities*, but also parts of the *Jewish War* and the *Life*) and Philo (the two treatises *In Flaccum* and *Legatio ad Gaium*), along with occasional references in Cicero and other Roman writers. In a few cases, the troubles centered on the actions of authorities from outside the local area, for example, the seizure of Jewish Temple funds in Asia Minor by the Pergamene king Mithridates (88 BCE), or the efforts by Roman officials to conscript

Excerpted from *Journal for the Study of the New Testament* 64 (December 1996): 101–124. Copyright by Sheffield Academic Press Limited. Reprinted by permission.

Jews from Asia Minor into the republican army during the Civil War period.[1] In most instances, however, the conflicts resulted from tensions between the Jewish community and the local citizen-body and/or their leaders.

IDENTIFYING THE OPPONENTS

Our primary source of information about the troubles in Asia Minor is the series of edicts and decrees by Greek and Roman officials that Josephus cites in books 14 and 16 of his *Jewish Antiquities*.[2] The historical reliability of these decrees has been questioned, but most investigators have accepted their authenticity despite a number of mistakes by Josephus and/or subsequent copyists.[3] By carefully reading between the lines, we can recover at least a general outline of the circumstances that gave rise to these decrees.

A helpful analysis would begin with a recognition of the *ethnic* dimensions of these conflicts. Most analysts have described the Jews' opponents in these disputes as 'Gentiles', framing the problem in 'Judeocentric' terms as one of 'Jews' versus 'non-Jews'. This approach founders on the fact that, in social terms, there was simply no such thing as a 'Gentile' in the ancient world. The use of the term 'Gentiles' (ἀλλοφύλοι or ἔθνη) to designate all non-Jews represents a 'social construction of reality' developed by a particular people-group (the Jews) in a concrete historical situation.[4] Those whom the Jews lumped together as 'Gentiles' would have defined themselves as 'Greeks', 'Romans', 'Phrygians', 'Galatians', 'Cappadocians', and members of various other ethnic populations. We simply cannot assume that the Jews of antiquity related the same way to each of these groups wherever they happened to live, nor that every conflict pitted the Jewish community against 'Gentiles' (i.e. non-Jews) in general. To speak of 'Jewish-*Gentile* conflicts' in antiquity is to confuse social analysis with ideology.

So who *was* causing so much trouble for Jews in the cities of Asia Minor in the late first century BCE? The edicts cited by Josephus offer no clear answer. In Parium and Miletus, the text of the decree specifies that the local citizen-body had

---

[1]On Mithridates at Cos, see *Ant.* 14.110–13. A similar episode occurred later (62–61 BCE) when the Roman governor L. Valerius Flaccus seized funds bound for the Jewish temple from four cities in western Asia Minor (see Cicero, *Pro Flacco* 66–69). For the decrees of Lentulus (49 BCE) and Dolabelia (44–43 BCE) exempting Jews who were Roman citizens from military service, see *Ant.* 14.223–34, 238–40. An earlier decree of the Pergamene senate (*Ant.* 14.247–55, late second century BCE) objecting to Seleucid mistreatment of the Jews also involved aggression by an outside party.

[2]Philo refers to some of the same edicts in *Leg. Gai.* 156–157, 291, 311–16, and cites an additional letter from Augustus (offering no new information) in 315.

[3]The most significant recent challenge was issued by H. Moehring. 'The *Acta Pro Judaeis* in the *Antiquities* of Josephus', in J. Neusner (ed.), *Studies for Morton Smith at Sixty: Judaism before 70* (Leiden: Brill, 1975), III, pp. 124–58. For a balanced review of the evidence, see T. Rajak, 'Was there a Roman Charter for the Jews?'. *JRS* 74 (1984), pp. 107–23.

[4]The term 'social construction of reality' is used here in the sense made famous by Peter Berger in *The Sacred Canopy: Elements of a Sociological Theory of Religion* (Garden City, NY: Doubleday, 1967).

voted to outlaw certain Jewish practices.[5] Similar actions are implied in the cases of Ephesus, the cities of Ionia, and Sardis, but the texts are less specific.[6] In Laodicea, Ephesus, and Halicarnassus, various forms of non-official opposition seem to be in view.[7] In other places, the circumstances remain unclear.[8]

When Josephus himself is narrating the conflicts, however, a clearer picture emerges. In book 16, while introducing his second set of pro-Jewish Roman decrees, Josephus offers the following overview of the troubles in Asia Minor:

> Now the Jews of Asia and those to be found in Cyrenaean Libya were being mistreated by the cities there, although the kings had formerly granted them equality of civic status (ἰσονομία); and at this particular time the *Greeks* were persecuting them to the extent of taking their sacred monies away from them and doing them injury in their private concerns. And so, being mistreated and seeing no limit to the inhumanity of the *Greeks,* they sent envoys to Caesar about this state of affairs (*Ant.* 16.160–61, Loeb translation; emphasis mine).

In this passage, the term 'Greeks' (Ἑλλήνεζ) is used to describe those who are 'persecuting' the Jews in Asia Minor and Cyrenaica. The same designation appears in Josephus's description of the problems in Ionia in 14 BCE, the only conflict in Asia Minor that he actually narrates.[9] The litany of charges against 'the Greeks' in this passage agrees fully with the more allusive references in the decrees. The Jews are being hindered from observing their laws, and are forced to appear in court on the Sabbath. The funds that they have collected for the Jerusalem Temple have been confiscated by city officials. Their sons are being conscripted into military service. Some of them have even been forced to expend their own funds for public service (λειτουργίαι).[10]

These references to 'the Greeks' as the primary oppressors of the Jews in Asia Minor become especially significant when we recall that such references actually

---

[5]*Ant.* 14.213–16 (Parium), 14.244–46 (Miletus). In both cases it is the 'magistrates, council, and people' of the city who are said to have forbidden certain activities.

[6]In *Ant.* 14.263–64 (Ephesus), the reference to 'fines' seems to imply an official action that is hereby reversed; in *Ant.* 12.125–26, 16.27–65 (Ionia), the practices cited are mostly 'official' in nature; in *Ant.* 16.163–64 (general), a mix of official actions (judicial procedures, seizing Temple funds) and unofficial conduct (stealing books) is proscribed; in *Ant.* 16.168 (Ephesus), the brief reference to the judicial system aims to overturn an official practice; in *Ant.* 16.171 (Sardis), official prohibitions are implied; in *Ant.* 16.172–73 (Ephesus), the 'interference' cited by the proconsul appears to be legal in nature.

[7]In *Ant.* 14.242 (Laodicea), the identity of the 'Trallians' who object to special privileges for the Jews in Laodicea is not further specified; in *Ant.* 14.258 (Halicarnassus), the possibility is raised that a 'magistrate or private citizen' might interfere with Jewish rights; in *Ant.* 16.167–68 (Ephesus), the issue is theft rather than official confiscation of Temple funds.

[8]In *Ant.* 14.227, 230 (Ephesus), the text is rather vague as to whether any offenses beyond the attempted military conscription are in view; in *Ant.* 14.235 (Sardis), the question is whether the privileges that are here 'maintained' by the Romans have in fact been challenged at the local level; in *Ant.* 14.260 (Sardis), nothing is said about who had abrogated the Jewish rights that were recently 'restored' by the Romans.

[9]*Ant.* 16.27–65 (cf. 12.125–27). The mention of 'the Greeks' appears in 16.58. In *Ant.* 12.125, they are simply 'the Ionians'.

[10]Election to public office was limited to citizens in the Greek cities, but 'liturgies' seem to have been imposed across the entire (upper-class) population, according to A.H.M. Jones, *The Greek City from Alexander to Justinian* (Oxford: Clarendon Press, 1940), p. 175.

run counter to Josephus's apologetic interests.[11] In a well-known passage at the end of his second collection of Roman decrees in book 16, Josephus states that he is writing primarily for 'the Greeks' of his own day, to encourage them to adopt a more favorable stance toward the Jews, whom he insists share the Greeks' fundamental concerns for justice and goodness.[12] If this is Josephus's intention, then it certainly would not be in his interest to label the Jews' opponents as 'Greeks' unless the facts warranted it. We should therefore accept Josephus's statement that it was 'Greeks' who sought to restrict Jewish rights in Asia Minor in the late first century BCE.[13]

GREEKS AND BARBARIANS

But who were these 'Greeks'? What did the term 'Greeks' mean when applied to people in western Asia Minor around the turn of the era? Asia Minor was the home of a highly diverse population with varying degrees of exposure to 'Greek' culture.[14] Some of its residents, such as the Lydians and Carians on the west coast, had long since adopted Greek culture in place of their own. Others, such as the Galatians, Isaurians, and Phrygians, retained a strong sense of their historic identity. The peoples of northern and inland Asia Minor had hardly been touched by Hellenism.[15] No educated person in antiquity (including Josephus) would have used the term 'Greek' to refer to the general non-Jewish population of Asia Minor.

---

[11]Philo is even more consistent than Josephus in pursuing his apologetic interests: the instigators of the Alexandrian pogrom are called 'Egyptians' throughout Philo's account, even though both Isidorus and Lampo had served as gymnasiarchs, the chief guardians of Greek culture in the city. See the discussion in K. Goudriaan, 'Ethnical Strategies in Greco-Roman Egypt', in P. Bilde *et al.* (eds.), *Ethnicity in Hellenistic Egypt* (Aarhus: Aarhus University Press, 1992), pp. 81–86.

[12]The passage, from *Ant.* 16.174–78, is worth quoting: 'Now it was necessary for me to cite these decrees since this account of our history is chiefly meant to reach the Greeks in order to show them that in former times we were treated with all respect and were not prevented by our rulers from practicing any of our ancestral customs but, on the contrary, even had their co-operation in preserving our religion and our way of honouring God. And if I frequently mention these decrees, it is to reconcile the other nations to us and to remove the causes for hatred which have taken root in thoughtless persons among us as well as among them' (Loeb translation). Apparently it never occurred to Josephus that the decrees he cites actually undercut his position, since they refer to occasions when 'rulers' (i.e. the governing officials of the Greek cities) did in fact prohibit groups of Jews from following their 'ancestral customs'.

[13]A similar ambiguity can be seen in the language Josephus uses to describe the conflicts at Antioch, Caesarea, Alexandria, and other cities (see nn. 3 and 4 for references). Here the opponents are styled sometimes 'Greeks', sometimes 'Syrians' or 'Antiochians' or 'Alexandrians'.

[14]On the ethnic and cultural diversity of Asia Minor, see Jones, *Greek City*, pp. 27–29, 41–46, 67–72; S.K. Eddy, *The King is Dead: Studies in the Near Eastern Resistance to Hellenism, 334–31 BC* (Lincoln: University of Nebraska Press, 1961), pp. 164–67; M. Avi-Yonah, *Hellenism and the East: Contacts and Interrelations from Alexander to the Roman Conquest* (Ann Arbor, MI: University Microfilms for the Institute of Languages, Literature and the Arts, the Hebrew University, 1978), pp. 169–72.

[15]According to W.M. Ramsay, *The Letters to the Seven Churches of Asia and their Place in the Plan of the Apocalypse* (New York: A.C. Armstrong & Son, 1905), pp. 120–21, the native languages of western Anatolia had mostly died out and been replaced by Greek by the first century CE, except in the inland regions. But in other areas, native languages survived into the third and fourth centuries CE.

But the cities were different. From archaic times, colonists from the Greek mainland had established cities (πόλειζ) with full Greek constitutions on the west coast of Asia Minor. The Seleucids founded numerous 'Greek' colonies and cities in the same area to secure their political and military control.[16] For centuries these cities, both old and new, served as the chief outposts of Greek civilization in a largely 'barbarian' world. The cities were also where most of the Jews lived. But no one in antiquity would have used the term 'Greeks' to designate the non-Jewish population of these cities. Whether founded in archaic or more recent times, the Greek *polis* guarded its historic identity by reserving the term 'Greeks' (Ἑλλήνεζ) for the enrolled body of citizens, which normally meant people of demonstrable Greek ancestry.[17] In addition to these 'Greeks', a typical city would have included (1) members of the local native population, whose ethnic identity varied from region to region; (2) the various resident alien communities, temporary and permanent settlers from such places as Italy, Egypt, Syria, and of course, Judaea, and (3) the slaves, whose origins were as diverse as the military conquests of the ruling powers.[18] To use modern terminology, the Greek city was a highly 'multiethnic' enterprise. To understand the conflicts between 'Jews' and 'Greeks' in the cities of Asia Minor, we must explore the *ethnic* implications of the terms 'Jew' and 'Greek' in the late first century BCE.

'JEWS' AND 'GREEKS' AS ETHNIC GROUPS

Modern studies of race and ethnic relations give us a useful framework for analyzing the 'ethnic' significance of the terms 'Jew' and 'Greek' in antiquity.[19] But we must be clear what we mean by the term 'ethnic'. Contemporary social theorists define 'ethnicity' not as a fixed quality that inheres in some objectively identifiable population group, but rather as a fluid aspect of individual and group

---

[16]Most of the Seleucid foundations were originally military colonies, but many of them were elevated to *poleis* with the passage of time. The Seleucids also refounded many 'barbarian' cities as *poleis* with full Greek constitutions.

[17]Other individuals, whatever their ethnic backgrounds, could gain acceptance as 'Greeks' if they fully embraced Greek culture, and could even be enrolled as citizens by a special vote of the citizen body.

[18]A fourth group, the Romans (many of them actually Italiote Greek businessmen from southern Italy), could be found organized into communities (*conventus Civium Romanorum*) in the major cities of Asia Minor, but probably not in the lesser centers.

[19]Several recent studies have recognized the heuristic value of modern race and ethnic studies for analyzing intergroup relations in the ancient world. See Bilde *et al.* (eds.). *Ethnicity*: E. Hall, *Inventing the Barbarian: Greek Self-Definition through Tragedy* (Oxford: Clarendon Press, 1989): E.T. Mullen, Jr. *Narrative History and Ethnic Boundaries: The Deuteronomistic Historian and the Creation of Israelite National Identity* (Atlanta: Scholars Press, 1993): G.G. Porton, *GOYIM: Gentiles and Israelites in Mishnah-Tosefta* (BJS, 155: Atlanta: Scholars Press, 1988).

self-definition that can be either highlighted or ignored as circumstances warrant.[20] In cases where it is activated, ethnic identity typically serves as a status marker to distinguish superior 'insiders' from inferior 'outsiders', who are often derided in stereotypical terms.[21] Certain boundary markers are regularly used to distinguish ethnic 'insiders' from 'outsiders'. The most common are (1) a belief in a *shared history*, often grounded in a story or myth of common origin; (2) a *common culture*, with special stress on features that distinguish the group from the broader society, including language and/or religion; and (3) some form of *physical difference* that sets group members apart from others (bodily appearance, hairstyle, dress, and so forth).[22] Where these three items receive special attention within a group or a society, one can be reasonably sure that the people in question are defining themselves (and others) in 'ethnic' terms.

There is ample evidence to indicate that both 'Jews' and 'Greeks' regarded themselves as distinctive 'ethnic groups' within the broader Graeco-Roman world. Whether scattered throughout the Diaspora or at home in Judaea, the people called 'Jews' (or 'Judaeans', Ἰουδαῖοι) thought of themselves as a *single people* united by a *common history* and a *shared culture* (derived for the most part from their sacred Scriptures), and set apart from their neighbors by the *physical mark* of circumcision.[23] Accompanying these shared symbols was a deep sense of mutual devotion and loyalty to others in their ethnic community, a devotion derided by outsiders as 'clannish' and 'misanthropic'.[24] Non-Jews (including 'Greeks') were typically classed together as 'Gentiles' (ἀλλόφυλοι or ἔθνη), a term that carried a host of negative connotations within the Jewish community.

---

[20]See especially the discussion in A. Royce, *Ethnic Identity: Strategies of Diversity* (Bloomington: Indiana University Press, 1982), pp. 1–33. Royce's definitions include several helpful distinctions: 'An "ethnic group" is a reference group invoked by people who share a common historical style (which may be only assumed), based on overt features and values, and who, through the process of interaction with others, identify themselves as sharing that style. "Ethnic identity" is the sum total of feelings on the part of group members about those values, symbols, and common histories that identify them as a distinct group. "Ethnicity" is simply ethnic-based action' (p. 18). Henri Tajfel's broader definition of 'social identity' is also useful here: 'that *part* of the individuals' self-concept which derives from their knowledge of their membership of a social group (or groups) together with the value and emotional significance attached to that membership' (*Social Identity and Intergroup Relations* [Cambridge: Cambridge University Press; Paris: Editions de la Maison des Sciences de l'Homme, 1982], p. 2).

[21]In the highly influential judgment of F. Barth (*Ethnic Groups and Boundaries: The Social Organization of Culture Difference* [Boston, MA: Little, Brown & Co., 1969]), maintaining boundaries between 'insiders' and 'outsiders' is the key issue for all ethnic groups: 'The cultural features that signal the boundary may change, and the cultural characteristics of the members may likewise be transformed, indeed, even the organizational form of the group may change—yet the fact of continuing dichotomization between members and outsiders allows us to specify the nature of continuity, and investigate the changing cultural form and content' (p. 14).

[22]Condensed from the list provided by W.W. Isajiw, 'Definitions of Ethnicity'. *Ethnicity* 1 (1974), pp. 111–24, which summarized the definitions used in twenty-seven recent studies of ethnicity. According to Royce (*Ethnic Identity*, p. 7). 'No ethnic group can maintain a believable (viable) identity without signs, symbols, and underlying values that point to a distinctive identity'.

[23]Apart from the (normally hidden) mark of circumcision, the Jews of antiquity could not be visually distinguished from their neighbors.

[24]G. Theissen (*Social Reality and the Early Christians: Theology, Ethics, and the World of the New Testament* [trans. M. Kohl; Minneapolis: Fortress Press, 1992], pp. 216–19, 274–76) points out that this ingroup solidarity across political boundaries (what he calls 'supraregional communication') actually heightened Greek suspicion of the Jews, since it helped to preserve the identity of the Jews and thus hindered their assimilation into Greek culture.

In reality, of course, none of these factors proved wholly reliable as markers of Jewish identity. Jews in Judaea and the Diaspora had in fact experienced quite different local histories, and had developed their own rather distinctive cultures over time. Circumcision marked the identity of males only, and perhaps not for all of them in the Diaspora. There were also many converts within the Jewish community who could never claim to have participated in the literal history of Israel, and many native 'Jews' who failed to follow Torah and became otherwise absorbed in Greek culture.[25] Yet 'the Jews' were still a distinct and identifiable people-group in the eyes of their Greek and Roman neighbors, as one can see from the extensive anti-Jewish literature of antiquity.

By the time of the Seleucids, the term 'Greek' was also being used as an ethnic self-designation in the cities of Asia Minor. The word Ἑλλήν ('Greek') first rose to prominence in the fifth century BCE as a political rallying cry to unite the fractious city-states of the Greek peninsula in a common military effort against the Persian threat. Under Alexander and his successors, the term took on a broader meaning. With the spread of Greek culture and Greek rule across the eastern Mediterranean, a 'Hellene' came to mean someone who spoke flawless Greek and embraced Greek culture and institutions, regardless of national origin.[26] But it would be wrong to conclude from this that the term 'Greek' was now stripped of all ethnic significance. Most of the people who identified themselves as 'Greeks' in the cities of the East could still trace their family-trees back to Hellas when required, as when the wealthier families went to enroll their sons in the local gymnasium. In most cases their ancestors had left their Greek homeland to start a new life in one of the many new cities established by Hellenistic monarchs throughout Asia Minor, Syria, Babylonia, and Egypt.[27] Here they laid aside their historic differences as they embraced the duties of citizenship in a new *polis*. Here they pursued the traditional 'Greek' way of life, with all of the social, economic, and political institutions that distinguished Greek cities from their oriental counterparts. And here, surrounded by a sea of 'barbarians', they nurtured a deep sense of 'Greek' identity that included a profound disdain for the native population.[28]

---

[25]Several examples of the latter practice are cited in J.D. Sevensler, *The Roots of Pagan Anti-Semitism in the Ancient World* (NovTSup, 41; Leiden: Brill, 1975), pp. 72–75.

[26]The often-quoted statement of Isocrates on this theme (*Paneg.* 50) is actually earlier than Alexander: 'So far has our city [Athens] distanced the rest of mankind in thought and in speech that her pupils have become teachers of the rest of the world, and she has brought it about that the name "Hellenes" no longer suggests a race but an intelligence'. But even Isocrates remained an implacable foe of all things 'barbarian': in the very same text he speaks of the need to 'reduce all the Barbarians to a state of subjection to the whole of Hellas' (*Paneg.* 131).

[27]The continued importance of physical descent from 'Greeks' is also evident in the efforts by both 'Greeks' and natives to 'discover' Greek origins for non-Greek civilizations and cities, usually by linking them in some way with the myth of Deucalion or the peoples of the Homeric epics: see Bickerman, 'Origines Gentium', *Classical Philology* 47 (1952), pp. 401–17; Diller, *Race Mixture*, pp. 32–56; Jones, *Greek City*, pp. 49–50.

[28]Cf. Walbank, *Hellenistic World*, p. 634; Green, *Alexander*, p. 319; Rostovtzeff, *Hellenistic World*, p. 1071; Hengel, *Jews, Greeks and Barbarians*, pp. 58–59. Greeks and Macedonians made up less than 10 per cent of the population of the Hellenistic kingdoms, according to S.M. Burstein ('Greek Class Structures and Relations', in M. Grant and R. Kitzinger [eds.], *Civilization of the Ancient Mediterranean: Greece and Rome* [New York: Charles Scribner's Sons, 1988], p. 545. Avi-Yonah (*Hellenism*, p. 131) has an even lower estimate: one million Greeks surrounded by fifteen to twenty million natives. Even this figure is probably too high.

But the wall of prejudice that separated 'Greeks' from natives was by no means impermeable. Most cities experienced chronic shortages of 'Greeks' to fill administrative positions, leaving the door open for Hellenized natives (normally from the local aristocracy) to find a niche in the local political economy. After two or three generations, the Greek-educated descendants of these former 'barbarians' might gain acceptance as 'Hellenes', including grants of citizenship. Moving in the opposite direction were an untold number of 'Greeks' (generally of lower social status) who married into the local population and slowly abandoned their 'Greek' identity. Through this process the boundaries of the 'Greek' ethnic community became more porous during the Hellenistic period, but the basic content of what it meant to be 'Greek' (i.e., the 'identity markers') remained largely unchanged,

'JEWS' AND 'GREEKS' IN CONFLICT

From at least the third century BCE, members of 'Greek' and 'Jewish' ethnic communities lived together (along with other peoples) in the cities of western Asia Minor.[29] Yet we hear of no conflict between them until the late first century BCE. Why? Here again modern studies of race and ethnic relations serve as a valuable heuristic tool. Recent studies in comparative ethnic relations have shown that interethnic *cooperation* is more common in settings where relations between groups are highly structured; where they occupy different (and/or complementary) socioeconomic or territorial niches; where political power is distributed in a mutually acceptable (though not necessarily equal) manner; where they have equally long histories of residence in the same area; or where they share a common language and worldview and a similar set of values. Ethnic *conflict* is more likely in places where groups are competing for scarce social, economic, or territorial resources; where there are discrepancies or changes in the size or political power of competing groups; where one group has migrated into the territory of another; where there is a history of conflict between groups; or where groups in the same geographical area possess discordant systems of personal and social values.[30]

When we ask where 'Jews' and 'Greeks' fit into this schema, we find their relationship to be low on the qualities that normally support intergroup harmony, and high on the scale of intergroup conflict. The problem areas can be summed up under two headings, 'social relations' and 'political relations'. (1) As individuals, Jews and Greeks could be found at every level of the socioeconomic structure of the Greek cities, where they competed for scarce jobs and resources. The distinctive beliefs and practices of the two groups would have been apparent (often irritatingly so) as their members interacted daily in the workplace and marketplace. Because the Jews believed that their 'ancestral customs' (τὰ πάτρια ἔθη) had come directly from God, they could not easily abandon those practices that ran counter

---

[29] On the early presence of Jews in Asia Minor, see Safrai and Stern (eds.), *Jewish People*, I, pp. 143–55; Trebilco, *Jewish Communities*, pp. 5–8.

[30] Compiled from Barth, *Ethnic Groups*, pp. 19–21; LeVine and Campbell, *Ethnocentrism*, pp. 36–40, 216–23; and especially R.A Schermerhorn, *Comparative Ethnic Relations: A Framework for Theory and Research* (New York: Random House, 1970), pp. 40–43, 68–73, 77–83, 238–42.

to the cultural prejudices of their Greek neighbors, such as Sabbath-observance, dietary restrictions, and circumcision. Nor did individual Greeks see any reason to lay aside those beliefs and practices that sustained their identity as 'Greeks' in the midst of a sea of 'barbarians'. Though there were certainly individual Jews and Greeks who sought to understand and affirm one another's cultures. The historically strong ethnic identity of both groups meant that the door was always open for misunderstanding and conflict. (2) The political relationship between the two groups was also rather ill-defined, and was a frequent source of conflict throughout the region. Both Jews and Greeks had at one time immigrated to Asia Minor, but the Greeks had arrived first (in most cases) and occupied a privileged position in the sociopolitical structure of the cities via their status as citizens (πολῖται).[31] But whereas the Greek population in the cities had leveled off by the first century BCE, the Jewish presence continued to grow through immigration from Palestine and a high birth rate.[32] This relative increase in the size of the Jewish community would have been a cause of concern for many 'Greeks'. Jews and other foreigners were viewed as 'barbarians' whose residence and status in the city was dependent on the goodwill of the citizen-body.[33] As an association of non-citizens, the Jewish community required permission from the civic authorities to own communal property (e.g., a synagogue), to hold public meetings, to maintain kosher food markets, and to adjudicate their own affairs. If the authorities decided to withdraw this permission, the political structure of the city offered no basis for appeal.[34] This inherent imbalance of power made the cities a fertile breeding ground for tensions between 'Jews' and 'Greeks'.

But these factors alone cannot account for the wave of nearly simultaneous actions by 'Greeks' against the Jews of western Asia Minor in the late first century BCE. Further stimuli were needed to raise these simmering tensions to the level of open conflict. Unfortunately, our sources tell us little about the circumstances leading up to these troubles. But a brief review of the political situation in western Asia Minor around the middle of the century can alert us to several probable causes.

The earliest of these conflicts coincided with the unsettled circumstances of the Roman Civil Wars, when opposing generals sought to bleed dry the treasuries of the Greek cities of Asia Minor. Both Rome and the provinces had experienced a shortage of currency since at least the 60s BCE,[35] and the cities of western Asia

---

[31]Only male citizens could vote for (and serve in) the assembly and/or governing council of a Greek city, and citizens jealously guarded their civic rights and privileges against non-citizens.

[32]Traditional Jewish values encouraged the production of large families, while many Greeks sought to control their family size via abortion and exposure of infants.

[33]According to Josephus, the Jews of Ionia, Antioch, Caeserea and Alexandria claimed the rights of citizenship by virtue of their ancestors' relations with the royal founders of the cities, but their claims were rejected by the broader citizen-body, which in a Greek *polis* was by definition 'Greek'. Scholars generally agree that Josephus was mistaken.

[34]Thus the Jews were forced to appeal outside the civic structure to the Roman authorities when the cities sought to restrict their privileges, as in the decrees cited in nn. 14 and 15.

[35]In 63 BCE, the Roman Senate acted to stem the currency crisis by prohibiting the export of gold and silver from Italy; the Roman governor L. Valerius Flaccus extended the prohibition to the province of Asia the following year. Much of the shortage in Asia can be traced to the punitive fines imposed by Sulla after the first Mithridatic war (88–86 BCE), which produced massive outflows of currency (in addition to ordinary taxes) over the next two decades.

Minor were now forced to contribute massive resources to keep competing Roman armies in the field.[36] Under these circumstances, it was inevitable that conflicts would arise over the Jewish practice of sending funds to Judaea to support the Jerusalem Temple. In a time when currency was scarce, exporting money from a city only increased the economic hardship of the local population. Those who did so would have met with disapproval and resistance from the people most concerned with the welfare of the city, that is, its 'Greek' citizens. The documented efforts of civic officials to prohibit such transfers and to expropriate Jewish funds represent an attempt to resolve an economic crisis, not a hatred of Judaism per se.[37]

On a more fundamental level, the political instability of the Civil War period opened up new opportunities for social unrest in the cities of western Asia Minor. The Roman Republic had long followed a two-pronged policy toward the Greek cities of the East: local officials were allowed substantial control over the internal affairs of the community, but authority was vested in a small number of wealthy upper-class 'Greek' families whose members alone could serve as magistrates and members of the city council (βουλή). Active decision-making power was in this way transferred from the democratically elected popular assembly to the oligarchic city council, which could be counted on to order civic affairs in a manner acceptable to Rome.[38] Direct Roman involvement (apart from times of crisis) was limited to the activities of Roman tax-collectors, businessmen, and governors who enriched themselves at the expense of the cities.[39] This Roman intervention in the affairs of the *polis* was deeply resented by the majority of 'Greek' citizens, whose social, political, and economic power was effectively eroded under Roman rule. Private clubs and associations became the forum of choice for anti-aristocratic and anti-Roman sentiment in the cities.[40] While Roman policy normally discouraged

---

[36]Crippling exactions continued throughout the decades of the 40s and 30s. In 49–48 BCE, the Pompeian general Q. Metellus Scipio seized vast sums from the province of Asia through new taxes and enforced 'loans' from local aristocrats and Romans alike. After a brief respite under Julius Caesar, the cities of Asia were muleted again by Caesar's partisan P. Cornelius Dolabella in 43 BCE. The heaviest exactions came in 42 BCE, when Marcus Brutus and Gaius Cassius ordered the cities to give them ten years' of taxes in advance, and 41–40 BCE, when Mark Antony demanded nine more years of levies as a penalty. The invasion of the Parthians in 40–39 BCE under the Roman renegade Q. Labienus brought another round of crushing impositions. The cities of Asia were also forced to contribute heavily to the maintenance of Antony's armies in the East until the battle of Actium in 31 BCE. Only under Octavian did the cities finally find relief.

[37]Whether the same can be said for the unknown individuals later accused of stealing Jewish funds and books (*Ant.* 16.163, 168) remains uncertain.

[38]According to M. Grant (*World of Rome*, p. 102), 'The Assemblies were only retained to "elect" to office by acclamation, the lists of candidates proposed by the Council, and to pass decrees ratifying what the Council had resolved'. Movement in this direction had begun already in the Seleucid period (*World of Rome*, p. 100), but it was the Romans who made the changes formal and irreversible.

[39]While Asia had the occasional good governor, most officeholders viewed the post as an opportunity to replenish the wealth they expended to gain high political office in Rome. On Roman taxation in the cities of the East, see Jones, *Greek City*, pp. 138–39, and B.D. Shaw, 'Roman Taxation', in Grant and Kitzinger (eds.), *Civilization*, pp. 809–28. For the financial effects of these 'ordinary' exactions, see Magie, *Roman Rule*, pp. 162–66, 216–17, 246–58; Rostovtzeff, *Hellenistic World*, pp. 812–19, 937–38, 955–74; Jones, *Roman Economy*, pp. 117–21; and especially Broughton, 'Roman Asia Minor', pp. 535–78.

[40]Anti-aristocratic and anti-Roman sentiment was no doubt reinforced by memories of the class warfare that wracked the cities of Asia Minor in the late second and early first centuries BCE: see Eddy, *The King is Dead*, pp. 171–72, 177–81; Grant, *World of Rome*, pp. 100–103; E.S. Gruen, *The Hellenistic World and the Coming of Rome* (Berkeley: University of California Press, 1984), II, pp. 592–603.

and even outlawed such groups, the turmoil of the Civil War period left the cities with only sporadic Roman oversight. Meanwhile the financial rapacity of the Roman army commanders added further fuel to local resentments.[41]

Attacking the Romans directly, however, was out of the question. But attacking Roman clients was not.[42] Since at least the late second century BCE, the Romans had developed a policy of protecting the religious rights of Jews in the cities of western Asia Minor as part of their strategy to limit the expansion of Seleucid power.[43] The popular impression must have been that the Jews (under Roman protection) had been granted a favored status within the cities, superior even to the citizens. To the average 'Greek', this was a blatant violation of all that the city stood for, and a constant reminder of his city's subjection to Rome.[44] Thus it comes as no surprise that the 'Greeks' of this area should take action against the Jews as Roman surrogates once Roman officials became distracted by the Civil Wars. As city after city acted to deprive the Jews of their established rights to assemble for worship, to provide for their dietary needs, to be excused from court on the Sabbath, and to manage their own affairs, the Jewish communities sent envoys to various Roman officials seeking protection and restoration of their rights.[45] The Romans, in their usual conservative manner, dutifully reaffirmed these rights in a

---

[41]For a summary of these exactions, see n. 56.

[42]Cf. G. Theissen, *Sociology of Early Palestinian Christianity* (trans. J. Bowden: Philadelphia: Fortress Press, 1978), pp. 91–92: 'Aggression against the Romans was transformed into aggression against a minority who could be identified with the Romans on the grounds of their privileges, but the Romans did not identify themselves with the Jews in any degree that might have made them feel that an attack on the Jews was an attack on them. Even in antiquity, the Jews were an ideal scapegoat.' So also Sevenster, *Roots*, pp. 145–46. Not only were the Roman armies an inhibiting influence, but the harsh Roman response to Asiatic support for Mithridates (including the reported slaughter of 80,000 Roman civilians in 88 BCE, probably an exaggeration) had surely not been forgotten.

[43]The decree from Pergamum preserved by Josephus in *Ant.* 14.247–55 (late second century BCE) refers to a recent *senatus consultum* by which the Romans adjured the Seleucid 'King Antiochus, son of Antiochus' to cease plundering the territory of Palestine in view of the Romans' Maccabean-era alliance with the Jews (cf. 1 Macc. 8.1–32, 12.1, 14.24; Josephus, *Ant.* 12.414–19, 13.163–65, 227). In response, the Pergamenes promised as 'allies of the Romans' to 'take care that these things are done as the Senate has decreed' (251) and to 'do everything possible on behalf of the Jews in accordance with the decree of the Senate' (253). Since the Pergamenes had no influence in Palestine, one can assume that they were referring to the Jews in their own territories, which included western Asia Minor. The author of 1 Maccabees (15.16–23) refers to a similar letter sent from Rome to a long list of cities around the Mediterranean world, including several in Asia Minor. Most scholars assume that Jewish rights in the cities of Asia Minor were guaranteed already by the Seleucids (cf. *Ant.* 12.119, 148–53), and perhaps by the Persians before them.

[44]Feldman (*Jew and Gentile*, pp. 422–23) speaks of a 'vertical alliance' with the outside power that protected the Jews while alienating the citizens. Blanchetière ('Le juif', p. 52) speaks similarly of 'les privilèges obtenus de l'extérieur, alors que les cités se montraient si jalouses de leurs droits' et de leur apparente autonomie' as a prime reason for anti-Jewish activity. Apparently this popular resentment of Jewish privileges reached into the upper levels of society, since by this time all legislation had to be initiated by the (aristocratic) city council.

[45]As H. Conzelmann notes concerning the Romans. 'Legal rights were not based on a permanent alliance, but were granted by Rome and could be revoked' (*Gentile, Jews, Christians: Polemics and Apologetics in the Greco-Roman Era* [trans. M.E. Boring; Minneapolis: Fortress Press, 1992], p. 24). In a period when the loyalties of Roman officials themselves were constantly changing, the Jews might have sought confirmation of their rights even if they had not been challenged by the cities. After a decade of governors who supported the First Triumvirate (61–50 BCE). Asia was governed in rapid succession by partisans of Pompey (50–48 BCE), Caesar (48–44 BCE), the conspirators (44–42 BCE, and Antony (41–31 BCE).

series of *ad hoc* decrees addressed to local officials.[46] Not until the period of Augustus, however, did Roman authorities regain sufficient control to enforce these decrees, and even then violations were slow to cease.[47] The entire episode was ironic: the very legal protections that the Jews had earlier received from the Romans set them apart from other immigrant groups as a focal point for anti-Roman hostility.

PAUL, 'GREEKS' AND 'JEWS'

With these events in mind, it requires little imagination to understand why anti-Jewish propaganda flourished in the Graeco-Roman world around the turn of the era, nor why much of it was produced by 'Greeks' from the cities of the East. Though our sources report few open conflicts (outside of Egypt) in the decades of Paul's missionary travels, these deep-seated interethnic tensions did not simply vanish with the passing of time. Instead they went underground, shaping attitudes and relationships in more subtle ways, until a new provocation should arise to fan them again into flame. The previously mentioned series of 'Jew-Greek' conflicts that broke out in the Levant in the 30s CE and continued sporadically until the great Diaspora revolt of 115–117 CE offers painful proof of this fact.

In any event, the apostle Paul, raised as a Jew in a prominent 'Greek' city of Asia Minor, would have been aware of the anti-Jewish sentiments of many 'Greeks' in the eastern Mediterranean basin, and had probably experienced discrimination himself at their hands. He was also aware of the inevitable tensions that would result from his efforts to unite 'Jews' and 'Greeks' into a novel social institution, the Christian house-church. Thus when he affirms that 'in Christ there is . . . neither Jew nor *Greek*' (Gal. 3.28), he *means* 'Greek', not 'Gentile'. When he argues that 'we were all baptized by one Spirit into one body, whether Jews or *Greeks*' (1 Cor. 12.13), he again has real 'Jews' and real 'Greeks' in mind.[48] Both Jewish and Greek converts brought heavy loads of ethnic prejudice with them into the

---

[46]Most of the decrees bear the names of Roman governors, but many other officials are represented: a Roman consul (L. Lentulus Crus); a proconsul with special *imperium* over the provinces of the East (Marcus Agrippa): two provincial legates (T. Ampius Balbus and M. Pupius Piso): a provincial pro-quaestor (L. Antonius): the governor of Syria (P. Cornelius Dolabella, who spent the winter in Asia after murdering its governor): and even the emperor himself. Where the decrees are issued by city officials, they invariably refer (at least indirectly) to some form of Roman initiative.

[47]While most of the Roman and civic decrees date from the Civil War era, the Jews of Ionia were still protesting their mistreatment before Marcus Agrippa in 14 BCE (*Ant.* 12.125–26, 16.27–65), and two years later the emperor Augustus was forced to issue a general decree protecting Jewish rights in Asia (*Ant.* 16.162–65: the choice between 12 BCE and 2–3 CE as the date for the decree depends on how one dates the 'Gaius Marcus Censorinus' referred to in 16.165). The letter of the proconsul Julius Antonius to the city of Ephesus (*Ant.* 16.172–73) seems to indicate that the Jews of Asia were still being abused in 7/6 BCE.

[48]Additional references to 'Jews' and 'Greeks' can be found in Rom. 1.16, 2.9–10, 3.9, 10.12; 1 Cor. 1.22, 1.24, 10.32; cf. Col. 3.11. Christian commentators have routinely overlooked the ethnic implications of such juxtaposed references to 'Jews' and 'Greeks' in early Christian literature due to their theological (and ahistorical) assumption that 'Greek' means the same as 'Gentile' wherever the term occurs.

new Christian house-churches. In Paul's view, such attitudes were simply inconsistent with the Christian's new social identity 'in Christ', and should be laid aside.

A more thorough examination of the subtle rhetorical strategies by which Paul sought to defuse the tensions between 'Jews' and 'Greeks' in his fledgling congregations must be left for another time. Certainly the handful of passages in which he expressly refers to 'Jews' and 'Greeks' could be fruitfully analyzed along these lines. Some of his comments about the relative status of Jews and *Gentiles* in the divine plan could also prove helpful, as could his ideas about the new identity of believers 'in Christ'.

A more difficult question is whether Paul really understood the power of ethnic identity to shape the attitudes and actions of both groups and individuals.[49] It would surely be instructive to compare Paul's social and rhetorical strategies with the methods suggested (and tried) by modern social scientists, in order to estimate how successful Paul might have been in his appeals for interethnic cooperation and unity in his mixed Jewish-Greek churches. Our own century bears painful witness to the deep-seated power of racial and ethnic prejudice in the Christian church, even after centuries of rehearsing Paul's appeals for love and self-sacrifice within the body of Christ. Whatever we think of his methods, however, we should give Paul credit for his halting attempts to address a burning problem that many modern Christians would rather ignore.

The Praxis of Coequal Discipleship

Elisabeth Schüssler Fiorenza

The contemporary discussion linking Gal. 3:28 and the household-code tradition seems to point to a historical-political dynamic that does not come to the fore when it is forced into the oppositions of "order of creation" and "order of redemption" on the one hand, and of "enthusiastic excess, or gnostic heresy" and

---

[49]The Stoics had long used similar language to express their vision for a unified Greek society, but to little avail. For references, see H. D. Betz, *Galatians* (Hermeneia: Philadelphia: Fortress Press, 1979), pp. 189–201.

From *In Memory of Her: A Feminist Reconstruction of Christian Origins*, Elisabeth Schüssler Fiorenza, New York: Crossroad Publishing, 1992. Copyright by The Crossroad Publishing Company. Reprinted by permission.

"Pauline theology and New Testament orthodoxy" on the other. Commentaries on Galatians "have consistently denied that Paul's statements have political implications."[1] Such commentaries are prepared to state the opposite of what Paul actually says in order to preserve a "purely religious" interpretation. In doing so, they can strongly emphasize the reality of equality before God sacramentally and at the same time "deny that any conclusions can be drawn from this in regard to the ecclesiastical offices (!) and the political order"—all of which, I would add, rest on the assumed natural differences between the sexes institutionalized in patriarchal marriage.

ANALYSIS AND INTERPRETATION OF GALATIANS 3:28

Form critical analyses converge in the delineation of Gal. 3:26–28 and its classification as a baptismal confession quoted by Paul.[2]

    i. 3:26a For you are all children of God

   ii. 3:27a For as many as were baptized into Christ

       b have put on Christ

  iii. 3:28a There is neither Jew nor Greek

       b There is neither slave nor free

       c There is no male nor female

  iv. 3:28d For you are all one

> Reinforced by dramatic gestures (disrobing, immersion, robing), such a declaration would carry—within the community for which its language was meaningful—the power to assist in shaping the symbolic universe by which that group distinguished itself from the ordinary "world" of the larger society. As a "performative utterance" it makes a factual claim about an "objective" change in reality that fundamentally modifies social roles. New attitudes and altered behavior would follow—but only if the group succeeds in clothing the novel declaration with an "aura of factuality."[3]

Such new behavior wa engendered by this baptismal declaration, at least with respect to women who exercised leadership roles in the house churches and mission of the early Christian movement. A letter of Pliny to the Emperor Trajan confirms that at the beginning of the second century women "servants" (slaves?)

---

[1]H. D. Betz, *Galatians,* Hermencia (Philadelphia: Fortress, 1979, 189, p. 68.

[2]W. A. Meeks, "The Image of the Androgyne: Some Uses of a Symbol in Earliest Christianity," *History of Religions* 13 (1974): 165–208; see also H. D. Betz, "Spirit, Freedom, Law: Paul's Message to the Galatian Churches," *Svensk Exegetisk Arsbok 39 (1974):* 145–60, and his *Galatians,* 181–201; J. Becker, Auferstebung der Toten im Urchristentum, SBS 82 (Stuttgart: Katholisches Bibelwerk, 1976), 56f.; H. Paulsen, "Einheit und Freiheit der Söhne Gottes— Gal. 3:26–29," ZNW 71 (1980): 74–95, for literature.

[3]Meeks, "Image of the Androgyne," 182.

were ministers in the church of Bithynia.[4] Around the same time, Ignatius writes to the bishop Polycarp of Smyrna, telling him not to set free either male of female slaves at the expense of the church (4:3). This exhortation presupposes that slaves who joined the Christian community expected their freedom to be bought by the church.

Such expectations were supported by the Christians' belief that they were truly set free by Christ. Such formulas occur again and again in the Pauline letters: "You were bought with a price, do not become human slaves" (1 Cor. 6:20; 7:23). Or "For freedom Christ has set us free . . . do not submit again to a yoke of slavery" (Gal. 5:1). The goal of Christian calling is freedom: "You were called to freedom" (Gal. 5:13), because "where the Spirit of the Lord is there is freedom" (2 Cor. 3:17). To argue that Christian slaves who understood their call to freedom had only "a superficial understanding of the gospel[5] is to minimize the impact of this language in a world where slavery was a commonly accepted institution. Liberation from the slavery of sin, law, and death, from the conditions of the "present evil age" (Gal. 1:4), has "freedom" as its purpose and destiny. "As a result, *eleutheria* (freedom) is the central theological concept which sums up the Christian's situation before God as well as in this world."[6] Therefore, a slave woman who became a Christian in the first century heard this baptismal pronunciation as a ritual, "performative utterance," which not only had the power to shape the "symbolic universe" of the Christian community but also determined the social interrelationships and structures of the church.

That such an expectation of free status on the grounds of baptism was not merely excessive enthusiasm is apparent if we look at the first opposites of the baptismal formula—Jew/Greek. One could show that Paul's whole work centered around the abolition of the religious distinctions between Jew and Greek. "For there is no distinction between Jew and Greek. The same Lord is Lord of all and bestows his riches upon all who call upon him" (Rom. 10:12). Equality among all those who call upon the Lord is based on the fact that they have all one and the same master who shares his wealth with all of them (cf. also Rom. 3:22). That such "religious equality" had social-ecclesial consequences for the interrelationship between Jewish and gentile Christians is apparent from the Antioch incident, which seems to have been well known in the early church.[7] Peter and Barnabas had entered into table sharing with the gentile Christians in Antioch but, after pressure from Jerusalem, discontinued it. They again adhered to the Pharisaic Christian purity rules against eating together with the "unclean." Paul publicly confronts Cephas and the Jewish Christian group around him because "they did not act in

---

[4]Pliny *Epistles* 10.96. According to A. N. Sherwin-White, "Pliny treats the *diakonoi* as these 'servants' evidently were, as slaves, whose evidence was commonly taken under torture. The torture of freeborn witnesses in ordinary criminal procedures was an innovation of the Late Empire. . . . Pliny stresses that many of 'every age, every class, and of both sexes are being accused . . .'" (*The Letters of Pliny: A Historical and Social Commentary* [Oxford: Clarendon Press, 1966], 708).

[5]Cf. J. E. Crouch, *The Origin and Intention of the Colossian Haustafel.* FRLANT 109 (Göttingen: Vandenhoeck & Ruprecht, 1972), 127.

[6]Betz, *Galatians*, 255.

[7]For literature and discussion, cf. ibid., 103f.

consistency with the truth of the gospel" (Gal. 2:14). The whole letter to the Galatians is written to make the same point. It is not circumcision or uncircumcision that counts, but the new creation.

This struggle of Paul for equality between gentile and Jewish Christians had important ramifications for Jewish and gentile Christian women alike. If it was no longer circumcision but baptism which was the primary rite of initiation, then women became full members of the people of God with the same rights and duties. This generated a fundamental change, not only in their standing before God but also in their ecclesial-social status and function, because in Judaism religious differences according to the law were also expressed in communal behavior and social practice. While one was *born* into Judaism—even the full proselyte could not achieve the status of the male Israelite—the Christian movement was based not on racial and national inheritance and kinship lines, but on a new kinship in Jesus Christ.[8] In baptism Christians entered into a kinship relationship with people coming from very different racial, cultural, and national backgrounds. These differences were not to determine the social structures of the community, nor were those of family and clan. Therefore both Jewish and gentile women's status and role were drastically changed, since family and kinship did not determine the social structures of the Christian movement.

This seems to be stated explicitly in the final pair of the baptismal pronunciation: "There is no male and female." This last pair differs in formulation from the preceding two, insofar as it does not speak of opposites but of man *and* woman. Exegetes have speculated a good deal over the fact that "male and female" are used here, but not "man and woman."[9] It is often argued that not only "the *social differences* (roles) between men and women are involved but the *biological* distinctions" as well.[10] Therefore, as we have seen, it is conjectured that the formulation is gnostic and advocates androgyny. Paul does not repeat the formulation in 1 Cor. 12:13—according to this argument—because he had special problems in Corinth due to the gnostic or enthusiastic consequences women drew from Gal. 3:28. However, such a conjecture is based on the unproven assumption that the behavior of Corinthian women was determined by gnostic beliefs and not by early Christian prophetic experiences.

The argument, moreover, overlooks the fact that designations of the sexes in the neuter can simply be used in place of "woman and man." Such designations do not imply a denial of biological sex differences.[11] The reference here probably alludes to Gen. 1:27, where humanity created in the image of God is qualified as "male and female" in order to introduce the theme of procreation and fertility.

---

[8]This is stressed by R. Loewe: "The sociological basis on which Christianity rests is not the tie of kinship as in he case of Judaism, but that of fellowship—fellowship in Christ" (*The Position of Women in Judaism* [London: SPCK, 1966], 52).

[9]See especially H. Thyen, "'. . . nicht mehr männlich und weiblich . . .' Eine Studie zu Galater 3.28," in F. Crüsemann and H. Thyen, eds., *Als Mann und Fran geschaffen* (Gelnhausen: Burkardthaus-Verlag, 1978), 109f.

[10]Betz, *Galatians*, 195.

[11]For documentation, see M. de Merode, "Une théologie primitive de la femme?" *Revue Théologique de Louvain* 9 (1978): 176–89, esp. 184ff.

Jewish exegesis understood "male and female," therefore, primarily in terms of marriage and family. In early Christian theology the expression also evokes the image of the first couple, and not that of an androgynous being, as can be seen from Mark 10:6. "No longer male and female" is best understood, therefore, in terms of marriage and gender relationships. As such, Gal. 3:28c does not assert that there are no longer men and women in Christ, but that patriarchal marriage—and sexual relationships between male and female—is no longer constitutive of the new community in Christ.[12] Irrespective of their procreative capacities and of the social roles connected with them, persons will be full members of the Christian movement in and through baptism.

In antiquity not only were sexual or gender roles considered to be grounded in biological nature but also cultural, racial, and social differences. Religious, social, racial, and sexual properties were not differentiated in antiquity as much as they are today. Although most would concede today that racial or class differences are not natural or biological, but cultural and social, sexual differences and gender roles are still proclaimed as given by nature. However, feminist studies have amply documented that most perceived sex differences or gender roles are cultural-social properties. We are socialized into sex and gender roles as soon as we are born. Every culture gives different symbolic significance and derives different social roles from the human biological capacities of sexual intercourse, childbearing, and lactation.[13] Sexual dimorphism and strictly defined gender roles are products of a patriarchal culture, which maintain and legitimize structures of control and domination—the exploitation of women by men.[14] Gal. 3:28 not only advocates the abolition of religious-cultural divisions and of the domination and exploitation wrought by institutional slavery but also of domination based on sexual divisions. It repeats with different categories and words that within the Christian community no structures of dominance can be tolerated. Gal. 3:28 is therefore best understood as a communal Christian self-definition rather than a statement about the baptized individual. It proclaims that in the Christian community all distinctions of religion, race, class, nationality, and gender are insignificant. All the baptized are equal, they are one in Christ. Thus, taken at face value, the baptismal declaration of Gal. 3:28 does not express "excessive enthusiasm" or a "gnosticizing" devaluation of procreative capacities."

---

[12]For a similar exegetical argument but a different systematic conclusion, see also B. Witherington, "Rite and Rights for Women—Galatians 3:28," *NTS* 27 (1981): 593–604. According to Witherington, the "Judaizers may have been insisting on the necessity of marriage and propagation, perhaps as a way of including women into the community and giving them an important role. . . ." But he insists that the mere fact that Paul speaks here of such sexual, racial, religious, and class distinctions means Paul recognizes quite well that exist. "He wishes not to obliterate them but to orient them properly. . . . Thus he rejects their *abuse* and not their proper *use*" (601f.). However, such a conclusion cannot be derived from the text.

[13]See especially M. Zimbalier Rosaldo, "The Use and Abuse of Anthropology: Reflections on Feminism and Cross-Cultural Understandings," *Signs 5* (1980): 389–417: and chap. 1 of Elisabeth Schüssler Fiorenza, *In Memory of Her: A Feminist Theological Reconstruction of Christian Origins* (New York: Crossroad, 1983).

[14]For the delineation of sex and gender, see A. Oackley, *Sex, Gender and Society* (New York: Harper & Row, 1972), 158ff.

We do not know the social effects initiation into Judaism had upon women, but we have some indication that it could spell "freedom" for slaves. The manumission or setting free of the slave was an act of the slave owner performed with the assent of the synagogue. The slave gained complete freedom except for the requirement to attend the synagogue. Connected with the act of manumission was a second washing that corresponded so closely to proselyte baptism that both could be seen as one and the same. Against the background of oriental cultic and Jewish religious manumission practices it is obvious that slaves would expect freedom from their initiation into the Christian community.[15] Paul seems to assume this when he sends the baptized Onesimus back to Philemon "no longer as a slave" but as a beloved brother "both in the flesh and in the Lord," that is, socially as well as ecclesially, as a human being as well as a Christian (Philem. 16). Paul has neither the legal ability to set Onesimus free himself nor the authority to *command* Philemon to do so. But by sending Onesimus back as a new member of the church in Philemon's house, he expects Philemon to acknowledge the new *status* of the former slave as a "brother."

Insofar as the Christian community did not withdraw from society, as the Epicurean Garden or the Jewish Therapeutae did, it provided an experience of an alternative community in the midst of the Greco-Roman city for those who came in contact with it. As an alternative association which accorded women- and slave-initiates equal status and roles, the Christian missionary movement was a conflict movement which stood in tension with the institutions of slavery and the patriarchal family. Such conflict could arise not only *within* the community but even more within the larger society, since Christians admitted to their membership women as well as slaves who continued to live in pagan marriages and households. This tension between the alternative Christian community and the larger society had to cause conflicts that demanded resolution, often in different ways. The Pauline exhortations and the household-code tradition within the New Testament testify to these tensions.

Yet unconsciously these injunctions of men, which demand the subordination of slaves, women, and children, may also express the interests of the "owner and patron class"[16]—as well as reflect the interests of husbands and masters, the heads of families, who felt that their prerogatives were being undermined. Of course, it is difficult for us to decide whether or not such motivations played a role in the modifications of the Christian baptismal self-understanding, that is, which admonitions to subordination were due to a genuine concern for the Christian group's embattled situation and which arose from a defense of patriarchal dominance couched in theological terms. The theological counterarguments by slaves or women have not survived in history.

Conversion and baptism into Christ for men, therefore, implied a much more radical break with their former social and religious self-understandings—especially for those who were also wealthy slave owners—than it did for women

---

[15]See Crouch, *Colossian Haustafel*, 126–29.
[16]E. A. Judge, *The Social Pattern of the Christian Groups in the First Century* (London: Tyndale Press, 1960), 60.

and slaves. While the baptismal declaration in Gal. 3:28 offered a new religious vision to women and slaves, it denied all male religious prerogatives in the Christian community based on gender roles. Just as born Jews had to abandon the privileged notion that they alone were the chosen people of God, so masters had to relinquish their power over slaves, and husbands that over wives and children. Since these social-political privileges were, at the same time, religious privileges, conversion to the Christian movement for men also meant relinquishing their religious prerogatives. It is often argued that it was possible for the tiny Christian group to abolish the institution of slavery and other social hierarchies. That might have been the case or it might not. However, what is often overlooked is that relinquishment of religious male prerogatives within the Christian community was possible and that such a relinquishment included the abolition of social privileges as well. The legal-societal and cultural-religious male privileges were no longer valid for Christians. Insofar as this egalitarian Christian self-understanding did away with all male privileges of religion, class, and caste, it allowed not only gentiles and slaves but also women to exercise leadership functions within the missionary movement.

PAUL'S MODIFICATIONS OF GALATIANS 3:28

The introduction to 1 Corinthians 7 clearly states that Paul is responding here to matters about which the Christians had written him. Although all the problems raised seem to refer in one way or another to marriage and the relationship between the sexes, Paul also mentions in 7:17–24 the question of circumcision/uncircumcision and slave/free. Since he also speaks in this section about the Christian calling by God, he clearly had the baptismal formula in mind when elaborating the general theological foundation for his advice in chapter 7. His reference to circumcision/uncircumcision in particular indicates that he has the three pairs Jew/gentile, slave/free, male/female in mind, since this reference to circumcision does not quite fit the tenor of the whole chapter, that is, it is not the social situation in which one finds oneself as a Christian that determines one's Christian standing, but rather living according to the will of God.[17] Exegetes misread Paul's advice to Jewish or gentile Christians, when they argue that Paul here means to say that they should remain in the social state and religious role they had when they heard the call to conversion. Paul clearly does not advise the former Jew or the former gentile to remain in their Jewish or pagan state. Rather he insists that the religious/biological sign of initiation to Jewish religion is no longer of any relevance to Christians.

Similarly, the advice to slaves cannot mean that slaves should remain in the state in which they were called. The advice in 7:21 is difficult to understand, since it is not clear whether they should "use" freedom or slavery to their advantage, if

---

[17]For a different interpretative emphasis, see H. Conzelmann, *1 Corinthians*, Hermencia (Philadelphia: Fortress, 1975), 126: "And grace embraces the world and holds me fast in my worldliness. No change of status brought about by myself can further my salvation."

they have the possibility of being set free.[18] Although most exegetes and translators assume that slaves were to remain in the state of slavery when they became
Christians, in my opinion the context speaks against such an interpretation. The
injunction of v. 23—"You were bought with a price, do not become slaves of people"—prohibits such an interpretation. The advice Paul gives to Christian slaves,
then, seems best understood as: "If you still must live in the bondage of slavery,
with no possibility of being freed, even though you were called to freedom, do not
worry about it. However, if you have the opportunity to be set free, by all means
use this opportunity and live in accordance with your calling to freedom. Those of
you who were slaves when called to become a Christian are now freedwomen and
freedmen of the Lord, just as those of you who were freeborn have now a master
in Jesus Christ." Paul argues here, then, that both slaves and freeborn are equal in
the Christian community, because they have one Lord. Therefore, it is possible to
be a Christian even as a slave, if no possibility of becoming free exists. Of course it
is more in line with one's calling to freedom to live as a free person. Much would
be gained by a change in social status, if such a change is possible. Regardless of
one's social status, however, the decisive thing is to continue in the calling to freedom which one has heard and entered into in baptism.[19] Thus it seems clear that
Paul had the baptismal declaration of Gal. 3:28 in mind when addressing the problem of the relationship between the sexes in chapter 7, even though the reference
to the first two pairs of the formula is made only in passing.[20]

Paul's theological advice with respect to the relationship between the sexes
is basically similar to the advice given to slaves. It is quite possible to live a Christian life as a married person, if that was the state in which one lived when becoming a Christian. However, Paul explicitly bases his argument not on the social
order, but on a word of the Lord that prohibits divorce. The eschatological ideal of
Jesus' declaration on marriage is here turned into an injunction of Jesus against divorce. However, despite this explicit instruction of the Lord, wives—who are
mentioned first and with more elaboration in 7:10f.—still have the possibility of
fleeing themselves from the bondage of patriarchal marriage, in order to live
a marriage-free life. If they have done so, however, they must remain in this
marriage-free state. They are allowed to return to their husbands, but they may
not marry someone else.

It is not only remarkable that Paul insists on equality and mutuality in sexual
relationships between husbands and wives, but even more that he advises Christians, especially women, to remain free from the marriage bond. This is often overlooked because Paul's option for celibacy has become "the higher calling" in
Christian tradition. However, in the first century, permanent abstinence from sexual relations and remaining unmarried were quite exceptional. The discoveries of

---

[18]See S. Scott Bartchy, *First-Century Slavery and 1 Corinthians 7:21*, SBLDS 11 (Missoula, Mont.: Scholars Press, 1973), 6–7, for a synopsis of the interpretations of 1 Cor 7:21.

[19]For a similar interpretation, see also P. Trummer, "Die Chance der Freiheir: Zur Interpretation des
mallon chr[emacron]sai in 1 Kor 7,21," *Biblica* 56 (1975): 344–68.

[20]See, e.g., D. Cartlidge, "1 Cor. 7 as a Foundation for a Christian Sex-Ethic," *Journal of Religion* 55
(1975): 220–34; W. Schrage, "Zur Frontstellung der paulinis chen Ehebewertung in 1 Kor 7.1–7," *ZNW*
67 (1976): 214–34; and the commentaries for bibliographical reviews.

Qumran and Philo's description of the community of the Therapeutae give evidence of such an ascetic lifestyle within Judaism, but it was lived in isolation from the mainstream urban culture. Temporary chastity was known in most oriental cults; castration was practiced in the worship of the Great Mother, and in Rome the Vestal Virgins remained chaste for the thirty years of their service; but virginity was a privilege and not a right according to Roman law.

> The lives of the Vestals were severely regulated but in some respects they were the most emancipated women in Rome. As noted in our discussions of unmarried goddesses, the most liberated females are those who are not bound to males in a permanent relationship. . . . Further evidence of the freedom from the restrictions of ordinary women is to be found in the privileges enjoyed by the Vestals. . . . These privileges had such implications of status that the "rights of Vestals" were often conferred upon female members of the imperial family, who were frequently portrayed as Vestals on coins.[21]

The privileges of virginity were not open to "ordinary women" in the Roman empire. In order to strengthen the traditional Roman family, Augustus had introduced severe marriage legislation and openly used religion to promote his marriage ideals.[22] In order to increase the birthrate, he granted freeborn women with three children and freedwomen who had given birth to four children emancipation from patriarchal tutelage. However, since he gave this privilege to his wife, the Vestal Virgins, and soldiers who could not marry during their time of service, other women who had not fulfilled the prescribed number of births also acquired this privilege. The rate of birth and the number of children were of great political concern, however, to the patriarchal establishment of the empire. The emperor levied sanctions and taxes upon those who were still bachelors. Moreover, widowers and divorcees of both sexes were expected to remarry after a period of one month. Widows at first were expected to remarry after a one year period, but, following protests, this period was extended to three years. Only those who were over fifty years of age were allowed to remain unmarried. Although these laws were probably not strictly kept throughout the empire, they evidence the general cultural ethos and the legal situation with respect to a marriage-free state. At the end of the first century, the emperor Domitian reinforced the Augustan marriage legislation particularly in order to strengthen the leading families of the empire.

It is therefore important to note that Paul's advice to remain free from the marriage bond was a frontal assault on the intentions of existing law and the general cultural ethos, especially since it was given to people who lived in the urban centers of the Roman empire. It stood over and against the dominant cultural values of Greco-Roman society. Moreover, his advice to women to remain nonmarried was a severe infringement of the right of the *paterfamilias* since, according to Roman law, a woman remained under the tutorship of her father and family, even

---

[21]S. B. Pomeroy, *Goddesses, Whores, Wives, and Slaves* (New York: Schocken Books, 1975), 213f.

[22]See N. Lewis, *Roman Civilization* (New York: Columbia University Press, 1955), 52ff.; P. E. Corbett, *The Roman Law of Marriage* (Oxford: Oxford University Press, 1930), 106–46:120f.

after she married. Paul's advice to widows who were not necessarily "old"—since girls usually married between twelve and fifteen years of age—thus offered a possibility for "ordinary" women to become independent. At the same time, it produced conflicts for the Christian community in its interaction with society.

Paul's theological argument, however, that those who marry are "divided" and not equally dedicated to the affairs of the Lord as the nonmarried, implicitly limited married women to the confines of the patriarchal family. It disqualified married people theologically as less engaged missionaries and less dedicated Christians. It posited a rift between the married woman, concerned about her husband and family, and the unmarried virgin who was pure and sacred and therefore would receive the pneumatic privileges of virginity. One can only wonder how Paul could have made such a theological point when he had Prisca as his friend and knew other missionary couples who were living examples that his theology was wrong.

Thus Paul's impact on women's leadership in the Christian missionary movement is double-edged.[23] On the one hand he affirms Christian equality and freedom. He opens up a new independent lifestyle for women by encouraging them to remain free of the bondage of marriage. On the other hand, he subordinates women's behavior in marriage and in the worship assembly to the interests of Christian mission, and restricts their rights not only as "pneumatics" but also as "women," for we do not find such explicit restrictions on the behavior of men qua men in the worship assembly. The post-Pauline and pseudo-Pauline tradition will draw out these restrictions in order to change the equality in Christ between women and men, slaves and free, into a relationship of subordination in the household which, on the one hand, eliminates women from the leadership of worship and community and, on the other, restricts their ministry to women.

CHRISTIAN MISSION AND THE PATRIARCHAL HOUSEHOLD

As we have seen, the early Christian vision of the discipleship of equals practiced in the house church attracted especially slaves and women to Christianity but also caused tensions and conflicts with the dominant cultural ethos of the patriarchal household. True, women as well as men, slaves as well as free, Asians as well as Greeks and Romans, participated fully in the cult of the Great Goddess; and in such a religious context the baptismal confession of Gal. 3:28 was not utopian. However, in contrast to the public cult of the goddess, in the Christian context, the public religious sphere of the church and the private sphere of the patriarchal house were not clearly separated. Insofar as Christians understood themselves as the new family[24] and expressed this self-understanding institutionally in the house church, the public-religious and private patriarchal spheres were no longer

---

[23]If this practical tension in Paul's writings is overlooked, then Paul is alternately condemned as a "chauvinist" or hailed as a "liberationist."

[24]For a survey of NT writings, see R. Hamerton-Kelly, *God the Father: Theology and Patriarchy in the Teaching of Jesus* (Philadelphia: Fortress, 1979), 82–99.

distinguished. In fact, it was the religious ethos—of equality—that was transferred to and came in conflict with the patriarchal ethos of the household. The
Christian missionary movement thus provided an alternative vision and praxis to
that of the dominant society and religion.

Colossians, written by a disciple of Paul,[25] quotes Gal. 3:28 but changes it
considerably. Moreover, he balances it out with a household code of patriarchal
submission. The relationship of Jews and gentiles was no longer a great problem
and concern for the author. The separation between the Jewish and Christian communities probably had already taken place at the time of his writing. In quoting
the baptismal formula[26] Colossians mentions Greeks first and elaborates the second member of the pair circumcision and uncircumcision with "barbarian and
Scythian," in order to stress that national and cultural differences and inequalities
are overcome in the new humanity of Christ. Since Scythians were the proverbial
boors of antiquity, it is obvious that the author of Colossians is especially interested in the opposite pair Greek and barbarian. While the third pair of Gal. 3:28—
male and female—is not mentioned at all, Col. 3:11 also dissolves the slave-free
polarization that defines the social-political stratifications of institutional slavery.
Col. 3:11 no longer juxtaposes slave-free as opposite alternatives but adds them to
the enumeration and elaboration of those who are uncircumcised: barbarian,
Scythian, slave, freeborn.

Although the letter to the Colossians still refers to the baptismal liturgy and
theology of the Asian churches,[27] it celebrates not so much the restoration of
human equality in the new community but rather "a cosmic event, in which the
opposing elements of the universe were reconciled to each other." The so-called
enthusiastic theology ascribed to Paul's opponents in Corinth is fully expressed
here. Baptism means resurrection and enthronement with Christ in heaven, "strip-
ping away the body of flesh" (2:11), and life in heaven rather than on earth (2:1–4;
cf. 2:12, 20). The baptized are delivered from "the dominion of darkness" and
transferred into "the kingdom of his beloved son" (1:13). They are "dead to the
cosmos," have received a secret mystery (1:26f.; 2:2–3), and have the assurance of
an inheritance among the "holy ones" in the realm of light. The writer of Colossians agrees with his audience on this theology of exaltation but disagrees with
some of the Colossians on how this baptismal "symbolic universe" and drama
should be remembered and made effective. While some in the community of
Colossae believed that the "removal of the fleshly body" and the "new humanity"
in baptism must be realized in ascetic practices and elaborate ritual observances,

---

[25]See E. Lohse, *Colossians and Philemon,* Hermeneia (Philadelphia: Fortress, 1971), 177–83, for a comparison of Colossians and Pauline theology; see also J. L[amacron]hnemann, *Der Kolosserbrief* (Gütersloh: Mohn, 1971), 11–28, 153–82.

[26]Lohse (*Colossians and Philemon,* 142–47) argues that the series has been adopted from tradition. But
whereas the tradition insists that the "new humanity" or "new creation" realized in the Christian community has "cut through distinctions of social position," Colossians understands the "putting on of the
new human" in moral terms.

[27]See especially W. A. Meeks, "In One Body: The Unity of Humankind in Colossians and Ephesians," in J. Jervell and W. A. Meeks, eds., *God's Christ and His People: Studies in Honor of Nils Alstrup
Dahl* (Oslo: Universitatsvorlaget, 1977), 209–21.

the author insists on the finality of Christ's reconciliation and unification. The new "angelic religion" and the life in heaven are not to be realized by ascetic and ritual practice but in ethical behavior and communal life.[28] Since they have been raised with Christ, they are to "seek the things that are above," and to set their "minds on the things that are above." They do so "by putting away" anger, wrath, malice, slander, and foul talk and by "putting on" compassion, kindness, lowliness, meekness, and patience, forbearing one another and forgiving each other. Above all, they should "put on love, which binds everything together in perfect harmony" (3:5–17). They should behave wisely to outsiders and be able to answer everyone (4:5f.).

This is the context of the household code (3:18–4:1), the first and most precise form of the domestic code in the New Testament. The basic form of this code consists of three pairs of reciprocal exhortations addressing the relationship between wife and husband, children and father, and slaves and masters. In each case, the socially subordinate first member of the pair is exhorted to obedience to the superordinate second. The formal structure of such a household code, then, consists of address (wives), exhortation (submit to your husbands), and motivation (as is fitting in the Lord). The only Christian element in the Colossian code is the addition "in the Lord."[29] However, the author of Colossians quotes the code here, not because he is concerned about the behavior of wives, but that of slaves.

The expansion of the code's third pair, slave-master, indicates that the obedience and acceptance of servitude by Christian slaves are of utmost concern.[30] Colossians asks slaves to fulfill their task with single-mindedness of heart and dedication "as serving the Lord and not men" (3:23). It not only promises eschatological reward for such behavior but also threatens eschatological judgment and punishment for misbehavior (3:24f). The injunction to masters, in turn, is very short and has no Christian component except the reminder that they, too, have a master in heaven. Slave behavior is likened here to the Christian service of the Lord, while the "masters" are likened to the "Master" in heaven. It is obvious that the good behavior of slaves, according to the author, is the concrete realization of Gal. 3:28, insofar as both slaves and freeborn have one Lord in heaven, Christ, and belong to the new humanity, now "hid with Christ in God" (3:3). What we hear in these injunctions is "the voice of the propertied class."[31] We have no way of determining whether "those who are your earthly masters" are only pagan or also Christian masters. The injunction to the masters presupposes that they still have slaves who might or might not have been Christian.

In taking over the Greco-Roman ethic of the patriarchal household code, Colossians not only "spiritualizes" and moralizes the baptismal community understanding expressed in Gal. 3:28 but also makes this Greco-Roman household

---

[28]For the many attempts to identify the "opponents" of Colossians, see F. O. Francis and W. A. Meeks, eds., *Conflict at Colossai*, SBLSBS 4 (Missoula, Mont.: Scholars Press, 1973).

[29]However, Lohse (*Colossians and Philemon, 156f.*) argues that this addition is not a "mere formal element. Rather the entire life, thought and conduct of believers is subordinated to the lordship of the Kyrios."

[30]See Crouch, *Colossian Haustafel,* 150f.

[31]Judge, *The Social Pattern of Christian Groups,* 60, 71.

ethic a part of "Christian" social ethic. However, it is important to keep in mind that such a reinterpretation of the Christian baptismal vision is late—it did not happen before the last third of the first century. Moreover, it is found only in one segment of early Christianity, the post-Pauline tradition, and had no impact on the Jesus traditions. The insistence on equality and mutuality within the Christian community that seems to have been expressed by slaves as well as by women is not due to later "enthusiastic excesses"[32] or to illegitimate agitation for emancipation. The opposite is true. Colossians shows how a so-called "enthusiastic" realized eschatological perspective can produce an insistence on patriarchal behavior as well as an acceptance of the established political-social status quo of inequality and exploitation in the name of Jesus Christ.

In discussing the *Sitz im Leben* of the household code form, exegetes have arrived at different interpretations. While a few scholars think that the demands for the obedience and submission of wives, children, and slaves are genuinely Christian, the majority sees the domestic code as a later Christian adaptation of a Greco-Roman or Jewish-Hellenistic philosophical-theological code.

Most recently scholars have pointed to the treatises on economics and politics that reflect a form already codified by Aristotle and at home in the philosophical schools and morals of the first century C.E. The moralists of the early empire sought to formulate an ethics that would find a balance between the absolute traditional demands of subordination and obedience to the *paterfamilias* and the ideals of equality formulated in the Hellenistic age. What comes to the fore in the household code form of the New Testament is the option for "an ethically softened or humanized notion of domination and rule."[33] The right order of the house and economics are intertwined because in antiquity the household was economically independent, self-sufficient, hierarchically ordered, and as such the basis of the state. Therefore, the three *topoi*, "concerning the state," "concerning household management," and "concerning marriage," were closely interrelated.[34]

Aristotle, who has decisively influenced Western political philosophy as well as American legal concepts,[35] argues against Plato that one must begin the discussion of politics with thoughts about marriage, defined by him as a union of "natural ruler and natural subject."[36] When slaves are added to the family, it can be called a "house." Several households constitute a village and several villages a city-state, or *politeia*:

> The investigation of everything should begin with its smallest parts, and the smallest and primary parts of the household are master and slave, husband

---

[32]See Crouch, *Colossian Haustafel*, 141.

[33]K. Thraede, "Zum historischen Hintergrund der 'Haustafeln' des NT," JAC Ergänzungsband 8 (1981): 359–68:365.

[34]F. Wilhelm, "Die Occonomica der Neupythagoreer Bryson, Kallikdratidas. Periktione, Phintys," *Rheinisches Museum* 70 (1915): 161–223:222.

[35]Cf. especially S. Moller Okin, *Women in Western Political Thought* (Princeton, Princeton University Press, 1979), 234–304.

[36]For this whole section, see ibid., 15–96, on Plato and Aristotle; and David L. Balch, *Let Wives Be Submissive: The Domestic Code in 1 Peter*, SBLMS 26 (Chico, Calif: Scholars Press, 1981), 33–38. For the translation on Aristotle's Politics, see H. Rackham, LCL (Cambridge, Mass.: Harvard University Press, 1926).

and wife, father and children. We ought therefore to examine the proper consti-
tution and character of each of the three relationships, I mean that of master-
ship, that of marriage and thirdly the progenitive relationship. [*Politics* I.1253b]

It is part of the household science to rule over wife and children as freeborn. However, this is not done with the same form of government. Whereas the father rules
over his children as a monarch rules, the husband exercises republican government over the wife:

> for the male is by nature better fitted to command than the female . . . and the
> older and fully developed person than the younger and immature. It is true
> that in most cases of republican government the ruler and ruled interchange in
> turn . . . but the male stands in this relationship to the female continuously. The
> rule of the father over the children on the other hand is that of a king. [*Politics*
> I.1259b]

Against those who argue that slavery is contrary to nature, Aristotle points to the
rule of the soul over the body.

> It is manifest that it is natural and expedient for the body to be governed by the
> soul and for the emotional part to be governed by the intellect, the part pos-
> sessing reason, whereas for the two parties to be on equal [*ison*] footing or in
> the contrary positions is harmful in all cases. . . . Also as between the sexes, the
> male is by nature superior and the female inferior, the male ruler and the
> female subject. And the same must also necessarily apply in the case of hu-
> mankind generally; therefore all human beings that differ as widely as the soul
> does from the body . . . these are by nature slaves for whom to be governed by
> this kind of authority is advantageous. [*Politics* I.1254b]

These "natural" differences justify the relationships of domination in household
and state.

> Hence there are by nature various classes of rulers and ruled. For the free rules
> the slave, the male the female, the man the child in a different way. And all pos-
> sess the various parts of the soul but possess them in different ways; for the
> slave has not got the deliberative part at all, and the female has it but without
> full authority, while the child has it but in an undeveloped form. [*Politics*
> I.1260a]

Interestingly enough, Aristotle acknowledges one exception when women can
rule with "authority." Usually the relationship between husband and wife is that
of "aristocracy" but when the husband controls everything it becomes an "oligarchy," "for he governs in violation of fitness and not in virtue of superiority."
"And sometimes when the wife is an heiress, it is she who rules. In these cases,
then, authority goes not by virtue but by wealth and power, as in an oligarchy"
(*Nicomachean Ethics* VIII.1160b).

Since, however, every household is part of the state, the state is jeopardized
if the different forms of household rule are not exercised faithfully.

The freedom in regard to women is detrimental both in regard to the purpose of the *politeia* and in regard to the happiness of the state. For just as man and wife are part of a household, it is clear that the state also is divided nearly in half into its male and female population, so that in all *politeia* in which the position of women is badly regulated one half of the state must be deemed neglected in framing the law. [*Politics* II.1269b]

Such was the case in Sparta, where women controlled their own wealth. Although the Spartans did attempt to bring their women under the law, they gave up when the women resisted. Therefore, they loved and respected wealth and were under the sway of their women. The women controlled not only many things but also ruled their own rulers! These remarks make it clear that Aristotle knows of a historical state that was differently constituted.

Although the negative influence of Aristotle on Christian anthropology is widely acknowledged today,[37] it is not sufficiently recognized that such an anthropology was rooted in Aristotle's understanding of political rule and domination. Just as he defined the "nature" of slaves with respect to their status as property and to their economic function, so Aristotle defined the "nature" of woman as that of someone who does not have "full authority" to rule, although he is well aware that such rule was an actual historical possibility and reality. The definition of "woman's nature" and "woman's proper sphere" is thus rooted in a certain relation of domination and subordination between man and woman having a concrete political background and purpose. Western misogynism has its root in the rules for the household as the model of the state. A feminist theology therefore must not only analyze the anthropological dualism generated by Western culture and theology, but also uncover its political roots in the patriarchal household of antiquity.

Aristotle's political philosophy was revitalized in neo-Pythagorean and Stoic philosophy.[38] It was also accepted in Hellenistic Judaism, as the writings of Philo and Josephus demonstrate. Philo insists that Jews are not impious, they respect father and mother, and wives must be in servitude to their husbands (*Hypothetica* VIII.7.14). In discussing the *politeia* of Moses and comparing it to that of Romulus, Josephus stresses that Jewish laws do not teach impiety but piety, not the hatred of others but the communal life. They oppose injustice and teach justice, they deter from war and encourage people to work. Therefore, there can be nowhere a greater justice, piety, and harmony than among the Jews. In their marriage laws and the birth and upbringing of children Jews fulfilled the laws of Romulus's *politeia*, which the Romans had imposed on the whole empire. Jewish women were good Roman citizens:

The woman, says the Law, is in all things inferior to the man. Let her accordingly be submissive, not for her humiliation, but that she may be directed, for the authority has been given by God to the man. [*Against Apion* II.201]

---

[37]See, e.g., K. E. Børresen, *Subordination and Equivalence: The Nature and Role of Women in Augustine and Thomas Aquinas* (Washington, D.C.: University Press of America, 1981).

[38]D. L. Balch, "Household Ethical Codes in Peripatetic, Neopythagorean and Early Christian Moralists," *SBL Seminar Papers* 11 (1977): 397–404.

Alongside this Aristotelian ethics of submission and rule, a marriage ethos developed which stressed the harmony between the couples.[39] Plutarch describes the ideal marriage as a copartnership:

> It is a lovely thing for a wife to sympathize with her husband's concerns and the husband with the wife's so that, as ropes, by being intertwined, get strength from each other, thus . . . the copartnership may be preserved through the joint action of both. [*Conjugal Precepts* 140e]

Plutarch also emphasizes that the wife should not only share her husband's friends but also his gods. She must therefore "shut the front door tight upon all queer rituals and outlandish superstitions. For with no god do stealthy and secret rites performed by a woman find any favor" (140d). Thus it is apparent that in antiquity rules of the household are part of economics and politics, as are religious rites and ancestral customs. The well-being of the state and the religious observance of the laws and customs of the patriarchal family are intertwined. Slaves and wives who do not worship the gods of the *paterfamilias* violate not only their household duties but also the laws of the state.

The praxis of coequal discipleship between slaves and masters, women and men, Jews and Greeks, Romans and barbarians, rich and poor, young and old, brought the Christian community into tension with its social-political environment. This tension, engendered by the alternative Christian vision of Gal. 3:28, and not by "enthusiastic excesses," became the occasion for introducing the Greco-Roman patriarchal order into the house church. Colossians and Ephesians testify that realized eschatology, rooted in the dualism between this world and the world above, is responsible for developing a theological justification of the patriarchal order.

---

[39]Thraede, "Zum historischen Hintergrund," 364; see also his article "Gleichheit," in *RAC* 10 (1978), 122–64.

Chapter 2

The Dispute about Slavery in America

The Biblical Anti-Slavery Argument of the Decade 1830–1840

Caroline L. Shanks

In the first half of the nineteenth century, those "tedious and tragic old times, before it had been discovered that hell was a myth," the divine inspiration of the Bible and its consequent authority over the mind and heart of man were generally accepted tenets. In Germany and England scholars were just beginning to apply the historical method to the Sacred Book, but on both sides of the Atlantic the vast majority still firmly believed that all parts of Scripture were equally channels of truth. To them, "The Bible says," was synonymous with "God saith." They regarded the authors of the Bible as only the agents, the pens, so to speak, of the Holy Spirit. Certainly in the United States the authority of scripture was

Excerpted from *Journal of Negro History* 16 (1931): 132–157, copyright by The Association for the Study of African-American Life and History, Inc. Reprinted by permission.

unquestioned—at least by the respectable portion of the community. Free-thinkers there were, but they were without the pale. All Christians both north and south agreed that the Scriptures were consistent with themselves and formed a "perfect rule of duty"[1]; the conflict came over the formulation of this "perfect rule."

What was the Bible teaching in regard to the burning question of the day—slavery? Was that institution actually sanctioned by the Old Testament and permitted by the New, as the Southerners maintained, or was it a direct violation of the precepts of the Gospel as the Northerners insisted? The point of divergence in this controversy, then, was not the authority of Scripture, on which all were agreed, but its interpretation. Both sides felt that the Biblical arguments were the most potent that could be adduced[2] and both found in the Bible ample support for their opinions—unmindful that each, instead of deriving his case from the Bible was trying to make the Bible subserve a ready-made system. Once in a while a devout brother was acute enough to perceive this bias. For instance, the Rev. John Paxton, a Kentucky anti-slavery man, complained that "the extent to which their previous opinions influence persons as to the meaning of Scripture, is greater . . . than most are aware of,"[3] but need we add that he applied this criticism only to his opponents?

Before taking up in detail the Biblical arguments of the abolitionists, it is well to get some conception of the opposite point of view. Starting with the premise that the moral law is immutable and, therefore, what it did not condemn as wrong formerly cannot, be wrong now, slavery champions interpreted such passages from the Old Testament as Leviticus 25:44–46[4] as sanctioning and legislating for slavery. Certainly, they reasoned, it is impious to say that God at any time or in any place gave his express sanction to sin. Their arguments from the New Testament were based on the apostolic injunctions to obedience and submission on the part of slaves,[5] as implying permission of the relation, and they pointed triumphantly to the Epistle to Philemon as teaching by Paul's example the duty of apprehending runaways and returning them to their masters. From such passages as these, the apologists for slavery deduced the principle that the relation of master and slave was in itself innocent and on the same footing as that of parent and child or husband and wife. All these relations, they said, are equally lawful and equally designed to be permanent. The evils which exist, and such men as

---

[1] Richard Fuller and Francis Wayland, *Domestic Slavery*, 49:170–171.

[2] "And here [after Biblical argument] I might close its defence; for what God ordains, and Christ sanctifies, should surely command the respect and toleration of man." J. H. Hammond, "Letters on Slavery" in *The Pro-Slavery Argument*, 108. "The word of God, rightly understood, must settle the matter." *Slavery vs. The Bible. A correspondence between the General Conference of Maine, and the Presbytery of Tonbecbee, Mississippi*, 31.

[3] John D. Paxton, *Letters on Slavery*, 60; see also Beriah Green, *The Chattel Principle*, 26, 27.

[4] "Both thy bondmen and thy bondmaids, which thou shalt have, shall be of the heathen that are round about you; of them shall ye buy bondmen and bondmaids.

"Moreover of the children of the strangers that do sojourn among you, of them shall ye buy, and of their families that are with you, which they begat in your land; and they shall be your possession.

"And ye shall take them as an inheritance for your children after you, to inherit them for a possession; they shall be your bondmen forever: but over your brethren the children of Israel ye shall not rule one over another with rigour."

[5] Col. 3:22; Eph. 6:5–8; I Peter 2:18.

Chancellor Harper granted freely that great evils did exist,[6] come not from the institution of slavery but from the abuse of the relation of master and slave. They were always anxious therefore to get the discussion on the plane of the abstract question, and decried the tendency of the abolitionists to emphasize the abuses of the system.[7]

The abolitionists replied that the matter must be discussed as it existed in the United States—not as a theoretical case. "Abstract slavery," they said, "never did and never can exist,"[8] and in their turn they took the sling and stone of the Scriptures to slay this Goliath of iniquity. The first of the anti-slavery Davids in point of scholarship was Francis Wayland, the president of Brown. The section on violation of personal liberty in his *Elements of Moral Science* (1835) was accounted one of the strongest abolition arguments of the day, and in his published correspondence with the Rev. Richard Fuller[9] the Biblical anti-slavery argument is so well arranged and clearly presented that one can easily forgive the prominence given to the syllogistic method. A teacher of logic might be expected to argue in terms of the major and minor premise. But the effect of these writings of President Wayland was, in the opinion of most abolitionists, neutralized by the section on slavery in his *Limitations of Human Responsibility* (1838), in which he comes to the general conclusion that neither as citizens of the United States nor as human beings under the law of God had Northerners a right to do anything whose direct intention was the abolition of slavery.[10] With the setting of truth before man, he says, our responsibility ceases. "We have no right, to force our instructions upon them (the Southerners) either by conversation, or by lectures, or by the mail."[11] This theory, if accepted, would have struck a death-blow at the whole system of organized abolitionism.

Of the scriptural dissertations published from 1830–1840, one of the most popular was written by Theodore D. Weld, who was already known as an eloquent abolitionist orator when *The Bible against Slavery* appeared in 1837. The subtitle of this essay, *An Inquiry into the Patriarchal and Mosaic Systems on the Subject of Human Rights* sufficiently indicates its scope. Weld's wife and sister-in-law, Angelina and Sarah Grimké, were also known both as authors and lecturers. The former emphasized the sinfulness of slavery and its opposition to Christian principles in her *Appeal to the Christian Women of the South* (1836), while the latter in an *Epistle to the Clergy of the Southern States*, published in the same year, goes over many of the stock abolitionist arguments, such as the dissimilarity between Jewish servitude and American slavery, and the equality of all men because they are

---

[6]William Harper, "Memoir on Slavery" in *The Pro-Slavery Argument*, 28 et seq.

[7]For the southern Biblical argument see *Slavery vs. The Bible*, 11–21; Fuller and Wayland, *Domestic Slavery*, 170–230; Hammond, "Letters on Slavery" in *Pro-Slavery Argument*, 105–109; Harper, "Memoir on Slavery" in *Pro-Slavery Argument*, 51; Thornton Stringfellow, *A Brief Examination of Scripture Testimony on the Institution of Slavery*.

[8]*First Annual Report*, New England Anti-Slavery Society (1833), 15.

[9]*Domestic Slavery considered as a Scriptural Institution:* in a correspondence between the Rev. Richard Fuller, of Beaufort, S.C., and the Rev. Francis Wayland, of Providence, R.I. 1845.

[10]Wayland, *Limitations of Human Responsibility*, 163.

[11]*Ibid.*, 185.

made in the likeness of God. Both of these pamphlets abound in apt texts and quotations from Christian authors; they are pervaded by a Biblical atmosphere as befits the writings of those who expounded the word of life to their Quaker brethren.

The appeal to the Scriptures was by no means confined to those books that dealt exclusively with Biblical arguments. There is little abolition literature in this earlier period that does not show the influence of this point of view and some of the best presentations of this phase of the subject are to be found in works that aim at covering the whole field of anti-slavery argument, such as Phelps' *Lectures on Slavery and its Remedy*. Paxton's *Letters on Slavery* is especially thorough for the Biblical argument; Bourne's *Picture of Slavery* contains essays on "Slavery Opposed to the Law of God and Man" and "Incompatible with the Gospel" and Rankin devotes nearly a third of his *Letters* to showing that "the modern system of slavery is prohibited by the book of inspiration."[12] The reports of the various anti-slavery societies and their addresses to the public also rely to a great extent on the authority of Scripture.

Most of the abolitionist commentators refused to admit that anything like American slavery had ever been practiced by the Jews, and even those who granted a limited form of Hebrew bondage denied that it had divine approbation. In discussing the arguments by which they attempted to prove this thesis, this paper will first take up the arguments based on the Old Testament, then those based on the New, in each case giving first the abolitionist explanation of the Biblical passages which apparently favored slavery, and secondly, the passages which were interpreted as opposing slavery.

It was a favorite theory of the Southerners that the Negroes as descendants of Ham were consigned to perpetual slavery by the curse which Noah had pronounced on Canaan, the son of Ham: "Cursed be Canaan; a servant of servants shall he be unto his brethren."[13] Most of the abolitionists who questioned this genealogy at all contented themselves with demanding proof that the Africans were indeed the offspring of Canaan and not of some other son, but John Rankin went so far as to record a doubt that they were the bona fide descendants of Ham.[14] The most usual explanation of this passage was that it was a prophecy, not a command or rule for moral action. The fulfillment of such a prediction would no more excuse those who executed it than the prophecies of Christ's death justified his murderers. "It must needs be that offences come; but woe to that man by whom the offence cometh!"[15]

More difficult of satisfactory elucidation was the practice of the Hebrews. There was plain Scripture testimony to the fact that Abraham, the father of the

---

[12]John Rankin. *Letters on American Slavery.* 73.

[13]Genesis 9:25. The black skin of the Negro was sometimes asserted to be the mark of Cain. The abolitionists countered this assertion with the reminder that the posterity of Cain were all drowned in the deluge. Weld, *The Bible Against Slavery*, 66; Child, *Oration in honor of Universal Emancipation in the British Empire*. 10.

[14]Rankin, *Letters*, 76.

[15]Matt. 18:7. For a discussion of the curse of Canaan, see Wright, *Does the Bible Sanction Slavery?* 3; Rankin, *Letters*, 73–76; A. Grimke, *Appeal to the Christian Women of the South*, 3; Paxton, *Letters*, 92; Edwards, *The Injustice and Impolicy of the Slave Trade, and of the Slavery of the Africans*, 9–10.

faithful and the friend of God, held servants or slaves, as many translated the Hebrew;[16] the Mosaic code laid down strict rules for the treatment of bond-servants;[17] nay, more, the Jews were actually directed to take servants from the surrounding nations.[18]

Patriarchal servitude, the abolitionists declared, was voluntary. They alleged as proofs that it was customary for a poor man to sell himself as a servant,[19] and that the pastoral mode of life would have made escape easy. Furthermore, Genesis 14:14 relates that Abraham led 318 armed servants on an expedition, and surely slaves could not have been trusted with arms. This they considered as conclusive evidence that the word commonly translated "servants" really meant subjects of a prince, i.e., members of the tribe like the armies of Saul and David. Those of a philological turn of mind bolstered up this position by lengthy and recondite examinations of the various Hebrew words denoting servitude, while Rankin raised Biblical exegesis to the realm of pure romance with the theory that Abraham, being benevolent as well as rich, made a practice of redeeming miserable captives of war who then rendered him willing and voluntary service.[20] Of more weight than any of these attempts to explain away patriarchal servitude was the argument that if slavery was to be justified by the example of Abraham, lying and concubinage might be justified in the same way.[21]

The admonition to the Hebrews to make bondmen of the surrounding nations was explained by the abolitionist expounders as referring only to the seven nations particularly mentioned in the seventh chapter of Deuteronomy, who for their sins had been devoted to destruction. The Jews in this case were selected as instruments to execute God's judgment. They held a divine commission to invade the land of the Canaanites and slay the inhabitants, some of whom Moses allowed them to spare as servants,[22] even as he allowed divorce for the hardness of their hearts. But the relation of the Hebrews and the Canaanitish tribes was constituted by an original and peculiar grant which was made to one people and had respect to one people. It was in force at no other time and with respect to no other people, even for the Hebrews.[23] Such a limited permission certainly neither implied approbation of the system nor justified slavery in the nineteenth century. "When the slave-holders of the present day have obtained of the same Author of Rights a *license* to deal in the bodies and souls of men, then, and not till then, will we admit any comparison of Hebrew bondage with American slavery."[24]

In addition to their theory of special permission as an explanation of Hebraic servitude, the abolitionists averred that this servitude was by no means a system

---

[16]Gen. 14:14–16; 24:35.

[17]Exod. 21:2–11; Lev. 25:39–55.

[18]Lev. 25:44–46.

[19]Gen. 47:19; Lev. 25:47.

[20]Rankin, *Letters*. 78. See Gen., Chap. 24.

[21]James G. Birney, *Second Letter*, 3. On the subject of patriarchal servitude, see also Wright, *Does the Bible Sanction Slavery?*, 4, 5: Weld, *The Bible Against Slavery*, 32–34; Phelps, *Lectures*, 70–74; Barnes, *Inquiry*, 64–70.

[22]Exod. 23:23; Deut. 7:2; Josh. 9:24, 27, II Chron. 8:7, 8; Phelps *Lectures* 75–79.

[23]Fuller and Wayland, *Domestic Slavery*, 50; *An Appeal on the Subject of Slavery*, 31.

[24]*Address of the Starksborough and Lincoln Anti-Slavery Society*, 7, 8.

of involuntary, unending slavery. From an examination of the various ways mentioned in the Mosaic code by which persons could be legally reduced to bondage, crime, poverty, capture in war, purchase from the heathen, and birth from bond-women,[25] they concluded that the Negroes had not been enslaved by any of these methods. They had been stolen and sold like Joseph, and man-stealing was a capital crime, indeed the only capital robbery under the Mosaic law.[26]

The bond servants held by the Jews were racially of two different classes, those of their Hebrew brethren who, as they had sold themselves, were parties to the bargain and voluntary servants, and those whom the Jews had obtained from the heathen round about them. It was generally admitted by both Northerners and Southerners that the first class served only till the seventh year, or till the year of jubilee, and were to be liberally provided for when they left their master's service.[27] It was about the second class that the controversy raged. Were they absolute slaves or not?

The Southerners took their stand firmly on Leviticus 25:44–46.

The answer to this took several different lines. It was contended, in the first place, that the Hebrew word *olem* translated "forever" stood for various durations of time, according to the subject to which it referred.[28] In this case it was intended to express only forty-nine years, or, in other words, the law of liberty was meant to apply to all the inhabitants of Judea. When the jubilee trumpet sounded on the great day of atonement every fiftieth year, both the man who had voluntarily sold himself and the heathen who had been sold to a Hebrew master were set free, the one as well as the other. The law was purposely designed to prevent the possibility of perpetual servitude existing among the chosen people of God.[29]

Some went even further and argued that the law giving freedom to the Hebrew servants in the sabbatical year really applied to all servants whom the Jews could legally retain. Those obtained from abroad as well as those born in the house must be circumcised and made partakers of the covenant. This rite was a kind of naturalization and carried civil liberty with it. Those who submitted to it were thus joined to the Lord and as brethren and sons of Abraham could be held in bondage no longer than six years.[30]

Besides the law of liberty, the abolitionists cited the ordinances governing the treatment of servants as further evidence that Hebrew bondage offered no analogy to American slavery. The Mosaic code protected the servant from violence, or, if it did not always prevent cruelty, it at least made amends by restoring freedom;[31] the fourth commandment secured the Sabbath rest to the servant; and at the three great annual feasts of the Hebrews, the Passover, the Feast of Weeks,

---

[25]Exod. 22:3; Lev. 25:39, 40; Deut. 20:14; Lev. 25:44; Exod. 21:4.

[26]Exod. 21:16; Bourne, *Picture of Slavery*, 19; Weld, *The Bible Against Slavery*, 11–17.

[27]Exod. 21:2; Lev. 25:10, 39, 40; Deut. 15:13, 14.

[28]Rankin, *Letters*, 82; Paxton, *Letters*, 86.

[29]A. Grimke, *Appeal to the Christian Women of the South*, 7–10; Barnes, *Inquiry*, 143 et seq.

[30]Gen. 17:13; Number, 15:15, 16. Paxton, *Letters*; 79–83; Weld, *The Bible against Slavery*, 28; Ralph Wardlaw, *The Jubilee: a sermon preached in Glasgow, August 1, 1834, the memorable Day of Negro Emancipation in the British Colonies*, 9.

[31]Lev. 25:43; Exod. 21:20, 21, 26, 27. Phelps, *Lectures*. 75.

and the Feast of Tabernacles, master and servant united in the celebration.[32] In religious observances, the bond and free stood on common ground. Even more frequently quoted was the law which shielded fugitives from recovery: "Thou shalt not deliver unto his master the servant which is escaped from his master unto thee"[33]; and finally, as one industrial compiler pointed out, there was a total lack of proof that bond-servants could be sold or alienated in any way.[34] From these various restrictions the abolitionists drew the inference that servitude in Palestine under the Mosaic code was a comparatively mild system utterly unlike American slavery. In a large proportion of cases it consisted merely in the payment of tribute,[35] and where personal service was due, the servitude was altogether of a domestic character. Master and slave worked together; there was no broad line of distinction between classes.[36] Slaveholding in the modern sense of the term abolitionists declared to be inconsistent with the Mosaic economy, the tendency of whose institutions was ultimately to abolish all bondage. This, they thought, had been accomplished by Jesus' time, and if the Jews then held slaves they did so in flagrant violation of the law.[37]

While the Biblical interpretation given above was the orthodox abolitionist doctrine, there were opponents of slavery—mighty men in Zion too—who either from a sounder scholarship or a less biased judgment held the attempt to deny the existence of slavery among the Jews utterly foolish.

The opinions of such anti-slavery men on the relation of the Mosaic law to slavery were summed up by Horace Bushnell in an address on "The Growth of Law" given before the Yale alumni in 1843. He characterized the Mosaic ordinances as "permissive statutes" which had no permanent significance and were "liable to be superseded" under the evolution of law. In other words, slavery was unquestionably a part of the Mosaic code but was subject to elimination by the growth of moral sentiment.[38]

In such statements as well as in Paxton's belief that we have "more light than the ancients,"[39] and Wayland's theory of a progressive revelation,[40] there is a kind of evolutionary idea which found frequent expression in such reasoning as this: Polygamy and divorce are now granted to be evils, yet they as well as slavery were permitted under the Mosaic code. Is Hebrew example warrant for one if not for the other? Or, as Wayland phrased it: Would the Mosaic code of laws be a

---

[32]Deut. Chap. 16.

[33]Deut. 23:15. This was quoted by practically all the anti-slavery writers. See, e. g., Weld, *The Bible against Slavery*, 29; Wright, *Does the Bible Sanction Slavery?* 7; A. Grimke, *Appeal to the Christian Women of the South*, 9; Paxton *Letters*, 77; Phelps, *Lectures*, 75. Other passages cited as teaching the duty of aiding fugitive slaves were "hide the outcasts; bewray not him that wandereth." (Isa. 16:3), and "Thou shalt not oppress a stranger: for ye know the heart of a stranger, seeing ye were strangers in the land of Egypt," (Exod. 23:9).

[34]Weld, *The Bible against Slavery*, 34.

[35]I Kings, 9:21; Phelps, *Lectures*, 75.

[36]Weld even expresses a belief that the "bought" servants were as a class superior to the hired. *The Bible against Slavery*, 80 et seq.

[37]Green, *The Chattel Principle*, 60–62.

[38]Theodore T. Munger, *Horace Bushnell,* Preacher and Theologian, 297.

[39]Paxton, *Letters*, 64.

[40]Fuller and Wayland, *Domestic Slavery*, 52–55.

sufficient reason for abolishing trial by jury in case of accidental homicide?[41]—an argument from analogy similar to that noted under patriarchal servitude.

The positive evidence against slavery from the Old Testament was of two different kinds, first, "text," direct quotations that were wrenched bodily from their context and made to denounce the "sum of all villainies" and secondly, historical instances in which the Jews and heathen nations had been punished for holding slaves. Slavery the abolitionists branded as sin, an open defiance of the eighth commandment: "Thou shalt not steal," and indirectly condemned by the tenth: "Thou shalt not covet . . . anything that is thy neighbor's," for, they asked, did not the slave-holder covet his neighbor's liberty and withhold it from him?[42] The passages which forbade man-stealing and trading in the persons of men[43] were excellent abolition texts, as were all injunctions against fraud and oppression.[44] Jeremiah, pronouncing a woe upon him "that useth his neighbor's service without wages"[45] was hailed as an anti-slavery prophet and one of the incendiaries of his age.[46] In regard to the treatment of Negroes, the many exhortations to pity and compassion on the needy[47] were invoked, as were those passages which were thought to teach equality by tracing the origin of races to a common stock, e.g., "So God created man in his own image."[48] This last piece of reasoning may seem a bit forced, but it is no more startling than the logic which deduced from the phrase, "All souls are mine,"[49] the doctrine that God had reserved the right to control man exclusively to Himself and that the slave-holder therefore "usurps the prerogative of Jehovah," an expression which found its way into the platform of the national anti-slavery society.[50]

Of the various historical events cited to prove that slavery was offensive to Jehovah the classic example was of course the plagues inflicted on the Egyptians for enslaving God's peculiar people. In this connection it is interesting to note that while most of the anti-slavery arguments insist that servitude among the Jews was not slavery, they are equally sure that the Egyptian bondage of the Jews was slavery.[51] Among the curious analogies traced between Hebrew bondage in Egypt and

---

[41]*Ibid.*, 54, 55.

[42]*An Appeal on the Subject of Slavery*, 40–45; Weld, *The Bible against Slavery*, 10, 11.

[43]"And he that stealeth a man, and selleth him, or if he be found in his hand, he shall surely be put to death." Exod. 21:16. "Thus saith the Lord: For three transgressions of Israel, and for four, I will not turn away the punishment thereof, because they sold the righteous for silver, and the poor for a pair of shoes" Amos, 2:6.

[44]Deut. 24:14; Isa. 58:6; Jer. 21:12.

[45]Jer. 22:13.

[46]Wright, *Does the Bible Sanction Slavery?* 8.

[47]e.g., Lev. 19:33, 34; Deut. 27:19; Exod. 23:9; Job 31:13, 14. Prov. 31:8, 9 was justification enough for many an abolition sermon.

[48]Gen. 1:27; *Proceedings of the Rhode Island Anti-Slavery Convention* (1836), 8.

[49]Ezek. 18:4.

[50]*Proceedings of the Anti-Slavery Convention* (Dec. 1833), 13. This same idea is developed in *Proceedings of the first annual meeting of the New York State Anti-Slavery Society* (1836), 9; *Address of the Starksborough and Lincoln Anti-Slavery Society* (1824), 7; A. Grimke, *Appeal to the Christian Women of the South*, 3; Phelps, *Lectures*, 91–92; etc., etc.

[51]Charles Elliott, *The Bible and Slavery*, chap. 2 and 3. Others, like Weld, argued that the condition of the Hebrews in Egypt was that of a tributary nation; individuals were not enslaved. *The Bible against Slavery*, 56–58.

Negro slavery in the United States was the resemblance in numbers of the enslaved. The number of those whom Moses led out of the "iron furnace" was computed at about three millions,[52] while in 1840 there were some two and a half million slaves in the United States.

Very different from the punishments meted out to the Egyptians was the blessing pronounced upon Cyrus, the "Lord's anointed"—the only heathen so called—because he had let his Israelitish captives go without price or reward.[53]

Another case in which Jews had been reduced to slavery was the capture of Judah by Samaria,[54] a glaring instance of enslavement of brethren. The condemnation of this act by the prophet Obed and the return of the two hundred thousand captives to Jericho were pronounced by the Rev. John Paxton a signal example of faithful discharge of duty by a minister and obedience on the part of his listeners.[55] Mr. Paxton's own flock, alas! did not prove so dutiful as that of the prophet, and he was compelled to leave his parish for the expression of views far milder than those of Obed.

Jeremiah and Nehemiah both rebuked the Jews for practicing slavery,[56] while the minor prophets give several instances of the punishment of heathen for this iniquity, particularly the destruction of Tyre, which seems to have been a center of the slave-trade.[57] This was taken as proof that slavery was a moral sin, as the heathen had no special prohibition against it. The Old Testament evidence is thus summed up in the sounding phrases of the Rev. George Bourne: "Jehovah is the great exemplar of all abolitionists. He exterminated slavery in Egypt to Pharaoh's cost; he abolished it in Babylon."[58]

One deduction from these historical instances quite in keeping with the rigid theology of the day was the doctrine of divine recompenses—that God in His dealings with individuals and nations will recompense them according to their works. Such passages as the one in Revelation that is supposed to refer to the fall of Babylon: "Reward her even as she rewarded you, and double unto her double according to her works: in the cup which she hath filled fill to her double"[59] were interpreted in this sense. So far, said an expounder of this merciless religion, we seem to have escaped the dreadful retributions that were visited on Egypt and Judah, on Tyre and Rome for slave-holding, but the injured morals of our people and the declining prosperity of the slave-states are "no dubious tokens of God's displeasure."[60]

When it came to a question of New Testament exegesis, the task of the abolitionist expounder of Scripture was much more arduous. Whatever the condition

---

[52]Barnes, *Inquiry*, 96. The basis of Barnes's calculation was one adult male for every five of the population. cf. Exod. 12:37, 38.

[53]Isaiah 45:2–4.

[54]II Chron. 28:8–15.

[55]Paxton, *Letters*, 103.

[56]Jer. 34:8–22; Neh. 5:5 et seq.

[57]Amos 1:6–9; Joel, 3:4–8; Ezek. 26:13.

[58]Bourne, *Picture of Slavery*, 180; 21.

[59]Rev. 18:6.

[60]Paxton, *Letters*, 185.

of bondmen under the laws of the Hebrews, under Roman laws the slaves were certainly the absolute property of the master and atrocities in their treatment were known to have occurred. There was the famous case of Pedanius Secundus; four hundred of his slaves had been slain because their master had been found murdered and no one knew who was guilty of the crime.[61] Such acts were legal and still Jesus and His apostles had said nothing in condemnation of so monstrous a system. Taking it for granted that Jesus was familiar with Roman slavery, the pro-slavery men considered this silence a tacit permission,[62] and as all permissions under the gospel dispensation were unlimited, not given like the Mosaic law to one people, but to the whole human race and for all time,[63] the inference was that slavery was intended to be perpetual. According to this view, Paul and Peter recognized the relation of master and slave as established by their admonitions to both as to their reciprocal behavior; and Jesus Himself in such expressions as, "The disciple is not above his master, nor the servant above his lord,"[64] took the existing social order for granted.

As a concrete illustration of this conception of New Testament teaching take the pro-slavery explanation of the Epistle of Philemon. Onesimus, they averred, was a runaway slave who had been converted by Paul and sent back to his master, Philemon, with this letter of commendation. Paul expected that Onesimus would remain with Philemon forever, as his slave, and the solicitude for kind treatment displayed by the apostle was accounted for on the theory that an easy pardon of Onesimus might have had a bad effect on Philemon's other slaves.[65]

In contrast with this view, the abolitionists protested that there was no certain evidence that Onesimus was a slave. As in the Old Testament argument, they appealed to textual criticism, arguing that *doulos*, the Greek word used by Paul, was generic, that it specified no particular kind of servitude and might be translated "servant" as well as "slave." It would be ridiculous to say, "Paul, a slave to Jesus Christ,"[66] or "Thou good slave—have thou authority over ten cities,"[67] yet *doulos* was used in both these cases. Further, from Philemon 18, "If he hath wronged thee, or oweth thee aught, put that to mine account," it was contended that the relation could not have been that of an American master and slave as then Onesimus could not have "owed him aught." Birney considers it probable that Onesimus was a menial, though not a slave, who had committed a theft from his master for which he was liable to be prosecuted.[68] The epistle then would amount to nothing more than an appeal to Philemon not to bring criminal action against his servant. Finally, if Onesimus were a slave, Paul's request that Philemon should receive him "Not now as a servant but above a servant, a brother beloved . . . both

---

[61]Tacitus, Ann., 14, 42–45. This incident is quoted, among others, by Samuel Edmund Sewall, *Remarks on Slavery in the United States*, 11 (note); Bacon, Slavery, 40.

[62]Dew in *Pro-Slavery Argument*, 452; Hammond, *ibid.*, 158.

[63]Fuller and Wayland, *Domestic Slavery*, 78, 194.

[64]Matt. 19:24.

[65]Fuller and Wayland, *Domestic Slavery*, 195–196.

[66]Romans, 1:1.

[67]Luke, 19:17.

[68]Birney, *The Sinfulness of Slave-holding*, 52.

in the flesh and in the Lord,"[69] was declared to mean that he should be received not as a mere spiritual brother, but as a real brother; i.e., it was equivalent to a requisition to set him free.[70] The letter, says the Rev. Beriah Green, was "read in the light of '*liberty*'" and "contained the principles of holy freedom, faithfully and affectionately applied."[71]

In the other Pauline epistles there are several passages where the apostle, in exhorting the various classes of society to the particular duties devolving upon their stations, makes mention of masters and servants. As the general content of these passages is the same, admonitions to obedience on the part of servants and kindness on the part of masters, it will be sufficient to quote only one as an example: "Servants, obey in all things your masters according to the flesh; not with eye-service, as men-pleasers; but in singleness of heart, fearing God." "Masters, give unto your servants that which is just and equal; knowing that ye also have a Master in heaven."[72]

Such instructions to servants, the abolitionists said, taught patience, meekness, fidelity, and charity—duties incumbent on all Christians. Masters were to be obeyed, not because they had a right to obedience as parents had to the obedience of children, but for the gospel's sake. It was pointed out, moreover, that the relation demanded a reciprocity of benefits. The master must "forbear threatening" and do "that which is just and equal"; and justice and equality on the one hand and slavery on the other are mutually subversive. "No abolitionist," says Beriah Green, "however eager and determined in his opposition to slavery, could ask more than these percepts, once obeyed, would be sure to confer."[73] Resorting to analogy again, it was argued that Paul recognized the position of the father as head of the family under the Roman law, but that no Christian nowadays would thereby justify unjust divorce or selling one's children into slavery.[74] Lastly, nowhere in prescribing the duties of masters and servants do the apostles utter a syllable in which they concede the right of the master to hold slaves.[75] Indeed, Paul in one place hints to the Corinthian converts that they should escape if possible: "Art thou called being a servant? care not for it; but if thou mayest be made free, use it rather."[76] The lack of more open condemnation of slavery was attributed to the fact that the Christians were under the Roman government and justly feared the accusation of instigating a servile war.[77]

While the New Testament contains no provision for slavery like the Old Testament ordinance: "Both thy bondmen and thy bondmaids, . . . shall be of the heathen that are round about you; of them shall ye buy," neither does it contain any

---

[69]Phil. 16.

[70]Green, "Slavery not in the New Testament" (*Sermons and Other Discourses*, 285).

[71]*Ibid.*, 279. In addition, see Barnes, *Inquiry*, 318 et seq.; *An Appeal on the subject of Slavery.* 30; Oliver Johnson, *Address delivered in Middlebury* 15, 16. Rankin, *Letters*, 85.

[72]Col. 3:22; 4:1. See also Eph. 6:5–9; I Tim. 6:1–2; I Peter 2:18; I Cor. 7:20–24.

[73]Green, *The Chattel Principle*, 54, 55. See also Fuller and Wayland, *Domestic Slavery*, 81; Wright, *Does the Bible Sanction Slavery?* 11.

[74]Birney, *Second Letter*, 8.

[75]Fuller and Wayland, *Domestic Slavery*, 81.

[76]I Cor. 7:21.

[77]Birney, *The Sinfulness of Slave-holding*, Chap. 7.

censure of the practice like the law of Exodus: "he that stealeth a man . . . shall surely be put to death."[78] The nearest approach to this is Paul's reference to manstealers, whom he classes with liars and murderers as those for whom the law was made.[79] Even the abolitionists had to admit that the New Testament passages which they quoted as opposing slavery did so only indirectly. The gist of their arguments was that the system of slavery was repugnant to the whole tenor and meaning of the Gospel, which breathed a spirit of kindness and love. How could the proposition that man can hold property in man be made to square with a religion founded on the Sermon on the Mount? "Therefore all things whatsoever you would that men should do to you, do ye even so to them: for this is the law and the prophets."[80] The Golden Rule and the second great commandment: "Thou shalt love thy neighbour as thyself," were characterized by the abolitionists as the summary expression of all the particular precepts enjoined in the New Testament. The law here inculcated, they said, does not mean merely that we should do to our slaves as we would be done by if we were slaves, as the pro-slavery men argue. No, the rule goes deeper. We must test the relation of master and slave itself by it and see if that relation is consistent with the Saviour's maxim. And can anyone seriously maintain that a system founded on force where the benefits are all on the side of the oppressor is not contrary to a rule based on the natural equality of all mankind?[81]

Another precept of Jesus that was often referred to as bearing on slavery was, "The labourer is worthy of his hire,"[82] one of the few utterances of the Master to which any economic significance can be imputed. Those passages that held up service as the true standard of greatness, such as, "whosoever of you will be the chiefest, shall be servant of all,"[83] were also occasionally alluded to. But more often quoted than any of these, except the Golden Rule, was the injunction to "Search the scriptures, for in them ye think ye have eternal life: and they are they which testify of me."[84] This obligation to search the Scriptures was binding on all men, but the slaves could not fulfill it because the laws of the southern states forbade teaching them to read under heavy penalties. Slavery then compelled its victims to commit this sin of omission.

To infer a condemnation of slavery from such passages as these is, to say the least, a forced construction. That the abolitionists felt the weakness of their argument is shown by the urgency with which they pressed the view that Jesus' failure to condemn slavery was due to his lack of experience of the system, just as his silence in regard to the gladiatorial contests could be traced to his want of contact with them. Even when He healed the centurion's servant He did not enter the house where the sick man lay.[85] Christ's mission was to the poor and needy. How

---

[78]Exod. 21:16.
[79]I Tim. I:10.
[80]Matt. 7:12.
[81]Wright, *Does the Bible Sanction Slavery?* 9–12; Green, *The Chattel Principle*, 25.
[82]Luke 10:7.
[83]Mark 10:44.
[84]John 5:39.
[85]Matt. 8:5–13; Luke 7:2–10; Bacon, *Slavery*, 33–34.

could He have daily come in contact with slaves and kept silence? As hired servants are mentioned in the New Testament, e.g., in the story of the prodigal son where they apparently are the lowest menials, it was supposed that slaves were not numerous in Judea and that those who were held belonged in the main to the Gentiles, the Roman officers.[86] This view of the number of slaves held by the Jews is probably substantially correct, for while one may not believe with Birney that slavery had been nearly extinguished among them by the "abolition principles of Moses' laws,"[87] the poverty of the Hebrews in Jesus' time must have been prevented their holding many slaves.[88]

Turning to the teaching of the apostles, we find there the same condition that we noted in Jesus' teaching, the inculcation of sublime moral lessons, that, whatever may have been the indirect result of their application, could be made to express disapprobation of slavery only by perversion. The precepts most frequently cited by the abolitionists were such as taught that respect should be paid to all men, e.g., "Honor all men," and "If ye have respect to persons, ye commit sin."[89] Peter's vision of the clean and the unclean animals taught the same truth.[90] Such exhortations to useful labor as "Let him that stole steal no more; but rather let him labor, working with his hands the thing which is good, that he may have to give to him that needeth"[91] were also quoted. This last was, of course, used as a direct admonition to the slave-holder, as was Jesus' denunciation of those who withheld the hire of the laborer,[92] and Paul's prophecy that extortioners should not inherit the kingdom of God.[93]

But when the abolitionists abandoned their quarrels over *olem* and *doulos* and took the broad ground that slavery was prohibited by the spirit of Christianity, they could present a much more convincing argument. This, they said, was the characteristic way in which Jesus and His apostles taught. Instead of laying down specific rules they had instilled such ethical truths as the equality of all before God and the law of brotherly love, ideals which had effected an entire revolution in the value of the individual, and if consistently applied would be found hostile to slavery. Such principles were the fruitful seed from which the tree of liberty had grown.[94]

One other argument that must be noted was that based on the general description of the primitive church found in Galatians.[95] From this it was deduced

---

[86]Green, *The Chattel Principle*, 60–62; Rankin, *Letters*, 89–90.

[87]Birney, *Second Letter*, 3.

[88]Gerald D. Heuver, *The Teachings of Jesus Concerning Wealth*, 79.

[89]I Peter 2:17; Jas. 2:9.

[90]Acts, chap. 10. See John Woolman, *Considerations on Slavery*, 4.

[91]Eph. 4:28.

[92]James 5:4.

[93]I Cor. 6:10.

[94]Fuller and Wayland, *Domestic Slavery*, 92–105; Barnes, *Inquiry*, 246–249; Green, *The Chattel Principle*, 55, 56. Dew acknowledged the force of this reasoning: "With regard to the assertion that slavery is against the spirit of Christianity, we are ready to admit the general assertion," *Pro-Slavery Argument*, 451.

[95]Gal. 3:28. See also Acts 2:44; 4:32.

that during the early ages of Christianity slavery could nowhere have prevailed under the sanction of the church.[96] The less radical abolitionists granted, however, that the equality of the early church was only a religious equality. They acknowledged that slavery existed in Corinth and elsewhere.

The application of these various Biblical arguments was obvious. It was the duty of all Christians "unbiased by interest" and "unawed by persecution"[97] to carry out the principles of the Gospel. They must not desist if accused of imprudence or over-zeal. Had not the apostle Paul himself been charged with meddling in politics and preaching doctrines which tended to change the existing order? The duty of bearing witness to the truth was especially incumbent upon ministers. As the Whig ministers had preached politics during the Revolution when their own rights and liberties were at stake, so must ministers now fulfill their duty when the rights of others are in question.[98] Many sermons were addressed to the delinquent southern clergymen. Northerners who shirked the duty of testifying against slavery came in for impressive reproof. They were warned that those who will be doomed in the last judgment will not be charged with inflicting positive injuries on the helpless but with not exerting themselves to relieve suffering.[99]

These labored efforts to solve a modern problem by Biblical precedents seem almost ridiculous to us. We no longer ask of the Bible what it cannot give us. We recognize that the Jewish patriarchs were not exemplars of modern morals and that Jesus did not try to revolutionize the social institutions of the Roman world. But standards were different a century ago. What the abolitionists were trying to do was to justify a profound moral sentiment by the highest authority which they knew, and through all their arguments we must recognize this ethical element—a grasping after that righteousness which exalteth a nation, a longing to rid their country of sin which is a reproach to any people.

---

[96]Green, *The Chattel Principle*, 32–36.

[97]Fuller and Wayland, *Domestic Slavery*, 107.

[98]Paxton, *Letters*, 15–21.

[99]Matt. 25:42–45; Green, "Slavery not in the New Testament" (*Sermons and Other Discourses*, 272–274.) Further references for the Biblical anti-slavery argument are George Bourne, *Man-Stealing and Slavery denounced by the Presbyterian and Methodist Churches. Together with an address to all the Churches*; Samuel Crothers, *The Gospel of the Typical Servitude*; John Hersey, *An Appeal to Christians, on the Subject of Slavery*, 52–87; Onesimus (pseud.), *Disquisition on Egyptian, Roman and American Slavery*; Leicester Sawyer, *Dissertation on Servitude: embracing an examination of the Scripture Doctrines on the subject, and an inquiry into the Character and Relations of Slavery*; "The Bible Argument" (*Emancipator*, March 1836, p. 3); "Did not Paul Sanction Slavery?" (*Emancipator*, May 19, 1836); *Slavery against the Bible: a correspondence between the General Conference of Maine, and The Presbytery of Tombeebee, Miss.*, 33–125; LaRoy Sunderland, *Anti-Slavery Manual*, 33–49; *An Appeal on the Subject of Slavery; addressed to the members of the New England and New Hampshire conferences of the Methodist Episcopal Church. Together with a Defence of the Said Appeal, in which is shown the Sin of Holding Property in Man*, 31–34; *Letter to a Member of the Congress of the United States of America, from an English Clergyman.*

The Curse That Never Was (Genesis 9:18–27)

Gene Rice

Of all the passages of the Bible none is more infamous than Genesis 9:18–27. Many a person has used this text to justify to himself and others his prejudice against people of African descent. Indeed, it has been widely used to claim divine sanction for slavery and segregation. Often the location of the passage is unknown and one is not familiar with the details, but with the certainty of unexamined truth it is asserted that the Bible speaks of a curse on Black people. And this notion has exercised so powerful an influence precisely because its adherents by and large have been "good Church people." While the hey-day of this understanding of Gen. 9:18–27 was during the last and early part of this century, it persists to this day. Whether wittingly or unwittingly a recent article by F. W. Bassett of Limestone College, Gaffney, South Carolina, lends aid and comfort and helps to perpetuate it.[1] It is time that the misunderstanding and abuse of this passage come to an end.

I.

Rarely have such clear and unambiguous claims been made of so obscure and difficult a passage. Its complexity is apparent from the outset. It begins by naming the sons of Noah who went forth from the ark, namely, Shem, Ham, and Japheth, but goes on to add in a statement that takes one completely by surprise: "Ham was the father of Canaan." And this information is repeated in v. 22. By its position immediately following the account of the flood, it is implied that the episode of 9:18–27 took place shortly thereafter. Moreover, the account gives the impression that Noah's sons have not yet set up separate households but are still unmarried and living with their father in the family tent. This impression is strengthened by

Gene Rice, "The Curse That Never Was (Genesis (9:18–27)," from *The Journal of Religious Thought 29*, no. 1 (Spring–Summer 1972): 5–27. Copyright © 1972 by the School of Religion, Howard University. Reprinted with the permission of The Permissions Company, P.O. Box 243, High Bridge, NJ 08829, USA on behalf of Howard University Press. All rights reserved.

I would like to express appreciation to Kingsley Dalpadado, Samuel L. Gandy, Jack H. Goodwin, and Frank M. Snowden, Jr. without whose generous help this article in its present form would not have been possible.

the fact that one of the sons is designated as "the youngest" (v. 24). Also the offense against Noah is the kind one might expect from a teen-ager but hardly from a mature, married man. Yet the two references to Ham as the father of Canaan presuppose that Noah's sons have left their father's tent, set up separate households, and that a number of years have passed in the course of which Canaan, who is Ham's fourth son (Gen. 10:6), was born and has become either a teen-ager or a young adult.

While the reference to Ham as the father of Canaan is awkward in every respect, one can infer from the context that it was introduced because later on Canaan is cursed for the misdeed of Ham. But instead of clarifying matters this only creates another problem. Why should Canaan be cursed for the wrong of his father? The biblical text provides no answer to this question.

The attentive reader of Gen. 9:18–27 is confronted, in the third place, by two different conceptions of the extent of Noah's family. Genesis 9:19a states that from Shem, Ham, and Japheth "the whole world was peopled." But according to 9:25–27 the sons of Noah all live in the land of Palestine.

In the fourth place, there is the perplexing fact that the sons of Noah are listed in the order Shem, Ham, and Japheth in 9:18 and on the basis of Gen. 5:32 this is most naturally understood as the order of their birth. In 9:24, however, the offender against Noah is expressly identified as Noah's "youngest" son. From the order Shem, Ham, and Japheth, the youngest son is Japheth. But Japheth is not cursed.

This brings us to the fifth and most enigmatic of all the difficulties of Gen. 9:18–27. In 9:24–25 Noah identifies the offender against him both as his youngest son and as Canaan: "When Noah awoke from his wine and knew what his youngest son had done to him, he said, 'Cursed be Canaan; a slave of slaves shall he be to his brothers.'" Then in vs. 26–27 Noah names the two brothers to whom Canaan is to be slave: "Noah also said: 'Blessed be the LORD, the God of Shem; and let Canaan be his slave. God enlarge Japheth, and let him dwell in the tents of Shem; and let Canaan be his slave.'" Thus whereas the sons of Noah are Shem, Ham, and Japheth in 9:18, they are Shem, Japheth, and Canaan in 9:24–27.

II.

All the tensions of Gen. 9:18–27 are resolved when it is recognized that this passage contains two parallel but different traditions of Noah's family. In one tradition Noah's family consists of Shem, Ham, and Japheth and these three are the ancestors of all the peoples known to ancient Israel. This tradition is universal, catholic in scope. It is found in Gen. 9:18–19a (and elsewhere in 5:32; 6:10, 7:13; 10:1; I Chron. 1:4). In the other tradition Noah's family consists of Shem, Japheth, and Canaan and they all live in Palestine. This tradition is limited, parochial in scope. It is found in 9:20–27 (and seems to be presupposed in 10:21 where Shem is referred to as the elder brother of Japheth).

The understanding of Gen. 9:18–27 is so confused because the text in its present form represents an effort to minimize the discrepancy between these two traditions by equating Ham in the one with Canaan in the other. This was done by the notation in 9:18b, "Ham was the father of Canaan," and by adding in 9:22a, "Ham the father of" before Canaan. When these two harmonizing notes are recognized as such the two different traditions of Noah's family stand out sharply: vs. 18–19a reflect one tradition, vs. 20–27 embody the other. Instead of trying to harmonize them, each should be considered in its own right. When this is done it becomes clear that Noah's discovery of wine and his cursing and blessing of his sons is an independent, coherent narrative in which the offender against his father as well as the one cursed in Canaan. This becomes graphically clear if the harmonizing notes are placed in brackets or removed as in the following citation of the text:

> [20]Noah was the first tiller of the soil. He planted a vineyard; [21]and he drank of the wine, and became drunk, and uncovered himself in his tent. [22]And ... Canaan saw the nakedness of his father, and told his two brothers outside. [23]Then Shem and Japheth took a garment, laid it upon both their shoulders, and walked backward and covered the nakedness of their father; their faces were turned away, and they did not see their father's nakedness. [24]When Noah awoke from his wine and knew what his youngest son had done to him, [25]he said,
>
> > "Cursed be Canaan;
> > a slave of slaves shall he be to his brothers."
>
> [26]He also said,
>
> > "Blessed be the LORD, the GOD of Shem;
> > and let Canaan be his slave.
>
> [27]God enlarge Japheth,
> > and let him dwell in the tents of Shem;
> > and let Canaan be his slave."[2]

This is not a new interpretation. It was first proposed by J. Wellhausen in 1876.[3] Among those who have subsequently adopted and defended it are: K. Budde (who devotes ninety pages to Gen. 9:18–27!),[4] A. Kuenen,[5] A. Westphal,[6] W. R. Harper,[7] B. Stade,[8] H. Holzinger,[9] B. W. Bacon,[10] C. H. Cornill,[11] W. E. Addis,[12] E. Kautsch,[13] D. S. Margoliouth,[14] J. E. Carpenter and C. Hartford-Battersby (with reserve),[15] H. Gunkel,[16] S. R. Driver (with reserve),[17] W. H. Bennett,[18] E. Meyer,[19] A. R. Gordon,[20] C. F. Kent,[21] J. Skinner,[22] F. Böhl,[23] R. Smend,[24] C. Steuernagel,[25] O. Procksch,[26] H. E. Ryle,[27] W. Eichrodt,[28] J. R. Dummelow,[29] W. M. Patton,[30] E. S. Brightman,[31] A. S. Peake,[32] O. Eissfeldt,[33] S. Mowinckel,[34] R. H. Pfeiffer,[35] W. Zimmerli,[36] E. G. Kraeling,[37] C. A. Simpson,[38] G. von Rad,[39] A. Lods,[40] E. B. Redlich,[41] J. Chaine (with reserve),[42] A. Clamer,[43] C. T. Fritsch,[44] J. Heemrood,[45] A. Halder,[46] L. Hicks,[47] J. H. Marks,[48] A. H. McNeile and T. W. Thacker,[49] R. Graves and R. Patai,[50] G. Fohrer,[51] E. H. Maly,[52] and T. E. Fretheim.[53] A variation of this interpretation is represented by A. Dillman,[54] J. Hermann,[55] and L. Rost[56] who maintain that originally the passage had to do only with Canaan (Dillmann) or with Canaan and Shem (Herrmann, Rost) and that the reference to the other brother(s) has been added later.[57]

The above roster of scholars is sufficient to indicate that after its introduction in the 1870's the interpretation presented above quickly won the assent of the majority of authorities and has maintained that position to the present. And it would be difficult to draw up a more distinguished company of scholars. Nevertheless this interpretation has not lacked for opposition nor have there been wanting vigorous defenders of an alternative point of view.

III.

Among those who assume the unity of Gen. 9:18–27 and therefore regard Ham as the offender are: A. Köhler,[58] C. A. Briggs,[59] Franz Delitzsch,[60] W. H. Green,[61] H. L. Strack,[62] J. Halevy,[63] C. J. Ball,[64] T. K. Cheyne,[65] M. Dods,[66] A. Ehrlich,[67] W. Möller,[68] L. Murillo,[69] E. König,[70] P. Heinisch,[71] B. Jacob,[72] H. C. Leupold,[73] U. Cassuto,[74] H. Junker,[75] H. Frey,[76] A. Richardson,[77] W. M. Logan,[78] R. H. Elliott,[79] J. de Fraine,[80] and F. W. Bassett.[81] To these may be added a small group of scholars who take the position that there is only one tradition of the sons of Noah, namely, Shem, Ham, and Japheth, but that part or all of the cursing of Canaan and the blessing of Shem and Japheth is later than the story about Noah's discovery of wine. Among these are: B. D. Eerdmans,[82] J. Hoftijzer,[83] H. W. Wolff,[84] and D. Neiman.[85]

Perhaps the most serious obstacle to those who defend the unity of 9:18–27 is the fact that Ham is regularly named as Noah's second son whereas the offender is specifically designated as Noah's youngest son (v. 24). One of the oldest and simplest expedients to avoid this difficulty is to accept the order Shem, Ham, and Japheth as the proper one chronologically but to construe the adjective, young, not as a superlative but as a comparative. That is, in relation to Shem, Ham is Noah's "younger" son.[86] Not two but three sons are compared, however, and when this is the case the proper construction is the superlative.

There is an old and well represented tradition, on the other hand, that the order Shem, Ham, and Japheth is not chronological and that Ham actually was Noah's youngest son.[87] This understanding is arrived at by construing Gen. 10:21 to read, "Shem, the brother of Japheth, the eldest" and by taking "youngest son" in 9:24 to refer to Ham. But almost all authorities are agreed that the proper construction of Gen. 10:21 is "Shem . . . the elder brother of Japheth." And if the "youngest son" in 9:24 is Ham the cursing of Canaan is completely unmotivated and without meaning.

Still others would solve this problem by contending that "youngest" in 9:24 should not be understood chronologically but morally in the sense of "the least, the contemptible."[88] But there are a number of words in the Hebrew language better suited to express moral condemnation and it is difficult to see why so ambiguous a term would have been chosen in this context.

Accepting that "youngest son" is to be understood chronologically and that the reference is to Canaan, some have sought a way out of the dilemma by calling attention to the fact that son is sometimes used in the sense of grandson.[89] Such usage is attested but never in conjunction with son used in the literal sense as in the present passage.

A few scholars assert that the original text consistently referred to Ham as the offender and as the one cursed and that Canaan is a later addition to the text.[90]

But this is pure speculation for which there is no firm support in the ancient texts and versions. This position is rendered completely untenable, moreover, by the statements, "Ham was the father of Canaan," and "Ham the father of." If Ham was the consistent reading of the original text these statements are superfluous and unintelligible. And if someone added Canaan to the text why did he not remove all references to Ham?

Various explanations are offered to account for Canaan being cursed for the offense of Ham. Some find here the working of a principle of retribution: as Noah suffered at the hands of his youngest son, Ham, so Ham is afflicted in the person of his youngest son, Canaan. But nowhere is such a principle enunciated in the Bible nor is an example to be found where the guilty father is passed over and his son punished in his stead.

Others account for the cursing of Canaan on the grounds that one whom God had blessed (Ham in Gen. 9:1) could not be cursed. Equally valid is the principle that the innocent should not be cursed for the misdeed of the guilty.

Still others would account for the presence of Canaan in the curse because Canaan was the nearest and best known of Hamitic peoples to the Israelites. Rather, that only Canaan is mentioned in the curse most naturally suggests that all other Hamitic peoples are excluded from it. And if Ham is the guilty party, the text provides no answer as to why only Canaan and not all Hamitic peoples should be cursed.

Finally, it has been maintained that both Ham and Canaan are guilty, that Canaan first saw Noah's nakedness and Ham told his brothers. There are also traditions that either Ham or Canaan (or a lion) rendered Noah impotent (or attacked him homosexually) and that this was what "his youngest son had done to him" (v. 24). But the context indicates that the disrespectful seeing itself was the offense done to Noah.[91] And if both father and son are guilty, why is the father treated as less responsible than the son?

A completely different tack is taken by Bassett. On the basis of the usage attested in Lev. 18 and 20 that to see a man's nakedness may have the idiomatic meaning of having sexual intercourse with his wife, Bassett interprets the passage to mean that Ham committed incest with his mother and that Canaan was cursed because he was the fruit of this illicit union. Bassett thinks that the case of the Reubenites who lost their preeminence among the tribes of Israel because of Reuben's affair with his father's concubine, Bilhah, and the midrashic traditions that Ham's offense against Noah was one of castration (which also has to do with displacing one's father) support his understanding of the passage. In order to maintain this interpretation, however, Bassett has to delete 9:23 as the later addition of a redactor or editor who "missed the idiomatic meaning"[92] of the seeing of Noah's nakedness.

Bassett overstates the case for the sexual implications of nakedness. E. A. Speiser points out on the basis of Gen. 42:9, 12 that nakedness in the first instance "relates to exposure" and "does not necessarily imply sexual offenses" (cf. Gen. 2:25; Ex. 20:26; II Sam. 6:20).[93] In a passage that may have been formulated under the influence of Gen. 9:18–27, Hab. 2:15,[94] drunkenness and nudity are associated with each other without any sexual overtones (cf. also Lam. 4:21).

Furthermore, the proper idiomatic expression for intercourse is to uncover the nakedness of another. Except for one instance, "uncover" is consistently the verb of the idiom for intercourse in Lev. 18 and 20. In Lev. 20:17 "uncover" and "see" are used in parallelism to each other, but this usage of "see" is clearly exceptional for the parallelism with "uncover" has to be made explicit. Bassett cites no other passages where to see the nakedness of another means to have sexual intercourse. Nor do the standard lexicons give this as a meaning for *r'h*. Still more damaging to Bassett's argument is the fact that "uncover" and "see" are used in adjoining sentences in Gen. 9:18–27 (vs. 21, 22) but there is no effort to relate them to each other and here they clearly are not synonymous. Canaan does not uncover Noah; Noah uncovers himself.[95] In short, Bassett has not established a case for the general usage of the expression to see the nakedness of another as meaning sexual intercourse. Nor does the context in Gen. 9:18–27 support such a usage. Quite simply the text states that Noah uncovered himself and Canaan witnessed him in this state.

Not only does Bassett overstate the case but he is inconsistent. He asserts on the one hand that "the idiomatic interpretation is so firmly established in Leviticus that it should be accepted as the normal one unless some other meaning is demanded by the context" yet maintains that Gen. 9:23 was added "by someone who did not understand the idiom"![96] On the one hand, Bassett commits himself to the limited, parochial tradition of Noah's family in that he takes 9:20–27 to be an ethnological tradition "designed to discredit the Canaanites and justify the Israelite and Philistine hegemony over them." The major burden of the paper, on the other hand, is to defend the catholic tradition of Noah's family according to which the sons are Shem, Ham, and Japheth (pp. 234ff.).

Critical to Bassett's position is his assertion that 9:23 is secondary. There is no evidence in the ancient texts and versions to support this claim. No other scholar has found reason to regard only this verse as alien to its context. Rather, the blessing of Shem and Japheth is unintelligible apart from some such meritorious act on their part as reported in v. 23. And if v. 23 is integral to its context it is fatal to Bassett's theory. For, as Cassuto observes, "if the covering was an adequate remedy, it follows that the misdemeanour was confined to seeing."[97] For that matter, v. 22 stands in great tension with Bassett's position. If Ham committed incest with his mother, it is likely that he would come outside and tell his brothers?

There are other flaws in Bassett's interpretation. If Ham's offense was incest it is difficult to see how Noah could curse by name the issue of this union at the time of conception and completely ignore the perpetrators of the deed. There is a persistent and often bitter polemic against the Canaanites in the Old Testament. Had Canaan's origin been an incestuous one it almost certainly would have been exploited (cf. Gen. 19:30–38) but nowhere is there any reference to it. Finally, Bassett's position leaves unsolved the questions that arise in connection with "youngest son" in v. 24.

Almost three hundred years ago a position essentially identical with that of Bassett was put forward by Hermann von der Hardt.[98] It received prompt rebuttal[99] and has since enjoyed the oblivion its deserves.

Unsatisfactory also is the attempt to master the difficulties of Gen. 9:18–27 by separating the curse and blessing from the preceding narrative. The following structure is transparent in the text:

Introduction: Noah's vineyard and drunkenness

I. The behavior of Noah's sons
   A. Canaan's disrespect and shamelessness
   B. The respect and piety of Shem and Japheth
II. Noah's response to his son's behavior
   A. Curse on Canaan
   B. Blessing on Shem and Japeth.[100]

The two parts of the passage correspond symmetrically and necessarily to each other. And this correspondence is unmarred by literary seams, formal dislocations, or other incongruities.

Those scholars then who defend the unity of Gen. 9:18–27 or who maintain that there was only one tradition of Noah's sons have not presented an interpretation that does justice to the text. They are at odds with each other and cannot agree on a common understanding. None of them has taken seriously the conflict between the catholic and parochial conceptions of Noah's family standing in juxtaposition to each other. In short, no satisfactory explanation of Gen. 9:18–27 has been given on the assumption that it is organic literary unity speaking with a single voice, nor, on this assumption, is one possible.

IV.

The earliest evidence of a racist interpretation of Gen. 9:18–27 is found in Bereshith Rabbah, an expository commentary on Genesis utilizing the work of rabbis from the second to the fourth centuries and probably completed in the early fifth century.[101] Alluding to a tradition that Ham castrated Noah, Rabbi Joseph has Noah say to Ham: "You have prevented me from doing something in the dark (cohabitation), therefore your seed will be ugly and dark-skinned."[102] "The descendants of Ham through Canaan therefore have red eyes, because Ham looked upon the nakedness of his father; they have misshapen lips, because Ham spoke with his lips to his brothers about the unseemly condition of his father; they have twisted curly hair, because Ham turned and twisted his head round to see the nakedness of his father; and they go about naked, because Ham did not cover the nakedness of his father."[103] And according to Pesahim, 113b of the Babylonian Talmud, "Five things did Canaan charge his sons: Love one another, love robbery, love lewdness, hate your masters and do not speak the truth."

This view gained no prominence in the ancient world, however, which by and large was free of color prejudice.[104] Moreover, in the Middle Ages when the wise men came to be regarded as three it was apparently with conscious reference to the three sons of Noah, and one of them, Melchoir or Balthasar, was depicted as black.[105] Nevertheless, the racist interpretation of Gen. 9-18-27 remained alive[106] and gained new life with the colonial expansion of Europe and the development of slavery in America. Emphasis was now placed on all Black people as being descended from Ham and/or Canaan and by that fact condemned to perpetual servitude because of Noah's curse. While this understanding only became a popular notion in the nineteenth century, it was intellectuals, often within the Church, who "sold" it to an age that found it expedient to exploit it.[107]

The proper clarification of Gen. 9:18–27 was not possible until the composite character of the Hexateuch was established and this was not until the time of Wellhausen in the 1870's. Even so, the interpreter has never been without ample resources for arriving at a non-racist interpretation of the passage. From the fact that the biblical text explicitly identifies Canaan—and only Canaan—as the one cursed one may reasonably infer that the other sons of Ham, Cush (Ethiopia), Egypt, and Put (Libya), who are African peoples properly speaking, were not cursed.

Secondly, the immediate context forbids a racist understanding of Gen. 9:18–27. Genesis 10 has to do with all the peoples of the world known to ancient Israel and since this chapter immediately follows the episode of Noah's cursing and blessing it would have been most appropriate to express here any prejudicial feelings toward African peoples. Not only are such feelings absent, but all peoples are consciously and deliberately related to each other as brothers. No one, not even Israel, is elevated above anyone else and no disparaging remark is made about any people, not even the enemies of Israel. Indeed, the point of Gen. 10 is that the great diversity and multiplicity of peoples is the fulfillment of God's command to Noah and his sons: "Be fruitful and multiply, and fill the earth" (Gen. 9:1). As God inspected his creative work in Gen. 1 and found it good, so in Gen. 10 he approves and rejoices in mankind in all its manifestations.

Had the ancient Israelites been conscious of some taint upon African peoples one would expect Abraham to have alluded to it when he went down to Egypt because of a famine in Canaan. Nor do Abraham and Sarah have any qualms about Hagar because of her Egyptian origin. They are glad to use her to get an heir and so secure through their own efforts God's promise of a great posterity (Gen. 16). While Miriam and Aaron spoke out against Moses because of his Cushite wife, the context clearly shows that what they are really protesting is Moses' authority (Nu. 12:1ff.).

The prophet Isaiah is very critical of Egypt, which, incidentally was ruled over by an Ethiopian dynasty during the latter part of his ministry, because he wants to dissuade Israel from relying on Egypt in its bid for independence from Assyria. But nowhere does he appeal to some ancient curse. He does make a few disparaging remarks about Egypt's help (cf., e.g., Is. 19:11ff.; 30:5, 7; ct. 18:1ff.), but his point to Judah is: "The Egyptians are men, and not God; and their horses are flesh, and not spirit" (31:3).

It is surely not without significance that Aaron's grandson, who is regarded as the ancestor of the Zadokite priesthood (Ex. 6:25; Nu. 25:6ff.; Josh. 22:30; 24:33; I Chron. 6:4, 50: Ezr. 8:2; Ps. 106:30), and one of the sons of Eli (I Sam. 1:3; 2:34; 4:11, 17: 4:3) were given the Egyptian name, Phinehas, which means literally, the

Nubian. Nor is it without important implications for the understanding of Gen. 9:18–27 that the introduction to the prophecies of Zephaniah tells us that his great, great grandfather was (King) Hezekiah and that his father was Cushi, that is, the Ethiopian.

Psalm 87 contains a vision of Zion as the spiritual mother of all men and among these African peoples are explicitly mentioned. Is. 19:24–25 anticipates the time when "Israel will be the third with Egypt and Assyria, a blessing in the midst of the earth, whom the LORD of hosts has blessed, saying, 'Blessed be Egypt my people, and Assyria the work of my hands, and Israel my heritage.'"

Simon from the North African city of Cyrene (Lk. 23:26) was not regarded as unworthy to bear Jesus' cross. Nor did Philip feel it incumbent upon himself to discuss Gen. 9:18–27 with the Ethiopian minister of Candace (Acts 8:26ff.). In short, nowhere in the Bible is there any support for the idea that people of African descent are under a curse. On the contrary, there is much evidence that they were regarded without prejudice and on an equal basis with other people.[108]

While Gen. 9:18–27 may well be the most misunderstood and abused passage of the Bible this is not a reflection on the Bible itself. Rather this misuse and abuse attest to what perversity the human spirit and intellect can sink and with what pains and ingenuity man finds ways to justify to himself and to others his sin.

Notes

1. "Noah's Nakedness and the Curse on Canaan: A Case of Incest?" *Vetus Testamentum* 21 (1971), 232–237.

2. This translation follows the RSV except at two points. In v. 21 the RSV has "lay uncovered" instead of "uncovered himself." The rendition adopted above is defended in note 95 of this study. "Blessed be the LORD" in v. 26 is given as an alternative translation in a footnote by the RSV and of the two alternatives it is closest to the Hebrew text.

3. "Die Composition des Hexateuchs," *Jahrbücher für Deutsche Theologie* 21 (1876), 403–404. This was the first of three long articles published in the above periodical (the third article was published in vol. 22, 1877). They were reprinted in the fourth edition of F. Bleek, *Einleitung in das Alte Testament* (Berlin, 1878), pp. 181–267 and published (unchanged) by Wellhausen in book form in 1885 under the same title as above.

4. *Die Biblische Urgeschichte* (Giessen, 1883), pp. 290–370; 506–516.

5. *An Historico-Critical Inquiry into the Origin and Composition of the Hexateuch* (translation of the 2nd Dutch ed. of 1885; London, 1886), p. 234.

6. *Les sources du Pentateuque*, I (Paris, 1888), p. 243.

7. "The Pentateuchal Question. I. Gen. 1:1–12:5," *Hebraica* 5 (1888/89), 61–62.

8. *Geschichte des Volkes Israel*, I (Berlin, 1889), p. 109.

9. *Genesis erklärt* ("Kurzer Hand-Commentar zum Alten Testament") (Leipzig, 1889), p. 91 and *Einleitung in den Hexateuch* (Leipzig, 1893), p. 141.

10. "Notes on the Analysis of Genesis I–XXX," *Hebraica* 7 (1890/91), 223 and *The Genesis of Genesis* (Hartford, 1893), pp. 114, 115, 231.

11. *Introduction to the Canonical Books of the Old Testament* (translation of the 5th German ed. of 1905; New York, 1907; 1st ed., 1891), pp. 86, 87.

12. *The Documents of the Hexateuch* (London, 1892), pp. 14–15.

13. *Die Heillge Schrift des Alten Testaments: Beilagen* (Leipzig, 1894), p. 154.

14. "Ham," *A Dictionary of the Bible*, II (ed. by J. Hastings: New York, 1899), pp. 288–289.

15. *The Hexateuch*, II (New York, 1900), pp. 14–15.

16. *Die Genesis übersetzt und erklärt* ("Göttinger Handkommentar zum Alten Testament") (3rd ed., Göttingen, 1910; 1st ed., 1901), pp. 78–81, 84, 87 and *Die Urgeschichte und die Patriarchen* ("Die Schriften des Alten Testaments") (Göttingen, 1911), p. 88.

17. *The Book of Genesis* ("Westminster Commentaries") (15th ed., London, 1948; 1st ed., 1904), pp. 109, 111–112.

18. *Genesis* ("Century Bible") (Edinburgh, 1904), p. 155.

19. *Die Israeliten und ihre Nachbarstämme* (Halle an der Saale, 1906), pp. 219–222.

20. *The Early Traditions of Genesis* (Edinburgh, 1907), pp. 3–4, 240, 260, 263.

21. *Narratives of the Beginning of Hebrew History* (New York, 1908), p. 60; cf. p. 69 and *The Heroes and Crises of Early Hebrew History* (New York, 1908), pp. 47–48, 51.

22. *A Critical and Exegetical Commentary on Genesis* ("International Critical Commentary") (2nd ed., Edinburgh, 1930; 1st ed., 1910), pp. 182, 184, 186, 195, 202, 219.

23. *Kanaanöer und Hebräer* (Leipzig, 1911), pp. 6, 68.

24. *Die Erzählung des Hexateuch* (Berlin, 1912), pp. 17–18, 21, 27, 28.

25. *Lehrbuch der Einleitung in das Alte Testament* (Tübingen, 1912), p. 140.

26. *Die Genesis* ("Kommentar zum Alten Testament") (2nd and 3rd ed., Leipzig and Erlangen, 1924; 1st ed., 1913), pp. 71ff.

27. *The Book of Genesis* ("Cambridge Bible") (Cambridge, 1914), pp. 127, 128, 129.

28. *Die Quellen der Genesis von neuem untersucht* (Giessen, 1916), pp. 118–119; cf. 145.

29. "Genesis," *A Commentary on the Holy Bible* (ed. by J. R. Dummelow, New York, 1916), p. 16.

30. *Israel's Account of the Beginnings* (New York, 1916), pp. 107–108.

31. *The Sources of the Hexateuch* (New York and Cincinnati, 1918), p. 38.

32. "Genesis," *Peake's Commentary on the Bible* (ed. by A. S. Peake, 2nd ed., New York, 1937; 1st ed., 1919), p. 145.

33. *Hexateuch-Synopse* (Leipzig, 1922), pp. 7, 8; cf. 89, 14*–15*, 256* and "Genesis," *Interpreter's Dictionary of the Bible*, II (New York, 1962), p. 372.

34. *The Two Sources of the Predeuteronomic Primeval History (JE) in Gen. 1–11* (Oslo, 1937), pp. 15–16.

35. *Introduction to the Old Testament* (2nd ed., New York, 1948; 1st. ed., 1941), pp. 274–275.

36. *1. Mose 1–11* (2nd ed., Zürich, 1957; 1st ed., 1942), pp. 355–356.

37. "The Earliest Hebrew Flood Story," *Journal of Biblical Literature* 66 (1947), 291.

38. *The Early Traditions of Israel* (Oxford, 1948), pp. 63–64, 451–452, 498 and "The Book of Genesis: Introduction and Exegesis," *Interpreter's Bible*, I (New York, 1952), pp. 555–556, 560.

39. *Genesis, a Commentary* ("Old Testament Library") (Philadelphia, 1961; 1st German ed., 1949), pp. 131–132.

40. *Historic de la Littérature Hébraïque et Juive* (Paris, 1950), pp. 174, 175.

41. *The Early Traditions of Genesis* (London, 1950), pp. 113–114.

42. *Le Livre de la Genèsis* (Paris, 1951), pp. 144, 145.

43. *La Genèsis* ("La Sainte Bible") (Paris, 1953, pp. 201–203.

44. *The Book of Genesis* ("Layman's Bible Commentary") (Richmond, 1959), pp. 46–47.

45. "Kanaän Vervloekt," *Het Heilig Land* 12 (1959), 129–130.

46. "Canaan," *Interpreter's Dictionary of the Bible*, I (New York, 1962), p. 494.

47. "Ham," *Interpreter's Dictionary of the Bible*, II (New York, 1962), p. 515.

48. "Noah," *Interpreter's Dictionary of the Bible*, III (New York, 1962), p. 555.

49. "Ham," *Hasting's Dictionary of the Bible* (revised by F. C. Grant and H. H. Rowley, New York, 1963), p. 361.

50. *Hebrew Myths: The Book of Genesis* (Garden City, N. Y., 1964), pp. 121–122.

51. *Introduction to the Old Testament* (translated from the German ed. of 1965, New York, 1968), p. 162.

52. "Genesis," *The Jerome Biblical Commentary* (edited by R. E. Brown, J. A. Fitzmyer, and R. E. Murphy, Englewood Cliffs, N. J., 1968), pp. 16–17.

53. *Creation, Fall, and Flood* (Minneapolis, 1969), p. 127, n. 2.

54. *Genesis Critically and Exegetically Expounded*, I (translation of the 6th German ed. of 1892, Edinburgh, 1897), p. 302, cf. 306, 307.

55. "Zu. Gen. 9:18–27," *Zeitschrift für die alttestamentliche Wissenschaft* 30 (1910), 127–131.

56. "Noah der Weinbauer," *Geschichte und Altes Testament* (A. Alt Festschrift) (Tübingen, 1953), pp. 169–178.

57. R. H. Kennett in his, "The Early Narratives of the Jahvistic Document of the Pentateuch," *Old Testament Essays* (Cambridge, 1928), pp. 17–19 argues that the sons were Shem, Japheth, and Canaan but that Ham rather than Noah was their father.

58. *Lehrbuch der Biblischen Geschichte: Alten Testament,* I (Erlangen, 1875), pp. 54, n. 4, 66.

59. *Messianic Prophecy* (New York, 1886), pp. 79–81.

60. *A New Commentary on Genesis,* I (translation of the German ed. of 1887, New York, 1889), pp. 290ff.

61. "The Pentateuchal Question," *Hebraica* 5 (1888/89), 173 and *The Unity of the Book of Genesis* (New York, 1895), pp. 127–130.

62. *Die Bücher Genesis, Exodus, Leviticus und Numeri* ("Kurzgefasster Kommentar") (München, 1894), p. 28.

63. *Recherches Biblique,* I (Paris, 1895), pp. 174ff.

64. *The Book of Genesis* ("Sacred Books of the Old Testament") (Leipzig, 1896). p. 56.

65. *Traditions and Beliefs of Ancient Israel* (London, 1907), pp. 150–154. Cheyne attempts to master the problems of Gen. 9:18–27 by understanding Ham to be a North Arabian people. To achieve this understanding, however, he freely and arbitrarily emends the text.

66. *The Book of Genesis* ("Expositor's Bible") (Edinburgh, 1907), p. 78.

67. *Randglossen zur Hebräischen Bible,* I (Leipzig, 1908), pp. 41–42.

68. *Wider den Bann der Quellenscheidung* (Gütersloh, 1912), p. 106, n. 2.

69. *El Génesis* (Rome, 1914), pp. 408ff.

70. *Die Genesis* (Gütersloh, 1919), pp. 385–386.

71. *Das Buch Genesis* ("Die Heilige Schrift des Alten Testamentes") (Bonn, 1930) pp. 184–186.

72. *Das erste Buch der Tora: Genesis* (Berlin, 1934), pp. 258ff.

73. *Exposition of Genesis* (Columbus, Ohio, 1942), pp. 343ff.

74. *A Commentary on the Book of Genesis,* II (translation of the Hebrew ed. of 1949; Jerusalem, 1964), pp. 141ff.

75. *Genesis* ("Echter-Bible") (3rd ed., Würzburg, 1953; 1st ed., 1949), pp. 35–36.

76. *Das Buch der Anfänge* ("Die Botschaft des Alten Testaments") (Stuttgart, 1950), pp. 132–135.

77. *Genesis I–XI* ("Torch Bible Commentaries") (London, 1953), pp. 113–115.

78. *In the beginning God* (Richmond, 1957), pp. 69–73.

79. *The Message of Genesis* (St. Louis, 1961), pp. 70–71.

80. *Genesis* ("De Boeken van het Oude Testament") (Roermond enMasseik, 1963), pp. 95ff.

81. Cf. note 1 of this study. The unity of the passage is assumed but not defended by R. L. Hughes, *A Critical Study of the Meaning of 'RWR in Genesis 9:18–21* (unpublished doctoral dissertation, New Orleans Baptist Theological Seminary, 1956)

82. *Alttestamentliche Studien I: Die Komposition der Genesis* (Giessen, 1908), pp. 77–78, 84.

83. "Some Remarks on the Table of Noah's Drunkenness," *Studies on the Book of Genesis* ("Oudtestamentische Studiën," XII) (Leiden, 1958), pp. 22–27.

84. "Das Kerygma des Jahwisten," *Evangelische Theologie* 24 (1964), 87.

85. "The Date and Circumstances of the Cursing of Canaan," *Biblical Motifs* (edited by A. Altmann, Cambridge, Mass., 1966), pp. 113–134.

By a questionable interpretation of Gen. 10, R. Dussaud infers that Canaan, Shem, Ham, and Japheth are brothers and issue of the same father. It was the author of Gen. 9:18–27, he maintains, who put Canaan in a secondary role in relation to his brothers ("Cham et Canaan," *Revue de l 'Histoire des Religious* 59 (1909), 221–230.

86. Both the Septuagint and the Vulgate construe the adjective, young, as a comparative. This construction was defended among older scholars by Schumann, Ewald, Keil, and Schrader (cited by Dillmann, *op. cit.,* p. 306, n. 7). Leupold (*op. cit.,* p. 348) and Hughes (*op. cit.,* p. 117) are virtually alone among more recent scholars in adopting this position.

87. This view is already found in Bereshith Rabbah 26:2. Numbers Rabbah 4:8; Babylonian Talmud, Sanhedrian 69b; Josephus, Antiquities i.4.1, cf. i.6.3; Jubilees 7:10; Justin Martyr, Dialogue 139; Köhler, *op. cit.,* p. 54, n. 4, cf. p. 66; Möller, *op. cit.,* p. 106, n. 2; Murillo, *op. cit.,* p. 410; König, *op. cit.,* p. 386; Heinisch, *op. cit.,* pp. 184, 185; Cassuto, *op. cit.,* p. 165; Hoftijzer, *op. cit.,* pp. 23–24; de Fraine, *op. cit.,* pp. 97, 98.

88. Bereshith Rabbah 36:7; Targum of Pseudo-Jonathan on Gen. 9:24; the early Syrian Fathers; Rashi; Jacob, *op. cit.,* pp. 264–265; cf. pp. 291, 308.

89. Ibn Esra; Redak (cited by Jacob, *op. cit.,* p. 263); Dillmann, *op. cit.,* p. 307; J. E. Surfelt, "Noah's Curse and Blessing," *Concordia Theological Monthly* 17 (1946), 740.

90. König, *op. cit.,* pp. 386–387; Heinisch, *op. cit.,* p. 186; Junker, *op. cit.,* p. 35; de Fraine, *op. cit.,* p. 98.

91. "And it is the seeing itself, the looking, that is accounted by the refined sensitivity of the Israelite as something disgusting, especially when it is associated, as it is here, with an affront to the dignity of one's father" (Cassuto, *op. cit.,* pp. 151–152). Cf. also Dussaud, *op. cit.,* p. 222.

92. *Op. cit.,* pp. 233–234, cf. 237.

93. *Genesis* ("Anchor Bible") (Garden City, N. J., 1964), p. 61.

94. Cassuto, *op. cit.,* p. 152.

95. The reflexive nature of the verb in question, *wa-yithgal,* has not always been respected by translators and commentators. But grammatically the verb is a reflexive. Moreover, the context supports a reflexive construction. The heat from the wine would have caused Noah to uncover himself.

96. *Op. cit.,* p. 137.

97. *Op. cit.,* p. 151.

98. *Ephemerides philologicae* (Helmstadt, 1696), pp. 43–54.

99. C. Calvoer, *Gloria Mosis* (Goslar, 1696), pp. 244–264.

100. Gunkel, *Genesis übersetzt und erklärt,* pp. XXXIV, 78, 79; ct. p. 81. Cf. also Procksch, *op. cit.,* pp. 72, 73; Jacob, *op. cit.,* pp. 262–263.

101. So G. F.Moore, *Judaism,* I (Cambridge, Mass., 1927), p. 166.

102. *Midrash Rabbah,* I (translated and edited by H. Freedman and M. Simon; London, 1939), p. 293.

103. L. Ginzberg, *The Legends of the Jews,* I (Philadelphia, 1925), p. 169.

104. Cf. the excellent study by F. M. Snowden, Jr., *Blacks in Antiquity* (Cambridge, Mass., 1970).

105. Cf. the comment of Beda in his commentary on Matthew at 2:1ff. cited by Charles, *op. cit.,* p. 727, Friedel, *op. cit.,* p. 449, and A. J. Toynbee, *A Study of History,* I (New York, 1934), pp. 223–224; ct. R. Bastide, "Color, Racism, and Christianity," *Daedalus* 96 (1967), 316.

106. So current in the seventeenth century was the idea that the blackness of Africans was due to a curse (cf. Calvoer, *op. cit.,* p. 260 and earlier, G. Genebrardus, *Chronographiae libri quatuor* (Paris, 1580), pp. 26–27) that Sir Thomas Browne, physician, man of letters, and reporter-at-large for his age, devoted three chapters of his *Pseudodoxia epidemica* (1646) to an appraisal of it (*The Works of Sir Thomas Browne,* III (edited by G. Keynes; London, 1928), pp. 231–255; cf. 273–275). Cf. also D. B. Davis, *The Problem of Slavery in Western Culture* (Ithica, N. Y., 1966), pp. 450ff. and Jordan, *op. cit.,* pp. 17–20, 35–36, 60. It should be noted that there were those who held Ham was white. Cf. Allen, *op. cit.,* pp. 119, 162 and the depictions of Ham in the fifteenth century woodcuts of the Cologne and Lubec Bibles (figures 23 and 24 in Allen's work). More recently H. Heras affirms that "the Hamites belong to the white race" and cites three other scholars who share this view ("The Curse of Noe," *Catholic Biblical Quarterly* 12 (1950), 67, n. 21).

107. Cf. Charles, *op. cit.,* pp. 732ff. and Perbal, *op. cit.,* pp. 159ff. Both Charles and Perbal date the modern development of the racist interpretation of Gen. 9:20–27 from 1677 with the publication of *Curiosum scrutinum nigridinis filiorum Cham* ("Curious Inquiry into the Blackness of the Children of Ham") by J. L. Hannemann at Kiel. They also charge Martin Luther with responsibility, albeit inadvertently, for this development because Hannemann, a Lutheran, claims Luther as an authority for his position. Actually all that Luther said was that the scripture depicts Ham in the foulest colors ("*foedissimis coloribus depictus,*" Works, Weimar ed., vol. 44, p. 384). Allier traces the idea of blackness as a curse back to the Jewish rabbis of the third, fourth, and fifth centuries and thinks that Hannemann, who was born in Amsterdam, was influenced in his interpretation of Noah's curse by the Jew he had known there (*op. cit.,* pp. 16–19; cf. p. 7, n.1). Allier also emphasizes that not Hannemann alone but many contributed to the popularizing of the ancient Jewish interpretation.

108. For a more thorough treatment of the African presence in the Old Testament cf. R. A. Bennett, Jr., "Africa and the Biblical Period," *Harvard Theological Review* 64 (1971), 483–500. For a more general approach to a non-racist interpretation of the passage, cf. E. T. Thompson," The Curse Was Not on Ham," *Presbyterian Outlook* 137:10 (1955), 7, E. Tilson, *Segregation and the Bible* (Nashville, 1958), pp. 23–27, and T. B. Matson, *The Bible and Race* (Nashville, 1959), pp. 105–117.

House Readings and Field Readings: The Discourse of Slavery and Biblical/Cultural Studies

Jennifer A. Glancy

A headline in *The New York Times*, 10 May 1996: 'Bible Backed Slavery, Says a Lawmaker'. In the context of a debate over whether the Confederate flag should fly over the Alabama State Capitol, a first-term Republican State Senator named Charles Davidson wrote a speech defending the institution of slavery. According to Davidson, 'white, black, Hispanic and Indian slave owners' loved and cared for their slaves, who were the ultimate beneficiaries of the slave system. In addition, Davidson revived the argument that the Bible vindicated slavery; his textual allusions included Lev. 25.44 and 1 Tim. 6.1. 'The issue is not race', he said. 'It's Southern heritage. I'm on a one-man crusade to get the truth out about what our Southern heritage is all about.' Martha Foy, representing the Republican National Committee, expressed her 'shock' at Davidson's speech. The measure to approve official display of the Confederate flag was tabled, thus precluding Davidson from actually delivering his speech.[1] Criticism over Davidson's role in the incident caused him to drop out of a race for the US House of Representatives.[2]

This brief news item serves as a catalyst in my thinking about the convergence of biblical and cultural studies. Drawing on the political appropriation of biblical texts pertaining to slavery, this article considers two articulations of the conjuncture of biblical and cultural studies. The first approach follows the mandate of cultural studies to take the panoply of cultural productions as its subject matter, whether those productions are artistic, mercantile, pious, or, as in this case, political.[3] (These are not, of course, mutually exclusive categories.) Interpretation is political. This is true of all interpretation, regardless of its location: classroom, conference, journal.

From *Biblical Studies/Cultural Studies: The Third Sheffield Colloquium*, ed. Cheryl J. Exum and Stephen D. Moore, (1998): 460–477. Sheffield: Sheffield Academic Press, 1998. Copyright by Sheffield Academic Press Limited. Reprinted by permission.

[1] 'Bible Backed Slavery, Says a Lawmaker', *The New York Times* (10 May 1996, A20), column 4.
[2] 'Ala. State Sen. Forced to Quit U.S. House Race After Defending Slavery', *Jet* 90 (27 May 1996), p. 4.
[3] While some formulations of cultural studies focus on popular culture, to delimit the scope of inquiry in this way is to 'repeat and reproduce the boundary between high and popular culture' (Antony Easthope, *Literary into Cultural Studies* [London: Routledge, 1991], p. 108). See also the treatment of 'culture' in Raymond Williams, *Keywords: A Vocabulary of Culture and Society* (New York: Oxford University Press, 1976), pp. 76–82.

At least in the United States, however, biblical interpretation remains political in another, more overt sense. The Bible is a cultural icon, and both major political parties remain publicly deferential to biblical authority. As biblical and cultural studies converge, the function of the Bible in constructing and maintaining ideologies dominant in the US today emerges as an important area of investigation.

The second articulation of the conjuncture of biblical and cultural studies that I will consider is the movement to include a wider range of voices in the academic conversation of biblical studies. This movement acknowledges that, within the academy, a disparate if intersecting set of social locations informs and influences the readings of biblical scholars; it also acknowledges the legitimacy of readings and ways of reading of those who are not members of the guild of biblical scholars. Recent works by Fernando Segovia and Daniel Patte exemplify this trend within the field of biblical studies. I will argue that political readings of the biblical discourse on slavery point to some useful limits on the celebration of polyphonic hermeneutics.

HOUSE READINGS

> Let all who are under the yoke of slavery regard their masters as worthy of all honor, so that the name of God and the teaching may not be blasphemed. Those who have believing masters must not be disrespectful to them on the ground that they are members of the church: rather they must serve them all the more, since those who benefit by their service are believers and beloved. Teach and urge these duties . . . (1 Tim. 6.1–2, NRSV).

A state legislator in Alabama plans to give a speech defending the tradition of slavery in the American South, highlighting what he claims is biblical support for the institution of bond labor. When *The New York Times* picks up the story, the headline is not 'Contemporary Legislator Dares to Defend Slavery', nor is it 'Lawmaker Cites Bible in Political Debate'. Rather, the headline focuses on the legislator's assertion that the 'Bible backed slavery'. What is newsworthy here? Does *The Times* really dispute Senator Davidson's claim that a variety of biblical texts in some sense 'back slavery'? What would constitute a 'good' reading of 1 Tim. 6.1–2? As I read this brief news item, I try to reconstruct its implicit logic:

1. the Bible is normative for those of the Judeo-Christian tradition, perhaps even infallible;
2. slavery is wrong;
3. therefore, the Bible cannot 'back' slavery.

This logic is familiar to me from my own classroom. In a seminar I have taught on slavery and Christianity, many students cannot accept that the Bible (for them, a univocal and relatively uncomplicated text) tolerates slavery. Therefore, they are willing to argue, *the text must mean something other than what it obviously says.*

We could try to reconstruct some other underlying logic to the story in *The Times*. For example:

1. the Bible supports slavery;
2. slavery is wrong and offends against US democratic ideals;
3. we reject the Bible as a political guide.

In such a case, we would anticipate a headline focusing on the anomaly of an elected official citing the Bible in political debate. However, to challenge biblical authority is dangerous today in American politics. One may quibble with particular readings of the Bible, but in the context of political discourse, a more general rejection of biblical authority is not a viable option.

While I cannot share the surprise implicit in *The Times*'s headline over the assertion that biblical authority supported slavery, neither do I share Senator Davidson's hermeneutical perspective. Meaning is use, according to Wittgenstein's dictum,[4] and Davidson's interpretation of biblical teaching about slavery is inseparable from its use justifying the degradation of human beings in slavery. In the course of a discussion of the scope of cultural studies, Raymond Williams writes that we 'cannot understand an intellectual or artistic project without also understanding its formation; that the relation between a project and a formation is always decisive'.[5] Davidson tells us that his motivation for revisiting the issue of slavery is his one-man mission to convey 'the truth' about 'our Southern heritage'. Consideration of that context may help us, then, as we assess Davidson's biblical interpretation.

Davidson denies that race motivates his defense of Southern heritage, but at the same time he trivializes the violence African-Americans experienced under slavery with an allegation that contemporary housing projects stand witness to a hundred times the rates of rape and murder as were present in slavery. (Aside from methodological questions about Davidson's cliometrics, one notices that Davidson seems to be able to conceive of persons of African descent living only in slavery or in housing projects.) As Ronald Reagan once said, in his youth there was no race problem. The nexus of Davidson's racism and his interpretation of biblical texts as justification of *American* slavery should alert us to the more fundamental problem of the role of biblical allusion and authority in political discourse. After all, Davidson argues not only that the Bible approved of slavery in the ancient world; he extends that to an argument that the Bible therefore legitimates slavery in later and radically different historical circumstances. Davidson claims that those who find the legacy of American slavery morally reprehensible 'are obviously bitter and hateful against God and his word, because they reject what God says and embrace what mere humans say concerning slavery.[6]

---

[4]'[T]he meaning of a word is its use in language' (Ludwig Wittgenstein, *Philosophical Investigations* [trans. G.E.M. Anscombe; New York: Macmillan, 3rd edn, 1968], p. 20). See also Frank P. Ramsey, *Philosophical Papers* (ed. D.H. Mellor; Cambridge: Cambridge University Press, 1990): '[T]he meaning of a sentence is to be defined by reference to the actions to which asserting it would lead. . .' (p. 51). Wittgenstein names Ramsey (who died in 1930) as one of the two greatest influences on his abandonment of the project of the *Tractatus*.

[5]Raymond Williams, *The Politics of Modernism: Against the New Conformists* (New York: Verso, 1989), p. 151.

[6]'Ala. State Sen.', p. 4.

Biblical slavery is an embarrassment to many who claim the Bible as a normative text or collection. Davidson cites 1 Tim. 6.1–2, one of a number of passages in deutero-Pauline letters that direct slaves to submit themselves to their masters (Eph. 6.5–8; Col. 3.22–25; Tit. 2.9–10; see also 1 Pet. 2.18–25). Some commentators displace the difficulties of these passages by explaining them on the basis of Greco-Roman literary prototypes. In the Hermeneia commentary on Colossians, for example, Eduard Lohse writes, 'These rules for the household are not, insofar as their content is considered, "a genuinely Christian creation" and thus they cannot, without further ado, be considered to be "applied kerygma"'.[7] Alternatively, or additionally, commentators imply that the authors of the deutero-Pauline epistles had no choice but to advocate submission to the authority of slaveowners. Ralph P. Martin writes of Col. 3.22–25:

> If this tone of advice seems pedestrian and accommodating, we should respect the limitations of what could be said in urging both slaves and owners to maintain the social order. The incitement to revolt would have been suicidal, as the earlier slave uprisings, led by Spartacus in 73–71 BCE, had shown.[8]

Martin does not consider the possibility that the author of Colossians could simply avoid the question of slaves' obligations to masters, or that there could be alternatives to submission other than revolt. Perhaps more striking from a theological perspective is his repudiation of the possibility that a Christian author could or should give 'suicidal' advice. From a certain perspective, Jesus' injunction to his followers to take up their crosses is an invitation to suicide, as is the glorification of martyrdom throughout the book of Revelation.[9] Despite the tension biblical scholars exhibit when they turn to the slavery passages of the deutero-Pauline epistles, however, their interpretations of these writings support the contention that, in some sense, the Bible backs slavery.[10]

---

[7]Eduard Lohse, *Colossians and Philemon: A Commentary on the Epistles to the Colossians and to Philemon* (Hermeneia; Philadelphia: Fortress Press, 1971), pp. 154–55 n. 4. Material in quotation marks attributed to Karl Heinrich Rengstorf.

[8]Ralph P. Martin, *Ephesians, Colossians, and Philemon* (Interpretation; Atlanta: John Knox Press, 1991), pp. 128–29.

[9]See Tina Pippin, *Death and Desire: The Rhetoric of Gender in the Apocalypse of John* (Louisville, KY: Westminster/John Knox Press, 1992).

[10]Louis Montrose suggests that 'new historicism' tends to focus on the cultural politics of the past, while 'cultural criticism' tends to focus on contemporary cultural politics. Thus, a new historicist writing about Shakespeare would write about cultural issues in Elizabethan England, while a cultural critic would write about the uses of Shakespeare today. It seems to me that whatever boundary exists between new historicism and cultural studies is a permeable one, although I also think the question of this boundary deserves further consideration by biblical critics interested in either the new historicism or cultural studies. The present article focuses on modern uses of the discourse of biblical slavery, but I think it could be within the purview of cultural studies to consider the cultural production of those texts, as well as their cultural implications in the ancient world. See Louis Montrose, 'New Historicism', in Stephen Greenblatt and Giles Gunn (eds.), *Redrawing the Boundaries: The Transformation of English and American Literary Studies* (New York: MLA, 1992), pp. 392–418. For a relevant example of the usefulness of cultural studies in the analysis of historical instances of cultural change, see Homi K. Bhaba's discussion of the obstacles encountered by missionaries in India when they tried to preach the gospel, in Bhaba, *The Location of Culture* (London: Routledge, 1994), pp. 33–34.

In the nineteenth-century debate over the abolition of slavery in the US, both proslavery and antislavery forces invoked biblical authority to bolster their causes. Proslavery forces relied on direct exegesis of particular passages; antislavery forces avoided discussion of particular texts and cited instead general underlying truths that they found in their reading of Scripture.[11] Certain claims of the proslavery forces were hermeneutically egregious, especially their claim that Africans are cursed descendants of either Cain or Ham. Thornton Stringfellow, a Baptist minister from Virginia, cited Gen. 9.25–27 as he claimed, 'Here, language is used, showing the *favor* which God would exercise to the posterity of Shem and Japheth, while they were holding the posterity of Ham in a state of *abject bondage*' (emphasis in original).[12] Other than this notorious hypothesis situating the enslavement of Africans in an ancient curse, the proslavery forces were in fact able to marshal a range of textual evidence to support their claim that the Bible was tolerant of slavery, and even supported the institution. In debates with abolitionists, proslavery clerics would quote chapter and verse from both Old and New Testaments, and challenge their opponents to quote even a single biblical verse that referred to slavery that unequivocally condemned the institution. Abolitionists regularly bypassed this challenge.

Eugene D. Genovese, who has written extensively on the slave system of the American South, writes of the hermeneutical debate:

> Regrettably, such formidable southern theologians . . . sustained themselves in scriptural exegesis with the abolitionists. Orthodox theologians demonstrated that neither the Old nor the New Testament condemned slavery as sinful. The abolitionists, displaying no small amount of intellectual dishonesty, never succeeded in making the Word say what they said it did, and eventually they had to spurn the Word for the Spirit. In consequence, they virtually reduced the Holy Spirit to the spirit (the conscience) of individuals. I do not say that an antislavery Christian theology remains an impossibility . . . But as a historian, I do insist that the abolitionists failed to construct one . . . [13]

Like Senator Davidson, Genovese concludes that the 'Bible backed slavery'. Davidson's biblical interpretation assumes the Bible's normativity in moral and political discourse. Genovese, who is not tied to upholding the cultural authority

---

[11]Larry R. Morrison, 'The Religious Defense of American Slavery before 1830', *Journal of Religious Thought* 37 (1980), pp. 16–29; John R. McKivigan, *The War against Proslavery Religion: Abolitionism and the Northern Churches, 1830–1865* (Ithaca, NY: Cornell University Press, 1984), pp. 30–31.

[12]Thornton Stringfellow, 'A Scriptural View of Slavery', reprinted in Eric L. McKitrick (ed.), *Slavery Defended: The Views of the Old South* (Englewood Cliffs, NJ: Prentice-Hall, 1963), pp. 86–98, esp. pp. 86–87.

[13]Eugene D. Genovese, *The Southern Front: History and Politics in the Cultural War* (Columbia, MO: University of Missouri Press, 1995), pp. 10–11. Genovese ranks among the most influential historians of slavery: for decades, an intellectual and political commitment to Marxism informed his work. *The Southern Front* represents a retreat from that commitment for reasons he confronts in an epilogue, where he attributes some measure of guilt for atrocities committed by socialist and communist regimes to American leftists. Readers of the volume may be surprised by the extent to which Genovese's emotional reaction against his past informs the spirit of this work, especially in light of his vituperative attack on the expression of 'feelings' in 'objective' scholarly work (pp. 6–7).

of the Bible, identifies the biblical position on slavery as a flaw of Christianity. His evaluation of the quality of Christian debate over slavery in the nineteenth century points to the intellectual distortions that arise when the Bible dictates the parameters of cultural discourse: 'Not always skillfully or even honestly, the abolitionists interpreted the Bible as antislavery, and we may thank God and the big battalions that, whatever their sins against intellectual integrity, they prevailed.'[14]

While antislavery forces questioned the use of the Bible by proslavery forces, they gave their consent to the authority of the same volume, locating the moral problem not in the Bible but in their opponents: 'They have turned our Bible into a smith shop whence consecrated hands bring fetters for the feet and manacles for the mind. They make the Old and New Testament a pair of handcuffs: and the whole book a straight jacket for the soul!'[15] Trapped within the debate, Christians who fought over the slavery question were unable to recognize that the Bible itself, or at least its use as an arbiter of cultural practice, was the source of ambivalence and embarrassment.[16]

Senator Davidson located his defense of slavery in the context of what he called a one-man crusade to disseminate the truth about Southern heritage. The narrative of a Southern heritage has been a deliberate fiction throughout the twentieth century. D.W. Griffiths's *Birth of a Nation* supplied a genealogy for the Ku Klux Klan. Margaret Mitchell created a nostalgic plantation world where elderly servants were grateful to be in the presence of their owners; white men were too busy courting white women to rape black women. *Gone with the Wind,* along with other plantation epics, has perpetuated an image of genteel Southern life that generations of Americans (at least white Americans) have found both convincing and comforting. There are, however, other possible stories to tell about Southern history, from legends of slaves who organized slave revolts to biographies of the many Southerners (both white and black) who fought on the side of the Union in the Civil War. Davidson's rhetorical claim that he is disseminating 'the truth' about Southern heritage implies that Southern cultural traits pre-exist their representation.[17] However, as Stuart Hall argues, cultural identities are constructed 'within, not outside representation'.

> Though they seem to invoke an origin in a historical past with which they continue to correspond, actually identities are about questions of using the resources of history, language and culture in the process of becoming rather than being: not 'who we are' or 'where we come from', so much as what we might

---

[14]Genovese, *Southern Front,* p. 131.

[15]J. Blanchard and N.L. Rice, *A Debate on Slavery: Held in the City of Cincinnati, on the First, Second, Third, and Sixth Days of October, 1845* (Cincinnati: Wm. H. Moore, 1846; repr.; Detroit: Negro History Press, n.d.).

[16]This is not entirely true. The Garrisonian abolitionists challenged the infallibility of the Bible. However, to the extent to which the public perceived the Garrisonians as inimical to biblical authority, their influence was diminished. On the whole, more moderate antislavery rhetoric helped sway public opinion in the North against the institution of slavery.

[17]Bhaba warns that the 'representation of difference must not be hastily read as the reflection of *pre-given* ethnic or cultural traits set in the fixed tablet of tradition', *Location,* p. 2.

become, how we have been represented and how that bears on how we might represent ourselves . . . not the so-called return to roots but a coming-to-terms with our 'routes'.[18]

The fictive and poetic qualities of tradition and identity in no way lessen their effectiveness.[19] Tradition, like the Bible, functions as part of the cultural apparatuses that sustain dominant ideologies in the US.

Antonio Gramsci was instrumental in articulating the variety of ways that cultural forces (from the family to the arts) create a climate of consent that binds individuals and communities to a social order. Imprisoned by the Fascists in Italy, Gramsci studied the mechanisms by which political powers gain and reproduce their hegemony.[20] For Gramsci, hegemony 'is not limited to matters of political control but seeks to describe a more general predominance which includes, as one of its key features, a particular way of seeing the world and human nature and relationships'.[21] Gramsci recognized that certain organs of the State exerted control by coercion—the police, say, or the military. However, he understood that the threat of coercion is more effective as a crisis tactic than as the ordinary apparatus of social control. He argued that State and civil society are inseparable, and that civil society exercises its control through a variety of cultural apparatuses that operate not through coercion but through consent. Families, religious bodies, the media, schools and other cultural institutions elaborate and reiterate a vision of society that advances the interests of dominant powers. Hegemonic thinking unites interests that would otherwise be at odds. Inasmuch as individuals and groups within society participate in this vision, civil society has managed to exert control without the overt exercise of violence.[22] Working out of a Marxist background, Gramsci nonetheless emphasized the role of non-economic cultural forces in the ordering of society. He understood that hegemony was both an unstable and a conflictual achievement, always contested by emergent groups in society.[23]

Articulation of theory in Gramsci's writings is inseparable from his investigations into Italian realities. He cannot describe the particular forms that hegemonic struggles will take in other historical and geographical circumstances;

---

[18]Stuart Hall, 'Introduction: Who Needs "Identity"?', in Stuart Hall and Paul du Gay, *Questions of Cultural Identity* (London: Sage, 1996), pp. 1–17 (4).

[19]By describing tradition and identity as 'poetic', I hope to imply that we are not simply handed our identities or traditions, but that in interesting ways we *make* them.

[20]The standard collection of Gramsci's writings in English remains the *Selections from the Prison Notebooks* (trans. Geoffrey N. Smith and Quintin Hoare; New York: International Publishers, 1971). As one might infer from the title, these writings are occasional and often fragmentary.

[21]Summary of Gramsci's understanding of hegemony in Williams, *Keywords*, p. 117.

[22]Louis Althusser developed Gramsci's ideas in 'Ideology and Ideological State Apparatuses (Notes towards an Investigation)', in *Lenin and Philosophy and Other Essays* (trans. Ben Brewster; New York: Monthly Review Press, 1971), pp. 127–86. Although I have been influenced by Althusser, I find the larger framework of his thinking to be problematic, especially his ahistoricism and his faith in a clear division between ideology and science. For an accessible critique of Althusser, see Terry Eagleton, *Ideology: An Introduction* (New York: Verso, 1991), pp. 136–53.

[23]For a helpful discussion of Gramsci's continuing (or even increasing) significance for postmodern thought, see Marcia Landy, *Film, Politics, and Gramsci* (Minneapolis: University of Minnesota Press, 1994).

however, he does point to the real power that cultural productions and texts can exercise. The appropriation of the Bible in political discourse is a moment in a cultural struggle for hegemony—as is the invocation of regional tradition, or even a debate over whether the Confederate flag should fly over the statehouses of Southern capitals. Americans who may be utterly unacquainted with the Bible as text nonetheless consent in some vague way to its moral normativity. Senator Davidson's reliance on the Bible to bolster his argument for the vindication of the institution of slavery illustrates the difficulty that arises in contesting the authority of ideological apparatuses. Davidson's interpretation slips from the recognition that biblical texts do not challenge the institution of slavery in their own times to the implication that the Bible therefore legitimates slavery, and in an ahistorical manner. When the direct applicability of biblical teachings to today's circumstances is *assumed*, interpreters are put in the awkward and disingenuous position of denying that the 'Bible backed slavery'. What is at stake, however, is not a particular reading of the Bible on any single social issue, but the role of the Bible in ideological struggles in American political life.

Davidson's speech seemed to backfire, causing him to drop out of a race for the US House of Representatives. However, his campaign to spread the word of Southern heritage brought him 15 minutes of fame, which in turn allowed him to reach far more people with his ideas than he might have anticipated. Of greater relevance, by seeming to locate the moral problem solely in Davidson's speech and not in the biblical texts he quoted, *The New York Times* illustrates the unimpeachable status of the Bible as a moral and cultural authority in the US today.

FIELD READINGS

Fernando Segovia and Daniel Patte have recently set forth theories of reading that focus on the interplay between the interpreter's social location and his or her construction of meaning. Both theorists suggest that biblical critics need to honor the interpretations of 'ordinary' readers as valid. Gramsci's analysis of the role of intellectuals in cultural struggles for hegemony offers a framework in which to evaluate these recent forays by biblical critics into cultural studies. The discussion continues by considering Senator Davidson and his political reading of biblical slavery as an everyday intellectual offering an 'ordinary' reading.

In Gramsci's formulation, the agents of cultural change are intellectuals. In the struggle for hegemony, intellectuals participate as cultural workers advancing the interests not only of the left but also of the right. His understanding of intellectuals is slippery, but several points are clear:

1. 'All men are intellectuals ... but not all men have in society the function of intellectuals.' Each person 'carries on some form of intellectual activity, that is, he is a "philosopher", an artist ... he participates in a particular conception of the world, has a conscious line of moral conduct, and therefore contributes to sustain a conception of the world or to modify it'.[24]

---

[24]Gramsci, *Selections*, p. 9.

2. Traditional intellectuals locate themselves in the historical lineage of intellectuals, and thereby disguise the nature of their ties to dominant powers in society. Intellectuals construct for themselves a 'social utopia by which . . . [they] think of themselves as "independent", autonomous, endowed with a character of their own, etc.'.[25]

3. 'Organic' intellectuals are those members of emergent social groups who help to articulate a conception of the world that reflects the group's experience and helps the group to negotiate a position in society. Note: although Gramsci primarily linked organic intellectuals to economic classes, he understood that other cultural factors (such as regional location and urban or rural ties) shaped group affinities.

Gramsci does not use 'common sense' to refer to practical insights into everyday life. Rather, 'common sense' refers to a person's unreflective understanding of the world in which she or he lives. 'Common sense' includes knowledge of tactics necessary to make one's way through life; it also includes misconceptions, accretions from earlier cultural moments, subordination of original insights to hegemonic categories. Common sense is incoherent, reflecting piecemeal the ideas gleaned from participating in a variety of social and cultural environments. In other words, it is not reliable. But Gramsci's claim that everyone is an intellectual, a philosopher, highlights his respect for common sense as the grounds of a more critical understanding of the world. Common sense contains much that is true, much that is useful. In order to help people understand their realities so that they can begin to shape them, Gramsci believes that education is necessary. But the starting point for such an education is common sense:

> In the teaching of philosophy which is aimed . . . at giving him [the student] a cultural formation and helping him to elaborate his own thought critically so as to be able to participate in an ideological and cultural community, it is necessary to take as one's starting point what the student already knows . . . And since one presupposes a certain average cultural and intellectual level among the students, who in all probability have hitherto only acquired scattered and fragmentary bits of information and have no methodological and critical preparation, one cannot but start in the first place from common sense . . . [26]

In many ways this articulation of common sense serves as a positive introduction to the hermeneutical proposals advanced by Segovia and Patte. Gramsci acknowledges each person as an intellectual and a philosopher. Segovia states that for 'cultural studies . . . all readers and critics are theologians',[27] while Patte focuses on the 'legitimacy' of readings by ordinary readers. Gramsci writes, 'In acquiring one's conception of the world one always belongs to a particular grouping which is that of all the social elements which share the same mode of thinking and acting. We are all conformists of some conformism or other . . . [28] Likewise, Segovia and Patte emphasize that one's social location and cultural attachments form the

[25]Gramsci, *Selections*, p. 8.

[26]Gramsci, *Selections*, pp. 424–25.

[27]Fernando F. Segovia, 'Cultural Studies and Contemporary Biblical Criticism', in Fernando F. Segovia and Mary Ann Tolbert (eds.), *Reading from This Place* (2 vols.; Minneapolis: Fortress, 1995), II, pp. 1–17, esp. p. 12.

[28]Gramsci, *Selections*, p. 324.

grounds of interpretive activity. Gramsci's notion of common sense has a critical edge, however; common sense is as likely to lead a person to accept her circumstances as inevitable as it is to lead her see how to change those circumstances. For Gramsci, education is a necessary moment, helping everyday intellectuals become 'organic intellectuals' who are able to articulate the interests of their social groupings and to make alliances with others in society who share common interests. Without this critical edge, deference to the productions of common sense would simply reify existing realities.

Segovia sets forth an agenda for the conjuncture of biblical and cultural studies in his introductions to the first two (of a projected three) volumes of *Reading from This Place*.[29] These volumes include the papers from two conferences held at Vanderbilt University that were coordinated by Segovia and Mary Ann Tolbert. The volumes reflect the increasing diversity of social locations represented in the guild of biblical scholars, and highlight the influence of social location on the interpretive process.[30] Segovia's understanding of cultural studies is consistent with a trend to equate cultural studies with the 'theory and politics of identity and difference'.[31] His essays situate the emergence of cultural studies in an overview of biblical studies in the late twentieth century. The story he tells is familiar: in the 1970s new movements in literary criticism and social scientific criticism began to displace, or at least compete with, historical criticism. These various critical movements share the myth of the disinterested reader who sets aside his or her particular concerns when interpreting the text; meaning is not contingent on the location of the interpreter. Against these movements Segovia sets cultural studies, 'a joint critical study of texts and readers, perspectives and ideologies'.[32]

Segovia understands that readers read in all their historical specificity: 'Different readers see themselves not only as using different interpretive models and reading strategies but also as reading in different ways in the light of the multilevel social groupings that they represent and to which they belong.[33]

---

[29]Segovia and Tolbert (eds.), *Reading from This Place*. Volume 1 covers 'Social Location and Biblical Interpretation in the United States'; Volume 2 covers 'Social Location and Biblical Interpretation in Global Perspective'.

[30]I will primarily direct my remarks to Segovia's position papers on cultural studies. However, several questions about the conference and the larger project of cultural studies remain. First, does the arrangement of papers construct a 'problematic chain of equivalences, between, say, women, people of color in the US, people from the third world, lesbians, gay men . . . [that falsely implies] these groups are caught in the webs of postmodernity in analogous ways'? (Lata Mani, 'Cultural Theory, Colonial Texts: Reading Eyewitness Accounts of Widow Burning', in Lawrence Grossberg, Cary Nelson and Paul A. Treichler [eds.], *Cultural Studies* [New York: Routledge, 1992], pp. 392–408, esp. p. 393.) Secondly, how do we evaluate the participation of Two Thirds world scholars in a conference primarily designed for the edification of First World American scholars? What efforts are made to avoid viewing these scholars as 'natives' and 'providers of knowledge about their nations and cultures'? (Questions raised in another context by Rey Chow, *Writing Diaspora: Tactics of Intervention in Contemporary Cultural Studies* [Bloomington: Indiana University Press, 1993], p. 99.)

[31]Lawrence Grossberg, 'Identity and Cultural Studies: Is That All There Is?', in Hall and du Gay (eds.), *Questions*, pp. 87–107, esp. p. 87. Grossberg's article is a critique of the conflation of cultural studies with the study of identity/difference.

[32]Fernando F. Segovia, "And They Began to Speak in Other Tongues": Competing Modes of Discourse in Contemporary Biblical Criticism', in Segovia and Tolbert (eds.), *Reading from This Place*, 1, pp. 1–32, esp. p. 25.

[33]Segovia, '"And They Began"', p. 31.

Furthermore, every interpretation, every historical reconstruction, is a construct reflecting the position of a flesh-and-blood reader. Meaning is situated in the interchange between 'a socially and historically conditioned text and a socially and historically conditioned reader'.[34] This understanding of meaning renders 'the question of validity in interpretation as a problematic, since even the very criteria used for judgment and evaluation are seen . . . as themselves constructions on the part of real readers and hence as emerging from and formulated within specific social locations and agendas'.[35] Segovia insists that cultural studies cannot demand any special training for readers, since all readings, 'high or low, academic or popular, trained or untrained', are equally constructs.[36] Cultural critics are to regard readings emanating from marginal communities, such as base Christian communities or millennarian groups, just as they regard readings emanating from conventional scholars within the field of biblical studies: as social constructs reflecting the complex cultural locations of their authors.

Towards the end of his essay, 'Cultural Studies and Contemporary Biblical Criticism', Segovia raises a series of problems with the agenda he has proposed for cultural studies, promising to return to these problems on a later occasion. One question he raises is this: 'If no master narrative is to be posited or desired, how does one deal with the continued abuse of the oppressed by the oppressor, the weak by the strong, the subaltern by the dominant?[37] How does one deal, that is, with an interpretation of biblical texts on slavery that claims the Bible legitimates the practice of American slaveholding? If the criteria by which we judge interpretive validity develop in the same cultural matrices as the interpretations we thereby evaluate, on what grounds do we disqualify any interpretation? Senator Davidson's interpretation of biblical texts on slavery reflects his own social location, or at least the story he has created about that social location in his narrative of Southern heritage.[38] Senator Davidson might even claim a marginalized status for himself, since the narrative of a Southern heritage imagines the South as a

---

[34]Segovia, 'Cultural Studies', p. 8.

[35]Segovia, 'Cultural Studies', p. 11.

[36]Segovia, 'Cultural Studies', p. 12. In a footnote Segovia denies that he sees education as 'unnecessary and superfluous', identifying it instead as essential for movements of liberation. He goes on, however, to say that 'education and scholarship—a high socioeducational level—represent no privileged access to the meaning of a text . . . but are simply another constitutive factor of human identity affecting all reading and interpretation, and in this sense are no different from any other such factor' (p. 12 n. 20). Perhaps Segovia will clarify his understanding of this issue in the projected third volume of this series, which is to deal with pedagogy.

[37]Segovia, 'Cultural Studies', p. 17.

[38]In an article prepared for the Vanderbilt conference, Mary Ann Tolbert raises the question: 'what do we mean by "right," "legitimate," and "valid" in the context of biblical interpretation?' She sketches two readings of Mk 13.9–27, one a historical reconstruction of the interpretation of first-century Christians, and the other a version of a contemporary and conservative interpretation. After rejecting historical soundness as the chief criterion of interpretive legitimacy or validity, she notes that many scholars who would embrace liberationist readings would reject the readings of more conservative congregations. By what criteria, she asks, do we designate 'one modern community's appropriation of the Bible commendable and another's not?' Tolbert recognizes many of the interpretive problems I am struggling with here. However, she ultimately seems to conflate the question of validity in biblical interpretation and the validity of the Bible itself (Mary Ann Tolbert, 'When Resistance Becomes Repression: Mark 13.9–27 and the Poetics of Location', in Segovia and Tolbert [eds.], *Reading from This Place*, II, pp. 331–46, esp. pp. 339 and 343–46).

victimized geographic region occupied by an imperial power (the North, or the Union): *'no one has a monopoly on oppositional identity.* The new social movements structured around race, gender, and sexuality are neither inherently progressive or reactionary . . .'[39]

Senator Davidson, we might say, is an 'ordinary' reader, one who has not formed his readings in the crucible of the biblical field, who does not rely on the tools of the biblical field. His readings reflect his social location, or at least, his *interpreted* social context.[40] But his readings also correspond to textual elements that express acceptance of the institution of slavery. According to recent work by Daniel Patte on the ethics of biblical interpretation, those trained in the biblical field should accept the basic legitimacy of ordinary readings, and even assist ordinary readers in developing and defending their readings: 'the different readings proposed by ordinary readers should be welcomed and *affirmed* as legitimate by critical readers, whose task would be to discover the meaning-producing dimension of the text that is reflected by this reading'.[41]

Patte argues that critical readings are simply refined versions of ordinary readings.[42] He concludes that *'the goal of critical exegesis is the bringing to critical understanding of an ordinary reading'.*[43] Even the readings of fundamentalist evangelical interpreters are legitimate, Patte says, although he finds the attempt to *universalize* such interpretations to be illegitimate (as he would find any attempt to offer a universalizing interpretation). Patte suggests that critical readers have much to learn from ordinary evangelical readers about the power-authority of the text, which precedes and grounds the interpretive process.

Finally, Patte proposes that 'we ask each of the various legitimate interpretations the following questions: What is its relative value? Is it helpful? Is it harmful? Who benefits? Who is hurt?[44] We could apply these questions to the entire process of interpretation that Patte outlines. For example, would it be helpful or harmful for a critical reader to work with an ordinary reader such as Senator Davidson to help him articulate and defend his interpretation more clearly? And for whom would it be helpful or harmful? For when we turn to the real world, we will find many ordinary readers who share Davidson's agenda. Is it beneficial or harmful to emphasize the meaning-authority of the biblical text when we remember what the Bible actually says about slavery (not to mention issues of gender

---

[39]Kobena Mercer, '"1968": Periodizing Politics and Identity', in Grossberg, Nelson and Treichler (eds.), *Cultural Studies*, pp. 424–49, esp. p. 426.

[40]'How can one explain the difference between the reading of the Bible in the base communities and the reading of the Bible by popular Pentecostals who live in the same social context?' asks Paulo Fernando Carneiro de Andrade. He answers that 'the "social context" that characterizes the reading of the text must be always understood as "interpreted social context"' (P.F.C. de Andrade, 'Reading the Bible in the Ecclesial Base Communities of Latin America: The Meaning of Social Context', in Segovia and Tolbert [eds.], *Reading from This Place*, II, pp. 237–49, esp. pp. 246–47).

[41]Daniel Patte does not locate his 'ethics of interpretation' in the rubric of cultural studies: I include this discussion here because Patte's project coheres with the critical agenda Segovia has articulated explicitly for cultural studies. Daniel Patte, *Ethics of Biblical Interpretation: A Reevaluation* (Louisville, KY: Westminster/John Knox Press, 1995), p. 11; emphasis his.

[42]An insight that I find both valid and significant.

[43]Patte, *Ethics*, p. 74; emphasis his.

[44]Patte, *Ethics*, p. 125.

and sexuality)? And for whom would it be beneficial or harmful? Patte's stated purpose in his ethics of interpretation is to include in the conversation of biblical studies the voices of those who have often been excluded: the voices of women and ethnic minorities, for example, but also the voices of ordinary people sitting in the pews of their churches. Those ordinary people, however, are not necessarily without power. Although they may not have voices at meetings of the Society of Biblical Literature, they do have voices that are heard in letters to the editor, local politics, the Internet, and a variety of other locations. Assuming the basic legitimacy of a reading such as Davidson's and abetting its development seem to me a curious project, yet it seems to be the very project that Patte advocates.

The proposals advanced by Segovia and Patte raise fundamental questions for the conjuncture of biblical and cultural studies. Cultural studies analyzes the productions of popular culture, often turning a critical eye towards those productions and their function in society. Segovia and Patte, however, simply *assume* the basic legitimacy of the ordinary readings they advocate. Gramsci acknowledges each person as an intellectual, yet also notes that the 'common sense' that is the basis of most people's intellectual interactions with the world is an uneven mix of insights, prejudices, contradictions, and images imposed by hegemonic discourse. The lack of this critical edge in the acceptance of 'ordinary' readings perpetuates those prejudices, contradictions, and hegemonic impositions. A cultural studies agenda that defers to popular readings without *emphasizing* the effects of those readings in the social sphere is in danger of repeating and confirming the liabilities of those readings.

Senator Davidson is not a scholarly construct, but a real reader attempting to draw on the cultural authority of the Bible to promote his regressive political position. This authority transcends any particular interpretation of the Bible, and is thus a formidable weapon in ideological discourse. In the absence of other interpretive criteria, *power* determines which interpretations will gain a hearing: the power to manipulate the press, the power of those with access to the airwaves or the Internet, the power to convince racists that their racism has theological merit. We might raise, therefore, the pragmatic question: what does Davidson's biblical interpretation allow him *to do?* Davidson's biblical interpretation (like many other instances of biblical interpretation outside our ivy-covered towers) relies on the cultural authority of the Bible to persuade people to consent to a particular ordering of society. A pragmatic approach bypasses the question of truth or validity in interpretation and focuses instead on the consequences of adopting a particular interpretation, or indeed on the consequences of relying on biblical authority in political discourse.

Chapter 3

Ethnic Perspectives on the Bible

Reading Texts Through Worlds, Worlds Through Texts

Vincent L. Wimbush

For ye are all children of God by faith in Christ Jesus. For as many of you as have been baptized into Christ have put on Christ. There is neither Jew nor Greek, there is neither bond nor free, there is neither male nor female: for ye are all one in Christ Jesus. (Gal. 3:26–2B KJV)

Then Peter said unto them, "Repent, and be baptized every one of you in the name of Jesus Christ for the remission of sins, and ye shall receive the Holy Ghost. For the promise is unto you, and to your children, and to all that are afar off, even as many as the Lord our God shall call." (Acts 2:38–39 KJV)

Then Peter opened his mouth and said, "Of a truth I perceive that God is no respecter of persons: But in every nation he that feareth him, and worketh righteousness, is accepted with him." (Acts 10:34–35 KJV)

From *Semeia* 62 (1993): 129–140. Copyright by Vincent L. Wimbush. Reprinted by permission.

I

Readings of texts, especially mythic, religious texts, are seldom cultivated by the lone individual; they are generally culturally determined and delimited. The cultural worlds of readers not only determine what texts are to be read—viz. what texts are deemed of value or are included within the canon—how canonical texts are read and what they mean, they also determine the meaning of "text" itself. Cultural readings are, like cultures themselves, rarely static; they are almost always dynamic and complex. They can, for example, represent at one time the struggle of fledgling nation for self-definition and purpose, at another, the rhetorical arsenal for the reform and revitalization of a rather old nation. They can represent for a minority group the rhetorics and visions of resistance—against the new or the established nation state. Whatever the character of and motive behind particular readings of mythic and religious texts, such readings are defined, and receive their impetus from, socio-political contexts and circumstances, and in turn function as "readings" of those contexts and circumstances.

No more dramatic and poignant example of the nexus between "readings" of religious texts and the "readings" of world can be found in modernity than in the history of engagement of the Bible by African Americans. Their history of engagement of the Bible not only reflects a particular history of consciousness, but also a provocative hermeneutical challenge, especially regarding an understanding of and response to the "worlds" of the Bible, and the notion of "text" itself. About this more discussion below.

II

A comprehensive interpretive history of African Americans' "readings" of the Bible remains to be written. Such a history cannot be offered here. But a summary treatment that hints of important developments is in order.

African Americans' engagement of the Bible is a fascinating historical drama. It begins with the Africans' involuntary arrival in the New World that came to be known as the United States. That the drama of the engagement of the Bible among African Americans continues in the present time is a sign of the creativity and adaptability of the African world view, and of the evocative power of the Bible. From the beginning of their captive experience in what became the United States Africans were forced to respond to the missionizing efforts of whites. They were challenged to convert to the religions of the slavers. These religions or denominations, for the most part of the establishment or the landed gentry, did not have much appeal to the slaves. The formality and the literacy presupposed by the religious cultures of the slavers—in catechetical training and Bible study, for example—clearly undermined efforts to convert the Africans in significant numbers. Not only were the Africans, on the whole—given both custom and law—incapable of meeting the presupposed literacy requirements of those religions, they did not generally seem emotionally disposed toward the sensibilities and orientations of the devotees, their piety and spirituality (Cornelius: chap.4).

To be sure, the Bible did play a role in these initial missionary efforts. But that role was not primary: its impact was indirect. It was often imbedded within catechetical materials or within elaborate doctrinal statements and formal preaching styles.

The Africans' introduction to "the Bible," or "the Scriptures," by whatever agency in the New World, would have been problematic; cultures steeped in oral traditions generally find the concept of religion and religious power circumscribed by a book at first frightful and absurd, thereafter, certainly awesome and fascinating (Gill: 226f).

It was not until the late eighteenth century, with the growth of non-establishment, evangelical, camp meeting revivalistic movements in the North and South that African Americans began to encounter the Bible on a large and popular scale. Appealed to by the new evangelicals and revivalists in vivid biblical language and with earnest emotion and fervor, the Africans began to respond enthusiastically and in great numbers. They joined white evangelical camps and began throughout the South and North to establish their own churches and denominational groups. What did not go unnoticed among the Africans was the fact that the white world they experienced tended to explain its power and authority by appeal to the Bible. So they embraced the Bible, transforming it from the book of the religion of the whites—whether aristocratic slavers or lower class exhorters—into a source of (psychic-spiritual) power, a source of inspiration for learning and affirmation, and into a language world of strong hopes and veiled but stinging critique of slave-holding Christian culture. The narratives of the Old Testament, the stories of and about Jesus the persecuted but victorious one in the New Testament, captured the collective African imagination. This was the beginning of the African American historical encounter with the Bible, and it has functioned as phenomenological, socio-political and cultural foundation for the different historical "readings" of the Bible that have followed.

From the late eighteenth century through the late twentieth century African Americans have continued their "readings" of the Bible. These "readings" reflect major changes and nuances in the self-understandings and orientations of a major segment of African Americans. The founding of the independent churches and denominations beginning in the late eighteenth century historically postdates and logically presupposes the cultivation of certain identifiable African diaspora religious worldviews and orientations. The Bible has played a fundamental role in the cultivation and articulation of such worldviews and orientations. It was rediscovered as a language world full of drama and proclamation such that the slave or freedperson could be provided with certain rhetorics and visions.

The "reading" of the Bible that was most popular was developed in the nineteenth century and continued into the twentieth century. According to this "reading" the (Protestant, viz. mainstream or establishment) canon provided the more aggressive and overtly political rhetorics and visions of prophetic critique against slavery, and the blueprints for "racial uplift," social and political peace, equality and integration as ultimate goal in the era of Jim Crowism and beyond. In addition, steps toward personal salvation were a vital part of the "reading." It reflected the dominant socio-political views and orientations among African Americans in this period. This "reading"—of both the Bible and of American can culture—expressed considerable ambivalence: it was both critical and accommodationist: on the one hand, its respect for the canon reflected its desire to accommodate and be included within the American (socio-economic-political and religious) mainstream; on the other hand, its interpretation of the Bible reflected a social and ideological location "from below," as demonstrated in the blistering critique of Bible-believing, slave-holding, racist America. Important personalities—from Frederick Douglass to Martin Luther King, Jr., are among the powerful articulators of this "reading." But the popular sources—the songs, conversion narratives, poetry, prayers, diaries, and the like—most anonymous, are a truer, more powerful reflection of history.

That this "reading" reflected considerable ambivalence about being in America on the part of a considerable segment of African Americans over a long period of history is indisputable. That it reflects class-specific (and to some extent, perhaps, depending upon the historical period, gender-specific) leanings within the African American population is also indisputable. Those who continued to "read" the Bible and America in this way continued to hope that some accommodation should and could be made. Those most ardent in this hope on the whole saw themselves as close enough to the mainstream to make accommodation (integration) always seem reasonable and feasible.

The historical interest in the dramatic narratives of the Old Testament notwithstanding, there was a certain cluster of passages from the New Testament, especially Galatians 3:26–28 and Acts 2; 10:34–36, that provided the evocative rhetorical and visionary prophetic critique and the hermeneutical foundation for this dominant "mainstream" African American "reading" of Bible—and American culture. These passages were important on account of their emphasis upon the hope for the realization of the universality of salvation. They were often quoted and paraphrased in efforts to relate them to the racial situation in the U.S. by generations of African Americans—from the famous to the unknown.

III

Attention to the evocation and engagement of the major theme of one or two of these passages in selected literature is in order. Such attention can not only provide greater clarity about the impetus behind one of the most powerful, if not dominant, "readings" of the Bible and of American culture among African Americans, it can also illuminate the relationship between social location, consciousness, and orientation and interpretive presuppositions and strategies. More specifically, it can help illuminate the complex relationship between the reading of texts and the reading of worlds.

David Walker's famous Article III of his 1829 "Appeal in Four Articles . . . to the Coloured Citizens of the World," deals with the problem of religion that frustrates, instead of cultivating, racial unity and harmony. His understanding of Christianity as mandating racial justice and harmony is made clear throughout the essay. Such understanding is the presupposition for both biting prophetic critique against contemporary white Christianity and further cultivation of a type of African American spirituality. The quotation of and allusions to the motifs of the biblical passages quoted at the beginning of this essay are obvious:

Surely the Americans must believe that God is partial, notwithstanding his apostle Peter, declared before Cornelius and others that he has no respect to persons, but in every nation he that feareth God and worketh righteousness is accepted with him.—"The word," said he, "which God sent unto the children of Israel, preaching peace, by Jesus Christ, (he is the Lord of all.") [Acts 10:36]

How can the preachers and people of America believe the Bible? Does it teach them any distinction on account of a man's color? Hearken, Americans! to the injunctions of our Lord and master. . . . Go ye, therefore, and teach all nations, baptizing them in the name of the Father, and of the Holy Ghost . . . " [Matt.28:19]

I declare, that the very face of these injunctions appears to be of God and not of man. They do not show the slightest degree of distinction. . . . Can the American preachers appeal unto God, the Maker and Searcher of hearts, and tell him, with the Bible in their hands, that they make no distinction on account of men's colour?   (Walker: 191–192, 194)

Frederick Douglass (1818–1915), abolitionist and writer, was a most articulate critic of the slaveholding Christianity of his day. His critique was based upon his acceptance of Christianity as a moral force that had particular authority in the debate about slavery, and in the construction of a society of racial equality. So Douglass embraced, as he called it the "Christianity of Christ," as opposed to morally bankrupt slave holding Christianity. The former was understood to be "good, pure, holy . . . peaceable . . . impartial" (104). There is little doubt that the reference to Christianity as "impartial" is most significant. An allusion to the theme that runs through the New Testament passages quoted at the beginning of this paper, this reference reflects Douglass' (and his world's) conceptualization of the key, defining element for "true" Christianity. Without the emphasis upon impartiality—especially as regards the races—Christianity could not be pure. His inclusion of a parody of slaveholding religion written by a Methodist minister makes clear his and many others' sentiments. The last lines of each stanza, in which the sarcastic reference to "union" occurs, was probably the reason for selection of the piece; it makes the point that Christianity is understood above all to represent the unity of the races, that it fails most miserably when this unity is undermined:

> Come, saints and sinners, hear me tell
> How pious priests whip Jack and Nell,
> And women buy and children sell,
> And preach all sinners down to hell,
> And sing of heavenly union.
>
> They'll bleat and baa, dona like goats,
> Gorge down black sheep, and strain at motes,
> Array their backs in fine black coats,
> Then seize their negroes by their throats,
> And choke, for heavenly union.

> They'll church you if you sip a dram,
> And damn you if you steal a lamb;
> Yet rob old Tony, Doll, and Sam,
> Of Human rights, and bread and ham;
> Kidnapper's heavenly union.
>
> They'll loudly talk of Christ's reward,
> And bind his image with a cord,
> And scold, and swing the lash abhorred,
> And sell their brother in the Lord
> To handcuffed heavenly union. (Douglass: 107)

Reverdy Ransom's address entitled "The Race Problem in a Christian State, 1906" may be one of the strongest examples of the African American reading of the Bible and culture under discussion. The address focuses upon the racial problem in the United States in the early twentieth century. The perspective is that of a Ohio born, relatively well-educated, activist African American cleric. His entire professional life was devoted to "racial uplift." This required, according to Ransom's thinking, levelling prophetic critique against the abuses and weaknesses and perfidy of both white and African American churches (especially including his own, the African Methodist Episcopal Church).

The address, delivered in a Boston church, is fascinating on a number of scores. First, it fits the genre of public address, functioning as a type of social prophetic critique, befitting an activist cleric. Third, as social critique the address employs a wide range of appropriate rhetorical strategies, including Enlightenment ideas, references to events in world history, theological argumentation, allusions to denominational doctrine, and loose quotations of and allusions to the Bible. Fourth, as public address it exhorts and critiques the immediate audience and the United States in general as "Christian State," with all that such an entity implies for the issues raised.

Racism is of course the primary theme of the address. But it should be noted that racism is defined and accounted for with the use of biblical language. In Ransom's opening statements the biblical notion of the kinship of humanity figures as the historical, theological foundation of Christianity, and is the hermeneutical key to the interpretation of all Scripture and of Christianity:

> There should be no race problem in the Christian State. When Christianity received its Pentecostal baptism and seal from heaven it is recorded that, "there were dwelling at Jerusalem Jews, devout men, out of every nation under heaven. Parthians, and Medes, and Elamites, and the dwellers in Mesopotamia, and in Judea, and Cappadocia, in Pontus and Asia, Phrygia, and Pamphylia in Egypt, and in parts of Libya about Cyrene; and strangers of Rome; Jews and Proselytes, Cretes and Arabians." [Acts 2:5–11a]
>
> St. Paul, standing in the Areopagus, declared to the Athenians that, "God hath made of one blood all nations of men for to dwell on all the face of the earth." [Acts 17:26]

> Jesus Christ founded Christianity in the midst of the most bitter and intense antagonisms of race and class. Yet he ignoredthem all, dealing alike with Jew, Samaritan, Syro-Phoenician, Greek and Roman . . . God, through the Jew, was educating the world, and laying a moral and spiritual foundation. That foundation was the establishment of the one God idea. Upon this foundation Jesus Christ built the superstructure of "the Fatherhood of God," and its corollary, "the Brotherhood of man."
>
> The crowning object at which Jesus Christ aimed was, "to break down the middle wall of partition," between man and man, and to take away all the Old Testament laws and ordinances that prevented Jew and Gentile from approaching God on an equal plane. And this He did, "that He might reconcile both unto God in one body by the cross, having slain the enmity thereby, so making peace." [Ephesians 2:14–15] (Ransom: 296–97)

All of the above was applied to the racial situation in the Christian State that was the United States in 1906," . . . the first nation that was born with the Bible in its hands." (Ransom: 297) According to Ransom, the Christian State that does not seek to address concretely in the spirit of Jesus the challenge inherent in the ideal of the universal kinship of all humanity—an ideal accepted by the integrationist/accomodationist African American culture, including "mainline" African American churches, even becoming the motto of Ransom's church, African Methodist Episcopal—is a state that has failed to live up to its creed and calling. That the United States has so failed was clear to Ransom.

> . . . the history of our past is well known. The Race problem in this country is not only still with us an unsolved problem, but it constitutes perhaps the most serious problem in our country today. In Church and State, from the beginning, we have tried to settle it by compromise, but all compromises have ended in failure . . . American Christianity will un-Christ itself if it refuses to strive on, until this Race Problem is not only settled, but, settled right; and until this is done, however much men may temporize and seek to compromise, and cry "peace! peace!" there will be no peace until this is done. (Ranom: 298)

The final point made by Ransom is that the Christian State has an obligation to translate its theological heritage and foundations into social and political realities. This should require correspondence between the transcendence of God above worldly matters and the Christian state's transcendence over human or worldly, especially racial, accidents. This is understood to be the special burden and calling of the United States, which in spite of its history of slaveholding and institutionalization of racial inequality, is seen by Ransom (very much a squaring with the political and popular notions—among whites and African Americans—of the day) as a special, divinely inspired experiment with a divine manifest destiny.

> As God is above man, so man is above race. There is nothing to fear by forever demolishing every wall, religious, political, industrial, social, that separates man from his brotherman. God has given us a splendid heritage here upon these shores; he has made us the pioneers of human liberty for all mankind. He has placed the Negro and white man here for centuries, to grow together side

by side. The white man's heart will grow softer, as it goes out in helpfulness, to assist his black brother up to the heights whereon he stands, and the black man will take courage and confidence, as he finds himself progressing, by slow and difficult steps upward toward the realization of all the higher and better things of human attainment; thus will these two peoples one at last become the school masters of all the world, teaching by example the doctrines of the brotherhood of man. If the new Jerusalem tarries in its descent to earth, coming down from God out of heaven, then we, not like some foolish tower-builders upon the plains of Shinar, but taught from heaven in a better way, shall build upon the teachings of Jesus, with the doctrine of human brotherhood as taught by Him, until fraternity realized, shall raise us to the skies. (Ransom: 304)

Ransom's address is an interpretation of the world that he experienced in the early part of the twentieth century: post-slavery, post-war urban America sometimes in some places struggling with the racial problems, most times in too many places ignoring the racial problems altogether. As a part of the relatively privileged class among African Americans—with access to some educational opportunities, with some independence, on account of location within a relatively less oppressive urban environment—Ransom's reading of the world was class- and race-specific. The goal of full integration within American society made sense to those who defined themselves as those in the middle—close, but not close enough, to the acceptable type of American citizen.

The Bible was appealed to as one of the most important sources of authority in order to persuade different publics of the wisdom of the course of integration, the acceptance of all human beings as part of the American experiment. This type of use of the Bible was not unique in American history or for Ransom's times, especially in the context of discussions about racial matters. But clearly Ransom's position reflected a particular type of engagement of the Bible that assumed the key to its mysteries to be the truth of the inclusion of all human beings within God's economy.

So as Ransom used the Bible to read his world, to interpret and critique it, he also reflected a particular type of reading of the Bible. This readings in turn, reflected heightened consciousness of social location as determinant of engagement.

IV

The Bible may have been a most welcome and powerful ally of Ransom and others during the early part of the twentieth century. But what remains to be explained is how this could have happened, how the likes of Frederick Douglass, David Walker, Reverdy Ransom and many other women and men of color could come to embrace the Bible in the first place. This is now not the question about the mere historical events (Great Awakenings, founding of African American churches, etc) leading up to the works and careers of those discussed. The question is rather about how the phenomenon of African Americans' coming to engage the Bible at all developed. How can a people by tradition and sensibility steeped in oral tradition make the step toward psychic acceptance of a Book as source of authority and power and spirituality? How does a people enslaved by a people of a Book come to accept that Book as authoritative and legitimate? How can a people come to interpret their experiences in the world through a Book (with its narratives and codes) that has little to do with its origins and immediate historical experiences? Again, the question is not about the mere historical events or antecedents; it is about phenomenological and psychic changes.

The most defensible explanation lies in a meeting of "worlds"—similar ways of viewing the self in the world—between African Americans and the ("worlds" of the) Bible. With its arresting stories of underdogs surviving and conquering and of a Savior figure who is mistreated but who ultimately triumphs, it is little wonder that the Bible came to be embraced by African Americans. This was so not simply because of the proselytizing efforts and successes among whites or African Americans, but because of the identification of African Americans with the protagonists of the biblical dramas. Again and again the real situations of the heroes and heroines of the Bible appeared to be similar to those of the historical experiences of most African Americans. The oppressed of the New World heard themselves being described in the stories of the Bible. The Africans in the New World applied to themselves the inclusion of all humanity within the economy of God.

Only some such phenomenological event can be assumed and thus help explain how the likes of Douglass and others could engage the Bible. Only the Bible understood not as the road map to nation-building, but as a manifesto for the oppressed and the marginal could have been taken up by such persons. Only the assumption of a hermeneutic of and from the perspective of the racially oppressed can explain the history of African American engagement of the Bible. Only such a hermeneutic explains the particular version or gloss upon the historical engagements of African Americans by those figures discussed above. Their positions make sense only the extent to which they can be placed in the middle—between white (Protestant) mainline culture and sensibilities and African marginal culture and sensibilities.

The African American history of engagement of the Bible suggests the power and challenge of the nexus between social location and biblical interpretation, and of a consistent hermeneutic "from below." African Americans, by virtue of their dramatic history, challenge every reading of the Bible to be more honestly and explicitly (and provocatively) a reading of a world.

Even as the strength of the connection between social location and interpretation is established in African American religious history, it also becomes clear that the very notion of "text" undergoes a change: If the core or foundational hermeneutic among African Americans is—as I have suggested—primarily defined by commitment to defining the African presence in the New World, radical inclusiveness from below or from without emerging as the dominant principle argued and advocated by the majority of the African American religious, then there really is no separate "text"—out there"—with assumed universal authority; there is primarily a language and image world, a world of stories that dramatize the dominant principle (and explanatory words) necessarily accepted on account of a life situation, the principle personified by characters within that language world and by which the Christian God, the Christian Savior figure, and Christian traditions generally are judged. Only on the basis of commitment to these principles can the African Americans' "conversion" to Christianity be understood, and their engagement of that part of the tradition that is Holy Book be understood. The latter was fundamentally changed from "text"—understood as static source of eternal truth that required a certain authority (intellectual or ecclesiastical or doctrinal) to be engaged—to a language world that could easily, freely, with much creative play, be engaged "from below," or from the margins. Taking the Holy Book off its repository-of-truth pedestal was a radical phenomenological event and challenge, given the status of African Americans and the respect accorded to reading in the American culture (Isaac: 230f; Gill: 224–28). To view the Holy Book as full of stories illustrating the truth about the radical inclusiveness of God's economy of salvation was to explode the notion of canon as it was understood. Not meanings of texts, but interpretations of world, of socio-political and cultural events, became primary; texts functioned to supply rhetorics and images, helping African Americans—in the way of a prism—to see themselves and the world in different colors. The Bible became important because it was received as "world" that could interpret "world." The contribution of African American religious traditions to hermeneutical theory is its modelling of a radical and consistent adherence to the primacy of interpretation (determination) of everything, including religious texts, through (a particular) "world."

Developments in Biblical Interpretation in Africa
Historical and hermeneutical directions[1]

Justin S. Ukpong

INTRODUCTION

Africa can rightly be referred to as the cradle of systematic biblical interpretation in Christianity. The earliest such attempt can be traced to the city of Alexandria and to such names as Clement of Alexandria. Origen, and others who lived and worked there.[2] The foundation laid by this tradition, which was largely allegorical and uncritical in the modern sense, lasted in the western church till the onset of the Enlightenment. It was replaced by the historical-critical method in the eighteenth century followed by the literary approaches in the twentieth century. These methods, developed in the West, have today been well established and recognised as veritable scientific tools of modern biblical research. In Africa south of the Sahara, which is the focus of this essay, the impact of these modern methods began to be felt about the middle of the twentieth century. This corresponds with the period of political independence and the founding of African universities where these methods were taught. By the third quarter of the century, the use of these methods in academic interpretation of the Bible in Africa had become widespread.[3] Biblical scholarship in Africa today is therefore to some extent a child of these modern methods of western biblical scholarship.

In spite of this however, biblical scholars in Africa have been able to develop a parallel method of their own.[4] The particular characteristic of this method is the concern to create an encounter between the biblical text and the African context. This involves a variety of ways that link the biblical text to the African context such that the main focus of interpretation is on the communities that receive the text rather than on those that produced it or on the text itself, as is the case with the western methods. To be sure, there are two currents of academic readings of the Bible in Africa: one follows the western pattern, while the other follows the African pattern of linking the text with the African context. Many African authors publish in both patterns. However, this essay is interested only in the latter.

The purpose of this essay is to show the developments that have taken place in this method of biblical interpretation in Africa. I shall focus mainly on academic interpretation excluding apartheid and popular uses of the Bible, and shall begin from the 1930s when one of the pioneering studies was first published. Within these parameters. I find it convenient to divide the development of biblical interpretation in Africa into three phases as follows:

Phase I (1930s–70s): reactive and apologetic, focussed on legitimising African religion and culture, dominated by the comparative method.

Phase II (1970s–90s): reactive-proactive, use of African context as *resource* for biblical interpretation, dominated by inculturation-evaluative method and liberation hermeneutics (black theology).

Phase III (1990s): proactive, recognition of the *ordinary reader,* African context as *subject* of biblical interpretation, dominated by liberation and inculturation methodologies.

---

[2]Joseph W. Trigg, *Biblical interpretation* (Wilmington: Michael Glazier, 1988) 21–23.

[3]N. Onwu, "The current state of Biblical studies in Africa", *Journal of religious thought* 41, no. 2 (1984–85) 35; J. H. le Roux, *A story of two ways: thirty years of Old Testament scholarship in South Africa* (Pretoria: Vita Verba, 1993).

[4]Knut Holter, "Ancient Israel and modern Nigeria: some remarks from sidelines to the socio-critical aspect of Nigerian Old Testament scholarship". Paper read at the annual conference of the Nigerian Association for Biblical Studies, Owerri, Nigeria, October 1995; G. LeMarquand, "The historical Jesus and African New Testament scholarship", *Whose historical Jesus?*, eds. William E. Arnal and Michael Desjardins (Waterloo: Wilfrid Laurier University Press, 1997) 163.

It must be emphasised that the above division is made to facilitate discussion and not to parcel biblical interpretation in Africa into compartments. It is also important to note that the seeds of one phase are sown in the previous phase, and the emergence of a new phase does not mean the disappearance of the former.

PHASE ONE: 1930–70s

The beginning of modern biblical studies in Africa, what I have called Phase I, was in response to the widespread condemnation of African religion and culture by the Christian missionaries of the nineteenth and twentieth centuries. African religion and culture were condemned as demonic and immoral and therefore to be exterminated before Christianity could take roots in Africa. In response to this, some westerners who were sympathetic to the African cause and later on Africans themselves, undertook research that sought to legitimise African religion and culture. This was done by way of comparative studies carried out within the framework of Comparative Religion. It took the form of showing continuities and discontinuities between the religious culture of Africa and the Bible, particularly the Old Testament. Since the New Testament shares the same cultural world-view as the Old Testament, the consequence of such comparison was considered to extend to the New Testament too.[5] These studies were mainly located in western, eastern and central Africa.

COMPARATIVE STUDIES

The comparison by Joseph John Williams, the earliest of such studies that was widely known, sought to illustrate a possible physical contact with the ancient Hebrews and therefore a borrowing from them. However, later studies did not have this intention and were merely meant to illustrate similarities in patterns of thought and feelings, and to show how certain basic notions have been expressed by people in different places and times.[6] The focus of early comparative studies was on the Old Testament, but there have been comparisons involving the New Testament.

Joseph John Williams' *Hebrewism of West Africa* published in 1930 represents the earliest, widely known, example of comparative studies. In the study, the author seeks to show a correlation between the Hebrew language and the Ashanti language of Ghana based mainly on similarities in sound. He also points to a similarity between the worship of deities apart from *Yahweh* in the Old Testament, and the Ashanti worship of God and the divinities. These similarities lead him to argue for the possibility of either the descent of the Ashanti of Ghana from the

---

[5]K.A. Dickson, *Theology in Africa* (London: Darton, Longman and Todd; Maryknoll; Orbis, 1984) 181.

[6]T. H. Gaster, *Myth, legend and custom in the Old Testament*, 1970 preface, cited in K. Dickson, *Theology in Africa*, 180.

Jewish race or a very early contact between the Ashanti and the Jews.[7] Williams' methodology has been shown by modern scholars to be superficial and weak. His conclusions have not been shared by later generations of scholars.

It was not until the 1960s that Williams' method was improved upon by later researchers who employed the methodology of Comparative Religion, and focussed on religious themes and practices rather than on mere extrinsic resemblance. Kwezi Dickson[8] has done many studies in this area pointing to what he calls the Old Testament "atmosphere" that makes the African context "a kindred atmosphere". He has shown similar elements in both cultures like sense of community, pervasive nature of religion, and so on. I have also done a comparative study of the sacrifices of the traditional religion of the Ibibio of Nigeria and those of the book of Leviticus.[9] In a similar study, S. Kibicho has shown the existence of a continuity between the African and the biblical conceptions of God.[10] John Mbiti has also made a comparative study of the New Testament and African understandings of eschatology.[11]

There have been objections to this type of study based on the fact that ancient Israel and contemporary Africa are far apart in both space and time.[12] Such studies are however justified on the grounds that only existential and not essential continuities are sought. Besides, in the field of linguistics, a similar method involving the study of semantic parallels of diverse languages has been successfully used.[13] The main weakness of this approach however is that it does not involve drawing hermeneutic conclusions, and does not show concern for secular issues which have become important today in theological discussions in Africa. Besides, such studies are generally apologetic, and sometimes polemical. Their value therefore is mainly heuristic.[14]

An important result of comparative studies is that African traditional religion came to be seen as "Africa's Old Testament". African culture and religion came to be recognised as a *praeparatio evangelica* (a preparation for the gospel) that is, a fertile ground for the gospel. Also, these studies have helped to articulate the values of African culture and religion for the appropriation of Christianity. To this extent, they remain foundational to all biblical studies that link the biblical text to the African context.

---

[7]J. J. Williams, *Hebrewisms of west Africa: from Nile to Niger with the Jews* (London: George Allen and Unwin: New York: Lincoln MacVeach/The Dial Press, 1930) 35.

[8]K. A. Dickson, "The Old Testament and African theology", *The Ghana bulletin of theology* 4, no. 4 (1973) 5, 141–184.

[9]J. S. Ukpong, *Sacrifice, African and Biblical: a comparative study of Ibibio and Levitical sacrifices* (Rome: Urbaniana University Press, 1987).

[10]S. Kibicho, "The interaction of the traditional Kikuyu concept of God with the Biblical concept", *Cahiers des Religions Africaines.* 2, no. 4 (1968).

[11]J. Mbiti, *New Testament eschatology in an African background: a study of the encounter between New Testament theology and African traditional concepts* (London: London University Press, 1971).

[12]Erich Isaac, "Relations between the Hebrew Bible and Africa", *Jewish social studies* 26, no. 2 (1964) 95.

[13]Gaster, *Myth, legend and custom in the Old Testament*, preface.

[14]Dickson, *Theology in Africa*, 181.

PHASE TWO: 1970S–90s

Phase II, the period covering the 1970s–90s, has been one of the most dynamic and rewarding periods of biblical studies in Africa. In it we notice that the reactive approach of the first phase gradually gives way to a proactive approach. The African context is used as a resource in the hermeneutic encounter with the Bible, and the religious studies framework characteristic of the former phase gives way to a more theological framework. Two main approaches, which can be identified as inculturation and liberation, crystallise. The comparative approach had led to the recognition of African culture as a preparation for the gospel. However, Christianity was still being looked upon as a foreign religion expressed in foreign symbols and idiom. This generated the desire to make Christianity relevant to the African religio-cultural context and gave rise to the inculturation movement in theology. In terms of biblical studies, the inculturation approach is expressed in two models which I refer to as the *Africa-in-the-Bible* studies and *evaluative* studies. Also, during this period, owing to the influence of socialist ideology, there arose greater consciousness about the need for theology to show concern for secular issues. Out of this background arose the liberation movement in theology which seeks to confront all forms of oppression, poverty and marginalisation in society. The liberation approach to biblical interpretation is expressed in *liberation hermeneutics, black theology* and *feminist hermeneutics.*

AFRICA-IN-THE BIBLE STUDIES

Africa-in-the Bible studies investigate the presence of Africa and African peoples in the Bible and the significance of such presence. The overall purpose is to articulate Africa's influence on the history of ancient Israel and Africa's contribution to the history of salvation, as well as to correct negative interpretations of some biblical texts on Africa. These studies were developed in part as a way of establishing African historical and geographical links with the biblical world following on the comparative approach, and in part to correct the tendency in western scholarship that de-emphasised Africa's presence and contribution in the biblical story. They belong to the same category of studies as those which, in the field of philosophy, have been able to show the contribution of ancient African nations to world culture.[15] In cartography, a map of the world supposed to be quite old, that places Africa not Europe at the centre, was discovered and popularised earlier in the century. Research of this type is often inspired by the movement referred to as "Afrocentrism" which seeks to articulate the role and contribution of Africa in world history.

Two main directions may be identified in these studies. One is concerned with correcting negative images about Africa and African peoples embedded in

---

[15]Cheikh A. Diop, *The African origin of civilization: myth or reality?* (Westport: Lawrence Hill, 1974); C. Williams, *The destruction of black civilization: great issues of a race from 4500BC to 2000AD* (Chicago: Third World Press, 1976).

certain traditional readings of some biblical texts. An important theme in this regard which has appeared in different versions is the so-called curse of Ham[16] whose descendants are listed in Genesis 10:1–14 and 1 Chronicles 1:8–16 as the Cushites (Ethiopians), Mizraimites (Egyptians), Phutites, and Canaanites. In Genesis 9:18–27, Ham sees the nakedness of his drunken father Noah, but instead of covering him, reports this to his two brothers Shem and Japheth who cover their father. According to Hebrew tradition, Ham had committed an act of great disrespect towards his father. When Noah wakes up and learns of the actions of his children, he pronounces a curse not upon Ham but upon Canaan, Ham's son. A fifth century AD midrash on this narrative places Noah's curse directly on Ham and states: "Your seed will be ugly and dark-skinned".[17] Also, the sixth century AD Babylonian Talmud states: "The descendants of Ham are cursed by being black and are sinful with degenerate progeny".[18] From these interpretations of the text came the idea that Africans are black because of the curse of Ham. It is very clear from the biblical text itself that the above interpretations of the narrative are purely ideological, for it is Ham's son Canaan and his descendants that were cursed. That Canaan (who was not yet born) was the one cursed seems based on the later experience of Israels subjugation of Canaan. The argument that Ham is thereby also cursed does not seem to follow any logic. This mythic interpretation of the biblical text whose foundation is purely ideological was forcefully used by the whites in South Africa and the southern USA as a support in their subjugation of the blacks. There has therefore been research today that shows up such an interpretation as having no foundation in the text and as based on the ideology of dominance.[19]

The second approach seeks to identify the presence of Africa and African peoples in the Bible as well as examine their contribution in biblical history. This is a direct reaction to the de-emphasis and exclusion, in western scholarship, of Africa and its contribution to the biblical story. Such de-emphasis shows itself for example in that Egypt is often considered in biblical studies to belong to the ancient Near East rather than to Africa. Also in the introductory courses in the Old Testament, the ancient Near East and Mesopotamia are focussed upon without much attention to the nations in Africa that made contributions to biblical history. Besides, some modern scholars have claimed that in the table of nations in Genesis 10, "the Negroes" are not mentioned because the author had not come in contact with them.[20] These studies have provoked reactions in terms of research that seeks to confirm Africa's presence and influence in the Bible, Temba Mafico has shown evidence of African influence on the religion of the patriarchs (and matri-

---

[16]T. Peterson, *Ham and Japhet: the mythic world of whites in the antebellum South* (Metuche and London: Scarecrow Press, 1978).

[17]Gene Rice, "The curse that never was (Genesis 9:18–27)", *Journal of religious thought* 29 (1972) 17, 25.

[18]Ephraim Isaac, "Genesis, Judaism and the Sons of Ham", *Slavery and abolition* 1, no. 1 (1980) +5.

[19]*Stony the road we trod: African American Biblical interpretation*, ed. C. H. Felder (Philadelphia: Fortress Press, 1991); David T. Adamo, "The table of nations reconsidered in African perspective (Genesis 10)", *Journal of African religion and philosophy* 2 (1993) 138–143; M. Prior, *The Bible and colonialism* (Sheffield: Sheffield Academic Press, 1997).

[20]P. Heinish, *History of the Old Testament* (Collegeville: Liturgical Press, 1952); W. F. Albright, "The Old Testament world", *The interpreter's Bible* (New York: Abingdon Press, 1952).

archs),[21] and in a number of studies, David T. Adamo has focussed on this theme.[22] Like the comparative approach, this model is not involved in the search for the theological meaning of the text; it however plays a very important and foundational role in creating awareness of the importance of African nations and peoples in the biblical story.

EVALUATIVE STUDIES

Evaluative studies focus on the encounter between African religion and culture, and the Bible, and evaluate the theological underpinnings resulting from the encounter. They go beyond studying similarities and dissimilarities between African religion and the Bible to interpreting the biblical text on the basis of these similarities and differences. The aim is to facilitate the communication of the biblical message within the African milieu, and to evolve a new understanding of Christianity that would be African and biblical. Generally, the historical-critical method is used for the analysis of the biblical text, and anthropological or sociological approaches are used in analysing the African situation. Studies within this model often include, in their title, such phrases as: "in the light of . . . ", "in the context of . . . ", "biblical foundations for . . . ", "against the background of . . . ". Up to five different approaches may be isolated within this model. Very often however, elements of one approach are combined with those of another, and sometimes elements of the comparative model are found in some of these approaches. However, in each study, the principal elements of one approach are generally predominant.

The first approach seeks to evaluate elements of African culture, religion, beliefs, concepts or practices in the light of the biblical witness, to arrive at a Christian understanding of them and bring out their value for Christian witness. The historical-critical method is used in analysing the biblical text. The belief or practice is analysed in its different manifestations and its values and disvalues are pointed out against the background of biblical teaching. Examples of such studies include Patrick Kalilombe's "The salvific value of African religions: an essay in contexualized Bible reading for Africa"[23] and Ernest A. McFall's "Approaching the Nuer through the Old Testament."[24]

The second approach is concerned with what a biblical text or theme has to say in the critique of a particular issue in the society or in the church's life, or what

---

[21]T. L. J. Mafico, "Evidence for African influence on the religious customs of the Patriarchs". *Abstracts: American Academy of Religion/Society of Biblical Literature* 1989, eds J. B. Wiggins and D. J. Lull (Atlanta: Scholars Press, 1989) 100.

[22]David T. Adamo, "The black prophet in the Old Testament", *Journal of Arabic and religious studies* 4 (1987) 1–8; "Ethiopia in the Bible", *African Christian studies* 8 (1992) 51–64.

[23]P. Kalilombe, "The salvific value of African religions: a contextualized Bible reading for Africa", *Christianisme et identité Africaine: point de vue exegetique—actes du ler congres des biblisles Africains, Kinshasa, 26–30 Decembre 1978,* eds A. Angang et al. (Kinshasa: Facultes Catholiques de Theologie, 1980) 205–220.

[24]Ernest A. McFall, *Approaching the Nuer through the Old Testament* (Pasadena: William Carey Library, 1970).

lessons may be drawn from a biblical text or theme for a particular context. It is similar to the first above but with the difference that in the first approach the contextual realities studied are assumed to be values or at least to contain values whereas in this one they are presented as liabilities to be challenged with the biblical message. The study involves analysing the biblical text and pointing out the challenge it issues to the context or drawing its implications for the context. Generally, historical-critical tools are used for the study. For example, Andrew Igenoza[25] has offered a biblical critique of the practice of medicine and healing in African Christianity, Chris Manus[26] has studied Paul's attitude towards ethnicity in a critique of the situation of ethnic discrimination in Nigeria, Gabriel Abe[27] has shown the relevance of the Old Testament concept of the covenant for the Nigerian society, and Nlenanya Onwu[28] has studied the parable of the unmerciful servant against the context of the erosion of the traditional idea and experience of brotherhood in Africa.

In the third approach biblical themes or texts are interpreted against the background of African culture, religion and life experience. The aim is to arrive at a new understanding of the biblical text that would be informed by the African situation, and would be African and Christian. Historical-critical tools are used in analysing the biblical text. The basis for this approach is the realisation that any interpretation of a biblical text or theme is done from the socio-cultural perspective of the interpreter. Approaching a theme or text from an African perspective is therefore expected to offer some fresh insights into its meaning even though the tools of interpretation still remain western. For example, Daniel Wambutda has offered some fresh insight by examining the concept of salvation from an African perspective[29] and Bayo Abijole has given an African interpretation of St. Pauls concept of "principalities and powers" that is different from western interpretations.[30]

The fourth approach has to do with erecting "bridgeheads" for communicating the biblical message. This means, making use of concepts from either the Bible or African culture, with which Africans can easily identify, to show the continuity between African culture and Christianity, for the purpose of communicating the biblical message. For example, in exploring the subject of Christology in an African context, John Pobee has shown that for the Akan of Ghana, from whose perspective he writes, Jesus' *kinship* as presented in the gospels is a key concept for underscoring his humanity. Also, he has used the anthropological concept of "the

---

[25]Andrew O. Igenoza, "Medicine and healing in African Christianity: a biblical critique", *African ecclesial review* 30 (1988) 12–25.

[26]Chris Manus, "Galatians 3:28—a study on Paul's attitude towards ethnicity: its relevance for contemporary Nigeria", *Ife journal of religion* 2 (1982) 18–26.

[27]G. O. Abe, "*Berith:* its impact on Israel and its relevance to the Nigerian society", *Africa journal of biblical studies* 1 (1986) 66–73.

[28]N. Onwu, "The parable of the unmerciful servant (Matt 18:21–35)", *Gospel parables in African context*, ed. Justin S. Ukpong (Port Harcourt: CIWA Publications, 1988) 43–51.

[29]Daniel N. Wambutda, "Savannah theology: a reconsideration of the biblical concept of salvation in the African context", *Bulletin of African theology* 3, no. 6 (1981) 137–153.

[30]B. Abijole, "St. Paul's concept of principalities and powers in African context", *Africa theological journal* 17, no. 2 (1988) 118–129.

grand ancestor", with which Africans can readily identify, to describe Christ.[31] John Mbiti also pointed out that the New Testament images of Jesus as miracle worker and risen Lord, (*Christus Victor*) are images Africans can easily identify with, because they show Jesus as the conqueror of evil spirits, disease and death, which Africans fear most.[32] These concepts serve as "bridgeheads" for communicating to Africans the role of Christ in the human community.

The fifth approach has to do with the study of the biblical text to discover biblical models or biblical foundations for aspects of contemporary church life and practice in Africa. Generally, such studies use the tools of historical-critical research in analysing the biblical text. For example, Balembo Buetubela has studied the relationship between the mother churches in Jerusalem and Antioch, and the mission churches they founded in early Christianity, and has shown how the relationship was marked by the autonomy of the mission churches rather than by their dependence on the mother churches.[33] He offers this as a model for the development of the autonomy of the young churches in Africa today. I have analysed the biblical foundations for inculturation of Christianity.[34] Joseph Osei-Bonsu has pointed to some New Testament antecedents of contextualisation of Christianity that form the basis for the contextualisation of Christianity in Africa today.[35]

The evaluative approach is the most common approach in biblical studies in Africa today. It is based on the classical understanding of exegesis, as the recovery of the meaning of a text intended by the author through historical-critical tools, and of hermeneutics, as the application of the meaning so recovered to a particular contemporary context. Its basic weakness is that it does not give attention to social, economic and political issues which have become important today in theological discussion. However, as a result of this research, African culture and religion have been seen to be not just a preparation for the gospel, as in the comparative method, but *indispensable resources in the interpretation of the gospel message* and in the development of African Christianity.

LIBERATION HERMENEUTICS

Liberation hermeneutics in general uses the Bible as a resource for struggle against oppression of any kind based on the biblical witness that God does not sanction oppression but rather always stands on the side of the oppressed to liberate

---

[31]John S. Pobee, *Toward an African theology* (Nashville: Abingdon Press, 1979) 88–94

[32]J. Mbiti, "Some African concepts of christology". *Christ and the younger churches,* ed. George F. Vicedom, (London: SPCK, 1972) 54.

[33]B. Buetubela, "L'autonomie des jeunes eglises et les Actes", *Les Actes des Apôtres et les jeunes eglises: actes du deuxieme congres des biblistes Africains, Ibadan, 31 Juillet-3 Aout, 1984,* eds W. Amewowo et al. (Kinshasa, 1990) 77–105.

[34]J. S. Ukpong, "Inculturation and evangelization: Biblical foundations for inculturation", *Vidyajyoti* 58, no. 5 (1994) 298–307.

[35]J. Osei-Bonsu, "The contextualization of Christianity: some New Testament antecedents", *Irish biblical studies* 12, no. 3 (1990) 129–148.

them. Here we shall focus on political and economic oppression in general. Because of the specific theological response to racial oppression (apartheid) in South Africa and oppression against women, these are treated separately below under the headings: "black theology" and "feminist theology" respectively.

The story of God's political liberation of the Hebrews in the book of Exodus is the ground text for the hermeneutics of political liberation. God's call on Israel to take special care of the poor among them, and deal justly with all (see Ex. 23:11, Amos 2:6–7, 5:21–24), and Jesus' sympathetic attitude to and teachings in favour of the poor (see Luke 4:18–19, 6:20–21) provide the grounding for the hermeneutics of economic liberation. Throughout the Bible, the message is that while the poor are to be loved and cared for, there should be commitment to action aimed at eradicating poverty and oppression. Thus Jean-Marc Ela asserts that "Africa today is crucified", and if the Bible is read from this perspective, Christians will be able to link their faith with commitment to transform society.[36] C. Banana uses Marxist analysis of the biblical text to show how the Bible not only condemns economic exploitation and political oppression, but also points the way to economic and political transformation of society.[37]

BLACK THEOLOGY

Black theology is a form of liberation hermeneutics focussed on the issue of apartheid racial discrimination that prevailed in South Africa until 1994. Its point of departure is the ideology of black consciousness whereby the blacks are made critically aware of their situation of oppression based on their skin colour, of the need to analyse the situation and to struggle against it. It uses the Bible as a resource for this struggle. The understanding of "black" here covers all who were discriminated against in the apartheid system, and this includes ethnic blacks, Indians and coloured people. Two strands may be discerned in this theology. One seeks to interpret the Bible in the light of the apartheid experience, and to reflect on this experience in the light of the biblical message.[38] Because the Bible had been wrongly used as an instrument to entrench the apartheid system, it remains central to black theology in its struggle for liberation. Its point of departure is that the Bible basically contains a liberating message, that apartheid is diametrically opposed to the central message of the Bible which is love of the neighbour, and that God is always on the side of the oppressed and therefore in support of the black liberation struggle.[39] Liberative themes in the Bible are studied as a resource of empowerment for the liberation struggle.

---

[36]Jean-Marc Ela, "Christianity and liberation in Africa", *Paths of African theology*, ed. R. Gibellini (Maryknoll: Orbis Books, 1994) 146–147.

[37]C. Banana, *The gospel according to ghetto* (Gwero: Mambo Press, 1981) 44–51; *Theology of promise* (Harare: College Press, 1982) 21.

[38]Basil Moore, "Black theology revisited", *Bulletin for contextual theology* 1 (1994) 7.

[39]Desmond Tutu, "The theology of liberation in Africa", *African theology en route*, eds Kofi Appiah-Kubi and Sergio Torres (Maryknoll: Orbis Books, 1979) 166; Alan Boesak, *Black and Reformed: apartheid, liberation and the Calvinist tradition* (Johannesburg: Skotaville Press, 1984) 149–160.

The other strand starts from the position that the Bible cannot be uncritically accepted as a resource for the liberation struggle. This is because the Bible itself was written by the elite to serve their interests. It is steeped in the ideology of the elite, is oppressive and in places mutes the voices of the oppressed. It is for this reason that it was used by the apartheid regime to suppress the blacks in South Africa. To make it serve the interest of the black struggle, it must first be liberated from that ideology. This is the position strongly articulated by Itumeleng Mosala.[40] He proposes the use of the historical-materialist analysis of the biblical text for his purpose.

Black theology has made an immense contribution to the demise of apartheid in South Africa. This is epitomised in the *Kairos document* issued in 1985 by a number of concerned theologians in South Africa on the issue of apartheid. The document, which in many ways exercised the international community, focussed on the ethical and theological impropriety of apartheid. Apart from this, black theology has contributed an important dimension to theological reflection in Africa by focussing on the issue of socio-political and economic relations which some of the other theologies on the continent lack. In spite of the abolition of apartheid and the resultant spirit of reconciliation, unity and solidarity in South Africa, a theology of liberation still has relevance in that country. For one thing, it will take a long time for the legacy of apartheid to disappear. For another, the liberation struggle must be seen as an ongoing exercise involving the marginalised in society. However, black theologians will need to re-evaluate their approach and emphasis in view of the changed situation. The task is no longer liberation from apartheid but liberation from the legacy of apartheid which is multifaceted. This includes the entrenched psychological distance between the different racial groups, poverty, marginalisation etc. The direction must be total liberation for fullness of life, reconciliation and integration.

FEMINIST HERMENEUTICS

Feminist hermeneutics is liberation hermeneutics focussed on the oppression of women. It uses the Bible as a resource for the struggle against the subordination of women in contemporary society and church life. Because the Bible has been used to support such subordination, a feminist critique of the Bible and of the conventional mode of biblical interpretation forms part of feminist hermeneutics. At least five approaches to feminist hermeneutics by African theologians are discernible. These are not mutually exclusive and very often a number of them are used in combination.

The first approach according to Mercy Oduyoye,[41] is a challenge to the conventional hermeneutics by which scripture and the history of Christianity are interpreted in androcentric terms. For example, it is presumed that God is male, and

---

[40]Itumeleng J. Mosala, *Biblical hermeneutics and black theology in South Africa* (Grand Rapids: Eerdmans, 1989) 13–42.

[41]M. A. Oduyoye, "Violence against women: a challenge to Christian theology". *Journal of inculturation theology* 1, no. 1 (1994): 47.

instances in the Bible where God is described with feminine attributes are ignored. Biblical translations, as a rule, render Gods name with the male pronoun. Feminist theologians refer to such hermeneutics as imprisonment of God in maleness. This approach is foundational to all feminist hermeneutics.

The second approach seeks to critique or reinterpret those biblical texts that are oppressive to women or portray them as inferior to men through "a close rereading" of such texts "in their literary and cultural contexts". Thus Teresa Okure has shown that the creation of Eve from Adams rib, far from denoting a situation of inferiority as is often understood, denotes their identity in nature, their destined marital status and their equality.[42] Similarly, concerning some sexist Pauline texts, Mbuy-Beya has pointed out that Paul was dealing with specific situations of disorder that needed establishing "a certain hierarchy for the sake of order".[43] He was therefore not giving a universal and timeless directive. The third approach focuses on texts that show the positive role of women in the history of salvation or in the life of the church. Some of these are explicit while others are implicit. Thus through an analysis of Jesus' teachings, parables and miracles, Anne Nasimiyu-Wasike has shown Jesus' attitude to women to have been positive.[44] Joyce Tzabedze has also studied the positive role of women in the early church as reflected in 1 Timothy and Ephesians,[45] and Mbuy-Beya has highlighted the role of women in the history of Israel, some of whom were unnamed like the widow of Zarephath (1 Kings 17:8).[46] Their lives have become an inspiration for contemporary women in their struggle in a male dominated world.

The fourth approach enquires into the basic biblical theological orientation that can function as a guide to interpreting both the negative and positive biblical texts about women. Mercy Oduyoye identifies the theology of creation which affirms the basic equality of man and woman created in the image of God, and the theology of community which calls for the exclusion of violence and discrimination in society.[47] Both theologies, she argues, are fundamental to all biblical teaching. And the last approach seeks to interpret biblical texts from the perspective of African womens experience. Rereading the stories of polygamy in the Old Testament from African women's experience of polygamy, Anne Nasimiyu-Wasike is able to show that the Old Testament itself contains a critique of this institution, contrary to the common assumption that it extols it.[48]

---

[42]T. Okure, "Biblical perspectives on women: Eve, the mother of all the living (Genesis 3:20)", *Voices from the Third World* 8, no. 3 (1985) 82–92.

[43]Marie Bernadette Mbuy-Beya. "Doing theology as African women". *Voices from the Third World* 13, no. 1 (1990) 155–156.

[44]Anne Nasimiyu-Wasike, "Christology and an African woman's experience". *Faces of Jesus in Africa*, ed. Robert Schreiter (Maryknoll: Orbis Books, 1991) 73–80.

[45]Joyce Tzabedze. "Women in the church (1 Timothy 2:8–15, Ephesians 5:22)". *New eyes for reading biblical and theological reflections by women from the Third World*, eds. J. Pobee and Barbel von Wartenberg-Potter (Geneva: WCC, 1986) 76–79.

[46]Mbuy-Beya, "Doing theology as African women".

[47]Oduyoye, "Violence against women", 48–51.

[48]Ann Nasimiyu-Wasike, "Polygamy: a feminist critique". *The will to arise*, eds. Mercy A. Oduyoye and Musimbi R.A. Kanyuro (Maryknoll: Orbis Books, 1992) 108–116.

The above shows that there are two main concerns in feminist hermeneutics—a critique of the androcentrism both of earlier interpreters of the Bible and of the Bible itself, and a recovery of the forgotten and muted voices, the images and contributions of women in the biblical text. Using a vast array of critical tools, including the tools of historical and literary criticism, and other disciplines like sociology and anthropology, it has succeeded in calling scholarly attention to many things that were taken for granted in the Bible.

PHASE THREE: 1990s

In the third phase, covering the 1990s, biblical studies in Africa become more assertive and proactive, daring to make an original contribution. The two main methodologies of *inculturation* and *liberation* which had crystallised in the second phase are carried forward with new orientations. One is the orientation that recognises the *ordinary African readers* (that is, non-biblical scholars) as important partners in academic Bible reading, and seeks to integrate their perspectives in the process of academic interpretation of the Bible. This is exemplified by Gerald West's *contextual Bible study* method.[49] The other is the orientation which, apart from recognizing the role of the ordinary readers, seeks to make the African context the *subject* of interpretation of the Bible. This is exemplified by my *inculturation hermeneutics*. Thus in this phase the African context is seen as both, providing the critical resources for biblical interpretation and the subject of interpretation.

CONTEXTUAL BIBLE STUDY

In contextual Bible study, the Bible is read against a specific concrete human situation, in this case, the situation of racial oppression and poverty in South Africa, within the context of faith, and with a commitment to personal and social transformation. In this, it shares the same goal as black theology except that the starting point of black theology is black consciousness. However, its specific feature is that it recognises the importance of the approach, the perspectives and concerns of the ordinary African readers of the Bible. It seeks to empower them for critical study of the Bible in relation to their life situation and for personal and societal transformation. It operates at the interface between academic and ordinary readings of the Bible and thus seeks to bridge the gap between academic and ordinary readings of the Bible. The procedure involves interaction between academic and ordinary readers of the Bible such that the ordinary readers are helped to develop critical awareness and identify and use local critical resources in their reading of the Bible. In developing the hermeneutics for this approach to Bible reading, the resources of the people's culture and historical life experience are used as complementary to conventional critical tools of biblical exegesis. This recognition, by

---

[49]Gerald O. West, *Contextual Bible study* (Pietermaritzburg: Cluster Publications, 1993).

the academic community, of the place of the ordinary reader's in the scheme of things, regarding the appropriation of the biblical message makes academic biblical scholarship relevant to the community of believers. According to Gerald West, a principal exponent of this approach, "If we are serious about. . . relating biblical studies to ordinary readers. . . then the contextual Bible study process provides the framework in which to read the Bible".[50]

INCULTURATION HERMENEUTICS

One criticism that runs through most of the inculturation models discussed above is lack of attention to social issues like poverty, political oppression, etc., while lack of attention to specifically African religio-cultural issues such as belief in ancestors, the spirits, spirit possession, witchcraft, etc. is the criticism of the liberation models. Inculturation hermeneutics discussed here seeks to redress the situation by adopting a *holistic approach to culture* whereby both the secular and religious aspects of culture are seen to be interconnected and as having implications one for the other, and the Bible is read within the religious as well as the economic, social and political contexts of Africa.[51] The second feature of this approach is that it operates at the interface of academic and ordinary readings of the Bible. The characteristics of ordinary readers here include that they are strongly influenced by the world-view provided by their indigenous culture as opposed to the world-view of the western technological culture, and that they are poor, oppressed and marginalised. The third feature is that the African context forms the *subject* of interpretation of the Bible. This means that the conceptual framework of interpretation is informed by African socio-cultural perspectives. Therefore, rather than the biblical text being read through a western grid and the meaning so derived applied in an African context, this model is concerned that the biblical text should be read through a grid developed within the African socio-cultural context. In this way the people's context becomes the *subject* of interpretation of the biblical text. The goal of interpretation is the actualisation of the theological meaning of the text in todays context so as to forge integration between faith and life, and engender commitment to personal societal transformation.

Certain basic assumptions that belong to the root paradigm of African culture inform the interpretive framework. Among these are, the unitive view of reality whereby reality is seen not as composed of matter and spirit, sacred and profane but as a unity with visible and invisible aspects, the divine origin of the universe and the interconnectedness between God, humanity and the cosmos, and the sense of community whereby a person's identity is defined in terms of belonging to a community. The basic hermeneutic theory at work is that the *meaning of a text is a function of the interaction between the text in its context and the reader in his/her*

---

[50]West, *Contextual Bible study* 58–61, 74.
[51]J. S. Ukpong, "Towards a renewed approach to inculturation theology". *Journal of inculturation theology* 1 (1994) 3–15.

context. Thus, there is no one absolute meaning of a text to be recovered through historical analysis alone. Also there are not two processes, consisting of recovery of the meaning of a text through historical analysis and then applying it to the present context, but one process of a reader who is critically aware of his/her context interacting with the text analysed in its context. For procedure, the general pattern for Third World hermeneutics is followed. The starting point is analysis of the contemporary context against which the text is to be interpreted, and analysis of the context of the text. The text is then read *dynamically* within the contemporary context that has been analysed. This involves entering into the text with a critical awareness about the contemporary context and allowing it to evoke in the reader appropriate reactions, responses and commitments about the context. The Bible is seen as a *sacred classic*—a book of devotion and norm of morality as an ancient literary work worth attention beyond its time. I have done two studies in this model, one clarifying the methodology, and the other applying the methodology to a particular biblical text.[52]

CONCLUSION

Modern biblical interpretation can conveniently be grouped into three main approaches.[53] One is the *historical-critical approach* that focuses on the history of the text, its author and original audience. In this approach, the meaning of the text is identified with the meaning intended by the author. Second, the *literary approaches* focus on the text and its underlying structure, meaning as attained in decoding the text; or they focus on the reader in interaction with the text, seeing the meaning of the text as emerging in the encounter between the reader and the text. Closely associated with this is the third, the *contextual approach* which focuses on the context of the reader in relating it to the text. It uses the reader's context in various ways as a factor in making the meaning of the text. All the approaches to biblical interpretation in Africa discussed above (and indeed all Third World approaches to biblical interpretation) belong to the last approach. Their point of departure is the context of the reader, and they are all concerned with linking the biblical text to the reader's context.

Given the diversity in the African cultural, religious, political, social and economic terrain, and the strategy of linking the biblical text to the African context, the contribution of modern Africa to biblical interpretation promises to be significant. The developments so far point to the two models of inculturation and liberation, gradually cross-fertilising each other such that both will be concerned with religious as well as secular issues in society. The importance of the ordinary reader will

---

[52]J. S. Ukpong, "The parable of the shrewd manager (Luke 16:1–13): an essay in inculturation hermeneutics", *Semeia*, no. 73 (1995) 189–210.

[53]See G. O. West, *Biblical hermeneutics of liberation: modes of reading the Bible in the South African context*, second edition (Pietermaritzburg: Cluster Publications; Maryknoll: Orbis Books, 1995) 131.

gradually come to the fore, because academic reading of the Bible in Africa will no longer afford to ignore the concerns and perspectives of the ordinary reader. Since African biblical scholarship focuses on the community that receives the text, any continued ignoring of the ordinary readers will lead to sterile scholarship. African questions are now being put to the Bible and African resources are being used in answering them. No longer then shall we have from the Bible answers to questions not asked by Africans.[54] Biblical interpretation in Africa has made bold strides which can be said to place it at the threshold of maturity as we enter the third millennium. However, the real test of this maturity will be the extent to which it will sustain the African context as the *subject* of interpretation of the Bible so that the hitherto muted voices and concerns of ordinary readers will come alive in the academic forum.

Life in the Midst of Death:
Naomi, Ruth and the Plight
of Indigenous Women

Dalila Nayap-Pot

INTRODUCTION

> A man offered to marry Maria and give her a house in the capital if she signed over her small piece of land to him. She did this, but he did not keep his promise, but instead, threw her off the property.

As in other countries in the world, for three decades, brutal warfare has enveloped large portions of Central America. Tens of thousands of innocent peasants and indigenous people have lost their lives—particularly in Guatemala, El Salvador and Nicaragua. Hundreds of thousands more have been pushed off their lands,

---

[54]Desmond Tutu, "Whither African theology", *Christianity in independent Africa*, ed. E. W. Fashole-Luke et al. (London: Rex Collins, 1978) 336.

---

bombed out of their homes and have fled to neighbouring countries, including Belize, my birthplace, and Costa Rica, my adopted homeland, women and children suffering the most. They have been raped, murdered and taught to kill. They have fled from their homes and small plots of land to an unknown destiny. It is made worse by the impact of natural disasters—drought, earthquakes, typhoons, volcanic eruptions and others—upon large segments of the population, particularly in these economically poor nations. The exodus of masses of people completes the destruction of families that warfare and disaster have set in motion. In the lands where they end up 'temporarily', they are usually herded into camps. Those that are fortunate enough to be allowed to settle in homes, are usually greeted with suspicion and even hostility. This was the fate of Salvadorans and Nicaraguans in Costa Rica during long years of exile, until most of them were allowed to return to their homelands to an uncertain future.

One part of my ministry is devoted to the women of an indigenous reservation many hours away (by bus and horseback) from my home. This has made me very aware of the cultural and spiritual creativity of many exiles, and of indigenous women who are excluded within their own lands. The quotations in this paper are taken from a report that I wrote on the situation of the indigenous women with whom I work.

My personal situation is very different (I arrived in Costa Rica to study for the Christian ministry). Having lived and pastored there for more than eighteen years, I can understand what it feels like to be uprooted from one's land and family, to be displaced and to have to adapt to a new culture and language,[1] to be discriminated against and marginalized as an indigenous Christian woman. Yet a handful of women like me here and there, have been able to move on, despite these limitations. In the process, the Bible has been our most powerful tool and starting point.

As I began to reflect upon my situation and that of many other women in the light of the Bible, I found special significance in the experience of Naomi and Ruth. First, I have asked myself, who is the real heroine of this little book? Are heroines recognizable for being first? In the first chapter of this book, it seems to be Naomi. Ruth comes into the story almost incidentally, the last person to join the family. Yet it is Ruth who gets her name attached to the book. Indeed, in the patriarchal context of the development of the Biblical canon, is it not remarkable that we find included a book with the name of a woman—and a pagan at that, the daughter of a cursed race?[2] The biblical record states: 'No Amonite nor Moabite may enter the sanctuary, even after the tenth generation. For they did not welcome you with food and water when you came out of Egypt and hired Balaam to pronounce a curse' (Deut. 23.3–4).

---

[1] English is spoken in Belize and Spanish in the rest of Central America.

[2] Women in the Biblical record, from every walk of life, responded to God's call and related to their own people in diverse ways. But only four of them—Ruth, the Moabite, Esther, the queen of Persia, Judith and Susannah, the heroines of inter-testamental times—were honoured by documents named after them which eventually acquired canonical or deutero-canonical status. Is it only a coincidence that these same three women, living in a patriarchal society, placed their own sexuality at the service of God and their people?

Remarkable also is the way in which the book joins the life of this woman to that of a descendant of another 'pagan' woman, Rahab, the prostitute of the cursed city of Jericho. Together, they become the progenitors of the Jewish Messiah, thus pointing the way to hope in the midst of desperation.

In our time, the message of the book of Ruth is downplayed by both liberal scholarship—which reduces it to an interesting piece of popular literature—and conservative evangelicalism. The latter sees in Ruth little more than an Old Testament preamble to the Jesus story.[3] This does not, however, do justice to the real message of this story. Not satisfied with these deductions, I have decided to learn from these women within their own cultural context. 'Long ago when judges ruled in Israel . . . ' (1.1) places the narrative in a concrete historical period. Following this lead, my reflections on Ruth are rooted in the culture, spirituality and socio-political situation of the indigenous people of Central America at a particular moment in history—the end of the second millennium.[4]

Who was Ruth and what extraordinary things did she do? What can she say to us, women and men, today? More importantly, what clues does she give to women who are involved in survival situations and family crises? To persons who are forced to make choices of identity, faith and commitment, does the plight of Elimelech's family, fleeing Judea to find a better life in an alien environment speak today? Ruth challenges us in many ways, but I will mention four ways, hoping by this, to affirm our hope for those who have been uprooted and to invite those who have not experienced it, to be in solidarity with those who have. In so doing, we will join in the building of God's Kingdom. As I reflect upon Elimelech, Naomi and Ruth, I cannot help but remember my neighbours in Costa Rica, Daniel, Zinia and their children.

It happened on Thursday. As he did every working day, Daniel, the breadwinner of the family, left his house very early to do what he knew best, repair heavy machinery. As on any other day, he called his wife to see how she was doing and to enquire about his family. Little did he realize that this was going to be his last day on earth. A few hours later, a call from the hospital made his wife realize that she would not see him alive again. As so often happens in Latin America, workers are not insured. His boss refused to accept responsibility for this accident, even denying that Daniel worked for him. A wife and five children were left husband and fatherless and without economic protection.

I wrote the following poem to Daniel and his family. It was his birthday, and a gift was to be laid on his tomb—a rose. His wife did not allow anyone to accompany her but me, her close friend—not even her relatives, friends or children. She wanted to be with him, yet needed someone who would help her bear the pain.

---

[3]Cf. Ralph Earle, *Beacon Bible Commentary* (Kansas City: Beacon Hill Press), p. 28. Commentaries such as this one, published by my own Church of the Nazarene, pay little attention to the role of Ruth, a peasant woman, and to her significant contribution to the history of salvation.

[4]Whereas in indigenous society, everything is conceived and experienced as in or through the equilibrium of the whole, not individually but in community, 'modern' society separates religious from political life.

Someone who would understand her and also connect her with her loved one through prayer.

> Daniel, this is your birthday. We come to be with you
> and to give you this Rose;
> it was always our birthday gift to each other.
> It is here today, as you were here with us,
> and tomorrow it will be with you.
>
> We have come to tell you that,
> although you are in a different state,
> you are still a part of us.
> We come to wish you peace, love and rest.
> Like a Rose, you were born, you bloomed and you died.
> Isn't this, after all, what life is all about?
> An ancient indigenous sage once said:
> 'I break this egg and a man, or a woman, is born.
> Together they will live and together they will die.
> But they will live again. They will be born, die and be re-born.
> They will unceasingly be reborn, because death is a lie'.
>
> You are still alive, Daniel,
> because while we live you live, and life goes on:
> your sons and daughters are students, they are proud of you.
> Your wife struggles and gets ahead.
> You are an example to us your friends; and
> we testify to the fact that you and your house are getting ahead.
> Onward, Daniel, rest where you are, because we are here
> carrying your banner with joy. Thanks for being alive!

A CULTURAL CHALLENGE: RUTH IS A BRIDGE BUILDER

Elimelech and his family broke cultural stereotypes by throwing themselves upon the mercy of their ancient enemies. Yet it was only after his death, that his sons took a step farther by marrying two Moabite women. However, Ruth goes even further when she decides to become part of an enemy people and include in her world a family which descended from a people who had cursed her own race. In her own way, she seems to challenge life, particularly of those who seem to forget their past.

Moab and Judah descended from the same family tree, though history had divided them. Moab was born out of the union of Lot and his eldest daughter (Gen. 19.37). And while the Moabites allowed the Israelites to cross through their territory, they did not permit them to follow the kings' highway (Deut. 2.29; Num. 21.21–30; Judg. 11.17). For this grave cultural breach, they became an accursed people. Today we are seeing dramatically how ancient conflicts and profound cultural and religious perceptions are dividing people and bringing death upon millions in Rwanda, Bosnia, Sri Lanka and Latin America. We are in need of bridge builders. What should be their characteristics?

The bridges that cross the mountain chasms should be firmly anchored at both ends. Otherwise, they are useless and even dangerous. Also, they are meant for two way communication, which appears at the very end of this story. Useful bridges are not ornaments; they are meant to be trodden on. They are usually taken for granted—like Ruth was in this story. Her bridge building was what challenged her culture and affirmed her spirituality, redeeming her past and her future into the present. This though is not enough, but only a beginning.

AN IDEOLOGICAL CHALLENGE: RUTH BREAKS STEREOTYPES

> Paulina has a very special husband. But he complains that his strength is giving out. 'I am very thin from sickness and concern for my wife. What is going to happen to us with so many negative things that surround us?'

HUNGER IN THE MIDST OF ABUNDANCE

Famine and migration (1.2) are familiar to millions of people around the world. Ironically, there was famine in Bethlehem, a 'house of bread', in Ephrata, 'fruitful land'. This had traditionally been a land where wheat grew abundantly. But drought, foreign invasions, civil conflict and who knows how many other disasters, both natural and man-made, had upset the natural order of things. Then and now disasters and other natural disorders were accepted without question as a punishment of God for sins.[5] In Central America many 'very good Christians' are bound by a pagan fatalism. With all the natural wealth that there is in our countries, why is it that so many people accept poverty and deprivation as the will of God? At the same time, more and more victims are beginning to question the inevitability of their suffering and to ask questions regarding the human actions which are often the cause of 'natural disasters'. Central American coastlands become flooded every rainy season because of the senseless destruction of giant trees in the nearby mountain ranges. Changes in the ecological balance bring hurricanes which destroy even more trees.

THE GOD WHO IS ABSENT AND YET PRESENT

The God of Israel seems to be absent in this story, a curious fact. In the book of Judges, every time the people got into trouble, they called out to Yahweh and were rescued (cf. Judg. 3.7–9). Nothing is said about this in the book of Ruth. Is Yahweh allowing the protagonists to choose their own destiny, and to face the consequences of their decisions? Did Elimelech and his family give up too soon and head for

---

[5]The Biblical record tells us that the time of the Judges, when Ruth's story took place, was one of particular apostasy and sin (Judg. 2.11–17).

Moab before God could intervene on their behalf? Or is this a case of 'God's salvation through human intervention'. Whatever the case, they opted to leave the land of 'the chosen people', and thus—according to the superstitions of the time—were on their own in the territory of strange gods. But was God really absent? Yahweh travelled with them. Their lengthy period of self-exile became a painful time of learning, of which we can only surmise by reading between the lines. We can be sure, however, that Yahweh was present as their teacher and companion.

As I try to understand Naomi from my own perspective and cultural context, I can sympathize with her reasons for agreeing to move with her husband and family to greener pastures. We indigenous people, when left alone, will do anything to defend the integrity and welfare of our families. However, once Naomi lost her immediate family, her will to struggle seemed to vanish. Yahweh had abandoned her. Perhaps if she returned to Bethlehem—she must have reasoned—where there was abundance she could find her God again. So, there was still hope. Yes, she would find protection under the law of Israel in the land of her ancestors.

LIFE IN THE MIDST OF DEATH

Is this a contradiction in terms or a dynamic tension? In the middle of the loss of dear ones, or in the death of a lifetime relationship, it is difficult to see the hand of the God of life. Naomi, a refugee and a victim, found it almost impossible to understand how her God could bring something positive out of circumstances that seemed to be the end of her world. In times like these, we who suffer loss and marginalization in our own circumstances, need to stop to question our attitudes. Is it correct to blame God when we do not comprehend the totality of human circumstances and relationships and God's purposes in them? Significantly, the very poor in Latin America seem never to lose their faith in God. With perhaps exaggerated fatalism, they trust that God who knows best will see them through, unaware of the opportunities that God may provide to them to begin changing their lives. At the other extreme, people who do not suffer marginalization and privation fail to understand their complicity in the sufferings of others. They also turn to God to help them in their projects, without assuming responsibility for their actions and the consequences.

How do we resolve the tensions and contradictions inherent in a world of injustice and death? We can blame God. It can alleviate our consciences and be less threatening than inexplicable contradictions. One way of avoiding contradiction is to place people and ideas that we fear into neat stereotypes, which end up paralysing us at every level of human relationships, and even in relationship with the Creator. However, we should neither avoid contradictions nor allow them to become the cause of violent conflict. Dynamic tension produces energy in the midst of which God can be revealed and problematic situations confronted with the possibility of transformation. God is full of paradoxes. Divinity does not fit easily into any boxes. Yahweh is a god of contradictions—in fact, dynamic tensions. We find in the book of Ruth several dynamic tensions and God at work among them.

YAHWEH IS A GOD OF LIFE

Famine in Judah, the death of the three male bread-winners of the family, who died one after the other, seemed too much for Naomi and later on for the other two women who were left widowed. These are the kind of questions that always haunt us when death stands at our doors. *Without a doubt,* pious people of the time, *as always,* could have concluded that God was punishing them for having left the 'land of promise'. And weren't the sons being punished for marrying two women of the curse. The fact that Elimelech's name is not mentioned after his death makes me wonder whether this is not a hint that Naomi had erased him from her mind, perhaps because she blamed him for having taken them far from the land of her ancestors. Am I reading too much between the lines? The author of this book allows readers to know only a few details so that they can reach their own conclusions and learn their own lessons. Nonetheless, these questions help readers develop their own theology of life. Is it life just for the present or does it continue even after our corporal bodies are extinguished? Can there be the possibility of Ruth discovering this truth even before Naomi who kept moaning over her loved one and forgot to seek renewal in death from another perspective?

A CHALLENGE TO COMMUNITY: RUTH PRACTICES SOLIDARITY

> Either women have been raped or they give themselves in exchange for a pair of shoes, a dress, or for someone to teach them Spanish.

NAOMI WAS ACCEPTED, IN SPITE OF HER SELF-REJECTION (1.8; 3.1)

In spite of all her loss, Naomi still had a lot to be thankful for. She had a family who cared for her. Her daughters-in-law had not abandoned her; they were working with her in the fields of Moab when the news of the end of the famine in Bethlehem reached Naomi. She had their support and conversely must have felt a certain responsibility toward them. Is this what she had in mind when she advised her daughters-in-law to return to their own families and gods? Naomi's arguments were accepted by Orpah. I work mainly with women, many of whom continue to be trapped in impossible situations because they accept what seems 'logical' and 'realistic' instead of being willing to take risks. I am not so much commenting upon Orpah's actions as questioning the facile and unthinking acceptance of 'givens' instead of taking charge of our lives in the name of Yahweh. 'Taking charge', of course, works out differently in each culture.

Jewish culture had taught Naomi that she belonged to 'the chosen people of Yahweh'. Having left her people years before and become part of a new family in an alien culture, Naomi's main concern was to return to her traditional roots, even if this meant leaving her new family behind. She was so embittered at the loss of her three male loved ones that she forgot to care for the two women in her adopted family! Self-rejection causes us to reject others, even those we love and who love us. While Naomi offered the young women their freedom, perhaps with a sense of guilt at having involved them in her family tragedy (1.13), she did not offer them the possibility of sharing the risk of a new life with her in a different land, *just as she herself had done years before.* Could she have been concerned that the two Moabite women might be ostracised by zealous Jews. Perhaps she was not up to this added problem, just as many of us women sell ourselves short because we feel inferior and end up missing the opportunity to create new communities. Or maybe she felt superior to her 'pagan' daughters, as so many 'good Christians' do. Such feelings can also break community.[6] Whatever the case, Naomi was about to learn a profitable lesson from Ruth.

OUT OF MARGINALIZATION SOLIDARITY (1.19, 20; 2.2)

In this story, God is revealed through an alien woman. The God of the poor and oppressed, the widows and orphans, takes the form of a 'pagan' woman in order to bring faith to a 'pious' Jewess. Ruth is a humble woman, herself a widow, who chooses to share the risks of an uncertain future with another woman, who wrote her off.

To begin with, Ruth could have rejected a family of strangers, of refugees from an enemy nation (in much the same way in which refugees and aliens are being turned away or evicted today by richer nations). In marrying into a Jewish family she demonstrated a willingness to leave any tribal feelings of superiority (or inferiority) aside in favour of starting a new life. From her husband, she must have learned about Yahweh, the God of Israel. So now that her mother-in-law intended to leave her behind, she refused. Her life had been altered and even though her husband had gone, she needed to continue learning about this God of Israel. Ruth did not get discouraged even when Naomi seemed not to appreciate her loyalty and sacrifice. Upon their arrival in Bethlehem, Ruth the alien was not taken into account by the women who made a big fuss over their old friend Naomi. She might be rejected by others, but Yahweh had accepted her, as the story makes plain (cf. 1.19 and 22). Even though Naomi, used her, one might think, to resolve their economic situation (3.1–5), it was Ruth herself who decided to become the breadwinner for this little family of two women (2.1, 2).

Because Ruth gave of herself she also received. Her faith carried her forward even though she was no longer under any formal obligation to her mother-in-law. Today we need to learn from Ruth's unselfish attitude if we are to share God's life with others and build a better world for ourselves and for our children. We can learn from marginalized people; we can profit from the experience and values of people of other faiths. Together we can search for those things that we have in common. When we give we receive. When we empty ourselves we are filled.

A NEW KIND OF FAMILY

The context in which this story takes place is ripe for conflict, and conflict does happen. We meet an Israelite family, united by blood but divided by the socio-economic and political situation. As family, they seek refuge in a divided family

---

[6]From personal experience, I sense that many First World feminists feel this way toward their 'less liberated' sisters from the Third World.

lineage. For their part, Israelites were not encouraged to marry outside of their own race and religion, and least of all with citizens of a cursed race.[7] Ruth experiences the depth of a family relationship, not just in being with her husband in life but also beyond death. When given the opportunity to begin a new family, she does it differently. In the process, she finds a new code of family wholeness. It is a new model of family that goes beyond traditional relationships, that follows an unconventional God who is ready to break stereotypes.[8]

THE CHALLENGE OF SPIRITUALITY: WHEN THE PROFANE BECOMES SACRED

> A very high index of pregnant single women have been abandoned by their men and rejected by their communities. Trying to find a solution, they place themselves under the protection of another man; but when they become pregnant again they are thrown out.

Indigenous women have an amazing creativity which comes out of generations of coping with adversity. In this they remind me of Ruth. She was not one to moan over her losses. She found comfort in serving Naomi who had lost far more. Even in a strange land, she did not sit back and wait for her new God to act, as Naomi seemed to be doing with Yahweh. She took the initiative in finding work to support them both by becoming a humble peasant gleaner.[9] In the process, she discovered a very surprising God: one who acts within human customs and traditions but also breaks cultural taboos. Although it was Naomi who, after Ruth met Boaz, immediately saw the possibilities of availing themselves of the levirate custom,[10] she counselled Ruth to break a sexual custom in order to attract Boaz's attention. Breaking taboos may also be an act of holiness![11]

---

[7]This was the case for many years in Latin America, where 'mixed marriages' between Protestants and Catholics were prohibited by both sides. Such alliances were called 'worldly' in the context where I grew up, ignoring the fact that a growing number of formal marriages were actually defunct.

[8]In Latin America, an increasing number of mistreated and abandoned women have, understandably, become cynical about marriage. Various kinds of single parent, unmarried parents or polygamous relationships are more and more openly practised, often with the kind of love that may be actually absent in formal marital relationships. What these situations require is not a moralistic attitude, but a pastoral spirit of love and compassion that communicates hope.

[9]Gleaning along the edges and in the corners of fields was established by ancient Israelite law (Lev. 19.9, 10) and practised as well in other agrarian societies. It was a way of socializing wealth, of sharing the earth's bounty with the poor.

[10]The levirate tradition among people of the Middle East required that the closest male relative to a childless widow marry her and that their first born carry on the name of the dead brother. If the brother refused to fulfil this obligation, the woman was allowed by custom to place a mark of scorn upon him. This is the context of Tamar's extraordinary action toward her father-in-law (Gen. 38.13–25). In order to gain Ruth, Boaz also appeals to the levirate law, along with a related tradition pertaining to the redemption of property (cf. Deut. 25.5–10, Lev. 25.25 and Ruth 4).

[11]The world of the sacred, according to William E. Paden, is not limited to the supernatural. 'For its members, a religious world is simultaneously a) a set of objects imbued with transhuman power or significance *and* b) a matrix of obligations which upholds the world of those objects.' By merely focusing on the first aspect, revelation, students of religion have ignored the second aspect: the sacrality of

What follows is a rather sexy romance, Hebrew style. Following Naomi's knowledgeable advice, Ruth bathes and perfumes herself at the end of a day of gleaning, then draws close to the kinsman Boaz (who may now be a little drunk, 3.3), 'uncovered his feet and lay down' (3.6, 7). The action, even if taken literally, may be a Hebrew euphemism for a little higher up in a man's body.[12] The point is that Ruth makes herself sexually vulnerable, and available to her hoped-for benefactor, out of personal need and solidarity with Naomi.[13] This is very much an indigenous trait, where women will give their bodies even to enemies to protect their loved ones. Unlike in the Christian tradition, 'sex' was not a dirty word in Judaism, nor is it in my own indigenous tradition. It is a divine gift to be celebrated, enjoyed, talked about, shared, and even risked on behalf of others.

> Maya feminine spirituality begins in the liberation and reproduction of life. This is sacred to them since it stems from the Giver of Life, and then from us, women, as portrayers of life . . . Throughout history [indigenous women] have managed to survive by obeying their masters. . . having lots of children by many different Spanish men was not their choice nor their will, yet they were prepared to outlive them . . . to resist the Spanish oppression by having children—multiplying their race in order to avoid extinction. . . While Maya women are by nature very modest with strangers, within the extended family they are remarkably liberated . . . unwed mothers are not marginalized as in Western societies.[14]

The biblical narrative seemingly highlights Boaz's high-mindedness and generosity in fulfilling the role of 'kinsman redeemer' (cf. Deut. 25.5–9). But there may be some irony here. Reading between the lines, Boaz is obviously attracted to Ruth—and she to him! He is not above resorting to some manipulation to achieve

---

all systems, and the need we all feel to uphold their integrity against violation. In religion, both have to do with 'holiness'. But sacred order can be oppressive, dealing in punishment and death for those who violate it. 'Sacredness then becomes identified with the process of deprofanising the religious life from its contamination with false contexts and values—and "purity" becomes a matter of backing out of the pollution of profane order'. William E. Paden, 'Sacrality and Integrity: "Sacred Order" as a Model for Describing Religious Worlds', in Thomas A. Indinopulos and Edward A. Yonan (eds.), *The Sacred and its Scholars: Comparative Methodologies for the Study of Primary Religious Data* (Leiden: E.J. Brill, 1996), pp. 3–18.

[12]Amy-Jill Levine, 'Ruth', in Carol A. Newsom and Sharon H. Ringe (eds.), *The Woman's Bible Commentary* (Louisville, KY: Westminster/John Knox Press, 1992), p. 82.

[13]The boundaries between 'sacred' and 'profane' in the human body are eating and sexuality. Particularly in patriarchal societies, 'bodily openings are border zones', according to Veikko Anttonen in 'Rethinking the Sacred: The Notions of "Human Body" and "Territory"', in Thomas A. Indinopulos and Edward A. Yonan (eds.), *The Sacred and its Scholars: Comparative Mythologies for the Study of Primary Religious Data* (Leiden: E.J. Brill, 1996), pp. 52, 53.

[14]Dalila C. Nayap Pot, *Spirituality of Maya Women and Grassroots Protestantism: Sources for Dialogue and Development,* dissertation presented in partial fulfillment of the Master of Theology Degree, New College, University of Edinburgh, Scotland (September, 1993), pp. 18, 20, 22. See Charles Gallenkamp, *Maya: The Riddle and Rediscovery of a Lost Civilization* (New York: Viking, 1985), pp. 128, 129; cf. Silvanus G. Morley, *The Ancient Maya* (London: Oxford University Press, 1946), p. 34; see also Paul Sullivan, *Unfinished Conversations: Mayas and Foreigners Between Two Wars* (New York: Knopf, 1989), pp. 40, 41, 112–14, 338 n. 19; and cf. Barbara Tedlock, *Time and the Highland Maya* (Albuquerque: University of New Mexico Press, 1992), p. 74.

what he wants.[15] We see Yahweh thus working through human sexuality and using human ingenuity to bring justice and protection to two women in distress, and not incidentally, happiness to a man and a woman.

Would the story have ended differently if Ruth and Naomi had sat back to wait for God to act? How often do we expect God to do our 'dirty work' for us? How many times do we pray and sit on our hands, or fail to recognize God at work in seemingly 'profane' actions? There may be times when God expects us to break barriers and taboos even when this means acting counter to social mores.

In the end, Ruth is fully accepted by Naomi and by her people. And Yahweh's actions have become manifest through the unassuming and unorthodox ministry of Ruth. She is called 'virtuous' by her future husband, and of more worth than seven sons, by the women who had earlier ignored her (cf. 1.19; 3.11; 4.14, 15). She is also accepted as co-inheritor of Elimelech's property (4.5). The closing verses tell us that Boaz and Ruth (both of 'questionable' ancestry) generate Obed, whose descendants are David and—as we learn much later—Jesus Christ the redeemer. They are part of a genealogy of Jesus (Mt. 1) that includes many flawed males and several 'impure' and ostracized women, some of whom are linked to this story. This is a preview of the life and ministry of Jesus, who consciously identified himself with marginalized people, and in particular, with outcast women.[16]

CONCLUSION

The plight of Naomi and Ruth, surviving within a patriarchal society with all its impositions, is not new to indigenous women in Latin America. Like Ruth, who begins as a secondary figure, but is first in the book that bears her name, many indigenous women have managed to survive despite their problems of not being recognized and valued. In the book of Ruth, there is no mention of God yet we cannot say that God was not present. We can say the same within indigenous culture and communities. Expecting to hear our name for God will be another form of imperial imposition where we are judged by the language we use rather than by the contribution we make to our communities.

It was not only Ruth who was called to unite her lineage. As human beings, we also should feel the responsibility to claim our heritage as human beings, which is, to join in the creation and recreation of humanity.

---

[15]The fact that manipulation was involved here, by both Naomi and Boaz to achieve their respective aims, with Ruth as the pawn, may account for the perceptive—perhaps ironic—blessing by the town elders in which Ruth is likened to Rachel, Leah and Tamar, also women who have been manipulated by men. Rachel and Leah (Ruth 4.11) were used by their father to trick Jacob (Gen. 29.15–28). Tamar (4.12) slept with Judah, her father-in-law, to regain her lost patrimony which belonged to her by the levirate custom (Gen. 38.6–30). Cf. Newsom and Ringe (eds.), *Women's Bible Commentary*, pp. 82, 83.

[16]Albert Nolan, *Jesus Before Christianity* (Maryknoll, NY: Orbis Books, 1992 [1976]), p. 144.

Chapter **4**

Christian Anti-Judaism in Biblical Interpretation

The Challenge of Hebrew Scriptures in Jewish-Christian Relations

Arthur E. Zannoni

I. COMMON SCRIPTURAL HERITAGE

One of the common heritages shared by both Jews and Christians is their love of stories.

> God decided to select a nation to be God's chosen people. First God inter-viewed the Greeks. "If I were to be your God and you were to be my people, what could you do for me?" God asked.
> "O God," the Greek people replied, "If you were to be our God and we would be your people we would honor you with the finest art and the loftiest systems of thought. Our great thinkers would extol you in their great writings."
> "Thank you for your offer," God said.

Excepted from *Introduction to Jewish/Christian Relations*, ed. Michael Shermis and Arthur E. Zannoni, copyright © 1991. Used with permission of Paulist Press. www.paulistpress.com

Next God visited the Romans. "If I were to be your God and you were to be my people, what could you do for me?"

"Great ruler of the universe," the Romans said, "we are a nation of builders. If you were to be our God and we were to be your people we would erect great buildings in your name and wonderful road systems so that your people could travel to worship in these great buildings."

God seemed pleased with the offer, and thanked the Romans.

From Rome God went all over the world interviewing one nation after another. Finally, God interviewed a mideastern group, the Jews, who had a reputation for being astute traders.

Once again God asked the question. "If I were to be your God and you were to be my people, what could you do for me?"

"God," the Jewish people said, "we are not known for our power or our art or our buildings. However, we are a nation of storytellers. If you were to be our God and we were to be your children we could tell your story throughout the whole world."

God, who also had a reputation for being a wise trader, said, "It's a deal!"[1]

The sacred book that records the many faith stories of the Jewish people is known by Jews as the Hebrew scriptures and by Christians as the Old Testament. Both Jews and Christians consider themselves "people of the book." This not only means that over the centuries they have preserved a relatively stable collection of religious writings, but also that each generation of believers has held that the teachings found in "the book" are inspired by God, or, for Orthodox Jews, the word of God. For this reason they have looked to these writings for their religious identity and inspiration. Since these two religious communities hold some of the same religious traditions in common, one might wonder why they do not always agree on their interpretation. The reason for this difference, as will be discovered later, is found in the way various traditions work within the respective communities.

As stated above, the sacred scriptures function as religious literature. This does not mean that they contain merely religious themes, but, more importantly, that they work as an agent informing a religious consciousness. A formative influence in the development of this consciousness is the actual experience of the individual group. Because this reality can be significantly different for religious groups, the same literature can be understood in quite diverse ways. An explanation of this might serve to clarify this point.

The Jewish community of the first century of the common era continued to perceive itself, as it had for centuries before, as the chosen people of God. (The term "common era" should be understood as the era Jews and Christians share in common. It is an inclusive term replacing the terms B.C. and A.D. where calendric dating was based entirely on the Christ event.)

The earliest Christians came from the same community and shared that self-perception. When this Jewish community split over the identity of Jesus, both factions continued to claim that they were the people of God and thus interpreted their religious traditions (the Hebrew scriptures) in such a way as to support their own claims. Hence, the same scriptures came to be understood in quite different ways by these two believing communities.

One of the major challenges that Christianity faced during the second century concerned the relevance of the Old Testament (Hebrew scriptures). Marcion, one of Christianity's staunchest critics—eventually condemned as a heretic—did not believe that this first Testament (Hebrew scriptures) had any religious value for Christians. His rejection of the Hebrew traditions went to such an extreme that he accepted as scripture only those Christian writings that he could interpret as repudiating the first Testament (Hebrew scriptures). Marcion's denigration of the Old Testament has remained a serious option within Christianity, or at least on its borders. Although the church denounced this position, Christian interpreters continued to struggle to understand the relationship between the Testaments.

Today, no one can deny that the entire Bible—both the Old and the New Testaments—has had a profound impact on world civilization. Its epic stories, sensitive prayers, and powerful language and images have left their imprint on human society and history, especially in cultures touched by Judaism and Christianity. In a sense, the Bible is a common heritage of both of these religious traditions.

Although the Bible is bound together under one cover and bears a single title, the Bible is *not* a single, unified book. It is a library of books composed by different authors, using very different styles and perspectives, compiled over several centuries. The gathering of these diverse writings into a single library collection or "book" (which is the literal meaning of the word "Bible") was itself a long-term, complicated, and laborious process. The technical term used to designate which books belong to the Bible is the "canon" (which means "a measurement").[2] Both Judaism and Christianity had to make choices about which books to include and which books to exclude from their respective "Bible." Judaism would not make any official decision about which books belonged to its "Bible" until the end of the first century of the common era. Jews and Christians have a different table of contents for their respective "Bibles." Christians include in their "Bible" the twenty-seven books of the New Testament. Jews do not. The actual naming of the major divisions of the books of the Hebrew scriptures, which Christians call the "Old Testament," differ.

However, before we look at this difference, it is important to speak about a problem that arises with the use of the expression "Old Testament."[3] It is the usual or normal way for Christians to refer to the first and largest section of their Bible. Yet for Jesus of Nazareth it was by no means an "Old Testament"; for him it was the *only* Bible, the living word of God. Recently the suggestion has been made by scholars that the terms "Old" and "New" Testaments be replaced with either the terms "first Testament" and "second Testament" or "Hebrew scriptures" and "Christian scriptures" or "Hebrew scriptures" and "apostolic writings." If this suggestion is not accepted, then the term "Old" when applied to one section of the Christian "Bible" cannot mean "displaced" or "antiquated," but rather should be seen to mean "prior" or "earlier" or "basic." The challenge is to be both respectful of and sensitive to both Judaism's and Christianity's vocabulary.

Jews call their Bible either "the holy scriptures" or *Tanak*. The consonants in *Tanak* come from the first letters of three Hebrew words: *Torah* (or law and instruction), *Neviim* (or prophets), and *Kethubim* (or writings). These three words are the titles for the three major parts of the Hebrew Bible. Or put more simply, *Tanak* is an acronym like, for example, AMA which stands for the American Medical Association.

For Christians the books of the Old Testament are subdivided (a) the Pentateuch and historical books, (b) the wisdom books, and (c) the prophetical books.

The arrangement of the Christian canon is an adaptation of the Jewish Bible that was produced in Alexandria in Egypt, before the common era. In the second and third centuries before the common era the Jewish *Torah* was translated into Greek by Jews in Alexandria. The reason for this translation was that, following the conquest of Alexander the Great a century earlier, Jews living in Alexandria had become thoroughly influenced by the Ptolemy kings and the Greek culture that existed in Alexandria. The Alexandrian Jews consequently needed to read their sacred scriptures in their own language, Greek. And so the *Torah,* the prophets, and the writings (*Tanak*) were translated into Greek from the original Hebrew. The name of this translation is the Septuagint. (The Roman numeral LXX is used to symbolize the Septuagint because according to the tradition there were seventy Jewish scribes who came from Jerusalem to Alexandria in order to engage in that particular translation process.) You will note that the books in both lists are arranged differently but they are the same books for Jews and Christians—a common scriptual heritage.

If we compare the official list of the Hebrew scriptures or Old Testament in Roman Catholic editions of the Bible with that of Jewish and Protestant editions we will notice seven more books in the Roman Catholic list: Tobit and Judith, 1 and 2 Maccabees among the historical books; Wisdom and Sirach among the wisdom books; Baruch among the prophetical books. Parts of the books of Esther and Daniel are also not shared by Protestant and Jewish editions of the canon. Roman Catholics call these sections that are not found in Jewish and Protestant editions the "deuterocanonical" books: Protestants use the word "apocrypha" for the same books. The term "deuterocanonical" means the "second" or "wider" canon; "apocrypha" means "concealed" or "hidden." These books were either unknown or later under dispute by some sectors of Jews and/or Christians. What is important to know, however, is that they were Jewish books.

The books of the apocrypha represent several different literary forms and were written at different historical times. However, they were seen to have their origin within the Jewish religion. Even though these extra books do not appear in the *Tanak* (the Hebrew Bible) they are nonetheless Jewish writings that Christians have chosen to use as Christian scripture. They are not used as Jewish scripture.

There are other writings that were produced around the same time as the biblical writings and the apocryphal writings, a whole collection of what we call the pseudepigrapha. Pseudepigrapha means "false writings." They are so called because these writings are falsely ascribed to Jewish leaders of the past, to the heroes of the past, for example, the Apocalypse of Daniel, the Testament of Adam, the Testament of Abraham, the Book of Enoch, the Apocalypse of Zephaniah, the Book of Jubilees, and many others.[4] So the ancient world that produced our sacred scriptures that we share in common as Jews and Christians was a world that was teeming with literary products, cultural artifacts that the ancient

Jews had produced. And many of these cultural artifacts became a part of the sacred canonical tradition of the Jews and also of the Christians. We share much in common.

II. DIFFERENT INTERPRETATIONS

Christians have a tendency to look at the Hebrew scriptures through the eyes of the New Testament. The New Testament becomes for Christians the principal collection of sacred scripture. Christians make the claim that the word of God is revealed in both Testaments, but in practice the New Testament has taken a position of priority over the Old Testament, and so Christian practice is to interpret the Old Testament in light of the New Testament.

Within Judaism, sacred writings did not cease when they had produced the *Tanak.* They continued to produce other writings such as the apocryphal books and the pseudoepigraphical books mentioned above. That tradition of writing sacred literature continued until eventually they produced works that were given the status of canonical literature alongside of the *Tanak.* This literature is called the *Mishnah,*[5] a massive collection of Jewish law based upon the *Torah.* The *Mishnah* developed the legal traditions from the *Torah* to new levels of understanding and observance. The *Mishnah* was assembled and published around 200 C.E. The production of Jewish literature continued: there were commentaries on the *Mishnah,* and eventually all the commentary and discussions about the *Mishnah* produced what is known as the *Talmud.* There were two different editions of the *Talmud,* one produced in Jerusalem, completed around 400–500 C.E. and another *Talmud* produced in Babylonia where there was a very significant Jewish community around 500 or 600 C.E.

Jews interpret *Tanak* with the aid of the *Mishnah* and the *Talmud.* Christians interpret the Old Testament through the eyes of the New Testament. Hence we frequently arrive at different interpretations for the same passages of sacred scripture that we share in common.

On the Christian side the tendency has been to give the prophets a place of prominence in the Hebrew scriptures (Old Testament). The prophets are looked upon as being the most important part of the Old Testament by many Christians. Christians have found in the prophets passages they believe are prophecies of the coming of the messiah. The reason Christians consider the prophets the most important part of the Old Testament is because they see Jesus as the messiah and maintain that the prophets predicted his messiahship. A good example of this is the gospel of Matthew which often quotes from the prophetic books to substantiate its interpretations about Jesus (see Mt. 1:23; 2:6, 18; 3:3).

To be a Christian, to make a confession of Jesus Christ as the messiah, is the principal basis of interpretation. That causes Christians to approach the Old Testament (Hebrew scriptures) section of the prophets in a different way than Jews approach them. To be Jewish, one is called to be observant. And in Jewish tradition, *Tanak,* especially the *Torah,* as interpreted by the sages (rabbis), forms a commentary on everyday life and may be used as a guide to doing God's will and attaining salvation.

On the Jewish side the practice has been to give the pre-eminent position to the *Torah*, first part of the *Tanak*, because it is in the *Torah* that Jews find the basis of their worldview and the way of life they have developed over the centuries. This view came to a more complete expression in the *Mishnah* and the *Talmud*. Jews begin with the *Mishnah* and the *Talmud* to find the foundation of their worldview and way of life which has become so important to them. To be a Jew means primarily to be observant of that way of life. This has been the emphasis over the centuries. To embrace that way and to live that way is what it is to be called a Jew. To do that, Jews must necessarily turn to the *Torah* in order to be observant and to the interpretation of *Torah* in *Midrash, Mishnah,* and *Talmud*. Through the careful reading of the holy scriptures, the rabbis located eternal truths. They had a name for the process, *midrash*, derived from the root *darash*, "to seek," "to investigate."

The tendency to be selective of which part of the Old Testament that we use in our appropriation of tradition for our respective Christian and Jewish lives can be illustrated by showing how we have developed differing views of redemption. The temptation story of the garden of Eden in Genesis 3 in the Old Testament (Hebrew scriptures) illuminates our Jewish and Christian differences on the point of redemption.

In the Christian view this is a story of the fall. Here is the beginning of sin in human life. There has been much discussion about original sin beginning with Adam and Eve and then transmitted through generations so that all of humankind is infected with the condition of sinfulness. If human beings are innately sinful, they cannot redeem themselves because they do not have that which is necessary for their own redemption. They must necessarily rely upon the act of God to deliver them from the bondage of sin and death. The messiah is the one who has been sent, in the Christian tradition, in order to break those bonds of sin and death and to effect the work of redemption—something human beings could not accomplish by themselves. Christians look upon the garden of Eden story as a story of a fail, and many texts in the New Testament reflect upon Adam and Eve as great sinners. This is where sin came into the world according to the Christian view. Sin is therefore a universal phenomenon and all humankind participates in it.

When we turn to the Jewish view of the garden of Eden story, Christians are astounded that Jews don't see in that story evidence of a fall as such. They don't see there the basis for the view that all humankind is innately sinful. But rather Jews see in that particular story two things. The rabbis from antiquity had a creative way of interpreting how those texts should be understood and they wrote down their understanding in the *Mishnah* and *Talmud*. They looked at the garden of Eden story because the Christians were claiming it was a story of Innate sinfulness and the rabbis noticed that the Hebrew telling of that story was different.

The rabbis discovered that where it says God "formed" Adam from the clay of the earth, God shaped Adam and breathed into him the breath of life, he became animated. The word in Hebrew that was used for "formed" is a word that can be transliterated normally *yatzar* with one "y." Wherever that word *yatzar* appears in the Old Testament (Hebrew scriptures), it is written with one "y." In this particular case (Gen 2:7), for some reason, it was written with two "y's," and the rabbis said that it was surely significant that *Tanak* has two "y's" here. And the rabbis asked why are there two "y's" when the text is talking about the forming of humankind. Their interpretation was that it is to tell us that every human being has two *yetzers*. *Yetzer* is the Hebrew word for "inclination" or "tendency." According to rabbinic interpretation every human being has within himself or herself two tendencies. One is the tendency for good and the other is the tendency for evil. And so this story is designed to teach us about the tendency for either good or evil. It does not say that humankind is innately evil. Human beings can go either way. God has so endowed each and every individual with the innate capacities that a person needs in order to be good. God has created everyone in the Image of God, and that is good; and that possibility of being good is open to every human being even after the garden of Eden. So the garden of Eden is a constant reminder that the possibility of being good is real. Hence, the rabbis see this story in a considerably different way.

If there is no general or universal condition of human sinfulness of an innate nature, then there is no particular need for a messiah to come and rescue these people from the bondage of sin and death. If human beings have within themselves the capacity to live the good life, to be ethical, and to be moral, then they can uphold the *Torah;* they can live according to the law; they can be observant doing what God wants them to do. So beginning with this particular story we can see differing views of human nature unfold: one, the Christian notion of the "fall"; the other, the Jewish notion of the two tendencies. And there are other views about, God, creation, the messiah, to mention but a few, that Jews and Christians look at somewhat differently.

III. REFLECTIONS ON THE CHRISTIAN CHURCH'S INTERPRETATIONS OF THE HEBREW SCRIPTURES

Writing from a Berlin prison cell in 1943, awaiting an uncertain fate at the hands of the Nazi regime whose downfall he had sought, German Lutheran theologian and pastor Dietrich Bonhoeffer expressed to his friend and fellow pastor Eberhard Bethge that he was experiencing a breakthrough to the Old Testament in his reading of scripture. "My thoughts and feelings seem to be getting more and more like those of the Old Testament and in recent months I have been reading the Old Testament much more than the New. . . . In my opinion it is not Christian to want to take our thoughts and feelings too quickly and too directly from the New Testament.[6] Bonhoeffer's concern about "the Christian significance of the Old Testament" is a timely one, because it was Bonhoeffer who at the end of his road of resistance to the most furious attempt to eliminate the Jewish people—the holocaust—was able to break through to a new and profound grasp of the revelation of Israel's God in the Bible.

The position of this essay is that the Christian grasp of the Hebrew scriptures has been continuously weakened and distorted by the relationship of hostility between Christianity and Judaism, for whom these writings are authoritative revelation. The prevailing Christian anxiety to develop a view of the Old Testament which would *exclude* its use as sacred scripture by Judaism has blinded the church in a variety of ways to the real message of the Old Testament (Hebrew scriptures).

It is at this point that we encounter the perennial problem of the shared canon of scripture. The Hebrew scriptures, *Tanak* for Jews, Old Testament for Christians— serves as a "root metaphor"[7] for both faiths. By "root metaphor" I mean the controlling story of a religious tradition: in the case of Judaism the exodus story, in the case of Christianity the Jesus story. Hence, each religious tradition must regard its rights to that document as inalienable. A denial of these rights would mean disinheritance and consequently disillusionment. Therefore, defense of its "root metaphor" seems essential to the continuing existence of each believing community. Judaism and Christianity, however, interpret their "root metaphor" in contrasting ways. For Jews, *Tanak*, is a covenantal document, establishing a relationship between God and the people with two foci, law and the land. For Christians, on the other hand, the Old Testament is read as a history of human sin and divine redemption that culminates in the coming of Jesus as the messiah. Since the Christian gospel, especially as interpreted by Paul, appears to leave concern with the law and the land behind. Christianity seems bound to insist that these themes cannot be truly central in the Hebrew scriptures, and for precisely that reason, Judaism insists on their centrality. The two interpretative communities, then, have developed mutually exclusive interpretations of their common "root metaphor." If one is right, must the other be wrong? And if that is so, then the community that offers the "false" interpretation is a usurper, a standing danger to the true community.

Social theorists have coined the term "nihilation" to describe the conflict that results from such a situation.[8] The intellectual leaders of Christianity, who were responsible for interpreting the scriptures and defending the faith, were compelled by this competitive relationship not only to find Christ and the church in the Old Testament, but also to eliminate any basis Jews might have for finding the law and the land as the central focus. To reduce the Jewish interpretation to nothing— to "nihilate" it—required either a thoroughgoing reinterpretation of the Old Testament in exclusively Christian terms, or else a change in the status of the Old Testament in the Christian canon, which would neutralize the potentially Jewish elements. Throughout the history of Christianity, various strategies and different degrees of nihilation were often a major shaping force in Christian analysis of the Old Testament. As a result the church's understanding of the Old Testament has been diminished.

IV. SPIRITUAL INTERPRETATION OF THE OLD TESTAMENT (HEBREW SCRIPTURES)

From the beginnings of Christianity there was another understanding that would be the dominant one for an entire millennium. In this interpretation, the Old Testament was accepted fully as part of the Christian Bible, but only as interpreted spiritually, that is, in a way that demonstrated its immediate relevance to the gospel. The Christian movement arose within Judaism and needed to justify itself to the Jews by means of the Hebrew scriptures. Therefore, a way of understanding the scriptures that would warrant the conviction that Jesus Christ was the goal and ful-fillment of God's revelation was needed. There are indications that the earliest Christian apologetic writings, which may underlie portions of the New Testament, consisted of collections of Old Testament *testimonia,* which gave witness to Jesus as the messiah.[9] Sometimes these passages were taken in a simple prophetic sense (e.g. Is 7:14); but increasingly the events and characters of the Old Testament were seen as types or shadows of Christ, the church, and redemption. (Paul's use of Sarah and Haggar as types of two communities in the history of redemption—see Gal 4:21–31—is an example of such typological interpretation, as is the symbolic use of Melchizedek and the tabernacle in the epistle to the Hebrews—see chapters 7–9.)

Eventually this method of analysis was extended from specific passages to the Old Testament (Hebrew scriptures) in general. Borrowing from the surround-ing Greco-Roman culture the technique of allegory—by which a passage of an-cient sacred literature could be read as speaking in a hidden way about current concerns of philosophy or morality—Christian analysts fashioned a unique and powerful tool for discerning a witness to Christ throughout the Old Testament. Allegory continued to be an important weapon in the Christian arsenal against the Jews. For nearly all the Christian analysts before the reformation, allegory in some form was the dominant mode of interpreting scripture.

Over this long period of development the origins of spiritual interpretation in the controversy with the Jews remained evident even when its use had become less directly polemical. An interpretation that did not lead to Christ, which was merely literal or historical, was held to be "Jewish," and hence decrepit, out-moded, transcended, Jewish analysis of the Hebrew scriptures, apart from Christ, could produce only superstition and legal ceremonial excess. Henri de Lubac summarizes the prevailing view in the middle ages; ". . . those Jews who, by re-fusing to recognize Jesus Christ, refused to recognize the New Covenant, lost their understanding of Scripture itself."[10]

Once again, the strategy of nihilation is evident. The Christian interpretation of scripture must exclude and destroy the Jewish interpretation. As a conse-quence, elements in the text of the Hebrew scriptures that cannot be interpreted christologically are problematic. There is a strong temptation either to force such passages into a christological framework, through fair means or foul, or to ignore them altogether. Both solutions serve to weaken Christian analysis: first by mak-ing the entire method of spiritual interpretation implausible, and second by placing certain portions of scripture out-of-bounds for Christianity.

V. DIALECTICAL INTERPRETATION OF THE OLD TESTAMENT (HEBREW SCRIPTURES)

Despite their considerable diversity in detail, the two views just considered (nihi-lation and spiritual interpretation) have in common one major feature: they take the Old Testament (Hebrew scriptures) in its entirety, viewing it as a single, non-reflective, non-historically conditioned entity in relation to a New Testament con-ceived in a similarly static and uniform fashion. In reality, however, the two parts of the Christian canon are each collections containing considerable variety. The New Testament contains the epistle of James as well as those of Paul. John's gospel as well as Matthew's. Likewise, the Hebrew scriptures (Old Testament) from an historical point of view consist of documents representing more than a millenium of Israelite religious and secular history. As a collection it presents tensions on fundamental issues: the relative importance of temple-cult and morality, the function and significance of a monarchy, the centrality of Jerusalem, the criteria for recognizing true prophecy, and so on. Hence, the possibility arises that a Christian appropriation of the Hebrew scriptures (Old Testament) might need to take into account this dynamic process: all biblical texts are culturally and historically conditioned, forging a link between the Testaments through historical developments. This process is more accurate than the pre-conceived teachings of Christianity, which are known as dogmas, namely a body of doctrines concerning faith or morals formally stated and authoritatively proclaimed by a church.

These doctrinal interpretations of the Hebrew scriptures (Old Testament) were less prominent before the rise of historical consciousness during the enlightenment, although they were not wholly absent. Yet the breakthrough in the historical understanding of the Hebrew scriptures which occurred during the eighteenth and nineteenth centuries of the common era forced many Christian theologians to consider seriously whether a static, dogmatic understanding of the Old Testament would be an appropriate interpretation. Within this context, Julius Wellhausen's[11] presentation of the "Documentary Hypothesis"—the view that the first five books of the Old Testament are the product of an evolutionary process in Israelite religion and thus contain material representing different ages of that evolution—held enormous appeal and soon came to dominate the work of "critical" Old Testament scholars, much as the views of Charles Darwin were becoming dominant in the natural sciences. Wellhausen viewed the evolution of Israel's religion as an ongoing process. But this evolution developed in a series of stages from the primitive to the more advanced. Even in the latter phases of development, it was possible for ancient Israel to lapse into superstitious or legalistic forms of religion. Other forms of Old Testament religion, more primitive than the prophets, led, if anywhere, to rabbinic Judaism, which Wellhausen regarded as a dead-end.

Wellhausen's hypothesis continued to be accepted in broad outline by succeeding generations of scholars. Among the most important syntheses of Old Testament theology, which took the dialectical approach as a basic point of departure was Walther Eichrodt's *Theology of the Old Testament*.[12] Eichrodt employed the concept of "covenant" as an organizing concept for the ideas of the Old Testament. Ancient Israel's faith, in his view, centered around the covenant of God with the nation, and its spiritual journey became manifest in the evolution of the covenant-concept through its history. The covenant in Eichrodt's hands becomes a tool for tracing the dialectical movement within the history of ancient Israel, through which ancient Israel's understanding of God was continually challenged, corrected, and enriched by the pattern of God's activity in relation to the nation. It was in "the manifestation of Christ" that this dialectical movement reached its climax and fulfillment.[13]

The selectivity inherent in this approach, by which some elements of the Hebrew scriptures are declared enduring and others transitory, is employed by

Eichrodt and other similar interpreters who argue that the "Jewish" interpretation is mistaken from the outset, and hence religiously irrelevant.[14] All that classical rabbinic Judaism has to offer—the legal traditions which led to the *Mishnah* and the *Talmud,* and the collections of the *Midrashim*—are declared null and void for Christian interpreters. It is worth asking whether such Christian analysis in its zeal to hear the witness of the Old Testament through the filter of the New Testament, and not also through the insights of the other believing community that has endeavored to remain faithful to the Hebrew scriptures, has not stiffed some crucial understandings of revelation.

VI. TOWARD A CONSTRUCTIVE ALTERNATIVE

All the strategies of Old Testament interpretation which we have considered here have in common a fundamental starting point: the conviction that there is in the Old Testament a "surplus" of meaning which cannot be immediately reduced to or assimilated by a theology based exclusively on the New Testament. Whatever label is given to this concept—legalism, primitivity, or national particularism—it is regarded as an alien element whose presence within the biblical canon must be accounted for or counteracted. Marcion and his theological disciples demoted the Hebrew scriptures to an inferior status within the Christian canon, or excluded them altogether. The allegorical interpreters contrived an analysis that would transpose the alien elements into a more familiar christological interpretation. Dialectical interpreters saw certain elements of the Hebrew scriptures as dead-ends, bypassed by the dynamic moment of Israel's history, and hence not of direct or positive significance for Christian analysis. Whether the problematic elements are excluded, transposed, or bypassed, the outcome is eventually the same: the witness of the Old Testament (Hebrew scriptures) to the saving power of God is in some respect muted, distorted, or impoverished.

This impoverishment is perhaps most clearly visible in a loss of a sense of concrete engagement with the world for Christian preaching and instruction. When the New Testament message of salvation is not understood in continuity with Israel's traditions, there is a danger that the church will forget some part of God's claim on the whole world, and the will of God is reduced to the sphere of individual piety. This means that the salvation of the individual takes on overwhelming importance, and the realization of God's will in the world is pushed into the background or forgotten.

The continued presence of the Hebrew scriptures in the Christian canon is an implicit recognition by the church that it cannot finally cut itself off from the "worldly" roots of its own gospel. The Hebrew scriptures are the Jewish roots of the Christian faith. Yet sacred scripture must be interpreted and applied in order to be meaningful. The development of a hermeneutic (method of interpretation) that does justice to the Old Testament within the context of the whole canon is a task of the church with no less urgency today than two millennia ago. The following challenges are offered as a possible alternative method of interpretation.

The God of Abraham, Isaac, Sarah, Rachel, and Jesus Christ must be at the center of any Christian interpretation of the Hebrew scriptures to be significant for Christian preaching and instruction. The analysis of the Hebrew scriptures by Christians must interpret the proclamation of salvation through the God of Jesus Christ. The status of the Hebrew scriptures in the canon of the Christian church is predicated on this assumption. The church needs to be theocentric (God-centered) in its interpretation of the Hebrew scriptures.

Further, the Hebrew scriptures are not to be subjected to the New Testament as a criterion of interpretation, for Christ is *not* identical with the New Testament. The notion that the New Testament as a document stands in a more immediate relationship to Christ than the Hebrew scriptures, and must therefore serve as the key to the interpretation and the authority of the Hebrew scriptures, has no basis in scripture and must be resisted.

> We should not deal with any passage of the Old Testament in order to show that in it we find only the type or shadow of what later becomes reality or light in the New Testament . . . we should not treat the Hebrew Scriptures in any way that suggests Christianity has superseded or displaced Jews and Judaism in the covenant with God, in God's love or favor. 'Supersede' is derived from two Latin words *super* ("on" or "upon") and *sedere* ("to sit"). It refers to the act in which one person takes a seat that has been vacated by another, thus preventing that person from sitting there again. All the ways in which we should not deal with the Old Testament are ways of claiming that Christianity has superseded, taken the place of, Judaism and the Jewish people in God's grace.[15]

The New Testament, which portrays explicitly the fact of Christ and the consequences of his appearance and work, must inevitably sharpen our Christian perspective on the Old Testament. Yet, since the world which God loves and Christ redeems is the world of the penultimate, the "things before the last," the Old Testament is *not* to be superseded by the New Testament. Any view of the Old Testament that regards its "this-worldliness" as a "barrier" that must be overcome if we are to strive toward the New Testament has stripped away from the center the context which gives it meaning. Rather, "the Old Testament's love for life and the earth forms the context within which the Christian resurrection hope can alone be properly interpreted and lived."[16]

All of the foregoing challenges imply that a Christian interpretation of the Hebrew scriptures need not—must not—exclude the Jewish understanding from consideration. The significance of the law (*Torah*) and the land as focal points of Hebrew scriptures for Judaism, as well as the interpretations found in the *Mishnah* and *Talmud*, may constitute an ultimate difference between Jewish and Christian analysis. But within the context of the penultimate, this-worldly boundaries of the Hebrew scriptures, the scene of the sanctification of the world before God, through the law (*Torah*) and within the land, as well as the *Mishnah* and *Talmud*, is an irreducible given that must be more deeply understood, respected, and celebrated by Christians if they are to fully grasp the meaning of the Christ event. Neither believing community can absolutize its interpretation of the sacred scriptures, for the God who is revealed through these inspired texts is both *greater* than, and not *limited* by, *either* Judaism or Christianity's interpretation. For the freedom of God's activity is greater than any human interpretation.

Since the task of teaching and instruction is carried out in the church not first of all by theologians but by pastors and lay people, a sympathetic knowledge of Judaism and an ability to encounter and benefit from the Jewish reading of sacred scripture should become a component of minimal literacy in the church. Admittedly, the barriers to realizing this ideal are serious. But for the sake of its own mission and for the sake of the truth, Christianity can no longer afford to make Judaism into a marginal element, alienated or trivialized, within its own consciousness.

Whenever the Hebrew scriptures have been used as a barrier between the church and synagogue, Christians have discovered their own grasp of the Bible made alien or trivial (i.e. the unwarranted notion that the God of the Old Testament is the God of wrath and judgment that robs Christians of the beauty of God's compassion in the Hebrew scriptures). "Then let us no more pass judgment on one another, but rather decide never to put a stumbling block or hindrance in the way of a brother" (Rom 14:13 NAB). "Behold how good it is and how pleasant, where brethren dwell at one" (Ps 133:1). Making the Hebrew scriptures into a bridge between church and synagogue is a vital step in recovering their meaning for Christians, Jews, and the world whose redemption we await in common.

Notes

1. Paraphrased from William R. White. *Stories for the Journey* (Minneapolis: Augsburg, 1988), p. 32.

2. "Canon" is a transliteration of a Hebrew word (*kaneh*) for "reed" or "stalk" which grows in swampy areas and when cut and trimmed was used at times as a yardstick or ruler; from this came the transfer to what was a "norm" or "rule" of faith and prayer. For an extensive treatment of the issue of canonicity see "Canonicity" in *The New Jerome Biblical Commentary*, edited by Raymond E. Brown, Joseph A. Fitzmyer, and Roland E. Murphy (Englewood Cliffs; Prentice-Hall, 1990), pp. 1034–54. For a brief explanation of the Jewish understanding of the process of canonization see S. Daniel Breslauer, "Bible: Jewish View" in Leon Klenicki and Geoffrey Wigoder, eds., *A Dictionary of Jewish-Christian Dialogue* (New York: Paulist Press, 1984), pp. 16–19.

3. Commenting on the use of the term "Old Testament" John T. Pawlikowski states:

> The time has come to eliminate the term 'Old Testament' from the Christian vocabulary about the Bible. Though admittedly the word 'old' can connote 'reverence' or 'long-standing experience,' used in reference to the first part of the Bible it tends to create an attitude that these pre-Christian books are inferior and outdated in their religious outlook when compared with passages of the New Testament. In such a context the Hebrew Scriptures at best appear as a foreword to the fullness of faith found in the Gospels and Epistles and at worst as works motivated by legalism and spiritual shallowness which Christians can ignore without in any way impoverishing their spirituality. Continued use of the term 'Old Testament' tends to keep Christians from the realization that the Hebrew Scriptures contain rich spiritual insights vital in their own right. It likewise continues to give credence to the discredited contrast between Christianity as a religion of love with Judaism as a faith perspective marked by cold legalism.

John T. Pawlikowski, "Jews and Christians: The Contemporary Dialogue," in *Quarterly Review*, 4 (Winter 1984), pp. 26–27. Paul M. van Buren suggests that instead of the terms "Old" and "New" Testament we speak of Hebrew scriptures and the apostolic writings. The merit of van Buren's suggestions is that the terms "Old" and "New" Testament do not themselves occur anywhere in the scriptures. Van Buren's suggestion, therefore, has the merit of appropriateness. See Paul M. van Buren, *A Theology of the Jewish-Christian Reality, Part I: Discerning the Way* (San Francisco: Harper & Row, 1980), pp. 122ff. For discussion and use of the term "Prime Testament" for "Old Testament", see André

Lacocque, "The Old Testament in the Protestant Tradition" in Lawrence Boadt, Heiga Croner, and Leon Klenicki, eds., *Biblical Studies: Meeting Ground of Jesus and Christians* (New York: Paulist, 1980), pp. 120–43.

4. For a complete treatment of the pseudepigrapha, see James A. Charlesworth, ed., *The Old Testament Pseudepigrapha*, 2 vols. (Garden City: Doubleday and Co., Inc., 1983).

5. Commenting on the meaning of *Mishnah* and *Talmud*, Jacob Neusner, in *Between Time and Eternity: The Essentials of Judaism* (Encino: Dickenson Publishing Co., 1975). pp. 53, 63, states:

> The *Mishnah* is the first and most important document of Rabbinic Judaism. It reached its present form at about the beginning of the third century, C.E. and is based upon traditions at least two hundred years older than that. . . . The *Mishnah* is essentially a law code. It is divided into six major parts, called *Sedera* or *Orders*, encompassing the vast themes of "reality" covered by the Oral *Torah*. These are, first, agricultural law; second, Sabbath and festival laws; third, family laws; fourth, civil and criminal laws; fifth, laws concerning sacrifices in the cult; and finally, laws concerning purities.
>
> To use more general language, *Mishnah* deals with the *Torah*'s governance of the economy and means of production, the material basis of life (agriculture); the organization and differentiation of time into the holy and profane (Sabbath and festivals); the structure and definition of the family, in particular the rights of women: the regulation of society and human interactions and transactions outside of the family; the mode of service to the divinity through sacrifice and cult; and the regulation of the unseen world of purity and impurity as these affect the cult, society, the economy, and the home. The "theory" of the *Mishnah*, therefore, is that all of reality is to be suitably organized and rationally governed through the law of *Mishnah*.
>
> . . . the great and authoritative commentary to the *Mishnah* is the *Gemara*, which also is simply called the *Talmud*. This is a compilation of materials relevant to a given paragraph of *Mishnah*, developed from the third through the fifth centuries C.E. In point of fact, two *Talmuds* exist for the same *Mishnah*, one edited in Palestine, called the Palestinian or Jerusalem *Talmud*, the other edited in Babylonia, and called the Babylonian *Talmud*. It is the latter that is widely studied to this day and which supplies the authoritative interpretation of *Mishnah*.

6. Dietrich Bonhoeffer, letter to Eberhard Bethge, 5 December 1943. See Eberhard Bethge, *Dietrich Bonhoeffer* (New York: Harper and Row, 1970), p. 360.

7. For a treatment of the stories that serve as root metaphors for both Judaism and Christianity see Michael Goldberg, *Jews and Christians, Getting Our Stories Straight: The Exodus and Passion-Resurrection* (Nashville: Abingdon Press, 1985).

8. See Peter Berger and Thomas Luckman, *The Social Construction of Reality* (Garden City: Doubleday, 1966), pp. 114ff for a lucid discussion of this concept.

9. See C.H. Dodd, *According to the Scriptures* (London: Nisbet, 1952) for an exposition of this view.

10. Henri de Lubac, *The Sources of Revelation* (New York: Herder and Herder, 1968), pp. 90f.

11. Julius Wellhausen, *Prolegomena to the History of Israel* (New York: Meridian, 1957).

12. Walther Eichrodt, *Theology of the Old Testament*, 2 vols. (Philadelphia: Westminster Press, 1961.)

13. Eichrodt, *Theology of the Old Testament*, 1. p. 26.

14. Ibid., 63, 133, 168ff.

15. Clark M. Williamson, *When Jews and Christians Meet: A Guide for Christian Preaching and Teaching* (St. Louis: CBP Press, 1989), pp. 15–17. Also see Rolf Rendtorff, "The Jewish Bible and Its Anti-Jewish Interpretation," *Christian-Jewish Relations* 16 (1983), 3–20, and Joseph Blenkinsopp, "Tanakh and the New Testament: A Christian Perspective" in Lawrence Boadt, Helga Croner, and Leon Klenicki, eds., *Biblical Studies: Meeting Ground of Jews and Christians* (New York: Paulist, 1980), pp. 96–119.

16. Martin Kuske, *The Old Testament as the Book of Christ: An Appraisal of Bonhoeffer's Interpretation* (Philadelphia: Westminster, 1976), p. 106.

The New Testament:
Confronting Its Impact
on Jewish-Christian Relations

Michael Cook

I. INTRODUCTION

Jews receive frequent mention in the Christian scriptures, commonly called the New Testament. But the tenor of these references is usually disparaging, and many of the criticisms lodged against Jews or their religious practice are, regrettably, ascribed to Jesus personally. Aside from rare reports of camaraderie between Jesus and the Jews' leaders, the gospels generally show him chiding, sometimes even maligning, the scribes and Pharisees, priests and Sadducees. And these authorities, in turn, are regularly depicted as bent on embarrassing or tricking Jesus and, particularly toward the end of his ministry, even on destroying him. Nor is such malevolence limited to the leaders; sometimes the Jews as a people are also thus portrayed, especially once they too seem to join in clamoring for Jesus' execution.

Negative depictions of Jews punctuate not only the four gospels but also the book of Acts, and appear occasionally in Paul's epistles as well. It is hardly difficult, therefore, to surmise the likely impact of these texts on the history of Jewish-Christian relations: over the centuries, not only have many Jews come to consider the New Testament a virtual catalogue of anti-Judaism, but many Christian readers have been unable to ignore how consistently the Jews come across as villainous. Moreover, since the figure of Jesus serves as a role model for Christians, they may naturally assimilate as their own those same disapproving attitudes toward Jews apparently advanced by Jesus himself.

II. SAMPLE PASSAGES AND STEREOTYPES

Most scholars view the "scribes" and "Pharisees" as having been forerunners of the rabbis, who, a generation after Jesus' death, began laying the foundations of Judaism as it has evolved even to the present day. It becomes especially instructive, therefore, to observe how the New Testament depicts Jesus in relation to these two groups in particular, for his assessments of them were undoubtedly determinative of how many later Christians, readily appropriating his sentiments, came to relate both to the Jews and the Judaism of their own day.

The gospels show us Jesus addressing these scribes and Pharisees with hostility, often accusing them of "hypocrisy." One well-known chapter, Matthew 23,[1] features Jesus relentlessly berating or belittling these groups.

In the synoptic gospels (Mark, Matthew, and Luke), only the Jews' chief priests and other leaders are cast as orchestrating Jesus' arrest and trial, and plotting his execution; ultimately, however, the Jews as a people are themselves enlisted in urging Pontius Pilate, the Roman governor, to "crucify him! . . . crucify him!" (Mk 15:13–14). And Matthew, for good measure, adds the infamous "blood curse," wherein the Jews, already collectively to blame for Jesus' death, now also eagerly foist responsibility on their offspring as well: "Let his blood be on us and on our children!" (27:25). In Mark and Matthew, the Jewish masses need to be "stirred up" (Mk 15:11) or "persuaded" (Mt 27:20) by their priests to demand Jesus' death, but in Luke they require no encouragement whatsoever.

While in the synoptic gospels it is only near the conclusion of Jesus' ministry that the Jews as a people emerge actively as his adversaries, in the gospel of John they surface in this capacity far earlier. John's frequent use of the collective term "the Jews"—seventy-one times compared to but five or six times in each synoptic gospel—suggests his desire not only to cast "the Jews" as Jesus' enemies, but to do so *throughout* Jesus' ministry, not merely at its end.

Thus, John informs us (italics added) that *"the Jews* persecuted Jesus" (5:16), and that *"the Jews* sought all the more to kill him" (5:18; also 7:1). Some who accepted Jesus as the Christ dared not admit it publicly "because they feared *the Jews"* (9:22; also 7:13). Joseph of Arimathea had to ask for Jesus' body secretly "for fear of *the Jews"* (19:38). The disciples' doors were kept shut "for fear of *the Jews"* (20:19). Strangely, John even has Jesus denounce Jews *accepting* of him: they are of their "father the devil . . . a murderer from the beginning . . . a liar and the father of lies" (8:44), with the reason why they do not hear the word of God being that they "are not of God" (8:47).

This antagonism, so intense in John, may even obscure from readers Jesus' Jewish identity and that of his inner circle. John 10:34, for example, presents Jesus as saying to Jews (italics added): "Is it not written in *your* law?" (why not *"our* law"?); John 13:33 has Jesus address his disciples (italics added): "as I said to *the Jews* so now I say to you" (why not "as I said to *our fellow* Jews"?). Such texts may only reinforce an already erroneous impression that Jesus somehow perceived himself as *outside* the Jewish people.

When viewed most broadly, the New Testament appears to have spawned negative stereotypes persisting for centuries—in some circles, even to the present day: that the Jews are responsible for crucifying Jesus and, as such, guilty of deicide; that their tribulations throughout history constitute God's punishment of them for killing Jesus; that Jesus originally came to preach only to Jews but, when they rejected him, he urged their abandonment in favor of Gentiles (non-Jews) instead; that Christianity (typified by Jesus and his teachings) emphasizes love, while Judaism (typified by the Pharisees and the "Old" Testament) stands for an oppressive legalism, stern justice, and a God of wrath; that, by Jesus' day, Judaism had entirely ceased to be a living faith: and, above all, that while the children of Israel were God's original chosen people by virtue of an ancient covenant, in rejecting Jesus they forfeited that chosenness—and now, through a new covenant, Christians (the "new" Israel) have replaced the Jews as God's chosen people, with the church now becoming the people of God.

III. THE MODERN LEGACY

The legacy of these themes and developments remains influential today because the New Testament continues to serve as such a vibrant stimulus of Christian teaching: aside from regular scripture readings in church (wherein the selections frequently happen to include anti-Jewish verses), and textual sermons (many based on passages targeting the Pharisees as models of what *not* to be[2]), the New Testament is also the central focus of thousands of books as well as university courses, not to mention adult education and sectarian training in churches and religious schools. Added to these is the seemingly endless citation of New Testament texts heard on an ever-growing number of radio and "televangelism" programs on national broadcasting networks.

Jews today frequently encounter expressions of the New Testament's anti-Jewish bias. Naturally they sometimes expect that Christians, in addition to looking askance, unjustifiedly, at the Jews of *Jesus'* day, will also carry this over when viewing *modern* Jews as well. This suggests that the ways in which the New Testament refers to Jews and Judaism may continue to set much of the tenor of Jewish-Christian relations in the future even as they have in the past—that these texts still constitute an imposing *obstacle for Jews* and a serious *quandary for Christians* interested in improving Jewish-Christian relations today.

IV. THE NEW TESTAMENT: HOW IT BECAME AN OBSTACLE FOR JEWS

When most Jews think of Jesus, the image they readily conjure up is not that of the actual historical figure but rather of the gospel portraits of him completed long after his ministry. The difference is notable, for there is no reason to believe that the historical Jesus was himself anti-Jewish, even though his later gospel image indisputably *is*.

It was this latter depiction that first induced Jews to dismiss Jesus as an apostate, i.e. as someone who had turned against his own religion, Judaism. And because missionaries sought to draw Jews into Christianity in Jesus' name, the rabbis condemned Jesus himself for attempting to deceive the Jewish people and lead them astray. It is probable that the proliferation of Christian writings toward the end of the first century catalyzed the rabbis into "closing" the Jewish Bible so as to prevent any such "external books" from gaining acceptance among the Jewish populace at large.

Of course, religious opinions of one age are not always consequential for subsequent eras. But the rabbis' disaffection with the New Testament did, in point of fact, set the trend for centuries of later Jews who, identifying the historical Jesus by the New Testament's depiction of him, came to relate to Christianity accordingly.

The New Testament's anti-Jewish Jesus also determined the attitudes of many Christians. During the middle ages, by which time the church had established a virtual monopoly on European learning, gospel teachings in particular conditioned the mindset of the masses against Jews. And since the laity was generally illiterate, church art became employed to teach that the Jews were accursed, with the "synagogue" depicted as either blindfolded or literally blind (cf. 2 Cor 3:14ff).[3]

Since, moreover, the gospels held the Jews as a people responsible for Jesus' execution, they gave rise to the epithet that Jews were "Christ-killers." This identification often inflamed popular passions against Jews in Christian Europe, who lived with perpetual anxiety that the gospels' accusations would become pretexts for pogroms (massacres of Jews). Nor was their fear without good reason: during the various crusades (beginning in 1096), Christian armies, trekking through Europe to recapture Jerusalem from the Muslim "infidel," routinely ransacked Jewish communities en route and murdered the inhabitants—justifying these actions by appeals to the gospels' own assessments of Jews as murderers of Jesus and infidels themselves. Other pogroms were triggered by outrageous "blood libels," to the effect that Jews were regularly reenacting their execution of Jesus by kidnaping Christian children to secure blood Jews supposedly needed to bake Passover *matzah* (unleavened bread).[4]

Etched even deeper into the modern Jewish psyche, after centuries of such continual prejudice, was Nazism's malicious exploitation of the New Testament's supersessionist theology. This conviction—that Gentile Christians had superseded the Jews, displacing and replacing them as God's chosen people—was now manipulated by Hitler's ideologues to suggest that the persistence of Jews into the twentieth century was an anomaly, a quirk or mistake of history, that they were a fossil meant to have disappeared far earlier. Such a ploy lessened potential resistance to Hitler's "final solution," the plan to exterminate the entire Jewish people.

Since Christian anti-Judaism has thus been such a source of anxiety for Jews over the centuries, it should come as no surprise how many Jews today continue to bristle or flinch, even to cringe, upon hearing the name of Jesus, and to view the New Testament with varying degrees of dismay and distrust, if not dread. This explains why these Christian texts loom up for Jews as such a fundamental and imposing obstacle in interfaith relations today.

V. THE NEW TESTAMENT: HOW IT POSES A QUANDARY FOR CHRISTIANS

It should be obvious now that these texts likewise pose a serious dilemma for Christians committed to interfaith relations. Their quandary is inescapable: what to do when their scriptures, sacred repository of their cherished teachings, also seem to generate such intensely anti-Jewish sentiment?

Their responses have usually resolved themselves into at least three different avenues of approach: (1) a *denial* that the New Testament itself is anti-Jewish; or (2) an acknowledgment of anti-Jewishness in the New Testament, but mainly in terms that tend to *minimize* its importance or otherwise explain it away; or (3) an open recognition that the New Testament is profoundly anti-Jewish and that this is a serious problem requiring full *confrontation*. It is important to recognize that these three categories of response are largely incompatible with each other: that is to say, either the New Testament is not anti-Jewish (#1) or it *is*, and if it *is*, either this problem is not especially serious (#2) or it is definitely so (#3). Agreement in these regards may be a necessary pre-condition for achieving any significant progress in Jewish-Christian relations in the future.

AVENUE #1—DENIAL THAT THE NEW TESTAMENT IS ITSELF ANTI-JEWISH

Christians espousing this approach believe interfaith relations will improve once Jews and Christians come to view the New Testament itself as neither a source nor a cause of Christian anti-Judaism. In the service of this viewpoint, at least a four-fold argument has been advanced:

a. Inspired by God, the New Testament reflects the ultimate revelation of divine love and could in no way have been intended to encourage the contempt of any people. Jesus himself spoke this language of love: he preached the turning of the other cheek, even the love of one's enemies. Therefore, those recording his spiritual teachings, and deeply committed to him themselves, could hardly have written works that are anti-Jewish.

b. The New Testament's apparently harsh language against the Jews is not anti-Judaism at all but simply prophetic rebuke out of love. Just as the Hebrew prophets of old, reprimanding the Israelites in their day, are surely not to be judged anti-Jewish, neither then should Jesus' criticisms of Jews be so construed. Diatribes against the Jews—whether by Jesus or Paul—were only a kind of oratorical style or a literary device intended not to be final but merely to shock people into repentance before it was too late.

c. The gospels and the book of Acts show us, approvingly, thousands of Jews accepting Jesus' message, or at least eager to hear what he had to say. How then, when the New Testament so *approvingly* presents so many Jews so positively disposed, can modern Jews consider it anti-Jewish?

d. Though, in subsequent eras, Christian theology did evolve along anti-Jewish lines, this later orientation toward Jews should not be confused with that in the New Testament itself, where such bias is not evident, even latent. Denunciations of Jews by church fathers, especially in the third century and following, were a function of a time long after the New Testament was completed, when Christian preachers were forging new weapons for the church in the church's ongoing conflict with Judaism. Interpreting the sacred gospel, the church fathers added their own errors and prejudices against Jews to the holy, eternal, and infallible truths of the New Testament itself. Thus, it is misunderstandings by *later* Christian interpreters which must be confronted, not sentiments of the New Testament writers themselves.

ASSESSING AVENUE #1

This first category of approach—*denying* as it does that the New Testament is anti-Jewish—strikes me as serving no constructive purpose; well-intentioned as it may be, it nevertheless depends on arguments which, from a Jewish point of view, are simply not compelling:

a. Respecting the first argument advanced—that the New Testament reflects the ultimate revelation of divine love—I do not wish to respond insensitively. But since Jews do not include the New Testament among their sacred texts, any argument proceeding, as if self-evidently, from the New Testament's divine inspiration is not seen as persuasive. Moreover, that Jesus himself spoke this language of love hardly guarantees that all those committed to him (including the later gospel authors) did so as well.

b. I welcome the second argument, that the admittedly harsh language against the Jews in the gospels, Acts, and Paul's epistles is only prophetic rebuke out of love. But I also experience a nagging sense that these reprimands far exceed any rebuke I know of by the Hebrew prophets of old. After all, were not the prophets acting out of love for and loyalty to the Jewish people, with their message designed to *solidify* the covenantal bonds between God and the Jewish people? Yet many censures of Jews in the New Testament predict that God will choose *others* to replace them! While Jesus himself may well have scolded some fellow Jews out of love, the particular intensity and animosity characterizing rebukes attributed to him by the gospels most likely reflect interjections by the gospel authors themselves, not the sentiments of the historical Jesus personally. And given the prominence of this editorial element, the New Testament, while sacred to Christianity, is nonetheless unavoidably to be construed as *itself* anti-Jewish.

c. How should we address the argument that, since it represents approvingly so many Jews as having accepted or at least having been open to Jesus, the New Testament cannot itself, therefore, be considered anti-Jewish? While the gospels, Acts and Pauline epistles are not biased against *all* Jews, they are biased against Jews not accepting Jesus. Not biased against Christian Jews (those accepting Jesus as the "messiah," or "Christ"), they *are* biased against *non*-Christian Jews. Since, in terms of Jewish theology, a Jew who professes belief in Jesus as the messiah has thereby, by definition, become a Christian—and is no longer a Jew[5]—in effect the only persons mentioned in the gospels with whom modern Jews can readily identify is with those not accepting Jesus, and the New Testament *is* hostile toward these Jews. It *is* therefore anti-Jewish.

d. In terms of the fourth argument cited—that anti-Jewish stereotypes originated in later Christian theology but not in or with the New Testament itself—my own reading of New Testament texts leaves me unpersuaded by the argument for this defense. I still feel that the four evangelists themselves have conveyed anti-Jewish sentiment in the very process of describing Jesus' ministry in their gospels.

AVENUE #2—THE NEW TESTAMENT'S ANTI-JEWISHNESS IS ACKNOWLEDGED, BUT MAINLY IN TERMS THAT TEND TO MINIMIZE ITS IMPORTANCE OR OTHERWISE EXPLAIN IT AWAY

Christians espousing this general approach, while acknowledging the New Testament's anti-Judaism, hope nonetheless to reduce its impact. They offer a variety of mitigating interpretations, or suggest a number of extenuating circumstances, which make that bias appear to be of only minor consequence. Their intent is to induce Jews to feel less offended by New Testament texts, and to move Christians themselves to take these texts less seriously. Arguments reflecting this position are quite varied, and not necessarily consistent with one another:

a. The Christian scriptures were hardly unique in attacking opponents; other religious or philosophical literatures of that age partook of this same tendency, and New Testament polemics even turn out to be relatively *mild* by comparison. This realization may help blunt any current-day effects of the New Testament's rhetoric by robbing it of "its capacity for mischief"[6]—since now Jews as well as Christians, identifying these diatribes as but the convention of a bygone era, will be able to dismiss them as inconsequential for the modern day.

b. It would be beneficial if Jews apprised themselves of the polemical nature of their *own* ancient literature! The Hebrew Bible itself, for example, abounds in condemnation of Israel's enemies. The first century Jewish historian Josephus, meanwhile, considers hostile Gentiles "frivolous and utterly senseless specimens of humanity,"[7] and caricatures his opponent, Apion, for having "the mind of an ass and the impudence of a dog, which his countrymen are wont to worship."[8] The first century Jewish philosopher Philo terms his Gentile opponents in Egypt "a seed bed of evil in whose souls both the venom and the temper of the native crocodiles and wasps are reproduced."[9] Moreover, rabbinic literature as well engages in considerable invective, directed even—it should be noted—against Christians and Christianity! In fact, if Jews themselves had ever become a majority presence, would not anti-Christian sentiment, imbedded within their own tradition, have occasioned the same kind of predicament for *them* vis-à-vis Christians as is now faced by Christians vis-à-vis Jews?

c. Also constructive would be the realization that authors of New Testament writings were not consciously contributing to a new corpus of scripture. In their day, their only Bible, recognized or envisioned, was the *Jewish* Bible. Had they imagined the importance their writings might someday assume, or surmised the detrimental effect of a "New" Testament on the Jewish people, such authors—themselves good Christians—may well have been more judicious in their presentations of Jews.

d. Anti-Judaism, moreover, hardly began with the New Testament since Jews had already become negatively perceived by many pagans well before these writings even emerged. This suggests that influxes of pagans into Christianity may have played a significant role in the introduction of anti-Jewish bias into Christian traditions. Thus, while the New Testament's anti-Judaism may now be admitted, its substantial origin *outside* Christianity should also now be more widely acknowledged—in the hope both of lessening resentment toward the New Testament among modern Jews and of weakening the attachment of modern Christians to prejudices so at variance with truly Christian ethics.

e. Conceivably, Jews whom the New Testament attacked were not all "the Jews" but only a *segment* of them, or perhaps even a group *outside* them altogether! When Jesus denounced the Pharisees, for example, he may have been targeting only a minority of "hypocrites" amongst them—or only the disciples of Shammai.[10] Alternatively, what appear to be anti-Judaic diatribes could actually have been rebukes only of particular Christians called "Judaizers."[11] Whichever the case, *modern* Jews, themselves akin neither to disreputable Pharisees nor to partisans of Shammai, and still less to Christian Judaizers, need in no way feel attacked by New Testament censures which only inadvertently became misapplied to them. And all the more so, therefore, should modern Christians understand that Jesus' and Paul's criticisms were in no sense applicable to all Jews of the first century, still less to those of later times.

f. The most formidable argument falling within this general approach offers an alternative way of viewing matters. The apparent anti-Jewish polemic in the New Testament was actually only *intra*-Jewish: admittedly intense, it was nevertheless only "in-house squabbling" between one segment of Jews (who had accepted Christianity) over against another (who had not). If what appears to be anti-Jewish rhetoric is thus merely recorded argument against those within the *same* family, then those scolding the Jews turn out still to be Jews *themselves*—with their condemnations therefore ceasing to be *anti*-Jewish in any meaningful sense.

ASSESSING AVENUE #2

The sentiments of this second approach also are well-intentioned. But do they effectively address our problem? Several arguments strike me as not genuinely relevant; and some, possibly relevant, may be unfounded.

a. Yes, the New Testament's invective was hardly unique; perhaps it was even relatively mild. But how many Christians today are sufficiently conversant with the conventions of ancient polemic to bring them to bear in an evaluation of the New Testament's anti-Judaism? Moreover, for Christians the New Testament, in sharp distinction from most other ancient writings, is *sacred* literature: as such, its polemics, whether comparatively tame or not, command authority as the inspired word of God. This sanctified status of their scripture accords its censures of Jews a compelling quality, and thus more than compensates for what is supposedly the *comparative* mildness of its anti-Judaism.

b. Yes, Jews too were certainly polemical in their own literature and should at the least consider whether, had they themselves become dominant in history, a Christian minority might not have suffered accordingly. But conjecture must pale before reality: Christianity, not Judaism, has been dominant, and Jews the victims of persecution fueled and justified by recourse to New Testament texts.

c. Yes, New Testament writers may have been unaware that their criticisms of Jews would become enshrined in a new corpus of scripture. To suggest, however, that such an awareness would have induced them to abstain from abusive language, or at least to tone it down, is again conjectural, and not relevant to realities at hand.

d. Yes, Jews were disliked by other peoples even prior to the rise of Christianity. Yet, for most Christian readers, would not such an awareness tend to *universalize* the New Testament's polemic rather than neutralize it? Arguing that other peoples (prior to and independent of Christians) also disapproved of Jews may have the unintentional effect of reinforcing if not validating the New Testament's prejudice by seeming to suggest that it was somehow justified or warranted.

e. Were the New Testament's rebukes against Jews actually directed only against a minority among them, or even persons outside them altogether? I am unconvinced. Even if correct, however, such speculation would render us little assistance in coping with the modern-day effects of these censures which especially after centuries of Christian preaching are still often *heard* today as attacks on *all* Jews of the first century (if not now as well).

f. Finally, I must take issue with the "in-house squabbling" argument which is sufficiently crucial to this discussion to require, at this juncture, an extended treatment.

Scholars holding to this theory usually accept the testimony of the book of Acts, which would have us believe that *early* Christianity had been swelled by "myriads" (literally, "tens of thousands"[12]) of Jews. This huge number of Jewish entrants feeds—or renders more plausible—the idea that, even in the post-70 era when the gospels were being composed, anti-Jewish polemics could have been essentially only "in-house" rebukes by one segment of Jews (accepting Christianity) against others (rejecting it). Gospel writers, assigned by this theory to the former category, would thus turn out to be polemicizing only against *fellow* Jews.

In responding, I feel that we must first dispense with one preliminary: at the least, let us not be misled by the *titles* of the gospels. While persons named Mark, Matthew, and John may indeed have been among Jesus' *Jewish*[13] contemporaries back around 30 c.e.,[14] these (together with Luke[15]) were not the actual authors of gospels written and ascribed to them so many years later. The four gospels apparently circulated initially as *anonymous* writings. Only belatedly, probably in the second century, did they come to be incorrectly attributed to contemporaries of Jesus.[16] Since we do not know the identity of the actual authors, certainly any names of *Jews* assigned to the gospel titles should not be enlisted in support of the "in-house squabbling" argument alleging that the gospels were written *by* Jews against *other* Jews. For some, possibly even all, of the actual authors could have been Gentiles themselves (i.e. of no Jewish extraction or affiliation)—and anti-Jewish ones at that.[17]

As for the "myriads" of Jews claimed originally to have joined Christianity's ranks, this is myth, not history. Paul's own epistles, dating from the 40s into the 60s, are not only far earlier than Acts (ca. the late 80s), but emanate from the very time frame when Acts insists "myriads" of Jews had *already* flocked to Christianity. Yet Paul advances a radically different assessment of Christian demography, expressing disappointment that so *few* Jews (only "a remnant" [Rom 11:5]) had become Christian. Most "were hardened" (2 Cor 3:14), resisting Christ and not attaining righteousness (Rom 9:31–33); "not enlightened" (10:2); a "contrary people" (10:21) who, in a "stupor," neither "see" nor "hear . . . *down to this very day*" (11:8; italics added), branches "broken off because of their unbelief" (11:20). Hence, Christianity's successful inroads, as early as Paul's own day, were already predominantly among *Gentiles*, hardly Jews.

Paul's statements should caution readers to be wary of Acts' alternative statistics and should prompt the question: Where is the huge critical mass of *Jewish-Christians* necessary to sustain the theory that the anti-Judaism of the post-70 gospels was only "*in*-house squabbling"? After 70 C.E., Christianity was no longer "in" the Jewish house at all—the "church" had severed itself from the "synagogue," with the Jewish revolt of 66–70 C.E. playing a crucial role in culminating this process (see below). Since the reality is that only relatively few Jews had become Christian at *any* time, surely the truth to be stressed is "not that some [Jews] accepted [the gospel], but that many rejected it," and that to "overemphasise the references to the conversion of the Jews . . . [is to get] hold of the wrong end of the stick."[18] The "in-house squabbling" argument, therefore, convenient and even comforting as it may be, is in my view simply not soundly-based.[19]

AVENUE #3—THE NEW TESTAMENT'S ANTI-JEWISHNESS IS RECOGNIZED AS A SERIOUS PROBLEM REQUIRING FULL CONFRONTATION

I personally not only espouse this third, remaining avenue of approach, but also believe the other approaches have now, regrettably, become part of our dilemma—for their orientation actually impedes our understanding of *why* the New Testament came to be anti-Jewish and our determination of how best to *cope* with this problem today. The remainder of this chapter is devoted to these two questions.

VI. WHY THE NEW TESTAMENT CAME TO BE ANTI-JEWISH

A GENERAL DYNAMIC

The New Testament may have *had* to be anti-Jewish. A new religion (Christianity), developing from its mother (Judaism) and wishing to establish a viable separateness, needed to justify its existence, and such self-justification actually necessitated expressions of negativity toward the parent. Especially since Christianity drew so heavily upon Judaism in terms of its ethics, scripture, and liturgy, as well as some of its theological teachings, would not the question naturally have surfaced: given Judaism, why Christianity?

One response by early Christians was a claim that *they* had supplanted the Jews in God's favor, that they had become the "new" Israel. Accordingly, for Christianity now to justify its worth, Judaism somehow had to be shown as possessing *less* value, and whatever value it was granted had to be explained as only a function of God's plan in preparing the world for *Christianity*. Since such a natural dynamic actually *required* Christian writers to express anti-Jewish sentiments, we should interpret many New Testament passages as precisely what they *appear* to be: namely, anti-Jewish. To deny the problem (Avenue #1) or even mitigate it (Avenue #2) thus becomes misleading, or at the least counter-productive.

SOME SPECIFIC DYNAMICS

We may surmise, as well, three more specific reasons why the New Testament came to be anti-Jewish:

(a) By insisting not only that Jesus was the messiah or "Christ," but also that others should agree, Christians inevitably became embroiled in acrimonious debate with *Jewish* adversaries, especially Pharisees, whose objections to the Christian message were sufficiently disconcerting to necessitate point-by-point refutations. As a vehicle for conveying and preserving these Christian rebuttals, stories arose of alleged controversies between Jesus and various Jewish leaders ("Pharisees," "scribes," "Sadducees," etc.), traditions which eventually achieved incorporation into the gospels themselves.

What is striking to realize, however, is that the early Christians mistakenly came to assume that their own immediate problems with Jewish opponents, for the most part *first* arising only in the decades *subsequent* to Jesus' death, had instead actually originated *during* his ministry itself, and that the answers to these problems were therefore discoverable in *his* words. That is to say, Christians naturally imagined that their omniscient Christ had anticipated all possible objections potentially confronting his followers after his death, and had therefore bequeathed to these followers the very responses they should emulate in disarming their critics. This explains why, later on in the gospels themselves, we find that harsh words silencing Jewish opponents—first surfacing only with the developing Christian tradition—are instead now attributed to *Jesus personally*, even though the issues being argued arose only after he died, and concerning them, in my view, the historical Jesus had no advance awareness.

By thus gaining inclusion in the gospels themselves, such depictions of Jesus vanquishing Jewish opponents generated the ineradicable image of his aversion to fellow Jews, and in this fashion markedly contributed to the New Testament's anti-Judaism. For centuries of later Christians, having no reason to question the authenticity of these gospel confrontations, naturally accepted what were heavily fictionalized[20] exchanges at face value instead. Thereby, they grew to dislike not only those Jews who had allegedly harassed Jesus himself, but also those who continued to vex generations of his later followers down to their own day.

What were these objections that Jews lodged against Christianity? In the main, they were attempts to refute claims of Jesus' messianic identity, and included the following: that Jesus had in no way resembled the *triumphant* messiah expected to overthrow Rome—his crucifixion therefore only *dis*confirmed his credentials (cf. Mk 15:29ff);[21] that Elijah, the herald of the Christ's coming, had yet to appear (cf. Mk 9:11);[22] that the messiah was not expected to come from *Galilee* (cf. Jn 7:41, 52), as did Jesus, who was neither born in Bethlehem of Judea, King David's birthplace,[23] nor was himself a Davidic descendant (cf. Jn 7:41–43; Mk 12:35–37); and that Jesus himself[24] had broken with the law of Moses, thereby abandoning the very essence of Judaism (cf. Mk 7:19; Jn 9:16; Acts 6:13ff). As for Jesus' resurrection, crucial to Christianity, Jews denied its occurrence, and dismissed the claim of the empty tomb as a hoax (cf. Mt 28:13–15).[25]

Naturally, given the Christian authorship, each gospel debate was resolved in favor of the Christian viewpoint (just as, in the writings of the pro-Pharisee and pro-Hillel rabbis, Pharisees out-debated Sadducees and the school of Hillel that of Shammai). But the net effect of the controversy traditions, as far as centuries of later Christian readers and churchgoers were concerned, was an overwhelming impression of a relentless anti-Judaism on the part of Jesus himself.

(b) A second factor productive of the New Testament's anti-Judaism was the emergence of severe tension between Christianity and *Rome,* a problem which the church found it most expedient to address by assuming an *anti-Jewish* stance. In 64 C.E., Emperor Nero had initiated a brutal persecution of Christians, whom he made scapegoats for a fire in Rome. Shortly thereafter, in 66 C.E., Jews in Judea launched a major revolt. This extraordinary act of sedition raised the ominous specter of Roman vengeance not only against Jews but against *Christians* as well. For in the eyes of Rome, the two were often confused since Christianity, arising from Judaism, perpetuated so many of its beliefs, teachings and practices. When the Jews revolted, therefore, it became imperative for Christians to distinguish themselves from Jews in such a way that Christians would also appear to be the allies of *Rome,* and in this fashion be able to deter any further persecution of Christians at Roman hands.

The major hurdle, however, was that Jesus had been *crucified,* a Roman punishment meted out notably to subversives. A crucified Jesus inevitably invited speculation that not only had Christianity's founder and Lord been himself a seditionist,[26] but that this same stigma adhered to his later followers as well.

Faced, then, with the urgency of establishing Jesus' loyalty, Christian tradition could hardly depict *Rome* as culpable in Jesus' execution. Responsibility had to be shifted, assigned to some other party. In view of the later antipathy being directed at Christianity by the Jewish community, it is not surprising that Jewish leaders (and, ultimately, "the Jews") became saddled with the blame in *substitution* for Rome—especially since Jewish opposition to later Christians was easily assumed to have originated as opposition to Jesus himself. This replacement of Rome by "the Jews" was accomplished through a literary device—a fictional trial of Jesus before the Roman governor—wherein the normally ruthless Pontius Pilate (symbolizing Roman officialdom) was now presented as actually desiring Jesus' exoneration but forced instead to yield to pressure *by the Jews* to crucify him.[27] Complementing this picture was the introduction of various other traditions suggesting harmony, or at least compatibility, between Jesus and Rome,[28] along with the story of another fictional, but earlier, trial in which Jesus had been condemned by judges of a specifically *Jewish* sanhedrin.[29] When viewed against the backdrop of the great Jewish revolt (66–70 C.E.), the sum effect of all these factors was to ally Christians with Rome, and to present the Jews as the enemies of *both.* Thus, paradoxically, did a Jew put to death by Romans become, instead, a Christian put to death by Jews.

(c) As previously mentioned in another connection, prejudice against Jews had already existed in *pagan* circles even prior to Christianity's emergence; accordingly, Gentiles entering Christian ranks may naturally have brought this antecedent bias into Christianity along with them. The reasons for such prejudice were varied: Jews in the Diaspora (lands outside Palestine) understandably tended to settle together, set apart from, rather than interspersed among, Gentiles;

this apparent unsociability intensified xenophobia, fear or dislike of foreigners (both of Jews, by Gentiles; and of Gentiles, by Jews). Not to go unmentioned, of course, was the Jews' refusal to worship the gods of the Greco-Roman pantheon, even though the God of Israel had received hospitable welcome. In addition, Jews observed what struck others as bizarre customs: circumcision, for example, and seemingly curious dietary laws; these only alienated them further in the eyes of some outsiders. One can well imagine, moreover, that whatever preferential treatment Jews received from Rome[30] only aggravated Gentile resentment.

The Jewish revolt of 66–70 C.E. must itself have played a profound role in intensifying this antipathy and thereby in stimulating anti-Judaism in gospel traditions. The auxiliary forces Rome drafted to crush the revolt in Judea were drawn from neighboring regions, particularly Syria. Many Gentile recruits died in putting down what their families probably considered only a needless disturbance by a fanatic upstart people. The casualties sustained fanned hatred of Jews especially by natives of Antioch, Syria's major city, which had a large Jewish population.[31] Josephus informs us that Jews in Antioch were harassed, even murdered, by Gentiles, who libeled them, spread rumors of Jewish plots, and asked the Roman general Titus to expel Jews, or at least revoke their privileges.[32]

With Gentile passions in Antioch now so inflamed against anyone Jewish, whether Jews per se or Christians of Jewish extraction, the latter must have realized how precarious it was to be viewed by others as still having *Jewish* ties. They may therefore have sensed it expedient to shed Jewish associations and instead to submerge their identity within Antioch's *Gentile*-Christian Church—whose members no doubt harbored some of the same anti-Jewish biases then typifying Antioch's wider Gentile community. These considerations may largely explain the extreme anti-Jewish bitterness permeating the gospel of Matthew, produced, I believe, in Antioch's Gentile-Christian community in the 80s.[33]

VII. COPING WITH THIS PROBLEM TODAY

It was Nazi exploitation of Christian anti-Judaism which first drove home to many modern Christians the critical need to confront their scripture, stimulating in turn not only a large number of church declarations disavowing anti-Semitism, but also hundreds of books and essays on the problem. Several noteworthy contributions deserve special mention, even within the confines of this brief chapter.

The Second Vatican Council's *Declaration on Non-Christian Religions* in 1965 delineated specific dimensions of biblical and theological study requiring revision, with the particular end in view of enhancing of Catholic-Jewish relations. Roman Catholics (and, by extension, all Christians) were now urged to recognize the Jewish ancestry of Jesus, his mother, and closest followers; to understand Christian faith in terms of its continuity with Judaism rather than its displacement of it; to realize that Jesus' death, as recorded in the gospels, should not be blamed upon all Jews then living, without distinction, nor upon Jews of today;[34] to view Jewish scripture in such a way that it not seem to espouse only legalism, fear, and justice devoid of love of God and humanity; and generally to achieve familiarity with how Jews themselves understand their own Bible and religion.

Rosemary Ruether's seminal volume, *Faith and Fratricide*,[35] published in 1974, is still considered by many the most important impetus in bringing Christians and Jews to their current state of progress in Christian-Jewish dialogue. Ruether argued that the presence of anti-Jewish bias in the New Testament is blatant and undeniable, and asked us to believe, moreover, that this bitter dialectic of christology and anti-Judaism is rooted not simply in the period of the gospels' composition (after 70 C.E.), but rather far earlier, in the days of Christianity's very emergence. (Also controversial was her conjecture that Jesus' disciples, mortified by their abandonment of him, had compensated for their sense of guilt by projecting blame upon the Jewish authorities instead.)

Christians view the New Testament as sacred, but does this sanctity inhere in the texts themselves or rather with the *interpreters* thereof? Some religious outlooks profess to root their sole authority in what their scriptures say: yet in practice they rely additionally on a tradition of interpretation that clarifies how these texts are to be understood, and prioritizes them in terms of importance. What has often resulted in the history of religions is that sacred written texts do not actually command in practice the degree of authority laid claim to by the texts themselves. As applied to the topic at hand, the *influence* of New Testament passages biased against Jews could well be more a function of what modern Christian interpreters will *allow* than of the scriptural texts in and of themselves.

Many Christians recognize that the Bible ("Old" and New Testament together) expresses some attitudes that, in the modern day, seem quite objectionable—e.g. passages endorsing animal sacrifices, condoning slavery, maligning homosexuals, or demeaning women. Yet despite their genuine presence in the Bible itself, such views are usually routinely ignored by many Christians who, not feeling constrained by *these* attitudes, could likewise be induced to dispense with the New Testament's anti-Judaism as well.

Posing the matter differently, what should be done when we encounter a conflict between sacred literature and religious *values?* Many interpreters of Matthew, for example, have asserted that included among the sacred values of Christianity are the mandates to turn the other cheek and to love one's enemies (5:39, 44). What, then, do we do with the text, found in the same gospel, which presents Jesus assailing the Pharisees as children of hell (cf. Mt 23:15)? A sacred image in Christianity is often said to be a "God of *love*": how is this to maintain itself alongside a prophecy that a wrathful God will destroy *Jerusalem to avenge the Jews' rejection* of Jesus (Mt 22:7)? Does there not devolve upon interpreters of Christian values a responsibility to declare anti-Jewish passages devalued?

Undoubtedly, the most formidable obstacle we face is unawareness on the part of the Christian laity of the role of *historical conditioning* in the formation of the New Testament's anti-Jewish passages. I have consistently argued that developments reflecting decades well after Jesus death were stimuli of anti-Judaism erroneously attributed to Jesus personally. *The anti-Jewish Jesus who emerges from the gospels is thus the product of writers who conceptualized him in the light of what had become their own anti-Jewish orientation, often a function in turn of whatever such views were current among their own constituencies.* In this fashion, emphases and attitudes in no way congenial to Jesus came to be associated with him. And it was to this retrojected gospel image of Jesus that Jews of later generations inevitably responded in kind, feeding a spiral of negative interchange between Christian and Jew over the centuries. This is why it is vital that modern readers of the gospels come to understand that the historical Jesus and the Jesus of the gospels are simply not one and the same. Reminiscent of a painting overlaid by later retouchings, or of two movie projectors showing simultaneously on the same screen, what we have in the gospels is one Jesus-image superimposed upon another.

VIII. CONCLUSION

It is important for Christians to recognize that while Jews today may urge changes[36] and new understandings, Jews cannot themselves do anything by way of actual implementation other than appeal to Christians of good will. For anti-Judaism, as much as it has affected Jews, is, in one major sense, not a *Jewish* problem but a *Christian* problem: only Christians, not Jews, can genuinely undertake the measures necessary to resolve it.

Nor will devising these means be easy. Several years ago, for example, I was invited to participate with a group of well-meaning Christians who intended to retranslate the New Testament so as to delete its anti-Jewish elements. Since I sensed this should be a *Christian* enterprise only. I felt it inappropriate for me personally to participate. But I also expressed my doubts about the wisdom of attempting erasures from what is deemed by most Christians *sacred* scripture.

Most assuredly, the scratches marring the history of Jew and Christian with one another can never be erased, regardless of how well-meaning the intent. Our task, rather, seizing the opportunity, accepting history for what it has been, is to fashion from our scars something redemptive. It is my hope that the foregoing analysis may contribute in some way to the transformation of our wounds into a positive resolve—a commitment, from now on, for joint endeavor in hastening the day when "the Lord shall be one and the Lord's name one" (Zec 14:9).

Notes

1. Scriptural citations follow *The Oxford Annotated Bible with the Apocrypha: Revised Standard Version* (New York: Oxford University Press, 1965).

2. Even though Jesus may well have been a Pharisee himself; cf. my essay. "Jesus and the Pharisees: The Problem As It Stands Today," *Journal of Ecumenical Studies* 15 (1978): 441–60.

3. Cf. Wolfgang Seiferth, *Synagogue and Church in the Middle Ages,* trans. by Lee Chadeayne and Paul Gottwald (New York: Frederick Ungar, 1970).

4. Cf. R. Po-chia Hsia, *The Myth of Ritual Murder* (New Haven: Yale University Press, 1988).

5. Cf. Dennis Prager, "Is There Such a Thing as a 'Jew for Jesus'?" *Ultimate Issues* 5 (1989): 6–7; also my article, "Anti-Judaism in the New Testament," *Union Seminary Quarterly Review* 38 (1983): 135, n.2.

6. Quoted from Luke Johnson's insightful essay, "The New Testament's Anti-Jewish Slander and the Conventions of Ancient Polemic," *Journal of Biblical Literature* 108(1989): 441. He suggests (pp. 434–35) the examples cited below, nn. 7–9.

7. *Against Apion* 1.25 §225–6; trans. by Henry St. John Thackeray, *Josephus* (Cambridge: Harvard University Press, 1926).

8. Ibid. 2.7 §86.

9. *Embassy to Gaius* 26.166.

10. An apparently arrogant teacher whose views were criticized later in the literature of rabbinic Judaism itself, where he is often contrasted with his contemporary, Hillel, reputed to have personified patience and loving-kindness.

11. These elicited the scorn of some fellow Christians for insisting that Gentiles accepting Christianity should nonetheless "live like Jews," as, e.g., by accepting the Mosaic law as binding and incorporating Jewish observances into the practice of their Christian faith.

12. "Myriads" literally means "tens of thousands," but some scholars understand the term as "thousands" only. Cf. Acts 2:41; 4:4; 5:14; 6:7; 21:20.

13. Church tradition considers Mark to have been Peter's (Jewish) interpreter and associate in Rome, and locates Matthew within Jesus' inner circle of twelve Jewish followers. *John is also often identified as among the twelve.*

14. "C.E." ("common era") is a more inclusive formulation than "A.D." (*anno Domini*, "in the year of our Lord"), a Christian theological term.

15. Luke is usually identified as Paul's (Gentile) physician.

16. Cf. Norman Perrin, *The Resurrection According to Matthew, Mark, and Luke* (Philadelphia: Fortress, 1977), p.x: "All the [gospels] were written and circulated anonymously. Names were attributed to them only in later ecclesiastical tradition."

17. This could have been the case even with the author of Matthew, the gospel most frequently cited as "Jewish"; cf. my article, "Interpreting 'Pro-Jewish' Passages in Matthew," *Hebrew Union College Annual* 54 (1983): 135–47.

18. Stephen Wilson, *The Gentiles and the Gentile Mission in Luke-Acts* (Cambridge: At the University Press, 1973), pp. 232–33.

19. Why then does Acts exaggerate the number of Jews joining early Christianity? The author was disturbed by the anomaly that, while Jesus' preaching naturally extended the essence of *Judaism,* Jews affirming Christianity in the author's day (ca. the late 80s) were embarrassingly few. How explain that Christianity's intuitively obvious truths had been rejected by those most expected to have intuited them? His explanation: while Christianity's truths were not perceived by Jews in his own late day, by no means had they been lost on Jews of a bygone age; for when Christianity had first emerged, Jewish entrants had numbered even in the (tens of) thousands! Only subsequently, upon beginning to experience rebuffs by Jews, did Christian missionaries turn to Gentiles instead; and it was their phenomenal success among Gentiles that accounted for the disconcertingly high percentage of Gentile-Christians in the church of the author's own day. Cf. my chapter, *"The Mission to the Jews* in Acts: Unraveling Luke's 'Myth of the "Myriads,"'* "in *Luke-Acts and the Jewish People: Eight Critical Perspectives,* edited by Joseph Tyson (Minneapolis: Augsburg, 1988), pp. 102–03, 152–58.

20. I am not denying that Jesus engaged in controversies with religious opponents, only that the gospels can be confidently used to confirm *specific* disputations during his ministry, reconstruct their *exact* substance, or even identify *precise* disputants. See my volume, *Mark's Treatment of the Jewish Leaders* (Leiden: Brill, 1978), pp. 15–28.

21. Rejoinders by the church, attesting that Jews lodged this objection, include: Jesus *expected* execution (Mk 10:33f); he could have prevented it but *chose* not to (Mt 26:53); he died to *fulfill* scripture (Mt 26:54). Stated in more modern terms, the objection would be that Jesus died without bringing the messianic age, typified by an end to war, oppression, and ill-will.

22. The church's attempted solution: cf. 9:13; Mt 17:13.

23. His birth was later assigned to Bethlehem to neutralize this Jewish objection. Cf. Raymond Brown, *The Birth of the Messiah* (Garden City: Doubleday, 1979), pp. 412ff., and Appendices 3 and 7; Howard Teeple, "The Historical Beginnings of the Resurrection Faith," *Studies in New Testament and Early Christian Literature: Essays in Honor of Allen P. Wikgren,* edited by David Aune (Leiden: Brill, 1972), p. 109.

24. Jews did not realize that it was developing Christianity (not Jesus) which broke with the law and then attributed the break to Jesus. The oft-cited, "Think not that I have come to abolish the law . . ." (Mt 5:17ff), is not relevant here; this reflects not words of Jesus but rather of *Matthew,* who casts Jesus as a lawgiver modeled on Moses.

25. They alleged that the disciples had stolen the body and proclaimed it resurrected. Matthew's reaction was to insist that a stone had been sealed and a guard set (27:66; cf. 28:11ff.), so an undetected theft was impossible. John responded by having the resurrected Jesus standing near the tomb (20:14ff). The empty tomb tradition is unmentioned and, I submit, unknown by Paul. Since the author of Mark (unlike that of Matthew) seems unaware of Jewish rebuttals, the story must have *first* surfaced either with Mark himself (ca. 70), or only shortly before him. This means that, while early Christians believed in Jesus' resurrection, they did not do so initially on the basis of any empty tomb tradition, which only originated as a Christian response to Jews and possibly others denying Jesus' bodily resurrection.

26. The gospels themselves may inadvertently preserve tell-tale clues of Jesus' possible subversive image: his "cleansing" of the temple (which must have involved *some* militancy); his followers' possession of weapons (on a holiday, no less; cf. Lk 22:36ff); his crucifixion between seditionists (the Greek, *lestes,* meaning, in this context, "seditionist," not "thief"); the title atop the cross: "king of the Jews" (worded from Rome's perspective and indicating that sedition, not "blasphemy" [Mk 14:64], was the actual reason for Jesus' arrest).

27. That this trial is fictional is accepted by many scholars today, especially after their recourse to Tacitus, Josephus, and Philo, ancient sources attesting to Pilate's ruthlessness and to his execution of opponents without trials.

28. E.g. Jesus' dicta, "render to Caesar the things that are Caesar's" (Mk 12:17) and "all who take the sword will perish by the sword" (Mt 26:52)—whether originating with Jesus or not—became useful in persuading Rome of Jesus' harmlessness and in downplaying any suggestion of his incompatibility with Roman interests.

29. Such sanhedrins could be legally convened by Jewish leaders only with the Roman governor's express consent (Josephus, *Antiq.* 20:197–203). The gospels present us with a fiction that the Jewish leaders, here in the case of Jesus, acted *independently.* The intent of this tradition was at least threefold: to show that the Jews arrested and tried Jesus without Rome's direction; to demonstrate that Jesus was formally condemned only by a specifically *Jewish* body; and to substitute "blasphemy," a non-significant offense in Roman eyes, for "sedition," the actual reason for Jesus' crucifixion (by Rome).

30. Jews were excused from participation in the cult of the emperor and could both administer their own funds (including export of dues to the Jerusalem temple) and settle their own legal affairs in civil suits involving one Jew against another. Some correctional authority may also have been conceded their communal leaders. Additionally, Jews were exempted from military service and court appearances on the sabbath. Cf. my article, "Judaism, Hellenistic," *The Interpreter's Dictionary of the Bible* Suppl. Vol. (Nashville: Abingdon, 1976), pp. 505–06.

31. Conjectured today at having been anywhere between 22,000 and 45,000.

32. *The Jewish War* 2 & 7.

33. Cf. "Interpreting 'Pro-Jewish' Passages."

34. Even this much-heralded statement, however, leaves gospel depictions essentially unchallenged since Roman involvement still goes unmentioned and Jesus' death remains solely the responsibility of Jews (only *fewer* of them).

35. Rosemary Ruether, *Faith and Fratricide: The Theological Roots of Anti-Semitism* (New York: Seabury, 1974).

36. I myself would urge the following: scriptural selections read in church should not contain anti-Jewish verses, and sermons vilifying Pharisees should no longer be preached; publishers of Christian textbooks should: (1) strip their texts of anti-Jewish material; (2) introduce positive treatments about aspects of Judaism mentioned in the gospels (e.g. Jewish holidays such as Passover, institutions such as the synagogue, and teachings such as the *Shema* [Mk 12:29]); (3) introduce positive statements about Judaism of no particular relevance to Christianity (treating, e.g., Judaism's ongoing vitality in the modern world); and (4) indicate the role Christian teachings have played in unsavory periods of Jewish history (e.g. the crusades, pogroms, the Spanish inquisition, expulsions of Jews, the holocaust, etc.).

PART IV

THE RHETORIC OF CLASS

Introductory Comment

When the industrial revolution emerged in many Western European countries during the late eighteenth and early nineteenth centuries, social and political analysts began to critically examine the changing economic stratification within their societies. The earlier feudal system, which had been primarily based on inherited wealth and status, disappeared. In its place emerged the capitalist structure of modern industrial societies, which stratified the population according to economic ownership, occupational prestige, power, educational status, and community status. The earliest and most influential observer of these developments, Karl Marx, argued that capitalist societies created a two-tier system: the owners of the "Means of Production" (the "bourgeoisie") and the "wage laborers" (the "proletariat"). This early, but comprehensive, analysis of class under the conditions of capitalism has been comprehensively criticized and extensively reformulated. The renowned notion—that class divisions in capitalist society develop from the surplus of capital, which, in turn, accumulates because of the system of wage labor and the competition among laborers—remains intellectually influential and politically powerful for understanding national and global dynamics of economic interaction under capitalist conditions.

Since the socio-political movements of the 1960s and early 1970s, which criticized the economic stratification of Western societies as well as the global economic interactions, biblical scholars also began to work on these questions. Researchers, influenced by Latin American liberation theologies, in particular, examined biblical books and chapters for understanding the economic conditions in Israelite society or the early Jesus movement in relation to their own time and place. Perhaps unsurprisingly, much biblical research on these issues emerged in countries outside the United States where discussions on class are often regarded as a taboo subject. The articles in this section on "The Rhetoric of Class" reflect this dynamic. Only three of the nine articles come from American authors, and one of them is written by a Native American scholar. The other six scholars are from Costa Rica, Nicaragua, South Africa, Germany, and Palestine. Although the selection is small due to the limitations of this one-volume anthology, the nine articles introduce major concerns about the reading of the Bible in light of questions on class and economic stratification.

The section is divided into three sets of articles, all of which illustrate, from a range of perspectives, the various discussions on class and the Bible. The first set, entitled "God and the Option for the Poor," includes two essays that examine biblical texts in light of poverty, wealth, and the divinity. The authors of the articles, Elsa Tamez and Jerry Itumeleng Mosala, argue that

God is on the side of the poor. They distinguish between God, as seen by the poor, and God, as seen by the rich, and relate the economic devastation in Third-World countries to biblical interpretation. Illustrating the liberation theological maxim of "God's preferential option for the poor," Elsa Tamez characterizes passages such as Luke 1:46–53 or Ezekiel 22:29 as fundamental criticism of poverty in many Latin American and other Third-World countries. To this Costa Rican scholar, the biblical God opposes rich people because their accumulation of wealth makes other people poor. God sides with the poor and their cause is God's cause.

Jerry Itumeleng Mosala explains why the characterization of the biblical God as "the God of justice" requires an antithetical relationship between the God of the poor and the God of the rich. Relating biblical texts about economic exploitation to the context of the Third World, this South African scholar identifies the liberation struggles of the biblical poor with the struggle of today's poor people everywhere. Both articles invite discussions on economic justice in light of the biblical admonition to eradicate the exploitation and economic oppression from societies everywhere. These articles raise a number of questions: What biblical texts as quoted by Tamez and Mosala support or oppose one's own class affiliation? Why do readers of the Bible in predominately wealthy countries, such as the United States, largely ignore or reject the idea that the biblical God opts for the poor? How does one's religious location silence or marginalize the issue of economic stratification among people, nations, and geographical regions? How can rich people participate in this biblical vision, as described by liberation theologians? What are the complicating factors?

The second set of articles, entitled "Economic Justice as a Biblical Concern," contains four essays that discuss selected biblical passages or books. Jon L. Berquist investigates Amos 5:18–27 in an effort to counter interpretations that see in this passage a call for advancing social justice in society, most famously articulated by Martin Luther King, Jr. Instead, Berquist maintains that the passage makes a statement about God. Justice and righteousness, he argues, are activities accomplished only by God rather than humanity. So, in the case of Amos, the people's inconsistent behavior, most prominently manifested in the contradiction between their worship and their societal behavior, is blasphemous to God and leads to the announcement of destruction. It is, however, God and not the people who restores societal justice and so, ultimately, supports the poor.

James L. Crenshaw focuses on the book of Proverbs and describes the inherent ambiguity of biblical wisdom literature on the issue of poverty and wealth. Accordingly, the analysis of this American scholar demonstrates that many passages in Proverbs express sympathy for the plight of the impoverished whereas other passages consider poverty or wealth as a detriment for spiritual growth. Crenshaw highlights the ambiguous position of the book of Proverbs regarding a person's economic status.

Luise Schottroff discusses the parable of the workers in the vineyard (Matthew 20:1–16) as a depiction about the goodness of God that fosters socio-political, economic, and religious solidarity among human beings. This German author also places the parable into the context of the larger gospel narrative to show that the Matthean community lacked this kind of solidarity, especially toward poor people inside and outside their group.

Jan Botha examines another well-known New Testament passage, Romans 13:1–7, in the context of the South African apartheid system. His article contributes to an understanding of socio-economic oppression in a more general sense than the previous essays. Comparing the historical situation of the Pauline community with the political situation in segregated South Africa, Botha documents that different social locations lead to different interpretations of the same text. Whereas Paul wrote Romans 13:1–7 to encourage Christian congregations of his time to blend into the larger societal hierarchies of the Roman empire, South African liberation theologians called for resistance and confrontation to the apartheid system by quoting the same text.

The four essays discuss specific biblical texts in order to illuminate economic and hierarchical stratification as practiced and theorized in different places and at different times. They raise several questions: What are the advantages and disadvantages of reading biblical texts with economic perspectives in mind? What interpretations seem to pose particularly challenging questions in regard to the contemporary status quo of the economic order? What are the difficulties for conclusively summarizing the biblical position about poverty and wealth?

The fourth set of articles, entitled "Liberation and Oppression in the Book of Exodus," offers three interpretations for one of the best known books in the Bible. Coming from the Latin American, Palestinian, and Native American perspectives, these essays demonstrate very effectively that social location drastically changes the interpretive result, particularly if the interpreter consciously relates context with text. To these three scholars, the issue of political, economic, social, and religious liberation stands in the foreground— although their individual interpretations differ enormously. George V. Pixley identifies the oppression of the ancient Israelites under Egyptian slavery with the oppressed and exploited people in Latin America. To Pixley, the book of Exodus is a story of liberation. Naim Ateek considers the situation of the Canaanites who, according to the biblical narrative, lost their land to the Israelites. Ateek parallels the situation of the Canaanites with the situation of the Palestinians, and so, to him, the Exodus narrative is a story of oppression. Robert Allen Warrior also identifies with the Canaanites, but from the perspective of Native Americans. Warrior postulates that peace and harmonious coexistence will never be realized, as long as the biblical God is simultaneously imagined as a god of liberation and of conquest.

One narrative, three readings—and if there was more space, countless other interpretations would be added. Consequently, this set of articles reinforces one of the most fundamental questions running through this anthology: How can interpretive multiplicity be reconciled with the quest for "truth", without loosing the diversity of views? A simple or quick answer is certainly not in sight, nor would it be desirable. The articles on the book of

Exodus as well as the other essays presented in this anthology give witness to this undeniably complex situation of biblical interpretation, and, in fact, of any interpretation, biblical or not. Is it not true that the wrestling with text *and* world provides an important opportunity to increase one's understanding of the Bible and the world? Indeed, once studied and read carefully, this anthology of biblical scholarship counteracts the popular notion all that is required of readers is to open the Bible and read what the Bible "says." Reading the Bible is unquestionably a much more complicated and intellectually more demanding task than generally recognized.

Christians, Jews, or people of other religious traditions or none, have rarely the chance to consider the complexities and promises of the Bible, not to mention the challenges of biblical interpretation, for their understanding of the world. The section "The Rhetoric of Class" concludes, but does not end, such considerations, demonstrating that biblical discourse has, indeed, much to say about the theory and practice of economic stratification in past and present societies.

Chapter 1

God and the
Option for the Poor

Good News for the Poor

Elsa Tamez

> I bring you good news
> of a great joy which will come
> to all the people [Luke 2:10].

In the first century A.D. the ordinary people of Palestine found themselves in extremely difficult circumstances. Like all Jews they had to pay heavy taxes to the Roman Empire; in addition, they suffered greatly from the inflation that was prevalent from Egypt to Syria. In the cities there was growing unemployment, and slavery was on the increase. For these reasons, slaves and farm workers abandoned their places and formed robber bands to prey on the caravans of traders and pilgrims.[1]

Meanwhile, there was another social class that did not suffer from this situation but, on the contrary, possessed economic and political power in Palestine and profited from inflation. These were the people who formed the council of elders (generally, men from the noble and powerful families), the chief priests, the great landowners, the rich merchants, and others who exercised some political and ideological control (the scribes, Pharisees, Sadducees). This class collaborated with the Roman Empire and acted in ways hostile to the masses of the people. Its members were the open enemies of the Zealots, a guerilla group that wanted to take power and drive out the Romans.[2]

It was in this historical context that the Good News came.

In Latin America there are also great masses of people who live in extremely difficult circumstances. Inflation is a very serious problem in almost all the countries of this part of the Third World, and it is evident that its effects bear most heavily on the masses, that is, the poor.

Other serious problems the poor have to face are unemployment, lack of housing, malnutrition, extreme indigence, exploitation.

On the other hand, there is a group that is small by comparison with the population as a whole, but that nonetheless has great economic and political power. Some in this group exploit the proletariat in order to accumulate capital; others derive great profit by becoming partners in foreign companies or by enabling the latter to operate freely in Latin America.

The ruling class, as in first-century Palestine, collaborates in the expansion of the wealthy nations. Latin American countries governed by the military receive weapons from abroad in order to put down the discontented masses. In some Latin American countries governments favor the entrance of the multinational corporations on the pretext that this will foster industrial development.

At the international level, the economies of the Latin American countries are dependent on foreign nations and are structured according to the interests of the wealthy nations of the world. As everyone knows, these nations see Latin America as a source of raw material and cheap labor.

In such a situation the poor feel oppressed; they are hard put to breathe and stay alive. Extreme poverty and exploitation are killing them. They are forced to rise up and fight for the life of the masses.

At this moment in history good news is urgently needed.

THE GOOD NEWS

The Good News takes a very concrete form. The central message is this: the situation cannot continue as it is; impoverishment and exploitation are not God's will; but now there is hope, resurrection, life, change. The reign of God, which is the reign of justice, is at hand.

We have often been told that the message contained in the Good News is that Christ came into the world to save us or free us from sin. But sin is identified with those actions that society considers immoral; drug taking, adultery, excessive drinking, and so on. Thus the gospel of life is reduced to a simple behavioral change.

But the Good News cannot be so reduced. After all, any non-Christian religion can propose that kind of moral teaching, which amounts to nothing but a set of patches designed to cover over the great sin that lies underneath: oppression at the national and international, the individual and collective levels.

The message of the Good News is of the liberation of human beings from everything and everyone that keeps them enslaved. That is why the Good News brings joy and hope.

Mary, the humble mother of Jesus, sang this song when she visited her cousin Elizabeth:

> My soul magnifies the Lord,
> and my spirit rejoices in God my Savior,
> for he has regarded the low estate of his handmaiden. . . .
> He has shown strength with his arm,
> he has scattered the proud in the imagination of their
>   hearts,
> he has put down the mighty from their thrones,
> and exalted those of low degree;
> he has filled the hungry with good things,
> and the rich he has sent empty away . . . [Luke 1:46–53].

Mary is here speaking not of individuals undergoing moral change but of the restructuring of the order in which there are rich and poor, mighty and lowly (vv. 52–53).

The priest Zechariah likewise saw the Good News as the fulfillment of the promise of liberation:

> Blessed be the Lord God of Israel,
> for he has visited and redeemed his people
> and has raised up a horn of salvation for us. . . .
> as he spoke by the mouth of his holy prophets from of old,
> that *we should be saved from our enemies,*
> *and from the hand of all who hate us* [Luke 1:68–71].

The news is therefore good news to the people; it is a reason for joy and gladness, since it gives the hope of a total change. In Luke 2:10 a messenger of the Lord tells the shepherds: "I bring you good news of a great joy which will come to all the people."

The Good News is evidently not so good for some people. King Herod was deeply concerned when they told him that the king of the Jews had been born. We are told that because he feared to lose his throne he ordered the killing of all children in Bethlehem who were less than two years old (Matt. 2:16).

The shepherds, on the other hand, rejoiced when they heard the News. The shepherds were men who lived in the fields and took turns watching over their flocks at night (Luke 2:10). They enjoyed little respect because they were part of the masses. When they received the Good News, they were glad; they listened to it and shared it with others.

The Good News that speaks of the liberation of the oppressed cannot be pleasing to the oppressors, who want to go on exploiting the poor. But the Good News is indeed good to those who want to change and to see a more just society.

For the most part, those who want to live in a society in which justice and peace reign are those who suffer hunger, oppression, poverty. For this reason the Good News is directed especially to the poor. Jesus himself said so when he read from the Book of Isaiah:

> The Spirit of the Lord is upon me,
> because he has anointed me
> to *preach good news to the poor.*
> He has sent me to proclaim release to the captives
> and recovering of sight to the blind,
> to set at liberty those who are oppressed,
> to proclaim the acceptable year of the Lord.
> [Luke 4:18–19]

Then he added: "Today this scripture has been fulfilled in your hearing" (Luke 4:21).

THE POOR

Knowing, then, that the Good News is addressed especially to the poor, let us reflect on who the poor are and why they are poor.

For many centuries now the biblical passages on the poor have been spiritualized and distorted. Poverty is regarded as a virtue, as an abstract quality that can be attributed to rich and poor alike. As a result, a rich person can be understood to be poor "in spirit," and a poor person rich "in spirit."

The beatitudes that Jesus addressed to the poor have been read as referring to something spiritual. In this distorted view, the "poor in spirit" may be:

1. those who have accepted (material) poverty voluntarily and without protest;
2. those who, though rich, are not proud but rather act humbly before God and their fellows (neither the riches nor the way they have been acquired are an *obstacle* to acting humbly);
3. those who are restless spirits and lack any element of the mystical in their religious outlook.

And yet, when Jesus reads the promise now fulfilled in him: "He anointed me to preach good news to the poor," he is referring to all those who lack the basic necessities of life. When he says: "Blessed are you poor" (Luke 6:20), he is referring to material poverty. The poor in spirit are the "poor of Yahweh," that is, they are the poor and oppressed who acknowledge their poverty, and who stand before God as poor people. In other words, they are not the kind of poor people who think, and try to live, as members of the bourgeoisie.

To sum up: the poor in the Bible are the helpless, the indigent, the hungry, the oppressed, the needy, the humiliated. And it is not nature that has put them in this situation; they have been unjustly impoverished and despoiled by the powerful.

In the Old Testament there are a number of Hebrew words that are often translated by "poor":[3]

1. *'ani* in its most fully developed use describes a situation of inferiority in relation to another. Concretely the *'ani* is one who is dependent. When used in combination with *dal* it describes an economic relationship. The contrary of the *'ani* is the oppressor or user of violence. God is protector of the *'anim* because they are people who have been impoverished through injustice;

2. *dal* is used in two senses: it may refer either to physical weakness or to a lowly, insignificant position in society;

3. *'ebion* often refers to those who are very poor and in a wretched state. Originally it meant someone who asks for alms, a beggar;

4. *rash* is the poor or needy person; its antithesis is the rich person. The social and economic meaning is the prominent one;

5. *misken* means "dependent," a social inferior.

I have listed these Hebrew words with their connotations in order to show that according to almost all of them the poor are individuals who are inferior to the rich or the powerful. Their situation is not the result of chance but is due to the action of oppressors. This point is brought out in many passages of the Bible: "They sell the righteous for silver, and the needy for a pair of shoes—they that trample the head of the poor into the dust of the earth, and turn aside the way of the afflicted" (Amos 2:6–7); "The people of the land [or: the landowners] have practiced extortion and committed robbery; they have oppressed the poor and needy, and have extorted from the sojourner without redress" (Ezek. 22:29).

There is evidently no need to reread the entire Bible in order to discover that poor persons are those who do not have the wherewithal to live because their means have been snatched away.

The authorities, for their part, frequently prove to be on the side of injustice. They close their eyes to the sinful activities of the powerful, and their role is, in fact, to maintain this order of things. Isaiah denounces them: "Your princes are rebels and companions of thieves. . . . They do not defend the fatherless, and the widow's cause does not come to them" (Isa. 1:23).

Orphans and widows were listed among the poor and helpless, because they had no one to defend them and no means of subsistence.

The accumulation of wealth is incompatible with Christianity, since any accumulation of possessions is at the cost of the very poor. The denunciation pronounced by Jeremiah is very clear: "Woe to him who builds his house by unrighteousness, and his upper rooms by injustice; who makes his neighbor serve him for nothing, and does not give him his wages" (Jer. 22:13).

The New Testament also launches a strong attack on those who heap up possessions:

Come now, you rich, weep and howl for the miseries that are coming upon you. Your riches [i.e., hoards] have rotted and your garments are moth-eaten. Your gold and silver have rusted, and their rust will be evidence against you and you will eat your flesh like fire. You have laid up treasure for the last days.

Behold, the wages of the laborers who mowed your fields, which you kept back by fraud, cry out; and the cries of the harvesters have reached the ears of the Lord of hosts. You have lived on the earth in luxury and in pleasure; you have fattened your hearts in a day of slaughter. You have condemned, you have killed the righteous man; he does not resist you [James 5:1–6].

At this point we are in a position to infer two points about the poor as seen by the Bible. First, poverty is regarded as something decidedly negative; it is "a scandalous condition" and the manifestation of "a degrading human condition.[4] Secondly, this situation of poverty is not the result of some historical inevitability nor is it "just the way things are"; it is, as we saw in Part I, the result of the unjust actions of oppressors.[5]

BLESSED ARE THE POOR

God, of course, is not indifferent toward situations of injustice. God takes sides and comes on the scene as one who favors the poor, those who make up the masses of the people. The Bible makes perfectly clear this divine predilection and option for the poor.

The poor alone are worthy to take part in the kingdom of God. Unless the rich break with their way of life, they cannot enter this kingdom. Zacchaeus, who was a chief tax collector and a very rich man, had to give half of his goods to the poor and pay a fourfold recompense to those he had exploited. We see a quite different response in the case of the rich young man whom Christ calls: he has the opportunity to share in the kingdom of God, but since he cannot detach himself from his possessions and give them to the poor, there is no place for him in the kingdom. With reason does Christ say: "Truly, I say to you, it will be hard for a rich man to enter the kingdom of heaven. Again I tell you, it is easier for a camel to go through the eye of a needle than for a rich man to enter the kingdom of God" (Matt. 19:23–24).

In Chapter 6 of Luke's Gospel we find contrasting but parallel statements that are part of Jesus' teachings to his followers:

Blessed are you poor, for yours is the kingdom of God [v. 20].
        But woe to you that are rich, for you have re-
        ceived your consolation [v. 24].
Blessed are you, that hunger now, for you shall be satisfied [v. 21].
        Woe to you that are full now, for you shall
        hunger [v. 25]
Blessed are you that weep now, for you shall laugh [v. 21].
        Woe to you that laugh now, for you shall
        mourn and weep [v. 25].

The reason why the Bible opposes the rich is not because they are rich, but because they have acquired their riches at the expense of their neighbors (James 5:1–6).

Chapter 5 of Matthew's Gospel contains further beatitudes for the poor:

Blessed are the poor in spirit, for theirs is the kingdom
of heaven.
Blessed are those who mourn, for they shall be com-
forted.
Blessed are the meek, for they shall inherit the earth.
Blessed are those who hunger and thirst for righteous-
ness, for they shall be satisfied.
Blessed are the merciful, for they shall obtain mercy.
Blessed are the pure in heart, for they shall see God.
Blessed are the peacemakers, for they shall be called
sons of God.
Blessed are those who are persecuted for righteousness'
sake, for theirs is the kingdom of heaven [Matt. 5:3–10].

God identifies himself with the poor to such an extent that their rights become the rights of God himself: "he who oppresses a poor man insults his Maker,
but he who is kind to the needy honors him" (Prov. 14:31); "he who mocks the poor
insults his Maker; he who is glad at calamity will not go unpunished" (Prov. 17:5).

It is clear that these many passages of the Bible in favor of the poor are in serious danger of being subjected to another kind of spiritualization: that of calling
upon the poor to be satisfied with their state, not of poverty as such, but of privilege in God's sight. This would be disastrous because then even the rich would
feel tempted to experience certain wants in order that they too might be God's
favorites. Then the situation of injustice that God condemns would be alleviated
in the eyes of the world.

We must always keep in mind, therefore, that poverty is an unworthy state
that must be changed. I repeat: poverty is not a virtue but an evil that reflects the
socioeconomic conditions of inequality in which people live. Poverty is a challenge to God the Creator; because of the insufferable conditions under which the
poor live, God is obliged to fight at their side.

In Latin America the poor are blessed, but the reason is not that they have re-
signed themselves to poverty but, on the contrary, that they cry out and struggle
and have their mouths shut for them on the grounds that "they are rebels and
have recourse to violence." They are blessed, but not because they voluntarily
seek to be poor, for it is the mode of production forced upon Latin America that
leads them to penury. They are blessed, but not because they have scorned riches;
on the contrary, it is they themselves who have been scorned by those who mo-
nopolize the world's riches.

The poor in Latin America are blessed because the reign of God is at hand
and because the eschatological promise of justice is drawing ever nearer to fulfillment and, with it, the end of poverty.

Notes

1. Fernando Belo, *Uma Leitura Política do Evangelho* (Lisbon: Multinova, 1974), p. 43. In English see
Belo's *A Materialistic Reading of the Gospel of Mark*, trans. Matthew J. O'Connell (Maryknoll, N.Y.: Orbis
Books, 1981).

2. Ibid., pp. 37 and 44.

3. Julio de Santa Ana, *Good News to the Poor: The Challenge of the Poor in the History of the Church,* trans. Helen Whittle (Maryknoll, N.Y.: Orbis Books, 1979), p. 10, n. 1.

4. Gustavo Gutiérrez, *A Theology of Liberation: History, Politics and Salvation,* trans. Sister Caridad Inda and John Eagleson (Maryknoll, N.Y.: Orbis Books, 1973), pp. 291–92.

5. Ibid., pp. 292–93.

The Biblical God from the Perspective of the Poor

Jerry Itumeleng Mosala

The emergence of liberation theology in Latin America and of black theology, feminist theology, and African theology in the United States and Africa, represents the unwillingness of the poor and oppressed people of the world to accept, as final, the definitions of Christian doctrines, not least the doctrine of God, emanating out of the context of the dominant classes of society. Although there is truth in the assertion that in every age the dominant ideas are the ideas of the dominant groups, there is equal validity in the view that nothing can stop the idea whose time has come. Within the framework of the business of *believing* among the politically and economically exploited people in the world, the impact of the history and experience of the poor on their faith represents an idea whose moment has arrived.

This chapter will attempt to show that God is as central to the faith of the poor as to the faith of the rich; but it will further seek to show that the God of the faith of the poor is not the same as the God of the faith of the rich. In point of fact, the two Gods stand in antithetical relationship to each other, reflecting the struggles between the rich and poor. If they did not, justice could not be a fundamental attribute of the God of the Bible as seen by poor people. The biblical God is mediated to the poor through a double process—of the historical experience of the poor of the Bible and the historical experience of the poor of today. Gustavo Gutierrez puts it aptly when he writes about these historical mediations: "Commitment to the process of liberation introduces Christians into a world quite unfamiliar to them and forces them to make what we have called a qualitative leap—the radical challenging of a social order and of its ideology and the breaking with old ways of knowing ('epistemological rupture')."[1]

Knowledge of God by the poor, therefore, is inextricably bound with their historical experiences as the poor. The importance of this for a Third World theological understanding of God cannot be overemphasized.

WHO ARE THE POOR?

It is necessary to say a word about who the poor are because of the way in which the basic contradiction of our international economic system has caused many Christians to mystify, in theological terms, the reality of poverty. The scandal of our economic system is that the increased process of accumulation of material goods for the benefit of a few develops in equal proportion to the increased immiserization of the masses of people in the world. Few people possess and control more and more, whereas more and more possess and control less and less.

As this has become more evident, theologians have responded by mystifying the reality of poverty. It is being claimed that poverty should not be reduced to a lack of material goods. This is called "only one side" of the coin of poverty. The other side is what is called spiritual poverty, emanating out of too many possessions and therefore expressing itself as a feeling of meaninglessness in the midst of plenty.

This is to psychologize poverty and fail to see the brutal violence that is inherent in the condition of the poor. Further, it is to read the Bible with the comfortably tinted lenses of middle-class society. The biblical texts that are normally adduced in support of the spirituality of poverty are those that evolve directly out of the hermeneutical crisis produced by the tragedy of exile, in the case of the Old Testament, and those that issue out of the hermeneutical context of early Christianity in the slave-based economy of the Roman Empire.

There is, therefore, no fundamental distinction between material and "spiritual" poverty in the Bible. What we do have is the difference in the hermeneutical contexts of poverty. To understand this difference it is well to keep in mind what J. A. Sanders says about "hermeneutic modes":

Behind whatever hermeneutic rules the biblical thinkers employed there were two basic modes: the constitutive and the prophetic, and both were valid. . . . At those historical moments when Israel was weak and needed reconstituting, the Bible in its canonical shape seems to indicate that the constitutive mode was proper: our father Jacob was a wandering Aramean (Deut. 26:5); maybe like him we mark another beginning and not the end of Israel. But if that same mode of rereading of the tradition about Jacob, or Abraham, was read at a time when Israel had power, and had somehow confused it with God's power, then Jeremiah and Ezekiel, as well as the other prophets, called it false prophecy. . . . At that historical moment the prophetic mode is indicated: it may be we must wander, once more, like Jacob, long enough to rediscover our true identity.[2]

Who, then, are the poor? Gustavo Gutierrez paints a dramatic but accurate picture of poverty and the poor:

What we mean by material poverty is a subhuman situation. As we shall see later, the Bible also considers it this way. Concretely, to be poor means to die of hunger, to be illiterate, to be exploited by others, not to know that you are being exploited, not to know that you are a person. It is in relation to this poverty— material and cultural, collective and militant—that evangelical poverty will have to define itself.[3]

The poor are the products of a historical process of dispossession and expropriation. In certain circumstances this process is natural, being brought upon a people through such disasters as earthquakes, floods, cyclones, etc. Very often, however, the historical process of dispossession and expropriation is man-made. It is the result of socioeconomic systems based on inequity and exploitation. The Deuteronomistic writer of the Old Testament describes, in a passage that is conveniently ignored by scholars and Christians alike, in vivid dramatic terms, how the tributary exploitative social relations of the Israelite monarchy would bring into existence a subhuman class of poor people:

> So Samuel told all the words of the Lord to the people who were asking a king from him. He said, "These will be the ways of the king who will reign over you: he will take your sons and appoint them to his chariots and to be his horsemen, and to run before his chariots; and he will appoint for himself commanders of fifties, and some to plough his ground and to reap his harvest and to make his implements of war and the equipments of his chariots. He will take your daughters to be perfumers and cooks and bakers. He will take the best of your fields and vineyards and olive orchards and give them to his servants. He will take your menservants and maidservants, and the best of your cattle and your asses, and put them to his work. He will take the tenth of your flocks, and you shall be his slaves. And in that day you will cry out because of your king, whom you have chosen for yourselves; but the Lord will not answer you in that day (1 Sam. 8:10ff. RSV).

This process of impoverishment had reached repugnant levels by the eighth century B.C.E. in Israel. As a result, the invectives of the prophets were directed against it:

> They covet fields, and seize them,
> and houses, and take them away;
> they oppress a man and his house
> a man and his inheritance (Mic. 2:2 RSV).

> I will not revoke the punishment;
> because they sell the righteous for silver
> and the needy for a pair of shoes—
> they that trample the head of the poor into the dust
> of the earth, and turn aside the way of the afflicted
> (Amos 2:6–7 RSV).

The historical process whereby a class of poor people is created is eloquently attested throughout the Bible. But perhaps the most impressive summary is the one given by the prophet Ezekiel:

> The leaders are like lions roaring over the animals they have killed. They kill the people, take all the money and property they can get, and by their murders leave many widows. The priests break my law and have no respect for what is holy. . . . The government officials are like wolves tearing apart the animals they have killed. They commit murder in order to get rich. The prophets have hidden these sins like men covering a wall with whitewash. . . . The wealthy cheat and rob. They ill-treat the poor and take advantage of foreigners (Ezek. 22:23ff. Good News Bible).

The history of the creation of the poor in the Third World, like the history of the poor in the Bible, is written in letters of blood and fire. The poor were first created through the process of colonization whose success depended on the existence of a landless class of former agriculturists and pastoralists. The process that E. P. Thompson describes aptly with respect to the creation of the poor in Britain is known to have been repeated with even greater brutality in the Third World. Thompson writes about Britain: "In agriculture the years between 1760 and 1820 are the years of wholesale enclosure, in which, in village after village, common rights are lost; and the landless and—in the south—pauperized labourer is left to support the tenant-farmer, the landowner, and the tithes of the Church. . . . In the mills and in many mining areas these are the years of the employment of children (and of women underground)."[4]

Describing the outcome of this process of dispossession, Colin Bundy paints an even dimmer picture with respect to the South African situation:

> There exists a vast and depressing body of evidence as to the nature and extent of underdevelopment in the Reserves (and particularly the Ciskei and Transkei) in the forty years that followed the 1913 (Land) Act: the details abound of infant mortality, malnutrition, diseases and debility, of social dislocation expressed in divorce, illegitimacy, prostitution and crime; of the erosion, desiccation and falling fertility of the soil; and of the ubiquity of indebtedness and material insufficiency of the meanest kind. The cumulative effect of these features is not easily described; life moulded by them was not lightly endured.[5]

In my country, as in many other Third World countries, the poor thus created were expected in the midst of their expropriation to believe that history, as it was happening to them, was consonant with the nature of the God of the Bible.

Having been dispossessed of their fundamental means of livelihood, the poor are kept poor from generation to generation through a process of creating a permanent "reserve army of labor," entry into and exit out of which is tightly controlled to ensure the continued existence of a class of poor, superexploitable people. Unemployment and poverty, at a time in history when technology has been developed to levels whereby all of mankind's needs can be met with relative ease, are not accidental. And the faith in and understanding of God of the poor of the world are hammered out of such a context.

THE BIBLICAL GOD IN THE PERSPECTIVE OF THE POOR

It is only in the context of active resistance and struggle for social justice that there emerges a new encounter between the poor and God. In Latin America, as in other parts of the Third World, the poor begin to reappropriate the biblical God in their own ways as they start to identify kindred struggles in the very pages of Scripture. The old ways of reading Scripture become obsolete and new ways evolve. Gutierrez has this in mind when he writes: "In this context the theology of liberation arose. It could not have arisen before the populist movement and its historical praxis of liberation had reached a certain level of maturity. The struggles of the common people for liberation provide the matrix for a new life and a new faith, both to be achieved through a new kind of encounter with God and our fellow human beings."[6]

The most basic point that Gutierrez is making, and that this chapter is also advancing, is that God of the poor is not predefined on the basis of certain metaphysical considerations. The poor are not given to metaphysics. That is the luxury of liberal and bourgeois theologians. On the contrary, the God of the poor, like the God of the Bible, is the fundamental *force* at the heart of history and is to be known and discovered only through a deliberate engagement in history.

This is the thread that runs through José M. Bonino's chapter, significantly entitled "Blessed Are the Doers," in his book *Christians and Marxists*.[7] Bonino starts this chapter by demonstrating that in the Bible to know God is to do justice. He shows how prophet after prophet in the Old Testament, and how the Gospel of John in the New Testament, attest to the fact that knowledge of God is knowledge of what God does in history to bring about justice. And then in a significant paragraph Bonino gives a biting criticism of the dominant modes of perceiving God: "Seen in the perspective of our dichotomising thought, this formulation (to do justice *is* to know God) smacks of an intolerable 'horizontalism'; it seems to be mere humanistic philanthropy, and naturally the interpreters try to supplement it with some 'religious' content. But what needs to be changed is not the Biblical formulation, but our perspective.[8]

For the poor of the world it is not necessary to change the biblical formulations. Their own contexts of social struggles enable them to see, without need for the harmonizations proposed by biblical critics, the true nature of the Bible as the product and the *site* of sociohistorical struggles. And their God, like the God of the Bible, is encountered in the crucible of these struggles. Historical engagement constitutes the theological epistemology of the poor. It is for this reason that the black South African migrant workers through the theology of the African independent churches have recaptured the social history of the precolonial societies as an epistemological tool by which to understand the biblical God in such a way that God is the supreme ancestor, while Christ is the *Nyanga* (Diviner). The metaphysical

God and Christ of missionary theology would not do since they are extrahistorical. The full significance of the doctrine of God in African independent church theology has not yet been explored by Christian theologians, most probably because it is erroneously assumed by the latter that no developed doctrine of God can emerge among such an illiterate mass of marginal mortals as that which makes up the membership of these churches.

Thus black theology, in line with other theologies of liberation, and as the weapon of theory of the practical faith of oppressed and poor black people of the world, posits that to know who God is in the Bible and in the life of black Christians one must ask: what is the history of Israel and what is the history of black people? Without knowledge of the history of the Israelites there is no knowing the God of the Bible, and without knowledge of the history of black people there is no comprehending the God of poor black people.

That being the case, the assertion is valid for black theology that "when the world beyond the truth has disappeared, we shall establish the truth of this world."[9] If black theology is right in this, as we contend that it is, then we must acknowledge first that the truth of this world is that humanity is radically divided into a small class of rich and powerful people and a majority of poor and exploited people, the most exploited of the latter being black people and women. Second, and of greater importance for us *believers*, any doctrine of God that is not based on a historical engagement, which this reality calls for, is heretical and false prophecy.

This chapter would, however, be grossly misrepresentative of the biblical text if it created the impression that the God of the poor is the sole or even central actor in the pages of the Bible. There are other gods in the Bible, just as there are classes other than the poor. In fact, although Yahweh, the God of the poor, could not be suppressed in the biblical texts, this is not necessarily the dominant God of the Bible. The biblical text is as much an *arena* of fierce social struggles—with gods taking opposing sides—as our own lives today are *sites* of conflicts. So that it is patently clear that even as the name of Yahweh is used as an ideological justification for the state apparatuses of the Israelite monarchy during the times of David and Solomon, other gods with completely different characters are meant.

Thus the onesidedness of this chapter in relation to the God of the poor is not a weakness, but a historical choice facing the poor of the world if they are to liberate the Bible so that the Bible can liberate them. It is a deliberate option for the one God among others in the Bible: Yahweh the God of justice. This option is a function of a hermeneutical class struggle in which the poor insist on a much more common-sensical and straightforward reading of what Jesus was saying and doing. When he speaks of emptying the prisons, they refuse to reduce this to "Spiritual prisons", since the cell blocks they and their friends and loved ones languish in are made of stone and steel. When he talks about cancelling debts, they think first of all not of infractions of social decorum but of their unpaid bills and the hot breath of their creditors. When he speaks of filling the hungry, they think not of communion wafers, but of rice and beans and bread: "Thy Kingdom . . . on earth."[10]

It must follow from this, therefore, that the poor neither know how nor have the propensity to talk of God ontologically. This is in line with the biblical God from whom they take their cue. Yahweh is the God who brings a people into being because Yahweh is the God of a people who bring themselves into being. The God of the poor is inseparable from the struggle of the poor for liberation. He/She precedes the poor because the poor precede him/her. He/She is both the cause and the product of a community struggling for a just society. He/She has no being apart from this community just as this community has no being apart from him/her.

Needless to say, the position advanced in this chapter must reveal that the God of the poor is different from the God of the rich, and that the gospel of Jesus Christ can only be properly proclaimed if this difference is recognized. Gone are the days when theologians and preachers declared like John Wesley that, notwithstanding the material differences between social classes, spiritually "there is at least equality of opportunity in sin and grace for rich and poor." What Thompson says about Wesleyan and Lutheran theology is particularly relevant for our understanding of the God of the poor: "And this reminds us that Lutheranism was also a religion of the poor; and that as Munzer proclaimed and as Luther learned to his cost, spiritual egalitarianism had a tendency to break its banks and flow into temporal channels, bringing thereby perpetual tension into Lutheran creeds which Methodism has reproduced."[11]

The poor are moving a step further. They are claiming that the God of the rich and powerful is under judgment from Yahweh, the biblical God of the poor:

> The Sovereign Lord says, "People of Israel, go to the holy place in Bethel and sin, if you must! Go to Gilgal and sin with all your might! Go ahead and bring animals to be sacrificed morning after morning, and bring your tithes every third day. Go ahead to offer your bread in thanksgiving to God, and boast about the extra offerings you bring! This is the kind of thing you love to do" (Amos 4:4ff.).

NOTES

1. Gustavo Gutiérrez, "The Hope of Liberation," *Mission Trends*, no. 3, (New York: Paulist Press, 1976), 64.

2. J. A. Sanders, "Hermeneutics," *IDB*, supplementary volume, (New York: Abingdon, 1976), 405.

3. Gustavo Gutiérrez, *A Theology of Liberation* (London: SCM Press Ltd., 1974), 289.

4. E. P. Thompson, *The Making of the English Working Class* (Harmondsworth: Penguin Books, 1963), 217.

5. Colin Bundy, *The Rise and Fall of the South African Peasantry*, (London: Heinemann, 1979), 221.

6. Gustavo Gutiérrez, "Liberation Theology and Progressivist Theology," *The Emergent Gospel*, eds. S. Torres and V. Fabella (New York: Orbis, 1978), 240.

7. José M. Bonino, *Christians and Marxists* (London: Hodder and Stoughton, 1976), 29ff.

8. Ibid., 35.

9. Karl Marx and Friedrich Engels, *On Religion* (New York: Schocken Books, 1964), 42.

10. Harvey Cox, Foreword, in G. Pixley, *God's Kingdom* (New York: Orbis Books, 1981), VIII.

11. E. P. Thompson, *The Making of the English Working Class*, 399.

Chapter 2

Economic Justice as a Biblical Concern

Dangerous Waters of Justice and Righteousness: Amos 5:18–27

Jon L. Berquist

I hate, I despise your festivals,
    and I take no delight in your solemn assemblies.

Even though you offer me your burnt offerings
    and grain offerings,
      I will not accept them;

And the offerings of well-being of your fatted animals
    I will not look upon.

> Take away from me the noise of your songs;
>> I will not listen to the melody of your harps.
>
> But let justice roll down like waters,
>> and righteousness like an overflowing stream.
>>> [Amos 5:21–24, NRSV]

Few passages have proven more important for recent understandings of the prophetic view of cult than Amos 5:21–24. In the same manner, this passage has been a fertile ground for many notions of social justice and its importance to prophetic religion.

Despite numerous minor disagreements among scholars, there exists today a general consensus regarding the meaning of Amos 5:21–24. According to this consensus, this God first condemns the people for participating in the wrong kind of worship and then commands them to perform justice and righteousness instead of the worship described in vv 21–23. By implication, the people should replace their worship with the proper ethics and social action (Paul: 188–93). Thus, the passage provides hope that humans can do what pleases God; the human performance of justice and righteousness in the world is possible and is clearly the divine preference.

Despite the extent of the current consensus, this interpretation arrived in relatively recent times. Earlier in this century, a very different interpretation of Amos 5:21–24 was common. According to this prior consensus, God pronounces judgment upon the people for their failings and condemns them to punishment. God announces the sending of divine judgment and punitive righteousness that will destroy the people like uncontrollable waters. The people practiced false worship, believing in other gods or worshipping YHWH in syncretistic ways. For this failing, God intends to purify the people through punishment, sending a small remnant into exile.

For many commentators, Amos was a prophet of doom, and Amos 5:21–24 simply announced that inevitable doom once more (Sellin: 194). The cultic failings had filled YHWH with displeasure, and now divine wrath would pour over the people, punishing their sins in a fitting judgment (Weiser: 223). Some interpreters thought that there was an implicit opportunity for change, and that thus Amos 5:21–24 was not a pronouncement of doom, but merely a threat of divine devastation if their sinful worship continued (Würthwein: 150–52). Sellin, Weiser, and Würthwein formed a strong tradition of interpretation, influencing much subsequent scholarship. In this view, Amos pronounced doom upon the people for their sins. Even though many writers now identify ethical failures as the cause for the divine wrath, they still explain Amos' prophecy as a firm statement that failed societies do not deserve to live (von Rad: 132; Blenkinsopp: 96).

The interpretation of Amos 5:24 as an announcement of punishment runs parallel to another exegetical trend in scholarship. William Rainey Harper offered an early exposition of this new opinion. He understood Amos 5:24 as "*an exhortation* to give up the old idea of religion, viz, a cultus, and adopt the new, viz, justice and righteous living" (136). Harper interpreted v 24 in opposition to the three previous verses. In his reading, Amos 5:21–23 described a situation in which humans were failing to approach YHWH, but v 24 offered to humanity a method for correcting the relationship with their God.

J. Philip Hyatt pushed this interpretation further. For him, v24 affirmed the possibility that human initiative could solve the problems of poor cult performance through non-cultic activities. Furthermore, this passage functioned as a promise of salvation if the conditions of justice and salvation were met (24). The concept of v 24 as punitive judgement was not present at all in Hyatt's interpretation; only the positive, ethical dimensions were highlighted. Amos 5:21–24 asserts God's desires, but the true focus of the passage is upon human performance.

Though James L. Mays discussed the possibility of Amos 5:24 as an announcement of YHWH's impending judgment, he immediately rejected this interpretation as "impossible." For Mays, justice and righteousness were not divine attributes or actions, but things that humans do: "Their execution belongs to the horizontal sphere of society" (108). Furthermore, he understood an even sharper opposition between vv 21–23 and v 24. Justice and righteousness would not cleanse the cult; in Mays' interpretation v 24 asserted that the cult must be abandoned entirely. The Israelites "are to desert their sanctuaries, renew righteousness by recognizing and fulfilling their responsibilities to their neighbors, and see that their rightness bears fruit in the justice of the courts" (108–09).

According to this consensus, God does not perform punitive justice. Instead, people do justice, or at least God desires that they do it, because justice is the human action that brings the world into the order that God intends. The progressive development of this consensus is striking. Harper understood the ethical dimensions of social justice as a way to re-establish the relationship with YHWH that proper cultic practices should have maintained. Hyatt's interpretation emphasizes the ethics and presupposes that God demands this type of behavior. Furthermore, God promised salvation if the people performed social justice. Ethics could solve the problems of the cult. For Mays, the cult was a failure *per se*, and only proper ethical action on the social plane would redeem the people from their cultic failings. Hyatt saw a word of hope that extended the means of freedom from cult alone to the inclusion of ethics; Mays understood ethics as the power that saves from cult.

In more recent scholarship, the widespread acceptance of this newer consensus can be seen clearly. Whereas Mays referred to the views represented by Sellin, Weiser, and Würthwein, most new commentaries do not mention any other opinion at all. For instance, John H. Hayes states simply that, in Amos 5:21–24, "Amos has the Deity condemn a wide array of cultic activities and then offer one exhortatory command" (172). YHWH presented the people with one positive demand on the human level: proper societal order, involving social justice. This interpretation of vv 21–24 is consonant with Hayes' general argument that Amos asserted YHWH's hatred of the dual feasts at Bethel and Gilgal, which were supported by different political factions.

Hayes' social thrust to Amos 5:21–24 disagrees with the approach of Francis I. Andersen and David Noel Freedman, who understand the reference as reflecting Amos' own life and thus state that "its pronouncements should not be absolutized into standing indictments of the cults as such" (529). Despite this very different orientation, they reach the same conclusions as Hayes regarding Amos 5:24. The earlier consensus receives no reference, and the entire focus rests with the limited indictment of the cult presented in vv 21–23 and the positive evaluation of human efforts for justice and righteousness in v 24. Just as Hayes understands the threat to the cult posed by national politics, Andersen and Freedman state that the national level of affairs (especially involving Jeroboam II) is important to understanding this conditional evaluation of the cult (540–41).

Though Shalom M. Paul avers that "it is not the cult per se that is under attack, but its practitioners" (188 n. 3), he argues that Amos 5:21–27 represents a vehement denouncement of all the practices of the official cult. Instead of the trappings of the cult, God requires "the basic moral and ethical actions of humans" as described in v 24 (192). YHWH requests that society receive the fresh and constant waters of human justice and righteousness in order to survive and flourish.

These three recent commentaries assume that justice and righteousness are human ethical events, not divine actions. Other recent works show the same direction in Amos 5:24, understanding the text as a commentary on the interrelation of cult and society. Often, interpreters argue that proper religion must contain reflections of the divine will in both spheres (Huffmon: 89). The emphasis, however, remains firmly fixed on the social implications of faith, especially in more popular writings (Craigie: 120; Heschel: 1:31–32; Limburg: 107–08).

Thus, recent scholarship has typically not treated v 24 in the same way that earlier scholarship did. Instead, the more recent authors focus on a different set of dominant questions, reflecting several specific assumptions; v 24 describes human activity that God prefers more than that in vv 21–23, justice and righteousness are human activities, and the main topic of the passage is the interrelationship between cult and society. This shift in assumptions has changed the nature of the debate over vv 21–24. Whereas the interpretation of the unit once reflected divine punishment for the people's failings, it now focuses on the unit's statement of YHWH's requirement of humans: justice and righteousness.

A close examination of Amos 5:24, within the context of vv 21–24, can result in a more nuanced understanding of this unit's intention. Both of the past consensuses, dealing with punishment or with ethical command, misinterpret the imagery of this sentence in ways that limit the interpretation of its meaning. Before commenting further on the theological ramifications of Amos 5:21–24, one must first investigate the syntax of the sentence as well as the use of water imagery and of the key words *justice* and *righteousness* in the eighth-century prophets. One must also interpret this *crux* from its context, rather than from the supposed "parallel" verses elsewhere in the First Testament.

THE SYNTAX OF AMOS 5:24

The first issue for examination is the meaning and function of Amos 5:24's first word, *weyiggal*, which is usually translated "Let [it] roll down." There are two significant questions about this word: the function of the copulative *w* and the function of the verb itself.

The prior consensus commonly understood the initial conjunction as the introduction to a new subunit, vv 24–27, which was usually identified as an announcement of impending punishment (Sellin: 195). In this interpretation, vv 21–23 provide the reasons for the divine action announced in vv 24–27. The connection between the two sections is causal: "Because you have failed cultically, *therefore* I will bring judgment." On the other hand, the more recent consensus understands the *w* as an adversative, contrasting the material of vv 21–23 with an antithetical climax in v 24: "You have failed cultically, *but now* do justice and righteousness." The majority of more recent scholars prefer this interpretation (Andersen and Freedman: 523, 539–42; Cripps: 26–28, 198; Duhm: 10–11; Hayes: 170; Kapelrud: 49, 65; Mays: 108–09; Melugin: 724; Newsome: 26–29; Smith: 187; Vesco: 500–01).

The verb *weyiggal* is usually understood to be jussive (*"Let* justice roll"), even though an imperfect ("Justice *will* roll") is equally possible. The recent consensus requires the jussive, which must take the force of an imperative ("*Make* justice roll"). On the other hand, if it is YHWH who performs the justice and righteousness, in agreement with the earlier consensus, then an imperfect becomes quite acceptable (Waltke and O'Connor: 568). Hyatt argued that "the verbal form at the beginning of v 24 should be translated as expressing purpose" ("I reject your worship *so that* justice will roll") rather than as an adversative. He understood a different kind of causal connection: the removal of the cult would cause the advent of justice and righteousness (18).

The argument favoring a jussive form assumes that the verb has the force of a command, perhaps as some type of "sapiential admonition" (Wolff: 261). "Let justice roll down" thus becomes "You should perform justice." However, this argues from negative evidence. The verb *weyiggal* most directly refers to the event and does not denote the subject who should perform it. The jussive form, when used with inanimate objects, is usually an instance of personification, emphasizing the thing done, not the one doing it (Waltke and O'Connor: 570). Had the intent of the verse been to direct someone to perform justice and righteousness, one would expect a continuation of the second person forms in Amos 5:21–23. Since v 23, in particular, contains a second person imperative ("take away . . . "), then the most likely phrasing for a command in v 24 would be another imperative. As it is, the jussive or imperfect in v 24 represents a change of syntax from the forms of vv 21–23. Though imperative force in jussive verbs is certainly possible and though it could occur in this case, the change in verb form must receive consideration. The interpreter's best course is to assume that the change of verb form represents a shift in thought, unless there are other factors at work. The verb *weyiggal* most likely is an imperfect ("Justice will roll"), not an imperative jussive ("Let justice roll" or "Make justice roll").

Thus, the older consensus is correct in seeing *weyiggal* as a reference to the advent of justice and righteousness, rather than as a jussive form that gives the audience a direct command to perform justice and righteousness. However, this shift in morphology from vv 21–23 does not provide sufficient argument for v 24 as the start of a new unit, and thematic connections as well as the language of the text still argue for a unit that includes vv 21–23 and v 24. In this, the more recent consensus is surely correct. Amos 5:24 is the climax of the unit (vv 21–24), but the interpreter must still determine the precise connection between this verse and the rest of the unit. This text presents justice and righteousness, not as human activities commanded by God, but as events that will happen to the people.

WATER IMAGERY

Justice will "roll down like water" and righteousness "like an ever-flowing stream" (Amos 5:24). How do these water similes affect the interpretation of this passage?

Sellin and the other representatives of the early consensus understood the water imagery as references to the myth of the flood as a time of disaster and destruction, as connected to the motif of *Unheilseschatologie* (Sellin: 196; Weiser: 223–24). In favor of this argument are texts such as Isa 10:22b that refer to disaster as the overflowing of righteousness (*[scaron]ôtep sedaqâh*). In that case, water is a disastrous force equivalent to a punitive righteousness. Contrary to this understanding, recent writings typically interpret the water imagery in terms of comfort and healing (Hyatt: 23; Koch: 58; McKeating: 46–47), of constancy and dependability (Andersen and Freedman: 528; Cazelles: 175; Cripps: 198; Huffmon: 112; Wolff: 259), or of volume (Hayes: 174; Propp). These recent works demonstrate a very different understanding of the water images, viewing them as positive metaphors instead of as negative, destructive images. The existence of two such sharply defined positions necessitates a fresh examination of the basic evidence for the use of water imagery in Amos 5:24.

The verb *gll*, "to roll down," is not common in the First Testament. In the niphal, it appears only twice. This rare term is combined in v 24a with the generic word for water, *mayim*. Without a range of other uses, it is dangerous to assert the meaning of Amos 5:24 with much certainty. Though the *translation* of the phrase is easily obtained, its precise *meaning* is much more difficult to determine. Does it refer to destructive flooding or peaceful watering? The other occurrence of *gll*, however, provides some assistance. In Isa 34:4, the verb refers, not to water, but to the blood of those slain by YHWH's anger. This suggests that the negative interpretation may be the better reading for Amos 5:24, but there must be caution within such a statement.

The second simile, *kenahal 'êtan*, offers a greater possibility for clarity. A *nahal* is a wadi, a small stream. Though wadis in Israel were typically irregular in their flow of water, the same term could apply to permanent streams. It is a common term, occurring in the First Testament in excess of 140 times and appearing with *'êtan* in several other places. Deut 21:4 seems to refer to a permanent stream, that is, one that exists year-round. Ps 74:15 refers to the power of God who dries up the permanent streams. In some places *'êtan* seems to mean "mighty." It is translated as "mighty" by the RSV in Job 12:19 and by "strong" in Jer 49:19, 50:44. In the other ten occurrences (Gen 49:24, Exod 14:27; Num 24:21, Deut 21:4, Jer 5:15, Amos 5:24, Mic 6:2, Ps 74:15, Job 33:19, Prov 13:15), this meaning is also possible. This suggests that the proper translation of *nahal 'êtan* in Amos 5:24 is "mighty stream," instead of "permanent stream." Quite possibly, both meanings are present within this metaphor; the stream is large and powerful, enduring throughout the year and straining to contain its fast-moving water.

To better understand the phrase and its function within this simile, the study of other water imagery in the eighth-century prophetic literature proves helpful. The eighth-century prophets demonstrate a variety of metaphorical usages of water imagery: dew that is impermanent and unfaithful (Hos 6:4, Mic 5:7), water in great abundance (Isa 11:9, Mic 6:7), raging water representing YHWH's wrath (Hos 5:10), water as comforting and healing (Is 12:3 [which refers to wells, not to moving water] and Hos. 6:3), destruction by flooding (Amos 8:7–8, 9:5–6; Isa 10:21–22, 14:23, 30:25), and violent cleansing of the land (Isa 4:4, 8:7–8, 36:6). Though a wide variety of clear options exists for water metaphors, a pattern emerges. Large amounts of open water typically appear in metaphors of danger, whether of YHWH's destruction or of ravaging cleansing. Even the more positive images of water, such as the pictures of healing in Isa 12:3 and Hos 6:3, depict a time of restoration *after* a period of divine purging.

In the great majority of cases among the eighth-century prophets, water imagery indicates danger, especially when the passage focuses on moving water. This provides the necessary clue for the interpretation of the images in Amos 5:24. Justice "rolls like water" and righteousness "like a mighty, permanent stream." Though these similes are lexically ambiguous, they most likely are consonant with the preponderance of metaphorical usages of water imagery in the eighth-century prophets. The justice and righteousness of this verse act in dangerous, possibly destructive ways. The image reinforces the notion of justice and righteousness as powerful forces beyond human control, just like wadis and flash-floods. Thus, YHWH calls justice and righteousness upon the people in destruction and purging. Though other interpretations are possible, this is most likely.

THE LARGER CONTEXT: AMOS 5:18–27

There is little consensus about the limits of the unit containing Amos 5:24. Recently, the most common position has been that Amos 5:18–27 forms one unit with three subunits: vv 18–20, 21–24, and 25–27 (Andersen and Freedman: 523; Duhm: 100–11; Hammershaimb: 86; Harper: 129–41; Hayes: 1700; Smith: 176–91; van der Wal: 110–11). A few scholars deal with vv 18–24 as a complete unit (Kapelrud: 75), and many interpreters (especially those within the older, German tradition of interpretation) take the unit to be vv 21–27 (Coote: 84–84; Jellicoe: 257; Paul: 188; Sellin: 192–97; S oggin: 96; Weiser: 221–29; Wolff: 258–68).

The delimiting of the unit can shift the theological interpretation of v 24, since the boundaries of the unit associate different materials with it (Auld: 66). If the unit is vv 21–27, then v 24 becomes the pivot, moving from the statements of divine displeasure in vv 21–23 to the punishment for human insufficiency (vv 24–27). In that case, the unit centers on what YHWH does to the people. On the other hand, if the unit includes vv 18–20, there is greater potential for emphasis on the actions of the people. Interpreters who include vv 18–20 in the unit containing vv 21–24 are more likely to perceive v 24 as a reference to positive human acts.

According to the growing consensus, Amos 5:18–27 forms a complete unit, which may well be part of a larger section within the book of Amos. Proposals for sections such as 5:7–6:12 (van der Wal: 110–11) or 5:1–6:14 (Andersen and Freedman: 519–44) do demonstrate merit, but 5:18–27 still exists as an independent unit. The cry of *alas* in v 18 balances the completion of the punishment in v 27, creating clear limits to the unit and providing coherence to its contents.

Thus, the unit deals with one theme in three parts.

I

18   "Alas, you who wait for the day of YHWH!
      What will the day of YHWH be for you?
      It is darkness, and not light;
19   Just as, when a man flees from the lion
         and the bear meets him;
      or he goes home, and he puts his hand on the wall,
         and a snake bites him.
20   Is not the day of YHWH darkness, and not light,
         gloom, and no brightness in it?

II

21   I hate, I despise your celebrations.
      I do not take delight in your assemblies.
22   Even if you sacrifice burnt offerings to me,
         I will not accept your gifts,
      And the celebratory offerings of your fatted calves
         I will not recognize
23   Remove from before me the noise of your songs.
      The tunes of your harps I will not hear.
24   Justice will roll like water,
         and righteousness like a permanent flash-flood.

III

25   Did you bring me sacrifices and gifts
      for forty years in the wilderness, O house of Israel?
26   And do you carry the canopy of your king
         and the palanquin of your images,
         the star of your god,
         which you made for yourself?
27   But I will exile you beyond Damascus,"
      says YHWH, whose name is God of Armies.

The context of this entire unit, Amos 5:18–27, is God's destruction of the people. The *alas*-utterance assumes that the destruction has already begun (Williams: 54–56), but the full measure of that destruction has not yet revealed itself. Thus, the purpose of this unit is to explain the extent of God's activity against the people.

Part I of the unit (Amos 5:18–20) begins with a statement about the day of YHWH. Amos' audience contains those who wait for such a day in hopeful expectation, but the prophet quickly dashes any such hopes. When this day of YHWH comes, it will be disastrous for the people. Despite much scholarly investigation of the YHWH's day motif, the exact nature of that day does not determine the meaning of this passage. Whether the day of YHWH is an event expected for the immediate future or an eschatological intervention, the unit's assertion is that it will harm those who await it.

This makes sense only if Amos is contradicting a popular expectation of a positive, beneficial day of YHWH. In that case, then Amos' audience has been experiencing the beginnings of their own destruction, but they have hoped in a coming day when God would intervene on their behalf. To these people, Amos' message is succinct: not even the day of YHWH can prevent the destruction that God is pouring upon you. Amos 5:18–20 emphasizes prophetic contradiction of the people's hope in a day of YHWH as a cure for their current distress.

In part II (Amos 5:21–24), the unit's attention turns to another source of popular hope: the sacrificial cult. Though many scholars understand these verses as an attack on the cult itself, such a reading is quite problematic. The only cultic elements mentioned here are the voluntary acts, which people performed in addition to their basic cultic obligations (Hayes: 173). Instead, these voluntary sacrifices were the celebrations of YHWH's goodness as manifested in human prosperity. Those with sufficient wealth could provide gifts to the deity in excess of the mandatory offerings, perhaps in lavish attempts to curry divine favor. These extra offerings receive sharp condemnation, though Amos does not mention the required cultic acts, in which all citizens would participate.

The seeking of divine favor through cultic excess appears so futile that God asks the people to desist (v 23), emphasizing the utter impossibility of cultic influence upon divine actions. No matter how impressive the people's worship is, they will not prevent God's justice, which comes like powerful waters to sweep away the people, even as they perform their cultic acts. This part of the unit emphasizes the inevitability of divine judgment, regardless of cult.

Nevertheless, the harsh divine justice of this unit is not punishment *per se*. There is no condemnation of wrongdoing, but only an assertion of the futility of seeking divine favor. The justice brings no vengeance upon sinners, but sweeps away all people like a flash-flood. The older consensus of punitive judgment is as misleading as more recent agreement about justice as human activity. God's intention is the presence of justice, not the punishment of a sinful humanity. On the other hand, God shows no interest in human activities that might render them acceptable. To the contrary, this passage asserts the futility of human attempts to earn God's favor through any means, especially through acts of worship.

Part III (Amos 5:25–27) follows quite naturally upon the prior verses, returning to the subject of gifts (v 25). The connection is indirect, however; the subject functions, not as repetition of the same theme, but as a transition to the next topic. Though the people did not bring gifts to YHWH during their wilderness experience, they do carry the standards of their king. The language of v 26 has proven difficult to translate, but interpreters usually render it in terms of the worship of foreign deities. Hayes' argument that this verse refers to political processions honoring the king is convincing on linguistic grounds, rendering a translation similar to the one above (176–77). In this view, the people were participants in a grand royal processional. Similar to the ancient Near Eastern processionals, it exalted the king and the power of the state. Participants celebrated the ability of the state to save them from danger.

Following this reminder of the people's reliance on the state for salvation, YHWH announces an approaching exile (Amos 5:27). In contrast to the political certainty provided by the king, YHWH asserts that the people are subject to political destruction. The exile will take the people far away from their homeland, offering little possibility for survival. YHWH's activity is inevitable, and even the great political prowess of the nation cannot avert it. Likewise, no celebrations of royal might can offer any hope against YHWH's decision to act.

Amos 5:18–27 progresses through three parts to present its highly unified theme of inevitability (Kapelrud: 71–72). First, an approaching day of YHWH will prove disastrous to the people, who had hoped for YHWH's intervention to be salvific (vv 18–20). Second, even the most generous cultic acts cannot save the people from God's powerful, flowing justice and righteousness (vv 21–24). Last, political power and pride cannot avert the coming political destruction of the exile (vv 25–27). In each case, the inevitability of God's destructive activity overwhelms human attempts at safety, whether in hope, in cult, or in politics.

Recent scholarship typically assumes that this passage opposes cultic worship and ethical society, commanding the people to forego cult in favor of social responsibility. Thus, the people should avoid the cult, whether because of a rejection of cultic syncretism (Barstad: 116–18), a negative reaction to some aspect of cultic practice, but not to the cult *per se* (Huffmon: 110; King: 89), or a complete rejection of all types of cultic practice (Blenkinsopp: 95; Hammershaimb: 89–90). This interpretation is problematic, however, since Israelite thought stresses the integration of cult and society. Soggin correctly states that an opposition of cult and society, "apart from being wrong, seems intrinsically absurd, given that in the ancient world, both East and West, a society that was not founded on religion and cult was inconceivable" (99; see also Koch: 56). Against the current consensus, Amos 5:18–27 does not command human social action, but instead makes a statement about the justice of God's action.

Likewise, the earlier consensus of divine punishment against an inadequate cult fails. Since the day of YHWH and the exile cannot, then, be divine reactions against the cult, they are not punishment (Gevirtz: 267–76). The unit does not depict a cause-and-effect relationship, but it does deny the expected cultic production of divine beneficence. The earlier consensus of justice's rolling as YHWH's punishment upon the people is as inappropriate in this context as the newer consensus of justice as the required human activity. This unit does not give the reason for the coming exile and for the day of YHWH; it proclaims their coming and their inevitability.

The divine potential is nonetheless present throughout this unit. Despite the divine protestations, YHWH is still aware of sacrifices, and mandatory sacrifices are not disallowed. In v 25, the wilderness tradition of YHWH's unmotivated care-giving is mentioned. The result of YHWH's activity will be justice and righteousness, which are clearly to be desired despite the cost. Justice and righteousness, though destructive, are reasons for hope (Huffmon: 115–16; Hyatt: 24). This agrees with the rest of Amos' thought: YHWH's rule will be made manifest, despite the cost that it carries to the people (Hayes: 194–228; van Leeuwen: 132–34).

JUSTICE AND RIGHTEOUSNESS

In Amos 5:24, justice (*mišpat*) and righteousness (*s^edaqâh*) refer to acts of God that result in the people's destruction. This destruction is, however, not punitive, since it does not result from a divine rejection of specific human actions, as presented in Amos 5:18–27. But what is the precise nature of this divine justice and righteousness? This issue has been prominent in scholarship (Booth; Cazelles; Kaiser; Koch 50–62; Schmid; Weinfeld), but these works have assumed either punitive judgment or human social action. A sensible place to begin investigation of justice and righteousness in Amos 5:24 is the other uses of these terms in the book of Amos. The words justice and righteousness appear in parallel three times in Amos: 5:7, 24; and 6:12. Additionally, justice alone appears in Amos 5:15.

At first, Wolff's argument that Amos uses justice (*mišpat*) for human action appears to be accurate (264). Amos 5:15 seems obvious: the audience receives a direct command to establish justice in the gate, a presumed reference to local law and associated ethics. Further investigation of this verse brings difficult questions, however. The verb to *establish* (*ysg*) is much rarer than typical word for establishing, and its meaning is much less clear. The exact connotation is crucial. If God commands the people to establish justice in the gate, then human performance of justice is possible. In the sixteen occurrences of this verb, a pattern appears (Gen 30:38; 33:15; 43:9; 47:2; Exod 10:24; Deut 28:56; Judg 6:37, 7:5, 8:27; 1 Sam 5:2; 2 Sam 6:17; Jer 51:34; Hos 2:5; Amos 5:15; Job 17:6; 1 Chr 16:1). A more accurate translation would be "to set aside" or "to create a protected space for [something]." In Amos 5:15, then, people should set aside a space for justice. Humans do not perform justice; they only allow it. Amos does not claim that human just action is ontologically impossible, but the prophet refrains from depicting any human action as just. Probably Amos would have agreed that humans *can* perform justice, but the prophet never finds cause to claim that humans actually do so. Amos engages in social critique, not metaphysical conjecture.

In Amos 5:7 and 6:12, the prophet castigates the audience for their damage to justice and righteousness. It follows that the human audience could degrade these qualities, but it is not logically consequent that humans perform them. The ability to destroy does not necessarily imply the ability to create. Though Amos 5:7 and 6:12 make clear the presence of justice and righteousness within the human sphere, these passages do not necessitate Wolff's assertion that these terms refer to human *actions*.

Justice and righteousness also appear within the wider range of literature from the eight-century prophets. The recent consensus often understands Amos 5:21–24 as roughly equivalent to Hos 6:4–6 and Mic 6:6–8. All three texts refer to justice and/or righteousness and disparage cultic practices. However, the passages are not precisely parallel. In Hos. 6:6, YHWH desires loyalty and knowledge of God, not justice or righteousness. Instead, Hosea's justice refers to God's action with disastrous results for the people (v 5). Mic 6:8 is quite different in its use of justice, presenting it as the desired result of human activity. Thus, in these two thematically similar units within the eight-century prophets, the apparent meaning of justice is quite different. There exists no unified understanding of justice and righteousness in these prophets that would determine the sense of Amos 5:24.

Perhaps the most relevant comparative texts for Amos 5:21–24 are to be found in the writings attributed to Isaiah of Jerusalem. If Hayes' recent proposals are correct, then Isaiah and Amos should be considered as approximate contemporaries, with Amos in 750 B.C.E. and Isaiah in 759 B.C.E. and following (Hayes: 13, 38–39; Hayes and Irvine: 34–40, 108–10). Isa 5:13–17 parallels justice and righteousness, with exile as a dominant theme (cf. Amos 5:25–27). Human humility contrasts with the divine glory that will produce peaceful prosperity. In this context, the exaltation of YHWH is in justice and in righteousness (v 16). As such, justice and righteousness seem to be attributes or activities of the deity, rather than the result of human accomplishment. Though it is possible that this text connotes God's enthronement on human justice, just as God is enthroned on Israel's praises (Ps 22:3), such does not seem to be likely in connection with Isaiah's extreme reduction in the status and ability of humanity (v 15).

The most extended treatment of justice and righteousness in Isaiah comes in the first chapter. The first occurrence of justice is in Isa 1:17, where the people are commanded to seek justice (*diršu mišpat*). Again, this reference is ambiguous; it is not clear whether humans should seek to *do* justice or should seek to *find* the divine actions of justice in the world. In v 21, the faithful city is described as full of justice and as the place where righteousness dwells. This too can reflect either human or divine justice and righteousness. The city will be called "the city of righteousness," after YHWH places proper leaders within the city (v 26). Thus, righteousness is the result of divine action, though the result is indirect, through divine appointment of people who do righteousness, or who at least avoid the prevention of righteousness. Similarly, the last reference in Isaiah 1 places justice and righteousness in parallel (v 27) and asserts that Zion and its inhabitants will be redeemed by justice and righteousness. This will be accompanied by the destruction of the sinners by YHWH, and so it seems best to understand the redemption of the city to refer to YHWH's activities and not the actions of humans.

In short, though Isa 1 presents a degree of ambiguity, the overall connotation is that justice and righteousness are activities of the deity rather than of humanity. Despite the variety and the uncertainty inherent in these eighth-century prophetic texts, this understanding emerges as the most frequent concept of justice and righteousness. Hayes states that justice and righteousness "are a special concern and responsibility of God and the king, who establish and uphold justice and righteousness" (161; cf. Paul: 192). But the role of the king in justice and righteousness, emphasized in Isaiah, is generally lacking in Amos, and so God is the only one who performs justice and righteousness in Amos.

TOWARD A THEOLOGY OF JUSTICE AND RIGHTEOUSNESS

Amos 5:24 is a statement of the coming of YHWH's justice and righteousness, not an imperative or an exhortation for humans to perform justice. This syntactic conclusion agrees with the tendency of water imagery in the eighth-century prophetic writings to connote divine purging or destruction and with the meaning of the rest of Amos 5:18–27. Thus, a new interpretation of Amos 5:24 can be advanced. As the tradition of Sellin and others has stated, justice and righteousness are activities of YHWH that result in the destruction of the people. However, the divine purging is not punitive, since it does not result from divine displeasure at the cult. Instead, the text emphasizes that even voluntary cultic practices cannot change the divine intention, nor can politics or any human intervention. In agreement with some of the more recent works on Amos, justice and righteousness are for the benefit of the people, but they benefit the people at the cost of societal stability.

Amos 5:18–27, therefore, does not assert that God is angry at the cult *per se*. In fact, there is no evaluation of worship's rightness at all. Instead, the text insists that God now decides not to let the cultic practices of the worshippers sway the divine intention. At one level, Amos 5:18–27 assumes that God's typical, expected reaction would be to honor worshippers' requests; this expectation sets up the contrast implicit within this text. The key phrase is that God will not accept the offerings and sacrifices (v 22), not that God hates sacrifices in some categorical fashion (v 21). Ancient Israel's prophets never argued against all cult worship, but here Amos insists that God's intention cannot be distracted even by the most extravagant worship. The prophet argues that cultic excess is not effective in the face of God's decisive wrath, but there is no discussion of the sacrifices required by Pentateuchal law. Amos in no way denigrates such normative worship practice. Instead, God's decision to act responds to a cause very different from temple worship.

Soggin correctly notes that unequal distribution of wealth and power is at the root of the problems here. Since the part of the population that controls worship has been taking advantage of legality, the inconsistency between cult and societal justice results in blasphemy (Soggin: 100; Huffmon: 111). Though the cost will be great and though the exile will destroy the accepted society of Israel, such destruction will be necessary to accomplish YHWH's goal. God's willingness to destroy the people in order to restore right society is shocking. The flood imagery is natural, recalling an earlier time of God's destruction of an evil humanity. The coming exile beyond Damascus will be similar to that ancient deluge; it will sweep away the people and set the stage for a world that responds to God's will. Amos thus combines a typical prophetic concern for equal distribution of social goods and privileges with an imagery of destruction more expected from apocalypticists of a later era.

In this sense, Amos' prophecy was extremely countercultural: it identified the destruction of known society with the fulfillment of divine intention. Such is probably a mark of prophetic alignment with a disenfranchised group. For such a group, societal destruction is not so much a loss as it is for the entrenched classes. The disadvantaged could witness societal devastation and perceive YHWH's justice and righteousness. These poor would have lost little through the destruction of society's institutions. Furthermore, these poor would not have been the ones begging to be spared from the destruction. The cultic excesses depicted in Amos 5:21–24 would have been extraordinarily expensive, and none of the poor could have participated in them. The poor were unable to plead for salvation through these special means, but they were also unwilling to ask for the aversion of destruction. Instead, the poor would have welcomed the removal of the upper classes, so that they could live their lives unfettered in the land.

In this context, Amos' prophecy echoed the desire of these poor and needy: "Let justice roll down like waters, and righteousness like an everflowing stream." The powerful had blocked God's justice from achieving its ends on earth. Divine intention remained unfulfilled, as the society's leadership oppressed the poor. In Amos 5:18–27, God announces a new action. No longer will the rich be able to block justice; instead, God's justice and righteousness will overwhelm the leaders like a flash-flood. Certainly, this means destruction for those who resist, but this flood of justice results in an outpouring of righteousness for the poor, who need it most. God's concern is the provision of justice and righteousness for all people, especially for the poor. But this justice and righteousness seem to require the cooperation of humans. At least, it is possible for humans to block justice, and God has not intervened. Now, Amos announces that God will provide such a flow of justice and righteousness that the leaders will not be able to stop it. In this flood, there will be darkness in YHWH's day, and the leaders will be washed away, beyond Damascus. Justice and righteousness will arrive like dangerous waters.

Works Cited

Andersen, Francis I. and David Noel Freedman. 1989. *Amos: A New Translation with Introduction and Commentary.* Anchor Bible 24A. Garden City, NY: Doubleday.

Auld, A. G. 1986. *Amos.* Old Testament Guides. Sheffield, UK: JSOT Press.

Barstad, Hans M. 1984. *The Religious Polemics of Amos.* Supplements to Vetus Testamentum 34. Leiden, The Netherlands: E. J. Brill.

Blenkinsopp, Joseph. 1983. *A History of Prophecy in Israel from the Settlement in the Land to the Hellenistic Period.* Philadelphia, PA: Westminster Press.

Booth, Osborne. 1942. "The Semantic Development of the Term *Mi[sbreve]pat* in the Old Testament," *Journal of Biblical Literature* 61:105–10.

Cazelles, H. 1951. "À propos de quelques textes difficiles relatifs à la justice de dieu dans l'ancien testament," *Revue biblique* 58:169–88.

Coote, Robert B. 1981. *Amos among the Prophets: Composition and Theology.* Philadelphia, PA: Fortress Press.

Craigie, Peter C. 1984. *Twelve Prophets. Volume 1: Hosea, Joel, Amos, Obadiah, and Jonah.* Daily Study Bible. Philadelphia, PA: Westminster Press.

Cripps, Richard S. 1929. *A Critical and Exegetical Commentary on the Book of Amos.* London, UK: SPCK.

Duhm, B. 1911. "Anmerkungen zu den Zwölf Propheten," *Zeitschrift für die alttestamentliche Wissenschaft* 31:1–43.

Gevirtz, Stanley. 1968. "A New Look at an Old Crux: Amos 5:26," *Journal of Biblical Literature* 87:267–76.

Hammershaimb, Erling. 1970. *The Book of Amos: A Commentary*. New York, NY: Schocken Books.

Harper, William Rainey. 1905. *A Critical and Exegetical Commentary on Amos and Hosea*. International Critical Commentary. New York, NY: Charles Scribner's Sons.

Hayes, John H. 1988. *Amos: The Eighth-Century Prophet. His Times and His Preaching*. Nashville, TN: Abingdon Press.

Hayes, John H. and Stuart A. Irvine. 1987. *Isaiah: The Eighth-Century Prophet*. Nashville, TN: Abingdon Press.

Heschel, Abraham J. 1962. *The Prophets*. 2 vols. New York, NY: Harper & Row.

Huffmon, Herbert B. 1983. "The Social Role of Amos' Message," *The Quest for the Kingdom of God: Studies in Honor of George E. Mendenhall*, ed. H. B. Huffmon, F. A. Spina, and A. R. W. Green. Winona Lake, IN: Eisenbrauns, 109–16.

Hyatt, J. Philip. 1956. "The Translation and Meaning of Amos 5:23–24," *Zeitschrift für die alttestamentliche Wissenschaft* 68:17–24.

Jellicoe, Sidney. 1949. "The Prophets and the Cultus," *Expository Times* 60:256–58.

Kaiser, Otto. 1985. "Gerechtigkeit und Heil bei den israelitischen Propheten und griechischen Denkern des 8.-6. Jahrhunderts," *Der Mensch unter dem Schicksal: Studien zur Geschichte, Theologie und Gegenwartsbedeutung der Weisheit*, ed. O. Kaiser. Berlin, Germany: de Gruyter, 24–40.

Kapelrud, Arvid S. 1956. *Central Ideas in Amos*. Oslo, Norway: Aschehoug.

King, Philip J. 1988. *Amos, Hosea, Micah—An Archaeological Commentary*. Philadelphia, PA: Westminster Press.

Koch, Klaus. 1982. *The Prophets. Volume I: The Assyrian Period*. Philadelphia, PA: Fortress Press.

Limburg, James. 1988. *Hosea-Micah*. Interpretation. Atlanta, GA: John Knox Press.

Mays, James Luther. 1969. *Amos: A Commentary*. Old Testament Library. Philadelphia, PA: Westminster Press.

McKeating, Henry. 1971. *The Books of Amos, Hosea, and Micah*. Cambridge Bible Commentary. Cambridge, UK: Cambridge University Press.

Melugin, Roy F. 1988. "Amos," *Harper's Bible Commentary*, ed. J. L. Mays. San Francisco, CA: Harper & Row, 720–25.

Newsome, James D. 1984. *The Hebrew Prophets*. Atlanta, GA: John Knox Press.

Paul, Shalom M. 1991. *Amos: A Commentary on the Book of Amos*. Hermeneia. Minneapolis, MN: Fortress Press.

Propp, William Henry. 1987. *Water in the Wilderness: A Biblical Motif and Its Mythological Background*. Harvard Semitic Monograph 40. Atlanta, GA: Scholars Press.

Schmid, Hans Heinrich. 1968. *Gerechtigkeit als Weltordnung: Hintergrund und Geschichte des alttestamentlichen Gerechtigkeitbegriffes*. Beiträge zur Historischen Theologie 40. Tübingen, Germany: Mohr (Siebeck).

Sellin, Ernst. 1922. *Das Zwölfprophetenbuch übersetzt und erklärt*. Kommentar zum Alten Testament 12. Leipzig, Germany: A. Deichert.

Smith, Gary V. 1989. *Amos: A Commentary*. Library of Biblical Interpretation. Grand Rapids, MI: Zondervan.

Soggin, J. Alberto. 1987. *The Prophet Amos: A Translation and Commentary*. London, UK: SCM Press.

van der Wal, Adri. 1983   . The Structure of Amos," *Journal for the Study of the Old Testament* 26:107–13.

van Leeuwen, C. 1974. "The Prophecy of the *Yom YHWH* in Amos V 18–20," *Language and Meaning: Studies in Hebrew Language and Biblical Exegesis*, ed. A. S. van der Woude. Leiden, The Netherlands: E. J. Brill, 113–34.

Vesco, Jean-Luc. 1980. "Amos de Teqoa, défenseur de l'homme," *Revue biblique* 87:481–513.

von Rad, Gerhard. 1965. *Old Testament Theology, Volume II*. New York, NY: Harper & Row.

Waltke, Bruce K. and M. O'Connor. 1990. *An Introduction to Biblical Hebrew Syntax*. Winona Lake, IN: Eisenbrauns.

Weinfeld, Moshe. 1982. "'Justice and Righteousness' in Ancient Israel against the Background of 'Social Reforms' in the Ancient Near East," *Mesopotamien und seine Nachbarn*, ed. H.-J. Nissen and J. Renger. Berlin: Dietrich Reimer, 491–519.

Weiser, Artur. 1929. *Die Profetie des Amos*. Beihefte zur Zeitschrift für die alttestamentliche Wissenschaft, 53. Giessen, Germany: Alfred T[omacron]pelmann.

Williams, James G. 1977. "Irony and Lament: Clues to Prophetic Conciousness," *Semeia* 8:51–74.

Wolff, Hans Walter. 1977. *Joel and Amos: A Commentary on the Books of the Prophets Joel and Amos*. Hermeneia. Philadelphia, PA: Fortress Press.

Würthwein, Ernst. 1947. "Amos 5, 21–27," *Theologische Literaturzeitung* 72:143–52.

Poverty and Punishment
in the Book of Proverbs

James L. Crenshaw

The Book of Proverbs has always stood as a didactic obstacle in the path of biblical salvation faith. Israel's priests and prophets saw Yahweh served when the rich and powerful upheld the rights of the poor. Her sages, however, examined wealth and poverty as if they were separate moral states, in some cases mandated by God. Poverty, like wealth, had a purpose. A look at proverbs concerned with the rich and the poor can provide a counterweight to the claim that there is a single biblical outlook on poverty. In the process, we will also expose the ancient roots of some current economic views.

RETRIBUTION AND ITS DOWNFALL

The poor fit badly in the scheme of things devised by the authors of Proverbs, Job, and Ecclesiastes, who enjoyed the privileges bestowed on society's influential leaders. As advisors to kings, friends of aristocrats, and professional teachers, the wise lived a protected existence. They even convinced themselves, and perhaps others also, that such luxury was their proper reward for the virtuous lifestyle they had adopted. This line of reasoning necessarily implied a less than enviable existence for those unfortunate persons who chose a way of life contrary to that of the teachers. These fools exhibited lack of morality that was matched by a shortage of the things that contributed pleasure and at least a modicum of happiness.

The argument went in the other direction, too. People who found themselves in a miserable situation must surely have possessed some character flaw, sometimes visible but often concealed from public scrutiny. Conversely, individuals who rose high in social standing and acquired the advantages of rank were naturally thought to have superior moral character.

The fundamental premise that produced these conclusions was theological. The creator of the universe took an active interest in its just order, punishing iniquity and rewarding virtue. Ethical decisions affected the essential order of the universe, either threatening its inner harmony or contributing to its stability. Choosing a pattern of life that elicited divine favor transformed the pursuit of pleasure, eudaemonism, into religious performance.

Over the years this conviction became dogma, for sufficient evidence of both aspects of the theory seemed present in society generally. The teachers who promulgated this idea found sufficient data to substantiate their claims, for they were eager to confirm their own favored status, and in doing so they condemned those less fortunate than they. The ambiguous assertion that divine solicitude never fails deserving individuals (Ps. 37:25) cruelly dismisses the poor as morally deficient while at the same time lauding God's providential care for the wealthy.

In the end the teachers actually defended the poor, but not before their own world came crashing down. The story of Job's fall from an exalted position to the ash heap forced the wise to reassess both sides of the equation they earlier championed. It became painfully clear to them that notable exceptions to the theory of reward and retribution occurred at least on the side of virtue. That concession led them to revise their understanding of vice and to admit that not all miserable persons deserved what befell them.

Once the sages acknowledged exceptions, their entire scheme became problematic. Not every deserving person fared well, and not all villains received just punishment. The earlier simplicity and optimism vanished, for now every individual case required careful study to determine whether or not the person's character accorded with external circumstances. The collapse of a cherished conviction precipitated a religious crisis, one which pushed believers over the threshold into the comforting (?) arms of a theophanic creator (Job) and skeptics into the empty abyss of a distant despot (Ecclesiastes).

Thus Israelite sages viewed poverty in the light of a retributive world view, with the emphasis falling on a negative assessment of the poor. The teachers acknowledged an obligation toward the unfortunate, but they harbored suspicion that the poor deserved their misery, which resulted from indolence. Idealizing the poor as special favorites of God, as, for example, in Amos' identification of the righteous with the poor, and Jesus' pronouncement that the poor are blessed (Lk. 6:20), did not find expression in wisdom literature. The wise would hardly have rejoiced to be called Ebionites (the poor ones), as a later sect seems to have done.

This attitude to poverty and its victims remains relatively consistent with the different expressions of wisdom in the Hebrew Bible and the Apocrypha. Furthermore, that understanding of the poor coincided with the sages' teachings in Egypt and Mesopotamia. One exception is an Egyptian text, the Instruction of Ani. Social turmoil in Egypt produced this pious wisdom text, which comes perilously close to claiming a special relationship between the deity and individuals in humble circumstances.

THE POOR IN COLLECTIONS OF PROVERBS

The book of Proverbs gathers together several collections of sayings from various periods and localities. It contains at least three collections of foreign extraction (22:17–24:22; 30:1–14; 31:1–9), each of which has an identifying comment, in one instance mistakenly inserted into the initial saying (22:17). This small unit resembles the Egyptian Instruction of Amenemopet, an earlier text that has thirty chapters. The other two collections derive from Aramaic wisdom, the first from an otherwise unknown Agur and the second from the mother of a king whose name, Lemuel, is given but about whose rule no further evidence has survived.

The remaining collections are associated with the name Solomon, for the most part (1–9; 10:1–22:16; 25–29); exceptions are 24:23–34; 30:15–33; 31:10–31). The tradition in I Kings 4:29–34 [EVV] credits this monarch with exceptional literary productivity, but virtually nothing in the collections attributed to Solomon agrees in content with this description of proverbs about trees, beasts, birds, reptiles, and fish. Perhaps Solomon achieved this association with wisdom collections as a reward for sponsoring the wise, although the subject matter rarely relates to special interests of royalty. An alternative explanation for the tradition of Solomonic wisdom relates it to his vast wealth, which must have suggested to many that he was exceptionally wise. Such reasoning was inevitable so long as the theory of reward and retribution flourished. The close juxtaposition of wealth and wisdom in the closing observations of the story about the Queen of Sheba lend credibility to this hypothesis.

The specific origins of the several collections are obscure, although their probable provenance and relative dating seem reasonably clear. The oldest units (10:1–22:16; 25–29) derive from actual family contexts, for the most part imparting parental teachings. Nevertheless, the present form of these proverbs lends itself to wider use, possibly in Israelite schools, for which evidence has vanished, except for a single witness in the second century B.C.E. That sole example was Jesus Eleasar ben Sira, called Sirach for convenience. The latest collections in Proverbs (1–9; 31:10–31) differ immensely from earlier sentences, or aphorisms, employing elaborate paragraphs replete with imperatives, exhortations and threats, or using an alphabetic device that is known as an acrostic. One miscellaneous collection (30:15–33) makes generous use of numerical sayings, both as heightening ("Three things are too wonderful, for me, four I do not understand"), and an absolute number ("Four things on earth are small"). These collections have material that predates Israel's monarchy as well as some from as late as the post-exilic period.

Some interpreters have attempted to trace a growing religious influence on the sayings, assuming that the earliest sages were wholly secular. That effort has not been entirely successful, for a religious element probably existed from the very beginning, perhaps becoming more explicit in the latest extensive collection (1–9).

The astonishing thing in Proverbs 1–9 is its virtual silence about the poor. The lone exception, 6:6–11, for which there is a partial parallel in 24:30–34, describes the calamitous results of laziness—poverty will overwhelm the indolent one.

> Go to the ant, O sluggard;
> consider her ways, and be wise.
> Without having any chief, officer or ruler,
> she prepares her food in summer
> and gathers her sustenance in harvest.
> How long will you lie there, O sluggard?
> When will you arise from your sleep?
> A little sleep, a little slumber,
> a little folding of the hands to rest,
> and poverty will come upon you like a vagabond,
> and want like an armed man.

This sharp warning adopts a simplistic approach to the problem posed by needy members of society, a response that many citizens of our own time readily endorse. By this reasoning, the poor only get what they deserve, the just fruits of their own laziness. If 3:27 ("Do not withhold good from those to whom it is due, when it is in your power to do it") actually refers to someone who is destitute, from whom the withholding of promised assistance might have drastic consequences, the collection would escape the charge of unmitigated bias against the poor. Outside 1–9, only two sayings come close to this negative attitude toward the less fortunate. In 10:4 ("A slack hand causes poverty, but the hand of the diligent makes rich") the implies teaching of 6:6–11 becomes explicit; not only do the indolent suffer need, but the industrious acquire riches. Another explanation for poverty occurs in 21:17 ("He who loves pleasure will be a poor man; he who loves wine and oil will not be rich which notes the way individuals squander resources in pursuit of pleasure.

If we are correct in assuming that the students to whom these sayings were ultimately directed came from wealthy families in Judean society, one wonders why the teacher did not try to instill a sense of charity in these young men. (I assume that these students were all males, for they are enjoined to be faithful to the wives of their youth and to spurn the sweet seduction of the foreign woman.) On the assumption that the poor were simply malingerers, did teachers think they would incur God's wrath by helping lazy people? This sort of thinking certainly led to ambiguous attitudes toward physicians, at least in the early second century before the Christian era, contrary to the negative view implied in Sirach 38:15 ("He who sins before his Maker, may he fall into the care of a physician"). Ben Sira struggles mightily to defend the medical profession against charges of interfering with divine punishment for evil, namely that by endeavoring to cure the sick, doctors risked shortening the divinely decreed period of affliction that befell sinners.

ON KINDNESS TO THE POOR

That explanation for the absence in Proverbs 1–9 of any sense of obligation toward alleviating the circumstances of the poor—that they have personally merited their lowly status—depends on an increased emphasis on *individual* retribution, as opposed to a *social* retribution, that is, the poor must be seen as an aggregate of individual sinners, not merely as a more or less suspect segment of Israelite society.

In any event, the earlier "Solomonic" collections openly praise kind actions toward the poor. The profit motive surfaces in 19:17 ("He who is kind lends to the Lord, and he will repay him for his deed"), a saying that presupposes the act/consequence scheme and uses it to good advantage. Those who do a good deed on behalf of the poor, the proverb insists, put the Lord in their debt and eventually receive payment from above. Similarly, 28:27 states that gifts to the poor pay worthy dividends, and 28:8 even asserts that those who lend money on interest will lose it to those who show generosity toward the needy. Such a statement as 21:13 fails to escape charges of self-interest, for it claims that an attentive ear and appropriate action in the cause of the poor ensure the same result if the situation is ever reversed.

The highest stage of blessedness is promised those who show kindness to the poor. Two different verbs indicate the happiness resulting from such considerate action, the first emphasizing the personal disposition and the second stressing others' praise. In 14:21 the charitable person is assured happiness, whereas 22:9 suggests that the needy with whom one has shared bread will sing the praises of their benefactor. The remarkable woman whose praises are heralded in 31:10–31 includes the "poor and needy" in her list of persons who come under her care. For the sum total of her actions, this virtuous wife receives praise from her children and husband. Curiously, the only other use of this combination, "poor and needy," appears in another late collection, the sayings of Agur. Four sayings, each beginning with the word "Generation," describe loathsome individuals who dishonor their parents, practice hypocrisy, think too highly of themselves, and consume the poor and needy. A different word in the initial position does occur in 14:31, which announces that insulting the poor (*dal*) actually demeans the one who made that person, whereas showing compassion for the needy honors "him." Although the pronoun could refer to the needy person, it may also apply to God, for whom the Bible uses masculine pronouns. By deeds of kindness, one honors the Creator.

This tendency to associate God with the poor extends to specific behavior such as ridicule. Whoever mocks the poor insults that person's Maker, according to 17:5, and anyone cruel enough to rejoice when calamity strikes (presumably the same poor person) will pay for such malice. In some instances the wise came very close to urging love for one's enemies; perhaps the motive was conservative self-preservation, but whatever the reason, the teachers decried violence of any kind. The metaphor about heaping coals of fire on an enemy's head by acts of kindness (25:21) remains obscure, although an Egyptian ritual of repentance may throw light on it.

Not every linking of the poor and deity served to protect the lowly against potential oppressors. In 29:13 the neutral statement asserts that a single sovereign empowers both oppressor and victim. No moral judgment appears in the observation, but the larger context probably lends it some small degree of censure. The next verse promises that kings who dispense justice to the poor will reign for a long time. By implication, the heavenly ruler ought to favor the poor over an oppressor.

The wise realized the precarious situation in which poor people existed, particularly in times of unscrupulous or weak rulers. Not all kings subscribed to, or actually implemented, the lofty ideal put forth by Lemuel's Mother (31:9, "Open your mouth, judge righteously, maintain the rights of the poor and needy"). According to 29:7, the poor have certain inalienable rights, which good people recognize but wicked ones fail to grasp. Astonishingly, not all who numbered themselves among the ranks of the poor respected the rights of others in their own social class.

The situation that James abhors, rich Christians (5:1–6) oppressing the poor, is comprehensible if also reprehensible; a rapacious poor person is almost unthinkable. The rich oppressor resembles a torrential rain that destroys vital crops instead of assuring the growth of life-sustaining food. The implication is that a deficient yield would tempt harvesters to neglect the obligation to leave some produce in the fields so that the poor would glean like the ancestress of David in Boaz' grain fields.

The advantageous position of the wealthy was taken for granted, for everyone knew that lenders possessed power over borrowers (Prov. 22:7). A curious observation surfaces at the transitional point between the older "Solomonic" collection and the section resembling the Instruction of Amenemopet, where the warning against such conduct appears. The robbing of poor people is at issue here. One would think such action would result in nothing worthwhile, but poverty, like wealth, is relative. Furthermore, the poor offered little resistance, because they lacked access to legal redress. Hence the wise insisted that individuals who take advantage of the poor for personal benefit or who toady to the rich for the same reason will experience need themselves (22:16). The warning against depriving the poor of their meager resources (22:22) actually mentions the place of judicial action, the gate of the city or village. This text also uses the combination "poor and afflicted," the latter term being *'ani* rather than *'ebyonim.*

Some sayings reflect the adverse social ramifications of poverty. The rich do not lack friends, but the poor cannot even rely on faithfulness from relatives (19:7, "brothers"). On the principle of "How much more!" the teachers assert that if brothers of poor people abandon them, neighbors and friends will avoid the poor even more quickly (19:4; 14:20).

In general, the sayings about the poor acknowledge their desperate plight. Lacking sufficient financial resources to secure their existence, they have no hope (10:15; 13:8), in sharp contrast to the wealthy, who can ransom their lives by prudent use of vast resources. Inherent to their status as wealthy members of society, the rich ignore the pleasantries of polite company, but those who occupy the bottom rungs on the ladder of success are obliged to plead their case (18:23). Even in rare instances when the poor act productively, lawless people seize their profit for themselves (13:23). Such miserable circumstances might have deprived the victims of their integrity, but the teachers saw things otherwise. The lowly people functioned as an example that the proud of spirit would do well to imitate (16:19), and a poor person with integrity was better than a perverse or foolish rich liar (19:1; 28:6). One sentence actually registers approval of a poor individual over an untruthful person (19:22). The wise refused to accept the notion that all poor people were stupid; in fact, one saying asserts that a poor person's grasp of things can be superior to the self-delusion of the rich (28:11).

"NEITHER POVERTY NOR RICHES"

An intriguing text expresses the view that both wealth and poverty hinder the achievement of a healthy spiritual relationship (Prov. 30:7–9). That opinion corresponds to the teachers' general emphasis on moderation in all things, arising from fear that excessive conduct endangers life. A close look at this text seems appropriate at this time.

> Two things I ask of you,
>> do not withhold them from me before I die.
>
> Emptiness and a deceitful word keep remote from me;
>> give me neither poverty nor riches;
>> tear off for me my portion of bread.
>
> Lest sated, I lie, saying, "Who is Yahweh?"
>> or lest impoverished, I steal,
>> besmirching the name of my God.

The external similarity with Job's request that God do two things for him to enable him to appear before the divine tribunal has not escaped notice (Job 13:20), but the contexts differ greatly. In Proverbs, the request seems to be a prayer with no forensic setting intended, whereas Job seeks safe entry into God's courtroom.

The abrupt "two things" engenders expectation that a numerical sequence will follow ("three things"), or that one preceded ("one thing"). What follows as a request takes a peculiar form, for prompt action on God's part is required for the gift to make significant difference. Delaying its receipt until just prior to death makes no sense. The petitionary address implies vertical discourse (prayer, that is) even if this text is the sole example of that genre in Proverbs. Of course, one could direct this request to other human beings such as parents, teachers, or kings, but the probable addressee is the deity.

The first petition actually embraces both ideas that follow, and one has difficulty discovering two requests. Perhaps the person asks to be spared idle thought and destructive conduct. Clearly, the emptiness and deceit relate to denial of Yahweh's claim over one's existence, whereas the full stomach will make it unnecessary for persons to commit desperate acts to stay alive. As illustration of the importance of sociological conditions in shaping human values, the author reflects on the impact of wealth and its absence.

The danger concealed in excessive possessions is that their owner cultivates a false sense of security, thinking nothing can arise for which money does not have an answer (cf. Eccles. 10:19). Like the rich man in Jesus' parable, the hypothetical individual in Proverbs runs the risk of trusting in wealth and forgetting the ultimate owner of everything in the universe. The question, "Who is Yahweh?" amounts to practical atheism, for it implies absolute reliance on one's own resources. The Septuagint, or Greek translation of the Bible, understood the question differently, rendering it "Who sees me?" This reading accords well with the theme of practical atheism in some Psalms and easily derives from a Hebrew text that closely resembles the present one. From the reading in the Greek, one can more readily explain the strange allusion to lying. The question, "Who sees me?" functioned as an emphatic denial that anyone observed misconduct, an intellectual position that constituted a spiritual lie.

The problem with poverty was less intellectual, for a hungry stomach forces one to extreme action regardless of its consequences. The ambiguous wording in 6:30 leaves open the possibility that society condones theft resulting from hunger, although the context seems to compensate for the missing sign of the interrogative. I refer to the observation that the thief must pay heavily for lawlessness. The thief's offense may be a grasping after the sacred name without realizing its sanctity, but the nuance of besmirching fits the context better. The choice of the general name for God accords with the foreign nature of the text's origin, a usage softened by the personal pronoun "my".

The coolness of this petition is noteworthy, especially the absence of the vocative "O Lord," and direct address "you" instead of "the name of my God." The lack of a vocative may derive from someone who thought God was unfavorably disposed toward the worshiper, but another explanation seems preferable. The prayer for a comfortable existence on neither end of the social scale contains a stinging attack against Agur, who represents the privileged class of the wise. In light of Agur's blasphemous inanities, as this person saw them, the prayer makes sense. Because it hovers between discourse among humans and communion with God, the cool tone and distancing from the ardor of religious devotion are quite understandable. The speaker did not remain afar off but drew near to the flame and uttered profound truth: destitute conditions force individuals to behave criminally, and living in the lap of luxury tempts persons to imagine self-sufficiency. The first, poverty, forces one to sully the divine name; the second, riches, blinds one to the possibility of transcendence.

The prayer has no concluding "amen." Instead, a transition to human discourse occurs with the ambiguous allusion to servant and master. On one level, the warning against belittling a servant before a master could refer to God, the supreme Lord. On the other level, it connotes human beings.

Whoever wrote this profound prayer could hardly have subscribed to the notable viewpoint expressed in the portrait of personified wisdom, who held vast riches in her hand and invited young men to pursue her like a lover. This remarkable figure, which resembles the Egyptian goddess of truth and justice, Maat, claimed to have occupied a favored position with Yahweh before the creation of the world and to have participated actively in that event. She even boasted of being the plaything or artisan of Yahweh, bringing joy to the creator and rejoicing in the finished product. Her largesse also extended to human beings, for she promised to endow her lovers with riches (8:21).

The section of Proverbs that coincides with parts of the Instruction of Amenemopet expresses considerable reservation about the pursuit of wealth, regardless of its source. In that author's opinion, acquired riches quickly vanish, taking wings like an eagle and flying off into the heavens (the Egyptian text has geese).

CONCLUSION

This examination of attitudes toward poverty and wealth in the book of Proverbs has exposed the ambiguities inherent to both. Those who lacked a fair share of worldly goods often suffered the added indignity of society's scorn, for which religious arguments were advanced. People who held an abundance of possessions also basked in almost universal favor, and this attitude, too, was supported on religious grounds. At least one concerned citizen, the Queen Mother from Massa in Edom, urged her royal son to offer something other than religion as an opiate for the miserable and perishing members of society. That solution was booze (31:6–7), enabling people to forget their poverty by drinking. Such a judgment from one in a position of authority, and therefore having access to better means of reducing want, has been repeated many times over the centuries. Equally dubious was the refusal to take a stand against those in power, shrugging one's shoulders and observing that officials always look out for their own interests (Eccles. 6:8–9).

Rare imaginative individuals, recognizing the inadequacy of such attitudes, saw the plight of the poor among them as an occasion for demonstrating the reality of the faith they professed. If Yahweh championed the cause of widows and orphans, then those who claimed allegiance to this Lord were obliged to extend that compassion to all needy persons. For that grand step to occur, another one was essential: the cessation of placing blame on those who found themselves in lowly circumstances.

Selected Bibliography

Camp, Claudia V. *Wisdom and the Feminine in the Book of Proverbs.* Sheffield: Almond Press, 1985.
Crenshaw, James L. *Old Testament Wisdom.* Atlanta: John Knox, 1981.
—.*Ecclesiastes.* Philadelphia: Westminster Press, 1987.
—"Clanging Symbols." Forthcoming in *Justice and the Holy,* edited by Douglas A. Knight and Peter Paris. Philadelphia: Fortress Press, 1989.
—"A Mother's Instruction to Her Son (Prov. 31:1–9)," In *Perspectives on the Hebrew Bible,* edited by James L. Crenshaw, pp. 9–22. Macon, GA: Merrer University Press, 1988.
—"The Sage in Proverbs." Forthcoming in *The Sage in the Ancient Near East,* edited by John G. Gammie and Leo G. Perdue. Winona Lake: Eisenbrauns, 1989.
—"Proverbs." Forthcoming in *The Books of the Bible,* edited by Bernhard W. Anderson. New York: Charles Scribner's Sons.
Fontaine, Carole R. "Proverbs" In *Harper Bible Commentary,* edited by James L. Mays, pp. 495–517. San Francisco: Harper & Row, 1988.
Greenberg, Moshe. *Biblical Prose Prayer as a Window to the Popular Religion of Ancient Israel.* Berkeley et al.: University of California Press, 1983.
Gutierez, Gustavo, *On Job. God Talk and the Suffering of the Innocent* Maryknoll, NY: Orbis, 1987.
Lang, Bernhard. *Wisdom and the Book of Proverbs.* New York: Pilgrim, 1988.
McKane, William. *Proverbs.* Philadelphia: Westminster Press, 1970.
Oesterley, W. O. E. *The Book of Proverbs.* London: Methuen & Co., Ltd., 1929.
von Rad, Gerhard. *Wisdom in Israel.* Nashville: Abingdon Press, 1972.
Whybray, R. N. *Wisdom in Proverbs.* London: SCM Press, 1965.
Williams, James G. *Those Who Ponder Proverbs.* Sheffield: Almond Press, 1981.

Human Solidarity and the Goodness of God: The Parable of the Workers in the Vineyard

Luise Schottroff

THE SOCIAL AND LEGAL SITUATION IN THE PARABLE

PRESUPPOSITIONS DERIVED FROM THE PARABLE ITSELF

Like many other parables, the one in Matthew 20:1–16 tells a story from real life. A proper understanding of it requires, therefore, that the real-life situation be explained with as much detail and accuracy as possible. Above all, we must not tacitly appeal to modern relationships between worker and employer as we try to interpret the parable.

Detailed socio-historical information is extremely important because interpreters set the switches, as it were, for their interpretations precisely at the points at which they see the story as departing from everyday reality. For example, an interpreter who thinks that the continued hiring of laborers until late in the day is improbable in the case of an earthly employer will interpret the parable differently from an interpreter who regards this element in the story as plausible but considers full-time wages for a part-time worker to be improbable. In the one case, God's goodness comes into play in the hiring; in the other, it is manifested in the wages.

The parable itself reveals the following socio-historical presuppositions. First of all, it is an everyday occurrence for the owner of a vineyard to hire workers in the marketplace. Men seeking work wait there for jobs. The owner of the vineyard goes in person to look for workers; such a man is not, of course, a great landowner who assigns slaves in administrative positions to this kind of duty and does not himself pay much attention to the wine harvest. Pliny the younger was a landowner of this type, and there were some such in Palestine as well. Pliny complains:

From *God of the Lowly: Socio-Historical Interpretations of the Bible*, ed. W. Schottroff and W. Stegemann, 129—147. Maryknoll: Orbis, 1984. English rights kindly granted by Luise Schottroff. English translation right copyright © 1984 by Orbis Books. Reprinted by permission.

I have just been getting in the vintage—a slender one this year, although more plentiful than I had expected—provided I may speak of "getting in the vintage" when I have simply picked a grape here and there, glanced into the press, tasted the must in the vat, and surprised my town servants who are now supervising the rural workers and have left me to my secretaries and readers.[1]

The owner in Matthew 20 has less land than that; he does have a steward (Matt. 20:8) who supervises the workers and pays them their wages, but he nonetheless goes in person to the market place in order to hire temporary workers.

The day laborers evidently do not expect any long-term contract but only a job for the day. As the story develops, it becomes clear that there are more workers available in the marketplace than are needed and that unemployment, even at harvesttime, is the rule among rural workers. Matthew 20:7 explicitly says that these men are unemployed: "No one has hired us." The degree of unemployment may be gauged above all from the matter-of-fact way in which we are told of workers who are still standing around in the marketplace at 9 o'clock (3rd hour), noon (6th hour), 3 o'clock in the afternoon (9th hour), and 5 o'clock (11th hour).

There is still another sign of unemployment. Harvesttimes are the most work-intensive periods in a rural economy. Day laborers who find work during the harvests are not employed on the farms apart from these periods. We can only guess at how they support themselves. Either they have farms of their own, which are too small to support a family, or they belong to the uprooted whom hunger drives into the countryside at harvesttime but who at other seasons look for occasional work in the cities—and who often enough must beg as well. We should not read into the parable the idea that the laborers who still have no work at midday are lazy and that their claim to have found no employer is a lazy man's excuse. No, the situation of unemployment is clear from the story itself.

The agreements with the day laborers are varied and are reported in detail. With the long-shift workers—that is, those hired at the beginning of the day—an oral agreement on wages is made. The workers agree to the wage and the hours, and are then sent off to work. To judge by the parable, one denarius is evidently the usual day's wage in that area. No such detailed agreement is made with the four groups of short-shift workers. The first three groups are hired, and the amount of the wage is left unspecified: "Whatever is right I will give you." The story presupposes that the precise amount of the wage is not determined in advance. There is no reason to assume that the phrase "whatever is right" refers to a wage usual throughout the area in such cases.[2] For the unemployed are evidently in such a weak position that they go off to work without any clear agreement on wages and accept the risk of having the vineyard owner pay them less than what they hope for. Finally, there is no question of relying on his charitableness, either in the story or in reality.

In the case of the last group of short-shift workers, those hired at the eleventh hour, there is, consistently enough, no mention at all of a wage.

The long-shift workers expected that each group of short-shift workers would be paid less than they and that the wage of these groups would be proportioned to the amount of time spent at work or, more probably, would take the form of a meal and a minimal amount of money. The workday lasts from sunrise to before sunset. During the grape harvest in August or September the workday would be twelve or thirteen hours long.[3] Workers hired at the eleventh hour (of the workday) thus, in all probability, work only a good hour or so.

The story tells us that the vineyard owner hires his day laborers in five stages, but it does not lay any emphasis on this point. If such a procedure were inconceivable or even just unusual in everyday real life, the story would make this clear.

It is obvious enough that the wage given to the short-shift workers is an unusual one. The course of the story itself thus compels us to agree with J. Jeremias's conjecture that at harvesttime vineyard owners do what they can to complete the harvest by evening.[4]

The story speaks of five groups of day laborers, but the second, third, and fourth groups play only a secondary role. In the dispute about the wage paid, these groups make no appearance. There are obviously good artistic reasons for this. The essential thing is the dispute about the wage paid to the two groups furthest apart. To report on the wage paid to the other three groups would be to introduce a detail superfluous from the artistic viewpoint. These other groups have to be mentioned in connection with the hiring, because a vineyard owner would not wait until the eleventh hour to judge that he needs still more workers; instead, he would keep on top of the situation and bring in extra workers in several stages as he determines that those already hired are not enough.

The payment of wages in the evening is likewise taken for granted and is to be regarded as the rule for such day laborers, unless of course the employer is trying to cheat them of their wage (see Lev. 19:13; Deut. 24:15). The relationship between employer and day laborers is to be thought of as a very loose one; the workers do not expect that the same employer will be able to use them the next day.

The story makes it clear that the amount of the wage paid to the short-shift workers is utterly unusual, so unusual that the long-shift workers may well expect so kind an employer to show them the same generosity and pay them substantially more than the agreed wage. It is not said that they expect five or six times as much, in keeping with the length of time they have worked. If a denarius is the usual day's wage, then a wage five or six times greater would be improbably large and even ridiculous in the judgment of hearers. Furthermore, such a view of the matter presupposes that work was paid for by the hour, but this is something that cannot be simply assumed to have been the case in antiquity. It is obvious that the vineyard owner is free to give away what is his own. The unusual thing is that in fact he does so.

Such is the extent to which the story itself and its manner of relating events permits us to reconstruct reality and identify departures from it. The story is quite plausible in all its details; only the employer's generosity is unusual. The dispute that this generosity occasions is the point to which the parable is meant to lead.

SOCIO-HISTORICAL MATERIAL

Most of the observations made thus far can be confirmed by what we know of social history.

The fact that extra day laborers were hired during the various harvests is not attested solely by this parable, although we should not underestimate the value of the parable as a source of information about social history. The use of day laborers during harvests is also attested for the Roman rural economy; the testimonies so closely resemble those of the parable that the information in the two sources is mutually confirmatory. Consequently, in this particular question at least, we can draw upon Roman writers of agriculture in order to clarify further the situation in Palestine. In addition, the Book of Ruth shows a comparable situation. The reapers who work in Boaz's field and are supervised by an overseer (Ruth 2:3ff.) are probably harvest workers hired by the day, or else a crew hired for the harvest period, such as is known also from the Roman economy.[5]

Varro (116–127 A.D.) wrote his *Res rusticae* ("On Agriculture") when he was eighty years old. As far as the workers used in the rural economy are concerned, he is interested primarily in the overseer, and he offers the landowner advice on dealing with this overseer or steward in the interests of greater productivity.

What he says about rural workers themselves is said rather in passing:

> All agriculture is carried on by men—slaves, or freemen, or both: by freemen, when they till the ground themselves, as many poor persons do with the help of their families; or hired hands *(mercennarii)*, when the heavier farm operations, such as the vintage and the haying, are carried on by the hiring of freemen and those whom our people called *obaerarii* [those who are working off a debt], and of whom there are still many in Aisa, in Egypt, and in Illyricum. With regard to these in general this is my opinion: it is more profitable to work unwholesome lands with hired hands than with slaves; and even in wholesome places it is more profitable thus to carry out the heavier farm operations, such as storing the products of the vintage or harvest.[6]
>
> Cato (234-149 B.C.) also employed freemen as day laborers and recommended: "He [the landowner] must not hire the same day-labourer or servant or caretaker for longer than a day."

The point of this last recommendation is that the landowner should try to put day laborers in as weak a position as possible when it comes to wages. Other ways were also tried in an effort to reduce the wage of a day laborer.[7]

Columella (ca. 1–70 A.D.) writes that a farmer should plant various kinds of vines in separate plots:

> One who separates the various sorts by sections has regard to these differences [among vines] as to situation and setting. He also gains no small advantage in that he is put to less labour and expense for the vintage; for the grapes are gathered at the proper time, as each variety begins to grow ripe, and those that have not yet reached maturity are left until a later time without loss; nor does the simultaneous ageing and ripening of fruit precipitate the vintage and force the hiring of more workmen, however great the cost.[8]

With the aid of these sources, which could be supplemented by others, we can to a great extent reconstruct the social situation of day laborers.[9] The picture that emerges is the same as that given in Matthew 20:1–15. During the harvests, and especially the grape harvest, day laborers are hired on larger estates. Even less heed is taken of their health than of the health of slaves. A clever farmer sees to it that the pressures of the harvest do not force him to pay excessive wages to these day laborers.

Modern scholars sometimes assume that contracts with day laborers were of little importance in the Roman imperial age because it was chiefly slaves who did the work.[10] But in all likelihood there were local differences in the number and situation of day laborers. Columella, for example, supposes a dearth of such workers at harvest time, whereas Matthew 20:1–15 supposes an oversupply.

It is not surprising that little attention should have been paid (in the law, for example) to this group of men who were in fact less protected than were slaves. But we may not conclude from this that they were few in number. Their numbers would be directly dependent on the economic situation of the rural population of each time and place. As estates became larger, the number of day laborers would grow.

The fact that we are better informed about the wretched condition of slaves than about the even more wretched condition of day laborers is probably connected with the fact that to the landowners of antiquity slaves were an object of economic and legal concern. In the calculations of such owners the harvest worker and his distress played a secondary role. To this extent the picture usually given of a "slave-owning society" is incomplete, and reflects the consciousness of the ruling class in antiquity. The landowner had an interest in the productivity—that is, the capacity for work and the life expectancy—of his slaves. They were his property and he had to pay for their cost and yield a profit as well. If a slave died too soon or became incapable of work too soon, the owner lost his capital investment.

The day laborer, on the other hand, was a kind of slave at his own risk.[11] The information in Matthew 20:1 that day laborers receive a denarius is difficult to evaluate when we try to reconstruct their living standard. There were fluctuations in the value of money at this period; in addition, it is not easy to determine what a worker could buy for this money and how often he could count on such a wage. On the whole, the attempt made by A. Ben-David to figure out the daily caloric intake of a day laborer's family in the period of the Mishnah will apply also to the situation of the day laborers in Matthew 20:1–15.[12] Theirs too is a life lived at "the lower limit of human nutritional needs."

Jewish and Roman law also confirm our picture of the social situation of day laborers. In the Old Testament the law prescribes that day laborers are to be paid their wage on the evening of the same day (Lev. 19:13; Deut. 24:14–15). The point is that there were employers who tried to withhold a day laborer's wage even though the latter had immediate need of it. The day laborer and his family lived from hand to mouth. The Mishnah contains detailed regulations regarding the day laborer's right to board during the time he is working. For example, he is to be kept from demanding food of too high a quality or, as the case may be, from eating too much of the produce that he is harvesting.[13] On the other hand, the employer is also prevented from failing to provide such board as is customary in the area.

Like the Old Testament, the Mishnah also requires wages to be paid on the evening of the same day. However, the Mishnah allows the employer to withhold the wage if the worker does not ask for it (BM IX, 12b). This represents a serious alteration of the Old Testament prescription: at least such workers as might hope to be hired more frequently by the same employer would under these circumstances not always have the courage to demand their wages immediately. The plight of day laborers is made especially clear by the regulation in the Tosefta: "A worker may not spend the night working for himself and then hire himself out to work for another during the day, because by doing so he robs his employer [by not being able to work as energetically] in the work given to him."[14]

These legal prescriptions show us how compromised in many respects the day laborer's demands for wages really were and how desperate his social situation was on the whole. The oracle of the prophet Jeremiah was probably applicable to the whole of the ancient world: "Woe to him . . . who makes his neighbor serve him for nothing and does not give him his wages" (22:13; cf. Job 7:1; Sir. 34:22).

Legal questions do not arise in Matthew 20:1–15. The wage contract with the long-shift workers is indeed depicted as a legally correct oral contract. But it is doubtful whether in case of a dispute such workers could obtain a legal settlement. The agreement with the short-shift workers, in which no wage is mentioned, would probably not be a legal contract under Roman law,[15] but in Jewish law it seems to have been regarded as validated by the fact that the man begins the work.[16] In any event, the weak position of the short-shift workers in relation to their employer is clear, whether or not one judges that their position is also weak legally inasmuch as no contract has been made. In either case their position is such—and is so described—that the employer can unilaterally determine how much or how little he will give them.

It has sometimes been assumed that the short-shift workers had a right to a full day's wage because there was no payment by the hour in either the Jewish or the Roman economy.[17] A day's wage for hourly workers—it is said—must have been the normal rule.[18] As has been shown, the hiring of day laborers for a single day and not for several favored the employer in every respect. But in addition there was in fact a hiring for parts of a day, as can be seen, for example, from this phrase in the Edict of Diocletian: "A water-carrier who works for a whole day . . . " (VIII, 31–32). These words show that the obligation of a full day's work may not always be presupposed. In Jewish law, too, we find indications that there might be a hiring for only parts of a day (BM IX, 11; bBM 76b). Contracts for an hourly wage, such as those we are familiar with, probably did not exist.

The picture derived from other sources thus matches the one given in Matthew 20:1–15. As the grumbling of the long-shift workers indicates, they take it for granted that the short-shift workers will receive only part of a day's wage. The long-shift workers are not complaining because *her, as usually,* a part-time worker is being paid a full day's wage; they are complaining because *this particular* employer is not following the usual practice.

WHAT THE PARABLE IS INTENDED TO CONVEY

As we have now seen, the same picture emerges from the course of the story in Matthew 20:1–15 as from observation of the everyday world of day laborers. Matthew 20:1–15 presupposes this real-life situation of workers in every detail but one: the behavior of the employer when he pays the men their wages. This behavior is in sharp contrast with everyday reality. Workers would in fact be afraid that the average employer might ill-treat them by not giving them a wage proportionate to the time they had worked. Employers normally take every opportunity to reduce wages. The parable presupposes this, as do the Old Testament, Cato, and Columella, among others.

Now that the relationship of the parable to reality has become clear, I must try to explain the intentions of the parable as far as possible. To this end I shall begin by restricting myself to the text in Matthew 20:1–15 as a self-contained entity. Two crucial points emerge. The parable intends to speak of the *goodness* or *generosity of God* (see esp. v. 15) and of the *behavior of human beings toward one another* as contrasted with the goodness of God (e.g., the envy and grumbling of the long-shift workers).

Matthew 20:1–15 is meant as a parable of the reign of God (see v. 1). A Jewish listener will realize from the very first sentence that the householder is God. The metaphorical representation of God as an employer is quite popular in Judaism, and this is not the only Jewish parable to explain God's dealings with the human race in terms of the behavior of an employer.[19] The picture is clear. Two levels of representation are simultaneously present: the work world of everyday life and the "world" of God. Interpretation of the parables involves explaining the relationship between these two levels.

Radical answers to the question have not stood up to testing. This parable— and the same is true of many others in the synoptics—is not a "parable" as understood by A. Jülicher and R. Bultmann, nor is it an allegory.[20] The story does not remain on the level of the human picture; it is not connected with the intended reality simply by a *tertium comparationis* (Jülicher), a *single* thought, or a "judgement" (Bultmann), such as would be the case with a "parable" in the sense given this term by Jülicher or Bultmann. From verse 8 on, it is the action of *God* that dictates the logic of the story, whereas up to that point it is everyday reality that determines its logic.

The other radical answer to the question of how parables are to be interpreted is to conceive of a parable as an allegory; that is, to relate almost every detail of the picture to something else—namely, the world of faith. This kind of interpretation breaks down here as it does in many other parables. This insight of Jülicher has proved valid with regard to many of the synoptic parables. The marketplace is a marketplace and not, for example, a symbol of the world.

In my opinion, it is methodologically possible to make use of the (socio-) historical presuppositions that play a role in the development of the picture in order to explain the logic of the story as it unfolds *from sentence to sentence*. Another point to be kept in mind is that in the original historical context of the parables of Jesus, all hearers knew from the outset that they were listening to a parable—that is, that a story was being told that really had God for its object. As applied to Matthew 20:1–15 this means that in verses 1–7 the employer is a real employer, but the hearers know the story is meant to explain an action of God. From verse 8 on, the employer is a different "employer," at least when it comes to the payment of wages. The fact that he has a steward is derived from everyday experience. The employer is thus in certain respects an "employer in quotation marks"—that is, God.

The parable depicts the goodness of God. Because it depicts the goodness of God through the image of an employer, the parable makes it clear that God is different by showing his goodness to be the source of experiences not normally to be had amid life's hardships. The world of toil provides the dark backdrop for a luminous picture of God. The contrast with this backdrop is a further source of light. Even the everyday world becomes more clearly visible; one is better able to see what makes it such a grim place. Matthew 20:1–15 is not intended as social criticism, but as a discourse about the goodness of God. But the picture used in conveying this is not of something "neutral" (Bultmann); reflection on the goodness of God as highlighted in a parable from the work world will obviously shed light on the reality of life itself and cause it to be seen more clearly.

The goodness of God is not depicted as unconnected with anything else; rather its consequences for the life of human beings in community are immediately brought out, as the scene of the grumbling long-shift workers shows. These men have in fact done more than the short-shift workers have. It is not their desire as such for a just wage that puts them in the wrong, but the way in which they deal with this desire—that is, they turn their desire for a just wage into a weapon against others. They are envious (v. 15); they begrudge the short-shift workers their denarius; they would be satisfied if the short-shift workers were to receive significantly less than they themselves received. What is being criticized here is not any abstract views on wages or any demands for a just wage, but rather behavior that is uncompassionate and lacking in solidarity. God is kind and merciful; the long-shift workers lack solidarity and compassion.

These are all thoughts that can without difficulty be garnered from the parable. But what does it all mean concretely? Who are the grumblers? To what does the goodness of God refer? What behavior is singled out? The concrete application of the thoughts cannot be discerned in the parable itself when it is taken as a self-contained entity. A context is needed: the context provided by texts *and* the context provided by concrete life—that is, in this case the precise historical situation to which the parable is related.

The attempt is usually made to concretize the parable by locating it—and rightly so, in all probability—in the context provided by the situation of the historical Jesus. But before I attempt this kind of concretization once again, I must take a critical look at a widespread kind of interpretation. It can be said that the exegetical tradition in the interpretation of Matthew 20:1–15 that the theological emphases are in almost every case open to criticism, even if one finds oneself in agreement with many observations on details. Moreover, they are open to criticism not only from the theological viewpoint but also from the viewpoint of the story itself. The parable is almost always understood as being in principle a critique of the Jewish "concept of recompense" (*belohngedanke*) or even a complete rejection of this concept.[21] In all likelihood it is chiefly Paul Billerbeck's commentary on the New Testament with an explanation of "the teaching of the ancient synagogue on *recompense*" (v. 1:490ff., 495) and of "the thirst for *recompense* among the [Jewish] people" (pp. 496ff.) that has swayed many interpretations of the parable in this direction.

Here I can only assert that in such pictures of the Jewish religion completely inadequate categories are used that do neither theological nor historical justice to the reality. As far as the parable in Matthew 20:1–15 is concerned, this kind of interpretation can be subjected to detailed criticism. The parable is not concerned with the concept of recompense, however the latter may be concretely understood, but rather with the use of the sense of justice (which requires that recompense should match the work done) as a *weapon* against other human beings. In other words, the parable deals with a concrete function of the concept of recompense. The idea that the Pharisees are being attacked here, or that the Christian concept of God is being opposed to the Jewish concept is completely erroneous.

The development of the parable is clear: its ultimate intention is not to criticize persons like the long-shift workers. Its ultimate intention is rather to win hearers over, to address those whose behavior is reflected, in exaggerated form, in the behavior of the long-shift workers.[22] Those addressed are to be able to recognize themselves even in this negative guise and, because they see the depicted behavior to be wrong, to change their way of acting. The purpose of the parable is not negative (criticism) but positive: to teach solidarity.

To read into the parable a difference, of whatever kind, between "Judaism" and "Christianity" is to miss the point of the parable. The parable rather presupposes that "short-shift workers" live in close proximity within a community and that nothing divides them but a lack of solidarity on the part of certain "long-shift workers."

The parable is a Jewish parable, told to Jews by a Jew. It is based on the idea of God in the Old Testament and Judaism, and specifically on the notion of God's goodness that is found therein. "The lord is merciful and gracious, slow to anger and abounding in steadfast love" (Ps. 103:8; 86:15; Exod. 34:6). The comparison repeatedly made by exegetes between this parable and that of the short-shift worker in the Jerusalem Talmud (jBer 2, 3c; see Billerbeck 4:493) is misleading. The rabbinic parable is meant to show that the rabbi who dies prematurely is not at a disadvantage. He receives a full reward from God because he accomplished more in a short life than others do in a long life. The parable thus presupposes that God rewards accomplishments—but so does the parable of the workers in the vineyard! The intention of the two parables is so different, however, that a comparison of the two is irrelevant. The rabbinic parable is about the distress of a young man faced with death; Matthew 20:1–15 is about solidarity.

These observations on the intention of the parable and on the history of its interpretation can be summed up as follows. The parable has two focuses: the goodness of God and—as a consequence of this goodness—solidarity among human beings. The goodness of God is not being opposed to another picture of God in which God rewards according to works or results. What the good God is implicitly being contrasted with is the employer in everyday life who keeps his wages as low as possible. The theological statement made by this parable is not to be understood as a challenge to another theology but as a challenge to the lives of human beings. The parable seeks to foster solidarity among human beings who share the same idea of God as merciful.

The questions of what the concrete context of this solidarity is and of what accomplishments the short-shift workers lack can be answered only by placing the parable in a concrete historical context. One must, for example, look for the reality behind the statement of the long-shift workers: "You have made them equal to us." This search can be carried out, on the one hand, in the historical context of the earliest traditions about Jesus (or of the historical Jesus himself—the distinctions in one that need not be thematized here)[23] or, on the other hand, at the historical level of Matthew's gospel.

I shall first consider Matthew's application of the parable in the context of his gospel as a whole and in the context of the historical situation discernible in his gospel. This first step will make it easier to look then for the concrete meaning of the parable in the situation of the earliest Jesus movement, because we see that if we want to understand the parable we cannot neglect its concretization in Matthew. Matthew does not use the parable to explain general and even supratemporal theological ideas, but rather to cope with a painful and pernicious conflict within his own community.

THE MEANING OF THE PARABLE IN THE CONTEXT OF MATTHEW'S GOSPEL

As in the other gospels, so too in that of Matthew the tradition of the stories and sayings of Jesus that are taken from (for example) the gospel of Mark or the Logia source (Q) is made part of a train of thought that is new and relevant to the disciples of Jesus at the time of Matthew. First, then, I shall follow Matthew's train of thought in the proximate context of the parable (19:16–20:28). Then I shall look for substantive parallels in the total context, which is Matthew's gospel in its entirety, and I shall ask what the real meaning of Matthew 20:1–16 is for him.

MATTHEW 19:16–20:28

Matthew is here following the text in Mark 10:17–45, which includes: the story of the "rich young man"; the subsequent conversation with the disciples regarding the wealthy; the prediction of Jesus' passion; the desire of the sons of Zebedee to sit at Jesus' right and left; sayings about the order of precedence among the disciples. In Mark 10:31 as in Matthew 19:30 the conversation about the wealthy ends with the saying: "But many that are first will be last, and the last first." This saying evidently gives Matthew an opportunity to introduce into the Markan sequence an addition (Matt. 20:1–16) that ends with a slightly altered repetition of the saying about the first and the last (v. 16).

Interventions in the Markan text, which in themselves are to some extent minimal, profoundly alter Mark's original train of thought in the process of relating it to the situation of Matthew's community. The rich man is *young* only in Matthew, and, unlike in Mark and Luke (whom I cannot discuss here), he is pert and unserious in Matthew. The changes from Mark, slight though they seem when taken in isolation, give rise to a new story.

In Matthew the young man asks Jesus: "What good deed must I do . . . ?" Jesus answers by criticizing the question: "Why do you ask me about what is good? One there is who is good." For Matthew this response means: the question was a superficial one, because the necessary consequence of God's goodness is love of neighbor, and the concrete need of the neighbor shows what ought to be done at the moment (Matt. 25:31–46). The most powerful presentation in Matthew of the imperatives that God's mercy lays upon human beings in their relationships with one another is the parable of the scoundrelly servant (Matt. 18:23–35).

In Matthew's story Jesus continues: "If you would enter life. . . ." If you are serious, then keep the commandments. Again the young man responds with a question that really represents an intention of avoiding the burden of the commandments: "Which [ones am I to keep]?" This question is just as unserious as that of the lawyer in Luke 10:29 who asks who his neighbor is. Matthew is saying: this young man is trying to engineer a theological discussion on which commandments one should keep, instead of going off and practicing love of neighbor. Jesus sums up the commandments for him and then, in Matthew's story, explicitly adds: "And, You shall love your neighbor as yourself." The young man now makes a rash claim: "All these I have observed; what do I still lack?" Once again he tries to avoid the radical demands of love of neighbor by asking superficial questions. The claim that he is perfect—and this claim is implicit in his rhetorical question—anticipates God's finding at the last judgment. This is an intolerable act of religious arrogance in Matthew's eyes; in his view the final judgment will produce great amazement among human beings (Matt. 25:31–46). Jesus does not here, as he does in Mark, look at the young man with love, but simply answers him once again in a quite objective way: "If you would be perfect. . . ." If you want to set out on the way to perfection—for you are not yet at all on this way—then act as love of neighbor demands, "sell what you possess and give to the poor." Do not talk; act! (cf. Matt. 7:21 or 21:28–32).

Stories of pert young men whose prattling makes it clear to a teacher that they are not really serious were often told in antiquity. For example, it is told of Zeno that "to a young man who was indulging in a good deal of idle talk he [Zeno] said: 'Your ears have run together with your tongue.'"[24] Matthew calls the rich man a young man because he can thus characterize the role the man adopts in relation to Jesus: that of an impertinent questioner.

In Matthew, therefore, the young man is an unlikeable rich man. After he leaves, Jesus converses with his disciples about the rich (as he does in Mark). The assertion that it is difficult, even impossible, for a rich person to enter the kingdom of God does not make the same strong impression in Matthew that it does in Mark, who several times reports the dismay of the disciples at this severity. Matthew mentions their shock only once. Matthew 19:16–26 seems to reflect painful experiences of the Jesus community with the rich, although this problem does not receive as much attention from Matthew as it does especially from Luke.[25] For Matthew the rich are not an internal problem of the community.

As in Mark so in Matthew, after this depressing scene Peter speaks to Jesus about the disciples. In Mark there is an almost arrogant self-assertiveness ("We have left everything"), to which Jesus responds with a warning (Mark 10:28, 31). In Matthew, however, Peter's statement is followed by a question: "Lo, we have left everything and followed you. What then shall we have?" For Matthew this question is not an expression of arrogance, but a legitimate question to which Jesus gives a positive answer by his promise of twelve thrones (19:28). In Matthew the story ends with the statement that "many that are first will be last, and the last first"; in other words, those who in this world are rich and "first" will be last in the kingdom of God if, like the rich young man, they do not keep the commandments. On the other hand, those who are poor in this world because they have left everything for the sake of Jesus and who are therefore "last" as far as money and prestige are concerned, will be first in God's kingdom. Unlike the same statement in Mark 10:31, Matthew 19:30 is not a warning to the disciples but a warning to those who act like the rich young man and prove faithless to the commandment of love of neighbor.

In 20:1 Matthew takes up a new theme. The problem now is that some of Jesus' disciples want to be first in relation to the other disciples (20:1–28 deals with the theme of *protos en hymin,* "first among you"). The theme is proposed in the story that follows at this point in Mark (Mark 10:33–45; Matt. 20:20–28), and is evidently very important to Matthew. The theme is another that is illumined by the saying about the eschatological reversal of first and last (Matt. 20:16).

In Mark the sons of Zebedee had asked that in glory they might sit at the right and left of Jesus. Matthew seeks to shift the onus somewhat from the sons of Zebedee themselves. He has their mother ask the ugly question about a special reward for her two sons, an extra reward that will put them in an advantageous position in relation to the other disciples. Matthew does not want to show the two disciples themselves in this negative light, but he does regard as important the problem of the desire for religious privileges within the community. Consequently he can conclude the story taken from Mark with almost the identical words that Mark uses: "Whoever would be great among you must be your servant, and whoever would be first among you must be your slave (20:26–27).

Matthew 20:1–16 is already linked to this theme of the religious claims that Christians make at the expense of other Christians. Matthew 20:16 is a warning to those who should recognize themselves in the long-shift workers. The long-shift workers act like the mother of the sons of Zebedee, with whom the disciples are justly angry (20:24), because the desire of these two men for an extra reward is a form of opposition to the other disciples, with whom they are unwilling to live on equal terms.

In my opinion it is not possible to interpret 19:30 as another warning to the disciples and thus to create a more obvious connection between 19:30 and 20:1–16.[26] Matthew 19:28 militates against such an interpretation. The question that the disciples ask in 19:27 about their reward is not criticized but is given a positive answer. I must agree with E. Schweizer (in his commentary on this passage) in seeing a certain material difference between 19:30 and 20:16: Matthew 19:30 criticizes the rich young man and others like him; Matthew 20:16, on the other hand, criticizes persons like the mother of the sons of Zebedee and the long-shift workers.

LACK OF LOVE IN THE MATTHEAN COMMUNITY

Matthew 20:1–28 shows what an important place the gospel of Matthew gives to the problem of counteracting the desire of being *protos en hymin,* first in the community. There are some texts in Matthew that make possible a fuller picture of the lack of love in the Matthean community and of the way in which Matthew deals with this problem. I refer especially to Matthew 18:1–14 and 23:8–12. Each text might have as its title the bitter saying: "Most men's love will grow cold" (Matt. 24:12).

Matthew 23:8–12 is part of a lengthy discourse of Jesus against the Pharisees. Matthew puts a great deal of himself into it as he constructs it out of material in Mark and Q and perhaps in another tradition as well. It is directed against the Pharisees of Matthew's own time. There are grounds for thinking that Matthew is living somewhere in the Jewish Diaspora during the period after the destruction of Jerusalem. The Pharisees with whom he is at odds are probable Pharisees in the same Jewish Diaspora community (perhaps Antioch) to which the Matthean Christians belong.

The fact that Jews have persecuted the disciples of Jesus is for Matthew now past history; otherwise why should he have put the prediction of persecution by Jews (from Mark 13:9–13) into the mission discourse (Matt. 10:17–25)? This striking transposition can mean only that the persecution of the disciples by Jews is in the past. The condemnation of Israel (in Matt. 23:1ff), from Q, means this to Matthew: to the extent that the Jewish people persecuted Jesus and his disciples, it has since been punished by the destruction of Jerusalem. Matthew has sharp criticism for Judaism, but we must not lose sight of the fact that he and his "Christian" community are *also* Jews. The Christians are probably a kind of sectarian group within the Diaspora community and carry on a keen ideological debate with other Jews while emphasizing the fact that the followers of Jesus regard themselves as Jews, that the God of the Old Testament is on their side, and that they observe the law to the full (see 5:17).

It would be an error to think of the passage as one in which *Christians* are speaking against Jews. Christianity in this sense does not yet exist here. This is certainly true in the minds of the "pagans" who persecute "Christians" (Matt. 24:9b–14). Persecutors might indeed harass the disciples of Jesus, but because they were, for example, a messianic group of *Jews;* the Matthean community emphatically confesses Jesus as son of David. The disciples of Jesus understand the persecution as persecution for the sake of Christ (see, e.g., 24:9b), but the persecutors understand it as a measure aimed at counteracting the political danger that Jewish messianic movements represented to them.

The historical state of affairs just described is one with which we are quite familiar, even if not as one concretely related to the gospel of Matthew. In Eusebius, for example, there is a citation from Hegesippus that may serve as an illustration of this historical situation:

"And there still survived of the Lord's family the grandsons of Jude, who was said to be His brother, humanly speaking. These were informed against as being of David's line, and brought by the *evocatus* before Domitian Caesar, who was as afraid of the advent of Christ as Herod had been. Domitian asked them whether they were descended from David and they admitted it. . . ."

Then, the writer [Hegesippus] continues, they showed him their hands, putting forward as proof of their toil the hardness of their bodies and the calluses impressed on their hands by incessant labour. When asked about Christ and His Kingdom—what it was like, and where and when it would appear—they explained that it was not of this world or anywhere on earth but angelic and in heaven, and would be established at the end of the world, when He would come in glory to judge the quick and the dead and give every man payment according to his conduct. On hearing this, Domitian found no fault with them, but despising them as beneath his notice let them go free and issued orders terminating the persecution of the church.[27]

Of course, the special problem of the descent of some disciples of Jesus from David, as presented in this text, is not comparable to anything in Matthew, but the theological and political situation is indeed comparable. Matthew could well have used the same eschatology to defend himself against the accusation of political messianism.

In the framework of the polemic against the Pharisees in chapter 23—the historical situation of which I have been trying to elucidate—Matthew suddenly digresses in 23:8–12 to criticize his own people—that is, disciples of Jesus. Having criticized the Pharisees for preferring the places of honor at feasts (23:6–7), he turns directly to a criticism of the same phenomenon within the Christian community. There are Christians who like to be called "rabbi," "father," and "master" (23:8–10). They regard themselves as teachers of the community and demand a special precedence on this account. Jesus tells them: "You are all brethren," "You have one Father, who is in heaven," and "You have one master, the Christ." Preferential treatment, which is to be thought of as analogous to *protoklisia* ("places of honor," v. 6), and the social claim this expresses should not exist among Christians. This abrupt digression against Christians in the midst of a discourse against the Pharisees shows how important a role the claim to privilege plays in the Matthean community.

Matthew 18:1–14 gives a similar picture. Here Matthew is following Mark 9:33–37, 42–50. From there he takes the theme and the key terms, but he sets the emphases differently in dealing with the problems of the disagreement about status. In 18:10–14 Matthew is using material from the Logia Source (parable of the lost sheep) in order once again to discuss ill-treatment of the "little ones," a subject he had already raised in 19:6 where he is dependent on Mark 9:42. The disciples' question about who is the greatest in the kingdom of God is immediately criticized in Mark (9:35) and treated as the expression of a wrong attitude. In Matthew, however, it is answered in a more nuanced way.

First, we are told who are in fact the greatest in the kingdom of God: those who humble themselves and become childlike.[28] Then Matthew shows the wrong way of giving vent to a desire to be greatest in the kingdom of God: by causing the "little ones" to take scandal (which probably means: to leave the Christian community) and by despising the "little ones" (Matt. 18:6–9, 10–14). It would be better to mutilate oneself than to become a source of scandal (18:6–9); one ought to go after the "little ones" as one goes after a lost sheep.

For Matthew the "little ones" are those who are "low" on the social scale—that is, both in regard to social prestige and in regard to economic status: they are in need of active mercy. The *elachistoi*, or "least," in Matthew 25:31–46 are, from a social and economic standpoint, identical with the *mikroi*, or "little ones," of Matthew 18. This means that there are "little ones" both inside and outside the community. In 25:31–46 the "least" are not presented as coming solely from among Christians, for if they were, their benefactors would not be so astonished at the final judgment.[29]

Insofar as dealing with those who are "low" on the social scale are concerned, Matthew 18:1–14 and 25:31–46 may be summarized as follows. Within the community social distinctions *must* be eliminated (18:1–14); independently of whether or not they belong to the community, all who are in distress must be the recipients of active mercy (25:31–46). In Matthew's eyes the behavior of Jesus shows him to be the teacher of this kind of mercy. In the stories of miraculous healings he has pity on the sick; he has pity on the tax collectors and sinners; he has pity on the hungry disciples who pluck the ears of grain. All these stories about Jesus are for Matthew—and usually for him alone among the evangelists—stories about mercy (see 9:13; 12:7).

Within the community the "little ones" are obviously being treated as outsiders. The community to which Matthew belongs is not a community of the poor. Even the problems of the day laborers in 20:1–15 are not presented in such a way as to suggest that the readers had personal experience of them. Nonetheless the distress of human beings confronts this community—made up of persons who are not perhaps "rich" but who at least do not experience material want—with the question of truth: whether they are truly on the side of the Jesus who calls those "who labor and are heavy laden" (11:28–30); whether they are truly on the side of the God who takes pity on the "short-shift workers."

For Matthew, then, 20:1–16 means: there are Christians who claim privileges in God's sight because in fact they do more than the "little ones" in the community. Such are the teachers, who shape and maintain the public image presented by the community. Their claim to privileges before God and therefore in the community as well offends against solidarity. "You are all brethren." For Matthew, the measure of how seriously Christians take their faith is their behavior toward the lowly inside and outside the community.

THE MEANING OF THE PARABLE IN THE EARLIEST JESUS TRADITION

Although it is not possible to *prove* that Matthew 20:1–15 as a whole is older than the gospel of Matthew, there are nonetheless grounds for surmising that the parable stems from the earliest tradition about Jesus.[30] The most important indication that Matthew has taken the parable from another source is the abrupt transition from 19:30 to 20:1. The connective *gar* ("for") in 20:1 is meant to effect a transition, but its meaning can be grasped only from 20:1–28 as a whole. The statement that the first will be last has a different sense from the one it has in 19:30. The *gar* in 20:1 connects one meaning of the saying about the first and the last (its meaning when directed against the rich in 19:30) with its other meaning: a warning against claims to precedence within the community (20:16).

Matthew 20:1–15 yields a sense when placed in the context of the earliest tradition about Jesus. We may regard the pre-Markan stories about the plucking of the ears of grain on the Sabbath (Mark 2:23–27), about the tax collector's feast (Mark 2:13–17), and about the gospel of the poor (Luke 6:20–21; Matt. 11:2–5) as the central texts of the earliest tradition about Jesus and take them as our point of departure here.[31]

Matthew 20:1–15 would fit quite well into the situation of dialogue between the disciples of Jesus and the Pharisees as this is reflected in Mark 2:13ff. and 2:23ff. The disciples of Jesus are poor. They claim that their need takes precedence over the Sabbath. They refuse to be standoffish toward tax collectors and criminals. They do not deny that criminals are sinners, but they regard them as called by Jesus no less than are the righteous (Mark 2:17). The Pharisees should accept this attitude as a logical conclusion from the Torah and from God's mercy, for they attach as much importance to these as do the disciples of Jesus.

There must no longer be a separation within the life of the Jewish people between sinners and nonsinners. "You have made them equal to us": the grumbling of the long-term workers, precisely because it takes this extreme and alienating form, should bring home to the Pharisees the truth that their justified claim to have accomplished more may not be used as an argument against tax collectors and sinners. As elsewhere in the earliest Jesus tradition, theological thinking is directed by a vision of the Jewish people as destined to be remade before God as a new community to which *all* human beings belong.

As part of the discussion that went on between the disciples of Jesus and the Pharisees long before the destruction of Jerusalem, Matthew 20:1–15 is *not* a criticism of and attack on the Pharisees but an effort to bring them to the point of joining the disciples of Jesus and accepting solidarity with the poor, the tax collectors, and sinners. The point of entry at which this approach to the Pharisees is made is their conception of God as merciful. The discussion with the Pharisees in that earlier time is of an entirely different kind from the discussion that Matthew carries on with (a later) Pharisaism. Matthew 20:1–15 shows the same friendly courting of the Pharisees that is to be observed elsewhere in the earliest Jesus tradition.

Notes

1. Pliny the Younger, *Epistulae* IX, 20, 2.
2. In addition, there was a good deal of flexibility in calculating the "usual" wage to be paid when no prior agreement had been made; see bBM 87a.
3. See G. Dalman, *Arbeit und Sitte in Palästina* (Gütersloh, 1928ff.), 1:1, 44; 4:936. On the length of the workday, see also Ps. 104:22–23 and bBM 83a.

4. See J. Jeremias, *The Parables of Jesus,* S. H. Hooke, trans. (New York, rev. ed., 1973), pp. 136–37.

5. *Corpus Inscriptionum Latinarum* 8, Suppl. 11824.

6. Marcus Terentius Varro, *Res rusticae,* I, 17, 2–3, in *Cato and Varro: De re rustica,* W. D. Hooper and H. B. Ash, trans., Loeb Classical Library (Cambridge, Mass., 1960), p. 225. Cf. Columella, *Res rustica,* I, 7, 4 (note 8, below).

7. Marcus Porcius Cato, *De agri cultura,* 5, 4, in *Cato and Varro,* p. 15. The text is translated in W. Krenkel, "Zu den Tagelohnern bei der Ernte in Rom," *Romanitas,* 6/7 (1965) 141, with whose arguments against the interpretation of H. Gummerus, *Das römische Gusbetrieb* (Leipzig, 1903), pp. 26–27, I am compelled to agree.

8. Lucius Junius Moderatus Columella, *Res rustica,* III, 21, 9–10, in *Columella: On Agriculture,* vol. 1, books I–IV, H. B. Ash, trans., Loeb Classical Library (Cambridge, Mass., 1960), p. 347.

9. For further discussion, see the works cited in n. 7, above, and P. A. Brunt, "Die Beziehungen zwischen dem Herr and dem Land," in his *Zur Sozial- und Wirtschaftsgeschichte der späten römischen Republik* (Darmstadt, 1976), pp. 124ff., esp. 133–34.

10. Thus, for example, F. van der Ven, *Sozialgeschichte der Arbeit,* 1 (Munich, 1971), pp. 98–99. M. Kaser, *Das römische Privatrecht,* 1 (Munich, 2nd ed., 1971), p. 568, is more cautious.

11. On these questions, see Krenkel "Zu den Tagelohnern."

12. A. Ben-David, *Talmudische Ökonomie* (Hildesheim, 1974), pp. 300–301.

13. BM VII, 1–7. On the rabbinical interpretation of Deut. 23:26–27, see chap. 8, above.

14. Tosefta on BM (Zuckermandel, p. 387, line 25); German translation and further information in D. Farbstein, *Das Recht der unfreien und freien Arbeiter nach jüdisch-talmudischem Recht* (Frankfurt, 1896), p. 45, line 5.

15. *Corpus Iuris Civilis: Digesta,* 19, 2. 2; 19, 5. 22.

16. bBM 76a; on these questions, see also M. Silberberg, "Dienstvertrag und Werkvertrag im talmudischen Rechte" (dissertation, Frankfurt, 1927), p. 19.

17. E. Wolf, "Gottesrecht und Menschenrecht. Rechtstheologische Exegese des Gleichnisses von den Arbeitern im Weinberg (Mt 20, 1–16)," in H. Vorgrimler, ed., *Gott in Welt. Festgabe für Karl Rahner,* 2 (Freiburg, 1964), pp. 640–62; J. B. Bauer, "Gnadenlohn oder Tageslohn," Bib, 42 (1961) 224–28.

18. The Edict of Diocletian (A.D. 301) also assumes that "a rural worker" is hired "by the day and given his board" (VII, 1a). Further material on work by the day as normal case is to be found in Bauer, "Gnadenlohn"; Krenkel, "Zu den Tagelohnern," p. 141; T. Mayer-Maly, *Locatio conductio* (Vienna, 1956), p. 124.

19. See the parables in Billerbeck 4/1:492–93.

20. A. Jülicher, *Die Gleichnisreden Jesu,* 1 (Tübingen, 1910); R. Bultmann, *The History of the Synoptic Tradition,* J. Marsh, trans. (Oxford, 1963), esp. pp. 174, 198.

21. A (purely random) selection of interpretations that show the validity of this statement: G. Eichholz, *Gleichnisse der Evangelien* (Neukirch-en-Vluyn, 1971), esp. pp. 99–100; Jeremias, *The Parables,* esp. p. 139; H. Braun, "Die Auslegung Gottes durch Jesus, dargestellt an der Parable vom gleichen Lohn für alle," *Der Evangelische Erzieher,* 16 (1964) 346–56.

22. Eichholz, for example, rightly emphasizes this point.

23. See L. Schottroff and W. Stegemann, *Jesus von Nazareth—Hoffnung der Armen* (Stuttgart, 1978), chap. 1.

24. Diogenes Laertius, *De vitis . . . philosophorum,* VIII, 21; cf. VII, 22–23.

25. See Schottroff and Stegemann, *Jesus von Nazareth,* chap. 3.

26. Thus, e.g., Eichholz, *Gleichnisse,* pp. 101–3; H. Frankemölle, *Jahwebund und Kirche Christi* (Münster, 1974), p. 154. For a different interpretation, E. Schweizer, *The Good News according to Matthew,* D. E. Green, trans. (Atlanta, 1975), pp. 394–95.

27. Eusebius, *The History of the Church,* G. A. Williamson, trans. (Penguin Classics, Baltimore, 1965), pp. 126–27. The Latin word *evocatus* means "veteran," but the precise meaning here is not known.

28. The logion on self-humbling is used in Matt. 23:8–13 to convey the same point.

29. On these questions, see P. Christian, *Jesus und seine geringsten Brüder* (Leipzig, 1975).

30. The old argument of the form-critics that Matt. 20:16 is secondary in relation to Matt. 20:1–15 (and that the parable is thus from the pre-Matthean tradition), because in it Matthew has incorrectly turned the temporal sequence of payments in the parable into the key point, can no longer be maintained. As I have shown, 20:16, in the context of Matthew's gospel, has its own substantial content and accurately captures the meaning of the parables.

31. See Schottroff and Stegemann, *Jesus von Nazareth,* chap. 1. In what follows I draw especially on the interpretation given there of Mark 2:13–17 and the interpretation of Mark 2:23–27 that is given in chap. 7, above.@READ_DING:X

Creation of New Meaning: Rhetorical Situations and the Reception of Romans 13:1–7

Jan Botha

INTRODUCTION

Whether we like it or not, Romans 13 does influence values and actions of people significantly. One of the most eloquent opponents of apartheid, Allan A. Boesak, starts his essay titled *What belongs to Caesar? Once again Romans 13*,[1] with the following story:

> On 19 October 1977, I was visited for the first time by the South African Security Police. They stayed from 3:30 till 7:00. At one point I was challenged by the Security Police captain (who assured me that he was a Christian and, in fact, an elder of the white Dutch Reformed Church) on my persistent resistance to the government. "How can you do what you are doing," he asked, "while you know what Romans Thirteen says?" In the hour-long conversation that followed, I could not convince him. For him, as for millions of other Christians in South Africa and across the world, Romans 13 is an unequivocal, unrelenting call for blind, unquestioning obedience to the state.

Addressing a gathering of a million members of the (mainly black and apolitical) Zion Christian Church near Pietersburg in April 1985, the former South African State President, P.W. Botha, praised his audience as people who "love and respect their Bishop," who have "a sincere and healthy lifestyle" and who "respect law, order and authority." Later on in his speech he said:

> The Bible . . . has a message for the governments and governed of the world. Thus we read in Romans 13 that every person be subject to the governing authorities. There is no authority except from God. Rulers are not a terror to good conduct, but to bad conduct. Do what is good, and you will receive the approval of the ruler. He is God's servant for your good.[2]

Coming from *the* symbol of an oppressive government, addressed to a black audience, spoken only three months before the first State of Emergency was announced, these words had an ominous ring. In addition to many other reasons

---

From *Journal of Theology for Southern Africa* 79 (June 1992): 24–37. Copyright by *Journal of Theology for Southern Africa*. Reprinted by permission.

[1]Allan A Boesak "What belongs to Caesar? Once again Romans 13", in Boesak, A.A. (ed), *When prayer makes news* (Philadelphia: Westminster, 1986) p138–156.

[2]Address by former State President P.W. Botha on the occasion of the award of the Freedom of Moria on 7 April 1985. Issued by the Section Liaison Services, Office of the State President, Tuynhuys, Cape Town.

which can be given, the fact that Romans 13:1–7 was addressed to governed *and not to governors*, gives decisive motivation to rule out this type of abuse of the text by an authoritarian government.[3]

The problematic nature of Romans 13:1–7 is well known. Many examples can be cited of the (sometimes) disastrous influence of this text in political contexts during the whole of Christian history.[4] The remarks of Boesak and Botha seem to confirm its current topicality in the South African socio-political context.

New Testament scholars have the special responsibility to propose valid contextual interpretation(s) of this problematic passage in the Bible. A very valuable catalogue of possible "escapes" from an authoritarian reading of Romans 13:1–7 has been compiled by Fowler.[5] Yet, it still leaves the basic problem open: What shall we do with this passage? To use the terminology of Victor Furnish: is Romans 13 a "sacred cow" or a "white elephant" in contemporary Christians ethics?[6]

In this article I shall argue from the general hypothesis that the rhetorical situation in which a text is read has a direct influence on the meaning created during the act of reading. This thesis will be illustrated by an analysis of different rhetorical situations in which Romans 13:1–7 can be/is read. (The illustration also serves to point out some similarities and differences between the concepts "rhetorical situation" and "historical situation.") From such an analysis it will be possible to identify similarities and differences between readings in different rhetorical situations. The acknowledgment of the (inevitable) existence of such differences leads us to the conclusion that every new reading of this (any) text is a *new creation* of meaning. Although this conclusion is by no means a new insight in terms of the results of research in contemporary literary theory, this concrete example of the creative role of the reader might be illuminating.

---

[3]For an informative analysis of the abuse of Romans 13:1–7 in South Africa, *cf.* J. A. Draper "'Humble Submission to Almighty God' and its Biblical Foundation" *JTSA* 63 (1988) p30–38.

[4]*Cf.* U. Wilckens *Der Brief an die Römer" VI/3 (Rom 12–16) (Zürich: Benziger, 1982) p43–66*, for a comprehensive discussion of the *Wirkungsgeschichte* of Romans 13:1–7. He discusses the influence of Romans 13:1–7 on the stance of the martyrs toward the authorities during the age of persecution (p44–46), the problem of the fusion of church and state after Constantine (p45–47), the Medieval *Zwei-Schwerter* theory and Romans 13 (p47–49). Luther's interpretation, especially in the light of the revolt by the farmers led by Thomas Müntzer (p47–52), the struggle of other reformers like Zwingli (who himself had eventually died in a political struggle). Bucer and Calvin to come to grips with Romans 13 and the consequent influence of Calvin's interpretation on all the reformed confessions (p52–55), the role of this text in the 17th century church-state relationship debates in Europe and England (p55–58); the significant influence of the French revolution and the subsequent reception of Romans 13:1–7 and the subsequent interpretations by Kant, Hegel and Marx (p58–61); Karl Barth and the Barmen confession in the our century (p62–64); the catholic theory of state since the 18th century (p65–66) and finally a short word about Romans 13:1–7 and Liberation Theology (p66).

[5]Robert M. Fowler *Wriggling of the Hook: Strategies of Resisting Authoritarian Readings of Romans 13:1–7.* (Paper read at the 1988 SNTS Seminar on The Role of the Reader, Cambridge, England).

[6]*Cf.* Victor P. Furnish *The Moral Teaching of Paul* (Nashville: Abingdon, 1985) p13–23. According to the sacred-cow view, all the ethical teachings of Paul are in fact God's commandments and are thus eternally and universally binding. On the other hand, the terms "outmoded, irrelevant and ridiculous" have all been applied to Paul's moral teaching—it is seen as an anachronism, like an antique automobile: interesting only to antiquarians, but a real menace when driven out onto a modern expressway. This is the white-elephant view of Paul's moral teaching.

The rhetorical situations of two texts are analysed: Paul's text and Boesak's text on Paul's text. The text by Boesak was chosen because it was published in a book which had resulted from a particularly interesting rhetorical situation[7] and because the essay itself contains a number of explicit remarks about its particular rhetorical situation. It is the aim of this article to illustrate an aspect of the theory of interpretation in general and not to take issue with any particular reading as such.

METHODOLOGICAL CONSIDERATIONS: READER RESPONSE CRITICISM AND RHETORIC

The active and creative role of the reader or audience in any act of interpretation and, subsequently, a renewed emphasis on the importance of context, is widely recognised by scholars in literary criticism,[8] rhetorical criticism,[9] and biblical studies.[10] However, with regard to the theoretical and methodological explanation of this creative role of the reader, we have a situation of *quot homines tot sententiae,* with positions differing from "the reader is encoded in the text" to "the reader has full freedom to 'play' with free signifying texts in the sense-making process.[11]

A major distinction to be drawn in reader-oriented approaches is the one between firstly, a text-oriented (or normative, or hermeneutical) approach, and, secondly, a reader-oriented (or historical or empirical) approach. In a text-oriented approach the text itself is the primary study-object with the focus on "reader-clues" in the text,[12] while a reader-oriented approach focuses on the actual, empirical reception of the text in the history of its reading (in the case of the Bible:

---

[7]In 1985 a group of leading South African Christians issued a "Theological Rationale and a Call to Prayer for the End of Unjust Rule." In addition to controversy in the SACC on its involvement and the status of the Rationale, a media uproar broke out—therefore the title of the book which dealt with various aspect of the Rationale and the subsequent debates: *When prayer makes news* (cf. note 1).

[8]Well-known are the anthologies of Susan Suleiman & Inge Crosman (eds.), *The Reader in the Text. Essays on Audience and Interpretation* (Princeton: University Press, 1980) and Jane P. Tompkins (ed) *Reader-Response Criticism. From Formalism to Post-Structuralism* (Baltimore: John Hopkins University Press, 1980). Both give extended bibliographies. Robert C. Holub, *Reception Theory. A Critical Introduction* (London: Methuen, 1984) and, more recently, Elizabeth Freund, *The Return of the Reader. Reader-response criticism* (London: Methuen, 1987) are two excellent critical discussions of major trends and developments in literary criticism regarding the role of the reader in interpretation.

[9]*Cf.* T.S. Sloane "Rhetoric: Rhetoric in Literature" *The New Encyclopedia Brittanica.* 15th ed. vol 25 1975 p804: "a text must reveal its context"; "And for its twin tasks, analysis and genesis, (modern rhetoric) offers a methodology as well: the uncovering of those strategies whereby the interests, values, or emotions of an audience are engaged by any speaker or writer through his discourse."

[10]In the last decades numerous studies of New Testament literature were done, emphasizing the role of the reader. Jeffrey L. Staley *The Print's First kiss: A Rhetorical Investigation of the Implied Reader in the Fourth Gospel* (Berkeley: GTU Dissertation, 1985) p9–14, traces the history of the use of reader-response criticism in Biblical studies.

[11]*Cf.* Jan Swanepoel "Literêre analise van die Nuwe Testament" *Koers* 51 (1986) p90–130 for a discussion and comparative chart of modern literary approaches to the reading of texts.

[12]For an example of this approach *cf.* B.C. Lategan "Reader-clues in the text of Galations" *Journal of Literary Studies* 3 (1987) p47–59.

commentaries, sermons, etc.)[13] However, it will be an oversimplification to classify all reader-oriented studies simply into these two categories, since there are intermediate positions.[14]

Most of the studies in reader-response criticism in literary and biblical studies so far have followed the first mentioned approach and we have seen quite a number of fine studies in the last decade or so.[15]

Since reader-response criticism was developed in the first place with narrative texts in view,[16] it has been particularly useful in studying the narrative sections of the New Testament. In the case of the letters, however, matters are different because of the significant difference in the communicative situation of narratives and letters (although a so-called "reader-response commentary" on Romans was published recently.)[17] In terms of the distance between the sender and receptor in a communication situation (or "real author" and "real reader")[18] we have a sliding scale from a narrative to a letter to a speech—with the speech the closest and the narrative the furthest.

In the specific case of Romans the situation is even more complicated since Romans is relatively loosely related to the letter-genre.[19] Thus, because of the nature

---

[13]Wilckens' discussion of the *Wirkungsgeschichte* (*cf.* note 4 *supra*) can be cited as an example here. However, an empirical reception-critical approach is more than merely a "history of exegesis" of a particular text. The basic difference lies in the different premises: in traditional "history of exegesis" studies the readers or audiences were not seen as active participants in the sense-making process. *Cf.* also B.C. Lategan & J. Rousseau "Reading Luke 12:35–48: an empirical study" *Neostestamentica* 22 (1988) p391–413 and D.J. Smit, "Those were the critics, what about the real readers? An analysis of 65 published sermons and sermon guidelines on Luke 12:35–48" *Neotestamentica* 23 (1989) p61–82, for examples of empirical reader-response criticism.

[14]*Cf.* B.C. Lategan "Coming to grips with the reader. Some guide-lines for a discussion of reader-oriented approaches" (Paper presented at the SNTS-Seminar on the role of the Leader, 1985) for a discussion of a whole range of concepts and "the reader" of whom some are between the reader-in-the-text and the-empirical-reader positions.

[15]To mention just a few of the most familiar ones: Robert M. Fowler *Loaves and Fishes: The Function of Feeding Stories in the Gospel of Mark* (SBL Dissertation Series 54; Chico, CA: Scholars Press, 1981); *Ibid* "Who is the Reader in Mark's Gospel?" *SBL Seminar Papers* 1983 (Chico: Scholars Press 1983), 33–53 (and also the other papers in that edition); R. Allan Culpepper, *Anatomy of the Fourth Gospel: A Study in Literary Design* (Philadelphia: Fortress, 1983); Donald M. Mitchie and David Rhoads, *Mark as Story: An Introduction to the Narrative of a Gospel* (Philadelphia: Fortress, 1982); Charles Talbert, *Reading Luke: A Literary and Theological Commentary of the Third Gospel* (New York: Crossroads, 1982); Bas van Iersel, *Marcus* (Brugge: Tabor, 1986, Belichting van het Bijbelboek); Sjef van Tilborg, *Johannes* (Brugge: Tabor 1988, Belichting van het Bijbelboek) and Staley, *Print's First Kiss op cit.*

[16]Staley *Print's First Kiss op cit* p7: Reader-response criticism is "an approach in contemporary literary criticism which deals primarily with analysis of the modern novel," *Cf.* also Lategan *op cit* "Reader clues in the text of Galatians" p49: "As far as biblical material is concerned, most work from a reader perspective has been done on narrative texts."

[17]John P. Heil *Paul's letter to the Romans. A reader-response commentary* (New York: Paulist, 1987.) However, this commentary does not differ very much from more traditional commentaries. My impression is that the words "reader-response" were used in the title merely to attract attention.

[18]*Cf.* Staley *Print's First Kiss op cit* p39–47 for a definition and discussion of the terms "real author" and "real reader."

[19]For a discussion of the literary nature of Romans as well as its possible historical background, *cf.* the essays in Karl P. Don Fried, (ed), *The Romans Debate.* (Minneapolis: Augsburg, 1977) *Cf.* also David E. Aune, *The New Testament in its Literary Environment* (Philadelphia: Westminster, 1987) p219–221; Stanley K. Stowers, *Letter Writing in Greco-Roman Antiquity* (Philadelphia: Westminster, 1986) p125–128 and A.J.M. Wedderburn, *Reasons for Romans* (Edinburgh: T & T Clark, 1988) p6–11.

of the text, some of the concepts as well as the methodology offered by reader-response criticism, seem to be less useful, although, of course, not totally irrelevant.[20]

This is where rhetorical criticism comes into play. Among others, George Kennedy,[21] Hans Dieter Betz[22] and Wilhelm Wuellner[23] are to be credited with the introduction of rhetoric (classical as well as new rhetoric) to New Testament studies in recent times.[24] Although traditionally linked with speeches, rhetorical criticism need not be limited to speeches, since, as Sloane has demonstrated, "All discourse falls within the rhetorician's purview."[25] Two interrelated aspects characterise a literary study along the lines of rhetorical criticism, namely a study of the text's discursive techniques, and secondly a study of the functioning of these techniques to provoke, or to increase the support of minds on the part of readers, to the action or value presented for approval.[26] Rhetorical criticism focuses on the interaction between an encoded author and his audience.[27] Therefore, we may say that rhetorical criticism has its eye specifically on the audience or readers. Kennedy claims that "The primary object of rhetorical criticism is to understand the effect of the text."[28] Suleiman maintains that "To the rhetorical critic . . . what matters primarily is the ethical and ideological content of the message. He seeks not only to

---

[20]*Cf.* for example the study of Patrizia Violi "Letters" (in T.A. van Dijk, (ed) *Discourse and Literature. New Approaches to the analysis of literary genres,* Critical Theory Vol 3) p149–168 in which the bearing of the concept of the implied reader on the analysis of letters is illustrated.

[21]George A. Kennedy *New Testament Interpretation through Rhetorical Criticism* (Chapel Hill: University of North Carolina Press, 1984).

[22]*Cf.* his essay "The Literary Composition and Function of Paul's Letter to the Galatians" *NTS* 21 (1975) p353–379; his book *Galations. A Commentary on Paul's Letter to the Churches in Galatia* (Hermeneia: Philadelphia: Fortress, 1979); and his essay "The Problem of Rhetoric and Theology according to the Apostle Paul" in *L'Apotre Paul* (BETL 73; ed. A. Vanhoye, Leuven: Peeters/Catholic University Leuven) p16–48.

[23]*Cf.* W. Wuellner "Paul's Rhetoric of Argumentation in Romans" in *The Romans Debate* p152–174 (originally published in *CBQ* 38 (1976) p330–351); *ibid* "Greek Rhetoric and Pauline Argumentation," in *Early Christian Literature and the Classical Intellectual tradition* (R.M. Grant *Festschrift;* ed. W.R. Schoedel and R.L. Wilken; Paris: Beauschesne, 1979) p177–188, *ibid* "Paul as Pastor. The Function of Rhetorical Questions in First Corinthians" in *L'Apotre Paul op cit* p49–77 and *ibid* "Where is Rhetorical Criticism taking us? *CBQ* 49 (1987) p448–463. In addition to the work of Kennedy, Betz and Wuellner, James D. Hester has also made a significant contribution to the application of rhetorical criticism to New Testament interpretation. *Cf.* his "The Rhetorical Structure of Galations 1:11–2:14" *JBL* 103 (1984) p223–233; "The Use and Influence of Rhetoric in Galations 2:1–14" *ThZ* 42 (1986) p386–408; and "Placing the Blame: The Presence of Epideictic in Galatians One and Two" (unpublished). *Cf.* also Elizabeth Schüssler-Florenza "Rhetorical Situation and Historical Reconstruction in 1 Corinthians" *NTS* 33 (1987) p386–403. For more literature on this topic, *cf.* Duane F. Watson "The New Testament and Greco-Roman Rhetoric: a bibliography" *JETS* (Dec 1988) p465–472.

[24]Although Wuellner himself credits the Mullenberg School with the recent revival of interest in rhetorical criticism in Old Testament studies. Cf. Wuellner "Where is Rhetorical Criticism taking us?" p451. However, rhetorical criticism as practiced by people like Wuellner, Betz, Kennedy, Staley and Hester is decidedly different from the work done by the Muilenberg-school, which had focused primarily on so-called stylistic figures in the Old Testament.

[25]Sloane "Rhetoric" *op cit* p804.

[26]W. Wuellner "Rhetorical criticism and its theory in culture-critical perspective: the narrative rhetoric of John 11": In P.J. Hartin & J.H. Petzer (eds), *Text and Interpretation. New approaches in the criticism of the New Testament* (Leiden: Brill, 1991) p171.

[27]L. Thurén *The rhetorical strategy of 1 Peter. with special regard to ambiguous expressions; (Abo Abo: Akademis Förlag, 1990) p42–46.*

[28]George A. Kennedy *op cit* p33.

formulate the set of verbal meanings embedded in a text, but above all to discover the values and beliefs that make those meanings possible—or that those meanings imply."[29] Taking specific cognisance of the reader, including special attention to the values and beliefs involved in the communication process, rhetorical criticism might offer a substantial contribution to the problem of possible implications of Romans 13:1–7 in its contemporary as well as modern-day communication situations.[30] It might perhaps become even more valuable when the *same* rhetorical "method"[31] for interpreting Romans 13:1–7 is also used to interpret *modern texts on Romans 13*, such as the one by Boesak.

Kennedy proposes a model of rhetorical criticism, based on classical rhetoric, which consists of five methodological steps, namely, 1) the definition of the rhetorical unit, 2) the identification of the rhetorical situation, 3) the identification of the rhetorical disposition or arrangement, 4) the identification of rhetorical techniques or style and 5) the identification of rhetorical criticism as a synchronic whole.[32] For the purpose of this experiment I shall confine myself to the first two steps.

Before we get into this, one final remark about the nature of rhetorical criticism is very important: rhetoric is not merely stylistic (reduced to stylistic features such as *tropae* or *schemata*), or only formal logical dialectic, or irrational emotional devices used to promote an uncritical acceptance of a message which is not necessarily "true"—although this might be what many of us understand when we hear the word "rhetoric." (Think for instance about our commonly used expression, "it is mere rhetoric.")[33] In the light of the claims of Wuellner, Sloan, Kennedy and Suleiman) quoted above) on the primary object of rhetorical criticism and the possibilities opened up by this approach, and for the rest of this article, it will become clear that such a traditional view of what rhetoric is, is very limited. For instance, although Kennedy proposes as a third step in a rhetorical analysis "the identification of rhetorical techniques or style," this is by no means the dominant aspect of rhetorical criticism. The notion of "rhetorical situation" (step 2) corresponds roughly to classical rhetoric's concept "invention," and already in classical rhetoric, *inventio* was at least as important as *elocutio*, if not more important.[34]

---

[29]Susan Suleiman "Introduction: Varieties of Audience-Orientated Criticism" in Susan R. Suleiman & Inge Crosman (eds) *The Reader in the Text* p8. In this introduction to varieties of audience-orientated criticism, Suleiman mentions rhetorical criticism as one of the six varieties or approaches available for a reception critical study.

[30]Wuellner's "Where is rhetorical criticism taking us?" is of major importance for future methodological developments in New Testament studies. He discusses some of the major concepts in rhetorical interpretation and applies it to I Corinthians 9.

[31]"Method" is placed in inverted commas since Wuellner "Rhetorical criticism and its theory in culture-critical perspective *op cit* p178ff argues convincingly that rhetorical criticism is more than a method.

[32]Kennedy, *op cit* p33–38. *Cf.* also A.H. Snyman "Retoriese kriliek en die Nuwe Testament. Die bydraes van en verband tussen Kennedy en Pereiman" *Acta Classica* p1–18.

[33]*For a discussion of what he calls the "false preoccupations" of the traditional view of rhetoric cf.* Lauri Thuren, *The rhetorical structure of 1 Peter p47ff. Cf.* also A.H. Snyman "On studying the figures (*schemata*) in the New Testament Biblica 69 p93–107.

[34]*Cf.* J. Botha "On the 'reinvention' of Rhetoric" *Scripture* 31 (1989) p14–31 for an elaborate plea for a broader conception of rhetoric.

PAUL'S TEXT: ROMANS 13:1–7

THE DEFINITION OF THE RHETORICAL UNIT

The function of this first step in rhetorical criticism is simply to delimit the section that is to be analysed. The rhetorical unit is in all respects the same as a literary unit except that it defines a text unit as an argumentative unit affecting the reader's reasoning or the reader's imagination.[35]

Romans 13:1–7 as a unit satisfies Kennedy's definition of the rhetorical unit: "In rhetorical criticism it is important that the rhetorical unit chosen has some magnitude. It has to have within itself a discernible beginning and ending, connected by some action or argument.[36] The inner logic of Romans 13:1–7 is completely self-contained. Though linked with its context within the Romans paraenesis, the passage is in many respects an isolated unity and can therefore be treated as an independent rhetorical unit.[37]

However, it might be worthwhile to consider for a moment the broader textual rhetoric of our text. Wuellner has analysed the textual rhetoric of Romans as follows: The argumentative thought (1:1–11:36) (*exordium* 1:1–15 and *probatio* 1:16–11:36) is followed by an argumentative appeal to commitment (or *paraenesis*) 12:1–15:13, with 15:14–16:27 as *peroratio*.[38] Regarding the textual rhetoric of the paraenesis-section, Friedrich, Pöhlmann and Stuhlmacher[39] offer the following analysis:

- 12:1–2 Programmatic preamble
- 12:3–16a First paraenetic main section: The life of Christians as ἐννλησία
  12:6–8 List of charismata
  12:9–13 Catalogue of virtues
- 12:16b–13:7 Second paraenetic main section: The life of Christians in worldly relations
- 13:8–10 Recapitulation of all the previous admonitions

The second main section (12:16b–13:7) differs in style from the first section. The first section consists of "exemplarischen und katalogartiger Formen der Ermahnung" without motivations, while the second edition has an "argumentierend-begrundendem paränetischen Still."[40] The admonition "Let everyone be subject to the governing authorities" (Rom 13:1a), is followed by the longest motivational argumentation (Rom 13:1b–7) of all the admonitions given in 12:16b–13:1a. This extended argumentative motivation for the admonition in Rom 13:1–7 further supports the identification of the passage as a distinctive rhetorical unit.

---

[35]Wuellner "Where is rhetorical criticism taking us?" *op cit* p455.
[36]Kennedy *op cit* p34
[37]J.I.H. McDonald "Romans 13:1–7: A test case for New Testament interpretations" *NTS* 35 (1989) p542, comes to the same conclusion.
[38]Wuellner, "Paul's Rhetoric of Argumentation in Romans" *op cit* p157–174.
[39]Johannes, Friedrich, Wolfgang Pöhlmannn & Peter Stuhlmacher "Zur historischen Situation und Intention vom Rom 13, 1–7" *ZThK* 73 (1976) p151.
[40]*Ibid* p153.

RHETORICAL SITUATION OF ROMANS 13:1–7

The Book *The Romans Debate*[41] illustrates how difficult it is to come to a consensus on the historical situation of Romans. Friedrich *et al* rightly speak of the unsolvable problem of the historical situation of Romans 13.[42] In this context Wuellner has offered rhetorical criticism as a new way to make some progress in the interpretation of the letter. According to him the important thing to realise is that

> The rhetorical situation differs both from the historical situation of a given author and reader and from the generic situation or conventions of the *Sitz im Lebem* of forms or genres in one point: the rhetorical critic looks foremost for the premises of a text as appeal or argument.[43]

In order to determine these premises, the rhetorical situation must be (re)constructed. Bitzer defines the rhetorical situation as

> a complex of persons, events, objects, and relations presenting an actual or potential exigence which can be completely or partially removed if discourse, introduced into the situation, can so constrain human decision or action as to bring about the significant modification of the exigence.[44]

What Bitzer means by "exigence" is "a situation under which an individual is called upon to make some response: the response made is conditioned by the situation and in turn has some possibility of affecting the situation or what follows from it."[45] According to Wuellner tradition rhetoric defined a text's rhetorical situation in three distinct ways: 1) in the notion of a text's *status* (or basic issue); 2) in the notion of a text's underlying *topoi* (or *loci*, the "places" or "material" where the "content" of the argument can be found) and 3) in the notion of a text's rhetorical

---

[41]*Ct.* note 19 *supra.*

[42]Friedrich *et al op cit* p156. More recently Wedderburn still found it necessary to publish a monograph (*The reasons for Romans* 1988) on this topic, concluding that the (historical) reasons why Romans was written are a cluster of different interlocking factors: the presence of both Judeizing and Law-free Christians in the church there, the present situation of the church in Rome and the present situation of Paul, the visit to Jerusalem now being undertaken and the prospect of a future visit to Rome (p142). Although extensively and well-argued, Wedderbum still does not escape the confinements of a *historical* line of questioning.

[43]"Where is rhetorical critism taking us?" *op cit* p456. For a definition and discussion of the rhetorical situation, cf. Lloyd F. Bilzor "The Rhetorical Situation" *Philisophy and Rhetoric* 1 (1981) p1–24 and Alan Brinton "Situation in the Theory of Rhetoric" *Philosophy and Rhetoric* 14(1981) p234–248. Cf. also James D. Hesler "The Uso and Influence of Rhetoric in Gatalians" *op cit.*

[44]Bitzer "The Rhetorical Situation" *op cit* p6. For the subsequent debate on the concept of the rhetorical situation, cf. R.L. Larson "Lloyd Bitzer's 'Rhetorical situation' and the classification of discourse: problems and implications" *Philosophy and Rhetoric* 3 (1970) p165–168; R.E. Vatz "The myth of the rhetorical situation" *Philosophy and rhetoric* 6 (1973) p154–161; S. Consigny "Rhetoric and its situations" *Philosophy and Rhetoric* 7 (1974) p175–186 and A. Brinton "Situation in the theory of rhetoric" *Philosophy and Rhetoric* 14 (1981) p234–248. Bitzer's response to this debate was published in 1980: "Functional communication: a situational perspective" in E.E. White (ed) *Rhetoric in transition, Studies in the nature and uses of rhetoric.* (University Park, PA: Pennsylvania State University Press, 1980) p21–38.

[45]Kennedy, *New Testament Interpretation through Rhetorical Criticism op cit* p35.

genre (forensic, symbouleutic or epideictic.)[46] For the purpose of this article, however, I shall not analyse the rhetorical situation of Romans in terms of this scheme,[47] but rather work with Bitzer's conception of the rhetorical situation.

In the case of the letter to the Romans as a whole, we can say with Wuellner[48] that Paul feels it exigent to write a letter to the Christian community(ies) in Rome in the light of two major concerns:

1. his calling as agent of the gospel for the nations—which concerns his travels to Jerusalem "in the priestly service of the gospel of God" (1:1–5; 15:15–22), and to the ends of the earth, to Hispania (15:24); and

2. his calling as agent of the gospel to the church(es) at Rome (ct. 1:6–15; 15:23f., 29;12:1–15:13). These concerns relate to Paul's claim for support and for authoritative teaching.

Thus,

1. he is expecting support from them for his continuing priestly services to the nations and

2. he is expecting mutual encouragement and refreshment from them.

And all of this, in turn, is predicted on what Paul seems to understand as the common faith (cf. 15:24b, 32 in the light of 15:24a.)[49] A customary component of this kind of authoritative teaching was the so-called paraenasis (12:1–15:13.)[50]

Part of the paraenesis of Romans is the exhortation "let every person be subject to the governing authorities." (13:1a)

In the light of this construction of the rhetorical situation of the letter, why did Paul include the Romans 13:1a command (unique in all letters)[51] in the paraenesis?

The problem to define the historical situation which might have prompted Paul to write Romans 13:1–7 can be illuminated by considering briefly three different proposals, namely Christian enthusiasm, Roman taxes and Jewish nationalism.

---

[46]Wuellner "Where is Rhetorical Criticism taking us?" *op cit* p456. To these three, Wuellner (following Kennedy), adds also the *rhetorical problem*, that is the special challenge faced by the speaker in a given rhetorical situation (which could also be called "the inventional strategy" of a given rhetorical unit, cf. Wuellner "Where is Rhetorical Criticism taking us?" p456; Kennedy *New Testament Interpretation through rhetorical Criticism*, chapter 1.

[47]A full treatment of the rhetorical situation of Romans 13 will take us well beyond the limits of this paper. In addition to that, the notions of *status* and *lopoi* are both on the hand very complicated and, on the other hand, very extensively treated in classical rhetoric; *cf.* Kennedy *New Testament Interpretation through Rhetorical Criticism op cit* p18–19; *cf.* also A.D. Leeman & A.C. Braet *Klassieke relorica. Haar inhoud, luctie en betekenis* (Groningen: Wolkers-Noordhol/Forsten, 1987) p76–84; A.C. Braet, The classical doctrine of status and the rhetorical theory of argumentation. *Philosophy and rhetoric* 20 (1987) p79–93; and Hester "The Use and Influence of Rhetoric" *op cit* note 23. On the identification of the *status* of Romans as well as its rhetorical genre, we are confronted with a number of different opinions. *cf.* Aune *The New Testament in its Literary Environment op cit* p219–220.

[48]Wuellner "Paul's Rhetoric of Argumentation" *op cit* p158.

[49]*Ibid* p161.

[50]*Cf.* Aune *The New Testament in its Literary Environment op cit* p189, 191, 194–197, 219; Abraham J. Malherbe *Moral Exhortation: A Greco-Roman source book* (Philadelphia: Westminster, 1986) p124–129.

[51]There are also no direct Jewish or Hellenistic-Roman parallels for the admonition to pay taxes *cf.* Friedrich et al op cit p153–4.

Käsemann[52] argues that there were "enthusiasts" in Rome who propagated that obedience to earthly societal structures had become irrelevant for them since they had become Christians, citizens of the heavenly *polis*. Against this background Paul warns in 12:3 against pompousness (a possible allusion to the enthusiast) and urges his readers in 12:6 to humbleness. In 13:1–7 he explicitly warns them that they still have to live and function within earthly structures.

Friedrich, Pöhlmann and Stuhlmacher[53] argue from a remark of Tacitus[54] that Nero had made major tax reforms in 58 C.E., that there were problems and tensions in the practice of the Indirect taxes (τὸ τέλος), during the immediately preceding years—that is, the time when Paul wrote his letter to the Romans. These problems were caused by the abuses of the revenue collectors. Some of the people of the Christian communities were of the commercial class[55] and would have been exactly those most affected by the revenue abuses of the middle fifties. Friedrich *et al* argue that Paul is urging his readers in Rome to pay all the taxes for which they were obligated, the direct taxes (ὁ φόρος) as well as the controversial indirect taxes (τὸ τέλος), in order that they may not suffer (again) an expulsion from Rome as had happened to the Jews a few years earlier (49 C.E.) under edict of Claudius. He did this because he was eager to get to Rome—the capital of the world of the first century—and to be received by the Christians there, because of his recognition of the importance such a visit would have for his own mission.[56]

Borg[57] explains Romans 13:1–7 against the background of Jewish nationalism. When the Letter to the Romans was written (55–56 C.E.) conflict had already been simmering for decades and in 66–70 it finally exploded in the Roman-Jewish war. The edict of Claudius in 49 C.E. ordering all Jews to leave Rome, gives evidence that the Jews in Rome were also causing trouble. It is possible that Jewish messianic expectations (according to which the Jews would be liberated from the Roman oppression) where promulgated by Jewish nationalists in Rome. Since Judaism and Christianity were at this stage still closely interwoven (for which there is much evidence in the Letter to the Romans), it was hardly possible for Christians to escape the Roman-Jewish conflict—although they did not any longer share the political and violent messianic expectations of the militant Jewish groups. If the Roman authorities act again against the Jews, as they did in 49, that

---

[52]E. Käsermann "Principles of the Interpretation of Romans 13" in *New Testament questions of today* (Philadelphia: Fortross, 1969) p196–216.

[53]"Zur historische Situation und Intention von Rom 13, 1–7" *op cit* p153—59; followed by Furnish, *The Moral Teaching of Paul* p132–143. It is important to emphasize here that this proposal for the historical background of Rom 13:1–7 is but one of many possibilities cf. *inter alia* Juan V. Picca *Romanos 13, 1–7. Un texte discutido* (Rome: LAS, 1980) p181–206; Willem C. van Unnik "Lob und Strate durch die Obrigkeit. Hellenischtisches zu Röm 13, 3–4" in E.E. Ellis & E Grasser (eds) *Jesus und Paulus* (fs. W.G. Kümmel, Göttingen: Vandenhoeck & Ruprechl) p334–343; M. Borg "A new context for Romans XIII" *NTS* 19 (1972) p205–218. Yet, it is necessary to underscore the basic premises of this kind of rhetorical analysis that it is *not* in the first place interested in the historical circumstances of a text, although the two aspects (rhetorical and historical situations) are very closely related. Matters of historical nature are only of secondary importance in relation to rhetorical situation.

[54]Annales, XIII p50.

[55]Cf. Wayne A. Meeks *The First Urban Christians* (New Haven: Yale University Press, 1983.)

[56]Furnish, *The Moral Teaching of Paul op cit* p133–134.

[57]M. Borg "A new context for Romans XIII" *NTS* 19 (1973) p205–216.

would also seriously harm the Jewish and Gentile Christians in Rome. Therefore, for their own good as well as for his own missionary ideals which involved the Roman Christians, Paul warned them in Romans 13:1–7 to conform with rather than to confront the Romans authorities.

Historical (re)constructions such as these, however, can usually be criticised on a number of points. For example, Käsemann's hypothesis is based on the highly problematic assumption which Lyons[58] had dubbed "mirror-reading," that is, using the text as a reflection from which a real situation could be read. Regarding the taxes-hypothesis of Friedrich *et al*, we may say that the inner logic of the argumentation in Romans 13:1–7 does not create the impression that the payment of taxes was indeed the main issue at stake.[59] It is mentioned at the end of the passage as an example and practical illustration of the basic exhortation, namely to be subject to the governing authorities.

In order to construct the exigence for Romans 13:1–7 without losing sight of the exigence of the rhetorical situation of the letter as a whole, we may perhaps envision a combination of these (and other?) possibilities. Although historical study will always remain an important aspect of the New Testament critic's works, historical inferences such as these, can hardly lead to definite conclusions.

Let us consider for a moment another (less "historical") construction of the rhetorical situation of Roma 13:1–7: if we accept Kraftchick's proposal[60] that one of the functions of paraenesis in Paul's letters may be establish the *ethos* of the author, we can come to quite another explanation for the presence of this specific command in Romans. Aristotle (*Rhet* 1, 2.3ff) identified *ethos, pathos,* and *logos* as the three basic artificial means of persuasion or proofs. *Pathos* is an appeal to the emotions of the audience, *logos* is the reasonable argumentation itself and *ethos* is the establishment of the trustworthiness of the speaker in the eyes of the audience: "The orator persuades by moral character when his speeach is delivered in such a manner as to render him worthy of confidence."

In the light of this, we might envision the following picture: since Paul was no known to the Christians in Rome, it was of particular importance for him to establish his ethos.[61] They should be persuaded that he was a man of character and that he shared their values and practices. Since submission to the authorities was an established part of Jewish as well as of the Hellenistic tradition,[62] it might well

---

[58]G. Lyons *Pauline autobiography* (Atlanta: Scholars Press, 1965.)

[59]*Cf.* for example McDonald's discussion of the inner logic of Romans 13:1–7 "A test case" p.542–543.

[60]Steven J. Kraftchick *Ethos and Pathos in Galation Five and Six: A Rhetorical Analysis* (Dissertation, Emory University, 1985).

[61]According to ancient rhetorical practice, the proper place for ethos-appeals was the *exordium*. H. Lausberg *Handbuch der literarische rethoric* (München: Max Hüber, 1973) p140–142. According to F. Schnider & W. Stenger *Studien zum neutestamentlichen Briefformular* (Lieden: Brill, 1987) p50–58, Romans 1:13–16 is a distinct form in the letter which they call the "selfrecommendation" of the author. This form (which can also be identified in all the other Pauline letters) primarily has the function to establish the *ethos* of the author. However, this does not mean that other parts of the letter can not have, *inter alia*, the function to establish an author's *ethos*. This seems to be particularly true of the paraenetic sections of letters.

[62]Convincingly demonstrated by E. Käsemann *Commentary on Romans* (London: SCM, 1980) p353.

be that it was already established practice of the Roman Christians. Whether or not that was indeed the actual life situation of the addresses of the letter, would be difficult to establish with any certainty today. However, in a rhetorical analysis, this is not the type of problem which is at issue in the first instance.[63] Nevertheless, it seems reasonable to assume that it might have been *Paul's perception* of the situation of his readers. Therefore, by "commanding" an existing practice, Paul used a rhetorical strategy which could strengthen his position among his readers: he could be sure of their assent and consequently their acceptance of him as "one of them". And this assent and acceptance are in accordance with the desired effect of argumentation of the letter as a whole. The fact that the content of paraenetic material tended to represent generally held views, seems to give further motivation for this construction. Malherbe[64] gives a number of example from Hellenistic authors to illustrate that paraenetic material was usually well-known traditional material and not new inventions by the author. Yet, small alterations to this material sometimes still reflected the values of the author who used it.[65]

By identifying the establishment of ethos as a possible function of the presence of paraenesis in Romans, one should not rule out any other functions it may have had. It also need not be contrary to the possible historical explanations for Romans 13:1–7 which we have considered. Neither does it rule out that Paul really meant the *logos* of his argumentation: that the Roman Christians in their concrete historical circumstances should submit to the Roman authorities. It may simply be an *additional* way to explain the presence and the function(s) of Romans 13:1–7 in the letter.

I admit that this rhetorical explanation for Romans 13:1–7 is also not a definitive conclusion, just as the possible (re)constructions of the historical situation above did not lead to exact information. But I would argue that it is not more or less possible than any of those historical (re)constructions. In the case of the second (re)construction of the historical situation considered earlier (the tax-issue), the argument is based on an inference made from a remark of Tacitus about tax reforms in A.D 58. In the case of his (re)construction of the rhetorical situation, the argument is based on an inference made from the presence of paraenesis in the letter, and the function of paraenesis to establish the *ethos* of the author. Yet, the explanatory power of the second possibility is clear. It is also a clear example of the differences as weel as the interrelatedness of the concepts "historical situation" and "rhetorical situation."

The difference is that, if one works with the notion of rhetorical situation, you define the effect of the text in terms of its *argumentative function:* Paul wants

---

[63]Concerning the relationship between the perception of the author and the real situation of the readers, J.N. Vorster *The purpose of Romans* (D.D.-dissertation, University of Pretoria 1991) p55 maintains:". . . the audience/readers is a construct of the speaker/author. How the audience "looks" and the role it is given, depends on the perspective of the author. If this is true in a face to face confrontation, the more where a letter has been written. Whether this construct corresponds to the real flesh and blood audience/readers is a further question which has to be asked. However, rhetorical criticism does not provide us with the answer to that question."

[64]Malherbe, *Moral exhortation op cit* p124–129.

[65]*Ibid.* p138.

his readers to accept him as one of them and support him in his missionary work. In order to accomplish this acceptance, he uses (among many other things, of course,) an admonition to submit to the authorities, to persuade them that he is indeed "one of them".

Now, how does this picture compare with the possible effect of Boesak's text on Romans 13? Let us consider briefly Boesak's text as a rhetorical unit as well as its rhetorical situation.

ALAN BOESAK'S TEXT: "WHAT BELONGS TO CAESAR? ONCE AGAIN ROMANS 13"

IDENTIFICATION OF THE RHETORICAL UNIT

Boesak's text is an article of 20 printed pages in the book *When prayer makes news.* There are also ten other essays in the book. Although some of them deal with related topics,[66] this is the only one dealing specifically and exclusively with Romans 13:1–7. For that reason, it is justifiable to work with it as a distinctive rhetorical unit.

THE IDENTIFICATION OF THE RHETORICAL SITUATION

We are in a position to (re)construct the rhetorical situation of this text more easily because it is clearly stated in the article itself. Boesak felt it exigent to write this article (to whoever reads the book) to challenge the widely shared view by Christians (in South Africa and all over the world) that Romans 13 is a command for absolute obedience and obedient submission to governing authorities, whoever they may be.[67] He gives important historical information as to why he has written it: in his persistent resistance to the South African government he was continually accused of acting in direct conflict with a "biblical command", and that he, as theologian, ought to know better.[68] The book itself, in fact, is the discourse reaction to the historical situation of a call for prayer for the end of unjust rule, issued by sections of the South African Council of Churches executive in 1985 and the ensuing controversy within the South African Council of Churches as well as the media in general.

Boesak's thesis is that Romans 13:1, "so often understood as the very basis for unquestioning obedience, is, in fact, not that at all but a salient point of sharp criticism on governmental power.[69] From this thesis he make two inferences: "First, it means that a government has power and authority *because, and as long as,* it reflects the authority of God." (my italics) "Second, this authority is given them by God and they must recognize it.[70] He uses the well-known rhetorical strategies of quoting authorities (John Calvin, R. Schippers, Karl Barth and Paul Lehman) to argue

---

[66]For instance "Prayer, Politics and False Piety" by John W. De Gruchy; "Jesus, Prayer, and the Kingdom of God" by William R. Domeris; and "On which side is God?" by Gabriel Setiloane.

[67]Boesak, "What belongs to Caesar?" by Gabriel Setiloane.

[68]Boesak relates three different instances of his personal clashes with governmental powers (p137–138).

[69]*Ibid* p141.

[70]*Ibid* p142.

that the intended effect of Romans 13 is *not* blind obedience and submission to authorities, whoever they may be. He emphasises the statements in Romans 13 that authorities are διάκονοι (vs4) and λειτουργοὶ ('vs 6) of God οοὶ εἰς τὸ ἀγαθόν—"for your good" (vs 4.)[71] Since the South African government was neither just nor good, it could no longer claim to be the "servant of God for your good.[72]

Utilising quite a number of *pathos* appeals, he shows why the South African government (which governed when his text was written) could not make this claim. For example, when the security police searched his house, they "stayed from 3 am to 7 am."[73] The actual time of the search is not directly relevant from the *logos* of his argument. However, by mentioning the time he makes an appeal to the emotions (especially the sympathy) of his audience, which in turn serves to persuade the audience to his point of view. Other examples of *pathos* appeals in Boesak's text are:

> What of the distribution of land, which gives 13 percent to black people and the rest is declared "white South Africa?" What of laws that make criminals of men and women who want to live together as husband and wife? How shall we judge detention without trial, torture and murder in South Africa's prisons and wanton violence in the streets by the police and army, when innocent men, women, and children are shot like dogs?[74]

This identification of *pathos*-elements of rhetoric (in terms of Aristotle's categories) in Boesak's text, of course, does not dismiss the reality of the suffering. On the contrary, it illustrates how masterly he handles a variety of aspects of rhetoric.

In the light of all these and many other arguments, utilizing rhetorical practice in all its variety and power, Boesak concludes: "It is our responsibility—indeed, our duty—to resist this government. It is for this reason that we are participating in the struggle for justice, peace and liberation in South Africa. And this we do, not *in spite* of Romans 13, but *because* of Romans.[75]

Boesak does not explicitly state who he envisions to be his addressees. It is an article in a book published by The Westminster Press in Philadelphia, Pennsylvania, in the USA, in 1986. It might thus be very interesting to speculate on who might be the audience he envisioned: suffering Christians in South Africa (enslaved partly due to a misconception of the implications of Romans 13:1–7), or anti-apartheid activists in the USA, or supporters of the South African government or government members themselves, or perhaps all these groups? A typical question of modern rhetorical criticism would be: What kind of person is going to buy this book in the first place? Which kind of audience does it intend to persuade?[76]

---

[71]*Ibid* p145.
[72]*Ibid* p151.
[73]*Ibid* p138.
[74]*Ibid* p151.
[75]*Ibid*.
[76]*Cf*. Wuellner "Rhetorical criticism and its theory in culture-critical perspective" *op cit* p179, on "the rhetoric of scholarship and E. Schüssler-Florenza "The ethics of interpretation: De-centering biblical scholarship" *JBL* 107 (1988) p3–17.

Regarding the implied audience in the light of the argumentation itself, it seems to me that a dual audience might perhaps be envisioned: he wants to persuade people who read Romans 13 as a command to absolute obedience to any government that this is in fact not the intention of the text, and, he wants to confirm for himself and for other people who are engaged in the struggle against the South African government, that their struggle is fully in accord with the intention of Romans 13.

On a different note, we may perhaps say that this text as a whole also has the function of establishing/enhancing the *ethos* (i.e. the good character, the credibility) of its author. By arguing against the authorities abuse of Romans 13, Boesak (once again) powerfully establishes himself as a leading activist, in other words, his *ethos* among anti-apartheid activists can be under no suspicion: he is "one of us." This is an aspect of his argumentation which is in principle analogous to that of Paul in Romans 13:1–7. It would of course be an injustice to Boesak to say that establishing his *ethos* was *primarily* the reason why he wrote this text. As we have already pointed out in the analysis of Paul's text, identifying such a (complementary) rhetorical function for a text, need not be in conflict with the *logos* of the argumentation. In addition to his strong *pathos* appeals and the quality of the *logos* appeals in Boesak's text, reading the text as a whole (also) as an *ethos* appeal, serves to enhance the power of its argumentation. The same might be true of the function which was identified for Paul's text earlier on: establishing his *ethos* need not be in conflict with the *logos*-persuasion of Romans 13:1–7. It all forms part of the rhetoric of the argumentation as a whole.

NEW MEANINGS CREATED IN THE READING PROCESS

If we accept, for the sake of our argument, that one of the effects of this text in its original communication situation was to establish the *ethos* of Paul, certain differences between the rhetorical situations of Romans 13:1–7 and Boesak's text become clear.

Whereas Paul's text wanted to orientate a small Christian community pragmatically in a specific situation for the sake of their continued existence and well-being[77] and for the sake of his own missionary ideals, *not* to stir the water, Boesak's text aims at exactly the opposite effect: it is a call for active resistance against a perceived illegitimate state. The pragmatic effect of Paul's text is *conformation*, that of Boesak's text is *confrontation*.

Whereas it can be doubted that Paul had any philosophy of the state and the nature of its authority in mind,[78] the premise for the call to resistance of Boesak's text is precisely a philosophy of the state derived from Romans 13:1–7 (i.e. authorities should do good, they are servants of God, etc).

---

[77]*Cf.* J.N. Vorster "Die vroeë Christene en die politiek" In C. Breytenbach (ed) *Church in context. Early Christianity in social context* (Pretoria: NG Kerkboekhandel, 1988) p112–113.

[78]Vorster "Vroeë Christene" *Ibid* p110 (with reference to the commentaries of Käsemann, Michel, Schiler and Wilckens) explicitly rejects the idea that Paul proposes a philosophy for the state in Romans 13:1–7.

None of these differences necessarily invalidate Boesak's reading, a reading which takes place in circumstances totally different from those in which Paul has argued. It does, however, underscore the basic thesis of this article: readers continually create new meanings when they read texts in new situations.

Important factors in Boesak's horizon of expectation which might have led him to this specific new creation of meanings, are (amongst others)[79]

- his own life experience (to which he explicitly refers),
- his previous reading experience (e.g. his references to Calvin and especially Lehmann's book on the Christian and revolution), and
- the role of the audience—not of the original text—but of the reading. He is not merely reading the text for himself. He also reads it for the group who shares his ideolect *as well as* the opposing audience (i.e. the Security Police captain and P.W. Botha, etc.)

In a complex process the interaction of many aspects on many levels of life and meaning and reading results in new creations of meaning whenever a text is read and reread, and when new texts are written of the basis of other texts. The *validity* of such new creations of meaning is another matter which is not under consideration here.

Although it was not the aim of this paper to propagate or evaluate any particular reading of Romans 13:1–7, it might be necessary to come clear on this matter. To my mind the content and the thrust of the argumentation of Romans 13:1–7, call for recognition that this text aims at conformation with state authorities on the part of its readers—provided that they are governed and not governors. Although I maintain that calls for absolute submission to an unjust and authoritarian state can definitely not be based on Romans 13:1–7, it also does not seem to be the best basis available for calls to active resistance against unjust authorities. For that purpose there are many other—better!—biblical texts available. As far as this aspect is concerned, Boesak has therefore, to my mind, overstated his case. His powerful argumentation—employing a wide variety of rhetorical devices and instruments of persuasion—against an understanding of Romans 13:1–7 as "an unequivocal, unrelenting call for blind, unquestioning obedience to the state" is, however, a valuable contribution to the debate on the interpretation of this text.

CONCLUSION

I would be very cautious about applying labels like "right" or "wrong" to new meanings created on the basis of an ancient text like Romans 13:1–7. The influence of a person's horizon of expectation in the specific creation of meaning can hardly be denied—this is clear from this analysis of different rhetorical situations of

---

[79]In a very informative essay. Lategan identifies six factors which contribute to a reader's horizon of expectation. "Reading Romans 13 in a South African context" In B.C. Lategan (ed) *Reception and beyond. Theory and practice in South African oriented studies.* Interdisciplinary project undertaken as part of the HSRC investigation into research methodology. 1989. The three factors quoted here are most directly relevant with regard to a possible explanation of Boesak's creation of meaning from Romans 13:1–7.

Romans 13:1–7. This need not imply, on the other hand, that "anything goes." Romans 13:1–7 does *not* discuss aeroplanes or computers!

However, merely pointing out that we should be careful with "right" or "wrong" labels but also not accepting that "anything goes," does leave us with a logical problem. In the current academic climate it is not popular to draw up hierarchies of readings and this is rightly so. After many centuries of authoritarianism (especially in the interpretation of biblical texts) this is an important phase in the development of the human sciences. I do suspect, however, that eventually we will once again become more and more involved in looking for new levels of systemisation in terms of which carefully nuanced hierarchies of readings can be drawn.

In the meantime New Testament interpretation should, to my mind, encompass *both* a meticulous study of the text and reader clues given in the text *and* the context of the interpreter.

Chapter 3

Liberation and Oppression
in the Book of Exodus

A Latin American Perspective:
The Option for the Poor
in the Old Testament

George V. Pixley

INTRODUCTION

This chapter seeks to establish just who the God of the Bible is. This might not seem necessary, as the question of who God is could seem to have been settled by the common understanding of our Western culture. God is the one perfect being, all-powerful and all-wise, creator of heaven and earth, whose goodness and justice never fail. But common understanding, in this as in so many other things, is deceptive. The long history of conflicts between Christians in Latin America has taught us that the common confession of one God hides different, and even opposing, ways of envisaging this all-powerful and all-wise creator God. The Bible takes great care to identify the God it speaks of, and does so using categories other than our common understanding. To simplify somewhat, but without distorting the matter in essentials, we can say that the God of the Bible is the God who led Israel out of Egypt and who raised Jesus Christ from the dead. This is the God who created heaven and earth, and this is the God whose perfection we have to postulate.

There is no reason to dispute the Western philosophical affirmation that for God's love to be perfect, it has to be universal. But this does need some qualification. The biblical narratives tell us that the concrete expression of this love favoured the slaves in Egypt and Palestine, and the poor of Galilee. God's love for Pharaoh was mediated through God's preferential love for the Israelite slaves. In the same way, God's love for the scribes and Pharisees was mediated through God's love for and solidarity with the fishermen and women of Galilee. And so the God whom the Bible calls creator of heaven and earth takes on specific characteristics.

So, having, we hope, established the importance of asking who the God of the Bible is, let us approach the question through the introduction to that admirable synthesis of law that we know as the Decalogue: 'I am Yahweh your God who brought you out of the land of Egypt, out of the house of slavery. You shall have no gods except me' (Exod. 20.2–3).[1]

The words are so familiar to us that we hardly pay attention to them, yet they contain affirmations that are far from obvious at first sight. In the first place, the God Yahweh displays a polemical tone with regard to other possible gods. The text neither denies nor affirms that there are other gods. Their existence or non-existence is not the case at issue. What is at issue is that *you*, Israelite, to whom the law is addressed, must base your justice on the prohibition to worship them or ask them for favours. In other words, any god who has not brought you out of the house of slavery cannot be your God.

All the commandments dealing with just conduct among people—'honour your father and mother . . . you shall not kill . . . you shall not steal', etc.—are presented as the direct and personal commands of *this* God, who 'brought you out of the land of Egypt, out of the house of slavery'. There is nothing to show that it had to be this way; at least, there is nothing in the common understanding of Western culture that would indicate this. But let us look at the text a little more closely:

(a) 'I am *Yahweh* your God.' The proper name Yahweh serves to ensure that those gods who cannot or will not save Israel from the house of slavery in Egypt cannot hide under the generic term *god*. It is not possible to make definite assertions about the origin of the name Yahweh.[2] Nevertheless, the Elohist and priestly traditions, two of the three great narrative traditions in the Pentateuch, agree in placing the revelation of this divine name within the context of the exodus. In the Elohist tradition, Yahweh revealed his proper name to Moses in the desert at the time he was persuading him to undertake the liberation of his enslaved people (Exod. 3.14–15). In the priestly tradition, he revealed his name to Moses still in

Egypt as a confirmation of his will to set the slaves free (Exod. 6.2–6). Both traditions coincide in having God already known to the patriarchs Abraham, Isaac and Jacob, though they did not know God's *name*. This was revealed only to the prophet who was to lead Israel in its liberation. So the name Yahweh asserts the singularity of God as liberator.

(b) 'I am Yahweh *your* God.' Because he brought Israel out of the land of Egypt, out of the house of slavery, Yahweh is the God of Israel. This liberation establishes a relationship of exclusive dependence on Yahweh. Yahweh cannot be adored except by those who confess themselves slaves liberated from the slavery in Egypt. To understand this, we have to be careful not to be confused by the patriarchal traditions. This *your* does not indicate a previous relationship independent of the liberation. The exodus formed the people of Yahweh. According to Exodus 12.38 (from the Yahwist tradition), 'people of various sorts' (*erev rav*) joined the Israelites on the march, showing that the unity of Israel had to be constituted on the basis of the exodus. What was ordained for the Passover shows how the nation was defined:

> No Alien may take part in it . . . Should a stranger be staying with you and wish to celebrate the Passover in honour of Yahweh, all the males of his household must be circumcised: he may then be admitted to the celebration, for he becomes as it were a native-born. But no uncircumcised person may take part (Exod. 12.43, 48).

In other words, for Yahweh to be *your* God, you have to unite yourself to those who are celebrating their liberation from slavery. And no one who shows solidarity with the liberated people, demonstrating it through the circumcision of his foreskin, will be excluded from the community that celebrates its liberation from Egypt. In Israel's later practice, things were not that simple, but this expresses an intention: Yahweh is *your* God.

(c) 'I am Yahweh your *God*.' Theology in the Old Testament is not organized round dogmatic themes. Strictly speaking, the Old Testament includes no Creed defining the nature of God. Its theology is narrative, and the great majority of the books that make up this collection of writings recognize the foundational character of the story of the exodus. Efforts at generalizing about the nature of God are based on this story:

> Yahweh your God is God of gods and Lord of lords, the great God, triumphant and terrible, never partial, never to be bribed. It is he who sees justice done for the orphan and the widow, who loves the stranger and gives him food and clothing (Deut. 10.16–18).

The God of the exodus account is a God who heard the cries wrung from the slaves by the slave-drivers of Pharaoh and so came down to set them free and lead them to a land flowing with milk and honey. Moses, the man chosen to lead this project, had gained his credentials by risking his high social position by killing an Egyptian who was maltreating a Hebrew (Exod. 2.11–15). So the exodus account clearly shows that justice means taking sides with the oppressed. The Yahweh of the exodus takes the part of the oppressed. From this our text draws the theological principle that God's impartiality makes God love the orphan and the widow with preference. Curiously, but nevertheless logically, not making exception of persons means making a preferential option for the oppressed in a situation of oppression.

These initial observations show that Yahweh, the God of the Bible, is characterized by his preferential option for the oppressed. The remaining sections of this chapter will examine some of the principal witnesses of the Bible concerning the way in which they appropriated this Yahweh God of the exodus. We need to remind ourselves here that the Bible is not one continuous work, but a collection of writings originating at different periods. This diversity of origin is also shown in the different ways it takes up the basic themes of Israel's tradition. Yahweh's option for the oppressed, as an integral element in the exodus narrative, which has a foundational character for Israel, exercised a basic influence over virtually all the books of the Bible (the notable exception being Proverbs, which we shall examine in due course as an expression of the teaching of 'wise men'). Our examination will seek to bring out the different shades with which God's preferential option for the impoverished and oppressed is presented.

THE EXODUS REVEALS YAHWEH AS LIBERATOR GOD: THE TEXT AND THE SOCIAL CONTEXT IN WHICH IT WAS PRODUCED

In the account of the exodus from Egyptian slavery under the inspiration of Yahweh and the leadership of Moses, Israel narrates its origins as a people and confesses that it owes these to Yahweh and is, in consequence, the people of Yahweh. Although the events narrated are earlier than the formation of Israel as a nation with its own language and identity, the account presupposes the existence of this nation. It is an 'official' account; and, like the official accounts of any nation explaining its origins, it hides some elements while revealing others. We therefore need to have some idea of the social history of Israel, the context in which the account was produced. So in this section we begin by reconstructing the probable origins of Israel, and go on to examine the exodus narrative and what it tells us about Yahweh and his choice of a nation for himself, showing how the social changes that came about in Israel altered the way in which the foundational events were understood.

Israel first appeared on the historical scene around the end of the thirteenth century BC. The name features on the steal of Memeptah, king of Egypt, in the context of his campaign in Palestine in 1208 BC. Although this text tells us no more than the existence of Israel in Palestine at this date, later texts tell us that it originated in the central mountains of Palestine, which, till the thirteenth century, had been the least populated area of Palestine. There is an extensive correspondence between the Egyptian court and the kings of Canaan, dating from the fourteenth and thirteenth centuries. Letters from Tel-el-Amarna indicate that the centers of population were the coastal plain and the valley of Yezreel, which crosses the mountain range by Mount Carmel. These were precisely the areas Israel did not control at the time of its origins, which is significant. Another important fact derived from these letters is that Egypt was unable to maintain stable control in Palestine, owing to continuous wars among the kings of the cities.

According to its own traditions of the early period, as recounted in the Book of Judges, Israel consisted of various peasant groups scattered around the mountain areas. The valleys and plains were controlled by hostile tribes, whose material culture was superior to that of the Israelites (they possessed horses and carts).

Around 1200 BC, archeology shows a vital transitional point in the material culture of Palestine, the introduction of iron tools. This must be the major factor leading at just this period to the clearing of mountain areas previously unserviceable for agriculture, producing the population shift that brought together groups who were to make up the nation of Israel.

All these facts are explained by the thesis that Israel arose in the thirteenth century BC from a process of internal migration in Palestine. Families and clans that had previously lived on the plain and in the valleys fled from the endless wars to seek a new life in the country that had become cultivatable through the introduction of iron tools. This movements is illustrated in the biblical tradition of the migration of the tribe of Dan from the cities of Zorah and Eshtaol to the extreme Northeast of Galilee (Judg., 17–18). These migrations also had a social effect. Those who migrated were peasants; not only did they escape the political conflicts; they also escaped the tributes they had previously paid to the lords of the cities. In their new hill areas they did not build cities because they were not city people. Archeological excavations have produced cases of cities destroyed at this period and rebuilt on a smaller scale, with humbler materials. The diminution of urban life can be explained by the incursion of peasant groups coming up from the plain. If this is the demographic origin of the clans that were to make up the nation of Israel, then one can talk of a movement of migration/uprising.[3]

These peasant groups were joined around 1200 BC by a group that came from Egypt, where it had carried out an uprising and an exodus into the desert under the leadership of Moses, a prophet of the God Yahweh. Their rebellion had been provoked by King Rameses II (1290–1224 BC), whose construction projects had placed an intolerable burden on the peasant population of Egypt. The social system obtaining in Egypt is described in Genesis 47.13–26: the people lived in their own villages and with their own families, but all the land belonged to the state and its produce was subject to a tax imposed by the Pharaoh. This was the same 'Asiatic' system as in Palestine, aggravated by the fact that the Egyptian state was far more powerful. The Hebrews who came out of Egypt understood that their success had been due to Yahweh, their God, being with them. The coincidence of this experience with that of the clans of Israel was noteworthy, and the clans gradually came to accept Yahweh as their God. The exodus of the Hebrews came to be the founding history of Israel.[4]

So the material basis of confession of faith in Yahweh was the diffuse peasant movement arising from the particular conditions in Palestine in the fourteenth and thirteenth centuries BC. Israelite society was made up of small villages organized by ties of blood relationship into families, clans and tribes. At the beginning, they had neither cities nor kings. The arrival of the Hebrew group gave the movement a political and social consciousness, the axis of which was confession of Yahweh as their only king.[5] The laws given on Sinai lent coherence to the movement and a consciousness of the group's difference from the 'Canaanites' who dwelt in the cities, subject to human kings and worshipping Baal. The Israelites spoke the language of Canaan (see Isa. 19.18), from where they had come. The telling of the exodus and their confession of faith in Yahweh gave weight to their consciousness of being different from the inhabitants of the valleys and the cities. They were people of Yahweh and had no kings 'like the other nations' (I Sam. 8.5).

Reflecting on the importance of their movement, the tribes of Israel gradually came to see its universal significance, and to recognize Yahweh as God *tout court*, not simply as the God of Israel. One tradition held that Yahweh had promised Abraham: 'All the tribes of the earth shall bless themselves by you' (Gen. 12.3). Deutero-Isaiah (sixth century) proclaimed that Israel, the servant of Yahweh, would be a 'light to the nations' (Isa. 49.6). So some biblical texts give universal value to the Israelite experience that God is a saviour of the oppressed. Logically, Israel also came to confess Yahweh as creator of heaven and earth. It also saw in Yahweh a companion to those who wander the face of the earth without a home, a God who gave them land in which to settle.[6] And so the people of Israel came to understand that the Yahweh of the exodus was the one God who governs all nations. This is the historical thesis we follow here.

After this brief reconstruction of the origin of Israel, let us turn to its founding text, the account of the exodus. The book of Exodus, like the whole of the Pentateuch of which it forms part, was not finally completed till the fifth century BC, eight hundred years after the events it recounts. During these eight centuries, several major changes took place in the life of Israel:

  i. For two hundred years, Israel existed as a loose grouping of clans and tribes of peasants, surrounded by cities under monarchical regimes, generally hostile to Israel (with some exceptions, such as Gibeon and Shechem).

  ii. Around the year 1000 BC, the attacks from the cities forced Israel to create its own monarchical state, which lasted some four hundred years.

  iii. After the destruction of the capital (587 BC), the Jewish people organized themselves as a religious nation led by a priestly caste, under the tolerant suzereignty of the Persian empire.

As the account of the exodus is the founding document of Israel, it was naturally revised in each of these three epochs. The final text of the book of Exodus contains elements from each of these revisions. So it is a text made up of superimposed layers, with differing interpretations of those events in Egypt in the thirteenth century BC.

The earliest stage of the account, probably exclusively oral, calls the people of the exodus 'Hebrews'. This term did not originally denote a race, but was a designation given to a various groups in several localities from Egypt to Mesopotamia. Such people were mercenaries, nomads, rebels; the name denoted the fact that they were not integrated into the broader framework of society, were outside the general rule of law.[7] When the exodus narrative was the foundational text of the Israelite tribes, the experience in Egypt was read as that of a group of peasants who had rebelled and placed themselves outside Egyptian law. Those who heeded the call of Yahweh and Moses to undertake a struggle that would set them free from slavery in Egypt were, therefore, 'Hebrews', people of various sorts' who decided to break with the Egyptian legal system, under which they had to hold their flocks, lands and bodies at the king's disposition.

The central feature of the account for the tribes of Israel was the part played by Yahweh in their liberation. They did not read the exodus as a secular revolutionary movement. Yahweh was on their side and guided the movement through his prophet Moses. The fact that they succeeded in escaping from their enforced serfdom despite the powerful Egyptian army showed that God, who took the side of the poor in Egypt, was the true God.

With the establishment of the monarchical state in Israel, the exodus narrative was taken up by the official scribes and converted into a national epic, together with the ancient traditions concerning the patriarchs Abraham, Isaac and Jacob. This process of adapting the Israelite traditions for the ends of the new monarchy probably took place at the court of Solomon. This produced the written version of the traditions that exegetes call the Yahwist version (known as J), the earliest writings that survive as part of the Pentateuch.

At this period, when the state was seeking to create a consciousness of national identity built up round the Davidic dynasty, it had to re-read the exodus as a national liberation struggle. The children of Israel, according to this re-reading, had been enslaved in Egypt after settling there to escape the famine in their own land of Canaan. A perverse king took advantage of their presence as guests, and the struggle that followed was between Egyptians and Israelites. The Israelites conceived the plan of 'returning' to the land of Canaan. In this way the account ceased to describe a social movement within Egyptian society and replaced it with a struggle between peoples, in which Yahweh took the side of Israel. Israel was an exploited people, but more importantly, it was the people of Yahweh, and this from before the time of its exploitation in Egypt. This is the emphasis in the Yahwist version:

> Go and gather the elders of Israel together and tell them, 'Yahweh, the God of your fathers, has appeared to me—the God of Abraham, of Isaac, and of Jacob; and he has said to me: I have visited you and seen all that the Egyptians are doing to you' (Exod. 3.16).

The children of Israel are shown as having a relationship with Yahweh going back to the time of their ancestors who lived in Canaan. They are his people and this is the reason Yahweh intervened to rescue them from their slavery. In this way the exodus lost a large part of its challenging content and could become useful for the monarchical aim of creating a national consciousness.

On the basis of this re-reading of the exodus, a theological reflection on the election of Israel as the special people of God was developed in the late monarchical period (seventh century BC):

> If Yahweh set his heart on you and chose you, it was not because you outnumbered other peoples: you were the least of all peoples. It was for love of you and

> to keep the oath that he swore to your fathers that Yahweh brought you out
> with his mighty hand and redeemed you from the house of slavery, from the
> power of Pharaoh king of Egypt (Deut. 7.7–8).

The exodus changes from Yahweh's option for the oppressed to being an in-
scrutable favour conferred by Yahweh in fulfilment of his promises to the patriarchs. This does not mean that the memory of the favour enjoyed by the poor in
Yahweh's eyes was lost, but it was carried on as part of a thought-process that en-
hanced Yahweh's special relationship with his people dating from commitments
entered into with the patriarchs.

The final re-reading of the exodus further overlaid the revelation of Yahweh
as the liberator God who showed his preference for the oppressed. This is the
reading made by the priests in the sixth century BC, when Judah existed as a national group within the Persian empire, internally led by the priestly caste. This re-
reading could not quite efface the privilege of the poor, but it changed the
emphasis so as to exalt the greatness of Yahweh. The following is an example:

> Yahweh said to Moses, 'See, I make you as a god for Pharaoh, and Aaron your
> brother is to be your prophet. You yourself must tell him all I command you,
> and Aaron your brother will tell Pharaoh to let the sons of Israel leave his land.
> I myself will make Pharaoh's heart stubborn, and perform many a sign and
> wonder in the land of Egypt. Pharaoh will not listen to you, and so I will lay my
> hand on Egypt and with strokes of power lead out my armies, my people, the
> sons of Israel, from the land of Egypt. And all the Egyptians shall come to
> know that I am Yahweh when I stretch out my hand against Egypt and bring
> out the sons of Israel from their midst' (Exod. 7.1–5).

In the earlier layers of the account, the blows delivered against Pharaoh were
to force him to let the Hebrews go. Every time Pharaoh hardened his heart, Yahweh visited a fresh plague on him so as to soften it. In the priestly re-reading, the
marvels have another purpose: to demonstrate the greatness of Yahweh. This is
why Yahweh himself hardens Pharaoh's heart so as to give himself new opportunities of showing his greatness.

In this priestly re-reading of the exodus, the desire to show the greatness of
Yahweh has grown to such an extent that it obscures—though it cannot completely erase—Yahweh's predilection for the poor and oppressed. So Yahweh's
option for the slaves and their liberation, the inspiration of pre-monarchical
Israel, was gradually weakened in later re-readings. The original vision was kept
in prophetic circles.

COULD ISRAEL HAVE KNOWN CLASS CONSCIOUSNESS?

Discussion of the origins of Israel as coming about through an uprising/migration
and repudiation of the structures of domination personalized in the kings of the
surrounding peoples raises a doubt: are we not imposing on these early years a
level of social consciousness that could not have existed two thousand years before Christ? This is a legitimate concern, and needs examination.

Obviously, there were no 'social sciences' either in Canaan or in Egypt in the thirteenth century BC. So there was no possibility of making a 'scientific' analysis of the structure of society and the dynamics of its reproduction. Hence if we raise the above question with reference to a kind of social consciousness grounded in social—scientific analysis, the reply has to be affirmative.

So let us put the question differently. Was it possible for groups of peasants to Canaan to arrive at a realization that their interests as peasant groups were being threatened by their subjection to the king of their cities—Dor, Megiddo, Bethshean? In a stable society, even though the king sequestered a large portion of agricultural produce and required significant labour quotas for state works, it is highly unlikely that a peasant class which had never known any other way of life would have hankered after alternative lifestyles. Furthermore, the king was not regarded as a man, but as a god, on whom they were dependent for such essentials as sun and rain.

Nevertheless, Canaan in the fourteenth and thirteenth centuries BC was going through a critical phase in the Egyptian domination, reflected in the continual wars among the kings of its cities. Such a situation would lead to each village undergoing changes of overload, besides interruptions to its crop production. One god/king would take the place of another as 'benefactor' responsible for giving life to the people of one place, without any internal change taking place within the people themselves. These changes would create the possibility of thinking of alternatives to the system of domination by kings. The peasants, well organized in large families on the local level, could come to realize that their interests were not identical with those of the city which demanded a quota of their produce. The presence of nearby virgin land, even if not as fertile as that of the plain, would have completed the process of 'conscientization' concerning the possibility of an alternative to their traditional subjection.

In Egypt, conditions that could have led to an alternative consciousness among the peasants were different. Here there was only one state, and it was a very strong state, with a very convincing religious underpinning. Conditions for a consciousness of oppression were created by the excessive exploitation of the peasant base of society for funerary constructions. It was natural to attribute these excesses of exploitation to abuses by the king's henchmen, which the king would correct if he knew the wrong being done his servants. That is, exploitation in itself would not have produced an alternative consciousness. As long as everyone continued to believe in the supreme god, whose goodness was shown in the richness of the country, irrigated every year by the flood waters of the great river Nile, the social structure was very secure. There was no alternative cultivatable land in the region. No one suggested the possibility of an alternative, and the wrongs suffered by a particular group of workers were a very localized incident compared to the overall riches of a land blessed by heaven.

Here, consciousness of an alternative must have come principally from an outside element introduced, undoubtedly, from the East, in the form of the God Yahweh, who appeared on the holy mountain. Yahweh had presented himself as a God of the poor, promising their liberation. It seems certain that very few peasants in the land of Egypt were prepared to receive such a message, though the conditions of exceptional oppression produced by the construction works of Rameses II would have led some to this extreme. So a small group of 'Hebrews' gathered round Moses, determined to understand their withdrawal from society as a repudiation of the oppression they now associated with Pharaoh, demystified for them by their acceptance of the God who had appeared to Moses with the promise of another land flowing with milk and honey.

Notes

1. Biblical quotations are taken from the Jerusalem Bible, adapted occasionally in accordance with the authors' own references to the original Hebrew and Greek.

2. J. Severino Croatto, 'Yavé, el Dios de la "presencia" salvífica: Exod. 3:14 en su contexto literario y querigmático' (*Revista Bíblica*, 43, 1981), pp. 153–63.

3. Though there are antecedents on the insurrectional theory of the origins of Israel, the definitive work is N. K. Gottwald, *The Tribes of Yahweh: A Sociology of the Religion of Liberated Israel 1250–1050 BCE* (Maryknoll, NY, Orbis Books 1979).

4. For a detailed examination of the texts, see J. V. Pixley, *On Exodus: A Liberation Perspective* (Maryknoll, NY, Orbis Books, 1987).

5. See Judges 8.22–3, and for an interpretation, J. V. Pixley, *God's Kingdom: A Guide for Biblical Study* (Maryknoll, NY, Orbis Books, 1981).

6. A good reading of the Pentateuch in the light of lack of land for Israel can be found in J. Severino Croatto, 'Una promesa aún no cumplida. La estructura literaria del Pentateuco' (*Revista Bíblica*, 44, 1982), pp. 193–206.

7. Much has been written on Hebrews/*'apiru*. See G. E. Mendenhall, 'The *'Apiru* Movements in the Late Bronze Age' in *The Tenth Generation: The Origins of the Biblical Tradition* (Baltimore, John Hopkins University Press, 1973), pp. 122–41; M. L. Chaney, 'Ancient Palestinian Peasant Movements and the Formation of Premonarchic Israel' in D. N. Freedman and D. F. Graf (eds), *Palestine in Transition: The Emergence of Ancient Israel* (Sheffield, Almond Press, 1983), pp. 39–90.

A Palestinian Perspective: The Bible and Liberation

Naim Stifan Ateek

The Spirit of the Lord is upon me, because he has anointed me to preach good news to the poor. He has sent me to proclaim release to the captives and recovering of sight to the blind, to set at liberty those who are oppressed, to proclaim the acceptable year of the Lord (Luke 4.18–19).

From *Justice and Only Justice*, 208–286 Maryknoll: Orbis Books, 1989. Reprinted by permission.

The purpose of this chapter is to explicate the major thrust of a Palestinian theology of liberation. Since nothing of its kind has been done before, I will attempt to lay the cornerstone for such a theology. It will not exhaust the subject; but I will try to raise the main theological issues as I have come to see them as a Palestinian Christian through my interaction with parishioners, colleagues, and other Christians during the last twenty years of my ministry.

THE TWO MAJOR ISSUES

The first major issue, which stands above all others and lies at the heart of the Palestinian problem, is justice. Since 1948 and the creation of the State of Israel, Palestinians everywhere have been talking about the injustice done to them—to young and old, educated and uneducated, rich and poor, male and female, religious and secular, Muslim and Christian—all talk about the problem of justice. All of them remember what happened in 1948 and 1967, and they relate both the story of the loss of Palestine and their own stories of personal loss.

I have heard some Jews in Israel say that there is a great difference between the Palestinian and the Jewish claim to the land. The Palestinian's concern is focused on the loss of his house, his home, his business, and maybe his village. Injustice to him has to do with the fact that he was deprived of his own private property. The Jew's concern is said to be with the whole of the land, not with a particular spot.

My experience shows that such a distinction is a specious attempt on the part of some Jews to give a greater weight to their claim, a rationalization that only the ignorant or the prejudiced would accept. When Palestinians talk about injustice, they are talking about the tragedy of Palestine. When they tell their own story, it is told in order to illustrate vividly and to substantiate the extent of the injustice and the dehumanization to which the people of Palestine have been subjected; when Jews do not tell personal stories of how they lost their homes or villages in Palestine, it is because they did not have them.

Any theology of liberation must of necessity address the issue of justice. It is, after all, the major issue for Palestinians regardless of their religious affiliation.

For Palestinian Christians there is a second major issue that needs to be tackled in a theology of liberation: the Bible. The Bible is usually viewed as a source of strength, offering solutions and leading people to faith and salvation. Strangely—shockingly—however, the Bible has been used by some Western Christians and Jews in a way that has supported *in*justice rather than justice. Liberation theologians have seen the Bible as a dynamic source for their understanding of liberation, but if some parts of it are applied literally to our situation today the Bible appears to offer to the Palestinians slavery rather than freedom, injustice rather than justice, and death to their national and political life. Many good-hearted Christians have been confused or misled by certain biblical words and images that are normally used in public worship; words that have acquired new connotations since the establishment of the State of Israel. For example, when Christians recite the *Benedictus,* with its opening lines 'Blessed be the Lord God of Israel, for he has visited and redeemed his people,' what does it mean for them today? Which Israel are they thinking of? What redemption? The eminent historian Arnold J. Toynbee comments:

> Within my lifetime the mental associations of the name 'Israel' have changed for those religious communities, the Jews and the Christians, in whose liturgies this name so often recurs. When, as a child, I used to take part, in church, in the singing of the Psalms, the name 'Israel' did not signify, for me, any existing state on the face of the globe. No state of that name was in existence then. Neither did the name signify the ancient Kingdom of Israel that was liquidated in 722 BC by the Assyrians. The history of Ancient Israel was familiar to me. But the name, when I recited it in the liturgy, meant a religious community of devout worshippers of Ancient Israel's God—the One True God in the belief of present-day Jews, Christians, and Muslims. 'Israel' signified 'God's people,' and we worshippers of God were living members of Israel, but members only conditionally. Our membership was conditional on our obeying God's commands and following His precepts as these had been declared by Him through the mouths of His Prophets.
>
> This traditional spiritual connotation of the name 'Israel' has been supplanted today by a political and military connotation. Today, if I go to church and try to join in the singing of the Psalms, I am pulled up short, with a jar, when the name 'Israel' comes on to my lips. The name conjures up today a picture of a small, middle-Europe type state, with bickering political parties like all such states, with a rigid—and unsuccessful—foreign policy with respect to its neighbours and with constant appeal to the Jews of the world either to send them money or to come themselves. This picture has now effaced that one in our minds. It has effaced it, whoever we are: Jews or Christians, diaspora Jews or Israelis, believers or agnostics. The present-day political Israel has, for all of us, obliterated or, at least, adumbrated, the spiritual Israel of the Judeo-Christian tradition. This is surely a tragedy.[1]

If this has been true among Western Christians, it has been more painfully true of Palestinian and other Christians in the Middle East. The establishment of the State of Israel was a seismic tremor of enormous magnitude that has shaken the very foundation of their beliefs. Since then, no Palestinian Christian theology can avoid tackling the issue of the Bible: How can the Bible, which has apparently become a part of the problem in the Arab-Israeli conflict, become a part of its solution? How can the Bible, which has been used to bring a curse to the national aspirations of a whole people, again offer them a blessing? How can the Bible, through which many have been led to salvation, be itself saved and redeemed?

These two concerns—justice and the Bible—will occupy most of our attention. Most of the other issues for a theology of liberation for Palestinian Christians, as we shall see, are derived from them. In fact, the two issues are very much interrelated. I will treat them in reverse order, beginning with the issue of the Bible; then in the next chapter, move to the issue of justice; and finally, consider the victims of injustice and the challenges that face them.

THE BIBLE: PROBLEM OR SOLUTION?

THE POLITICAL ABUSE OF THE BIBLE

For most Palestinian Christians, as for many other Arab Christians, their view of the Bible, especially the Hebrew Scriptures, or Old Testament, has been adversely affected by the creation of the State of Israel. Many previously hidden problems suddenly surfaced. The God of the Bible, hitherto the God who saves and liberates, has come to be viewed by Palestinians as partial and discriminating. Before the creation of the State, the Old Testament was considered to be an essential part of Christian Scripture, pointing and witnessing to Jesus. Since the creation of the State, some Jewish and Christian interpreters have read the Old Testament largely as a Zionist text to such an extent that it has become almost repugnant to Palestinian Christians. As a result, the Old Testament has generally fallen into disuse among both clergy and laity, and the Church has been unable to come to terms with its ambiguities, questions, and paradoxes—especially with its direct application to the twentieth-century events in Palestine. The fundamental question of many Christians, whether uttered or not, is: How can the Old Testament be the Word of God in light of the Palestinian Christians' experience with its use to support Zionism?

Closely involved in the question of the Hebrew Scriptures in our concept of God. With the exception of relatively few people within the Christian communities in the Middle East, the existence of God is not in doubt. What has been seriously questioned is the nature and character of God. What is God really like? What is God's relation to the new State of Israel? Is God partial only to the Jews? Is this a God of justice and peace? Such questions may appear on the surface trite and their answers may seem obvious. Nevertheless, they are part of a battery of questions that many Christians, both in Israel-Palestine and outside of it, are still debating. The focus of these questions is the very person of God. God's character is at stake. God's integrity has been questioned.

Generally speaking, the Church in Israel—Palestine has stood impotent and helpless before these questions. It is no wonder then that there is widespread apathy among many Christians toward the Church. The pervasive and crucial question for its leadership has been, and still is: How can the Church, without rejecting any part of the Bible, adequately relate the core of the biblical message—its concept of God—to Palestinians? The answer lies largely in the doing of theology. The only bridge between the Bible and people is theology. It must be a theology that is biblically sound; a theology that liberates; a theology that will contextualize and interpret while remaining faithful to the heart of the biblical message. Unless such a theology is achieved, the human tendency will be to ignore and neglect the undesired parts of the Bible.

Some Christians, clergy included, have found a way to deal with the text through allegorization. Others use what I call spiritualization. Although these and other methods can be helpful, they do not meet the challenge of the political abuse of the Bible. One observes, too, that especially in this century in the West, biblical scholarship has made real strides in the application of critical methods to the study of the Bible. These scientific tools can clarify many ambiguities and help the student to get as close as possible to the original text—its author, date, source, context, and so on. Unless these methods are guided and informed by a larger theological understanding, however, they tend to leave the text dissected and to confuse rather than clarify matters of faith.

Generally speaking, all these methods do not throw light on whether or not the text is the Word of *God*. For Palestinian Christians, the core question that takes priority over all others is whether what is being read in the Bible is the Word of *God* to them and whether it reflects the nature, will, and purpose of *God* for them. In other words, is what is being read an authentic insight from God about who God is? Is it an authentic insight from God about persons or relationships or about human nature and history? Conversely, is what is being heard a reflection of authentic human understanding about God at that stage of development? Is it an authentic statement of humans about other human beings or about human nature at that stage of development? Or, to put it bluntly, is it basically a statement from humans put into the mouth of God, that has become confused as an authentic message from God to people? Do the words reflect an authentic and valid message from God to us today? What is eternally true in the Bible and what is conditioned? What is lasting and what is temporal? These are important questions for Palestinian Christians, whose answers will ultimately determine what God is or is not saying to them in the Bible.

THE CENTRAL BIBLICAL HERMENEUTIC

Palestinian Christians are looking for a hermeneutic that will help them to identify the authentic Word of *God* in the Bible and to discern the true meaning of those biblical texts that Jewish Zionists and Christian fundamentalists cite to substantiate their subjective claims and prejudices.

The criterion that Palestinians are looking for must be both biblically and theologically sound, lest it in turn becomes a mere instrument to oppose Jewish and Christian Zionists and support subjective Palestinian claims and prejudices. The hermeneutic must ring true of a God whom we have come to know—unchanging in nature and character, dynamically constant rather than fickle and variable, responding to but not conditioned by time, space, or circumstances.

The canon of this hermeneutic for the Palestinian Christian is nothing less than Jesus Christ himself. For in Christ and through Christ and because of Christ, Christians have been given a revealed insight into God's nature and character. For the Christian, to talk about the knowledge of God is to talk about knowing God through Christ: this is the best source of the knowledge of God; this is the concept of God that has matured through the period of biblical history. For the Christian, it has found its fulfillment in Jesus Christ's understanding of the nature and character of God. This understanding of God was vindicated for us in the life, death, and resurrection of Jesus, whom we acclaim as the Christ, God incarnate. Jesus the Christ thus becomes—in himself and in his teaching—the true hermeneutic, the key to the understanding of the Bible, and beyond the Bible to the understanding of the action of God throughout history. In other words, the *Word* of God incarnate in Jesus the Christ interprets for us the *word* of God in the Bible.

To understand God, therefore, the Palestinian Christian, like every other Christian, begins with Christ and goes backward to the Old Testament and forward to the New Testament and beyond them. This becomes the major premise for the Christian.

Due to the human predicament of evil, however, one discovers that the use of this hermeneutic does not mean that all of our theological problems are solved automatically; but one can discover that the new hermeneutic (which after all is not new at all in the Church) is really liberating. The Bible for Palestinian Christians, then, can be retained in its entirety, while its contents would be judged by this hermeneutic and scrutinized by the mind of Christ.

To let the mind of Christ bear on situations and events is very important theologically. As C. H. Dodd explains:

> Perhaps one of the most striking features of the early Christian movement was the re-appearance of a confidence that man can know God immediately. . . . Jesus Christ, with a confidence that to the timid traditionalism of His time appeared blasphemous, asserted that He knew the Father and was prepared to let others into that knowledge. He did so, not by handing down a new tradition about God, but by making others shares in His own attitude to God. This is what Paul means by 'having the mind of Christ.' Having that mind, we do know God. It was this clear, unquestioning conviction that gave Paul his power as a missionary: but he expected it also in his converts. To them, too, 'the word of knowledge' came 'by the same Spirit.' He prayed that God would give them a spirit of wisdom and revelation in the knowledge of Him. Such knowledge is, as Paul freely grants, only partial, but it is real, personal, undeniable knowledge. In friendship between men there is a mutual knowledge which is never complete or free from mystery: yet you can know with a certainty nothing could shake that your friend is 'not the man to do such a thing,' or that such and such a thing that you have heard is 'just like him.' You have a real knowledge which gives you a criterion. Such is the knowledge the Christian has of his Father.[2]

This criterion gives Christians great confidence, and informs their approach to the various problems that they encounter.

Notes

1. E. Berger, *Prophecy, Zionism and the State of Israel,* Introduction by A. J. Toynbee (New York, American Alternative to Zionism, n.d.).

2. C. H. Dodd, *The Meaning of Paul for Today* (New York, Meridian, 1957), pp. 131–2.

A Native American Perspective:
Canaanites, Cowboys, and Indians

Robert Allen Warrior

Native American theology of liberation has a nice ring to it. Politically active Christians in the US have been bandying about the idea of such a theology for several years now, encouraging Indians to develop it. There are theologies of liberation for African Americans, Hispanic Americans, women, Asian Americans, even Jews. Why not Native Americans? Christians recognize that American injustice on this continent began nearly 500 years ago with the oppression of its indigenous people and that justice for American Indians is a fundamental part of broader social struggle. The churches' complicity in much of the violence perpetrated on Indians makes this realization even clearer. So, there are a lot of well-intentioned Christians looking for some way to include Native Americans in their political action.

For Native Americans involved in political struggle, the participation of church people is often an attractive proposition. Churches have financial, political, and institutional resources that many Indian activists would dearly love to have at their disposal. Since American Indians have a relatively small population base and few financial resources, assistance from churches can be of great help in gaining the attention of the public, the media, and the government.

It sounds like the perfect marriage—Christians with the desire to include Native Americans in their struggle for justice and Indian activists in need or resources and support from non-Indians. Well, speaking as the product of a marriage between an Indian and a white, I can tell you that it is not as easy as it sounds. The inclusion of Native Americans in Christian political praxis is difficult—even dangerous. Christians have a different way of going about the struggle for justice the most Native Americans: different models of leadership, different ways of making decisions, different ways of viewing the relationship between politics and religion. These differences have gone all but unnoticed in the history of church involvement in American Indian affairs. Liberals and conservatives alike have too often surveyed the conditions of Native Americans and decided to come to the rescue, always using *their* methods, *their* ideas, and *their* programs. The idea that Indians might know best how to address their own problem is seemingly lost on these well-meaning folks.

Still, the time does seem ripe to find a new way for Indians and Christians (and Native Americans Christians) to be partners in the struggle against injustice and economic and racial oppression. This is a new era for both the church and for Native Americans. Christians are breaking away from the liberal moorings and looking for more effective means of social and political engagements. Indians, in this era of 'self-determination,' have verified for themselves and the government that they are people best able to address Indian problems as long as they are given the necessary resources and if they can hold the US government accountable to the policy. But an enormous stumbling block immediately presents itself. Most of the liberation theologies that have emerged in the last twenty years are preoccupied with the Exodus story, using it as the fundamental model for liberation. I believe that the story of the Exodus is an inappropriate way for Native Americans to think about liberation.

No doubt, the story is one that has inspired many people in many contexts to struggle against injustice. Israel, in the Exile, then Diaspora, would remember the story and be reminded of God's faithfulness. Enslaved African Americans, given Bibles to read by their masters and mistresses, would begin at the beginning of the book and find in the pages of the Pentateuch a god who was obviously on their side, even if god was the god of their oppressors. People in Latin American base communities read the story and have been inspired to struggle against injustice. The Exodus, with its picture of a god who takes the side of the oppressed and powerless, has been a beacon of hope for many in despair.

GOD THE CONQUEROR

Yet the liberationist picture of Yahweh is not complete. A delivered people is not a free people, not is it a nation. People who have survived the nightmare of subjugation dream escape. Once the victims have been delivered, they seek a new dream, a new goal, usually a place of safety away from the oppressors, a place that can be defended against future subjugation. Israel's new dream became the land of Canaan. And Yahweh was still with them: Yahweh promised to go before the people and give them Canaan, with its flowing milk and honey. The land, Yahweh decided, belonged to these former from Egypt and Yahweh planned on giving it to them—using the same power used against the enslaving Egyptians to defeat the indigenous inhabitants of Canaan. Yahweh the deliverer became Yahweh the conqueror.

The obvious characters in the story for Native Americans to identify with are the Canaanites, the people who already lived in the promised land. As a member of the Osage Nation of American Indians who stands in solidarity with other tribal people around the world, I read the Exodus stories with Canaanite eyes. And, it is the Canaanite side of the story that has been overlooked by those seeking the articulate theologies of liberation. Especially ignored are those parts of the story that describe Yahweh's command to mercilessly annihilate the indigenous population.

To be sure, most scholars, of a variety of political and theological stripes, agree that the actual events of Israel's early history are much different than what was commanded in the narrative. The Canaanites were not systematically annihilated, nor were they completely driven from the land. In fact, they made up, to a large extent, the people of the new nation of Israel. Perhaps it was a process of gradual immigration of people from many places and religions who came together to form a new nation. Or maybe, as Norman Gottwald and others have argued, the peasants of Canaan revolted against their feudal masters, a revolt instigated and aided by a vanguard of escaped slaves from Egypt who believed in the liberating god, Yahweh. Whatever happened, scholars agree that the people of Canaan had a lot to do with it.

Nonetheless, scholarly agreement should not allow us to breathe a sigh of relief. For historical knowledge does not change the status of indigenes in the *narrative* and the theology that grows out of it. The research of Old Testament scholars, however much it provides an answer to the historical question—the contribution of the indigenous people of Canaan to the formation and emergence of Israel as a nation—does not resolve the narrative problem. People who read the narratives read them as they are, not as scholars and experts would *like* them to be read and interpreted. History is no longer with us. The narrative remains.

Though the Exodus and Conquest stories are familiar to most readers, I want to highlight some sections that are commonly ignored. The covenant begins when Yahweh comes to Abram saying, 'Know of a surety that your descendants will be sojourners in a land that is not theirs, and they will be slaves there, and they will be oppressed for four hundred years; but I will bring judgment on the nation they serve and they shall come out' (Gen. 15.13,14). Then, Yahweh adds: 'To your descendants I give this land, the land of the Kenites, the Kenizzites, the Kadmonites, the Hittites, the Perizzites, the Rephaim, the Amorites, the Canaanites, and the Jebusites' (15.18–21). The next important moment is the commissioning of Moses. Yahweh says to him, 'I promise I will bring you out of the affliction of Egypt, to the land of Canaanites, the Hittites, the Amorites, the Perizzites, the Hivites, and the Jebusites, a land flowing with milk and honey' (Exod. 3.17). The covenant, in other words, has two parts: deliverance and conquest.

After the people have escaped and are headed to the promised land, the covenant is made more complicated, but it still has two parts. If the delivered people remain faithful to Yahweh, they will be blessed in the land Yahweh will conquer for them (Exod. 20–3 and Deut. 7–9). The god who delivered Israel from slavery will lead the people into the land and keep them there as long as they live up to the terms of the covenant. 'You shall not wrong a stranger or oppress him [*sic*], for you were strangers in the land of Egypt. You shall not afflict any widow or orphan. If you do afflict them, and they cry out to me, I will surely hear their cry; and my wrath will burn, and I will kill you with the sword, and your wives shall become widows and your children fatherless' (Exod. 22.21).

WHOSE NARRATIVE?

Israel's reward for keeping Yahweh's commandments—for building a society where the evils done to them have no place—is the continuation of life in the land. But one of the most important of Yahweh's commands is the prohibition on social relations with Canaanites or participation in their religion. 'I will deliver the inhabitants of the land into your hand, and you shall drive them out before you. You shall make no covenant with them or with their gods. They shall not dwell in your land, lest they make you sin against me; for if you serve their gods it will surely be a snare to you' (Exod. 23.31b–33).

In fact, the indigenes are to be destroyed:

> When the Lord your God brings you into the land which you are entering to take possession of it, and clears away many nations before you, the Hittites, the Girgashites, the Amorites, the Canaanites, the Perizzites, the Hivites, and the Jebusites, seven nations greater and mightier than yourselves, and when the Lord your God gives them over to you and you defeat them; then you must utterly destroy them; you shall make no covenant with them, and show no mercy to them (Deut. 7.1,2).

These words are spoken to the people of Israel as they are preparing to go into Canaan. The promises made to Abraham and Moses are ready to be fulfilled. All that remains is for the people to enter into the land and dispossess those who already live there.

Joshua gives an account of the conquest. After ten chapters of stories about Israel's successes and failures to obey Yahweh's commands, the writer states, 'So Joshua defeated the whole land, the hill country and the Negeb and the lowland and the slopes, and all their kings, he left none remaining, but utterly destroyed all that breathed, as the Lord God of Israel commanded.' In Judges, the writer disagrees with this account of what happened, but the Canaanites are held in no higher esteem. The angel of the Lord says, 'I will not drive out [the indigenous people] before you; but they shall become adversaries to you, and their gods shall be a snare to you.'

Thus, the narrative tells us that the Canaanites have status only as the people Yahweh removes from the land in order to bring the chosen people in. They are not to be trusted, nor are they to be allowed to enter into social relationships with the people of Israel. They are wicked, and their religion is to be avoided at all costs. The laws put forth regarding strangers and sojourners may have stopped the people of Yahweh from wanton oppression, but presumably only after the land was safely in the hands of Israel. The covenant of Yahweh depends on this.

The Exodus narrative is where discussion about Christian involvement in Native American activism must begin. It is these stories of deliverance and conquest that are ready to be picked up and believed by anyone wondering what to do about the people who already live in their promised land. They provide an example of what can happen when powerless people come to power. Historical scholarship may tell a different story; but even if the annihilation did not take place, the narratives tell what happened to those indigenous people who put their hope and faith in ideas and gods that were foreign to their culture. The Canaanites trusted in the god of outsiders and their story of oppression and exploitation was lost. Interreligious praxis became betrayal and the surviving narrative tells us nothing about it.

Confronting the conquest stories as a narrative rather than a historical problem is especially important given the tenor of contemporary theology and criticism. After 200 years of preoccupation with historical questions, scholars and theologians across a broad spectrum of political and ideological positions have recognized the function of narrative in the development of religious communities. Along with the work of US scholars like Brevard Childs, Stanley Hauerwas, and George Lindbeck, the radical liberation theologies of Latin America are based on empowering believing communities to read scriptural narratives for themselves and make their reading central to theology and political action. The danger is that these communities will read the narratives, not the history behind them.

And, of course, the text itself will never be altered by interpretations of it, though its reception may be. It is part of the canon for both Jews and Christians. It is part of the heritage and thus the consciousness of people in the United States. Whatever dangers we identify in the text and the god represented there will remain as long as the text remains. These dangers only grow as the emphasis upon catechetical (Lindbeck), narrative (Hauerwas), canonical (Childs), and Bible-centered Christian base communities (Gutierrez) grows. The peasants of Solentiname bring a wisdom and experience previously unknown to Christian theology, but I do not see what mechanism guarantees that they—or any other people who seek to be shaped and molded by reading the text—will differentiate between the liberating god and the god of conquest.

IS THERE A SPIRIT

What is to be done? First, the Canaanites should be at the center of Christian theological reflection and political action. They are the last remaining ignored voice in the text, except perhaps for the land itself. The conquest stories, with all their violence and injustice, must be taken seriously by those who believe in the god of the Old Testament. Commentaries and critical works rarely mention these texts. When they do, they express little concern for the status of the indigenes and their rights as human beings and as nations. The same blindness is evident in theologies that use the Exodus motif as their basis for political action. The leading into the land becomes just one more redemptive moment rather than a violation of innocent peoples' rights to land and self-determination.

Keeping the Canaanites at the center makes it more likely that those who read the Bible will read *all* of it, not just the part that inspires and justifies them. And should anyone be surprised by the brutality, the terror of these texts? It was, after all, a Jewish victim of the Holocaust, Walter Benjamin, who said, 'There is no document of civilization which is not at the same time a document of barbarism.' People whose theology involves the Bible need to take this insight seriously. It is those who know these texts who must speak the truth about what they contain. It is to those who believe in these texts that the barbarism belongs. It is those who act on the basis of these texts who must take responsibility for the terror and violence they can and have engendered.

Second, we need to be more aware of the way ideas such as those in the conquest narratives have made their way into Americans' consciousness and ideology. And only when we understand this process can those of us who have suffered from it know how to fight back. Many Puritan preachers were fond of referring to Native Americans as Amelkites and Canaanites—in other words, people who, if they would not be converted, were worthy of annihilation. By examining such instances in theological and political writings, in sermons, and elsewhere, we can understand how America's self-image as a 'chosen people' has provided a rhetoric to mystify domination.

Finally, we need to decide if we want to accept the model of leadership and social change presented by the entire Exodus story. Is it appropriate to the needs of indigenous people seeking justice and deliverance? If indeed the Canaanites were integral to Israel's early history, the Exodus narratives reflect a situation in which indigenous people put their hope in a god from outside, were liberated from their oppressors, and then saw their story of oppression revised out of the new nation's history of salvation. They were assimilated into another people's identity and the history of their ancestors came to be regarded as suspect and a danger to the safety of Israel. In short, they were betrayed.

Do Native Americans and other indigenous people dare trust the same god in their struggle for justice? I am not asking an easy question and I in no way mean that people who are both Native Americans and Christians cannot work toward justice in the context of their faith in Jesus Christ. Such people have a lot of theological reflection to do, however, to avoid the dangers I have pointed to in the conquest narratives. Christians, whether Native American or not, if they are to be involved, must learn how to participate in the struggle without making their story the whole story. Otherwise the sins of the past will be visited upon us again.

No matter what we do, the conquest narratives will remain. As long as people believe in the Yahweh of deliverance, the world will not be safe from Yahweh the conqueror. But perhaps, if they are true to their struggle, people will be able to achieve what Yahweh's chosen people in the past have not: a society of people delivered from oppression who are not so afraid of becoming victims again that they become oppressors themselves, a society where the original inhabitants can become something other than subjects to be converted to a better way of life or adversaries who provide cannon fodder for a nation's militaristic pride.

With what voice will we, the Canaanites of the world, say, 'Let my people go and leave my people alone?' And, with what ears will followers of alien gods who have wooed us (Christians, Jews, Marxists, capitalists), listen to us? The indigenous people of this hemisphere have endured a subjugation now 100 years longer than the sojourn of Israel in Egypt. Is there a god, a spirit, who will hear us and stand with us in the Amazon, Osage County, and Wounded Knee? Is there a god, a spirit, able to move among the pain and anger of Nablus, Gaza, and Soweto? Perhaps. But we, the wretched of the earth, may be well advised this time not to listen to outsiders with their promises of liberation and deliverance. We will perhaps do better to look elsewhere for our vision of justice, peace, and political sanity—a vision through which we escape not only our oppressors, but our oppression as well. Maybe, for once, we will just have to listen to ourselves, leaving the gods of this continent's real strangers to do battle among themselves.

Biblical Reference Index

Hebrew Bible

New Testament

John

Acts of the Apostles

Romans

1 Corinthians